THE
ESSENTIAL CANON
OF CLASSICAL
MUSIC

THE
ESSENTIAL CANON
OF CLASSICAL
MUSIC

DAVID DUBAL

WITH DRAWINGS BY THE AUTHOR

NORTH POINT PRESS

A DIVISION OF FARRAR, STRAUS AND GIROUX

NEW YORK

North Point Press
A division of Farrar, Straus and Giroux
19 Union Square West, New York 10003

Copyright © 2001 by David Dubal
Distributed in Canada by Douglas & McIntyre Ltd.
Printed in the United States of America
Published in 2001 by North Point Press
First paperback edition, 2003

The Library of Congress has cataloged the hardcover edition as follows:
Dubal, David.
    The essential canon of classical music / David Dubal.
        p. cm.
    Includes bibliographical and discographical references and index.
    ISBN 0-86547-608-X (hc.)
    1. Music appreciation.   I. Title.

MT90 .D83 2001
780'.92'2—dc21

                                                          2001034268

Paperback ISBN 0-86547-664-0

Designed by Jonathan D. Lippincott

www.fsgbooks.com

3   5   7   9   10   8   6   4

林容光

For Jung Lin

the sunlight of my life

The study of the history of music and the hearing of masterworks of different epochs will speediest of all cure you of vanity and self-adoration.

—ROBERT SCHUMANN

Music is a higher revelation than all wisdom and philosophy.

—LUDWIG VAN BEETHOVEN

As neither the enjoyment nor the capacity of producing musical notes are
faculties of the least direct use to man in reference to his ordinary habits of
life, they must be ranked amongst the most mysterious with which he is
endowed. —CHARLES DARWIN

CONTENTS

ACKNOWLEDGMENTS

The creation of a book begins with the author, but its completion requires collaboration. I wish to thank Elisabeth Sifton for acquiring the book. I thank my editor, Lauren Osborne, for her true gifts as an editor, for her patience and perspicacity. I thank Catherine Newman, assistant editor, for her goodwill and grace. She worked hard and meticulously through many stages. I also extend my appreciation to Lisa Yui, who did various tasks. I also thank Janet Biehl, the copyeditor, who was fastidious to a high degree, as well as André Balog, a tireless fact-checker. My gratitude and love go to Jung Lin, who typed and retyped relentlessly and who inspired me to complete the work.

I also want to express my debt to the many writers from whom I have borrowed quotations and information. Their special insights have enriched my efforts. The poet Marianne Moore once said of quotations, "I've always felt that if a thing had been said in the *best* way, how can you say it better? . . . If you are charmed by an author, I think it's a very strange and invalid imagination that doesn't long to share it. Somebody else should read it."

THE
ESSENTIAL CANON
OF CLASSICAL
MUSIC

INTRODUCTION

The advent of the long-playing recording in 1948 generated a larger and more sophisticated listening audience for classical music. This audience was already substantial because of the development of FM radio, which had been invented by Edwin Armstrong in 1933 solely with serious music in mind. When stereophonic recording arrived in 1960, the number of recordings of the standard repertoire exploded, while much music, ranging from the Baroque to contemporary composition, was recorded for the first time.

For over two decades, I served as program and music director of WNCN, New York's twenty-four-hour classical music station. WNCN programmed a wide range of music and introduced thousands of listeners to the classical repertoire. For me, it was an enlightening experience to listen to so many works that were new to me, and to so many different performances of works I already knew. During those years, my musical hunger kept increasing. Even after business hours, I found myself exploring, for example, a previously unrecorded Janáček opera that I wanted to share with my audience. I happily devoted several months to the study of Janáček operas, concluding without doubt that this contemporary of Puccini was the equal of the great Italian. And so it would go—I devoted much time to Scriabin, Delius, Nielsen, and the then-obscure Baroque composers, whose music was being discovered and recorded daily, it seemed.

Before 1950, it was almost taken for granted that serious music began by some miracle with J. S. Bach, apart from a few earlier historical figures. Music composed since 1800 has had a much higher dissemination than that of earlier periods, and to make room for all of the new composers clamoring to be heard, a great deal of the past became obsolete. It is much easier than one would think for our artistic heritage to become lost. Nor did we know much about how music of the past was performed, as many of the instruments were no longer played or had been superseded. In the twentieth century musicologists have uncovered much astonishing music and allowed us to understand period instruments and their proper performance practice. Thousands of works that had never been published are now available. Even with new publications, however, a great deal of music would have remained dormant without Thomas Edison's invention of the phonograph: August 12, 1877, was a red-letter day in the history of music. (By his own admission, the quite unmusical Mr. Edison shouted into the mouthpiece of his new invention the insipid words "Mary had a little lamb." Although he expected to hear something in return, upon hearing his own voice he was startled: "I was never so taken aback in my life.")

In 1900, for example, Antonio Vivaldi was virtually unknown, and his music had hardly been published. Even in 1940 only one recording of his *The Four Seasons* was available, conducted by Leopold Stokowski. Today hundreds of recordings of his music are available, including about a hundred CDs of *The Four Seasons* alone. When Nadia Boulanger first made her now well known recordings of madrigals by Monteverdi in the mid-1930s, it was considered a bold step; few music lovers had heard of any composer who lived before J. S. Bach. Today we know that much "early" music is haunting and mysterious, and that early dance music is not only entertaining and rhythmically subtle but startlingly refreshing. But even with so famous a figure as Beethoven, devotees had to wait patiently from 1932 to 1939 for Artur Schnabel to complete history's first recorded traversal of the thirty-two piano sonatas. When completed, they added up to fifteen bulky albums, with more than 250 sides of then-current 78 rpm records. The price of the set was over $200, a small fortune during the Depression, and only a few dealers in larger cities stocked it.

By contrast, the amount of recorded art music available today is staggering. But most of the people who care for classical music listen to a very small portion of the literature. This restricted standard repertoire is what we hear over and over at recitals, operas, and symphony concerts, peppered occasionally by contemporary works. But although the international performing repertoire is exceedingly small, the recorded repertoire is constantly growing (as one sees from a brief perusal of the *Schwann Opus* catalogs). The music lover with a taste for Glazunov may indulge it to gluttony on recordings yet never hear a Glazunov piece performed live in a lifetime of concertgoing. Unfortunately, sales for such recordings are pitifully small—but they do exist, and for the more experienced classical music lover, they can open new vistas.

In music as in the other arts, we have been badly conditioned to the "masterpiece syndrome," or what the American composer Aaron Copland condemned as "a special stupidity of our own musical time; the notion that only the best, the highest, the greatest among musical masterworks is worthy of our attention." He had "little patience with those who cannot see the vitality of an original mind at work, even when the work contains serious blemishes." Of course, the so-called masterpieces of classic culture are indeed essential listening, but too much consumption and too many pedestrian performances of these works can make them stale, exhausting their immense spiritual energy. Yet a wealth of superb work by the masters is unhackneyed, work that has all the qualities of the "masterpieces" we love. In fact, only a fraction of the music of Handel, Schubert, Haydn, Mozart, and many others is known.

Nor can music lovers live only by the masters of the past. The twentieth century produced exciting sound explorers—Charles Ives, Edgard Varèse, Arnold Schoenberg, John Cage, Harry Partch, Elliott Carter, Michael Tippett, Pierre Boulez, and dozens more—each tingling with creative vitality. Their work satisfies our often-repressed curiosity to hear music of our time. An art is floundering if at least a small but passionate group is not devoted to the new in it. Fortunately, a great deal of twentieth-century and contemporary music is now available on compact disc.

In this book I hope to address two audiences at once. The first is those who are more or less new to classical music. The second is those who are already familiar with it but could use a source that codifies the essential canon and suggests a lifetime listening plan. During my years at WNCN, many listeners wrote or called to request that I write a book that might guide them through the classical music repertoire. Some of them were youngish parents who had grown up on the inevitable pop music but had begun to realize they had missed a vital musical experience. They wanted to give this missed experience to their children, and—sadly—they knew that public education could no longer be counted on to provide a new generation with any musical or artistic knowledge.

In the long run, understanding of art will enhance one's desire to go deeper into one's humanity. Over the years, I have gained the deepest respect for the impact of great music. If Beethoven mirrors our humanity and desire for transcendence, then for some of us a day without Beethoven's message is a day when we are not fully human. The eminent historian of Italian painting Bernard Berenson described music in a particularly wonderful way: "Music itself . . . conjuring up with wordless sound audible edifices as sublime as any architecture, disciplining, canalizing our emotions, and transporting them into realms as remote from our brutish beginnings as our animal present will permit! On the wings of music we soar above and beyond nature, farther than any

other vehicle can carry us, where some far-distant day we may reach the limit-
less ecstasy of infinitude."

Although classical music lovers occasionally go to concerts, the great majority depend for their musical nourishment upon recordings and radio. Amateur musicians are few, and the average music lover has no theoretical training
of any kind. When I asked my radio listeners what kind of book they wanted,
the answer was invariably the same. They wanted to know something about the
composer, his life, and his importance. They wanted to know something of his
essential works, and they wanted guidance in picking recordings of excellent
performances. Fulfilling this request is generally what I have attempted to do
in this book—to put within easy reach the established canon of great Western
music at the beginning of the twenty-first century.

The book covers 236 composers. The composers are grouped into five parts
representing the various epochs of music history: (1) the Medieval, Renaissance, and Elizabethan Ages, (2) the Age of the Baroque, (3) the Age of Classicism, (4) the Romantic Age, and (5) the Age of Modernism. Each part begins
with an introduction that gives an idea of the new forms of music that emerged
during that period. Sixty of the composers, from Handel to Britten, receive
long biographical essays, and many of their best-known works—followed by
suggested recordings—are discussed so as to whet the listener's interest in a specific score. These long essays appear first in each section; the less well known
composers follow, with shorter essays. Composers are listed chronologically
within their groups.

This is not a book of analysis; it does not offer program notes, or tell the listener where, when, and how the main themes go and what instruments are
used. Books of analysis were valuable in an earlier time, when many audiences
could read music and study the work at the piano or follow the score while listening to the recording. Unfortunately, this elementary musical literacy has all
but disappeared today. As I am stating what the book contains and does not
contain, I must add that I do not give synopses of operas, and I discuss an opera
only as a work within the permanent international repertoire.

Nor does this book review performances, weighing their merits and flaws.
Performance books—with their endless adjectives, too easily applied for hundreds of pages, giving almost no real information except which is a critic's favorite choice—tend only to confuse the novice or inexperienced consumer.
My criteria for selecting particular recordings are many, but first and foremost,
for each composition, I have chosen several interpretations that show varying
aspects of its potential. Great music always surpasses any one performance. In
the interest of space, each entry is given rather sparingly, with only last names
of performers and brief notations of the orchestra and record label—for exam-

ple, "New York Philharmonic Orchestra, Bernstein: Sony Classical, Number." (This abbreviated information is enough to locate the recording easily in a store or library.) Recordings are listed for each composer's essential works, and to avoid clutter, I have not listed other pieces that appear on the same CDs. Nevertheless, my choices have been influenced by what other music is on a CD; it may be another performance of an "essential work," which will reveal another side of the composition, or it may be another item in the repertoire that the listener may find value and pleasure in. I do not list the performances in any order of importance. I have included many recordings that represent older artists, some monophonic and some that are transfers from 78s. The recordings of Alfred Cortot, Pablo Casals, Elisabeth Schwarzkopf, George Szell, Wilhelm Furtwängler, Jascha Heifetz, Arturo Toscanini, and others are invaluable and immutable. Indeed, I recommend any and all recordings of these immortal artists. After listing performances of the essential works, I list the composer's other principal compositions. All of these are valuable, but I put an asterisk (*) next to works of particular interest and importance. This is the scheme for the sixty composers to whom I have given the most space.

The 176 remaining composers receive shorter essays, which appear grouped together at the end of each chronological section. (Because of the lack of reliable biographical information and the still-limited appeal of early music, no biographical essays appear on composers before the Baroque.) These short essays may contain some bits of biographical information, but their main purpose is to convey the composer's general importance in the context of the greater composers. Although these 176 composers are less known, their music is of enormous interest and serves to round out our understanding of their era. Each sketch includes a list of the composer's most famous, important, or characteristic scores and one or more suggested recordings. Again, however flawed or limited, these composers are important. Some masters, such as Max Reger, Franz Berwald, Carl Nielsen, Nikolai Medtner, Vincent d'Indy, Albert Roussel, Ferruccio Busoni, Arnold Bax, and Karol Szymanowski, are not memorable melodists. This is the main reason they are not performed frequently. All the world loves a good tune, but many composers would agree with Copland that "a melody is not merely something you can hum."

No devotees are more passionate than music lovers, and no people are more opinionated about their favorites. I am certain that, for whatever reason, readers will charge me with favoritism or aesthetic unawareness. Certainly the secondary masters are more often open to subjective evaluation. I have left out composers that some readers will miss. Some would prefer to see Peter Mennin, David Diamond, or William Schuman represent American symphonists rather than Walter Piston, while others think minimalism should be represented by John Adams or La Monte Young or Terry Riley rather than Philip Glass. But by and large, most everyone who really should be here is here.

Music is by far the most elusive of the arts to write about. Aldous Huxley observed: "Music 'says' things about the world, but in specifically musical terms. Any attempt to reproduce these musical statements 'in our own words' is necessarily doomed to failure. We cannot isolate the truth contained in a piece of music; for it is beauty-truth. . . . The best we can do is to indicate in the most general terms the nature of the musical beauty-truth under consideration and to refer curious truth-seekers to the original." But writing about music is by no means a fruitless effort, for it can at least spur interest in great music.

In this complex, harassed, and fragmented world, let us somehow make time for great music. Close the lights, sit back, calm the mind, and let the music unfold. Let the badly neglected instinctive-artistic side of the mind become *musicalized*. We won't find an oasis; we shall be entering paradise.

PART ONE

THE MEDIEVAL, RENAISSANCE, AND ELIZABETHAN AGES

We can only speculate about the origins of music, but its seemingly magical qualities must have been apparent early in human prehistory. Primitive music of some sort probably preceded speech by thousands of years. Those with unusual vocal abilities may have used their power in rituals or to convey messages over a distance. These ancient singers, like their brothers the cave painters, may even have been privileged members of the clan. But it was a long time before people started making vocal utterances in intervals, thus creating melodies that could be repeated again and again.

The first musical instrument, if you can call it that, was the pursed lips of a whistler (no doubt first used in an attempt to imitate bird calls). Early peoples thereafter developed banging, twanging, and scraping instruments, most of which were used, with the dance, to practice magical and sexual rites and to worship the sun and the moon. Charles Darwin was convinced "that musical notes and rhythm were first acquired by the male or female progenitors of mankind for the sake of charming the opposite sex."

As the concept of pitch developed, those with good musical ears could start to imitate sounds. The pitches they heard, however, were not those that we have come to know. Each area of the world developed a different vocabulary of sounds. We do not know who the first musical geniuses were, or when they first organized sound into a musical form. How interesting it would be to go back in time and hear the music used for prehistoric funeral and marital rites, or the humming and singing (if any) that accompanied hunting and gathering!

Our knowledge of music in ancient civilizations is unfortunately scanty. We know very little about Egypt, and only a little more about the strides made in

India, Persia, and the Far East. The five-tone or pentatonic scale was first developed in China around three thousand years ago. In ancient Greece music was almost held sacred, and the mythological musician Orpheus was feted. Pythagoras realized that music had healing agents, but Plato found it dangerous and enervating. The Greeks made great advances in musical theory, developing scales or modes, but only a few fragments of their music survive. This gifted civilization was probably the most musically expressive up to that time.

It was with the emergence of Christianity that the Western musical tradition began. Gregorian chant, named for Pope Gregory the Great (d. 604), had its roots in Jewish liturgical chants. In addition, psalmody, hymns, antiphons, and so forth became part of a common liturgy that spread through the Christian world. For several hundred years after Gregory, theory and practice slowly evolved together (for creativity could not blossom until theoretical problems were solved).

The Middle Ages saw the birth of polyphony, a revolutionary new form of music based on two or more parts, or melodic lines. Polyphony made possible the mass, the chief musical ritual of the Roman Catholic Church. It also saw the birth of a secular musical tradition, alongside the liturgical. Wandering minstrels, known as troubadours, based their popular melodies on poems of courtly love. They made creative use of new musical instruments to accompany their chivalric stanzas, which were usually written in the vernacular languages and not in Latin.

The vernacular was making rapid progress in the other arts, especially after 1300, when both Dante and Petrarch started to write verse in Italian. Their poems expressed emotional states not previously addressed by the arts. (Petrarch, for example, dedicated his sonnets to his lady love, Laura.) Music could not yet rival the flexibility of poetry, but Petrarch's contemporary Guillaume de Machaut brought music to a new rhythmic complexity through syncopation. Like other composers, he worked for the Church, but in his *ballades* he codified a new type of secular song in courtly language, accompanied by an instrument, with sections of ornamental freedom. The ballade form would retain its popularity for a century.

As it did with the other arts, Italy, the cradle of the Renaissance, developed a flourishing musical culture, especially after 1450. While Giovanni Bellini was painting his incomparable madonnas, Italians were reveling in madrigals, a mostly secular polyphonic form using two to as many as eight vocal parts. In the humanistic Renaissance, as one scholar put it, "music was not a set of compositional techniques but a complex of social conditions, intellectual states of mind, attitudes, aspirations, habits of performers, artistic support systems, intracultural communication, and many other ingredients which add up to a thriving matrix of musical energy." Beauty in art and craft was a highly valued element of life. The artist of the Renaissance was in fact more integrated into general society than he would ever be again.

Italian and English musicians were artists of the highest cultivation. Performances were constant and lively, and for the first time notated music was published. New instruments were created in abundance and were of exceptional beauty in their ornaments: organs, harpsichords, cornetti, shawms (forerunners of the oboe), sackbuts (early trombones), viols (cousins of the modern violin, cello, and viola), flutes, lutes, and dozens of others. Like many noblemen, Henry VIII of England, who considered himself a fine composer, had a splendid collection of instruments (nearly four hundred by 1530).

By the late sixteenth century, any person of rank or pretension was expected to have musical proficiency. Most were excellent sight-readers. The reign of Elizabeth (1558–1603) was a golden age for the arts, and music thrived in the home, at church, and in the theater. Shakespeare used song prolifically in his plays and showed not only his love for the art but his knowledge of it. He may have played the recorder. In his 128th sonnet, he wrote of "jacks," that part of the virginal (keyboard) action that makes possible the plucking of the strings:

> *I envy those jacks that nimble leap*
> *To kiss the tender inward of thy hand.*

In Italy madrigals continued to rule the secular musical scene in the later Renaissance. Both Claudio Monteverdi and Carlo Gesualdo provided greatness to this form. The madrigal is the neglected glory of the Renaissance. Two close contemporaries, Giovanni Pierluigi da Palestrina and Orlande de Lassus, were giants: Palestrina's masses, with their beautiful euphony, are among music's purest, most angelic manifestations. The versatile master Lassus fulfilled the motet form, the villanella, and the chanson. These and many composers in other lands—such as the Swiss Ludwig Senfl, the Dutchman Jan Pieterszoon Sweelinck, the Spaniard Tomás Luis de Victoria, and the Englishman William Byrd—make the sixteenth century a time of high musical adventurousness. Composers had never had more options in vocal and instrumental expression. During this time, conflicts between polyphony and melody grew. At the end of the sixteenth century, a group of Florentine dilettantes, poets, and musicians plotted the germ of a new art form. They rejected polyphony as unsuited to accompany song in drama. Jacopo Peri's *Dafne* (1598) may be called the first drama to be completely set to music. It signaled the birth of opera—and of the Baroque era.

GUILLAUME DE MACHAUT

(c.1300–1377) France

Machaut was perhaps the most famous composer of the fourteenth century. His music, both secular and religious, has been described as the most fully formed of the period. Ordained a priest, he led an adventurous and dangerous existence as secretary to the warring John of Luxembourg, king of Bohemia. Machaut, also a poet, used his own verse in composing secular ballades, rondeaux, and virelais. He has been called a fourteenth-century Romantic and a champion of medieval chivalric ideals. Machaut was one of the first composers to experiment with rhythmic syncopation.

Messe de Nostre Dame (mass) (c.1350)
Hilliard Ensemble, Hillier: Hyperion CDA 66358

GUILLAUME DUFAY

(c.1400–1474) France

Born at Cambrai, Dufay became one of Europe's best-known musicians. He worked in the early 1420s in Rimini and later in Rome, where he was a singer in the papal choir. For the rest of his life, he held important posts, mainly in Savoy and Cambrai, and his compositions were prized throughout Europe. His life's work sums up many of the musical aspirations of the fifteenth century, and he is often considered to be the most universal composer of his age, assimilating many styles. Dufay's masses became the foundation for the form, which was in rapid development in the second half of the century. In the field of secular music, his chansons were models, and their grace and elegance remain remarkable to modern ears.

Masses
Prague Madrigal Singers, Venhoda: Supraphon Collection 110637-2

JOSQUIN DESPREZ

(c.1440–1521) France

Josquin Desprez's work embodies the musical achievements of the fifteenth century. This contrapuntist's thirty masses, seventy chansons, and one hundred motets are among the most enduring music of his age, which marks the turning point from medieval to Renaissance. His work is infused with warmth and poignant sorrow. The *Missa Pange Lingua* (c.1500) is his most celebrated work, but his motets and chansons have been beautifully realized by many fine early music performers.

Missa Pange Lingua (mass) (c.1500)
Tallis Scholars, Phillips: Gimell CDGIM-009

THOMAS TALLIS

(c.1505–1585) England

Due to his prolific outpouring of church music in various forms, Tallis has been dubbed "the father of English cathedral music." The revival of Tallis and other Tudor composers began in England during the third quarter of the nineteenth century. Sadly, his name is best known through Ralph Vaughan Williams's *Fantasia on a Theme of Thomas Tallis*.

The Lamentations of Jeremiah (c.1560)
Deller Consort, Deller: Musique D'Abord HMA 190208

GIOVANNI PIERLUIGI DA PALESTRINA

(c.1525–1594) Italy

Although too little of Palestrina's exquisitely chaste church music is performed today, it expresses a radiant spirit. The composer Johann Fux, in his 1725 treatise *Gradus ad Parnassum*, considered him to be the greatest representative of sixteenth-century counterpoint, surpassing many other fine contrapuntists, including the Spanish mystic Victoria. Indeed, Palestrina created perfect models of devotional polyphony.

Nineteenth-century Romantics like Gounod felt that in Palestrina's music "one senses that the technique of the executing hand no longer counts, and the soul alone, immutably fixed upon a nobler world, endeavors to express in obedient and modest form the sublimity of its contemplation." Hans Pfitzner's massive post-Wagnerian opera *Palestrina* (1912–15) added to the legend of Palestrina's life and art: in this opera, Palestrina composes his most celebrated work, *Missa Papae Marcelli*, with angelic guidance.

Palestrina's output was large, including 104 masses and six hundred motets, psalms, madrigals, and other vocal works. He said of one group of his motets that they were "composed with continuous application and, so far as lies in me, polished with such art as I possess."

Missa Papae Marcelli (mass) (1567)
Tallis Scholars, Phillips: Gimell 454939-2
Pro Cantione Antiqua, Brown: MCA Classics MCAD-25191

ORLANDE DE LASSUS

(c.1532–1594) Flanders

Perhaps the most versatile composer of the sixteenth century, Lassus wrote some 1,250 works and was the most published composer of the age. Though his best works are motets, he traveled widely and absorbed all the current musical forms except the mass. He composed Italian madrigals, German part songs, French chansons, and many other forms. For more than three decades, he was *Kapellmeister* at the Bavarian Court Chapel in Munich. Under his direction, the court chapel became one of Europe's major music centers.

Choral Music
Christ Church Cathedral Choir, Darlington: Nimbus NI-5150

WILLIAM BYRD

(1543–1623) England

There is only a thimbleful of data on Byrd, giving us a scanty story of his life. He was a Catholic, which in sixteenth-century London was a constant trial. Fortunately, Elizabeth I was too fine a music devotee to make his station unbearable, and he attained a position at the Chapel Royal. We may know little of his life—yet from his art we may surmise the scope and richness of his being. Byrd, within the richly endowed world of Tudor music, is the most universal master; his range is the widest, his architectural scope the largest, his humanism the most Shakespearean. With equal success he composed motets, anthems, masses, and madrigals, and he charted the future of keyboard music in such anthologies as *My Ladye Nevells Booke* (forty-two pieces) and the *Fitzwilliam Virginal Book* (seventy-two pieces). The pianist Glenn Gould wrote, "Byrd, though the creator of incomparable music for the voice, is also the patron saint of keyboard writing. All of his prolific output for the keyboard is distinguished by a remarkable insight into the ways in which the human hand can most productively be employed upon it."

With advances in music scholarship and a wider general perception of music history, Byrd's position continuously rises. An appreciation of his many-sided genius takes exposure and patience; our ears are still primed for "modern" tonality, and Byrd is locked between an older modality and the system of tonality completed by J. S. Bach and his time. As with Shakespeare, Byrd's music becomes natural and forthcoming; after repeated listening, his drama and poetry penetrate to the core of our humanity.

In his 1588 publication *Psalmes, Sonets, and Songs,* Byrd wrote a charming preface: "Reasons briefely set downe by the auctor to perswade every one to learne to singe":

> First, it is a knowledge easely taught, and quickly learned, where there is a good master, and an apt scoller.
>
> Second, the exercise of singing is delightful to nature, and good to preserve the health of Man.
>
> Third, it doth strengthen all parts of the brest, and doth open the pipes.
>
> Fourth, it is a singuler good remedie for a stutting and stamering in speech.
>
> Fifth, it is the best meanes to procure a perfect pronunciation, and to make a good orator.
>
> Sixth, it is the onely way to know where Nature hath bestowed the benefit of a good voyce; which guift is so rare, as there is not one among a thousand, that hath it; and in many, that excellent guift is lost, because they want Art to expresse Nature.
>
> Seventh, there is not any musicke of instruments whatsoever, comparable to

that which is made of the voyces of Men, where the voyces are good, and the same well sorted and ordered.

Eighth, the better the voyce is, the meeter it is to honour and serve God therewith: and the voyce of man is chiefely to be employed to that ende.

Since singing is so good a thing, I wish all men would learne to singe.

Three Masses (in three, four, and five parts) (1592–95)
Deller Consort, Deller: Musique D'Abord HMA 190211

TOMÁS LUIS DE VICTORIA

(c.1548–1611) Spain

The late-Renaissance master Victoria has lived in the shadow of his contemporary Palestrina, but they differed in temperament and essence; the seraphic Italian possessed none of Victoria's visionary rapture. There remains no record of Victoria's early years in Spain, but he was born in Ávila, the birthplace of Saint Teresa, and both were mystical ascetics. He wrote 180 works, all religious. His masses and motets are the high-water mark of Spanish music at the beginning of the seventeenth century.

Masses
Westminster Cathedral Choir, Hill: Hyperion CDA 66129

GIOVANNI GABRIELI

(c.1553–1612) Italy

Giovanni and his uncle Andrea Gabrieli (1510–1586) inaugurated the grand style of Venetian music that would influence composers in Germany and the Netherlands for the next century. The Dutch master Jan Pieterszoon Sweelinck studied with Andrea, while that giant of seventeenth-century German music, Heinrich Schütz, was the adoring pupil of Giovanni.

Giovanni has become the more celebrated of the two Gabrielis, but Andrea was a multifaceted master of original genius who laid the foundation for a new conception of music at St. Mark's in Venice. His use of instruments in conjunction with choral music was one of the great innovations in music history. Giovanni expanded on his uncle's innovations with even more grandly conceived and sumptuous music for Venice's great church. Alfred Einstein wrote, "Palestrina and Lassus inherited and perfected an art which was nearing its maturity, but with Giovanni Gabrieli music seems to have burst into fresh bloom. . . . His music was brilliant, yet profound; festive, yet for the church—albeit a specifically Venetian church, full of power, romance, and wonderfully glowing color." With Giovanni the pomp and sweep of the early Italian Baroque was in full swing.

Canzoni for Brass Choirs (1600)

Canadian Brass (with additional brass players of the Boston Symphony and New York Philharmonic): Sony Classics 44931

Music of Gabrieli (canzoni, sonatas, and motets on period instruments)

Taverner Consort Choir and Players, Parrott: EMI Classics CDC 54265

CARLO GESUALDO

(c.1561–1613) Italy

Don Carlo Gesualdo lived and died in Naples during one of the more violent periods in Italian history. His family came from the highest-ranking nobility; a maternal uncle was Cardinal Carlo Borromeo, who was canonized in 1610. Far from saintly, Gesualdo, the hereditary prince of Venosa, partook of the violence of his time. After discovering that his young wife was unfaithful, he entered her quarters on the evening of October 16, 1590, and, with the help of paid assassins, murdered both her and her lover. As a prince, Gesualdo remained above the law, suffering no punishment for his hellish deeds. In his remaining twenty-three years, he continued to wreak havoc among those around him and developed a taste for being flogged by his servants.

Gesualdo's personality and behavior seem oddly incongruous with his astonishing musical genius, especially in his madrigals. Aldous Huxley felt that "Gesualdo's music is so strange and, in its strangeness, so beautiful, that it haunts the memory and fires the imagination." With Monteverdi, his contemporary, Gesualdo brought the art of the Italian madrigal to its apogee, one of the supreme but neglected accomplishments of the Renaissance. The Gesualdo madrigals in their poetic settings are exquisitely crafted to the polyphony of five human voices. In order to attain the freedom of expression necessary for his increasingly original music, he broke from the strict laws of modality into a harmonic freedom that allowed for greater emotional eloquence.

Madrigals (c.1600)

Les Arts Florissants Ensemble, Christie: Harmonia Mundi France HMC-901268
Consort of Musicke, Rooley: London 410128-2

JOHN DOWLAND

(1563–1626) England

Dowland was the finest lute virtuoso in Europe in an age when the lute, a difficult instrument to play well, was practiced considerably. Richard Barnfield's 1598 sonnet on Dowland praised his ability: "Whose heavenly touch upon the lute doth ravish human sense."

Little is known of his early life; possibly he was born in Dublin but most likely in London. He was well traveled and had firsthand knowledge of the most advanced music of France, Germany, and Italy, probably having encountered Gesualdo's extraordinary madrigals. From 1596 to 1606, he was a highly paid employee of King Christian IV of Denmark. In London Dowland mingled with Jonson, Marlowe, Donne, Shakespeare, Bull, Byrd, Thomas Morley, Orlando Gibbons, and the other luminaries.

Dowland was for the most part content to concentrate on the solo voice and lute; *Lachrimae or Seaven Teares* (1604) is his only purely instrumental score. His music was exceedingly popular in that eminently musical time, for it floats in exquisite, touching, anguished lyricism, often harmonically bold and rhythmically pliant.

The great English critic and composer Wilfrid Mellers wrote, "The position of John Dowland among the great masters is now assured. If his music is still not widely performed (and precious little of the great music of any age other than the eighteenth and nineteenth century can, alas, claim to be that), at least there is now a tacit recognition among musically responsible people that he is not merely the greatest English song-writer, but among the supreme song-writers of the world."

Lute Songs
Deller Consort, Deller: Harmonia Mundi France HMC 90244

CLAUDIO MONTEVERDI

(1567–1643) Italy

The colossal genius of Monteverdi linked the Renaissance to the Baroque: he brought the Renaissance madrigal to its zenith. Within a decade of the first primitive operas in Florence, he transformed opera into a form that possessed far-reaching dramatic flexibility and anticipated Alessandro Scarlatti. *L'Orfeo* (1607), Monteverdi's first opera, is one of the revolutionary works in music history. Orchestral music as we know it today was born from his operas, and in his instrumentation he incorporated several innovations, such as pizzicato and tremolo. Modern emotional melody may well have begun in such works as Arianna's lament, the only preserved section of Monteverdi's second opera, *L'Arianna* (1608). At its premiere, the audience wept profusely at its moving strains.

Throughout Monteverdi's music, including such church masterpieces as the *Vespers* (1610), the secular madrigals, and the greatest of his operas, *L'Incoronazione di Poppea* (1642), runs a dramatic impulse that is charged by revolutionary harmonic procedures and unresolved chords. He was virtually forgotten until the late nineteenth century, when Vincent d'Indy brought him to notice in France, and the twentieth, when the Italian composer Francesco Malipiero issued performing editions of his works and published his letters. Nadia Boulanger conducted a landmark recording of Monteverdi madrigals in 1937.

Madrigals: Book 8 (1638)
Deller Consort, Deller: Vanguard Classics OVC 2519

L'Incoronazione di Poppea (opera in three acts) (1642)
Augér, Jones, Hirst, Bowman, Reinhart, City of London Baroque Sinfonia, Hickox: Virgin Classics CDCC 59524
Donath, Söderström, Berberian, Esswood, Vienna Concentus Musicus, Harnoncourt: Telarc 2292-42547-2

GREGORIO ALLEGRI

(1582–1652) Italy

Allegri was born and died in Rome, giving his life to the service of the church. When he was a child, his sweet voice gained him a place as a chorister. After his voice broke, his smooth tenor was much in demand, and he obtained a position as singer at the chapel of Pope Urban VIII. He was said by temperament to be "of a singular gentleness and sweetness of soul and habit." His fame as a composer rests on the *Miserere* for nine voices in two choirs, a composition that was allowed to be performed only at the Sistine Chapel during Holy Week. The score was so relished for the delicacy and profundity of its sadness that for generations the manuscript was jealously guarded—copying it was a crime worthy of excommunication. During its Holy Week unveiling of 1770, the fourteen-year-old Mozart—perhaps nature's most perfect ear—rapidly notated it and broke the spell.

Miserere
German Bach Soloists: Christophers 74534
King's College Choir, Willcocks: EMI Classics CDC 47065-2

PART TWO

THE AGE OF
THE BAROQUE

The word *Baroque* is French (in Italian *Barocco*, in German *Barock*), stemming from the Portuguese *barroco*, meaning "misshapen pearl." The word was used most often in architecture, which during the Baroque period did indeed produce many a fantastic, misshapen structure: Baroque architecture is generally ornate, gilded, and grandiose. But there is a wide gulf between St. Paul's Cathedral and Versailles; the century and a half that passed between the first operas by Jacopo Peri and Claudio Monteverdi and J. S. Bach's *Art of the Fugue* saw many changes in art and society as well.

History of course is a complex, fluid process, and attempts to channel it into definite time periods are usually simplistic and often downright false. The arts do not evolve in tandem from country to country, and there are many overlappings. Is Monteverdi of the Renaissance or the Baroque? His *L'Orfeo* of 1607 is a revolutionary work, a primitive Baroque opera, while Shakespeare's *Hamlet* of 1601 is the zenith of Elizabethan Renaissance art. For most people, Bach represents Baroque music, but his sons merely considered him old-fashioned.

For convenience, however, we can generally divide the musical Baroque into three periods: the early Baroque (from, say, 1580 through 1620), the high Baroque (roughly 1620 to 1700), and the late Baroque (ending around 1750, with the last works of J. S. Bach, G. F. Handel, Domenico Scarlatti, Georg Philipp Telemann, and Jean Philippe Rameau).

During this century and a half, Europeans, recovering from the deadly plague, were procreating as never before. From a flat world, a global ocean way was opened. A new internationalism stirred as man painfully redefined a post-Copernican world. People no longer walked the earth as the center of the universe. All that had been previously known and believed in was either crushed or reevaluated, and long before Darwin, the shock of man's insignificance defined the future. Yet the Baroque age was basically optimistic, seething with change and teeming with men of genius. Indeed, one marvels at the frenzy of it all as humanity made the decision to swim upstream, to civilize itself, to make life fuller and more meaningful, to use awareness and creativity to operate in a seemingly senseless universe. As Renaissance formalism was shaken off, artistic knowledge increased and man was ready for his confrontation with science. The Baroque proved to be the dawn of the modern world, and what we most value stems from these first years of reason, when a flood of geniuses provided substance and faith.

What did all this mean for music? The Baroque era saw an immense expansion of music production. Patronage was ever increasing, and instrumental music flourished with new and perfected instruments. Fresh and vibrant forms were coming into being. Vocal writing was expanding with opera and oratorio. Chamber ensembles and small orchestras were rejoicing in concerti grossi and Baroque suites, with their variety of dance forms. Violin technique was fast expanding, as was organ technique. Harpsichord making was at its apogee, and Bach, François Couperin, and the French *clavecinistes* were creating a more sophisticated technique of harpsichord playing. Bach fulfilled fugal writing, the most demanding of the contrapuntal forms. A revolution in harmony was taking place, with rules for modulations (key changes) and a new availability of the twelve major and twelve minor keys. Our modern sense of tonal hearing was established in this period and must be considered one of Western civilization's supreme achievements.

The Baroque world came to fruition especially in France and had an almost hypnotic effect everywhere. The life of Louis XIV, the Sun King, spanned the high Baroque: he lived from 1638 to 1715 and had the longest reign in history, seventy-two years. The French call his reign the *grand siècle* and consider it their golden "classical age." From Louis's court radiated the etiquette and entertainments that we call civilization. Louis may claim the honor of being the grandest patron of the arts in history.

France was the most populous nation in Europe, with twenty million people ready to adorn themselves with the things of the good life. Paris became the capital of the Western world, and even seemingly minute advances there had long-lasting impacts. For example, in 1660 or thereabouts, napkins came to the table. Women's garments, coiffeurs, and perfumes were greatly admired and acquired. Thousands of other examples could be told. Indeed, the grand century is high civilization precisely because the minor arts and crafts were in demand. Hands were never at rest, always busy creating every sort of artifact. Nor was the body neglected. Louis adored the dance and made ballet the vogue, calling it "one of the most excellent and important disciplines for training the body." He also valued the theater as a stage for the transmission of ideas and the perfection of language. Molière, Racine, and Corneille forever changed the theater. Literature and literacy were in happy concord, from La Fontaine to Boileau.

Music was everywhere, at court and in the open air. The worldly energy emanating from Versailles and Paris made the public insatiable for opera and ballet. In the great salons, the princely harpsichord reigned, and one could listen to the insinuating performances of François Couperin "le Grand." Musicians had once been a lowly breed of vagabond, but Louis elevated his favorites, such as the Italian-born Jean-Baptiste Lully, to the nobility. When complaints arose at court, Louis told Lully, "I have honored them, not you, by placing a man of genius among them."

Nor was science neglected. Amidst firm reproach from the Church, the Académie des Sciences received its royal charter in 1666. If sculpture and painting produced lesser men, architecture was practiced on an unprecedented scale. We have come to equate Louis with the ultimate royal residence, Versailles, but as the historians Will and Ariel Durant pointed out, "It was . . . not so much a masterpiece of architecture as an invitation to live outdoors, amid a nature tamed and improved by art: to breathe the fragrance of flowers and trees, . . . to hear Lully and Molière under the open sky." It was in the *grand siècle* that the general status of women improved, and as the feminine influence leavened masculine harshness considerably, all countries took note. In women's fashionable salons, the arts and philosophy flourished. We still read the time-honored letters of Madame de Sévigné, in whose glorious style is distilled the sophistication of an age.

Across the Channel, we find England at the dawn of the Baroque concluding its mightiest period, with Shakespeare's death in 1616 and that of Byrd in 1623. The next decades would be a fallow period for the arts, as Oliver Cromwell and the Puritans held power, and a bleak time for creative endeavor. Theaters, previously a lifeline to ideas, were closed from 1642 until 1656. The only literacy that was encouraged was Bible reading, to avoid the fires of damnation. Although John Bunyan and John Milton both lived under Puritanism, Bunyan was heard to mutter, "I was of a low and inconsiderable generation." After twenty years of unrest and treachery, Charles II returned from exile, and the so-called Restoration began.

Charles, heavily influenced by the Sun King, soon brought French refinement to court, and everything bloomed. Nell Gwyn acted nightly at the Drury Lane Theatre. The horrific fire of 1666 in London wiped out two-thirds of the city, whereupon the architect Christopher Wren put the stamp of his genius on the city's new buildings. Sculpture and painting had been discouraged under Cromwell, so England had to import practitioners of these arts. Both Bunyan and Milton produced their greatest work during the Restoration, and *Paradise Lost*, completed in 1665, is the highest creation of the English Baroque.

Music, the most Dionysian of the arts, had been feared under Cromwell, and the majority of the populace had long forgotten their once-superb madrigal singing. But instrumental music was not so easily quelled. Samuel Pepys, the celebrated diarist, tells how important music was to him and his household, and during the great fire instruments of all sizes floated down the Thames, where their owners had thrown them in a desperate attempt to save them. Afterward organ building thrived. Charles and his successors incessantly demanded music while importing countless French and Italian musicians. Never before had music accompanied so many events, private and public, and always with splendid Baroque pomp.

During these years, England once again produced a musical genius in Henry Purcell, who was given only thirty-six years of life. Purcell codified all the Baroque forms in vocal and instrumental music. He put English opera on the musical map with his splendid *Dido and Aeneas*: Dido's lament "When I am laid in earth" still touches us. Dr. Charles Burney, the arbiter of musical taste in the eighteenth century, said that Purcell "so far surpassed whatever our country had produced or imported before, that all other musical compositions seem to have been instantly consigned to contempt or oblivion."

Within a short time, Purcell's achievements were obliterated by the English craze for Italian opera in general and by Handel's triumphant years in London. Indeed, England's native musical talent was demoralized by the might of Handel. The English language itself, however, was flourishing, and all able to read were devouring the work of Defoe, Addison, Steele, Swift, and others. The Royal Society of London for Improving Natural Knowledge was inaugurated in 1662, and it is noteworthy that poets and architects were among its elite charter members. Isaac Newton, a mystic-scientist, was the most thrilling scientific mind the world had yet seen. His *Principia* (1687) explained the force of gravity, and the human mind had never understood more. England, with a population of fewer than five million, was producing other elemental thinkers too, such as Hobbes and Locke. London became the hub of a fast-growing industrialization, with publications of all kinds democratizing the nation.

In the little Netherlands, there was also fervent activity, both intellectual and artistic. Spinoza, one of history's most influential philosophers, was born the same year (1632) as Locke. Vermeer's paintings showed a comfortable domestic world, while Hals portrayed the jollity of common life and Ruisdael the earthiness of Dutch landscape. Rembrandt, a colossus for the ages, produced an art of timeless universality. No important Dutch composer stood among them (the last Dutch master, Jan Sweelinck, died in 1621), but the Dutch were second to none in practicing music at home.

The Baroque in Spain also lacked musical genius; the high Renaissance master Victoria had died in 1611. The other arts were better represented, though, and in painting Velázquez loomed large. Spain's music lovers made up for their lack by importing Italian musicians like Domenico Scarlatti, whose greatest work was composed in Spain.

The Italian states had lost some of the luster and vitality of their fabled Renaissance years, but even in Counter-Reformation Rome, Bernini was busy sculpting throughout the city and the Vatican. Opera, which had been invented in Florence with Jacopo Peri's operas *Dafne* (1598) and *Euridice* (1600), became Italy's major form of entertainment, and operas by Alessandro Stradella, Alessandro Scarlatti, and dozens more, using castrato singers, were all the rage. In 1700 Venice alone had sixteen elaborate Baroque opera houses, all of which were filled nightly. Musical instruments were in heavy domestic demand. The violin began to supersede other stringed instruments in Lombardy during the seventeenth century. In Cremona the Amati, Guarneri, and Stradivari workshops created the instruments that spawned Italy's rich violin tradition and inspired the compositions of Antonio Vivaldi, Arcangelo Corelli, Giuseppe Tartini, Francesco Geminiani, Francesco Veracini, Pietro Locatelli, Gaetano Pugnani, and Pietro Nardini.

Instrumental music advanced, with such composers as Giovanni Vitali groping toward the thematic unity that eventually became classical sonata form. Corelli's *concerti grossi* constitute the link between the seventeenth and eighteenth centuries, and Handel and Bach's *concerti grossi* picked up where Corelli left off. Giuseppe Torelli in Bologna and Vivaldi in Venice gave scope to the solo concerto, with its rival soloist and orchestra in a tripartite structure. Vivaldi's rich instrumental coloring complements the sumptuous paintings of the last great Venetian painter, Tiepolo, who was working at the same time.

In Germany, the spirit of the Protestant Reformation still pervaded music of the early Baroque. The finest representative of this period is the highly endowed Heinrich Schütz, who had studied in Venice with Giovanni Gabrieli and later came into contact with Girolamo Frescobaldi. It was Schütz who brought the sumptuous Italian grand manner to Germany—and thereby brought Germany out of its musical provinciality. Schütz gave voice to the oratorio, an Italian form that had had a great impact on the work of Giacomo Carissimi, whose oratorios paved the way not only for Schütz but later for the vast fertility of Handel. Religious faith continued hand in hand with the rise of operas, oratorios, passions, and cantatas.

German high seriousness gave rise to an enormous instrumental wealth, and throughout the entire Baroque, German composers such as Johann Jacob

Froberger developed a cosmopolitan style based on the fugal works of Girolamo Frescobaldi and on the music of Jacques Chambonnières and Louis
Couperin (whom Froberger had met in Paris). The fusion of French dance
forms and Italian rhetorical flourish spurred a German organ and harpsichord
literature, by musicians such as Johann Pachelbel, Heinrich Biber, Johann
Reincken, Johann Kuhnau, and Johann Rosenmüller. This literature in turn
prepared the way for a more universal master, Dietrich Buxtehude, whose cantatas and especially organ music, utilizing the chorale, variations, preludes,
fugues, toccatas, and chaconnes, led to the supreme fulfillment of the Baroque
in the music of J. S. Bach, the most far-reaching composer to have yet been
born (and one of the greatest artists in any field). His work synthesized musical
thinking in all forms but the opera.

Aaron Copland observed, "What strikes me most markedly about Bach's
work is the marvelous rightness of it. It is the rightness not merely of a single individual but of a whole musical epoch . . . never since that time has music so
successfully fused contrapuntal skill with harmonic logic." So towering is Bach
that he has all but obliterated the other enormous achievements of his epoch,
as we are only beginning to appreciate in all of its manifold fullness. Music
needs an interpreter to gain life. Each new generation had removed important
works to make room for new ones, at least until musicology began to discover
what had been lost. Today listening freshly to music once thought dead, often
performed on "original" period instruments, has produced an exciting renova-
tion of the ear. More than ever, the Baroque is coming to light as one of the
great periods of musical history.

GEORGE FRIDERIC HANDEL

b. Halle, February 23, 1685

d. London, April 14, 1759

Whether I was in my body or out of my body as I wrote it, I know not. God knows.

— *after composing the "Hallelujah" Chorus*

Georg Händel, a successful barber-surgeon, was sixty-three when Georg Friederich (better known as George Frideric), the only son of his second marriage, was born. Georg considered music to be a low trade and forbade the boy to study it. With his mother's secret help, however, young George soon taught himself the clavichord and organ. By chance, a visiting aristocrat, the duke of Saxe-Weissenfels, heard the child of seven playing the organ and convinced his father that the boy had an unusual talent. The duke persuaded the elder Händel to let his son study with F. W. Zachow, an organist in Halle. After three rigorous years, Zachow felt he had nothing more to offer the boy, and Handel (as he later spelled his name) never needed another teacher. His father died when he was just eleven, and young Handel entered the university at seventeen, determined at first to honor his father's last wish that he should become a lawyer. But his musical gifts begged for expression, and in 1703 he abandoned the law and moved to Hamburg. There he procured a position as second violinist in the orchestra of the opera, whose powerful director was the well-known composer Reinhard Keiser.

It was in Hamburg that Handel's first opera, *Almira*, was successfully produced, on January 8, 1705. There, too, Handel's notorious temper first became noticeable. He fought a duel with an equally hot-headed young singer-composer, Johann Mattheson; fortunately, the duel was stopped before it became fatal. (This was only the first of many incidents; in 1723, in London, the celebrated prima donna Francesca Cuzzoni refused to sing one of Handel's arias. The composer, a giant of a man, had to be bodily restrained from throwing her out a third-story window.)

By 1706 the Hamburg Opera, plagued with petty squabbles, could offer Handel no more fresh opportunities. The young composer, always ready for adventure, set his sights on music-loving Italy, despite his complete lack of money, connections, or knowledge of Italian. For the next four years, Il Sassone (the Saxon), as he was called, divided his time among Florence, Rome, Naples, and Venice, making lasting impressions as an organist and harpsichordist and writing *Rodrigo*, the first of his many Italian operas. In Italy he developed a keen appreciation for painting and began what would eventually become a valuable collection of Italian masters and Rembrandts.

After these productive years, Handel was lured back to Germany in 1710 with an appointment as *Kapellmeister* to the Hanover court. (The *Kapellmeister* was the highest-ranking court musician, a prestigious and influential post.) Only months after his engagement began, he asked for a leave of absence: an invitation had arrived from the Queen's Theatre in London to compose an opera. The leave was granted, and in two weeks he wrote *Rinaldo*, which was produced to great fanfare in London and proved a resounding success. Although he resented returning to Hanover, he did so and stayed at his post until 1712. Restless and longing for a larger arena, he begged his employer, the elector of Hanover, to permit him to visit London once again, if only for a few weeks. Handel left and never returned. In 1714 that same elector ascended the British throne as George I. Much to Handel's relief, the monarch forgave him his delinquency.

Life in London was exciting. The English capital, on the brink of the industrial revolution, was bursting with vitality and commerce. Handel wrote orchestral music (including the famous *Water Music*) and became a clever opera impresario, with a keen eye for publicity that enabled him to make money easily. For the English aristocracy, Italian opera had for years been all the rage, and Handel composed numerous operas in Italian for some of the finest singers in history, including the castrati Nicolini and Gizzielo. The immortal Farinelli, alas, sang for the rival opera house. Handel developed a rivalry with the popular Italian composer Giovanni Bononcini, who was also in London. The rivalry has survived in John Byron's doggerel verse:

> *Some say, that Signor Bononcini,*
> *Compar'd to Handel's a mere ninny;*

> *Others aver, to him, that Handel*
> *Is scarcely fit to hold a candle.*
> *Strange! that such high dispute should be*
> *Twixt Tweedledum and Tweedledee.*

Arriving in London just seventeen years after the early death of Henry Purcell, Handel assumed musical leadership in a nation that had yet to produce another musician of the first rank. In 1727 he became a British subject and a source of national pride; calling him a German composer amounted to an insult.

But by the middle 1720s the English appetite for Italian opera had diminished, and a new populist form of theater was appealing to a wider audience. The year 1728 saw an unprecedented theatrical hit: *The Beggar's Opera* (with text by John Gay and arrangements of popular ballads by John Pepusch). Handel continued writing Italian opera but in the process went bankrupt. He needed a new vehicle. He had always been powerfully attracted to religious music, but in increasingly secular London, a mercantile society inspired by Enlightenment ideals, people did not turn out in droves for church music. Instead, he realized, religion had to be woven into the fabric of life. He hit on the idea of the oratorio—a vocal work based on biblical themes but sung in English and performed in a theater. In time his oratorios would far surpass his operas in popularity and provide him with financial comfort.

Handel's first oratorio in English was *Esther* (1732), but not until *Saul* and *Israel in Egypt* (both produced in 1739) did he perfect the form. From then on, Covent Garden heard a new Handel oratorio each season. In 1751, while he was composing *Jephtha*, he began to have trouble with his eyesight. He wrote on the manuscript, "I reached here on Wednesday February 13,—had to discontinue on account of the sight in my left eye." Ten days later he added, "Feel a little better, resumed work." After completing *Jephtha*, he underwent three unsuccessful operations by the same surgeon who had failed to save Bach's vision. (One can only imagine what such operations were like, in the days of primitive instruments and no anesthesia.) By 1753 Handel was completely blind and unable to compose. For the remaining six years of his life, he still played the organ and conducted. On April 6, 1759, he arrived at Covent Garden to conduct a performance of the already popular *Messiah*. The audience rose and gave the composer a thunderous and tearful ovation, but the strain was beyond him; he collapsed before completing the performance and was carried home to bed. He died eight days later, early on the morning of Saturday, April 14. He had wanted to die the day before, on Good Friday, "in the hope of rejoining my sweet Lord and Saviour on the day of the Resurrection."

All of England grieved. After almost half a century of residence, he had become a national treasure. More than three thousand mourners attended his
elaborate funeral. Above Handel's tomb in Westminster Abbey is a statue of the
composer at a table with the score of Messiah opened to "I know that my Re-
deemer liveth." His work was everything to Handel, and in fact little is known
of his personal life. He never married.

After his death and throughout the nineteenth century, Handel's oratorios
and choral works continued to resound and inspire Victorian society, and his
bracing optimism appeared to mirror English values. In the first quarter of the
nineteenth century, while J. S. Bach's music was almost forgotten, Handel's
complete works were published in London. In the last months of his life,
Beethoven received from the Philharmonic Society in London a gift of the
Handel publications. Beethoven had always admired Handel's music, but seeing it all together, he was astounded at the variety and wealth of his invention.
"To him I bend the knee," he proclaimed, "for Handel is the greatest, ablest
composer that ever lived. I can still learn from him."

But the twentieth century was not kind to Handel. Aside from seasonal air-
ings of Messiah, he is scarcely performed in any proportion to his voluminous
output and worth. His old-fashioned Baroque operas are rarely staged, and the
oratorios—once the mainstay of now-defunct choral societies—also lie dormant. A few of his orchestral works have fared better, but it is clear that for our
age, Handel's emotional directness, his healthy vigor, and his simple faith seem
no longer to stir us as they once did. Fortunately, large segments of his work are
preserved through recording, and one may listen to the gigantic range of his
art, from the touching arias in his forgotten operas to the wealth of church music, secular cantatas, anthems, Te Deums, chamber works, harpsichord suites,
organ concertos, and concerti grossi. His music is a sumptuous feast from the
late Baroque waiting for those who wish to listen beyond Messiah, Music for
the Royal Fireworks, and Water Music.

Water Music (1717)

In the summertime, King George I, like many wealthy Londoners, was fond of
lavish river excursions on the Thames. The excursions usually included music,
sometimes commissioned by the king himself. On July 17, 1717, newspapers
reported the premiere of a new Handel work on one such excursion: "On
Wednesday Evening at about 8, the King took Water at Whitehall in an open
Barge. . . . Many other Barges with Persons of Quality attended, and so great a
Number of Boats, that the whole River in a manner was cover'd." Fifty musi-

cians performed the hour-long score, and the musical monarch was so delighted that he listened to the piece three times that night. *Water Music* consists of three suites: ten selections in Suite I, five in Suite II, and four in Suite III. Handel's most majestic and fetching manner is on display, and *Water Music* is surely one of the most joyous orchestral scores of the early eighteenth century. It was widely performed in Handel's day.

English Baroque Soloists, Gardiner: Philips 434122-2
English Chamber Orchestra, Pinnock: Deutsche Grammophon 410525-2
Stuttgart Chamber Orchestra, Münchinger: London 417743-2

Twelve *Concerti grossi,* Op. 6 (1739)

These *concerti grossi* are resplendent representatives of this primary form of Baroque instrumental music. The form was crystallized around 1700 by Giuseppe Torelli, who made prominent use of the solo violin; then it was passed to Arcangelo Corelli, whose splendid *concerti grossi* Handel had heard and admired while in Rome in 1708. Handel's *concerti grossi* possess a marvelous inventiveness, often displaying lusty vitality and exhilarating energy. Italianate melodiousness and Handel's typical dignity and grandeur make these "grand" *concerti* a treasure of the Baroque (surpassing even the wonderful series of six *concerti grossi* in Op. 3). That they were composed in a continual stream of inspiration within thirty-one days in 1739 seems incomprehensible. With Bach's six *Brandenburg Concertos,* they are the supreme examples of the form.

English Chamber Orchestra, Leppard: Philips 426465-2
Academy of St. Martin in the Fields, Brown: Philips 410048-2

Messiah (1742)

In a 1743 letter, Horace Walpole wrote: "Handel's oratorios thrive abundantly. For my part, they give me an idea of heaven, where everybody is to sing whether they have voices or not." Handel's genius shines in the hundreds of pages of his oratorios. There is so much to admire in *Saul, Samson, Solomon, Theodora, Susanna, Esther, Hercules, Joshua, Belshazzar, Jephtha, Judas Maccabaeus,* and *Israel in Egypt* (which Romain Rolland called "the most gigantic effort ever made in the oratorio") that if *Messiah* had never been composed, these works would be far better known. But *Messiah* is overwhelming. It remains the oratorio of the ages. The impressive score was composed in twenty-four days of unrelieved labor and creative ecstasy. The overweight master barely ate and hardly slept. During its creation, he feverishly muttered to a servant, "I think I did see all Heaven before me, and the great God Himself."

After its initial performance in Dublin, it was introduced to London on March 23, 1743, with George II attending. Upon hearing the "Hallelujah" Chorus, the transfixed king rose to his feet, a gesture that has been followed ever since. *Messiah* abounds in famous choruses and arias, each unfolding with an awesome cumulative power in over two and a half hours of music. So popular did it become that in mid-nineteenth-century London, it was said that "there are at all times more than four thousand singers and instrumentalists capable of executing it from memory and without notes."

Augér, von Otter, Chance, Crook, English Chamber Orchestra and Concert Choir, Pinnock: Archiv (DG) 423630-2

Harper, Watts, Shirley-Quirk, Wakefield, London Symphony Orchestra and Chorus, Davis: Philips 438356-2

Te Kanawa, Gjevang, Lewis, Howell, Chicago Symphony Orchestra and Chorus, Solti: London 414396-2

Music for the Royal Fireworks (1749)

The *Fireworks* music was composed in 1749 to celebrate the Treaty of Aix-la-Chapelle, which ended the War of the Austrian Succession. Twelve thousand people heard it in rehearsal at Vauxhall Gardens on April 21. The music was intended to accompany a grand fireworks display in Green Park on April 27. The event was extremely popular—crossing London Bridge by carriage that day took up to three hours—but it turned into a fiasco when only twenty percent of the bombs and rockets ignited, and the structure built to launch the display caught fire. Fortunately, posterity has been blessed with Handel's music. The large-scale festive overture is ceremonial music at its best; the other movements, slighter in proportion, are a delight. They are Bourrée, La Paix (Largo alla Siciliana), La Réjouissance (Allegro), Menuet I, and Menuet II.

English Concert, Pinnock: Archiv 431707-2

English Chamber Orchestra, Leppard: Philips 420354-2

RCA Victor Symphony Orchestra, Stokowski: Victrola 7817-2-RV

Cleveland Symphonic Winds, Fennell: Telarc 80038 (original wind scoring)

OTHER PRINCIPAL WORKS

CHAMBER MUSIC
Six flute sonatas
Six recorder sonatas
Six violin sonatas
Various trio sonatas

CHURCH MUSIC
Dixit Dominus (1707)*
Eleven *Chandos Anthems* (1717–18)*
Coronation Anthems for George II (1727)*
Dettingen Te Deum (1743)

CONCERTOS
Sixteen concertos for organ and orchestra*

HARPSICHORD MUSIC
Twelve suites (No. 5 includes the air and variations known as "The Harmonious Black-smith")

ITALIAN CANTATAS FOR VARIOUS VOICES AND INSTRUMENTS
"Ah! crudel, nel pianto mio" (1707)*
Armida abbandonata (1707)*
Agrippina condotta a morire (1708)
Apollo e Dafne (1708)
"Cecilia, volgi un sguardo" (1736)

ORATORIOS
Esther (1732)*
Deborah (1733)*
Saul (1739)*
Israel in Egypt (1739)*
Samson (1743)*
Belshazzar (1745)*
Judas Maccabaeus (1747)*
Joshua (1748)
Susanna (1749)
Solomon (1749)*
Theodora (1752)*
Jephtha (1752)*

ORCHESTRAL MUSIC
Six *concerti grossi*, Op. 3*

OPERAS
Radamisto (1720)*
Ottone, Ré di Germania (1723)*
Giulio Cesare (1724)*
Alcina (1735)*
Serse (Xerxes) (1738)*

SECULAR CHORAL WORKS
Acis and Galatea (1718)*
Alexander's Feast (1736)*
Ode for St. Cecilia's Day (1739)*

JOHANN SEBASTIAN BACH

b. Eisenach, Germany, March 21, 1685

d. Leipzig, July 28, 1750

I was obliged to work hard. Whoever is equally industrious will succeed just as well.

Johann Sebastian Bach was born into the most prodigiously musical family of all time, one that produced gifted musicians from the sixteenth century through the eighteenth. The organist and humanitarian Albert Schweitzer wrote about them: "It appeared self-evident that one day a Bach must arise in whom all those other Bachs [would] live again and forever and in whom the portion of German music incarnate in this family [would] find its fulfillment. Johann Sebastian Bach is, to use Kant's language, a historical postulate."

Johann Sebastian's father, Johann Ambrosius, was a fine musician. Unfortunately, both he and his wife, Maria Elisabeth, died when Johann Sebastian was only nine. Sebastian was sent off to live with his eldest brother, Johann Christoph, the organist at Ohrdruf, who resented having an extra mouth to feed. Sebastian attended the local lyceum, where he studied Latin, Greek, history, geography, composition—and a smattering of music. Christoph was unwilling to extend the boy's musical education, but Sebastian was a survivor and learned to adapt to every circumstance—a trait that proved useful in a life filled with endless obligations.

From his earliest years, Johann Sebastian was deeply religious. His Lutheran faith and the purity of his religious spirit fed his all-consuming musical passion. When he was fifteen, he obtained a position as choirboy in a church school in Lüneburg, which enabled him to leave his brother's harsh household. His eyesight was already weakened from copying by moonlight manuscripts that his brother had forbidden him to study.

It was at this time that Bach's genius for the organ began to ripen. He often listened to the renowned organist Georg Böhm, who urged young Bach to listen to his own teacher, Johann Adam Reincken. Reincken, at eighty, still played the organ with fire. Bach was impressed and whenever possible made the thirty-mile trek to Hamburg to listen to the old master. Reincken appreciated the youngster's ability and was delighted by Bach's already prodigious improvisational skills. At eighteen, Bach took a post as organist at an important new church in Arnstadt. During the previous few years, he had begun composing, and on Easter Sunday 1704, his first cantata was performed at his church at Arnstadt.

Though Bach's appointment at Arnstadt was an important and prestigious one, he found the town limited and the church authorities, to whom he reported, rigid. Still in his teens, he was rebellious and eager to learn from great musicians in other towns. The magnificent organist Dietrich Buxtehude was in the twilight of his career, and in the fall of 1704 Bach asked his employers for a short leave to hear him perform at Lübeck. Bach, convinced that he had much to learn from Buxtehude, stayed away for four months. The church authorities were hardly sympathetic to their wayward organist—but neither was Bach pleased with their parochial attitude toward his development, and he did not hesitate to tell them so. Although Bach has often been thought of as a passive and pious musician, the real Bach could fight furiously for what he felt was his due in the highly competitive musical world.

His term at Arnstadt would be short-lived, however. Both Bach and the church council decided to terminate his stay, and in 1707 he became organist at Mühlhausen. At the same time, the twenty-two-year-old Bach married his second cousin, Maria Barbara. In 1708 he left Mühlhausen, to spend the next nine years at the ducal chapel in Weimar as chamber musician and court organist. The Weimar years were productive, especially of organ music, and Bach came to be known as one of the best organists of the time—perhaps the best. Some, however, considered the French organist Louis Marchand to be peerless. In 1717 both organists happened to be in Dresden, and a contest was arranged. On the morning of the appointed day, legend has it, the Frenchman heard Bach improvising and was so intimidated that he hurriedly left town.

Not long after, Bach became unhappy with his situation at Weimar. He was passed over when the court appointed a new *Kapellmeister*, and he began to look elsewhere. Prince Leopold of Anhalt-Cöthen, a devoted amateur musician, was deeply affected by Bach's ability and offered him the prestigious post of *Kapellmeister* at Cöthen. The duke of Weimar, piqued by Bach's defection from his contract, had him arrested, and Bach was imprisoned from November 6 until December 2, 1717. Once Bach regained his freedom, he moved his household to Cöthen. His great organ period was over.

Bach devoted the next five years at Cöthen mainly to composing instrumental music, which included the *Chromatic Fantasia and Fugue* (BWV 903), the two- and three-part inventions (BWV 772–786, 787–801), the *French Suites* (BWV 812–817), the *English Suites* (BWV 806–811), the partitas (BWV 825–830), and the first book of *The Well-Tempered Clavier* for harpsichord (BWV 846–869). For orchestra he composed concertos for various instruments, the four orchestral suites (BWV 1066–1069), and the *Brandenburg Concertos* (BWV 1046–1051). At court Bach conducted, while Prince Leopold often played in the orchestra.

Maria Barbara died in the summer of 1720, less than three years after the family had arrived at Cöthen. She left her husband with seven surviving children, all of them, as Bach noted with pride, "born musicians." Bach took special care with their musical education; then-six-year-old Carl Philipp Emanuel would grow up to become *Kapellmeister* to Frederick the Great and a more famous composer than his father—in his own time, that is. Bach was in desperate need of a new wife and mother for his children, and on December 3, 1721, he married twenty-year-old Anna Magdalena Wilcken, "a good clear soprano." Soon she would provide him with many more children to support.

Bach, who had been close to Prince Leopold, was now alarmed that "my gracious prince who both loved and understood music and in whose service I hoped to live out the rest of my days . . . grew rather lukewarm." The reason was his recent marriage to a frivolous princess, whom Bach saw as interfering with the court's musical life. The situation soon became intolerable, and Bach looked for new employment.

In 1723 he found it in Leipzig, as director of music and cantor (teacher) at the school affiliated with the Church of St. Thomas. His "audition" piece was no less than the *St. John Passion* (BWV 245, 1724; rev. 1725). Although Bach was well disposed to compose church music, he was upset that the position of cantor was lower in status than that of his previous position of *Kapellmeister*. After seven years in Leipzig, he complained to a friend that he wanted to seek his fortune elsewhere, because "1. the position is not nearly so advantageous as I had believed; 2. many of the incidental fees have been withdrawn; 3. this town is very expensive to live in; 4. the authorities are queer folk, little devoted to music, so that I have to endure almost constant annoyance, vexation, and persecution." He never left the Leipzig post, however, and toiled there for the twenty-seven years that remained to him, writing the *St. Matthew Passion* (BWV 244, 1727), the *Christmas Oratorio* (BWV 248, 1734–35), more than three hundred cantatas, the B minor mass (BWV 232, c.1747–49), the second book of *The Well-Tempered Clavier* (BWV 870–893, 1742), and much more. It was a staggering creative achievement.

Bach's eyesight continued to worsen, and by the end of 1749, he was nearly blind. An operation by an English surgeon, John Taylor, was an utter failure; it made Bach completely blind, and soon afterward a stroke partially paralyzed him. Ten days before his death, some vision returned, and he used the time to revise parts of *The Art of the Fugue* (BWV 1080). He was buried in St. John's churchyard, apparently with no headstone or inscription. As his music was forgotten, so was his grave. His wife Anna Magdalena lived for ten more years and then died in the town's poorhouse. It was not until 1894, during church renovations, that Bach's remains were located and identified with certainty.

Bach's only known assessment of his art is simply "I worked hard." In his time he was best known as an organist, and his compositions (only a few of which were published) were seldom heard after their first performance. He composed with an amazing intensity and concentration and appeared to hold no judgment about the worth of his works, nor to give any thought to their survival. Most likely he would be astonished at his leading place in music history.

Bach lived during a gradual change in European music, but he was unconcerned that his beloved polyphony, or counterpoint (the simultaneous use of several voices or melodies), was being replaced by simpler homophonic music (melody with accompaniment). He was essentially of the past, and the newer *style galant* and its forms meant nothing to him. His own sons considered him to be hopelessly old-fashioned, although they admired his general musicianship.

After his death a few connoisseurs and keyboard players knew a small portion of his work, and in the second half of the eighteenth century, several of his manuscripts were copied and circulated among discerning musicians. It was not until around 1830, through the efforts of Felix Mendelssohn and other musicians, that he became at all known. As the vast quantity of his work was finally published, it became apparent that this humble craftsman lived in the climate of the sublime—not at rare moments or in a few masterworks but throughout a lifetime of boundless creation. No other composer celebrates human potential the way Bach does—potential that is, for him, ruled by the eternal presence of God. Aldous Huxley wrote of Bach that his music is "a manifestation, on the plane of art, of perpetual creation, a demonstration of the necessity of death and the self-evidence of immortality, an expression of the essential all-rightness of the universe—for the music was far beyond tragedy, but included death and suffering with everything else in the divine impartiality which is the *One*, which is *Love*, which is *Being*. . . . Who on Earth was John Sebastian? Certainly not the old gent with sixteen children in a . . . stuffy Protestant environment!"

In every form Bach touched, he stands alone. There is no greater series of organ works. The harpsichord music is one of the towering achievements of the Baroque. One could call *The Well-Tempered Clavier* music's essential dictionary, and the *Goldberg Variations* show Bach as a supreme variationist.

Most likely Bach's ear was the most subtly attuned of any musician's. He was the mightiest contrapuntalist who ever lived, and his inconceivable mastery of fugue—the most cerebral of music's forms—ranks him among the greatest intelligences. Merely to copy out his music pushes the limits of one lifetime. No wonder Richard Wagner called him "the most stupendous miracle in all music."

Suites no. 1–4 for Orchestra, BWV 1066–1069 (dates unknown)

The four orchestral suites are majestic examples of the spirit of the late Baroque. They were composed for Prince Leopold of Anhalt-Cöthen during Bach's tenure at Cöthen from 1717 to 1723. Suite no. 2 in B minor and no. 3 in D major are the popular favorites. The first movements of the suites are of extraordinary vitality and majesty. After the overture, Bach proceeded to use various dance forms, such as the gavotte, forlane, polonaise, bourrée, and minuet. The Suite no. 2 is scored for flute and orchestra; the air from the D major suite is one of Bach's best-known movements.

Academy of St. Martin in the Fields, Marriner: London 430378-2
English Concert, Pinnock: Deutsche Grammophon 439780-2

Six Suites for Solo Violoncello, BWV 1007–1012 (c.1720)

The six cello suites are the cellist's bible. They demand unmitigated labor and devotion. Once again Bach's ability seems superhuman; he took the cello and pushed it far beyond its apparent limitations. The suites were a closed book until they fell into the hands of thirteen-year-old Pablo Casals, who in his memoir *Joys and Sorrows* tells of browsing in an old music shop in Barcelona, coming upon "a sheaf of pages, crumbled and discolored with age. They were unaccompanied Suites by Johann Sebastian Bach—For the Cello only! . . . For the following eighty years the wonder of my discovery has continued to grow on me. . . . I studied and worked at them every day for the next twelve years, and I would be twenty-five before I had the courage to play one of the Suites in public."

Casals: EMI Classics CDH 61028-2 and CDH 61029-2
Bylsma: Sony Classical S2K 48047
Fournier: Deutsche Grammophon 419359-2
Starker: Mercury 432756-2

Three Sonatas and Three Partitas for Solo Violin, BWV 1001–1006 (c.1720)

Demanding an indomitable will and a complete grasp of the violin as well as high musicianship, these six works for unaccompanied violin stand alone in the instrument's literature. The best-known movement of the group is the great Chaconne that concludes Partita no. 2, an awesome edifice built on four strings.

Milstein: Deutsche Grammophon 423294-2
Perlman: EMI Classics ZDCB 49483-2
Kremer: Philips 416651-2
Heifetz: RCA 7708-2-RG

Six *Brandenburg Concertos*, BWV 1046–1051 (1721)

Like the orchestral suites, the *Brandenburg Concertos* were composed for Prince Leopold. Bach called them "Six Concertos with Various Instruments." By an error of history, they received their present name because the only copies that survived were those Bach sent to Ludwig, margrave of Brandenburg. They were rediscovered after languishing there for 120 years.

The *Brandenburgs* are the apex of *concerto grosso* writing. Each one is in three movements and throbs with the pulse of genius. No. 5 possesses an elaborate and electrifying harpsichord part.

Of the concertos, Albert Schweitzer wrote, "The *Brandenburg Concertos* are the purest revelation of Bach's polyphonic style. Neither on the organ nor on the keyboard could he have worked out the architectonic structures of a piece with such vitality." One wonders what Bach really thought when he wrote to the margrave on March 21, 1721: "I humbly pray for you not to judge their imperfection by the severity of that fine and delicate taste which everyone knows you have for music, but rather to consider benignly the profound respect and humble obedience to which I have intended them to testify." The margrave obviously had no idea of the treasures that Bach had sent him.

Academy of Ancient Music, Hogwood: London 414187-2
Berlin Philharmonic Orchestra, Karajan: Deutsche Grammophon 415374-2

The Well-Tempered Clavier, Book I, BWV 846–869 (1722), and Book II, BWV 870–893 (1738–42)

The Well-Tempered Clavier is a landmark in the history of music. The keyboard instruments of the Baroque could not play in tune in all keys. They were tuned in the "mean tone" system, which was based on the slightly unequal division of intervals of string instruments. The "well-tempered" or "equal-tempered" system, by contrast, tuned the instrument to the fixed, equally divided pitches of the chromatic scale, so it would stay in tune in all the keys. The practicality and rigidity of equal-tempered tuning necessitated a loss of certain subtleties that are available to string players, such as the real difference between G sharp and A flat. But the advantages far outweighed the disadvantages, as the major and minor scales were becoming indispensable to the composition of harmonically implied music. Bach's advocacy of the twelve-tone chromatic system through these forty-eight preludes and fugues in the twelve major and twelve minor keys gave added prestige to equal-tempered tuning. *The Well-Tempered Clavier* laid the foundations of modern harmonic practice and, in the pianist and writer Ernest Hutcheson's words, is "a treasury of musical scholarship, giving final definition to instrumental counterpoint and fugue."

PERFORMED ON HARPSICHORD
Landowska: RCA 6217-2-RC and 7825-2-RC

PERFORMED ON PIANO
Gould: Sony Classical SM2K 52600 and SM2K 52603
J. C. Martins: Concord Concerto 1343-12019-2

Concerto in A Minor for Violin, BWV 1041 (1717–23)
Concerto in E Major for Violin, BWV 1042 (1717–23)

Written at Cöthen, for its discriminating court audience, these works are the finest German violin concertos of the period. They do not use the soloist as "prima donna"; in fact, they have nothing of the violinistic brilliance of the Italian violin concertos that were being written at that time by Vivaldi and others. Yet neither are they chamber music or *concerti grossi*. The A minor concerto is sober, while a driving exuberance propels the E major concerto, with its hushed Adagio slow movement.

Mutter, English Chamber Orchestra, Accardo: EMI Classics CDC 47005-2
Grumiaux, New Philharmonia Orchestra, De Waart: Philips 420700

Concerto in D Minor for Two Violins and Orchestra, BWV 1043 (1717–23)

Bach's concertos are modeled on Vivaldi's tripartate form of fast-slow-fast. They use *ritornello* form, in which an orchestral passage is stated complete at the start of a movement and then returns, either complete or in part, in between the solo areas. (The Italian word *ritornare* means "to return.") A *double concerto* is a concerto for two solo instruments; the contrapuntal skill and the magnificent dialogue between the two violin soloists make the D minor concerto the most profound of Bach's concertos. The first movement is proud, leading to a glorious Baroque slow movement. Here, the two violins answer each other in music of visionary illumination, against the orchestra's simple harmonic backdrop. The Allegro continues the concerto's contrapuntal pace of compelling motion but halts for a melody of simple and noble beauty.

Perlman, Zukerman, English Chamber Orchestra, Barenboim: EMI Classics CDC 47856-2
Szeryng, Hasson, Academy of St. Martin in the Fields, Marriner: Philips 422250-2

Organ Music (various dates)

If Bach had composed nothing but organ music, he would still be immortal. In his youth he played with unprecedented passion and ferocity. Members of the Arnstadt city council warned, "If Bach continues to play in this way, the organ will be ruined in two years, or most of the congregation will be deaf."

Since Bach's time, all organ composition has been defined by his contribution. After hearing Bach on the organ, Goethe wrote: "It is as though eternal harmony were converging with itself, as it may have happened in God's bosom shortly before He created the world."

Of the forty-six chorale preludes that make up the *Orgelbüchlein* (*Little Organ Book*), Albert Schweitzer wrote, "The *Orgelbüchlein* is not only of significance in the story of the development of the chorale prelude, but it is itself one of the greatest events in music." Among Bach's most frequently played organ works are the Passacaglia and Fugue in C Minor (BWV 582); Toccata, Adagio, and Fugue in C Major (BWV 564); Toccata and Fugue in D Minor (BWV 538); and the Fantasia and Fugue in G Minor (BWV 542).

Selected Organ Works
Biggs: Sony Classical SBK 46551
Koopman: Novalis 150036-2
Rilling: Denon 7809

Orgelbüchlein (BWV 599–644)
Preston: Deutsche Grammophon 431816-2

St. Matthew Passion, BWV 244 (1727)

A passion is basically an oratorio that is performed during Holy Week and that recounts the last suffering and death of Jesus Christ. Anton Ehrenzweig writes: "Bach's *St. Matthew Passion* is perhaps the most heart-rending mourning for the dying Christ in our art. There is no hint of the coming resurrection, no hope of rebirth; it is indeed the true emotional acceptance of death." The *St. Matthew Passion* was first performed on Good Friday in 1727. Words fail at the eloquence of this cosmic structure, in which Bach fuses his Lutheranism with much personal symbolism into a compassionate universe of feeling, controlled by an awesome mind.

Schwarzkopf, Ludwig, Gedda, Fischer-Dieskau, Berry, Philharmonia Orchestra and Chorus, Klemperer: EMI Classics ZDMC 63058
Schreier, Adam, Popp, Lipousek, Buchner, Holl, Leipzig Radio Chorus, Staatskapelle Dresden, Schreier: Philips 412527-2
Bonney, Monoyios, von Otter, Chance, Crook, Rolfe, Johnson, English Baroque Soloists, Monteverdi Choir, Gardiner: Archiv 427648-2

Goldberg Variations, BWV 988 (1741)

Today many think that Bach's keyboard music sounds best and most "authentic" on the harpsichord, but it is often performed on the piano. Bach was familiar with early pianos, but he had no true sympathy for them, so his keyboard music always intentionally favored the harpsichord. Claudio Arrau has summed up the problem this way: "Any shades of crescendo and diminuendo and other inflections which can only be achieved on a modern piano hinder Bach's meaning. These qualities of the piano creep into Bach whether you like it or not." Bach's keyboard music, however, will continue to be shared by both pianists and harpsichordists. The Six *English Suites*, the Six *French Suites*, the Six Partitas, the *Italian Concerto*, the *Chromatic Fantasia and Fugue*, and the two- and three-part inventions are of the highest importance to Baroque keyboard music.

The *Goldberg Variations* are the Mount Everest of Baroque variation writing. A Count Keyserling supposedly commissioned them from Bach. Goldberg was a pupil of Bach's employed by Keyserling, who suffered from insomnia. The story goes that poor Goldberg was often awakened by his master's call. "Dear Goldberg," said the count, "please come and play me one of *my* variations."

Musically speaking, the pianist and writer Charles Rosen asserts, "The elegance of the *Goldberg Variations* is its glory. It is the most worldly of Bach's achievements, with the Italian Concerto. . . . Except for the *St. Matthew Passion*, in no work is the depth of Bach's spirit so easily accessible, and its significance so tangible."

PERFORMED ON HARPSICHORD
Newman: Newport Classic NC 60024
Landowska: RCA 09026-60919-2

PERFORMED ON PIANO
Gould: The 1955 and 1981 versions
Sony classical 9699-87703-2)

Mass in B Minor, BWV 232 (c.1747–49)

The B minor mass is less personal in quality than the *St. Matthew Passion*, which defines its expression within the context of the aria. The B minor mass is more objective, with a tremendous use of the chorus. It is neither a conventional Catholic mass nor completely Lutheran in its theology. It stands alone as the spiritual journey of a man in awe of and humbled before his creator.

Augér, Murray, Lipovsek, Scharinger, Leipzig Radio Choir, Staatskapelle Dresden, Schreier:
   Philips 432972-2
Giebel, Baker, Gedda, Prey, Crass, New Philharmonia Orchestra, BBC Chorus, Klemperer:
   EMI Classics ZDMB 63364-2

OTHER PRINCIPAL WORKS

CHURCH MUSIC

Six motets, BWV 225–230 (1723–30)*
St. John Passion, BWV 245 (1724; rev. 1725)*
Magnificat in D Major, BWV 243 (c.1728–31)*
Christmas Oratorio, BWV 248 (1734–35)*
Easter Oratorio, BWV 249 (1732–35)
More than two hundred cantatas*

CONCERTOS

Seven concertos for harpsichord and orchestra, BWV 1052–1058
  No. 1 in D minor*
Concerto in C Minor for Violin, Oboe, and Strings, BWV 1060*
Three concertos for two harpsichords and strings, BWV 1060–1062
Two concertos for three harpsichords and strings, BWV 1063–1064*
Concerto in A Minor for Four Harpsichords and Strings, BWV 1065*

KEYBOARD WORKS

Fifteen two-part inventions, BWV 772–786 (1723)*
Fifteen three-part inventions, BWV 787–801 (1723)*
Six *English Suites*, BWV 806–811 (c.1715)*
Six *French Suites*, BWV 812–817*
Six partitas, BWV 825–830 (1726)*
Chromatic Fantasia and Fugue, BWV 903 (c.1720, rev. c.1730)*
Seven Toccatas, BWV 910–916 (1708–c.1738)*
Italian Concerto, BWV 971 (1735)*
The Art of the Fugue, BWV 1080 (c.1745–50)*

SOLO INSTRUMENT AND KEYBOARD WORKS

Six sonatas for violin and continuo, BWV 1014–1019 (1717–23)*
Six sonatas for flute and continuo, BWV 1030–1035 (1717–23)*

DOMENICO SCARLATTI

b. Naples, October 26, 1685

d. Madrid, July 23, 1757

Dear reader, whether you are a dilettante or a professor, do not expect to find in these compositions any profound intention, but rather, an ingenious jesting of the art, to prepare you for bold playing on the harpsichord. . . . Show yourself more human than critical, and thus you will increase your own pleasure. . . . LIVE HAPPILY.

—Scarlatti, from the preface to the first publication of his sonatas

Domenico Scarlatti was the sixth of ten musically gifted children of Alessandro Scarlatti, one of the most illustrious composers in Italy, known and respected throughout Europe. Alessandro was the most celebrated theatrical composer of his time, and his 114 operas were greedily produced at the height of the rage for Italian opera. For years Alessandro's great son Domenico tried to emulate him, then took another path.

The Scarlatti household was filled with music, and Domenico (called Mimo) learned through absorption. By his teen years, he was a fine organist and was quickly becoming a uniquely skilled harpsichord player. By the time Domenico was twenty, his father could write to his patron Ferdinando de' Medici, "This son of mine is an eagle whose wings are grown; he ought not to stay idle in the nest, and I ought not to hinder his flight."

Sometime in 1705 Domenico arrived in Venice, the destination of choice for many Italian and foreign musicians of the day. He was soon a regular fixture at the frequent musical gatherings hosted by the local nobility, and his harpsichord playing startled even this musically astute audience. The Neapolitan soon developed a warm friendship with Handel, who, despite his ornery and lusty personality, was attracted to the sweet-tempered Domenico. Early in 1709 the two young geniuses traveled together to Rome, where the presiding patron of the arts, Cardinal Pietro Ottoboni, pitted them in musical battle at his home.

The judges found Handel's harpsichord prowess formidable indeed but were convinced that Scarlatti's was even better. When the two contestants were at the organ, however, Handel was the victor. Scarlatti himself declared that Il Sassone was so good that "till he had heard him upon this instrument, he had no conception of its powers."

But Domenico now had to make a living in the teeming world of early-eighteenth-century music. His first position of importance was in Rome, where, from 1709 to 1714, he served in the private court of an exiled queen of Poland. Scarlatti's musical production from these years consisted of at least one cantata, one oratorio, and six operas. In 1713 he became *maestro di cappella* (chapel master) at the Basilica Giulia, but he was still living in the shadow of his father and producing little of merit.

A radical break was imminent. In 1719 Scarlatti left Italy and for the next ten years served the wealthy Portuguese court at Lisbon. One of his responsibilities was the musical education of the young princess, Maria Barbara, already an exceptional harpsichordist. It was Scarlatti's duty to compose for the insatiable musical appetite of his royal charge. This duty unleashed Domenico's creative powers, and he finally began to produce the works for which we remember him today. It was in this period that Domenico became for all the world the one and only Scarlatti. The Portuguese princess valued his services so highly that in 1728, when, at sixteen, she married Fernando, the heir to the Spanish throne, she took Scarlatti to Madrid with her. He remained in the Madrid court for the rest of his life.

In the age of castrati, mythological opera, oratorio, and large church forms, Scarlatti went against the custom, content to compose miniatures. When we think of the sonata, we often mean the Classical format (just emerging in Scarlatti's time) of C.P.E. Bach, Haydn, and Mozart. Scarlatti's nearly six hundred sonatas are instead simple binary structures in one movement, structures that the unpretentious composer merely called *Essercizi per gravicembalo* (*Exercises for Harpsichord*). In 1738 Scarlatti published thirty of his *Essercizi*, the only ones to be published in his lifetime. He diplomatically dedicated his epoch-making collection to the king of Portugal, who promptly knighted him.

Little is known of Scarlatti's personal life. He returned to Italy only twice, once in 1724 to visit his ailing father, and again in 1728 to marry a sixteen-year-old Neapolitan girl, Maria Caterina Gentili. Maria died in 1739, leaving the composer with five young children, and Scarlatti soon married again. His second wife, a Spanish woman called Anastasia, added four more children to the family, one of whom was named Maria Barbara, after Scarlatti's patroness.

In 1746 the Spanish monarch, Philip V, died. Fernando—married to Maria Barbara by then for seventeen years—finally became king. The royal couple remained childless, but the queen took comfort in her seven regal harpsichords and her productive composer. Although she had become grossly overweight, her technical prowess increased over the years, and Scarlatti composed hundreds of sonatas to fulfill her demands.

After Scarlatti's death, Dr. Charles Burney queried the great castrato singer Farinelli about him. Farinelli had lived in Madrid since 1738 as the king's music master and claimed to have known Scarlatti well. He told the historian that Scarlatti was "an agreeable man in society, but so much addicted to 'play' [gambling] that he was frequently ruined, and as frequently relieved in his distresses by his royal patroness, the queen of Spain, who was constant in her admiration of his original genius and incomparable talents." Her majesty was indeed constant, writing to "my music master who has followed me with great diligence and devotion." After his death she provided for Scarlatti's wife and children. Unfortunately, Maria Barbara died only one year after Scarlatti, at the age of forty-three.

When Scarlatti passed away, his manuscripts, like those of Bach, were discarded, and not one original Scarlatti manuscript is extant. But thanks to Maria Barbara, fifteen thick volumes of copies exist, written out at her behest. Bringing Scarlatti to universal recognition was and is a slow process. Not until 1838, when Carl Czerny, Beethoven's pupil, edited two hundred of his sonatas for publication, was Scarlatti's music available in quantity. In 1906–8 another three hundred sonatas were published under the editorship of the Italian pianist and composer Alessandro Longo. Since then another hundred or so have been published. At the time of the Longo edition, the harpsichord itself was being rediscovered, especially by Wanda Landowska, an ardent champion of Scarlatti's music. Many believe that Scarlatti, when played on his native instrument, has an added magic that is absent on the piano, a magic that is vitally intrinsic to his art. Whether his music is played on harpsichord or piano, however, Scarlatti clearly created a unique keyboard literature that palpitates with life. Sacheverell Sitwell called him "this greatest of keyboard composers and executants, always excepting Chopin and Liszt of whom he is the peer and equal," and Landowska wrote, "Spain fired the imagination of the great Neapolitan. . . . When we hear Scarlatti's music, we know that we are in the climate of sunlight and warmth. It is Italy, it is Spain—the spirit of the Latin countries and the god of the Mediterranean; we are in the presence of that deity who has been truly called 'the god who dances.' "

The Harpsichord Sonatas (various dates)

Scarlatti's work has no opus numbers, and both Alessandro Longo and the harpsichordist Ralph Kirkpatrick have cataloged Scarlatti, which has caused much confusion. The Kirkpatrick numbering, which is more chronologically accurate, has slowly usurped the Longo listing.

The sonatas vary greatly. Some have the tang of Naples, while others are bucolic; some are slow and lyrical, while others are devastatingly rhythmic. There are dozens of dance movements, martial-sounding sonatas, and dazzling high-speed virtuoso pieces producing an amazing variety of keyboard effects.

In his biography of the composer, Kirkpatrick sums up the sonatas as follows: "There is hardly an aspect of Spanish life, of Spanish popular music and dance, that has not found itself a place in the microcosm that Scarlatti created with his sonatas. . . . He has captured the click of castanets, the strumming of guitars, the thud of muffled dreams, the harsh bitter wail of Gypsy lament, the overwhelming gaiety of the village band, and above all, the wiry tension of the Spanish dance."

PERFORMED ON HARPSICHORD
Trevor Pinnock: Deutsche Grammophon ARC 419632-2
Anthony Newman: Newport Classic NCD 60080
Leonhardt: Sony Classical 61820

PERFORMED ON PIANO
Vladimir Horowitz: CBS MK 42410
Maria Tipo: Vox Box 2-CDX 25515
Pogorelich: Deutsche Grammophon 35855

OTHER BAROQUE COMPOSERS

GIROLAMO FRESCOBALDI

(1583–1643) Italy

Frescobaldi was one of the important instrumental composers of his day, and along with his pupil, Johann Jacob Froberger, he had a vast influence on the instrumental music that was rapidly developing in the seventeenth century. As an organist, he had unprecedented virtuosity. In 1608 he received the coveted position of organist at St. Peter's in Rome. So famous was he that, according to legend, thirty thousand people attended his first appearance.

Harpsichord Music
Tilney: Dorian DOR 90124

HEINRICH SCHÜTZ

(c.1585–1672) Germany

Schütz was one of the great masters of the early Baroque. In 1599 he became a choirboy at Kassel, where the landgrave of Hesse-Kassel was his patron. The youngster was well educated in a variety of subjects as well as in music. At the University of Marburg, he distinguished himself in legal studies. In 1609, with expenses paid by the landgrave, Schütz traveled to Venice, where he studied with Giovanni Gabrieli and immersed himself in the sumptuous Italian style. It was in Venice that Schütz produced his first set of Italian madrigals for five voices. He returned to Kassel in 1612, then two years later took a post in Dresden, where he concentrated on composing religious music for voices with and without instruments.

Another trip to Venice occurred in 1628 when Monteverdi was dominating the musical world there. It is likely that Schütz studied with him. After returning to Saxony in 1629, he published his influential *Symphoniae sacrae*. In years to come, his passions became widely known and made a deep impression on J. S. Bach. After the mid-1650s Schütz composed little, but in 1664 the seventy-nine-year-old composer had a burst of creativity and wrote the magnificent *Christmas Oratorio*.

In his music, Schütz combined elements of two diverse cultures: the high seriousness of Reformation Germany and the splendor of the Venetian Baroque. He was able to mesh reflective, sincere German expression with Italian ceremonial pomp and tonal color. His contribution was especially important in the swirling social and cultural conflicts of the transition from the Renaissance to the Baroque.

Psalms
Monteverdi Choir London, Gardiner: Philips 446116-2

Christmas Oratorio (1664)
Taverner Choir and Players, Parrott: EMI Classics CDC 47633

JEAN-BAPTISTE LULLY

(1632–1687) Italy

Lully, born near Florence, early struck out for Paris to create his career. The young Louis XIV heard his wonderful violin playing and made him a member of his celebrated "twenty-four violins," basking at the court of the Sun King. It was not long before no fête was complete without music by Lully. He amassed a fortune and four luxurious homes in Paris. Lully is often called "the father of French opera." His music has Italianate grace yet sounded specifically French to the ears of his time; he was an expert in fitting the French language to his graceful or highly rhythmic material. Lully's operas (the finest of which may be *Acis et Galatée*, 1686) and the comedy-ballets (on which he collaborated with Molière) hold many delights, as do some of his ceremonial and religious compositions. Madame de Sévigné wrote, "I do not believe that there is any sweeter music under heaven than Lully's." For later generations, the cause of his death became more celebrated than his music. As music master to the royal family, he wrote a *Te Deum* celebrating His Majesty's recovery from a foot injury. In his day, conductors beat time on the floor with a long bejeweled walking stick, which Lully gouged into his foot while conducting the *Te Deum*. Gangrene set in, and he died of blood poisoning.

Le Bourgeois Gentilhomme (comédie-ballet in five acts, selections) (1670)
Kweksilber, Yakar, Jacobs, La Petite Bande, Leonhardt: Editio Classica 77059-2-RG

DIETRICH BUXTEHUDE

(c.1637–1707) Denmark

A German composer born in Denmark, Buxtehude was the finest organist of his time. For the young Bach, it was imperative to hear the legendary Buxtehude play the organ at Lübeck, so imperative that he walked two hundred miles each way to hear him. Bach remained indelibly influenced, and at one time he was interested in succeeding Buxtehude at his post in Lübeck. Buxtehude required his successor to marry his daughter, and Bach (following Johann Mattheson and G. F. Handel) turned down the offer. Buxtehude's music, especially his organ works, is some of the finest of the German Baroque.

Various Organ Music
Koopman: Novalis 150 048

ARCANGELO CORELLI

(1653–1713) Italy

Corelli is an essential figure in the history of music. Not only was he the founder of a violin school in Rome, which flourished for over a century and a half, but he was an important composer, crystallizing the *concerto grosso* as an important Baroque form of instrumental music. Although he was an admirable contrapuntist, his composing was adapted to the exigencies of the emerging classical tonal system. Of his music, the violinist-conductor Yehudi Menuhin observed, "It looks deceptively simple, and yet it has an organic structure which is very closely knit. As soon as one begins studying a few bars, one finds an incredible complexity in terms of counterpoint, fugal elements, bass line, imitation, and other compositional devices." Corelli's music is direct and vigorously bracing in the fast movements and is highlighted by expressive slow movements, where the violin shines in song. His best-known work, the *Concerto grosso* in G Minor (Op. 6/8), is called the *Christmas Concerto*. He lived a good deal of his life in Rome, where he was cherished. After a regal funeral, he was buried near Raphael in the Pantheon. At the time of his death, Corelli was possibly the most famous musician in Europe.

Twelve *Concerti grossi* (published 1714)
English Concert, Pinnock: Archiv 423626-2
I *Musici: Philips* 426453-2

HENRY PURCELL

(1659–1695) England

Purcell was England's greatest Baroque composer. Although his life has been extensively researched, many facts remain unknown or controversial. Most likely he was a member of the highly musical Purcell family. With his beautiful singing voice, he was admitted to the Chapel Royal of Charles II at around eight years old. There he most likely came into contact with two of the best-known composers in London, Henry Cooke and Pelham Humfrey, who had known Lully in Paris and doubtless brought French influence to the young Purcell's hungry musical mind. When Purcell's voice broke, he probably stayed on at the chapel and continued his musical studies with the fine composer John Blow.

Purcell was a splendid organist and in 1679 took the position of organist of Westminster Abbey. Already he had been composing for Charles's court—anthems, songs, and instrumental works rushed from his pen. He married in 1681 and became a father the following year, when he was appointed organist at the Chapel Royal. The year 1683 marked his debut as a published composer, with *Sonnata's of III Parts*. He seems to have been heralded as a master from the beginning of his career. Especially noted was his talent for setting English words to music.

In 1689 Purcell wrote his only opera, *Dido and Aeneas,* based on Virgil. He wrote it for an amateur performance at Josias Priest's boarding school for young gentlewomen in Chelsea. English opera was in a primitive state and would have only a brief run of popularity before Italian opera obliterated it. *Dido and Aeneas* is a masterwork of vocal declamation. Besides the celebrated lament at the end of the opera, two other songs—"Ah! Belinda" and "Oft She Visits"—reveal the subtlety of expression that marks Purcell as characteristically English, as Couperin is characteristically French and Bach German.

The period of Cromwell (1653–60) had frowned upon music, and musical creativity had been at a minimum. Charles II restored to England not only the crown but the arts as well. Purcell, who came to maturity during the last years of Charles's reign, thought he was at the beginning of a new dawn in English music. As if the Elizabethan Age had not existed, he wrote, "Poetry and painting have arrived to perfection in this country; music's but yet in its monage. . . .

'Tis now learning Italian, which is its best master, and studying a little of the French air, to give it somewhat more gaiety and fashion."

Purcell wove all the elements of the European Baroque into the fabric of English music. He possessed a dynamic sense of form and rhythm, a fine contrapuntal technique, and above all a melodic genius with which he expressed a rich variety of emotions.

During the last decade of his short life, Purcell composed at a feverish pace, producing nearly five hundred compositions. Early in 1695 his eloquent anthem "Thou know'st, Lord, the secrets of our heart" was played at the funeral of Queen Mary. The anthem soon became famous and has since become a traditional piece for funerals at Westminster Abbey and St. Paul's.

Perhaps it was the strain of overwork that led to Purcell's death after a short illness at age thirty-six, on November 21, 1695. He was buried near the organ at Westminster Abbey with the inscription: "Here lyes Henry Purcell, Esq., who left this life, and is gone to that blessed place where only his harmony can be exceeded." Soon after his death, his teacher John Blow composed his beautiful "Ode on the Death of Mr. Henry Purcell."

Handel was only ten years old when Purcell died, but the German's arrival in England in 1712 greatly overshadowed Purcell's music. Not until 1876 was the Purcell Society founded, and it took until 1926 to compile the twenty-two volumes of his compositions. Purcell still sounds accessible to today's listeners. Indeed, the English critic Eric Blom wrote, "Masters as great as he had lived much earlier, but Purcell is the oldest whose music is capable of living in the affection of non-specialist musicians and music lovers today."

One may begin by looking into his sonatas and overtures, the G minor chaconne, the fantasias for viola da gamba, *Ode for St. Cecilia's Day* (1692), *Funeral Music for Queen Mary* (1695), *The Fairy Queen* (1692), and *King Arthur* (1691), which has a libretto by John Dryden, who deeply admired Purcell.

Dido and Aeneas (opera in three acts) (1689)

Norman, McLaughlin, Allen, English Chamber Orchestra, Ambrosian Singers, Leppard: Philips 416299-2

Chacony in G Minor for Four Strings (*London*)

Orpheus Chamber Orchestra: Deutsche Grammophon 429390

ALESSANDRO SCARLATTI

(1660–1725) Italy

At the height of his powers in 1710, Alessandro Scarlatti was the most illustrious vocal composer in Italy. Indeed, he was so celebrated that his son Domenico, the Scarlatti now known and loved, was but a mere embellishment to his fame.

Scarlatti was born to compose for the voice, and he worked relentlessly. He produced nearly seven hundred cantatas. But it was as the composer of sixty-six operas, produced at the height of the rage for Italian opera, that Scarlatti made his fame and fortune. He had little dramatic ability, but, as this quality was generally in short measure in Baroque opera, that lack was not a fatal one. His refined and sensuous melodies were a ready vehicle for the elaborate embellishments of the popular castrato singers. With his innovative *aria da capo*, Scarlatti influenced the ever-growing urge to centralize tonality. He also helped to establish the fast-slow-fast concept of the opera overture, which became a model for later generations.

La Griselda (opera in three acts) (1721)
Freni, Alva, Luchetti, Panerai, Naples Alessandro Scarlatti RAI Orchestra, Naples Scarlatti
Chorus, Sanzogno: Memories HR 4154/55

Cantatas
Picollo, Balconi, Bagliano, Collegium Pro Musica: Nuova Era NUO 7162

FRANÇOIS COUPERIN

(1668–1733) France

Couperin le Grand, as he was known, was born into one of the most distinguished of musical families. The Couperins produced generations of musicians, including François's uncle, Louis Couperin. In 1693 Louis XIV chose Couperin to provide and perform music as an official organist of the royal chapel. Ennobled by the Sun King, Couperin busily composed church and chamber music but above all harpsichord pieces, which he put into *ordres*, as he called them, or suites of pieces of original beauty. The twenty-seven *ordres* contain more than two hundred harpsichord pieces, many based on dance forms, and most of them with delightful titles like "La Voluptueuse," "La Tendre fanchon," "Les Plaisirs de Saint-Germain-en-Laÿe," "Les Tambourins," and "Les Guirlandes." These works, with their sumptuous profusion of ornamentation, form an alluring, insinuating art akin to the painting of Watteau in their grace, exquisite taste, and refinement.

Wanda Landowska said, "Couperin's language differs entirely from that of Bach or Handel. . . . But what is this elusive anguish that Couperin provokes in us? He does not speak of love, sensuousness, or sorrow, in the same manner as does Bach or Handel. Couperin's music permeates our subconscious, agitating its levels. . . . It burrows into the depth of our inner life."

L'Apothéose de Lully (sonata) (1725)
English Baroque Soloists, Gardiner: Erato 2292–45011-2ZK

Harpsichord Music
Gilbert: Musique D'Abord HMA 190359/60

TOMASO ALBINONI
(1671–1751) Italy

Albinoni was born in Venice to a wealthy family and was called *"dilettante Veneto."* But Albinoni, talented and prolific, was anything but a dilettante. Historically he may be placed between Corelli and Vivaldi. Bach admired his music and transcribed a few of his works.

Unfortunately he is now best known by the Adagio in G minor for Organ and Strings, an eight-minute piece celebrated out of all bounds—and unfortunately for many ears the very essence of Baroque music. In fact, it is a cleverly plush reconstruction of Albinoni sketches by Remo Giazotto, an Italian musicologist. In the 1960s the Adagio became popular as background music in movies and television commercials, ranking in ubiquity with Pachelbel's Canon. The real Albinoni was a composer of color and mastery. The zesty oboe concertos (Opp. 7 and 9) are true Baroque treasures.

Adagio in G Minor for Organ and Strings
Berlin Philharmonic Orchestra, Karajan: Deutsche Grammophon 419046-2

Concertos for Oboe and Strings, Op. 7 (1715)
Holliger, Bourgue, I Musici: Philips 432115-2

ANTONIO VIVALDI

(1678–1741) Italy

Little is known of Vivaldi's life. He was the son of a violinist in Venice. He studied with his father and would himself become an important violinist. Around 1703 he was ordained a priest, dubbed the Red Priest because of his flaming red hair. Like so many Italian composers, he wrote operas, all of which have been forgotten. Although he was famous in his time, he died in poverty.

For more than a century and a half after his death, Vivaldi's music languished in obscurity. In the early twentieth century, Italian musicians and scholars began to explore his work seriously. With the invention of the long-playing recording in the late 1940s, the Red Priest was recognized as one of the masters of the late Baroque and the greatest Venetian composer of the eighteenth century. His best music is charged with rhythmic vitality and sunny melody, sumptuous with the joyous Venetian love of abundant color.

The Four Seasons, his most popular work, consists of four violin concertos, nos. 1 through 4 from a set of twelve, titled *Il cimento dell'armonia e dell'inventione* (*The Trial between Harmony and Invention*, Op. 8). The four violin concertos—"Spring," "Summer," "Fall," and "Winter"—are grand tone paintings with appropriate seasonal effects masterfully integrated into the three-movement form.

The Four Seasons, Op. 8/1–4 (n.d.)

Standage, English Concert, Pinnock: Archiv 400045-2 (period instruments)
Kennedy, English Chamber Orchestra, Kennedy: EMI Classics CDC 49557
Mutter, Vienna Philharmonic, Karajan: EMI Classics CDC 47043

JAN ZELENKA

(1679–1745) Bohemia

After receiving his education at a Jesuit college in Prague, Zelenka stayed in Bohemia until 1710, when he became a member of the Dresden Court Orchestra as a double bass player. In 1715 he left to study with the renowned contrapuntist Johann Joseph Fux. During the remainder of his career, he took on various positions, including director of church music at Dresden. In his last years, he is said to have been disappointed with his lack of recognition. He excelled in both church and instrumental works. His sacred music possesses a stately seriousness, while his orchestral music has a regal quality.

Lamentationes Jeremiae Prophetae (1722)

Jacobs, de Mey, Widmer, Schola Cantorum Basiliensis, Jacobs: Editio Classica 77112-2-RG

Concerto à 8 for Orchestra (1723)
Collegium 1704 (no conductor): Supraphon SUP 0009

GEORG PHILIPP TELEMANN

(1681–1767) Germany

In late Baroque Germany, Telemann was far more famous than J. S. Bach. But like many others, he was soon forgotten, until the Baroque revival after World War II. For some listeners today, he represents all that is boring in Baroque music: a constant patter of mindless musical patterns, churned out ad nauseam. But others hear his musical "chatter" as pleasant and commodious, a soother of shattered nerves. Classical music radio stations constantly program Telemann as a pleasantry, or palliative, before or after more demanding fare. His output was prodigious, bringing Handel to comment that he could write a motet in eight parts as easily as another could write a letter. His smooth craft never fails, and one may be surprised by the many little audacities and poignancies that separate him from such contemporary composers as Reinhard Keiser, Johann Mattheson, Johann Adolf Hasse, and Carl Heinrich Graun, all of whom were also, in their day, considered greater than Bach.

Five Concertos for Oboe and Orchestra
Holliger, Academy of St. Martin in the Fields, Brown: Philips 412879-2

JEAN-PHILIPPE RAMEAU

(1683–1764) France

Rameau was the successor of Jean-Baptiste Lully, a friend of Voltaire, and the supreme composer and musical theoretician of France's late Baroque. He was the major arbiter of "modern" harmonic practice in France, based on the emerging strength of diatonic tonality. His treatise *Traité de l'harmonie*, finished in 1722, was indispensable reading for fledgling composers. Rameau is a complex composer who needs far more contemporary exploration than he has received. The most comprehensive musical thinker of the French Baroque, he utilized all the cross-currents of that elaborate age, crossing polyphonic and homophonic technique as magnificently as Handel.

Rameau firmly believed that music was not merely decorative but a path to higher human expression, and that harmony was the key to that path. "It is certain that harmony can arouse various passions within us, depending on the chords which we employ," he wrote. "There are sad, languishing, tender, agreeable, gay and surprising chords; there is also a specified sequence of chords to express particular passions." His treatise reads like a Romantic manifesto, and to his contemporaries his work was a revelation. At times his operas possess a spirit of grandeur that directly anticipates passages of Christoph Gluck.

Rameau was a master of contemporary dance forms, which are typically French in spirit and subtle gallantry. His orchestration, too, was far more progressive than was usual in his time. Voltaire needed little convincing that Rameau was the greatest composer of the age, and he wrote a libretto for Rameau's comedy-ballet *La Princesse de Navarre*, performed in splendor at Versailles in 1745. The composer's music was challenged by an Italian troupe called Les Bouffons, which in 1752 gave Paris lighter Italian fare, including Giovanni Pergolesi's *La Serva padrona*. In this Guerre des Bouffons between Italian and French styles, Grimm, Diderot, Rousseau, and a herd of journalists berated Rameau for his French formality. Soon after his death from typhoid fever, Rameau, who outlived J. S. Bach, Handel, and Domenico Scarlatti, was ousted from his preeminence by Gluck, whose *Orfeo ed Euridice* of 1762 rendered obsolete the entire repertory of both Italian and French opera since 1600.

If Rameau's stage works have not been revived, plenty of excerpts have been. He wrote high-level chamber music, and his fifty-three surviving keyboard works, with their harmonic verticality and wide keyboard scope, are superb for playing and listening. Claude Debussy, in his second piece of his first set of *Images* for piano (1905), wrote a sarabande that he called "Hommage à Rameau." Always an advocate of Rameau's importance, he maintained that "Rameau was lyrical, and that suits the French spirit from all points of view. . . . I fear that our ears have lost their power to listen with the necessary delicacy to the music of Rameau, in which all ungraceful noises are forbidden. Nevertheless, those who do know how to listen will be afforded a polite but warm welcome."

Castor et Pollux (opera in five acts) (1737)

Schéle, Scovotti, Leanderson, Souzay, Vienna Concentus Musicus, Harnoncourt: Teldec 42510-2

La Princesse de Navarre (comédie-ballet in three acts) (1745)

English Bach Baroque Orchestra, English Bach Festival Singers, McGegan: Erato ERA SEL 12986

ALESSANDRO MARCELLO

(1684–1750) Italy

BENEDETTO MARCELLO

(1686–1739) Italy

The Marcello brothers were two gifted Venetian composers contemporaneous with J. S. Bach; their wealthy father, like many fathers from time immemorial, thought the life of a musician was undignified and directed them to the law and public service, where Benedetto held respected government posts. In Venice he was a member of the council of forty. Both managed to produce a large amount of work, which expresses beautifully the Italian spirit of the late Baroque.

A. Marcello, Concerto for Oboe and Strings (1725)
Holliger, I Musici: Philips 420189-2

B. Marcello, Concerto for Recorders (c.1730)
Academy of Ancient Music, Hogwood: L'Oiseau-Lyre 436905-2

PART THREE

THE AGE OF CLASSICISM

Tradition and innovation are always at odds in the arts. The age of Classicism (which began developing in the 1720s) made radical departures from counterpoint and Baroque forms. In stark contrast to Baroque polyphony, its keynote was homophony, a single melody supported by progressions of chords (harmony) in accompaniment. Homophony, the opposite of polyphonic counterpoint, can be used in a wide variety of musical styles, from simple homely popular songs to the decorative *style galant* of the Rococo. It was a complex change of taste that affected all the arts. It rendered J. S. Bach's music too complex, even confusing, for listeners; polyphony in general was now considered to be dry and difficult to digest. Although Bach himself tolerated the new and simple music, even on occasion enjoying the "pretty tunes" at the opera, he little realized that he—like Handel, Couperin, Rameau, Lully, Telemann, Alessandro Scarlatti, and other composers of the late Baroque—had had his day.

This major shift in aesthetic systems had been brewing since the introduction of new instruments and the beginning of operatic music. Final refinements were made on the violin around 1600, and in the eighteenth century, this easily portable instrument resembling the human voice loomed large in popular, dance, and serious music. It became the standard-bearer of chamber music, which filled the homes of aristocrats and connoisseurs. Baroque music now seemed passé. Enlightenment had come to the scientific world, and it brought changes to the arts as well. Jean-Jacques Rousseau called for the abolition of counterpoint, and his "natural man" opted for melody and more melody. Even more preferable, the philosopher felt, would be harmonic accompaniments that lacked any complexity at all.

But thinking of changes in the arts as "progress" is detrimental. It has very often been said that "modern times" began with homophony. But in the name of progress, much wonderful music—what the nineteenth century called "ancient music"—was lost. In the twentieth century, the music profession found it necessary to create the discipline of musicology in order to study and resurrect music's past.

The Enlightenment spurred on a new spirit of classical secularism that made a gigantic leap forward in 1709, when Bartolomeo Cristofori invented the pianoforte (piano). (Cristofori's career coincided with that of Antonio Stradivari, maker of legendary violins.) It took quite some time after Cristofori's 1731 death for the piano to be improved, but by the 1770s many musicians realized that its expressive possibilities were perfectly suited to the restless and sentimental *Sturm und Drang* (Storm and Stress) movement then in vogue. Although Voltaire was convinced that the piano (an ironmonger's instrument, he called it) would never dethrone the majestic harpsichord, the sage of Ferney in this case was decisively wrong: the piano would totally eclipse the aristocratic harpsichord. The harpsichord's "plucked" mechanism offered a dry, crackled sound that was suited to counterpoint and the Baroque era; but the piano, through mere finger-pressure, could create true inflection, soft and loud and *crescendo* and *diminuendo*, with many degrees in between. Moreover, its pedal mechanism could create mellifluous tones and delicious harmonic coloration. In short, the piano was the ideal homophonic instrument.

Concurrently, the modern orchestra was developing. In the 1740s, Johann Stamitz, concertmaster of the court orchestra at Mannheim, contributed powerfully both to composition for orchestra and to orchestral performance. He was a chief progenitor of the sonata-allegro form (the first movement of a sonata) and its songlike slow movement. And he conducted his orchestra in performances whose carefully articulated crescendos created a sensation. Musicians had always been conscious of dynamics, but the Mannheim orchestra accomplished a new variety of tonal gradations, much like those of the piano. In Baroque performances, the dynamic range had been limited to alternations between loud and soft, in a layering or "terraced dynamics." But in Classical performances, the many degrees from very soft (*pianissimo*) to very loud (*fortissimo*) could be articulated, bringing unheard-of titillation to the nervous system and delighting an age of sensibility. Stamitz initiated the orchestra's long flight toward large-scale public performances in concert halls, which would later be constructed throughout the world.

At Leipzig in 1750, the blind Bach labored furiously to finish *The Art of the Fugue*, assigning it to no specific instrument. It was his summation of the polyphonic world and his farewell to the system that had nourished his genius. In

1824 the deaf Beethoven was gently turned around to face a weeping audience after conducting his Ninth Symphony, whose finale, a musical setting of Schiller's Ode to Joy, proclaimed brotherhood and freedom. These two moments mark, respectively, the end of the polyphonic era and the high peak of tonal homophony. They also sum up the three quarters of a century of transition in the social position of the musician: from a servant dependent on Church or nobility to the lonely artist creating, for society at large, "art for art's sake." A total upheaval had taken place in music.

The changes in society and art that led to Napoleon, Beethoven, and Byron were vast and can only be hinted at here. The industrial revolution and Europe's colonization of distant lands brought new wealth to England, France, Prussia, and the Austro-Hungarian Empire. That wealth encouraged a still-small but powerful landed gentry to contest the powers of the nobility, and a commercial and professional class was formed. In the age of reason, religious dogmas were attacked, and new, more liberal sects were coming into being (including Freemasonry, which so attracted Mozart). "The proper study of mankind is man," prescribed Alexander Pope. Latin had been undermined as the language of scholarship and diplomacy, and vernacular languages were coming into their own. French was now the international language of the educated. Upper-class circles cultivated manners and polished conversation as well as elegance in dress. Palaces with formal gardens and parks spoke of luxury. Sexual mores were considerably relaxed; Casanova's immortal memoirs were more accurate than not. Religious painting had long been in decline, and Watteau, Boucher, and Fragonard now portrayed the life of the senses. Canaletto promoted tourism in his photographic renderings of Venice and London; Reynolds and Gainsborough showed in their portraiture the smug contentment of the English upper crust. Canova's sculptures are marvels of the enlightened, sophisticated European; in every satisfied face, a smile tells us that man is a perfectable animal. Burns, Klopstock, and the young Goethe gave birth to modern lyric poetry, and Swift, Fielding, Sterne, and others wrote the precursors of modern novels. Modern Europe came of age.

Along with this fervent activity in the arts came further developments in instrumental music and in the sonata form, or the sonata-idea, as it may be called. The sonata is the form that dominated the minds of the greatest masters of the Classical era, from Haydn to Beethoven, and beyond the Classical era to Bruckner, Brahms, and Mahler. Compositions in the sonata form are of pure or "absolute" music—music without words, filling a long span of time, based entirely on the constructive principles of melody, rhythm, and harmony. In the Baroque era, an instrumental piece such as a dance or a prelude lasted only a few minutes, but Beethoven spanned forty-five minutes with his piano sonata

Op. 106, a miracle in the manipulation of abstract sound that fulfills the original meaning of the word *sonata*—"to be sounded" by an instrument (as opposed to *cantata*, "to be sung by voices"). The concept of organic instrumental music that continued for extended periods of time was a radical departure.

Since the late sixteenth century, the term *sonata* had been used for various musical formats, usually those of more than one movement. The Baroque sonatas of J. S. Bach are really suites, and the sonatas of Domenico Scarlatti are simple binary forms that use the name *sonata* in its original meaning of "sounded" (though Scarlatti himself called them "exercises"). A Baroque suite was basically a string of dance forms; a Baroque opera, a string of arias and duets. Opera composers attempted little dramatic consideration and architectural organization beyond the rudimentary, and music was grafted onto stereotyped librettos.

Let us look more closely at the sonata form as it developed from Stamitz and innumerable others. The sonata form is the same for all instruments: the piano sonata, the violin and piano sonata, and so on. In chamber music, the string quartet, string quintet, piano trio, and piano quartet all use sonata form. The sonata for orchestra is a *symphony*, and the sonata for piano, violin, cello, or any other instrument in conjunction with orchestra is a *concerto*. Concertos with a solo instrument have three movements with a *cadenza*, a solo display of three or four minutes near the end of the first movement (and sometimes in the third movement as well) that shows off the performer's technical prowess while utilizing the material of the movement. It had been the custom for the soloist to improvise this section, but composers eventually took control.

While the concerto usually uses a three-movement scheme, the symphony has four movements, as do string quartets and other chamber combinations. The piano and violin sonatas of Mozart are in three movements, although many "classical" sonatas have two movements and some Beethoven and Schubert piano sonatas have four.

The essential element of the sonata is its contrasting musical material. The most complex and usually the longest movement is the first movement, which is in what is called *sonata-allegro form*. It consists of three main divisions: the *exposition*, the *development*, and the *recapitulation*. (On occasion, particularly in Beethoven and Haydn, the exposition is preceded by an introduction, usually of a *grave* character.) The exposition itself is a dramatic contrast. It presents in the *tonic* (home) key its theme or themes. The opening material often possesses a certain dramatic urgency and has (simplistically) been called "masculine." After expounding this theme or group, a transition (or bridge passage) follows, moving to another key with a new subject, often of a lyric bent ("feminine"). This contrast sets up tension and opposition, which challenges the composer to work his way to the end of his exposition and arrive at the *dominant* key (the fifth note up the scale from the tonic). The ear is now suspended, waiting for the drama to continue. At the end of the exposition, a repeat sign appears in the score, telling the players to play it all again from the opening. Some performers ignore the sign, feeling the repetition is a redundancy, but today's practice is usually to obey it. Most likely, the reason for this was to clarify the themes for the listener.

After the exposition has been repeated, we arrive at the sonata's most difficult section: the development, where the composer throws new light and meanings on the character of his exposition material. He may develop or bend any fragment or part of the exposition material as well as introduce new material, all the while modulating freely into new and even distant keys. Although juxtaposing the material heightens the drama, the development section never finds a sense of fulfillment. But as it proceeds to its conclusion, it creates a conscious desire for fulfillment, which begins by bringing the listener back to the tonic (home key), with its original material intact.

We are now in the recapitulation, where the composer may modify the material only in small details. Although the material is the same, however, its psychological effect is different. The tensions of the exposition and the upheavals of the development now find comfort and peace in the home tonality of the tonic key. No matter how far the composer has traveled, he now takes us home. The "Classical style" is the story of manipulating tonality and finally achieving security. At the end of the recapitulation, a *coda* (tail or end) may be attached, using independent material or further finalizing and strengthening the home key. Beethoven greatly expanded the effect of the coda by using it to pound away his emphasis on the tonic.

The second movement of the sonata form is usually a slow movement, but as with the sonata-allegro first movement, there are always exceptions. The slow movement may be marked by various degrees of slowness (*andante, adagio, larghetto,* or *largo*). It is in a different key (tonality) from the first movement; if the first movement was in the major, the second is often in the corresponding minor key. Its structure is ternary: ABA. A typical A section displays the material complete; then the B section contrasts in mood and tonality. The second A section is a variant of the first. A slow movement can take a different form; for instance, Mozart liked his slow movements to be in sonata form without development, while Haydn and Beethoven often wrote a theme and variations as a slow movement. But regardless of its internal form, a slow movement is essential to the dramatic organic design of the sonata form as a whole. As the critic Donald Francis Tovey declared, "In the music of a master slowness means bigness." Haydn, Mozart, Beethoven, Schubert, Brahms,

Bruckner, and Mahler were all masters of "bigness." Their finest slow movements are monuments to the sonata idea and could never have been conceived simply as isolated movements.

For the third movement in a four-movement work, the usual plan is the *Minuet*. The Minuet was derived from the Baroque suite, largely because, of all the older dance forms, it fit best with mid-eighteenth-century manners. It gives off an aristocratic air; set in triple meter, it is lighter in style than the first two movements and serves as a necessary breathing space for the interior drama of the whole. The Minuet will have a contrasting *Trio* or middle section before returning to the dance proper. Haydn's Minuets can be quirky and unstable; Mozart's are suavely lyrical, with strong undercurrents of drama. Beethoven burst the bounds of the form and invented the *Scherzo* to replace the Minuet. Like the Minuet, the Scherzo moves in triple meter. Its name means "musical joke," and in Beethoven's Scherzos, humor may rage into ferocity: his Scherzos with Trios far exceed in scope the courtly world of the Minuet.

The finale of the four-movement sonata can take any of several forms. It is frequently a *Rondo*, consisting of an A theme that appears three or four times, alternating with several contrasting themes (for example, ABACA coda). A pure Rondo is generally sectional, with little thematic development, and it may be light and tuneful. A composer may, however, blend the Rondo with elements of the first-movement sonata form. Many finales use a modified sonata-allegro form or a set of variations based on the composer's own theme.

These are the most common usages of sonata form, but for every rule there are numerous exceptions, and in the hands of Haydn, Mozart, Beethoven, and Schubert, sonata form was living, flexible, and expanding. Musical theorists by no means wrote books about the form until long after its great days had passed.

By the last quarter of the eighteenth century, dozens of composers had achieved Classicism's basic tenets, among them clarity and elegance in form, classical restraint, tonal stability, and a modicum of cohesiveness. It was a high time for the small but musically hungry public. Never had society provided such a good living for so many productive composers. Unfortunately, many of them produced by the yard a nondescript, prettified, innocuous product, petrified in a scholastic, rule-bound shell. Almost none of this vast output has survived. (By contrast, a wealth of material survives from the minor masters of the Italian Baroque and from the many delectable Romantics and Romantic nationalists.) The great sonata-idea needed composers with great minds and hearts; without Haydn, Mozart, Beethoven, and later Schubert, the form would have remained the stereotype it became in lesser hands. Fortunately, these four composers brought the sonata to its intellectual and emotional fruition. In the case of Beethoven, the sonata appeared capable of infinite expansion, eventually synthesizing homophony, polyphony, and slow movements of every variety and bringing the art of variation writing to a new peak of creative complexity. In each new sonata, he formed an entirely new vision of the form's possibility. By contrast, in Muzio Clementi's excellent last piano sonatas, composed at the same time as Beethoven was composing his last three piano sonatas, the Italian composer was locked rigidly in battle with the sonata: the form mastered him. The same is true of Carl Maria von Weber's sonatas, in which the German poured his warm Romantic themes into a form that strangled their poetic impulse.

On his deathbed, Beethoven told his doctor that his day's work was done. He meant precisely that his lifelong journey within the sonata-idea was fulfilled. Much later, Brahms, waiting long and patiently to write his First Symphony, revealed his anxiety to the conductor Hermann Levi about "that great giant whose steps I always hear behind me."

The other great advance of the Classical age came in opera. Opera remained a never-ending challenge for composers, but by the middle of the eighteenth century, the form had become mere formula: Pietro Metastasio's more than eight hundred librettos were rehashed by dozens of composers. These stilted caricatures, retelling ancient history or myth, lacked dramatic substance and for a century had relied on great singers of unprecedented vocal virtuosity to achieve their effect. In 1740 the world's most famous musician in all areas of music was not a composer but the castrato singer Farinelli. But new and more sophisticated audiences needed more complex, psychologically interesting stories that they could relate to.

In fact, the rise of the sonata-idea stimulated opera composers to achieve dramatic unity by articulating their music through the characters' essential being and the exigencies of the texts. It would be a middle-aged Christoph Willibald Gluck whose "reform" operas paved the way for opera as a musical-dramatic entity. Significantly, his *Orfeo ed Euridice* of 1762 is the earliest opera that is still regularly staged. From Gluck, it was but a step to the greater operas of Mozart, whose training and mastery in all contemporary forms was faultless. In their rarefied spirit and dramatic organization, several of his operas are incomparable. The poet Schiller may have been thinking of Mozart when he wrote, "Man only plays when in the full meaning of the word he is a man, and he is only completely a man when he plays." Beethoven, primarily an instrumental composer, admired Luigi Cherubini's rather forced drama more than Mozart's all-seeing comedy of manners; he thought Mozart's *Don Giovanni* and *Marriage of Figaro* were licentious.

But Mozart's operas tower over those of other Classical composers. Haydn could never accommodate his instrumental art to opera and was saddled with perfunctory librettos. And Schubert, whose gift of melody was extraordinary, discovered that even that was not enough for a great opera. This last of the Classical masters wasted valuable time, in his short life, writing a dozen operas to miserable librettos. (Fortunately, Schubert found solace in lyric poetry and almost invented the song, or *Lied*, which would ignite the Romantic era.) And Beethoven labored bitterly over his only opera, *Fidelio*. An artist who was capable of achieving untold dramatic potency in his sonatas struggled to understand why he could not tame the opera form. Sonata form could in its essence pack far more dramatic power than the machinery of opera. In spite of his difficulties, though, Beethoven's *Fidelio* remained the greatest Classical opera after Mozart. And it was Beethoven's instrumental music that set the stage for the next era. Wagner (who overcame the libretto problem by writing his own) was the most penetrating student of Beethoven's instrumental work. In many respects, Wagner's *Tristan und Isolde* is a huge symphony, impossible without the discoveries of Beethoven. *Tristan* would haunt the music world with the same power that Beethoven's Ninth Symphony had.

CHRISTOPH WILLIBALD GLUCK

b. Erasbach, Upper Palatinate, July 2, 1714

d. Vienna, November 15, 1787

It is sometimes necessary to laugh at rules and to make one's own rules in order to produce good effects . . . sever the chains with which they wish to bind us, and try to become original in our own right.

Gluck grew up in a German-speaking Czech family that showed no trace of musical ability until he came along. His father, a rough fellow, was a hunter and forester who demanded physically Spartan feats of his two sons. He made them tramp barefoot through snow-covered Bohemian forests. Little is known of Gluck's early years, but the family moved frequently because of the father's various forester positions. By age eighteen, Gluck, who had a good singing voice and played a few instruments, was in Vienna attempting to make his way as a musician. He was often in dire need, and at those times he would join a band of roving musicians, singing and playing dance music for peasants.

But the ambitious Christoph Willibald had higher musical aspirations and a good deal of persistence. In the early 1730s he was displaying his talent at the homes of fabulously wealthy Viennese aristocrats. In Vienna he became associated with many of the capital's best musicians and profited from their advice. In 1735, at the palace of Prince Lobkowitz, the young man met Prince Melzi, an Italian nobleman who was delighted by his pleasing voice and fine cello playing. Deciding to take the twenty-three-year-old Gluck to Milan as a member of his palace orchestra, Prince Melzi arranged for him to study composition with Giovanni Sammartini, one of Italy's foremost composers. The callow

Gluck was happy with his teacher and well pleased with Italian life. In 1741, after diligent study, he presented Milan with the first fruit of his labor, his opera *Artaserse*, which brought his name to public attention.

During the 1740s, Gluck traveled in Italy, making occasional trips to Vienna and other German-speaking cities. He visited London in 1745 and struck up a friendship with Handel. The two lusty men ate and drank together voraciously; Handel taunted Gluck about the defects of his technique, telling his friend Susanna Cibber that Handel's own cook knew more about counterpoint than Gluck did. But along with the teasing came serious conversations, and Handel's dramatic oratorios made a deep impression on Gluck.

By 1750 Gluck was living in Vienna. In that year he married Marianna Bergin, the daughter of a recently deceased wealthy merchant. The composer took advantage of his wife's comfortable income to indulge in high living, all the while continuing to work. An opera he wrote for the San Carlo Theater in Naples in 1752, *La Clemenza di Tito*, became famous through a single aria, "Se mai senti spirarti sul volto," sung ravishingly by the celebrated castrato Caffarelli. Gluck's renown was spreading, and on his return from Naples he became *Kapellmeister* to the prince of Saxe-Hildburghausen, an influential Austrian field marshal. Gluck's activities brought him to the attention of the Empress Maria Theresa herself, who in 1754 appointed Gluck *Kapellmeister* for opera at the court theater. With this glamorous position, he was clearly on the rise both in society and in his profession.

It was a period of great personal development. Well aware of his lack of education and social polish, Gluck made full use of his new station in life, studying literature, learning French, and mingling with the many artists who had gravitated to the imperial city. The new opera manager, Count Durazzo, had brought together a dazzling array of talent. Gluck would become close friends with these artists, including the famous choreographer and dancer Gaspero Angiolini.

Most of Gluck's friends were bored with the regimentation of opera. In particular, *opera seria* had unyielding rules that limited the play of human drama and warmth. Reform was brewing, and the catalyst for change came in 1761 with the arrival in Vienna of Raniero da Calzabigi, a financial speculator, libertine, diplomat, and above all poet. Calzabigi wanted opera to be infused with reality, with real people, not statues. He wanted a unified drama, with music creating a constant commentary on the libretto. In short, he wanted to eradicate all conventions for the sake of dramatic integrity, simplicity, and nobility of style. Convinced that Gluck was the composer to initiate such reforms, Calzabigi beseeched him to stop writing arid and vapid scores. "I begged him," Calzabigi later wrote, "to banish . . . all the gothic, barbarous and extravagant things that have been introduced into our music." Calzabigi brought the composer his new libretto based on the Orpheus myth. Gluck, always a keen man of the theater, understood instantly and passionately: here was the possibility of transforming *opera seria* into true tragic music-drama. With *Orfeo ed Euridice*, he gave opera a transfusion. "I now strive to be a poet and a painter rather than a musician," he wrote.

The premiere of *Orfeo ed Euridice* took place at Vienna's Burg Theater on October 5, 1762. At first the opera baffled Maria Theresa and most of the audience, who had expected the usual stilted biblical or historical spectacle. But *Orfeo* quickly established itself. Gluck wrote of Calzabigi's influence, "I think it is my duty to recognize that I am beholden for it to him, since it was he who enabled me to develop the resources of my art."

Gluck's fame soared. He left his post at the court opera but retained his position as teacher to the royal family, instructing Maria Theresa's daughter, Marie Antoinette. In 1767 Gluck produced *Alceste*, a "reform" opera even more radical than *Orfeo*. In the preface to the published score, the composer stated his intentions: "I have striven to restrict music to its true office of serving poetry by means of expression of the sentiments and dramatic situations of a story, neither interrupting the action nor detracting from its vividness by useless and superfluous ornament. . . . Further I have thought that my greatest effort should be directed to the search of beauty in simplicity. . . . There is no academic rule that I have not willingly sacrificed to dramatic effect."

During the 1770s, Gluck divided his time between Paris and Vienna. His next vehicle, *Iphigénie en Aulide*, was composed for the Paris Opera (supported by the dauphin's wife, Marie Antoinette) and based on Racine's tragedy. Finding the performance standards deplorable, Gluck not only conducted but took part in every detail of production. Rehearsals lasted for six months. On April 19, 1774, the opera at last met Gluck's satisfaction—and took Paris by storm. That summer, Paris also heard his French version of *Orfeo*.

Although Marie Antoinette, now queen of France, was his ardent supporter, Gluck had powerful detractors who still wanted the old-fashioned, stilted style of Italian opera or the French tradition of Lully and Rameau. In 1777 the Parisian press, always ready for an intrigue, concocted one of the fiercest rivalries in theater history, between Gluck and the Italian composer Niccolò Piccinni. The public was fascinated: "Are you a Gluckist or Piccinnist?" became a question of pressing concern, and the controversy continued for several seasons. Gluck was gleeful as box-office receipts mounted. "I love money more than anything," he announced. "Then I love wine, and then glory. With money I buy wine, which inspires me to compose, and the opera brings me glory."

In Paris in 1776, while preparing the French version of *Alceste*, he was informed that his beloved niece, Marianne, whom he had adopted upon the death of his sister, had died in Vienna of smallpox. Gluck called Marianne, a remarkable singer, his "little nightingale." Inconsolable, he returned to Vienna. But he continued to work, completing *Armide*, which was first performed on September 23, 1777, in Paris, under Gluck's scrupulous direction. It was an even greater success than his previous "reform" operas. Writing to the Countess de Fries, he exclaimed, "No one has ever stirred up a more terrible and fiercely disputed battle than I with my opera *Armide*. By comparison, the intrigues against *Iphigénie*, *Orphée*, and *Alceste* were but little skirmishes. . . . I have seen people leaving with their hair disheveled and their clothes soaked, as if they had fallen into a river. You have to be French to pay this price for entertainment. There are six places in the opera that cause the audience to be carried away and lose self-control."

The incomparable American ambassador to France, Benjamin Franklin, himself an amateur composer, was delighted by the controversy, writing "Happy people! Thought I, you live certainly under a wise, just and mild government, since you have no public grievance to complain of, nor any subject of contention but the perfection and imperfections of foreign music." Did one of the founding fathers of the American republic really have no inkling of the tumultuous changes in the social order that would occur a dozen years later? Many others did.

Gluck would compose one more important opera. *Iphigénie en Tauride* was given to the world at the Paris Opera on May 18, 1779. The German author Friedrich von Grimm wrote, "I do not know whether this is song, but perhaps it is something more than that. . . . I forget that I am in an opera-house and think I am hearing a Greek tragedy." Gluck had succeeded in writing operas with a far wider perception of drama than ever before. As another German writer, Paul Bekker, said, "He thrust the doors open and allowed the daylight of human naturalness to fall upon the opera world of the time."

After a series of strokes starting in 1779, composing became nearly impossible. Gluck returned permanently to Vienna, where he was the reigning monarch of music. He kept in touch with his pupil Antonio Salieri and was enthusiastic about Mozart's 1782 *Entführung aus dem Serail* (*Abduction from the Seraglio*), inviting the composer and his wife to one of his lavish dinners. For the last six years of his life, his wife carefully watched him, imposing a stringent diet with no alcohol. But on November 15, 1787, at a dinner with friends from Paris, Marianna Gluck's eagle-eyed vigilance for once failed, and Gluck, in an alcoholic orgy, gulped down a full decanter of brandy. That evening the creator of modern opera died.

Gluck's fame was unique in his time. Not only did he change the face of opera, but he improved performance and production standards. Never before had a composer so successfully dictated his wishes to management, orchestras, even star singers. He insisted on training singers himself and on having "as many rehearsals as I shall consider necessary," for "the best-composed works, when badly executed, become the most insupportable of all." Gluck was a despot, often unpleasant, unable to stand any criticism—but in opera production he always seemed to get his way.

Well into the nineteenth century, Gluck was considered one of the major immortals of his art. A decline in his reputation was inevitable as Mozart's operas became more universally known and treasured, yet Gluck's influence and revolutionary impact on Luigi Cherubini, on Beethoven's *Fidelio*, and on the music-dramas of Hector Berlioz and Richard Wagner make him a heroic figure. Berlioz said that it was after hearing *Iphigénie en Tauride* that he definitively decided to become a musician. In his memoirs he relates, "I read and reread Gluck's scores. I copied them and learnt them by heart. I went without sleep because of them and forgot to eat or drink. An ecstasy possessed me." Thirty years later, after completing his opera *Les Troyens*, Berlioz proudly said of himself, "I believe that if Gluck were to return, he would say: 'This is my son.'"

Gluck is presently more neglected than performed; he is nevertheless an austere and noble master of dramatic music whose "reform" operas can be appreciated by audiences seeking music of nobility and stately grandeur. His work is the proudest representation of eighteenth-century opera-theater until Mozart's maturity.

Orfeo ed Euridice (1761–62)

Orfeo (Orpheus), the legendary Greek musician and poet, is allowed to bring his wife Euridice (Eurydice) back from death only if he can resist looking at her. But he succumbs to the temptation, and all is lost. Calzabigi's libretto deviates from the bleak finality inherent in the Greek tragedy, though, and Orfeo is told that the power of his love has inspired the gods. Orfeo sings Gluck's most celebrated aria, "Che farò senza Euridice," then instead of joining Euridice in death, he too is allowed to live, and both lovers return to the world. One of Gluck's reforms was his superb use of the chorus as a major factor in his drama, as it was used in Greek drama. The recitatives are accompanied not by the harpsichord but by the orchestra. Gluck's use of orchestral effects was unprecedented, as in the grotesque barking of the three-headed dog. Never had an orchestra been so stark as in Gluck's realistic presentation of the furies, demons, and other dark horrors of Hades. *Orfeo ed Euridice* is Gluck's most integrated work, and it is the earliest opera that is still widely performed today.

Moffo, Raskin, Verrett, Collegium Musicum Italicum Instrumental Ensemble, Rome Virtuosi, Fasano: RCA 7896-2-RG (Italian version)

Donath, Lorengar, Horne, Royal Opera House Orchestra and Chorus, Covent Garden, Solti: London 417410-2

McNair, Sieden, Ragin, English Baroque Soloists, Monteverdi Choir London, Gardiner: Philips 434093-2

OTHER PRINCIPAL WORKS

BALLET
Don Juan (1761)

OPERAS
Alceste (1767)*
Iphigénie en Aulide (1774)*
Armide (1777)*
Iphigénie en Tauride (1779)*

FRANZ JOSEPH HAYDN

b. Rohrau, Lower Austria, March 31, 1732

d. Vienna, May 31, 1809

Oh, God, how much is still to be done in this splendid art, even by a man like myself.

Haydn was born to poor parents in a hamlet in Lower Austria. His father was a wheelwright and played the harp by ear. His mother was a cook for an aristocratic household; she, too, had musical leanings. Haydn astonished his parents with his perfect pitch and his fine voice. (In 1737 his brother Michael, who would later become an eminent musician, was born.) When Franz was six, a distant cousin from Hainburg took him as a boarder and arranged for his musical education. Although Haydn later recalled that there had been "more floggings than food" at his cousin's home, he was nonetheless grateful for the training he received.

When Haydn was eight, Georg Reutter, *Kapellmeister* of Vienna's famous St. Stephen's Cathedral, paid a visit to Hainburg and happened to hear the boy's small but sweet voice. Reutter was impressed enough to take Haydn back to Vienna, where he became a hard-working chorister at Reutter's church. It was a splendid opportunity, without which Haydn might have had no musical future. In the eighteenth century, it was rare for someone of the lower class ever to move from his place of birth, let alone achieve international celebrity, as Haydn would.

When he reached adolescence, Haydn's voice started to change, which meant he would be dismissed from his post. Reutter (who in spite of his admiration for Haydn's talent had never particularly liked the boy) suggested that his voice—and thus his livelihood—might be saved by castration. The operation was then by no means a rarity, and the court chapel housed more than a dozen castrati, whose value in churches and opera houses was prized. Famous ones, like Farinelli, were idolized and royally paid. But Haydn, already susceptible to the charms of women, was horrified at the proposal. When his voice broke, he was dismissed from the cathedral choir.

Free now but practically starving, Haydn found himself singing for his supper on the street. With a small loan, he rented a dingy attic, bought a broken-down harpsichord, and acquired some pupils. Although he played the harpsichord well, he was, in his own words, "no conjuror on any instrument." Later in life he lamented the eight wretched years he spent teaching children. But he used those years well and studied everything in sight, from the composer Johann Joseph Fux's 1725 *Gradus ad Parnassum*, a treatise on counterpoint, to the most recent keyboard sonatas of C.P.E. Bach.

In due course, Haydn secured a position as valet and copyist to the eminent composer and singing master Nicola Porpora. This post gave him valuable contacts. In 1761, at age twenty-nine, he was hired as a court musician by Prince Paul Anton Esterházy, head of the wealthiest family in the Holy Roman Empire. Haydn was quite happy to leave Vienna for the prince's 210-room palace at Eisenstadt. Within a year Paul died, but his brother Nikolaus, "the magnificent," was pleased to retain Haydn as an official vassal of the court. His three-decade tenure as Nikolaus's *Kapellmeister* is the most eloquent example of noble patronage in an age of princely bounty.

A few years before going to Eisenstadt, Haydn had married a woman who caused him much unhappiness. The childless couple eventually separated, but Haydn continued to support his wife throughout her life. (As Catholics, they never divorced.)

Though Haydn occasionally missed Vienna and felt lonely, his circumstances at court suited him admirably. His duties were heavy and included the daily administration of the prince's considerable musical forces. But he was an efficient administrator, and his musicians affectionately called him Papa. Most important, Haydn was literally forced to compose music in great quantity. It was during these years that he, above all composers, codified the sonata form, which would become the most important means of expression for Mozart, Beethoven, and Schubert.

In 1766 Prince Nikolaus unveiled Esterháza, which after Versailles was the largest and most lavish palace in Europe, a veritable paradise set in "a delightful grove, containing a deer park, flower gardens and hot-houses, elaborately furnished summer-houses, grottoes, hermitages, and temples." There were as well two elegant theaters for drama and opera. Over the years, Haydn composed an abundance of symphonies, quartets, masses, and operas, and more than two hundred trios using the *baryton*, or *viola di bordone*, a now-obsolete string instrument that the prince loved to play.

No composer had ever been left to develop so peacefully and with so many resources at his command than Haydn, who acknowledged, "My Prince was always satisfied with my works; I not only had the encouragement of constant approval, but as conductor of an orchestra, I could make experiments, observe what produced an effect and what weakened it, and was thus in a position to improve, alter, make additions or omissions, and be as bold as I pleased. I was cut off from the world, there was no one to confuse or torment me, and I was forced to become *original*."

In 1790 Nikolaus died, and the Esterháza orchestra was disbanded. With freedom and financial security, Haydn was pleased to settle into an easier and more convivial life in Vienna. Although he had been cut off from the world at Esterháza, his music had traveled far and wide, and he found himself the most famous composer in Europe. Shortly after his return to Vienna, a London impresario, Johann Peter Salomon, offered Haydn a large commission: to compose six symphonies and conduct them in London. Haydn, who had never traveled, was thrilled with the prospect of adventure. Crossing the English Channel on a stormy night, the great composer arrived in London on New Year's Day 1791.

The evening before his departure, Haydn and Mozart, who had been close friends since 1781, dined together. As they departed, Mozart said, "We shall not ever meet again." Although Mozart had never visited Haydn at Esterháza, Haydn had usually gone to Vienna every year for a short visit. It is interesting that both masters wrote their finest music after their friendship began.

Haydn's eighteen months in England were like a fairy tale. Not since Handel's death more than thirty years before had the English so venerated a composer. His new symphonies were heralded as works of genius; articles and poems about him appeared in the press. Banquets were given in his honor. Nobility and musicians of every ilk flocked to him. Oxford gave him an honorary degree. The king and queen begged him to stay permanently. He enjoyed it all enormously, even though, as he once said, the humble composer "[preferred] people of [his] own class." The only blight during his London sojourn was the terrible news of Mozart's tragic early death on December 5, 1791.

Upon returning to Vienna in the summer of 1792, Haydn was besieged by commissions and social engagements, but he still found time to teach the recalcitrant young Beethoven, who had recently moved from Bonn to Vienna. Haydn now commenced work on a series of radiant masses. His church music was more joyful than pious, and when asked why, he replied, "Because whenever I think of God, I always feel so indescribably happy."

In the fall of 1793, London once again beckoned: Salomon asked for six new symphonies. Early in 1794 Haydn arrived in the British capital again, staying for another eighteen months. There he was awed by performances of Handel's oratorios. The seed had been planted, and on his return home, he started composing *The Creation*. "I knelt down every day and prayed God to strengthen me for my work," he wrote. On April 29, 1798, *The Creation* was heard publicly in Vienna. After the performance, Haydn wrote, "One moment I was cold as ice, the next I seemed to be on fire. More than once I was afraid I should have a stroke." Almost immediately he began work on another oratorio, and *The Seasons* had its premiere in the spring of 1801. *The Creation* and *The Seasons* would become the two most popular works of their genre after Handel.

But now Haydn was feeble and exhausted. "*The Seasons*," he declared, "gave me the finishing stroke." He was badly afflicted with rheumatism, his legs so painful and swollen that he could not walk. Composing ceased almost totally, which caused him terrible frustration. "I have only just learned in my old age how to use the wind instruments," he told a friend, "and now that I do understand them I must leave the world."

On March 27, 1808, Haydn, now Austria's major celebrity, was seen for the last time in public at a performance of *The Creation*, conducted by Antonio Salieri. After the first part of the work, overcome by emotion, Haydn had to be carried home. Beethoven, who had also attended the performance, rushed to the doors of the theater, passionately kissing the old master's hands and forehead.

In mid-May 1809, the French army occupied Vienna. When French officers paid Haydn a courtesy call, he asked his servant to carry him to the piano, where he proudly played his composition "The Emperor's Hymn," which became Austria's national anthem. Days later he was dead. Napoleon himself ordered an honor guard to surround his home. On June 15 Mozart's Requiem was sung in Vienna, and memorial services took place from Cádiz to St. Petersburg. No artist had lived a more fruitful or humble life. "I know that God has bestowed a talent on me," he said, "and I thank Him for it; I think I have done my duty, and been of use in my generation by my works."

Haydn was an innovator who consolidated, developed, and refined the Classical form's aesthetic and intellectual content, which places him in the forefront of eighteenth-century music. Mozart's contact with him greatly enriched the younger man, and Beethoven found his major early inspiration in Haydn's example.

To rank Haydn, as is often done, below Mozart and as Beethoven's necessary forerunner is a disservice to his greatness. This attitude has prevented performers from adequately exploring a staggering output of an amazingly consistent high quality. But Haydn, the obedient servant of the aristocracy, has come in through the servants' entrance for too long. The label *Papa*, in turn, conjures a picture of a benevolent old man who blithely wrote good-natured music. Never has a superficial image done more harm to a composer of such vitality, originality, and profundity. One critic wrote condescendingly, "Haydn compels our study just because he is so like other men, so amply representative of them within their own limitations." Such nonsense has caused Haydn, except for a few works, to be all but obliterated from public musical performance. The twentieth century concentrated mainly on its happy rediscovery of Mozart, and although Haydn research has taken great strides since 1950, he remains but a shadow in the performance world. Fortunately, recordings have preserved for us one of the most wonderful of all composers.

Six Quartets for Strings (*Erdödy Quartets*), Op. 76, H.III/75-80 (1797)

The listener new to Haydn has an embarrassment of riches in string quartets. One may choose to hear the Six *Sun Quartets* (Op. 20, 1772); the Six *Russian Quartets* (Op. 33, 1781); the rarely recorded Six *Prussian Quartets* (Op. 50, 1787); the *Tost Quartets* (Op. 64, 1790); and many others. The most famous are the Six *Erdödy Quartets* (Op. 76). No. 1 in G major is noted for its hushed slow movement, an Adagio sostenuto, mezza voce. No. 2 is called *Quinten* (*Fifths*) because of the intervals of falling fifths in the first movement. In No. 3, *Emperor*, Haydn used the melody (and variations on it) that he composed for Emperor Francis I, which became the Austrian national anthem. No. 4 is known as *Sunrise* because of its progression from dark to light in the first movement. In No. 5 Haydn, a great master of asymmetrical form, composed a slow movement that is almost as long as the other three movements together. No. 6 has a gray tone and is the most interpretively problematic of the series.

Amadeus Quartet: Deutsche Grammophon 415867-2
Takács String Quartet: London 421360-2 and 425467-2

Concertos (various dates)

Haydn wrote concertos for horn, organ, violin, oboe, keyboard, flute, violin, and other instruments. Four of his concertos are well known: the sparkling and smiling D major keyboard concerto (1784), the C major and D major cello concertos (c. 1761–65 and 1783, the most frequently played in the eighteenth-century repertory), and the cheerful, irrepressible Trumpet Concerto (1796).

Concerto in D Major for Keyboard, Two Oboes, Two Horns, and Strings, H.XVIII/9 (1784)

PERFORMED ON HARPSICHORD
Pinnock, English Concert, Pinnock: Archiv 431678-2

PERFORMED ON PIANO
Kissin, Moscow Virtuosi, Spivakov: RCA 7948-2-RC

Concerto in C Major for Cello and Orchestra, H.VIIb/1 (1761–65)
Du Pré, London Symphony Orchestra, Barbirolli: EMI Classics ZDMB 69707

Concerto in D Major for Cello and Orchestra, H.VIIb/2 (1783)
Harell, Academy of St. Martin in the Fields, Marriner: EMI Classics CDM 64326

Concerto in E-flat Major for Trumpet and Orchestra, H.VIIe/1 (1796)
Symphony no. 88, H.I/88
André, Zurich Chamber Orchestra, de Stoutz: EMI Classics CDC 54086
Schwarz, New York Chamber Symphony Orchestra, Schwarz: Delos DCD 3001
Marsalis, National Philharmonic of London, Leppard: CBS MK 37846

Sonatas for Piano (various dates)

Haydn's fifty-two keyboard sonatas are not as easy to assimilate as those of Mozart. They are diffuse, often brusque, wilder—indeed, often experimental. Haydn was less interested in singing memorable tunes on the keyboard than in creating "pure musical" expression. These sonatas, like the neglected keyboard trios, have an earthy passion. Haydn's devastating and often biting humor is irrepressible.

Sonatas no. 20, 28–33 for Piano
Kocsis, Hungaroton HCD 11618-19

Sonatas no. 2, 49, 52 for Piano
Bilson: Elektra/Nonesuch 78018-2

Sonatas no. 32, 34, 37, 40, 42, 48–52 for Piano
Brendel: Philips 4-416643-2

Symphonies (1763–89)

It is a pity that conductors choose to feast on so few of Haydn's symphonies. Each has a rare and individual quality. No. 13, *Jupiter* (1763); No. 22, *The Philosopher* (1764); No. 26, *Lamentatione* (1770); No. 30, *Alleluja* (1765); No. 31, *Hornsignal* (1765); No. 43, *Mercury* (1772); No. 44, *Trauer* (1772); No. 45, *Farewell* (1772); No. 48, *Maria Theresia* (1769); No. 49, *La Passione* (1768); No. 53, *L'Impériale* (1778–79); No. 55, *The Schoolmaster* (1774); No. 59, *Fire* (1769); No. 63, *La Roxelane* (1781); and No. 73, *La Chasse* (1782)—each of these nicknamed symphonies is wonderful fare for the Haydn admirer. Nos. 82 through 87 are the better-known Paris Symphonies, composed in 1785–86 for a concert society in Paris. Symphony no. 88 in G Major is one of Haydn's most beloved works. Every page contains novel beauties. Symphony no. 92, called *Oxford*, was composed in 1789 and was performed at the famous university when Haydn received an honorary doctorate, on July 7, 1791. It is a work of unblemished beauty, and the Adagio cantabile is one of the great slow movements of Classicism.

Symphony no. 88 in G Major (c.1787)
Berlin Philharmonic Orchestra, Furtwängler: Deutsche Grammophon 447439-2
New York Philharmonic Orchestra, Bernstein: Sony Classical SM2K 47563

Symphony no. 92 in G Major (*Oxford*) (1789)
Cleveland Orchestra, Szell: Sony Classical SBK 46332
Vienna Philharmonic Orchestra, Böhm: Deutsche Grammophon 429523-2

The London Symphonies (1791–95)

With the D major symphony, No. 93, we enter the hallowed realm of the tremendous dozen—the symphonies Haydn composed for London represent, along with Mozart's last symphonies, the high plateau of symphonic art before Beethoven. When Mozart heard that Haydn was to go to London, he worried for the old master's welfare: "Oh, Papa, you have no education for the wide world." Haydn, without knowing two words of English, emphatically declared, "But all the world understands my language." No. 93 was first played on February 17, 1792, with the impresario Johann Peter Salomon conducting.

No. 94 in G major is known as the *Surprise* because of a loud kettledrum stroke within the slow movement. This *fortissimo*, however, has no important meaning in the context of the movement except perhaps, in our louder world, to raise a smile. The symphony itself exhibits Haydn's usual lively imagination and formal mastery. The slow movement tune is known to every child as "Twinkle, Twinkle Little Star."

No. 95 in C minor is the only London Symphony that does not begin with a slow introduction—a procedure that Haydn frequently used to set up his sonata-allegro first movements. This introduction functions almost as an overture to the movement. The critic Edward Downes writes, "Haydn shows himself to be one of the masterful innovators of his era. Outwardly a lighthearted sonata allegro, this brisk finale incorporates techniques and style traits of the fugue."

No. 96 in D major, the *Miracle,* is so called because as Haydn was taking his seat at the harpsichord, a large crowd from the middle of the hall rose and gathered closer to see the great composer. At that moment, a gigantic chandelier crashed from the ceiling onto their empty seats. The astonished crowd shouted, "It's a miracle!" The word stuck, but it has always been applied to the wrong symphony. In fact, the incident took place before the performance of Symphony no. 102.

In the Symphony no. 97 in C Major, the Minuetto is especially felicitous, as Haydn deftly varied his orchestration. The slow movement, as usual with Haydn, is ample and subtle. The coda is a beautifully emotional episode, while the airy Presto assai is a finale that in its swiftness and dash could only have been composed by Haydn.

Symphony no. 98 in the sturdy key of B-flat major was an instant hit in London. One writer called it "one of the grandest compositions we ever heard, and it was loudly applauded; the first and last movements were encored." In an age when compositions were not frequently heard, the audience's favorite movement was often encored.

A close friend of Haydn's died while he was at work on the Symphony no. 99 in E-flat Major, which may account for the piercing grief of the slow movement. The Symphony no. 100 in G Major, known as the *Military,* is one of the most popular of all Haydn's symphonies. When it was first performed, London audiences were intrigued with the use of the triangle, bass drum, and cymbals to induce martial feelings. "Encore! Encore!" the first-night audience shouted after the second movement. After composing one hundred symphonies, the true miracle was that Haydn had never even vaguely repeated himself. Indeed, in Symphony no. 101, the *Clock,* the orchestral writing becomes richer than ever, while its final Rondo is more extended. The Symphony no. 102 in B-flat Major is less frequently performed though quite equal to its companions. The finale is unbuttoned Haydn, with all stops out.

The penultimate Symphony no. 103 in E-flat Major is called the *Drum*

Roll because of the timpani roll in the first movement. London audiences were once again enthralled with the richly colored composition, first performed on March 2, 1795. George III, a confirmed Handelian, and his musical queen, Charlotte, who had studied piano with Johann Christian Bach, begged the composer to stay permanently in London, even offering him rooms at Windsor Castle.

Symphony no. 104 in D Major, *London*, is Haydn's final and most majestic effort as a composer of symphonies. It begins once again with an Adagio, followed by an Allegro format of increasing intensity. The Andante is serene until the mood is shattered by a full orchestral blast. The vigorous Minuet releases itself into a lovely Trio, and the finale, marked *spiritoso*, has a folklike flavor using mostly one theme. With this symphony Haydn took leave of the form that he had made immortal.

Haydn's two visits to London were now over and he was amazed at the large amount of money he had made. On April 13, 1795, at King's Theatre, Haydn bade farewell to the English public, who were so receptive and gracious to him and who seemed to understand that they were listening to the greatest music of their age.

It is extremely refreshing to hear Haydn's music performed on period instruments. Roy Goodman conducts the Hanover Band in twelve volumes (Hyperion 66520 to 66531). Other period versions, by Christopher Hogwood and Trevor Pinnock, are equally tempting. The LP performances of Antál Dorati, a long-standing Haydn conductor, have been transferred to thirty-two CDs in eight volumes (London 430100-2).

Symphony no. 93 in D Major, H.I/93 (1791)
New York Philharmonic Orchestra, Bernstein: Sony Classical SM3K 47553
London Philharmonic Orchestra, Solti: London 417620-2

Symphony no. 94 in G Major (*Surprise*), H.I/94 (1791)
Academy of Ancient Music, Hogwood: L'Oiseau-Lyre 414330-2
Royal Concertgebouw Orchestra, C. Davis: Philips 442614-2

Symphony no. 95 in C Minor, H.I/95 (1791)
Royal Concertgebouw Orchestra, Harnoncourt: Teldec 9031-73148-2
English Chamber Orchestra, Tate: EMI Classics CDD 64286

Symphony no. 96 in D Major (*Miracle*), H.I/96 (1791)
Austro-Hungarian Haydn Orchestra, Fischer: Nimbus NI 5135
Scottish Chamber Orchestra, Schwarz: Delos DCD 3062

Symphony no. 97 in C Major, H.I/97 (1792)
Orchestra of the Eighteenth Century, Brüggen: Philips 434921-2
New York Philharmonic Orchestra, Bernstein: Sony Classical SM3K 47553

Symphony no. 98 in B-flat Major, H.I/98 (1792)
NBC Symphony Orchestra, Toscanini: RCA 60281-2-RG
Austro-Hungarian Haydn Orchestra, Fischer: Nimbus NI 5230-2

Symphony no. 99 in E-flat Major, H.I/99 (1793)
London Philharmonic Orchestra, Beecham: Pearl PEA 9064
Philharmonic Orchestra, Slatkin: RCA 09026-68425-2
Royal Concertgebouw Orchestra, Harnoncourt: Teldec 2292-46331-2

Symphony no. 100 in G Major (*Military*), H.I/100 (1793–94)
Vienna Symphony Orchestra, Sawallisch: Philips 422973-2
Academy of St. Martin in the Fields, Marriner: Philips 420866-2
New York Philharmonic Orchestra, Mitropoulous: Enterprise ENTLV 976

Symphony no. 101 in D Major (*Clock*), H.I/101 (1793–94)
Orchestra of St. Luke, Mackerras: Telarc CD 80311
New York Philharmonic Orchestra, Bernstein: Sony Classical SM2K 47557

Symphony no. 102 in B-flat Major, H.I/102 (1794)
New York Philharmonic Orchestra, Walter: Sony Classical SMK 64485
Hanover Band, Goodman: Hyperion CDA 66528

Symphony no. 103 in E-flat Major (*Drum Roll*), H.I/103 (1795)
Berlin Philharmonic Orchestra, Karajan: Deutsche Grammophon 410517-2
Lausanne Chamber Orchestra, López-Cobos: Denon CO 79729

Symphony no. 104 in D Major (*London*), H.I/104 (1795)
Royal Concertgebouw Orchestra, C. Davis: Philips 442611-2
London Symphony Orchestra, Solti: London 417330-2

The Creation, H.XXI/2 (1796–98)

The Creation is the world's most revered oratorio after *Messiah*. Before he visited London, Haydn knew little of the oratorio form, but he was deeply moved by Handel's *Messiah*, *Israel in Egypt*, and others. After returning to Vienna, he

vowed to write an oratorio himself. *The Creation*, in the words of the critic
C. G. Burke, "is the greatest splendor that innocence has ever worn. The deepest resources of a profound musical mind have been lavished to prove an absence of guile. This music has the obviousness of the very earth, the sweetness
of the south wind, the happiness of sunlight, the exultation of completeness. It
is the lyrical imagery of eyes that find nothing to question. It is cherubic, and it
cannot be doubted." Haydn's *Creation* (in three parts) is the most "pictorial"
music written before the nineteenth century. Part III brings together Adam,
Eve, and angels in benediction before "The Fall."

Janowitz, Wünderlich, Borg, Vienna Philharmonic Orchestra, Karajan: Bella Voce BLV 7204
Upshaw, Humphrey, Cheek, Atlanta Symphony Orchestra, Atlanta Chamber Chorus, Shaw:
    Telarc CD 80298
Seefried, Holm, Borg, Berlin Philharmonic Orchestra, St. Hedwig's Cathedral Choir, Marke-
    vitch: Deutsche Grammophon 437380-2

OTHER PRINCIPAL WORKS

CHAMBER MUSIC
Seventy-five quartets for strings*
Sixty-five trios for two violins and bass
125 works for *baryton* (string instrument), viola, and cello
Forty-three trios for piano, violin, and cello*
Six trios for flute, violin, and cello

CHURCH MUSIC
Fourteen masses (especially nos. 10, 11, and 14)*

CONCERTOS
Two flute concertos
Concertos no. 3 and 4 for Violin and Orchestra
Two horn concertos

OPERAS
Nine operas

ORATORIO
Die Jahreszeiten (The Seasons) (1801)*

ORCHESTRAL WORKS

104 symphonies*

Sixteen overtures

Twenty *divertimentos*

KEYBOARD WORKS

Fifty-two sonatas*

Andante with Variations in F Minor*

WOLFGANG AMADEUS MOZART

b. Salzburg, January 27, 1756

d. Vienna, December 5, 1791

People are wrong who think my art comes easily to me. I assure you, nobody has devoted so much time and thought to composition as I. There is not a famous master whose music I have not industriously studied through many times.

The most wonderful artistic prodigy of all time was born in Salzburg, an enchanting town where music was profusely practiced—a town that Mozart grew to detest. Mozart's mother, a sensitive, unassuming woman, gave her two children love and warmth. His father, Leopold, a composer and a fine violinist, proved to be a clever and demanding teacher for his wonder children. Wolfgang's sister, Maria Anna, five years older, showed an outstanding aptitude for music. Even at age three, Wolfgang listened enthralled to her lessons. It was soon apparent that his gifts of ear and coordination surpassed even those of "Nannerl," as Maria Anna was called. By five the child was composing harpsichord pieces that showed an instinct for elegance and flexibility. Some of Mozart's juvenilia are superior to many works by his mature colleagues.

Perhaps more from pride than for financial gain, Leopold could not resist showing his children off. He was entirely capable of supporting his family in comfort; he had an excellent court position in Salzburg, and his published violin method had attracted private students. It was an age of prodigies, but Leopold was convinced that Nannerl at eleven was already the finest harpsichordist in Europe, and his son a phenomenon the like of which the world had never seen. Wolfgang was just six when Leopold took his prizes to Munich, where they stunned the elector of Bavaria. Word spread quickly, and later in 1762 the children were presented in Vienna at the Schöbrunn Palace. The Imperial Court, including the royal family, was thrilled, and Wolfgang's childish charm and easy manner further endeared him to them. The ladies lost their heart to the little fellow. Gifts, jewels, and cash were lavished on the children as tokens of the high nobles' appreciation.

The family stayed in Vienna for about four months, during which time little Wolfgang contracted scarlet fever, a dangerous disease that often killed children. Fortunately Wolfgang was spared, and by January 1763 the family was able to return home to Salzburg. Leopold, now seething with worldly ambition, planned a longer journey. On June 9, 1763, the little troupe started out again for Munich, then proceeded to numerous cities and towns in southern Germany, to Brussels, and finally to Paris on November 18. Everywhere the tiny boy played not only harpsichord and violin but also the organ, at leading churches. On New Year's Day 1764, by invitation of Louis XV himself, the family dined at Versailles. During these exciting times, Mozart became spoiled for life.

All the while Leopold painstakingly taught him, and while they were in Paris, he had the child's early violin sonatas (K.6–9) printed. They left the French capital in April 1764 and arrived in London, where the family remained until the summer of 1765. As usual, the children caused a sensation, giving public and private concerts and becoming the darlings of George III's court. More important for the long term was Wolfgang's friendship with the talented youngest son of J. S. Bach, Johann Christian, then thirty years old and Queen Charlotte's music master. The "London Bach," as he was called, adored the child and frequently spent time with him, introducing him to the newest music of the *style galant* and playing for him his own sonatas on the pianoforte, a new instrument that was making a stir in London.

After nine months in the British capital, the family went on to Holland, where fever incapacitated Wolfgang for weeks. As soon as he recovered, the strenuous tour continued. The Mozarts traveled on primitive roads and under difficult conditions until they returned home in November 1766. The children had been away from their mother for nearly three and a half years. Mozart's musical growth during this difficult but stimulating time was phenomenal.

Unfortunately, Nannerl showed no such development—but then, she did not receive the same pedagogical attention. After the first grand tour, she began to recede into the background, and her inseparable childhood bond with her brother faded as his celebrity grew. (She was to marry at thirty-three. After her husband died in poverty in 1801, she took on music students. In her last years she was blind and poor. She died in 1829, outliving her brother by nearly forty years.)

After returning to Salzburg, Leopold continued to work his son hard on counterpoint exercises and digesting the method of the Austrian composer and theorist Johann Joseph Fux's celebrated 1725 treatise on counterpoint, *Gradus ad Parnassum*. In September 1767, after only eight months at home, the entire family traveled to Vienna, expecting to cash in on the various court festivities. Instead, a smallpox epidemic broke out, and the nobility, fearing infection, fled the capital for their country retreats. Both Mozart children came down with the disease, and their parents were mad with anxiety as Wolfgang became blind for nine nightmarish days, although Nannerl quickly recovered. They returned to Salzburg in January 1769.

After less than a year of further study and many more concert exhibitions, Leopold decided that his twelve-year-old son must conquer Italy, where opera and church music reigned supreme. It was an extraordinary tour, lasting from December 1769 to March 1771. The itinerary included Verona, Mantua, Cremona, Bologna, Florence, Naples, Rome, Milan, Turin, Venice, Padua, and Vicenza. In Milan, after hearing Mozart's music, the famous German composer Johann Adolf Hasse told his friend, "This boy will consign us all to oblivion." How right he was. In Bologna Wolfgang took a few lessons with Padre Martini, the church composer revered as the foremost counterpoint teacher in Europe. The old man and the teenager got along famously; Martini gave Wolfgang complicated exercises, which he dispatched with ease. In Florence he met and accompanied the violinist Pietro Nardini and had the only real friendship of his formative years with Thomas Linley, a fourteen-year-old composer of promising talent who would drown in 1778.

Father and son arrived in Rome during Holy Week 1770, and Mozart was excited to be able to hear the *Miserere* of Gregorio Allegri, performed exclusively at the Vatican. The score of Allegri's work was well guarded, and copies were forbidden. After a single hearing, Mozart wrote down the entire composition from memory. In Naples they were entertained by the English ambassador Sir William Hamilton and Lady Hamilton, herself a fine keyboard player. At the Naples Conservatory, Wolfgang gave a concert, but the superstitious Neapolitans were convinced that Mozart's miracles were due to a magic ring on his finger. To prove to them that it was not true, he removed the ring and continued playing; the audience gasped in astonishment and fear while crossing themselves.

During Mozart's teen years, he made two more Italian visits, from August to December 1771 and from October 1772 to March 1773. With these tours, Mozart's legendary childhood concluded. No longer would the world be astonished by the Wunderkind. At seventeen he was just another musician competing in a crowded field. Seldom did Mozart's contemporaries rank him higher than Antonio Salieri or the eminent violinist and composer Karl Ditters von

Dittersdorf. Publication was infrequent, middle-class concert life was in its infancy, and after its first performance, a new work was usually relegated to obscurity.

As his letters abundantly attest, Mozart never got over his unique childhood. Never one to suffer fools gladly, he found it difficult to bow and scrape as his father had. He knew well his superiority as a musician, and he was irritated by mediocrity and annoyed that the world no longer raved about him as an adult. He was a disaster as a court musician and was always at odds with the archbishop of Salzburg. In September 1777, at age twenty-one, he received a leave of absence from the archbishop and hoped to establish himself in Paris.

In October, this time accompanied by his mother, Mozart left for Paris by way of Mannheim. In Mannheim he fell in love with Aloysia Weber, a beautiful sixteen-year-old singer. Leopold was furious: the Webers were poor, and Wolfgang, he said, must concentrate on his career. For her part, Aloysia made it clear that her interest in Mozart was limited. Years after his death, she was asked why she had rejected his love. "I did not know," she replied. "I only thought he was such a little man."

After five months in Mannheim, mother and son traveled to Paris. The French capital paid Mozart little attention, and fashionable society, including his childhood acquaintance, Queen Marie Antoinette, was exclusively interested in the operatic war surrounding Piccinni and Gluck. To make matters far worse, in July 1778 Mozart's beloved mother died while they were in Paris. Grieved and defeated in finding employment, he left Paris in September, never to return.

In what was probably the most relaxed period of his life, he meandered for several months, giving a few concerts, then returned to Salzburg and his job at court on January 15, 1779. The archbishop required him to stay in Salzburg under his watchful eyes, a situation that Mozart could not tolerate. The break between them finally came on June 8, 1781, when the archbishop called his captive musician a vile name and the two hurled insults back and forth. To his father, Wolfgang wrote, "I will never have anything more to do with Salzburg. I hate the archbishop almost to fury."

At this propitious moment, Mozart made an unprecedented leap for freedom. For the final ten years of his short life, he was history's first important professional "freelance" musician. Instinctively he had understood the necessity, at all costs, of leaving the archbishop as well as Salzburg, a town where he would have no opportunity to compose operas or grow musically. Unconsciously he knew he had to separate from his domineering father, who watched and censored a great deal of his behavior. His feelings toward Leopold were loving and grateful, but were also filled with fear.

In the summer of 1781, Mozart left for Vienna, where he began the most difficult but also the most fruitful years of his life. There he once again met his former love Aloysia. This time, however, it was Aloysia's younger sister, eighteen-year-old Constanze—an attractive, flighty, and fun-loving spend-thrift—who caught his eye. Over the intense opposition of his father and sister, Wolfgang married Constanze on August 4, 1782. It was not an easy marriage, yet the couple persevered, through infant deaths, near poverty, infidelities, and quarrels, having many gay and frivolous times as well.

Mozart's last ten years were spent in a constant struggle to earn money. Both he and Constanze were poor money managers, and the couple was for-ever in debt. Mozart was forced to give piano lessons and to take in boarders, one of whom was the child prodigy Johann Nepomuk Hummel. But musically speaking, the decade was miraculous. The six great piano concertos Nos. 20 through 25 (K.466, 467, 482, 488, 491, 503) were composed from February 1785 to December 1786. During this time, he composed thirty other scores, including Le Nozze di Figaro (The Marriage of Figaro, K.492). Between June 26 and August 10, 1788, Mozart, at a low point in his finances and without a commission, composed his last three and greatest symphonies, Nos. 39, 40, and 41 (K.543, 550, 551). He never heard them performed. By 1790—in less than nine years—he had composed more than two hundred works. His opera Die Zauberflöte (The Magic Flute, K.620) was performed in Vienna in September 1791 to rapt audiences.

But Mozart was desperately tired and ill beyond repair. After receiving a commission from a mysterious stranger for a Requiem, he began writing his mass for the dead, which he said he was actually composing for himself (K.626). He was convinced that he was slowly being poisoned, thus giving rise to the later, unfounded accusation that his rival Salieri had killed him. The ac-tual cause of Mozart's death remains veiled in mystery. Possibly it was uremia, a failure of the kidneys, or perhaps his body was simply exhausted from a life of utmost mental toil, the toil of a creative spirit that would not rest.

No money was available for a proper funeral, and the service was held in the open air outside the church. On that day there was a furious thunderstorm, and Constanze and the little funeral cortège decided not to accompany Mozart to his pauper's grave. Soon after his death, the bulk of his output was forgotten.

Mozart died just before the dawn of the nineteenth century, an era that de-sired sterner stuff than his music; to nineteenth-century ears, his work sounded tame and rococo, and he seemed like a doll dressed in an outmoded costume. His elegance and formal beauty were noted, but often he was thought of as merely a predecessor of the more turbulently dramatic Beethoven. In The Will to Power (1886), Friedrich Nietzsche called Mozart "a delicate and lovable soul, but quite eighteenth century even when he is serious." Today, however, commentators vie to outdo each other in proclaiming his genius. Mozart— ironically, given his feelings about it—is responsible for the fame and economy of his native Salzburg. Liquors, candies, and music festivals in his name abound. During his life, he seldom heard any of his compositions performed twice, and he would be amazed at the monthly arrival of new CDs of performances of his music.

Today's complex world finds Mozart a balm for sagging spirits. For cynics who think human perfection is an impossibility, Mozart is always with us to prove otherwise. With him we may walk through the paradise garden. The English pianist Myra Hess, in the bleakest hour during the bombings of London in World War II, received a letter from the great scientist Albert Einstein that said, "We cannot despair about mankind knowing that Mozart was a man."

Writing on Mozart, the American novelist Saul Bellow says that "he learned for himself the taste of disappointment, betrayal, suffering, the weakness, foolishness, and vanity of flesh and blood, as well as the emptiness of cynicism. In him we see a person who has only himself to rely on. But what a self it is, and what art it has generated. How deeply (beyond words) he speaks to us about the mysteries of our common human nature. And how unstrained and easy his greatness is."

Concerto no. 5 in A Major for Violin and Orchestra, K.219 (1775)

The sound of his father's violin was probably the first music Mozart ever heard. Mozart played the instrument well and wrote more than forty violin sonatas. All five violin concertos were composed when he was nineteen. The Fifth Concerto, the richest in detail and rhythmical variety, is bewitchingly gracious. The finale, marked *rondeau: tempo di menuetto*, is the best-known movement. It uses an *alla turca* (Turkish) style, which was then fashionable in Vienna. A. Hyatt King, a music critic, wrote, "The whole concerto is an object lesson in the construction of melodies from the notes of the tonic chord."

Lin, *English Chamber Orchestra, Leppard*: CBS MK 42364
Oistrakh, *Berlin Philharmonic Orchestra, Oistrakh*: EMI Classics CDM 69064

Concerto no. 9 in E-flat Major for Piano and Orchestra, K.271 (1777)

In Mozart's early years, the Classical piano concerto was still in its infancy. With his uncanny ability to create perfect symmetry, Mozart arrived at a partnership of piano and orchestra that has never been equaled. In January 1777, the twenty-one-year-old master composed his Ninth Piano Concerto, calling for an orchestra of only strings, oboes, and horns. In length and depth, this majestic work, with its exquisite and complex slow movement, is unprecedented in Mozart's already-formidable output and remains one of his greatest concertos. Charles Rosen devotes seventeen pages to an analysis of this score in his book *The Classical Style*. He observes that "with a sense of proportion and dramatic fitness unsurpassed by any other composer, Mozart bound himself only by the rules he reset and reformulated anew for each work."

Hess, Perpignan Festival Orchestra, Casals: Melodram MEL 18024
Uchida, English Chamber Orchestra, Tate: Philips 432086-2
Perahia, English Chamber Orchestra, Perahia: CBS MK 34562

Sonata no. 8 in A Minor for Piano, K.310 (1778)

Penned during the tragically dark time when Mozart's mother died in Paris, the A minor sonata, with its pulsating content, is one of the great works for solo piano from the Classical period. The musicologist Eva Badura-Skoda wrote, "Suddenly with the A minor sonata, a new world opens up. The opening theme is indeed majestic . . . the texture is orchestral in fullness and the relentless pulsing of the accompanying chords suggest majesty of a demonic and sinister kind. The second movement . . . displays a restrained passion. . . . The presto is one of the darkest movements Mozart ever wrote, with its remarkable fluctuations between resignation and defiance."

Lipatti: EMI Classics CD 69800
Pires: Denon CO 8007
Schnabel: Grammofono 2000 GRM 78503

Sinfonia concertante in E-flat Major for Violin and Viola, K.364 (1779)

Mozart's consummate use of string tone is unparalleled. Here he used a string orchestra supported merely by horns and oboes. The violin and viola are integrated in dialogues of profound beauty. The *Sinfonia concertante* suggests both concerto and symphony at once and is a bold formal experiment, completed in the early autumn of 1779. It is a sublime example of Mozart's unique sensitivity to sound in general and to these instruments in particular. No other composer has quite captured his ability to shift mood from gaiety to sadness with no obvious preparation, with an abruptness so startling that the listener is left behind.

Spalding, Primrose, New Friends of Music Orchestra, Stiedry: Pearl PEA 9045
Heifetz, Primrose, RCA Victor Symphony Orchestra, Solomon: RCA 6778-2
Perlman, Zukerman, Israel Philharmonic Orchestra, Mehta: Deutsche Grammophon 415486-2

Concerto no. 17 in G Major for Piano and Orchestra, K.453 (1784)

This is a score of glowing youthfulness, with a leisurely first movement. The slow-movement Andante uses five themes and is cast into a complex form. It possesses an intensely rarefied beauty. The critic C. M. Girdlestone wrote, "No concerto andante of Mozart's had reached hitherto such fullness. There had been pathetic ones, even tragic ones; none had penetrated into the soul with such breadth and depth. What is admirable is not only the quality of the inspiration, but its variety." In the finale, Mozart leaves the usual Rondo form for a theme, five variations, and a coda. The soloist and orchestra (consisting only of flute, two oboes, two bassoons, two horns, and strings) blend together magically.

Anda, Salzburg Mozarteum Camerata Academica, Anda: Deutsche Grammophon 447436-2
Barenboim, Berlin Philharmonia, Barenboim: Telarc 73128

Sonata no. 14 in C Minor for Piano, K.457 (1784)
Fantasia in C Minor for Piano, K.475 (1785)

Six years separate the C minor sonata, composed in 1784, from the A minor sonata (K.310). In performance it is frequently preceded by the C minor fantasia, with which it has an affinity in mood. In the range of its emotional freedom, the fantasia is unique in Mozart's solo piano music. The C minor sonata is the most dramatic of Mozart's piano sonatas, with an almost symphonic spaciousness.

Pires: Deutsche Grammophon 429739-2
Moravec: VAI Audio VAIA 1096

Quartets no. 14–19 for Strings, K.387, 421, 428, 458, 464, 465 (1782–85)

Tchaikovsky wrote, "Christ inspires truly and exclusively the feeling of love . . . we pity Him, we love in Him His ideal human side. . . . Mozart I love as the musical Christ." These six quartets were all composed between December 1782 and January 1785. Mozart had fully studied Haydn's quartets; in them he saw the path to a richer quartet style, and he gratefully dedicated his new works to his older friend.

No. 14 (K.387), in G major, is light but subtle; the interplay of instruments reveals a new connectiveness within the highly wrought, contrapuntal textures. No. 15 (K.421), in D minor, shares its turbulent tonality with the Twentieth Piano Concerto and *Don Giovanni*. No. 16 (K.428), in E-flat major, is rather experimental in its layout. Perhaps it was the conclusion of a performance of this quartet that prompted Haydn's famous comment to Leopold, "I tell you that your son is the greatest composer known to me either in person or by name." No. 17 (K.458), in B-flat major, is known as *The Hunt* because the opening theme sounds like a hunting call. This earthy, engaging, and tightly packed composition is one of the most often performed of the set. No. 18 (K.464), in A major, lacks the ingratiating qualities that this key usually stirs in Mozart. Instead it has stately seriousness. As with all of Mozart's music, it has unsuspected qualities of strangeness, which come upon the listener only after repeated listening. No. 19 (K.465), in C major, the so-called *Dissonant* Quartet, opens slowly with what was then an almost alarming display of dissonant chromaticism. Even Haydn was somewhat shocked at its audacity. The fabric of the quartet writing itself exhibits an unusually intense brotherhood in its unity.

Quartets no. 14 and 15
Cleveland Quartet: Telarc CD 80297
Guarneri String Quartet: Philips 426240-2

Quartet no. 16
Smetana String Quartet: Testament 1117

Quartet no. 17
Emerson Quartet: Deutsche Grammophon 445598
Budapest String Quartet: Biddulph LAB 140

Quartet no. 18
Smetana Quartet: Testament 1117

Quartet no. 19

Talich String Quartet: Calliope CAL 6256
Guarneri String Quartet: Philips 432076-2
Melos String Quartet: Deutsche Grammophon 429818-2

Concerto no. 20 in D Minor for Piano and Orchestra, K.466 (1785)

The Six Piano Concertos, Nos. 20–25, are universally acknowledged to be among the most honored works in the concerto literature. No. 20 is the first of Mozart's piano concertos to be written in a minor key. Its reception was less favorable than Mozart had anticipated from the response to his other concertos. Perhaps the dark, brooding first movement was too demonic for his polite, aristocratic audience. The middle movement, marked *Romanza*, has a melody of which Beethoven remarked to his pupil Ferdinand Ries, "We will never get an idea like that." Unexpectedly the movement erupts in a caldron of dark passion, then subsides to its original serenity. The finale continues its turbulent attitude. Beethoven performed it in public and wrote two cadenzas for the concerto, which was the nineteenth century's best-known Mozart concerto.

Haskil, Lamoureaux Orchestra, Markevitch: Philips 456826
Serkin, Columbia Symphony Orchestra, Szell: Sony Classical SM3K 47207
Uchida, English Chamber Orchestra, Tate: Philips 416381-2

Concerto no. 21 in C Major for Piano and Orchestra, K.467 (1785)

No. 21 is a regal work with one of the most complex piano parts of the series. The dreamlike Andante, with its magnificent sustained lyricism, is loveliness personified. The scoring, fuller than usual, uses two oboes, two bassoons, two horns, two trumpets, kettledrums, and strings.

Anda, Salzburg Mozarteum Camerata Academica, Anda: Deutsche Grammophon 447436-2
Casadesus, Cleveland Orchestra, Szell: Sony Classical SM3K 46519
Rubinstein, RCA Victor Symphony Orchestra, Wallenstein: RCA 7967-2

Concerto no. 22 in E-flat Major for Piano and Orchestra, K.482 (1785)

At the premiere of No. 22, the central Andante movement had such instant appeal that the audience demanded that the composer repeat it. K.482 is one of the longest of the piano concertos, running to thirty-five minutes in performance. It is incomparable for its breadth, humor, and pathos. In his volume on the Mozart piano concertos, C. M. Girdlestone wrote, "Combining grace and majesty, the music unfolds like a sovereign in progress, the queen of the concertos." Mozart adds two clarinets to his flute, two bassoons, two horns, two trumpets, kettledrums, and strings.

Landowska, New York Philharmonic Orchestra, Rodzinski: Iron Needle IN 1336
Schiff, Salzburg Mozarteum Camerata Academica, Végh: London 425855-2
Richter, English Chamber Orchestra, Britten: Music & Arts CD 761

Concerto no. 23 in A Major for Piano and Orchestra, K.488 (1786)

K.488 is one of the most popular of the group. Its opening movement is radiant. The slow movement, a *siciliana*, is transparent, touching, and melancholy; Mozart's use of the clarinet is exquisite. Strangely, it is the only movement Mozart ever composed in F-sharp minor. The English critic Eric Blom wrote, "The Finale, *allegro assai*, is euphoric, though not without that after-tang of sadness which is always liable to make one suddenly feel that Mozart, even in his most light-hearted moods, is fundamentally never a singer of ingenuous happiness." In the A major concerto, Mozart used an orchestra without oboes, trumpets, or drums.

Curzon, London Symphony Orchestra, Kertész: London 433086-2
Horowitz, La Scala Orchestra, Giulini: Deutsche Grammophon 423287-2
Goode, Orpheus Chamber Orchestra: Elektra/Nonesuch 79042-2

Concerto no. 24 in C Minor for Piano and Orchestra, K.491 (1786)

K.491 touches the sublime. It is Mozart's only minor-keyed concerto besides No. 20 in D minor. A. Hyatt King wrote, "In its sustained imaginative power, in unity of conception and in the amazing structure of its first movement, devised to contain and resolve stark and tragic passions within formal bounds, it reaches heights of Sophoclean grandeur." The work employs Mozart's largest orchestra, including two horns, two trumpets, and two kettledrums.

Bilson, English Baroque Soloists, Gardiner: Deutsche Grammophon 447295-2
Uchida, English Chamber Orchestra, Tate: Philips 422331-2

Concerto no. 25 in C Major for Piano and Orchestra, K.503 (1786)

Sometimes called the *Jupiter* among his concertos, No. 25 rivals No. 24 in complexity and grandeur. Even the finale of this Olympian work possesses an unusual seriousness. In the Twenty-fifth Concerto, Mozart's contrapuntal skill reaches a high point. It spurns the radiant lyricism and transparency of No. 17 and No. 23, but its austere sphere commands awe. In the first movement we find a march in C minor. The slow movement is a dignified and spacious aria. The gavottelike finale is still somewhat remote, although the duet between piano and oboe is delectable. In this concerto, the air is so pure that we take no notice of the heights it attains. It has a majesty that is unconscious of itself.

Fleisher, Cleveland Orchestra, Szell: CBS MYK 37762
Perahia, English Chamber Orchestra, Perahia: CBS MK 37267

Le Nozze di Figaro (*The Marriage of Figaro*), K.492 (1786)

Beaumarchais's play *The Marriage of Figaro* rocked prerevolutionary France with the force of a tornado. When Mozart decided to write an opera on the play, it seemed necessary to tone down some of the social implications of the original. Lorenzo Da Ponte, an adventurous wastrel, was at the time the librettist for Salieri, Mozart's court rival. But after a fracas, the librettist was free to work with Mozart. He subsequently wrote Italian librettos for *The Marriage of Figaro*, *Don Giovanni*, and *Così fan tutte*, which the conductor Sir Thomas Beecham called "a long summer day spent in a cloudless land by a southern sea." (Da Ponte continued his adventures after Mozart's death, living to be eighty-nine and dying in New York in 1837. He was buried in Greenwood Cemetery in Brooklyn.)

In the hilarious *Marriage of Figaro*, Da Ponte gave Mozart tremendous scope to exercise his gift of musical characterization. With its high sophistication and dazzling arias, duets, and ensemble numbers, many consider *Figaro* the supreme "comic" opera. Brahms thought, "Every number in *Figaro* is for me a marvel; I simply cannot understand how anyone could create anything so perfect." W. J. Turner, a Mozart biographer, felt, "The characters in *Figaro* are not the characters of Beaumarchais' play at all: they are entirely the creation of Mozart and the expression of his own personality in every single respect . . . never has the dewy freshness, the sensitiveness, sensuousness, and ecstasy of the human heart in the first bloom of its youth had such perfect expression."

Te Kanawa, Popp, von Stade, Allen, Ramey, London Philharmonic Orchestra, Solti: London
  410150-2

Harper, Blegen, Berganza, Fischer-Dieskau, Evans, English Chamber Orchestra, John Aldis
  Choir, Barenboim: EMI Classics CDMC 63646

Don Giovanni, K.527 (1787)

The philosopher George Santayana thought "*Don Giovanni* [was] the best of operas. . . . I love the tragedy in farce, the exquisiteness in folly that make it up." With *Don Giovanni*, Mozart wrote the most cataclysmic opera of the eighteenth century. Writing to his friend Madame von Meck, Tchaikovsky attempted to warm her to Mozart, whom she disliked:

> *Don Giovanni* was the first music to produce an overwhelming effect on me and it aroused in me a holy ecstasy. Donna Anna is the most superb and wonderful human presentation ever depicted in music. . . . I am quite incapable of describing to you what I feel on hearing *Don Giovanni*, especially the scene where the noble figure of the beautiful, proud, revengeful woman appears on the stage. Nothing in any opera has ever impressed me so deeply. Afterwards, when Donna Anna recognizes Don Giovanni, the man who has wounded her pride and killed her father, and her anger bursts out like a rushing torrent in that magnificent recitative, and then the aria later on, where every note in the orchestra seems to speak of her wrath and pride, I actually quiver with horror—I could cry out and weep from the overpowering strain on the emotions. And her lament over her father's body, the duet with Don Ottavio where she swears vengeance, her arioso and the great sextet in the churchyard— These are incomparable, superb operatic scenes! . . . Even as I write you, I could shed tears of agitation.

Schwarzkopf, Sutherland, Frick, Sciutti, Alva, Wächter, Philharmonia Orchestra and Chorus,
  Giulini: EMI Classics CDCC 56232

Watson, Ludwig, Gedda, Ghiaurov, New Philharmonia Orchestra and Chorus, Klemperer:
  EMI Classics CDMC 63841

Quintet in G Minor for Strings, K.516 (1787)

In 1787 Mozart, deeply troubled by his father's illness, composed a string quintet that is among the great manifestations of his simultaneously elfin and Olympian spirit. The quintet is the open door to his final years. For J.W.N. Sullivan, "The G minor Quintet is the most poignant expression of his angelic anguish at his late discovery of this earth's pain." Tchaikovsky wrote, "In his chamber music Mozart fascinates me by his purity and distinction of style and his exquisite handling of the parts. . . . There are things that bring tears to my eyes. I shall mention only the *adagio* of the G minor String Quintet. No one else has ever interpreted so beautifully and exquisitely in music the feeling of resignation and inconsolable sorrow." Mozart finished the quintet on May 16; his father passed away twelve days later.

Heifetz, Baker, Primrose, Majewski, Piatigorsky: RCA 7869-2
Tokyo String Quartet, Zukerman: RCA 09026-60940-2
Primrose, Griller String Quartet: Vanguard Classics 8024

Eine kleine Nachtmusik, K.525 (1787)

This celebrated serenade in four gracious movements is light music of the highest quality, composed as *Don Giovanni* was being born. The score is dated August 10, 1787. The first movement, Allegro, has a simple, even commonplace theme that Mozart transforms magically. In the famous second movement, Romanza, the composer creates music of beguiling delicacy. The third movement is an Allegretto in tempo and a Minuet and Trio in form, both as fresh as a budding flower. The spirited Rondo is gracious, with a childlike simplicity.

Hanover Band, Goodman: Nimbus NI 5228-2
Columbia Symphony Orchestra, Walter: CBS MYK 37774
Academy of Ancient Music, Hogwood: London 411720-2

Symphony no. 38 in D Major (Prague), K.504 (1786)

Mozart's *Marriage of Figaro* had only four performances in Vienna, but Prague took the opera to its heart. The composer wrote, "Here they talk about nothing but *Figaro*; they play nothing, sing nothing, whistle nothing but *Figaro*; they go to no opera but *Figaro* and forever honor *Figaro*." During this *Figaro* madness, on January 18, 1787, Mozart composed and conducted his D major symphony, appropriating a theme from the opera for the last movement. The symphony is in three movements instead of the usual four, dispensing with the Minuet and its Trio. It is notable for its intensity of expression and its rousing finale, with its delightful contrapuntal ingenuity.

English Baroque Soloists, Gardiner: Philips 426283-2
Berlin Philharmonic Orchestra, Böhm: Deutsche Grammophon 429521-2

Symphony no. 39 in E-flat Major, K.543 (1788)
Symphony no. 40 in G Minor, K.550 (1788)
Symphony no. 41 in C Major (*Jupiter*), K.551 (1788)

Incredibly, in less than six weeks in the summer of 1788, Mozart wrote three symphonies. What prompted him to shut himself up and write works for which he had no commission? Like his contemporaries, Mozart wrote for money and immediate consumption, yet in his last alienated years he found himself writing from musical conscience. He never heard these works performed. In this respect, his spirit looked forward to the Romantic age and "art for art's sake." By the 1790s the novelist and composer E.T.A. Hoffmann and others were using the term *Romantic* to describe some of Mozart's music.

The E-flat major symphony, No. 39, is less often performed but is no less great than its companions. It is sunlit, cheery, heartfelt, witty, and comforting in mood. While composing it, Mozart, because of financial difficulty, was forced to move from his home to cheaper quarters.

How different is the Symphony no. 40 in G Minor, with its elusive and poignant sorrow! G minor is a despairing tonality for Mozart, and in each movement he touches painful issues. Leonard Bernstein said, "What a piece! No amount of analysis or explanation can prepare one for the overwhelming surprise of its existence when it is actually heard in performance. It is hard to think of another work that so perfectly marries form and passion."

The Symphony no. 41 was first called *Jupiter,* for its Olympian character, by the composer Johann Baptist Cramer, who heard it in London early in the nineteenth century. This is Mozart's most powerful symphonic creation; it inhabits a colder, more abstract region than its sisters. Its amazing formal construction embraces a dazzling contrapuntal technique.

Symphony no. 39
Bamberg Symphony Orchestra, Jochum: Orfeo 045901
Vienna Philharmonic Orchestra, Bernstein: Deutsche Grammophon 413776-2
London Classical Players, Norrington: EMI Classics CDC 54090

Symphony no. 40
Cleveland Orchestra, Szell: Sony Classical SBK 46333
Chicago Symphony Orchestra, Reiner: RCA 09026-62588-2
English Chamber Orchestra, Britten: London Classics 444323-2

Symphony no. 41 (*Jupiter*)
Bamberg Symphony Orchestra, Jochum: Orfeo 045901
Amsterdam Baroque Orchestra, Koopman: Erato 2292-45857-2

Die Zauberflöte (The Magic Flute), K.620 (1791)

For The Magic Flute, Mozart composed music both silly and mysterious. It is a work of art that is at once enigmatic and popular. Mozart was a committed Freemason in an Austria that looked somewhat askance at Freemasonry's liberalism, considering it a threat both to the state and to formally encrusted Roman Catholicism. The Magic Flute contains many symbolic allusions to Freemasonry's ideals of human brotherhood. It is partly a German Singspiel (song-play) with spoken dialogue. It also laid the foundation for German Romantic opera to come, with Weber. Mozart, always pressed for time and in his usual state of panic, completed the glorious overture two days before conducting the first performance on September 30, 1791. In little more than two months, he would be dead. On the day before he passed away, in a feeble voice, he attempted to sing Papageno's little aria "Der Vogelfänger bin ich ja." The conductor Wilhelm Furtwängler once wrote, "The Magic Flute is life itself. Mozart . . . as is becoming increasingly apparent is a cosmic phenomenon, simply Mozart, entirely sui generis."

Hendricks, Anderson, Steinsky, Hadley, Allen, Lloyd, Scottish Chamber Orchestra and Chorus, Mackerras: Telarc CD 80302

Lorengar, Deutekom, Burrows, Prey, Fischer-Dieskau, Talvela, Vienna Philharmonic Orchestra, Solti: London 414568-2

Concerto in A Major for Clarinet, K.622 (1791)

Mozart loved the clarinet and used it in his orchestration with unprecedented charm and effect. A friendship with the clarinetist Anton Stadler inspired the great Clarinet Quintet (K.581, 1789) and the Clarinet Concerto (his last completed work, except for the Cantata K.623). On the verge of death, Mozart wrote music full of sunlight, gentleness, and autumnal beauty.

Shifrin, Mostly Mozart Festival Orchestra, Schwarz: Delos DCD 3020

Marcellus, Cleveland Orchestra, Szell: CBS MYK 37810

Brymer, London Symphony Orchestra, Davis: Philips 420710-2

Requiem, K.626 (1791)

In the summer of 1791, Mozart received one half of a handsome fee from an anonymous person to commission a requiem mass. In early October, after he completed *The Magic Flute*, his health withered frightfully. He became convinced that he was writing his own requiem. As death approached, his primary concern was to complete the score and receive the rest of the payment for his family. Only hours before his last breath, he was in tears, singing in a faint whisper the "Lacrimosa." Death intervened before he could finish it, and the work was finished by his pupil Franz Süssmayr from his master's wishes and sketches. Fortunately, Süssmayr's contribution was inspired, as if for a moment he became possessed of Mozart's genius. In a letter to his father, Mozart had written,

> Since death, strictly speaking, is the true end and purpose of our life, for several years I have made myself so familiar with this true, best friend of men that his image holds nothing frightening for me anymore, but much that is calming and consoling. And I thank my God that he granted to me the blessing of providing me with the opportunity of recognizing in Death the real key to our true happiness. I never go to bed without considering that perhaps, as young as I am, I may not see the next day dawn.

Edvard Grieg observed, "The death of Mozart before he had passed his thirty-fifth year is perhaps the greatest loss the musical world has ever suffered."

Bonney, von Otter, Blochwitz, White, English Baroque Soloists, Monteverdi Choir London, Gardiner: Philips 420197-2

Cotrubas, Watts, Tear, Shirley-Quirk, Academy of St. Martin in the Fields, Academy of St. Martin in the Fields Chorus, Marriner: London 417746-2

OTHER PRINCIPAL WORKS

Note: Mozart used no opus numbers, and in the nineteenth century, the Austrian botanist Ludwig von Köchel catalogued his work in order of composition. The K. listings are now universally used for Mozart's works.

CHAMBER MUSIC

Forty-two violin and piano sonatas

Seven piano trios

Quintet in E-flat Major for Horn and Strings, K.407 (1782)*

Quartet in G Minor for Piano and Strings, K.478 (1785)*

Quartet in E-flat Major for Piano and Strings, K.493 (1786)*

Trio in E-flat Major for Clarinet, Viola, and Piano (*Kegelstatt*), K.498 (1786)*

Quintet in C Major for Strings, K.515 (1787)*

Trio in E-flat Major for Violin, Viola, and Cello (*Ein Divertimento*), K.563 (1788)*
Quintet in A Major for Clarinet and Strings, K.581 (1789)*

CHURCH MUSIC

Exsultate, jubilate (motet), K.165 (1773)*
Mass in C Major (*Coronation*), K.317 (1779)
Mass in C Minor (*The Great Mass*), K.427 (1782–83)*
Ave verum corpus (motet), K.618 (1791)*

CONCERTOS

Concerto no. 5 in D Major for Piano and Orchestra, K.175 (1773)
Concerto in B-flat Major for Bassoon and Orchestra, K.191 (1774)
Concerto no. 4 in D Major for Violin and Orchestra, K.218 (1775)
Concerto no. 7 in F Major for Three Pianos and Orchestra, K.242 (1776)
Concerto in C Major for Flute, Harp, and Orchestra, K.299 (1778)*
Concerto no. 1 in G Major for Flute and Orchestra, K.313 (1778)
Concerto no. 2 in D Major for Flute and Orchestra, K.314 (1778)*
Concerto in C Major for Oboe and Orchestra, K.314 (1778)*
Concerto no. 10 in E-flat Major for Two Pianos and Orchestra, K.365 (1779)*
Concerto no. 12 in A Major for Piano and Orchestra, K.414 (1782)*
Concerto in E-flat Major for Horn and Orchestra, K.417 (1783)*
Concerto in E-flat Major for Horn and Orchestra, K.447 (1784–87)*
Concerto no. 14 in E-flat Major for Piano and Orchestra, K.449 (1784)
Concerto no. 15 in B-flat Major for Piano and Orchestra, K.450 (1784)*
Concerto no. 19 in F Major for Piano and Orchestra, K.459 (1784)*
Concerto in E-flat Major for Horn and Orchestra, K.495 (1786)*
Concerto no. 26 in D Major for Piano and Orchestra (*Coronation*), K.537 (1788)
Concerto in D Major for Horn and Orchestra, K.412 (1791)*
Concerto no. 27 in B-flat Major for Piano and Orchestra, K.595 (1791)*

OPERAS

Bastien und Bastienne, K.50 (1768)
Lucio Silla, K.135 (1772)
Il Rè pastore, K.208 (1775)
Zaide, K.344 (1779–80)
Idomeneo, K.366 (1781)*
Die Entführung aus dem Serail (*The Abduction from the Seraglio*), K.384 (1782)*
Così fan tutte, K.588 (1790)*
La Clemenza di Tito, K.621 (1791)*

ORCHESTRAL MUSIC

Symphony no. 25 in G Minor, K.183 (1773)*

Symphony no. 29 in A Major, K.201 (1774)*

Serenata notturna, K.239 (1776)*

Serenade in D Major (*Haffner*), K.250 (1776)*

Symphony no. 31 in D Major (*Paris*), K.297 (1778)*

Symphony no. 33 in B-flat Major, K.319 (1779)

Serenade in D Major for Wind Instruments (*Posthorn*), K.320 (1779)*

Serenade in B-flat Major for Thirteen Wind Instruments, K.361 (1781–84)*

Serenade in E-flat Major for Wind Instruments, K.375 (1781)*

Symphony no. 35 in D Major (*Haffner*), K.385 (1782)*

Serenade in C Minor, K.388 (1782 or 1783)*

Symphony no. 36 in C Major (*Linz*), K.425 (1783)*

120 minuets

Forty contredanses

Fifty German dances

SOLO ARIAS WITH ORCHESTRA

Fifty-five works

SOLO PIANO MUSIC

Sonata no. 5 in G Major, K.283 (1775)*

Sonata no. 10 in C Major, K.330 (1781–83)*

Sonata no. 11 in A Major (*Turkish March*), K.331 (1781–83)

Sonata no. 12 in F Major, K.332 (1781–83)*

Sonata no. 13 in B-flat Major, K.333 (1783–84)*

Rondo in A Minor, K.511 (1787)*

Adagio in B Minor, K.540 (1788)*

Sonata no. 15 in C Major, K.545 (1788)*

Sonata no. 17 in D Major, K.576 (1789)*

TWO-PIANO WORK

Sonata in D Major, K.448 (1781)*

LUDWIG VAN BEETHOVEN

b. Bonn, December 16, 1770

d. Vienna, March 26, 1827

Blessed is he who has overcome all passions and then proceeds energetically to perform his duties under all circumstances careless of success! . . . for he who is wretched and unhappy is so only in consequence of things.

Beethoven spent his first twenty-two years in Bonn, a town of fewer than seven thousand people but with an exceptionally rich musical and literary life. His mother, Maria Magdalena, was kind and quiet, and Ludwig loved her deeply. Beethoven's father, Johann, a minor court musician, had hoped to exploit his eldest son's talent by producing a second Mozart. Although Ludwig was a child prodigy, his development was not rapid enough to bring his father the anticipated financial rewards. But Johann kept his son practicing "stupendously," as Beethoven later said, often awakening the boy when he arrived home after midnight, drunk. Ludwig learned piano, organ, viola, and violin, and from 1781 he was fortunate to have as a teacher Christian Gottlob Neefe, who nurtured him on a rare manuscript copy of Bach's *Well-Tempered Clavier*.

In 1787 funds were raised for a trip to Vienna, where the seventeen-year-old Beethoven was to study with the thirty-one-year-old Mozart. When Beethoven played for him, Mozart, impressed, supposedly told friends visiting him, "Keep your eyes on him; some day he will give the world something to talk about." After only a few weeks in Vienna, however, Ludwig received news that his mother was ill. He arrived back home barely in time to be with her when she died at age forty.

The next five years were crushing. Ludwig's father was by then a completely incapacitated alcoholic, and the youth was forced to take full responsibility for supporting his brothers financially. Beethoven was a callow and unsophisticated young man, but his talent, combined with an inner strength, won for him some firm friendships. During this difficult time, the Bonn household of the Breunings, whose children he taught, served as a refuge of gentle breeding and culture.

In 1792 Haydn, who was returning to Vienna from his London triumphs, stopped off in Bonn. He met Beethoven, heard his music, and encouraged him to come to Vienna for study. By mid-November of that year, with very little money, few clothes, and many manuscripts, Beethoven had arrived in the Hapsburg capital, where he was to live for the rest of his life. Before he left Bonn, Count Waldstein—an early patron who helped finance the move—wrote to him that if he worked hard, he would "receive the spirit of Mozart from the hands of Haydn."

In Vienna it was the richest hour of the titled aristocracy. As the American music critic Joseph Kerman notes, "Not Handel or Mozart in earlier times, nor Brahms or Stravinsky in theirs—have been so heartened by idealistic aristocrats predicting great conquests and mapping out ahead, with sufficient accuracy, the future course of music history." At first Beethoven entered Vienna's great houses through his piano playing. Never had Vienna heard a pianist of such emotional power. Johann Tomášek, who heard him in Prague in 1798, said, "Beethoven's magnificent playing and particularly the daring flights in his improvisation stirred me strangely to the depths of my soul; indeed I found myself so profoundly bowed down that I did not touch my pianoforte for several days."

Beethoven's first decade in Vienna was immensely fruitful. During the first two years, he studied with the composers Haydn, Salieri, Johann Albrechtsberger, and Johann Schenk. Refusing to accept an official post—he thought it would sap his creative energy—for the most part he depended on Vienna's titled elite for his living, dedicating his compositions to them, playing at their sumptuous residences, and tutoring their children. For them he improvised, preened, and complained, vented his fury and introduced his newest music, and through them he met many important people in the imperial city.

In the mere breath of time since Mozart's death in 1791, the world had already changed. The French Revolution, Rousseau's ideas, and Napoleon's audacity brought about a new and impervious spirit of individualism. Beethoven possessed in full the new image of the artist as hero. When Goethe bowed to the Empress Maria Theresa, Beethoven shouted that Goethe, too, was a king. At an earlier moment, Beethoven would have been booted out the back door. The pianist and educator Ernest Hutcheson wrote, "It is amazing that the cultured aristocracy of Vienna tolerated a disposition so uncontrolled. Tolerate it they did; his genius opened all doors to him. Stranger still, this ugly, uncouth little man exercised a singular fascination on the high bred ladies, who forgave his eccentricities for the force of his personality."

By the end of the century, Beethoven's confidence in his future was growing and his creative power was ever increasing. But disaster was impending; he found himself growing deaf. Deeply embarrassed, he tried to keep the affliction hidden. But his anguish was terrible. In 1802 he wrote, "It was impossible for me to say to men, 'Speak louder, shout, for I am deaf!' Ah! how could I proclaim the defect of a sense that I once possessed in the highest perfection — in a perfection in which few of my colleagues possess or ever did possess it? . . . But what a humiliation when one stood beside me and heard a flute in the distance and I *heard nothing*. Such incidents brought me to the verge of despair; but little more and I would have put an end to my life; only my art held me back. It seemed impossible to leave the world before I created all that I felt myself called upon to accomplish and so I endured this wretched existence."

Somehow Beethoven passed through this crucible with new fortitude, realizing he could live for art, and that through art he had a responsibility to the world. "I will take Fate by the throat," he exclaimed, undaunted by the onslaught of his disability.

Beethoven's so-called middle period, 1803 to 1810, saw the creation of a body of work that is at the core of international concert life. In that short span of time, Beethoven wrote the Third to Sixth Symphonies (Opp. 55, 60, 67, 68), the Violin Concerto (Op. 61), the Fourth and Fifth Piano Concertos (Opp. 58, 73), the opera *Fidelio* (Op. 72), the Three *Razumovsky* String Quartets (Op. 59/1–3), the A major cello sonata (Op. 69), the *Kreutzer* Sonata for violin and piano (Op. 47), the *Harp* Quartet (Op. 74), the overtures to *Coriolan* (Op. 62) and *Egmont* (Op. 84), and fourteen piano sonatas, including the *Waldstein* (Op. 53) and the *Appassionata* (Op. 57). Productivity on such a level staggers the imagination.

Bolstered by this immense creative strength, Beethoven felt that all was still possible. With the death of Haydn in 1809, he became the most famous composer in the world. But Vienna was now under Napoleonic siege, and his main patron and pupil, the Archduke Rudolf, temporarily fled the city. Shortly afterward two other important patrons died, and money was soon in short supply.

The years 1812 through 1817 were Beethoven's least productive. The often ill and lonely composer's need for love was sublimated to his desperate attempt to gain the guardianship of his nephew Carl after his brother's death, and Beethoven spent years in litigation against Carl's mother. With all his might, he had attached himself to a child who lacked the capacity either to understand his tumultuous and irascible uncle or to love him. It was an ill-fated match, culminating in Carl's attempted suicides, but it was Beethoven's only emotional attachment. Although he had proposed marriage to several different women, he had been refused every time. Conjugal bliss nevertheless seemed to him to be a state that would offer him ultimate fulfillment. He once wrote: "Love alone—yes only love can give you a happier life—O God—let me finally find one who will strengthen me in virtue, who will lawfully be mine."

Throughout these punishing years, Beethoven's frustrations mounted. Restless, he constantly changed his squalid lodgings; his clothes were in tatters, and his one pair of boots was full of holes. At the same time he was becoming increasingly intolerant of his fellow man, suspicious even of loyal friends and supporters. His intimate companion had always been his piano, but due to his hearing, his playing had pathetically declined. In 1815 the great violinist Louis Spohr heard him at a rehearsal of his *Archduke* Trio, where the composer still insisted on playing the piano part. In his autobiography, Spohr paints a tragic scene: "It was by no means an enjoyment for in the first place the pianoforte was woefully out of tune, which however little troubled Beethoven since he could hear nothing of it, and secondly, of the former so admired excellency of the virtuoso, scarcely anything was left, in consequence of his total deafness. In the *forte*, the poor deaf man hammered in such a way upon the keys that entire groups of notes were inaudible, so that one lost all intelligence of the subject unless the eye followed the score at the same time."

Sometime around 1817, with the composition of the Piano Sonata no. 29 (Op. 106), the *Hammerklavier*, a change began to take place within Beethoven's inner world. Even earlier he proclaimed, "Submission, absolute submission to your Fate . . . *there is no longer happiness except in thyself; in thy art.*" He appeared to be living two distinct existences, that of the man and that of the artist. The mathematician and scholar of Beethoven J.W.N. Sullivan writes, "Deep within himself the artist in him knew that his isolation was irretrievable. Personal relations that should give him a sense of completeness and satisfy his hunger, were impossible. . . . Beethoven's realization of his essential loneliness was terrible and complete. But we may suppose that even then he was becoming aware that his separation from the world was the entry into a different and more exalted region."

As the years passed, Beethoven's isolation became purified into a resignation that kindled the creativity of his "third period" to deeper levels of spirituality. Though not religious in a dogmatic or orthodox sense, he was deeply religious in a spiritual sense, as expressed in the *Missa solemnis* (Op. 123, completed in 1823) and the Ninth Symphony of the following year. His last years were occupied with composing the final string quartets, music that for years to come seemed enigmatic to most listeners. Sullivan, again, wrote, "He lived in a universe richer than ours, in some ways better than ours and in some ways more terrible, and yet we recognize his universe and find his attitudes towards it prophetic of our own. It is indeed our own universe, but as experienced by a consciousness which is aware of aspects of which we have but dim and transitory glimpses."

Late in 1826, after catching a chill, the debilitated composer took to bed. During the first months of the new year, he suffered terribly, becoming jaundiced. By mid-March four operations for dropsy had been performed in his filthy rooms. On March 14 he told the pianist Ignaz Moscheles, who had been preparing a piano score of *Fidelio,* "Truly, a hard lot has fallen to me! Yet I am resigned to what Fate has ordained." His physician, Dr. Andreas Wawruch, wrote, "No words of comfort could brace him up, and when I promised him alleviation of his sufferings with the coming of the vitalizing weather of spring, he replied with a faint smile, 'My day's work is finished.' " Few have uttered words of such true fulfillment.

The battle was over, and peace was at hand. In his Quartets in C-sharp Minor (Op. 131) and A Minor (Op. 132), Beethoven's art had achieved its final illumination. On the evening of March 26, violent thunderstorms shook Vienna. Beethoven, who had been lying in bed unconscious, seemed to be shaken by a mighty thunderclap. The deaf man lifted his head and looked upward with a fierce expression on his face. With fist raised, he fell back, dying seconds later. Vienna, his adopted city, mourned. Schools and shops were closed; nearly twenty-five thousand people attended the funeral, as crowds lined the road to the cemetery.

The musicologist Wilfrid Mellers wonders, "[H]ad we a Beethoven among us, would we so recognize and honor him? At least we honor the historical Beethoven now, since he is still present, and he may even be the most deeply significant composer of *our* time, since no man has approached with more unflinching honesty and fortitude the psychic turmoils of his and our divided and distracted age."

The American composer Aaron Copland best summed up Beethoven's greatness: "Beethoven brought three startling innovations to music: first, he altered our very conception of the art by emphasizing the psychological element implicit in the language of sounds. Secondly, his own stormy and explosive temperament was, in part, responsible for a dramatization of the whole art of music. . . . Both of these elements—the psychological orientation and the instinct for drama—are inextricably linked in my mind with his third and possibly most original achievement: the creation of musical forms dynamically conceived on a scale never before attempted and of an inevitability that is irresistible."

Thirty-two Sonatas for Piano
Featuring
No. 1 in F Minor, Op. 2/1 (1795)
No. 2 in A Major, Op. 2/2 (1795)
No. 4 in E-flat Major, Op. 7 (1798)
No. 7, Op. 10/3 (1798)
No. 8 in C Minor, Op. 13 (c.1798–99)
No. 14 in C-sharp Minor, Op. 27/2 (1801)
No. 21 in C Major, Op. 53 (1803–4)
No. 23 in F Minor, Op. 57 (1804–5)
No. 26 in E-flat Major, Op. 81a (1809)
No. 28 in A Major, Op. 101 (1816)
No. 29 in B-flat Major, Op. 106 (1817–18)
No. 30 in E Major, Op. 109 (1820)
No. 31 in A-flat Major, Op. 110 (1821)
No. 32 in C Minor, Op. 111 (1822)

If Mozart was practically lost to nineteenth-century taste, Beethoven was its chief obsession. Taking up the piano tradition from Clementi and Mozart, he enriched it with a larger compass and sonority. His own playing and improvising on the instrument possessed an emotionality never before heard. Beethoven launched the piano into its century of fulfillment. His sonatas, variations, and concertos for the piano are one of the great creative documents of the ages; their humanity and breadth are a perpetual challenge to the creative listener as well as the player. "The essence of Beethoven," wrote the pianist Louis Kentner, "perhaps the greatest artist ever produced by civilization, lies distilled in the Piano Sonatas." Hans von Bülow called Bach's *Well-Tempered Clavier* the pianist's Old Testament and the Beethoven sonatas the New Testament.

Each of the thirty-two piano sonatas is a landmark in the history of the sonata form. Getting to know them over many performances is a never-ending boon. Of the many highlights, one may point out the very first sonata, in F minor (Op. 2/1), where the storms of the first and fourth movements announce that Beethoven will soon change the world of music.

In the Second Sonata, he substituted the Scherzo for the traditional Minuet, and the Rondo is planned on a luxurious time-scale. Beethoven's many shades of humor are offset by movements of ferocity and gentleness. The crown of the Sonata no. 7 (Op. 10/3) is the long slow movement in D minor, with its tragic content and emotional power. It is one of the great movements in early Beethoven.

With the Eighth Sonata, *Pathétique* (Op. 13), Beethoven stood at the threshold of nineteenth-century Romantic emotionalism. The slow movement is an exquisite love song. The celebrated *Moonlight* Sonata (Op. 27/2) brings us into the nineteenth century. The plaintive lament of the famous first movement was something truly new. Liszt called the second movement, neither a Scherzo nor a Minuet, "a flower between two abysses" (*une fleur entre deux abîmes*). The finale is a surging sonata movement with its heated and frenzied upward arpeggio motion. The *Pathétique* Sonata introduced palpitating anxiety to music; the *Moonlight* Sonata's finale brought to music a new element of anger and ruthlessness.

The two great sonatas of the middle period, the *Waldstein* (Op. 53) and the *Appassionata* (Op. 57), are both perennial favorites. The *Waldstein* is framed in a two-movement form with a twenty-eight-bar Adagio molto—introduzione occupying the place of the slow movement. In the pianist Wilhelm Kempff's words, "It is a flash of genius, illuminating the twilight between minor and major. The Rondo theme is as radiant as a temple in the first light of dawn." The *Appassionata* in its burning passion marks the greatest musical explosion for the keyboard up to its time.

The celebrated *Les Adieux* Sonata (Op. 81a) was composed during a troubled period in Beethoven's life when important patrons either died or, like the Archduke Rudolf (to whom Beethoven is here bidding farewell), left town as Napoleon began the terrible bombardment of Vienna.

Six unhappy years elapsed before Beethoven entered his final period of the last piano sonatas, from 1816 to 1822. They present the most exalted music ever written for the instrument. Op. 101's first movement has an indescribable yearning, followed by an almost brutish, ironic march. The fugal finale is one of the most magical pieces in all contrapuntal writing. In his late music, Beethoven incorporated into his vast compositional equipment a counterpoint inspired by and absorbed from Bach, yet entirely his own.

Sonata no. 29 (Op. 106) is the mythic *Hammerklavier*, the longest (at forty-five minutes) of the sonatas. Beethoven was modest indeed when he said, "Now you have a sonata that will keep the pianists busy when it is played fifty years hence." "The immensity of this composition," wrote the pianist Ernest Hutcheson, "cannot fail to strike us with awe. We gaze at its vast dome like pygmies from below, never feeling on an intellectual or moral level with it." Its slow movement is the longest and most sublime in the history of instrumental art. Sullivan wrote of the finale, "The Fugue is an almost insensate outburst of unconquerable self-assertion. The Sonata Op. 106 remains startling to contemporary ears; it must have been incomprehensible to its few practitioners and listeners in Beethoven's day."

In the Sonata no. 30 (Op. 109), Beethoven has left behind his beleaguered spirit's long battle for human warmth, in a sonata of incomparable subtlety in its structure and lyricism. Beethoven's flexibility is now so great that each work is an entirely new invention in form and cannot be classified under any genre. In the Thirty-first Sonata (Op. 110), Beethoven's passion, humor, expressiveness, lyricism, and unity of design are combined in a magnificent fugue of a deep humane passion.

His ultimate piano sonata (Op. 111) is set in two movements: the first is somber and dramatic, and the second is a set of otherworldly variations. Here Beethoven capped off his struggle with the form that occupied him longer than any other.

The Complete Piano Sonatas
Arrau: Philips 432301-2
Schnabel: EMI Classics CDHH 63765
Kempff: Deutsche Grammophon 429306-2
Ashkenazy: London 425590-2

Fidelio, Op. 72 (1804–5)

By nature Beethoven was not an opera composer, but he was attracted to the theme of humanity's oppression. Florestan is unjustly imprisoned for political reasons, but the courage and devotion of his wife Leonore eventually free him from his chains. The theme was very close to Beethoven's spiritual center.

Fidelio is Beethoven's only opera, and accommodating his genius to the stage caused him much heartache and creative toil. He wrote, "This work has won me the martyr's crown." Two English authors (Thomas Love Peacock in the early nineteenth century and Stephen Spender in the twentieth) voiced their admiration for the deep humanity of this great work. Peacock wrote, after a performance in 1832: "Beethoven's *Fidelio* . . . combines the profoundest harmony with melody that speaks to the soul. It carries to a pitch scarcely conceivable the true musical expression of the strongest passions, and the gentlest emotion in all their heroism of devoted love. The rage of the tyrant, the despair of the captive, the bursting of the sunshine of liberty upon the gloom of the dungeon. . . . *Fidelio* is the sun among the stars." For Spender, the Prisoners' Chorus and the quartet in the prison cell of Florestan "[scale] the greatest heights of Beethoven's humanistic piety."

The many highlights include Leonore's Act I aria "Abscheulicher! Wo eilst du hin?"; the prisoners' "O welche Lust!"; Florestan's Act II "In des Lebens Frühlingstagen"; and the great Leonore Overture no. 3, a creation of white-hot passion. The first performance of *Fidelio* took place in Vienna on November 20, 1805. A revised version was first performed in Vienna on May 23, 1814. It was dedicated to Beethoven's benefactor, the Archduke Rudolf.

Flagstad, Patzak, Greindl, Vienna Philharmonic Orchestra and State Opera Chorus,
    Furtwängler: EMI Classics CDC 64901
Norman, Coburn, Goldberg, Dresden Staatskapelle and State Chorus, Haitink: Philips
    426308-2
Behrens, Ghazarian, Hofmann, Chicago Symphony Orchestra and Chorus, Solti: London
    410227-2

Thirty-three Variations on a *Waltz by Diabelli*, Op. 120 (1819; 1822–23)

In 1823 the publisher and composer Anton Diabelli asked fifty-one Viennese composers to write a variation on his theme. Beethoven called the innocuous tune a "*Schusterfleck*"—a "cobbler's patch"—but found it so rich with variational possibilities that he wrote thirty-three of them for piano. They remain the fundamental set of variations of the Classical epoch and equal in greatness Bach's *Goldberg Variations*, which are the summit of Baroque variation technique. In the *Diabelli*, Beethoven's point of departure for the piano writing is the texture of the string quartet. The composition, nearly one hour long, makes enormous interpretive demands on the pianist. Only an auditor concentrating with total awareness should try to enter into the labyrinths of Beethoven's mind.

Serkin: Sony Masterworks MPK 44837
Schnabel: Pearl PEA 9378
Gulda: Musique D'Abord HMA 1905127

The Five Concertos for Piano and Orchestra
No. 1 in C Major, Op. 15 (1795; rev. 1800)
No. 2 in B-flat Major, Op. 19 (1793; rev. 1794–95, 1798)
No. 3 in C Minor, Op. 37 (c.1800)
No. 4 in G Major, Op. 58 (1805–7)
No. 5 in E-flat Major (*Emperor*), Op. 73 (1809)

Each of the Beethoven piano concertos ranks high in the international repertoire. The first two are classically proportioned, optimistic, and outgoing, with
rollicking, humorous finales. No. 3, the C minor, presents emotional elements
of the composer's dark middle period. No. 4 is the most lyrical. The critic Donald Francis Tovey wrote, "All three movements demonstrate the aesthetic principles of Concerto form with extraordinary subtlety."

Beethoven gave the first performances of the first four concertos. By the
time of the *Emperor* Concerto, however, his hearing had badly deteriorated,
and he had to relinquish the pleasure of premiering it himself to his student
Carl Czerny. The *Emperor* is the grandest of the concertos and at the time the
longest concerto yet composed for the piano.

The Complete Piano Concertos
Fleisher, Cleveland Orchestra, Szell: CBS M3K 42445
*Schnabel, London Symphony Orchestra and London Philharmonic Orchestra, Sargent: Pearl
    PEA 9063*
Arrau, Dresden Staatskapelle, Davis: Philips 422149-2

Trio no. 6 in B-flat Major for Piano, Violin, and Cello (*Archduke*), Op. 97 (1811)

Of the more than twenty compositions that Beethoven dedicated to his friend,
patron, and student, the Archduke Rudolf, only the gigantic Piano Trio in
B-flat Major has popularly retained his name. The *Archduke*, in its size,
strength, and emotional amplitude, overshadowed Beethoven's other fine piano trios. For many, the *Archduke*, completed in 1811 and his farewell to the
form, is the greatest of all works for piano, violin, and cello.

Zukerman, Du Pré, Barenboim: Arkadia 2-589
Rubinstein, Heifetz, Feuermann: RCA 09026-60926-2
Kempff, Szeryng, Fournier: Deutsche Grammophon 429712-2

The Five Sonatas for Cello and Piano
No. 1 in F Major, Op. 5/1 (1796)
No. 2 in G Minor, Op. 5/2 (1796)
No. 3 in A Major, Op. 69 (1807–8)
No. 4 in C Major, Op. 102/1 (1815)
No. 5 in D Major, Op. 102/2 (1815)

Beethoven was very fond of the cello, and cellists are grateful for his superb contributions from all three of his periods.

The two sonatas in Op. 5 were completed in 1796, and Beethoven is known to have performed them in Berlin with King Friedrich Wilhelm's cellist Jean-Pierre Duport, receiving for his effort a princely gold snuffbox. Neither Mozart nor Haydn had composed sonatas for the cello, so Op. 5/1 and 5/2 may be called the first important cello sonatas. The Op. 69 sonata is well placed in Beethoven's middle period, being warm in tone, with a fine, singing slow movement.

The later sonatas are very different in style and form. Both are so tightly woven that it takes several close listenings to begin to perceive the new world that Beethoven was entering at this time, here and in the Piano Sonata no. 28 (Op. 101), which he would write directly after the last cello sonatas.

The Complete Cello Sonatas

Ma, Ax: CBS M2K 42446
Harrell, Ashkenazy: London 417628-2
Rostropovich, Richter: Philips 442565-2

The Ten Sonatas for Violin and Piano
No. 1 in D Major, Op. 12/1 (1797–98)
No. 2 in A Major, Op. 12/2 (1797–98)
No. 3 in E-flat Major, Op. 12/3 (1797–98)
No. 4 in A Minor, Op. 23 (1800)
No. 5 in F Major (*Spring*), Op. 24 (1800–1)
No. 6 in A Major, Op. 30/1 (1801–2)
No. 7 in C Minor, Op. 30/2 (1801–2)
No. 8 in G Major, Op. 30/3 (1801–2)
No. 9 in A Major (*Kreutzer*), Op. 47 (1802–3)
No. 10 in G Major, Op. 96 (1812)

The violin sonatas are the most important sonata literature for the violinist. Mozart's numerous sonatas gave the violin part but a fraction of what Beethoven's asked of the instrument.

The first three are beautiful pieces of Classicism, with the piano and violin in comfortable partnership. In 1800 Beethoven composed two finer and more individual sonatas. The terse A minor sonata (Op. 23) will always be less played than the gracious masterpiece in F major (Op. 24), beloved as the *Spring* Sonata; its vivaciousness has the freshness of spring, and it is in the same key as the *Pastoral* Symphony. The next year, Beethoven continued exploring the form with three even more brilliant violin sonatas. Op. 30/2, in his high-drama key of C minor, is the most frequently played of these three.

In 1803 he wrote the most monumental and richest of the series, the *Kreutzer*, named for the violinist Rodolphe Kreutzer. The work is grand in scale and presents both partners with difficult technical chores.

The first nine sonatas were all composed in a six-year period. Beethoven did not return to the form until 1808, when he wrote the G major sonata (Op. 96), which sounds a more inward note than the almost-flamboyant *Kreutzer* Sonata; the Adagio second movement is one of those noble and characteristic slow movements that are among the hallmarks of Beethoven's art. The finale is a contrasting set of variations, another form that Beethoven owned.

Zukerman, Neikrug: RCA 09026-60991-2

Menuhin, Kempff: Deutsche Grammophon 415874-2

Perlman, Ashkenazy: London 421453-2

Oistrakh, Oborin: Philips 412570-2

Concerto in D Major for Violin and Orchestra, Op. 61 (1806)

The D major is regarded by many as the greatest of all violin concertos. The violin writing itself is miraculous, building upon the violin sonatas (in which the composer had delved deep into the instrument's technical nature). The themes are of a rare inspiration; the orchestral balance is perfection. Donald Francis Tovey called it "mysterious in radiantly happy surroundings." In the first movement, Allegro ma non troppo, five solo timpani taps establish the rhythm that permeates the movement. It possesses a lyric tranquillity throughout, as well as a subtle motion that saves the beautiful themes from stagnation. In the Larghetto, peace and serenity fill the listener's mind and body as the music floats above human conflict. The Rondo, marked *allegro*, is spacious and dignified with some sparkling violin writing. The novelist Lawrence Durrell felt that "there's something of the same kind of terrifying pathology about the themes that there is in *Hamlet*. The fusion of the dream with reality."

Heifetz, NBC Symphony Orchestra, Toscanini: RCA 60261-2-RG

Kennedy, North German Radio Symphony Orchestra, Tennstedt: EMI Classics CDC 54574

Grumiaux, Royal Concertgebouw Orchestra, Davis: Philips 420348-2

Menuhin, Philharmonia Orchestra, Furtwängler: EMI Classics CDH 69799

The Nine Symphonies
No. 1 in C Major, Op. 21 (1800)
No. 2 in D Major, Op. 36 (1801–2)
No. 3 in E-flat Major (*Eroica*), Op. 55 (1803)
No. 4 in B-flat Major, Op. 60 (1806)
No. 5 in C Minor, Op. 67 (1807–8)
No. 6 in F Major (*Pastorale*), Op. 68 (1808)
No. 7 in A Major, Op. 92 (1811–12)
No. 8 in F Major, Op. 93 (1812)
No. 9 in D Minor (*Choral Symphony*), Op. 125 (1822–24)

In his memoirs, the biographer André Maurois wrote, "Everything that I had thought and been unable to express was sung in the wordless phrases of these symphonies—when that mighty river of sound began to flow, I let myself be carried on its waters. My soul was bathed and purified. . . . Beethoven called me back to kindness, charity, and love."

Beethoven was careful to bask for a long time in other branches of the sonata "idea" before giving the world his First Symphony in C Major (Op. 21), first performed when he was twenty-nine years old. Its Classical boundaries are denoted. The opening gives a nod to Haydn, who so often began his first movements with slow introductions. The third movement is called a Minuet but is much more in the nature of the bumptious Beethoven Scherzo. The Second Symphony in D Major (Op. 36) still looks almost longingly back to the late eighteenth century in style.

The dam would burst in 1803, with the might of the Third Symphony in E-flat Major (Op. 55), the *Eroica*. The work was inscribed to Napoleon, for whom Beethoven had developed a deep admiration. When told that his Republican ideal had crowned himself emperor, Beethoven, in a fit of rage, roared, "So just another tyrant! After all he is like the rest—he too will trample on the rights of men and indulge in monstrous ambition." In front of his loyal pupil, Ferdinand Ries, he tore up the title page. The symphony would soon be symbolically rechristened, "Composed to celebrate the memory of a great man."

Never had the sonata form been used for composition on such a vast scale as in the Third Symphony. Never had abstract music been so inexorably shaped. Writing to his daughter, the twentieth-century composer Ernest Bloch spoke of "the infallible logic that guides him. I have discovered (after 45 years of study) a thousand details that had escaped me . . . it is a whole world—and the *step* between the Second Symphony and this one is the greatest a composer has ever taken." Words remain silly tools to describe such feelings of grief as contained in the *Marche funèbre* slow movement.

The next symphony, No. 4 in B-flat Major (Op. 60), is a resting place in Beethoven's symphonic journey. He returns to modest proportions and gentle feelings in a work that Schumann called "a slender Greek maiden." The symphony nonetheless presents a great menu of moods and delights.

Beethoven struggled for over four years with the Fifth Symphony in C Minor (Op. 67), the most loved and widely performed symphony of all time. The work seems to exemplify the defiant spirit of the human race to continue to strive against adversity. Its opening theme, in its stark but pregnant simplicity, is emblematic of its defiance and is probably the most famous motif ever composed.

The Sixth Symphony (Op. 68), the *Pastoral*, had its first performance on December 22, 1808. Beethoven wanted to make certain that his auditors understood that the work was "more the expression of feeling than tone-painting." This symphony is an homage to nature, a major inspiration for Beethoven, whose perpetual walks were indispensable to the germination and working out of his compositions. In his notebook, he jotted down things like "[A]lmighty one, in the woods I am blessed. Happy everyone in the woods. Every tree speaks through thee." An entry from 1814 tells, "My miserable hearing does not trouble me here. In the country it seems as if every tree and rock said to me: Holy! Holy! Oh the ecstasy of the woods." In his last months he was haunted by and longed to see "our father Rhine" and the Rhine country of his youth. The symphony's five movements are titled: "Awakening of cheerful feeling on arriving in the country"; "Scene by the brook"; "Merry gathering of country folk"; "Thunderstorm—tempest"; and "Shepherd's song—Happy, thankful feelings after the storm."

The Symphony no. 7 in A Major (Op. 92) was called by Wagner "the apotheosis of the Dance," and its cosmic rhythm finds no rest. The Allegretto movement possesses a nonstop inner motion. In a great performance, this symphony is one of music's most exciting events. Somehow the increasingly deaf Beethoven conducted the premiere on December 8, 1813, for the benefit of war-battered Austrian soldiers.

The charming Eighth Symphony in F Major (Op. 93), like the Fourth, is a spiritual resting place, written while Beethoven was also composing No. 7. The third movement is a return to the courtliness of the minuet. After completing the Eighth in October 1812, Beethoven did not return to the symphony form until 1822.

The Ninth Symphony in D Minor (Op. 125), with its setting of Schiller's "Ode to Joy," is the mightiest of Beethoven's symphonies. It was finished in February 1824. Sitting in the midst of the orchestra at its first performance on May 7, 1824, the master heard nothing. The English pianist Denis Matthews observes, "For all its revolutionary aspect and impact the Ninth Symphony still owes much of its strength to Classical tradition. Its spirit has inevitably been linked with outside events, the aftermath of the French Revolution, the Napoleonic wars, the dignity of the individual, the sufferings and hopes of mankind, including Beethoven's own; and yet in simple musical terms it may be held as the greatest example of the triumph of the major over the minor key."

The Complete Symphonies
Royal Concertgebouw Orchestra, Haitink: Philips 442073-2
Hanover Band, Goodman: Nimbus NI 5144/48 (period instruments)
Cleveland Orchestra, Szell: Sony Classical SB5K 48396
Vienna Philharmonic Orchestra, Bernstein: Deutsche Grammophon 423481-2

Missa solemnis, Op. 123 (1819–23)

Beethoven's religious creed was undogmatic. In the *Missa solemnis*, he poured out his religious passion, which in its more subjective mold differs in degree from that of Bach, Handel, and Haydn. Perhaps his attitude was best summarized in a remark he made to the pianist-composer Ignaz Moscheles. Moscheles, while working for Beethoven on the vocal score of *Fidelio*, wrote at the conclusion, "Finished with God's help." Upon seeing this, Beethoven, slightly annoyed, shouted, "Oh man, help thyself."

In its metaphysical profundity, the *Missa solemnis* is one of the great works of the human spirit. (Incidentally, Beethoven was unfortunately unaware of Bach's unpublished Mass in B Minor and the *St. Matthew Passion*.) Beethoven, the master architect in one of the largest forms, attempts to make sense of the human experience and its existential dilemma. Aldous Huxley said of the Benedictus, "Blessed and blessing, this music is in some sort the equivalent of the night, of the deep and living darkness."

Moser, Schwarz, Moll, Kollo, Hilversum Radio Choir, Royal Concertgebouw Orchestra, Bernstein: Deutsche Grammophon 413780-2
Janowitz, Ludwig, Wunderlich, Berry, Berlin Philharmonic Orchestra and Vienna Singverein, Karajan: Deutsche Grammophon 423913-2

The Sixteen Quartets for Strings
Six Quartets, Op. 18 (1798–1800):
No. 1 in F Major
No. 2 in G Major
No. 3 in D Major
No. 4 in C Minor
No. 5 in A Major
No. 6 in B-flat Major
Three Quartets (*Razumovsky*), Op. 59 (1804–6):
No. 7 in F Major
No. 8 in E Minor
No. 9 in C Major
Quartet no. 10 in E-flat Major (Harp), Op. 74 (1809)
Quartet no. 11 in F Minor, Op. 95 (1810)
Quartet no. 12 in E-flat Major, Op. 127 (1823–24)
Quartet no. 13 in B-flat Major, Op. 130 (1825–26)
Quartet no. 14 in C-sharp Minor, Op. 131 (1825–26)
Quartet no. 15 in A Minor, Op. 132 (1825)
Quartet no. 16 in F Major, Op. 135 (1826)

Beethoven had closely studied the string quartets of Haydn and Mozart and was cautious about attempting to compose in so intimate and fragile a format. He led up to it with the fine string trios of Op. 9 (1797–98). In 1798 he began the serious work of writing the Six Quartets (Op. 18), which Beethoven's musically elite circle would understand to be an important step in the development of the string quartet.

The Op. 59 quartets were commissioned by the Russian ambassador to Vienna, Count Andreas Razumovsky, a great connoisseur of chamber music who had a resident quartet in his palace. They represent Beethoven at the height of his middle period. Beethoven had by now composed the *Eroica* Symphony, and he inevitably wanted to try to accommodate such expanded size and emotional content to the limitations of four string instruments. (When one violinist complained of the difficulty of some passages of the F major quartet, Beethoven retorted, "Do you think I worry about your wretched fiddle when the spirit speaks to me?") In the *Razumovsky* group, Beethoven accomplished his goal tremendously. These are works of symphonic energy. In them Beethoven also brought the drawing room into the sphere of public music making. The entire nineteenth-century production of quartets does not surpass the explosiveness and range of Op. 59.

Beethoven resumed string quartet writing in 1809 with the E-flat quartet

(Op. 74), called the *Harp* because of the arpeggiation in pizzicato in the first movement. Neither the *Harp* nor the following *Quartetto serioso* (No. 11 in F minor), although full of contrasts of all kinds, is as grandly conceived as the Op. 59 set.

Not until 1823 did Beethoven again compose a quartet. By then the perpetually ill, stone-deaf, disordered, and slovenly composer had written the last piano sonatas, the *Missa solemnis*, the *Diabelli Variations*, and the Ninth Symphony. For his valedictory utterances the composer was brought back to the lean abstraction of the quartet. A Russian prince, Nikolai Golitsyn, commissioned him, and Opp. 127, 130, and 132 are all dedicated to this discriminating aristocrat, an amateur cellist who as early as April 1824 in St. Petersburg organized the first complete performance of the *Missa solemnis*.

During his last four years, a time of earthly haplessness, the composer concentrated his thoughts on this medium. The *Grosse fuge* (Op. 133) was first attached to the B-flat quartet (Op. 130) as its finale, but Beethoven found it cumbersome and rightfully set it apart. Of Op. 131 in C-sharp minor, Sullivan wrote, "Even Shakespeare . . . never wrote his C-sharp minor quartet." Again in the words of Sullivan, "All art exists to communicate states of consciousness which are higher synthetic wholes than those of ordinary experience, but in these last quartets Beethoven is dealing with states for which there are no analogues in any other art." The poet Stephen Spender felt that in the late quartets "there was the exploration of a universe of pure melody, beyond suffering, oppression and difficulty."

Quartets no. 1–6 (Op. 18)
Quartetto Italiano: Philips 426046-2
Guarneri Quartet: RCA 60456-2-RG

Middle Quartets (Opp. 59, 74, 95)
Quartetto Italiano: Philips 420797-2
Guarneri Quartet: RCA 60457-2

Late Quartets (Opp. 127, 130–32, 135, *Grosse fuge*)
Tokyo String Quartet: RCA 09026-60975-2
Guarneri String Quartet: RCA 60458-2-RG
Quartetto Italiano: Philips 426050-2

OTHER PRINCIPAL WORKS

BALLET

Die Geschöpfte des Prometheus (*The Creatures of Prometheus*), Op. 43 (1800–1)

CHAMBER MUSIC

Trio in E-flat Major for Strings, Op. 3 (before 1794)

Three Trios for Piano, Violin, and Cello, Op. 1/1–3 (1794–95)

Quintet in E-flat Major for Strings, Op. 4 (1795)

Sextet in E-flat Major for Two Horns and String Quartet, Op. 81b (c.1795)

Quintet in E-flat Major for Piano and Winds, Op. 16 (1796)*

Serenade in D Major for String Trio, Op. 8 (1796–97)

Trio in B-flat Major for Clarinet, Piano, and Cello, Op. 11 (1797)

Three Trios for Strings, Op. 9 (1797–98)*

Quintet in C Major for Strings, Op. 29 (1801)

Two Trios for Piano, Violin, and Cello, Op. 70 (1808)*

CHORAL MUSIC

Christus am Ölberg (*Christ on the Mount of Olives*) (oratorio), Op. 85 (1803)

Mass in C Major, Op. 86 (1807)*

INCIDENTAL MUSIC

Egmont, Op. 84 (1809–10)

Die Ruinen von Athen (*Ruins of Athens*), Op. 113 (1811)

König Stephan (*King Stephen*), Op. 117 (1811)

ORCHESTRAL WORKS

Die Geschöpfte des Prometheus Overture, Op. 43 (1800–1)

Leonore Overture no. 2, Op. 72a (1804–5)*

Leonore Overture no. 3, Op. 72b (1805–6)*

Leonore Overture no. 1, Op. 138 (1806–7)

Coriolan Overture, Op. 62 (1807)*

Egmont Overture, Op. 84 (1809–10)*

König Stephan (*King Stephen*), Op. 117 (1811)

Wellington's Victory, Op. 91 (1813)

PIANO MUSIC

Twenty-four Variations on Righini's "Venni amore" (1790)

Rondo a capriccio in G Major, Op. 129 (1795)

Rondo in C Major, Op. 51/1 (c.1796–98)

Rondo in G Major, Op. 51/2 (c.1798)*
Seven Bagatelles, Op. 33 (1801–2)
Six Variations in D Major on an Original Theme, Op. 34 (1802)
Fifteen Variations and a Fugue on an Original Theme, Op. 35 (1802)*
Andante favori (1803)
Thirty-two Variations in C Minor on an Original Theme (1806)*
Fantasia in G Minor, Op. 77 (1809)
Bagatelle in A Minor ("Für Elise") (1810)
Polonaise in C Major, Op. 89 (1814)
Eleven Bagatelles, Op. 119 (1820–22)
Six Bagatelles, Op. 126 (1823–24)*

SOLO INSTRUMENT AND ORCHESTRA MUSIC
Romance in F Major for Violin and Orchestra, Op. 50 (c.1798)
Romance in G Major for Violin and Orchestra, Op. 40 (c.1801–2)
Concerto in C Major for Piano, Violin, Cello, and Orchestra (*Triple Concerto*), Op. 56
    (1803–4)*
Fantasy in C Minor for Piano, Chorus, and Orchestra (*Choral Fantasy*), Op. 80 (1808)

SONG CYCLE
An die ferne Geliebte, Op. 98 (1815–16)*

VOICE AND ORCHESTRA MUSIC
"Ah! Perfido" (scene and aria), Op. 65 (1795–96)*

OTHER CLASSICAL
COMPOSERS

FRANCESCO GEMINIANI

(1687–1762) Italy

In the first half of the eighteenth century, Italians were the great violinists of the world; Francesco Veracini, Giuseppe Tartini, Pietro Locatelli, and Geminiani dominated the field. Geminiani was a pupil of Corelli, and his 1730 treatise, *The Art of Playing on the Violin*, was revered. He was the link between Corelli and such violinists as Pietro Nardini, Antonio Lolli, and Giovanni Viotti. Geminiani's *Concerti grossi* are typically late Baroque in style and are important works of that tradition, composed in the year of Haydn's birth.

Twelve *Concerti grossi*, Opp. 2 and 3 (1732)
I Musici: Philips 438766-2

GIUSEPPE TARTINI

(1692–1770) Istria

Born in Pirano, Istria (now in Slovenia), Tartini, who moved to Padua when he was sixteen, is considered an Italian composer. As a composer for the violin, his great predecessors were Corelli, called the "master of masters," and Vivaldi, one of the main creators of the Baroque violin concerto. He began as a late Baroque composer but lived long enough to encompass the *style galant* and died the year Beethoven was born.

Tartini's career had its romantic touches. Quick-tempered and a master swordsman, he was often embroiled in duels. At only eighteen, he married a violin pupil, a Paduan lady of rank (much to the chagrin of both families). In the following few years, Tartini developed into the most brilliant violinist of his time. In 1745 he had a dream that produced his *Devil's Trill* Sonata. As he later told the great French astronomer Joseph Lalande, "One night I dreamed that I had sold my soul to the Devil. All went well; my new servant fulfilled all my wishes. I gave him my violin out of curiosity to see what he could do with it. To my amazement, I heard him play with consummate skill a sonata of exquisite beauty that surpassed the boldest flights of imagination. I was enchanted, my breath stopped, and I awoke. Seizing my violin, I tried to reproduce some of the sounds I heard in my dream. But in vain. The piece I then composed, although the best I ever wrote—(I call it the Devil's sonata) is but a far cry from what I heard in my dream." It is an irresistible story—the devil and his violin. The sonata itself is a magnificent work of violin wizardry.

Tartini's fame traveled through Europe. He founded a violin academy at Padua around 1728, and pupils flocked to him. He taught more than eight hours a day for decades. The American musicologist Boris Schwarz wrote, "In the history of violin playing Tartini is the mighty ancestor whose basic concepts of the instrument are still valid today: variety of bow articulation, sturdy left-hand technique both in double stops and fluent runs, and above all a singing cantabile style which he preached to all his students: *Per ben suonare bisogna ben cantare* (to play well one must sing well)." The indefatigable Tartini produced more than four hundred works.

Sonata in G Minor for Violin and Piano (*Devil's Trill*) (1745)
Milstein, Mittman: Biddulph LAB 055
Menuhin, Balsam: Biddulph LAB 046

Concerto in D Minor for Violin and Orchestra (1750)
Szigeti, New Friends of Music, Goehr: Biddulph LAB 064

THOMAS ARNE

(1710–1778) England

Arne was born the year Handel first came to England. He and William Boyce developed into the brightest native voices in a country musically dominated by the German composer. His masque *Alfred*—a theater piece with music first performed for Frederick, prince of Wales, in 1740—contains one of England's great patriotic songs, "Rule, Britannia." But Arne composed much else that is today once again being appreciated.

Six Concertos for Organ and Orchestra
Williams, Cantilena, Shepherd: Chandos CHAN 8604

GIOVANNI BATTISTA PERGOLESI
(1710–1736) Italy

Pergolesi's early death at twenty-six from tuberculosis occasioned many a false and romantic story, for it came after a high-spirited life. The composer was born near Ancona and was a sickly child, probably with a limp. The impoverished youngster received his musical training in Naples, where in 1732 his three-act *opera buffa, Lo Frate 'nnammorato,* achieved a fine success. That success, however, paled in comparison with the triumph he achieved on the night of September 5, 1733. The occasion was the first performance of an intermezzo he wrote, *La Serva padrona.*

For a quarter century, it had sometimes been the custom to relieve the tedium and stuffy artificiality of serious opera with a lighter theater piece between acts. These interludes, called intermezzos, often stole the show with their gaiety and naturalness. Pergolesi's *La Serva padrona (The Servant as Mistress),* in one act for three players, was designed as an intermezzo for his new *opera seria, Il Prigionier superbo.* The intermezzo "hit it big" and is the most famous of all intermezzos, forever enshrining its composer's name.

After Pergolesi's death, the little *opera buffa* traveled through Europe, where it charmed the populace and was hailed as a glory of the Italian spirit.

In 1752 in Paris, *La Serva* and a few other *opere buffe* spearheaded the Guerre des Bouffons, a war between the French and Italian styles. Pergolesi's piece seemed to repudiate the formality and conventionality of the operas of Jean Joseph Mondonville, Lully, and Rameau. More than fifty pamphlets were published over this musical storm. In his *Confessions,* Rousseau, himself the composer of an *opera buffa (Le Devin du village,* or *The Village Soothsayer),* tells us, "All Paris divided into two camps, whose excitement was greater than if they had differed over politics or religion. The more powerful and more numerous party, made up of the great, the rich, and the ladies, supported French music; the other, which was more active, more distinguished, and more enthusiastic, was made up of true music lovers, talented people, and men of genius." In his characteristic fashion, he reported, "Only *The Village Soothsayer* could stand the comparison and still please when played after even *La Serva Padrona.*"

As his end approached, Pergolesi retired to a Capuchin monastery in the town of Pozzuoli, where he feverishly completed his beautiful *Stabat Mater* (1736).

La Serva padrona (opera buffa) (1733)
Eisenfeld, Miljakovic, Süss, Berlin Staatskapelle: Berlin Classics BER 9114

Stabat Mater (1736)
Marshall, Valentini-Terrani, London Symphony Orchestra, Abbado: Deutsche Grammophon
    415103-2

WILLIAM BOYCE

(1711–1779) England

The names of Boyce and Thomas Arne are often linked together, though Arne had a reputation for dissipation and Boyce for a kind heart. But Arne's music is gentler and sweeter than Boyce's, which has greater weight and dimension. In recent decades, Boyce's vibrant symphonies have become popular listening. The composer, long associated with St. Paul's Cathedral, is buried beneath the center of the dome at that celebrated London house of worship.

Eight Symphonies
English Concert Orchestra, Pinnock: Archiv 419631-2 *(period instruments)*
Menuhin Festival Orchestra, Menuhin: EMI Classics CDK 65730

CARL PHILIPP EMANUEL BACH

(1714–1788) Germany

The second surviving son of J. S. and Maria Barbara Bach, the godson of Telemann, and for nearly thirty years the court composer to Prussia's Frederick the Great, Philipp Emanuel was the most important instrumental composer of his generation, which separates his mighty father from the mature works of Haydn. He was one of the chief progenitors of the sonata form. Alfred Einstein wrote of him, "This music presents the most luxuriant testimony of the age of sensibility, full of sighs, echoes and tearful effusions, yet in quick movements also full of surprises and unconventional, not to say, coquettish details." As adventurous as much of his *Sturm und Drang* music is, Philipp Emanuel has a tendency to be rudderless in form, leaving formal perfection and amplitude to Haydn and

Mozart. Both of these composers acknowledged their debt to him, and Mozart, who had also been as much influenced by the *style galant* of his half-brother Johann Christian Bach, described Philipp Emanuel as the father (and himself as the child).

Philipp Emanuel also wrote a still-valuable treatise, *The True Art of Playing Keyboard Instruments*, published in 1753. Beethoven, at his pupil Carl Czerny's first piano lesson, asked the young Czerny to purchase a copy. Beethoven wrote: "Of Emanuel Bach's pianoforte works I have only a few things, yet a few by that true artist serve not only for high enjoyment but also for study; and it gives me the greatest pleasure to play them to a few genuinely artistic friends." Philipp Emanuel was himself a deeply expressive keyboard player. One of his contemporaries, the music historian Dr. Charles Burney, reported that Philipp Emanuel's playing brought tears to his eyes in the slow movements.

Various Concertos for Flute and Strings
Haupt, C.P.E. Bach Chamber Orchestra, Haenchen: Capriccio 10104 and 10105

Magnificat in D Major, H.772 (1749)
Ameling, Collegium Aureum: Deutsche Harmonia Mundi 74321-26613-2

Sonatas for Keyboard
Bärtschi: Jecklin JD 683-2

Concerto in A Major for Cello and Orchestra, H.439 (1750)
Harrell, English Chamber Orchestra, Zukerman: EMI Classics CDK 65733

PIETRO NARDINI

(1722–1793) Italy

Nardini, an exceptional musician, was born in Livorno and trained in Padua. He studied violin with the great Tartini, becoming that master's most important pupil. After hearing him perform in 1763, Leopold Mozart, a man thrifty of praise, wrote, "The beauty, purity and equality of his tone, and the tastefulness of his cantabile playing, cannot be surpassed." From 1762 to 1765 he was orchestra leader at the ducal court in Stuttgart, and after 1770 he was music director at the ducal court of Tuscany.

Nardini is a proud member of Italy's extraordinary school of violin playing, which culminates with Nicolò Paganini. He was not a prolific composer and has been little recorded, but his music has a special grace and is highly representative of mid-eighteenth-century Italian instrumental music and the development of the sonata form. He died in Florence.

Concerto in E Minor for Violin and Orchestra
Elman, Vienna State Opera Chamber Orchestra, Golschmann: Vanguard Classics OVC 8033

ANTONIO SOLER

(1729–1783) Spain

The Spanish monk Padre Antonio Soler was born in Catalonia and died at the Escorial Monastery in Madrid. It is not known if he studied directly with Domenico Scarlatti, but he certainly came in contact with him, probably from 1753 until Scarlatti's death in 1757. Soler modeled his 150 sonatas on the Scarlatti binary form and infused them with all manner of Spanish sentiment and rhythms. Notwithstanding their resemblance to Scarlatti's, Soler's harpsichord sonatas are masterpieces on their own, and repeated listening will reveal their depths and individuality.

Sonatas for Harpsichord
Rowland: Nimbus NI 5248

Fandango for Keyboard, M.1A (1760)
Cole: Virgin Classics 59624

LUIGI BOCCHERINI

(1743–1805) Italy

Boccherini was born and educated in Lucca and died in poverty in Madrid. (Spain was his adopted country.) Unfortunately, the composer's fame rests almost exclusively on his delectable Minuet, known the world over as "Boccherini's Minuet," which is found in his E major string quartet (Op. 13/5, 1775). But this is only one of his compositions—there are close to one hundred string quartets among his five hundred instrumental compositions. Boccherini's music, which once graced the parlors and drawing rooms of amateur musicians, contains many piquant touches, such as the Spanish flavor he introduced in some scores.

Of the abundant eighteenth-century musicians writing in sonata form, Boccherini stands out as a true minor master. Admirers of classical chamber music can spend many pleasurable hours delving into the work of this affable and sensitive composer.

Concerto in B-flat Major for Cello and Orchestra
Ma, St. Paul Chamber Orchestra, Zukerman: CBS MK 39964
Du Pré, English Chamber Orchestra, Barenboim: EMI Classics CDC 47840

Quintets for Strings
Berlin Philharmonia Ensemble: Denon CO-2199

DOMENICO CIMAROSA
(1749–1801) Italy

Neapolitan-born Cimarosa was once regarded as a darling of his art, and his sixty operas were as popular as any of his age. *Il Matrimonio segreto (The Secret Marriage,* 1792) was performed for one hundred consecutive evenings. Haydn produced his work at Esterháza; Goethe translated and staged an opera in Weimar; Rossini never tired of singing his airs; and Catherine the Great invested him with the title of chamber composer at her court. Painters portrayed him, and he sat for a marble bust by Canova, who endowed his subject with the authority of a Roman senator. (The bust found a home in Rome's ancient Pantheon.)

Cimarosa was at his best, indeed at his most sparkling, in comedy. His is the authentic Italian *buffa* style. His melody is infectious, his wit delicious, his ensemble writing ebullient. His best piece, *Il Matrimonio,* was first produced in Vienna only weeks after Mozart's death.

Il Matrimonio segreto (The Secret Marriage) (opera in two acts) (1792)
Patterson, Williams, Banditelli, Eastern Netherlands Orchestra, Bellini: Arts 471172

MUZIO CLEMENTI
(1752–1832) Italy

Clementi, born in Rome four years before Mozart, was also a child prodigy of the first order. As a youngster, he was brought to England to live. By age twenty he was considered the best pianist in London, superseding J. S. Bach's youngest son, Johann Christian ("the London Bach"), who is credited with being the first musician to perform in public a piano solo (in 1768).

In 1781 Clementi encountered Mozart in Vienna, and the two early giants of the piano competed in a grueling pianistic duel for the pleasure of Emperor Joseph II. The outcome was a draw, but Mozart was piqued, calling all Italians charlatans and Clementi a mere mechanic without feeling or taste. Doubtless Mozart was irritated at the Italian's pianistic boldness, brilliance, and enlarged technique, which Clementi codified in the one hundred piano pieces titled *Gradus ad Parnassum*, published in three volumes in 1817, 1819, and 1826.

Between 1773 and 1820, he composed sixty-four piano sonatas—the longest career of any sonata composer. Had Beethoven not lived, Clementi's sonatas would represent a high-water mark in the history of the form. Beethoven admired Clementi's sonatas and kept a volume close at hand. The much-esteemed musician was buried at Westminster Abbey. On his tombstone is inscribed the finest epitaph he could have wished for: "the father of the pianoforte."

Sonatas for Piano
Horowitz: RCA 7753-2-RC

LUIGI CHERUBINI
(1760–1842) Italy

The Florentine-born Cherubini had a formidable career. He was well trained in his native land and attained international repute. He resided in Paris from 1786 on, and the premieres of his operas were major events, until the even more popular operas of François-Adrien Boieldieu and Daniel Auber surpassed them. Soon after the revolution, theatrical life flourished; Paris sported seventeen new theaters. Madame Cherubini remarked, "The guillotine was kept busy, and in the evening one could not get a seat in the theater."

Unfortunately, Napoleon preferred the operas of Cherubini's rival, Étienne-Nicolas Méhul, whose *Joseph* (1807) is his best work. Napoleon told Cherubini that his music was too loud, and the composer softly replied, "I understand; you like music which does not stop your thinking of state affairs."

Cherubini was associated with the Paris Conservatory from its inception in 1795. He became its autocratic director in 1822 and led the institution to the highest pinnacle of public musical education.

A prolific composer, he was primarily concerned with opera and sacred music. Perhaps his finest sacred composition is the Requiem in C Minor (1836); it is solid, serious, and splendid in technique, showing his rare skill as a contrapuntist. From 1780 to 1833, he wrote twenty-five operas. The best known were *Les Deux journées* (*The Two Days*, 1800) and *Médée* (*Medea*, 1797). *Médée* was reinstated into the repertoire in the 1950s through Maria Callas's fiery performances. Audiences were enchanted by the composer's portrayal of shrieking passion and hatred.

Beethoven was a staunch admirer of the Italian, and as late as 1823 he wrote to him: "In spirit I am often with you, in that I value, more than any other, your stage work. . . . I am filled with delight whenever I hear that you have composed a new work, and take as great an interest in it as in one of my own; in short, I honor and love you."

Today little is heard of Cherubini, an intriguing composer who built on Gluck's "reform" operas and linked the Classical world, through Beethoven's *Fidelio*, with the feverish elements of early Romantic operas such as Gaspare Spontini's *La Vestale* (1807) and Giacomo Meyerbeer's grand operatic spectacles.

He was commanding in skill, but was unfortunately denied the gift of melody. If his music is slighted today, thousands of visitors to the Louvre view his image each day in Ingres's celebrated portrait.

Médée (opera in three acts) (1797)

Callas, Scotto, Pirazzini, La Scala Orchestra and Chorus, Serafin: EMI Classics CDMB 63625

FRANÇOIS-ADRIEN BOIELDIEU

(1775–1834) France

French comic opera was a breath of fresh air that helped Parisians release the many tensions of the revolution, and no composer served his public with more delightful fare than did Boieldieu, from his first *opéra comique* in 1793 to his finest score, *La Dame blanche*, in 1825. In 1803 he was appointed to conduct the Imperial Opera in St. Petersburg, and he toiled in Russia for eight years, yearning for Paris all the while. In 1817 he became professor of composition at the Académie des Beaux-Arts, a highly prestigious appointment. At the time, Paris (and all of Europe, in fact) was smitten with Sir Walter Scott's novels. Fashionable Paris took to everything Scottish, and the whole town seemed to be wearing kilts and plaids. Boieldieu cleverly based an opera on two Scott novels, *The Monastery* and *Guy Mannering*. *La Dame blanche*, with a libretto by Eugène Scribe, was a stupendous success at the Opéra-Comique. Here all of Boieldieu's pleasing qualities were fulfilled, using a succession of Scottish tunes for spice. For contemporary listeners, the opera is clearly part of an important tradition.

La Dame blanche (opéra comique in three acts) (1825)
Sénéchal, Doniat, Héral, Legros, Paris Symphony Orchestra and Chorus, Stoll: Accord ACD 220862

Concerto in C Major for Harp and Orchestra (1801)
Moretti, Southwest German Radio Symphony Orchestra: Koch Schwann SCH 311422

JOHANN NEPOMUK HUMMEL

(1778–1837) Hungary

As a child, Hummel was a prodigy on the piano and lived in Mozart's home for two years as his pupil. After his prodigy years, he had one of the great careers in music.

By 1800 he was considered first among pianists and a rival to Beethoven in improvisation. Czerny, who idolized his teacher Beethoven, thought Hummel surpassed him in the clarity and elegance of his piano technique.

As a composer, Hummel foreshadowed Romanticism in several works, but like many others he could not overcome the stranglehold of conventional Classical forms. Chopin's early music and pianism clearly show his influence, and the young Pole once bragged that a friend thought his F minor concerto finer than a Hummel concerto. The Septet in D Minor (Op. 74), with its early Romantic aroma, created a sensation when introduced in Vienna in 1816. Occasionally he anticipated Schumann, who considered Hummel's F-sharp minor sonata (Op. 81) to be epic and titanic.

In 1819–22, Hummel was *Kapellmeister* at Weimar, where Goethe often heard him play and was inspired by his improvisations. He composed in all musical forms, and his contemporaries would be surprised that so little of his work has been preserved today. His brilliant Trumpet Concerto (S.49, 1803) is now his best-known composition. But Hummel has an important place in the history of piano playing, for he attempted to codify modern piano playing in such areas as trills and other ornamentation.

By 1830 his immaculately clean style, with sparse use of pedal, appeared dry; a larger, more colorful type of performance was becoming popular. Hummel's widow, Elisabeth, was astonished by Liszt's tremendous performance of her husband's Piano Concerto in B Minor (Op. 89, 1819) at Weimar in 1844, remarking that "my old man certainly never played it like that."

Concerto in E-flat Major for Trumpet and Orchestra, S.49 (1803)
Marsalis, National Philharmonic Orchestra, Leppard: CBS MK 37846
Hardenberger, Academy of St. Martin in the Fields, Marriner: Philips 420203-2

FERNANDO SOR

(1778–1839) Spain

Sor, a Catalan from Barcelona, was the key player of the guitar at the end of the eighteenth century. He was educated at the Escolanía at Montserrat and began composing opera and ballet early. It is his guitar music that remains, however.

The first treatise on the guitar was published in Barcelona as early as 1596, and the instrument over time became common in Spain. But Sor's presence as a performer and teacher in Paris, London, and even Moscow gave new interest to the guitar in Europe, where it suddenly became a household instrument. (One of Berlioz's first musical encounters was with the guitar, and Paganini was a virtuoso on it.)

Sor himself contributed a *method* for its performance, and his resourceful and attractive études considerably advanced its technique. His work remains in the repertory of those seriously interested in the instrument. He died in Paris, where his monument at the famed Montmartre cemetery should be refurbished.

Various Works for Solo Guitar
Fernández: London 425821-2

MAURO GIULIANI

(1781–1829) Italy

At the end of the eighteenth century, the guitar had become popular in Italy, and Giuliani, born near Bari, was a virtuoso on the instrument. In 1806, to improve his finances, he moved to Vienna, where his career as a composer and performer took shape. Little is known of his life and locales, but around 1814 Empress Marie Louise, Napoleon's second wife, made him *virtuoso onorario di camera*. He was prolific, producing nearly two hundred works, mostly for guitar. Many are salon puff pieces.

An important solo guitar work is the Grand Overture in A Major (Op. 61), which exhibits superb knowledge of the instrument. Concerto no. 1 (Op. 30) has gained popularity through recordings. The composer died in Naples, deep in debt.

Concerto no. 1 in A Major for Guitar and String Orchestra, Op. 30
P. Romero, Academy of St. Martin in the Fields, Marriner: Philips 420780-2

PART FOUR

THE ROMANTIC AGE

Most important movements in the arts come to fruition after tremendous social and political upheavals. The eighteenth and early nineteenth centuries were one such period of upheaval. The American and French revolutions brought individual rights to the fore. Napoleon electrified the world with his astounding personality; never had one person so dominated the world's thought. Rousseau's *Confessions* (1770) told of intimacies never before revealed and opened the gates to an endless stream of memoirs. Pre-Romantic novels, from Goethe's *The Sorrows of Young Werther* (1774) to the Marquis de Sade's novels of the 1790s, opened a Pandora's box. By the last quarter of the eighteenth century, Shakespeare's vast art had been translated into German and French, and the Bard's universal genius caused a revelation in those countries. Beethoven, when asked what his D minor piano sonata (Op. 31/2) meant, told the inquirer to read Shakespeare's *The Tempest*. Technological progress took off, and poets, writers, and painters (including Wordsworth) lauded the natural world that they feared would soon disappear. Painters left off portraying ordered landscapes and turned instead to tortured ones. Blake, both poet and painter, explored mysticism and the "divine vision." Goethe, E.T.A. Hoffmann, Novalis, and Hölderlin wrote of the supernatural and metaphysical. Many writers were intrigued by the growing scientific knowledge: Schiller wrote of the criminal mind, and a gruesome science gave birth to Mary Shelley's *Frankenstein* in 1818.

In the literary world, two of the major progenitors of Romanticism were Lord Byron and Sir Walter Scott. Byron's larger-than-life heroes (and his own Romantic life) and Scott's highly colored historical novels of romance and chivalry helped give the new age its name. Scott was the most-read novelist of the age; his *Waverley* novels (starting in 1814) were translated into every European language, and his works became grist for countless opera librettos.

Music—the art most tied to tradition and arduous training—had more difficulty making the leap into Romanticism. The older Classical forms (always excepting Beethoven and Schubert) were too rigid. Classicism stood for balance, unity, order, and homogenized forms. The Romantics longed to break rules, to engage in subjective fantasies, to enter realms of the exotic and strange, to explore the erotic, to delve into national origins. As Aldous Huxley best put it, "Mozart's melodies may be brilliant, memorable, infectious, but they don't palpitate, don't catch you between wind and water, don't send the listener off into erotic ecstasies." But various new forms, such as Schubert's songs, Chopin's preludes and ballades, Schumann's poetic piano cycles, Liszt's symphonic poems, and Wagner's music-dramas would soon appear. In 1820 Keats was correct: "Heard melodies are sweet, but those unheard are sweeter." But those unheard melodies were soon to be heard *molto appassionata*, and to this day they still resonate.

Beethoven was the spiritual father figure of musical Romanticism. Although he had fulfilled the Classical style, his music of the middle and later years was so suffused with expressive and elemental power that it haunted the nineteenth century. Beethoven, called the Napoleon of composers, became in the Romantic era a heaven-storming hero of mythic proportions. Napoleon had been defeated, but Beethoven was to be victorious.

The first composer to display the Romantic spirit was Carl Maria von Weber, who in many of his works could not wholly reconcile it with the Classical tradition. He explored new types of color in the orchestra and in the piano, and in 1819, with *Aufforderung zum Tanz* (*Invitation to the Dance*), he composed a glittering ballroom scene vibrating with waltz themes of undeniable erotic energy. In the next year, with *Der Freischütz* (*The Free-Shooter*), German national opera was born. Weber had accomplished something that others had not quite done—he had captured the special flavor and charm of a specific locale and landscape, permeated by folk-sounding melodies. He had breathed a mysterious, supernatural, Germanic spirit in this work. The time was ripe, and all of Europe knew it. From that moment, composers in every country that had a folklore and folk music would mine their national lore. It is still being done today.

The first generation of full-fledged Romantic composers flourished with Schubert, Donizetti, Berlioz, Bellini, Glinka, Mendelssohn, Schumann, Chopin, Liszt, Verdi, and Wagner, an amazing harvest of genius all born within only a decade and a half of one another. Schubert's songs and small piano pieces, his lyrically beautiful melodies, and his poignant harmony mark him as a transitional artist, with one foot in each age. Although Schubert did not invent the German art song, or *Lied*, his songs were the first to use the piano as equal partner, and as a new genre they constitute a landmark of the Romantic age. Like his fellow Romantics, Schubert was deeply moved by poetry and literature, and he responded by creating melodies of breathtaking beauty. His songs gave impetus to composers in every nation to exercise their talents through poetry.

The era of the Romantic art song coincided with the mature development of the piano and its dissemination in the homes of the rising middle class. The common presence of the piano in the home was responsible for the enormous song literature of the nineteenth century. Imagine a Schubert, Wolf, Mussorgsky, Rachmaninoff, or Fauré song with a harpsichord accompaniment! The harpsichord could not produce those extremes of human emotion that the various pressures of a more complex society generated; the harpsichord could not weep human tears or sing a melody. Romanticism depended on the piano, the most suggestive of all musical instruments. The sound the Romantics wanted was, in the pianist Arthur Loesser's words, "[a] vague, mellow tone-cloud, full of ineffable promise and foreboding, carrying intimations of infinity . . . harboring the mystical suspicion that anything might merge into everything." The piano could sigh or shiver, quiver or swoon, as no other instrument could. The public wanted virtuoso gods to sing upon it and show them the stars. By 1830 the piano could accomplish the lightning-quick changes from dark to light that the Romantics needed to express their passions. It was now ready for Mendelssohn, Chopin, Schumann, Liszt, and many lesser lights.

Chopin holds a central place in Romanticism. He arrived in Paris after the July Revolution of 1830, which installed Louis-Philippe as king. The city was boiling with new ideas, business enterprises, and feverish activity in all the arts. He made his Paris debut early in 1832 and knew that Paris was the city to nurture his genius. He had already finished writing most of his études, which have become for pianists the world over the standard for technical excellence.

As a harmonic innovator, Chopin contributed to the destruction of the older tonal system. The pianist and critic Charles Rosen goes so far as to say that "Chopin's music was as destructive of the tonic-dominant polarization of eighteenth century style as Schoenberg's of late nineteenth century chromaticism." Chopin was also the first Slavic nationalist, and although he resisted writing a "Polish" opera, he showed the world his pain, bitterness, and nostalgia for his tragic country in his mazurkas and polonaises. The historian Norman Davies wrote, "Chopin could appeal not only to listeners who were well attuned to his political message but equally to others who were totally oblivious.

There was no contradiction between the national and the universal aspects of his genius. The deliciously ambiguous emotional qualities of his bitter-sweet Polish melodies were woven into alternating moods of rousing protest and melancholic languor. For some, he translated Polish history into notes on the keyboard; for others, he conjured up poignancies of a purely personal and intimate character."

Paris was also the headquarters for the Hungarian composer Franz Liszt, who had been there since childhood pursuing a career as a piano prodigy. Liszt was perhaps the greatest pianist in history; his recitals and celebrity initiated the modern international performing career. In his Piano Sonata in B Minor, written in 1853, he created a huge one-movement form, incorporating aspects of the sonata that were not bound by its several separate movements. The Classical sonata had become stilted, and Romantic music (so much of which was inspired by literary sources) did not fit into it. In fact, it is surprising that it took so long after Beethoven's death to achieve a single-movement sonata format. Liszt's B minor sonata, whose themes are intricately transformed from the opening page, had far-reaching importance thematically and harmonically, and it must have been a powerful stimulus to Wagner, who in the late 1850s would compose *Tristan und Isolde*. Liszt also invented the symphonic poem, or tone poem for orchestra. His most famous is *Les Preludes*. Here finally was an orchestral vehicle that was free of stringent rules and flexible enough to portray the many moods desired.

Berlioz too was a fixture of Parisian artistic life, protesting the stilted forms and conservative notions in French music of the previous half century as well as the frivolity of conventional opera. He was the most radical presence in French music, a worthy colleague to Hugo in literature and Delacroix in painting. Deeply sensing the spiritual affinities of the arts, Berlioz was inflamed by Romantic literature and possessed a sense of the monumental. As Delacroix did in painting, Berlioz depicted in music the dramas *Romeo and Juliet*, *Faust*, and *Hamlet*, as well as works by Dante, Virgil, Byron, and others. With his *Symphonie fantastique* in 1830, he forged anew the modern orchestra, asking of its resources far more than Weber or Schubert had done before him, and paved the way for all later orchestral investigations. Berlioz, an alienated spirit fighting a conventional society, also fought ardently for advances in public perception and understanding of music. Like most of the Romantics, he was a prolific writer who propagandized his own theories in tireless polemics. His sparkling memoirs are still read with enjoyment and tell us a great deal about the Romantic movement.

Because of the superior training that the Paris Conservatory offered, many musicians gravitated to Paris to study there, such as the Belgian-born César

Franck, who wrote highly chromatic music that absorbed German influences, especially Bach, Beethoven, and Schumann. Franck felt that there was still vigor in the Classical forms, and his Symphony, Piano Quintet, String Quartet, and *Symphonic Variations* (all written in the 1870s and 1880s) had a large impact on his pupils d'Indy, Chausson, and others.

French composers were also busy writing Romantic operas, many of which were influenced by Wagner, especially after *Tristan* was produced in 1865. Wagner's influence on French musical culture was compelling and would curtail many talents too weak to resist it. Gounod and Chausson were influenced, and though Chabrier resisted to some extent, as did Saint-Saëns, they were smitten by him at the same time. Massenet, the opera composer best loved by the French public, wrote works of artistic charm that exhibited slight Wagnerian traits.

In Austria and Germany, other Romantic composers were hard at work, especially those who considered themselves the successors to their leading lights, Weber and Schubert. Felix Mendelssohn, born a generation after Weber and twelve years younger than Schubert, composed his Octet and *A Midsummer Night's Dream* Overture by 1826, before either Beethoven's or Schubert's death. His forty-eight *Songs Without Words* exuded a comfortable but poetic Romanticism and added to the prestige of amateur home music-making. Mendelssohn (who was a fine watercolorist) also invoked the Romantics' admiration of nature in splendid, evocative landscapes such as his *Hebrides Overture*.

Schumann idolized Mendelssohn, but Mendelssohn could not return the enthusiasm, for he found Schumann's music to be a maze of contradictions. Schumann's art is literary, autobiographical, love-starved, visionary, half-mad, idealistic. Schumann brought German Romanticism to its early fulfillment. His piano cycles, such as *Carnaval, Kreisleriana,* and *Kinderszenen,* are successful miniatures that are linked to the whole. In the field of the Romantic *Lied,* he was Schubert's worthy successor, and the Heine song cycle *Dichterliebe,* composed in 1840, is an incomparable expression of the essence of the Romantic spirit, dealing with despair, intimacy, and tenderness. The well-bred Mendelssohn may have repressed some of the more violent aspects of Romanticism, which Beethoven had flung upon the world, but in page after page of violent emotions, even as the grip of insanity began to strangle him, Schumann grappled with his demon.

For many music lovers, Wagner is the apotheosis of German and perhaps of all music. He absorbed every quality of Romanticism, clothing his music in plays filled with symbolism and based on myths that seemed to probe deeply into the psyche. Few were immune to his music, and those who hated him were drowned out by the world's Wagnerites. As late as 1925, the critic H. L. Mencken, a confirmed Brahmsian, could nonetheless write, "I believe that *Die Meistersinger* is the greatest single work of art ever produced by man. It took more skill to plan and write it than it took to plan and write the whole canon of Shakespeare." Never had an artist had such a hold on his audience, and Wagner fever spread through the world.

The earlier Wagner operas—*Rienzi, Der fliegende Holländer, Tannhäuser, Lohengrin*—extended the tradition of German Romantic opera. As Wagner himself confessed, "I have become a completely different fellow as a harmonist since my acquaintance with Liszt's compositions." But the transformation of opera into what Wagner would call "music-drama" was the result of a complex of elements, ranging from Greek drama to Schopenhauer, as well as his own considerable powers as a poet, dramatist, theorist, conductor, supreme orchestrator, and the most far-reaching harmonist of the period. Because of *Tristan*, the *Ring* cycle, and *Parsifal*, the system of tonal music practically came to a halt.

The music-drama was the most successful synthesis of the arts ever attempted, encompassing Wagner's notions of Beethoven's later style. His achievement was a new art form, and if today it lacks some of the emotional and spiritual impact that it had on the grandiose thinking of the nineteenth century, we must nevertheless attach to it the highest historical and artistic importance.

Although Wagner's demands on singers are technically horrific, the chief protagonist of his music-drama is the orchestra. Indeed, he invented music-drama as a safeguard to protect opera from the tyranny of singers. He saw that opera was destined to perish unless it had more far-reaching goals. In *Opera and Drama*, published as early as 1851, he outlined his thinking. Here, briefly summarized, are Wagner's prescriptions for music-drama:

1. A music-drama is not the work of a composer who rises to make his contribution after someone else (at best a Goethe, at worst a hack) has supplied a literary stimulus. A music-drama, rather, is the work of The Artist. It is intolerable that a musician who is a greater artist than any living poet or playwright or scene designer, as Beethoven was, should merely respond to others.

2. A music-drama is an amalgam of the arts (*Gesamtkunstwerk*), as Beethoven's Ninth Symphony implicitly was, although it used only music and words. Since music is the most powerful of the arts, the great artwork of the future will stem from music, and The Artist will be primarily a composer of music. At first music-drama, as ancient tragedy was for the Greeks, will be the communal expression of the German race, the ritual of a nation, until the new culture spreads beyond Germany.

3. In music-drama, music should not sound for music's own sake. Though Gluck, Mozart, Weber, and Beethoven achieved music-drama in *passages* of their operas, these works were marred by "set pieces" designed to display the caliber of the composer or the performers as musicians. "The error in opera has been that a means (music) has been made an end, while the end (drama) has been made the means." (Let the reader measure this judgment against *Tristan* and be glad that Wagner was primarily a musician.)

4. A music-drama proceeds on a scale like that of Beethoven's symphonies; it is not interrupted to accommodate choruses, ballets, airs, processions, and marches. Instead there is endless melody, which is maintained by the orchestra when the contribution of the actors must be speechlike or declamatory.

5. A music-drama, like a Beethoven symphony, is integrated by themes or motives. The chief among them (*Leitmotive*) bind not only music to music but also music to drama, for they are associated with persons, things, and ideas, like Siegfried, gold, and jealousy. As each act of a music-drama resembles a vast symphonic movement, the motives undergo transformation to suit succeeding moods and situations.

As influential as he was, Wagner of course did not have a monopoly on Austro-German Romanticism. Nineteenth-century Vienna offered a culturally rich environment; it was home to everyone from Wittgenstein to Freud to the perpetually loved Johann Strauss, Jr., the Waltz King. Bruckner also made his home there, and his massive symphonies evoke a special Romanticism, epic in tone, with mystical slow movements, rapt in contemplation. Although Bruckner's religious fever is entirely his own, the epic element of Wagner thrilled him to ever greater heights and lengths.

Vienna was also home to the Hamburg-trained Brahms, who did much to restore the city's prestige as a great musical center. Brahms was a giant among giants and Romantic to the core, though the old Classical division of movements suited his Romanticism better than Lisztian tone poems or Wagnerian opera. He was stimulated less by literature than by the desire to investigate all music before him. He was hardly a conservative; he merely went his own way writing masterpieces.

The generation of Wolf, Richard Strauss, and Mahler, all born in the 1860s, furnished Austro-German Romanticism with its last rites. Wolf's life's work was devoted primarily to *Lieder*, and his songs are in essence miniature music-dramas, with Wagner's orchestra becoming the piano. Draining to listen to, they brought a century of German song production to an astonishing conclusion.

Strauss and Mahler were both famous conductors with international careers. They may have been rivals, but both were orchestrators of genius. At the end of the nineteenth century, with his astonishing series of "realistic" tone poems, Strauss was the "progressive" who was worshiped by most young composers. If anyone was to find the solution for the demise of the tonal system, it would be Strauss. This seemed more than apparent in his early operas, *Salome* and *Elektra*. But instead, the Romantic composer that he actually was opted in his next opera (the delicious *Der Rosenkavalier* of 1911) for a neoclassical pastiche. He continued to compose operas, and his heartrending *Four Last Songs* of 1948 embody a Romanticism that could well have been composed in 1895.

Mahler's philosophical Romanticism centered upon the symphony. Great opera conductor that he was, he never ventured to compose an opera or to put himself into rivalry with Wagner. From Beethoven's Ninth, and from Bruckner and Schubert, he formed his monumental symphonies. Less radical harmonically than Strauss's *Elektra*, they were filled with every fin-de-siècle malaise. As he grew, Mahler was able to express even subtler states of emotion, as well as his own neurotic reactions to them. With Mahler the symphony (which had made a long journey from Haydn) became a dialogue between composer and the world itself.

During the Romantic era, Italy, a country that symbolized song and romance, continued to focus on opera. Italian orchestras were deplorable, and concerts and recitals were infrequent. Beethoven was hardly known there. In the early nineteenth century, the nation was in political disarray, beseiged by Metternich's Austria and Napoleon's France. Its opera houses gave Italy a sense of identity as well as a social life: here a gregarious people mingled and cheered on their favorite singers. Opera was Italy's chief cultural export, and its operas were in heavy demand in every corner of Europe, as were Italian singers.

In the 1810s and 1820s, Rossini was the king of opera, and he wrote quickly to fulfill the demand. His operas mingled straightforward, almost elementary diatonic harmony with Italian melodies that were easily remembered and overtures that moved at breakneck speeds. With *William Tell*, his last opera, Rossini enlarged the scope of Italian opera by using a more expressive drama and expanding the orchestra's participation. After Rossini, Donizetti made an international impact with both serious and comic operas. His comedies sparkled, but his public most loved his typically Italian portrayals of jealousy, guilt, betrayal, and romantic love in a long line of tragic heroines from Lucia di Lammermoor to Maria de Rohan. A serious blow to Italian opera was the early death of the idolized Vincenzo Bellini, whose melancholy melodies inspired the young Chopin and stirred the Romantic sensibility.

Rossini, Donizetti, and Bellini led the way, but the major figure of nineteenth-century Italian Romantic opera was Giuseppe Verdi, whose life (from 1813 to 1901) spanned the century. Verdi would become, along with such Romantic leaders of Italian unification as Garibaldi and Mazzini, a national hero, and he would write operas that stirred the national consciousness while cleverly avoiding censorship by its oppressors. He synthesized all aspects of Italian operatic drama, with an unusually varied subject matter. He was well loved by audiences in Italy and internationally, but critics often regarded his music as inferior to Wagner's subtle and progressive harmony, while the Wagnerian propaganda machine tore into "simple-minded" Italian opera in general.

As Verdi matured, his ever-growing genius for melody and characterization became incandescent. At the end of his career (with *Otello* and finally the comedy *Falstaff*), he organically integrated singer and orchestra, while the purest essence of Italian melody permeated their vast structures. Verdi, who thought each country should retain its national characteristics, never deviated from using vocal melody as his basis. He lived long enough to realize that music had to enter new stages and to worry that Italian composers would become artificial and overelaborate. Giacomo Puccini was Verdi's one major successor in songful opera, and he forms the epilogue to a tradition that began with the fragrant arias of Alessandro Scarlatti, Alessandro Stradella, and Giovanni Pergolesi. The Italians created bel canto, or "beautiful singing," and the finest work of Rossini, Bellini, Verdi, and Puccini is a proud cultural treasure, human as the voice itself.

Romantic Italy produced just one nonoperatic figure of importance. Nicolò Paganini symbolizes for all time the archetypal Romantic virtuoso. Images of his truly strange and eerie personality, his wasted spectral figure (playing the devil's own instrument, the violin), vibrate through the satanic dominion of nineteenth-century Romanticism.

In Russia, Romantic art music developed more slowly than in other countries, as Russia had had no Classical tradition nor much of a music education system. When it did arrive, it belonged almost exclusively to that subset of Romanticism, Romantic nationalism. Russians' musical diet in the early nineteenth century consisted of Italian opera and the occasional visit by a famous performer such as John Field, who was brought to Russia in 1803 to demonstrate the merits of Muzio Clementi's pianos. Field stayed in Russia for several decades and wrote pretty nocturnes, which were often played. He also gave some piano lessons to the semidilettante Mikhail Glinka, the first specifically Russian national composer, who is often called the father of Russian music. Glinka wrote both orchestral pieces and some pioneering operas. Today his music sounds relatively mild compared to that of his later compatriots, but his efforts gave confidence that a Russian school of music could emerge, showing the world a Russian landscape and character.

Another poorly trained musician, Mily Balakirev, dreamed of opera and song in the Russian language, whose subject matter would be drawn from the history and folklore of the Russian peoples, including the folk songs of the Transcaucasian countries and Central Asia (areas that European Russia called "Oriental"). Balakirev's most enduring work is the 1869 "oriental fantasy" *Islamey*, but his real influence was as the teacher of a group of gifted amateurs (César Cui, Alexander Borodin, Nikolai Rimsky-Korsakov, and Modest Mussorgsky), with whom he formed the "Mighty Handful" or the "Russian Five" and whose music became forever linked with their homeland.

Another type of Romantic influence was infiltrating Russia through a great teacher, the pianist and composer Anton Rubinstein, who founded the St. Petersburg Conservatory in 1862. Rubinstein was trained in Europe, and his influence on his pupil Peter Tchaikovsky was indelible. Tchaikovsky chromaticized and Russianized Rubinstein's essentially Mendelssohnian forms and harmonies. In turn, Tchaikovsky influenced his direct offspring, Sergei Rachmaninoff, whose chief appeal is musical nostalgia for his Russian roots. Rachmaninoff's exact contemporary, Alexander Scriabin, began his creative life as a Russian Romantic but became an avant-gardist, greatly contributing to the ferment of early-twentieth-century music.

In other countries, Romanticism merged with the nationalistic spirit after the 1848 revolutions. Smetana led a movement to opera in the Czech language. Dvořák used traditional forms that were flooded with Czech-like melodies, while the youngest of the Czech nationals, Janáček, studied the language patterns of his Czech-Moravian roots. In his operas and other forms, this isolated composer became increasingly original, ending his nationalistic art with one foot solidly in modernity, using discontinuity, nondevelopmental procedures, and irregular rhythm. His operas display an uncanny feeling for character and reality, but remain within a Romantic lyricism.

Norway had a few early composers who realized the value of its folk material, but Grieg's music by the end of his life was synonymous with his homeland. Similarly, Finland and Sibelius will forever be linked. Spain got on the nationalist bandwagon fairly late, and not until Albéniz's last years, with his piano cycle *Iberia* (1906), did he achieve an authentic Spanish style. Granados followed suit in his *Goyescas*, and the third of Spain's most gifted composers, Manuel de Falla, was as Romantic as his compatriots until World War I, when he developed a more astringent nationalism.

Ardent nationalism and the adaptation of folk material continued through the nineteenth and twentieth centuries in other countries, too, with the United States' Louis Moreau Gottschalk, Edward MacDowell, George Gershwin, and Aaron Copland; Hungary's Zoltán Kodály; Brazil's Heitor Villa-Lobos; Armenia's Aram Khachaturian; Romania's George Enescu; Poland's Karol Szymanowski; Australia's Percy Grainger; Argentina's Alberto Ginastera; and Mexico's Carlos Chávez.

And what, finally, of England? One of the few European nations to remain stable after the various revolutions of 1848, England remained stifled during the Romantic era. Bourgeois and mercantile values ruled, allowing little room for the supposedly frivolous pursuit of music (even making it almost national policy to cover the legs on the piano). Byron and Scott, an Englishman and a Scot, were key figures in generating the Romantic movement in poetry and literature, but England, alas, could not achieve the same in music. In fact, Chopin, visiting England in 1848–49, was shocked to discover that the English did not think of music as an art. No wonder the nation produced few important musicians, or that Edward Elgar emerged into the heat of Romanticism with his *Enigma Variations* in 1898, at the end of that era.

NICOLÒ PAGANINI

b. Genoa, October 27, 1782

d. Nice, May 27, 1840

I am neither young nor handsome, I'm ugly, but when the women hear me play, they come crawling at my feet.

Paganini was born in a squalid section of Genoa to parents who were poor but not destitute. Antonio, his father, was an amateur musician, and his mother, Teresa, sang well. They had five children, and Antonio taught the two boys, Carlo and Nicolò, guitar and violin. Carlo would become a violinist in the Lucca Orchestra.

One night Teresa had a dream that an angel would grant her any wish; she asked that Nicolò become the greatest violinist in the world. Her son loved her tenderly all his life, but his feelings for his father were another matter. As soon as Antonio discovered great talent in Nicolò, he became obsessed with turning him into a virtuoso violinist. He made the boy practice beyond endurance, and often locked him in a room and deprived him of food if he rebelled.

In just a year, Nicolò exhausted his father's teaching resources, and he was taken to study with Giacomo Costa, one of Genoa's leading violinists. It was not long before the amazed Costa presented the prodigy at a Genoa church, where his playing caused a sensation. His progress was so rapid that he outgrew Costa, too, in a short time. The twelve-year-old boy gave a concert to raise funds to go to Parma, where the celebrated violinist Alessandro Rolla lived.

In 1795, when father and son arrived at Rolla's home, they found the violinist still in bed. While waiting, the boy spied a manuscript of Rolla's new violin concerto. Looking at the practically illegible score, he began sight-reading it with such perfect intonation, style, and technique that Rolla jumped from his bed and exclaimed, "I can teach you nothing, you are wasting your time here!" The ever-watchful father and his son remained in Parma for a year. Rolla did give him a few lessons, but more important, the boy studied composition with the eminent opera composer Ferdinando Paer, who was just then at the peak of his fame.

In the winter of 1796, the Paganinis returned to Genoa, and for the next few years Nicolò practiced relentlessly, delving into the hidden resources of his instrument, exploring new avenues of technique and refinements of bowing. In 1800 he dispensed with playing from the score; playing from memory stunned his audiences.

In 1801, accompanied by his brother, the already well-known Nicolò performed at a festival in Lucca. This time Antonio stayed home. The concert again caused a sensation. This taste of freedom was exhilarating, and Nicolò decided to escape his father. His fame preceded him to every town where he wandered, yet his career as a concert artist was only at its dawn.

In those days, performers had no management or public relations experts, proper concert halls were few, and traveling was grueling and messy (the roads thick with mud after a rain). An artist usually entered a town, spent much time making contacts, and arranged what he or she could in the way of appearances, usually at the salons of the local aristocrats. Payment often came in gifts and meals, seldom in cash, unless it was a public concert; in that case, the soloist had to hire singers and frequently an orchestra, as the concept of a solo violin recital with piano accompaniment still lay far in the future. After paying everyone else, the "star" was lucky to have something left for his own pocket. A wandering virtuoso could live a sorry existence, and time to practice the instrument was scarce. Except for opera, Italy was far less developed in its concert life than many other European countries, and during this period, after Napoleon's conquests, Italy was in political turmoil.

For Paganini, the opening years of the nineteenth century were harsh, and the twenty-year-old violinist understandably succumbed to the charms and protection of an older Tuscan woman, who took him to her mountain estate, where they lived in total seclusion. The idyll lasted nearly three years, from 1801 to 1804. We know only that her name was Dida, and that Paganini used these years to begin sketching his caprices and perfect himself on the guitar, an instrument of which he was fond.

During this time, stories began circulating that Paganini had been imprisoned for murdering his mistress and fashioning fiddle strings from her intestines. Even as late as the 1830s, much to the violinist's chagrin, a print titled *Paganini en prison* was a popular seller in Paris. Paganini was himself a promotional genius, and no other performer in history was ever the object of so many rumors and so much malicious gossip.

After the passion of the Tuscan affair faded, Paganini returned to Lucca, which had become a stimulating city since Napoleon's sister, Princess Elisa Baciocchi, had become its ruler. She was a great patroness of the arts and was soon enthralled with the young violinist. They became romantically involved, and she gave him the post of opera director. After four years, the government moved to Florence, and Paganini, feeling like a lackey in the princess's service, broke with her. He needed his independence; he needed to perform, and the princess refused to make him *maestro di cappella*.

In 1809 he commenced performing and traveling much more extensively. In these years he learned how to please and titillate the public. He had the uncanny instincts of a born showman, and for each town he appeared to find the exact recipe for gaining adulation. His appeal involved more than his bag of tricks, his perfected ability to play only on the G string, and his electrifying, ever more breathless variations on familiar tunes. He also had a sinister, even sleazy magnetism, and he cast a spell on most of his audiences. Goethe heard him and found in him, as he did in Napoleon, demonic forces. Paganini himself wrote, "No one ever asks if you have heard Paganini, but if you have seen him."

Still, he was cautious and hesitant and put off his Milan debut until 1813. For his first concert at the great La Scala Opera House, he unveiled his *Le Streghe (Witches' Dance)* variations (Op. 8). The public had never seen or heard such speed and accuracy. The more superstitious members of the crowd were convinced that the devil was onstage invisibly directing his violin. On the streets, people crossed themselves when he appeared. Paganini gave no fewer than eleven concerts in Milan, and from that time his fame spread irresistibly.

His next several years were occupied with dissipation. Paganini was involved in numerous amorous escapades and gambled perpetually. But he performed constantly and composed a great deal, including the scintillating D major violin concerto (Op. 6, c.1817). He suffered long illnesses with poor medical treatment and long periods of recovery; all the while, his legend grew. He finally performed in Rome and Naples in 1819. In Rome pandemonium reigned at his concerts. The Austrian chancellor, Prince Metternich, heard him in the eternal city and begged the violinist to show himself in Vienna.

At a concert in 1824, Paganini met an attractive young singer, Antonia Bianchi, with whom he lived for four years. A son, Achille, was born in 1825. Paganini adored him and showered his son with attention for the rest of his life.

By 1828, the whole of Europe clamored to hear the great virtuoso. The time had come for a tour of Europe. Paganini, at age forty-six, took his seven

Stradivari violins and set out on a six-year tour. Vienna went wild, in more than a dozen concerts. Schubert, in his last tragic, poverty-stricken year, scraped together the money for an expensive ticket and was overwhelmed. "I heard the singing of an angel," he cried. Rossini sat stupefied and wept. It was the same in Prague, Warsaw, the German states, England, Ireland, and Scotland. In Berlin the often-stern critic Ludwig Rellstab, after hearing the Adagio of the D major concerto, wrote, "Never in my life have I heard such weeping. It was as if the lacerated heart of this suffering mortal were bursting with sorrow."

No soloist had ever been so triumphant, and the money Paganini made was exorbitant beyond his wildest speculations. Only Paris remained to be tackled. The city had been in the throes of the July Revolution of 1830, and he wisely waited until early 1831 to conquer the sensation-loving Parisians.

His debut took place at the Paris Opera on March 9. Ticket prices were tripled for the event, and le tout Paris turned out, including the artistic elite. The great showman always knew when and how to enter a stage. In Paris, with gaslights low, he rose from the trap door of the opera stage looking like a corpse. The audience was electrified. The poet Heinrich Heine, keen observer of human nature, said, "At last a dark figure which seemed to have arisen from the underworld, appeared on the stage. It was Paganini, a vampire with a violin, who, if not sucks the blood out of our hearts, at any rate sucks the gold out of our pockets."

Paganini gave twelve concerts in Paris, including one for charity, and earned an unprecedented 165,000 francs—at a time when a small apartment in Paris cost 200 francs a month and when Berlioz was content with his salary of 1,500 francs a year as librarian of the Paris Conservatory.

The thriving Paris school of violin playing was much impressed. From the older violinists Pierre Baillot and Charles Lafont (whom Paganini had crushed in a contest in Italy in 1816) to the younger ones such as Jean-Delphin Alard and Henri Vieuxtemps, the consensus was that he was supreme.

The painter Eugène Delacroix was enraptured and was inspired to paint the violinist as the very incarnation of an agonized, tortured soul, a cadaverous necromancer playing a violin capable of every kind of evil seduction. (The painting is now in the Louvre.) Paganini above all symbolized the satanic elements of the Romantic movement, an age that celebrated the lurid.

Chopin did not arrive in Paris until later in 1831, but the Pole had already heard the violinist in Warsaw in 1829, where Paganini doubtless inspired him to begin composing his Twenty-four Études. The twenty-year-old Liszt, who had been depressed and floundering, was literally shocked back to life. "What a man," he wrote, "what a violin, what an artist! Heavens! What sufferings, what misery, what tortures in those four strings." After the first concert, Liszt rushed home and began transcribing Paganini's caprices for the piano; he vowed to become the "Paganini of the piano."

Late in 1833 Paganini suffered a pulmonary hemorrhage, but recovered. He then had a painful operation on his jaw, which almost caused his death. In addition, he was suffering from tuberculosis and cancer. After six years of touring, he was exhausted beyond repair, and he and his inseparable companion Achille left for the estate in Parma that he had recently purchased. With sufficient rest, some of his strength returned. Parma was then ruled by Princess Marie-Louise of Austria, Napoleon's second wife and a discriminating lover of the arts. Under her protection, Paganini was given the task of reorganizing and improving Parma's orchestra. In general, Italy's orchestras were among the worst in Europe. In July 1836, he resigned because of intrigues against him, but he had already brilliantly accomplished his mission of making Parma's orchestra the finest in Italy.

With performance offers pouring in, the violinist once again took to the stage, appearing in Nice and Marseilles. But his strength was ebbing; after two benefit concerts in June 1837 in Turin, he left the concert stage forever.

For years, Paganini's voice had been a deadly whisper; now his larynx was paralyzed. His son communicated with him by reading his lips. In 1837 he invested a large amount of money in a reckless business venture in Paris that was to combine music and gambling, called Casino Paganini. It closed after two months. Besieged by lawsuits, he was forced to stay in Paris. Finally, in 1839, he moved to the warmer climate of Nice, at the time still an Italian city.

He died the next year. He refused to see a priest in his last moments, so the bishop of Nice forbade burial in a cemetery. Hours before he died, it was said, he was heard wildly improvising on the *Dies Irae*. For seven years his coffin lay in a cellar. Marie-Louise finally located it and had him buried at his villa in Parma. Then in 1876 he was interred in Parma's cemetery, where legend had it that each midnight in the cemetery, one could hear the sound of agonized violin playing. In 1896 his remains were reburied in the town's new cemetery, where an impressive monument was erected.

Unfortunately, a certain element of charlatanism has always tainted Paganini's name, and since his day, the musical world has been divided over the concept of "musician" versus "virtuoso." To some listeners, virtuosity is showing off superficial talents and is at odds with pure musicianship. Few can conceive of both qualities combined in a single executant.

With all the attention given to his virtuosity, Paganini's place as a composer and innovator should not be underestimated. Brahms thought that "Paganini's genius for composition was fully equal to his genius for the violin." As the creator of modern violin technique, he forged new directions for the instrument.

Historically he was the culmination of a glorious Italian violin tradition that sprang from Arcangelo Corelli and Antonio Vivaldi and continued with Giuseppe Tartini, Pietro Locatelli, Giovanni Viotti, and Alessandro Rolla. Paganini's concertos are engaging and spectacular showpieces that inspired a string of later concertos; and his magnum opus, the Twenty-four Caprices (Op. 1, 1804–9), is a manifesto of fantastic new effects for unaccompanied violin, which are still regarded as the Mount Everest of Romantic violinism.

As the English critic Wilfrid Mellers noted, "The sinister, cadaverous figure of Paganini haunts the nineteenth century, transforming romantic glamour into the spectral and demoniacal." Paganini continues to be a disturbing and endlessly fascinating personality, an essential artist of the Romantic age.

Twenty-four Caprices for Solo Violin, Op. 1 (c. 1805)

The publication of the Twenty-four Caprices in 1820 was a milestone in the history of violin playing. Paganini—who had admired the twenty-four caprices by Pietro Locatelli, published a half-century earlier—wrote, "They opened up a world of new ideas and devices that never had the merited success because of excessive difficulties." Locatelli's pieces are technically intriguing but musically arid; Paganini's are modeled on the art of Italian bel canto singing, including the prowess of great coloratura sopranos and the unnatural feats of the castrati, whom he had heard in his youth. And like the singers of his day, he improvised variants and all forms of embellishments that surrounded the written-down versions. Most likely they were of a difficulty that would astonish present-day violinists.

The caprices were written for an enormous hand, and there has been much speculation that Paganini had Marfan's syndrome, a connective tissue disorder. Some have also thought that he had an operation to remove the tendons between the fingers, making his joints hyperextensible and making possible the tremendous stretches necessary to perform his work. Violinists take special care in practicing Paganini, knowing that considerable injury to the hand can result.

Most of the caprices use double, triple, and quadruple stops, flying staccato, left-hand pizzicato, spiccato, chordal combinations, chromatic thirds, sixths, octaves, broken octaves, tremolos, undulating bowing, trills and arpeggios, and so forth: in short, they provided a new vocabulary for the instrument. The caprices offer an amazing diversity. The theme and variations of No. 24 in A minor inspired Franz Liszt, Witold Lutosławski, Boris Blacher, Johannes Brahms, Sergei Rachmaninoff, and others to write yet more variations on it. Violinists who can manage them all are rare, and it is fascinating to hear complete versions by such heroes of the instrument as Ruggiero Ricci, Salvatore Accardo, Shlomo Mintz, Paul Zukofsky, Michael Rabin, Victor Pikaizen, and Itzhak Perlman.

Accardo: Deutsche Grammophon 429714-2
Perlman: EMI Classics CDC 47171
Rabin: EMI Classics CDM 64560

Concerto no. 1 in D Major for Violin and Orchestra, Op. 6 (c.1817)

D major is the most felicitous key for violin playing. This concerto has been called a Rossini opera on a violin, and the comparison is apt. Rossini is reputed to have said that if Paganini turned to opera, he would be out of business. The first movement, Allegro maestoso, has a rather long orchestral prelude. The violin enters with a wonderful bravura sweep, followed by the lyric theme marked *dolce* ("sweetly"). The movement exhibits an astounding array of violinistics. The Adagio, composed in the relative key of B minor, is melancholy and opens in tragic grand opera style. Paganini supposedly was inspired by a scene in a play where a prisoner falls to his knees and asks God to end his earthly existence. The finale is a Rondo, marked *allegro spiritoso*, and is infectious in its sparkling vivacity and spine-tingling in its devil-may-care virtuosity.

Mullova, Academy of St. Martin in the Fields, Marriner: Philips 422332-2
Midori, London Symphony Orchestra, Slatkin: Philips 420943-2
Francescatti, Philadelphia Orchestra, Ormandy: Sony Classical SBK 47661

OTHER PRINCIPAL WORKS

VIOLIN OR VIOLIN AND ORCHESTRA WORKS
Le Streghe, Op. 8 (1813)*
Concerto no. 6 in E Minor, Op. posth. (c.1815)*
I Palpiti, Op. 13 (1819)
Moser Fantasy, Op. 24 (?1819)
Introduction and Variations on "Nel cuor più non mi sento" (c.1820)
Concerto no. 2 in B Minor, Op. 7 (1826)*
Concerto no. 3 in E Major (1826)
Maestoso sonata sentimentale, Op. 27 (1828)
Variations on "God Save the King," Op. 9 (1829)

Concerto no. 4 in D Minor (1830)*
Concerto no. 5 in A Minor (1830)*
Moto perpetuo in C Major, Op. 11 (after 1830)*

VIOLIN AND OTHER INSTRUMENT(S) WORKS
Six Sonatas for Violin and Guitar, Op. 2 (c.1805)
Six Sonatas for Violin and Guitar, Op. 3 (c.1805)*
Fifteen quartets for violin, viola, cello, and guitar (1818–20)
Terzetto concertante in D Major for Viola, Cello, and Guitar (1833)

CARL
MARIA
VON WEBER

b. Eutin, Germany, November 18, 1786

d. London, June 5, 1826

To judge a contemporary work of art correctly demands that calm, unprejudiced mood which, while susceptible to every impression, carefully guards against preconceived opinion or feelings. It requires a mind completely open to the particular work under consideration.

Carl Maria von Weber was born into a theatrical family. His father, Franz Anton, made a precarious livelihood as an actor-impresario with small traveling troupes. Carl and his siblings were often put to use backstage or onstage, in spite of Carl's congenital hip displacement (which made him unable to walk until he was four; he limped throughout his life).

This unsettled lifestyle did not permit consistent study of anything, but Franz Anton taught the boy music, and Carl quickly showed rapid development. He picked up more musical knowledge wherever he could, and at age eleven he spent a few profitable months in Salzburg, where he learned a great deal from Haydn's brother, the sixty-year-old Michael (who was also a fine composer). A few years later, in 1803, Carl studied with the Abbé Vogler, who was also the teacher of Giacomo Meyerbeer, in Vienna. Vogler quickly saw Weber's imagination and fired his interest in Romanticism, with its exotic subject matter and use of folksong.

Weber's personal life was reckless and adventurous. At one time, father and son were thrown into prison, accused of stealing ducal funds from the court of Württemberg, but the duo were soon acquitted. The slim and handsome youth, with his "Byronic" limp, was described by Philipp Spitta, a German music historian, as "a wandering minstrel . . . winning all hearts by his sweet, insinuating, lively melodies. . . . His person uniting in the most seductive manner aristocratic bearing with indolent dissipation, in all ways he resembled a figure from some Romantic poem." But somehow Weber also found time to develop his many talents—he was an excellent guitarist; he drew, painted, and wrote well; and he had a keen interest in lithography. (But one evening, upon arriving home, he mistook nitric acid—used in lithography—for wine and drank it, damaging his vocal cords. His fine baritone voice was ruined forever.) Weber also worked hard at his piano playing and became known as one of the great pianists of his generation.

While Weber was perfecting all these talents, he was also composing constantly. Before 1819 he produced two symphonies (J.50, J.51), the two clarinet concertos (Opp. 73, 74), the two piano concertos (J.98, J.155), the first three piano sonatas (J.138, J.199, J.206), the operas *Silvana* (J.87) and *Abu Hassan* (J.106), and an abundance of songs, many with a folk flavor. And though the songs of Schubert have eclipsed Weber's, Weber should receive much credit for the early development of this fertile Romantic genre. Maurice Ravel, a devoted admirer, was amazed that, by his time (nearly a century later), Weber's songs were never sung. He noted that "no more fruitful source fed German Romanticism. At a time when the Italian style was invading music Weber kept it at bay by discoveries which one could compare to Goethe's, finding in popular music the freshness which gave his *Lieder* a new form: the inner feeling, the drama, became the stuff of music."

From 1804 to 1806, Weber made his living as *Kapellmeister* in Breslau. After various posts in Karlsruhe, Stuttgart, Mannheim, Darmstadt, and Berlin, he became director of the Prague Opera in 1813. An outstanding conductor and director, he soon transformed the Prague Opera into one of the finest houses in Europe. In 1817 he took up heavy chores as director of the prestigious Dresden Opera, where his commanding personality, organizing ability, and meticulous productions forged standards of operatic performance that have been emulated ever since. In 1817, too, he married the singer Caroline Brandt, a union that produced two sons and personal happiness for the couple.

In 1821 Weber composed a seminal work of the quickly emerging Romantic spirit. The opera *Der Freischütz* (J.277) brought German Romantic opera to its maturity. It also caused a furor: Beethoven himself was stunned, exclaiming to a friend, "That usually feeble little man—! I'd never have thought it of him. Now Weber must write more operas, one after the other." Weber was the hero of the day. In *Freischütz* he crystallized Romantic myth and the supernatural, long prevalent in German literature and poetry, and combined them with folk imagery and folk-sounding melody. His next opera, *Euryanthe* (J.291), was produced late in 1823. The opera has wonderful music, but its terrible libretto has so blighted it that today only its overture is heard, with rare revivals of the opera itself.

Weber suffered from tuberculosis, and after *Euryanthe* he was an exhausted man. In 1824, knowing that he would not live long and desperately desiring to provide for his family, he accepted a new commission in spite of his poor health. The commission was to write a new opera for London's Covent Garden. Weber began an immediate and feverish study of English (in 153 lessons) to understand better every nuance of the English libretto. In just over a year, he composed the huge score. In February 1826, upon leaving Dresden for London with the score, he told a friend, "I am going to London to die"; his wife wept, "I heard the lid close upon his coffin." On the way to England, he visited Paris, where the crowds turned out to fete him in such numbers that the young Hector Berlioz, who wanted desperately to meet him, never got a chance. In London the many tiring rehearsals shattered Weber physically, yet he conducted *Oberon*'s premiere on April 12, 1826, as well as the following eleven performances. To Caroline he wrote, "It was the greatest success of my life. The emotion produced by such a triumph is more than I can describe. To God alone belongs the glory." *Oberon*, like *Euryanthe*, is plagued by a confused libretto and is difficult to stage, but the score contains some of Weber's most delectable music.

Within six weeks of the premiere, Weber, the first great master of picturesque Romanticism, was dead in London, not yet forty years old. For eighteen years, his remains stayed in England; not until 1844 were arrangements made for interment at Dresden. Late that year an English vessel bearing Weber's coffin docked at Hamburg. In the harbor, ships of many nations showed their colors as the Funeral March from Beethoven's *Eroica* was played. The coffin was then sent on to Dresden, where large crowds assembled to witness its return. Fittingly, thirty-one-year-old Richard Wagner—who had said, "In my youth, I had learned to love music by way of my admiration of Weber's genius"—was now a conductor at the Dresden Opera. Wagner composed commemorative music for the interment ceremony and eulogized Weber in 1844: "The Briton does you justice, the Frenchman admires you, but only the German can love you. You are his own, a bright day in his life, a drop of his blood, a particle of his heart." He concluded by calling Weber "the most German of all German composers."

No other composer's influence on Romantic music can compare to Weber's. For Schumann, he was a major role model, while Mendelssohn's airiest creations flow from Weber's magic wand. When Liszt first heard Weber's music, he was captivated, quickly adding the *Konzertstück* (concert piece) for piano and orchestra to his performance repertoire. Chopin, who cared little for others' music, captured the ballroom atmosphere of *Aufforderung zum Tanz* (*Invitation to the Dance*, J.260, 1819) in his own waltzes, and once, when listening to Weber's A-flat major piano sonata (J.199, 1816), cried out, "An angel passes through the sky." In France, Berlioz learned much from Weber's use of the orchestra and acknowledged his debt in his own coruscating orchestration of *Invitation to the Dance*. Not least, Wagner's *Der fliegende Holländer*, *Tannhäuser*, and *Lohengrin* might possibly not exist if not for Weber's operas.

Weber brought his Romantic impulses to bear on the explosive transition period from Classical to Romantic. As a harbinger of Romanticism, he was the best equipped of any musician of the period. Astonishingly, he was born sixteen years after Beethoven and eleven years before Schubert, the last two masters of Viennese Classicism, yet he died before either of them. He was born a full quarter century before those other great Romantics, Mendelssohn, Chopin, Schumann, Liszt, Wagner, and Verdi.

Weber's dramatic, picturesque, and poetic ideas were often strangled by pseudo-Classical structure, especially in his instrumental music. But his best work retains a dewy freshness and a youthful and chivalric verve that was absolutely new to the art. His music glows with a sense of wonder and pristine innocence that all but disappeared from music as the century grew more heated, sophisticated, and harmonically ambiguous. It was fortunate indeed that Weber's potent genius appeared at the dawn of a great movement.

Concertino in E-flat Major for Clarinet and Orchestra, J.109, Op. 26 (1811)
Concerto no. 1 in F Minor for Clarinet and Orchestra, J.114, Op. 73 (1811)
Concerto no. 2 in E-flat Major for Clarinet and Orchestra, J.118, Op. 74 (1811)

These are three of the most enduring and endearing works in the clarinet literature. And if Weber was here locked in combat with the demanding sonata form, he also provided a delicious vivacity, operatic flourishes, characteristically piquant turns of phrase, and dazzling variety. All three works are refreshment personified. By Weber's day, the clarinet had evolved to its mature state and had become his favorite wind instrument. His friendship with Heinrich Bärmann, the finest exponent of the clarinet in his day, spurred Weber to write these three works for him. In the slow movements, he exploits the dark register of the instrument, producing an early Romantic melancholia that is peculiar to Weber.

Shifrin, Padua and Venice Orchestra, Golub: Delos 3220
Johnson, English Chamber Orchestra, Tortelier: ASV 585
*Neidich, Orpheus Chamber Orchestra (without conductor): Deutsche Grammophon
    435875-2*

Aufforderung zum Tanz (Invitation to the Dance), J.260 (1819)

Composed six years before the birth of Johann Strauss II, the *Invitation*
launched the dance form of the century into the concert hall, and it remains
one of the world's great concert waltzes, forever young. In this piano work of
poetic virtuosity, Weber combined all the popular elements of Romanticism.
For decades it was one of the most-played piano works. It has become even better known in Berlioz's version for orchestra. Showing his Romantic colors, Weber devised a complicated programmatic scenario for it, but it is really a waltz
encased in a rondo form. *Invitation to the Dance* also had a history in the world
of ballet, retitled *Le Spectre de la rose (The Spirit of the Rose)* for the ballet
which was performed by Diaghilev's Ballets Russes on April 19, 1911. It was
one of Vaslav Nijinsky's greatest roles, as he soared outward and upward
through an open window, to the disbelief of audiences.

FOR PIANO
Ohlsson: Arabesque Z6584-2
Cortot: Biddulph LHW 002

FOR ORCHESTRA
Cleveland Orchestra, C. von Dohnányi: London 430201-2
Chicago Symphony Orchestra, Reiner: RCA 09026-68160-4
Detroit Symphony Orchestra, Paray: Mercury 434336-2

Der Freischütz (The Free-Shooter) (1817–21)

Weber was a master at recreating the mystery and magical spell of the forest,
bathed in an aura of ghostly moonlight and haunted by strange and fearful
creatures. No opera composer before him used the orchestra with such breadth
and dramatic cohesion. The Berlin premiere on June 18, 1821, changed the
face of opera forever. *Der Freischütz's* impact was immediate, not only in Germany but throughout Europe. The opera arrived in Paris late in 1824, and its
most discerning listener was the twenty-one-year-old Berlioz, who wrote in his

memoirs: "In my exclusive worship of Classical opera I had been intolerantly prepared to reject the new style; but to my surprise it delighted me. . . . There was a wild sweetness in the music that I found intoxicating. I must admit I was getting a little tired of the tragic music and her high solemnities. Here, in complete contrast was a wood-nymph of ravishing freshness and charm, a creature of instinct and mercurial fancy, naive, gay, pensive, passionate, melancholy, whose beauty overwhelmed me with a flood of undiscovered sensations."

The opera portrays a battle between the forces of good and evil, in a fine libretto by Friedrich Kind. The term *free-shooter* refers to an early German tradition of huntsmen who receive magic bullets that always hit their mark—except for one, which belongs to the devil. The Wolf's Glen scene remains one of the great descriptions of the sinister and terrifying. In the end, good triumphs over evil.

Seefried, Streich, Holm, Wächter, Bavarian State Radio Symphony Orchestra and Chorus, Jochum: Deutsche Grammophon 439717-2

Ziesack, Sweet, Schmidt, Hölle, German Symphony Orchestra and Berlin Radio Chorus, Janowski: RCA Red Seal 09026-62538-2

Konzertstück in F Minor for Piano and Orchestra, J.282, Op. 79 (1821)

John Warrack, in his biography of Weber, states the unique importance of this score: "The *Konzertstück* is a keystone work of romantic piano writing, crowning the bridge that leads from Dussek, Kalkbrenner, Prince Louis Ferdinand and their contemporaries into the mid-nineteenth century and Mendelssohn, Schumann, Chopin, and Liszt, while its influence was consciously acknowledged as late as 1929 by one of Weber's greatest modern admirers, Stravinsky, in his Capriccio." The *Konzertstück* was the first successful merging of individual sections into a one-movement forum and became a model for later Romantic concertos, most notably Liszt's two concertos. The score is wonderfully condensed, running less than eighteen minutes. The march movement leaves the piano out entirely, until a mighty *glissando* passage leads to a climactic ending. The finale is a perpetual motion, which Liszt at one concert played so fast that he could not keep the tempo. He solved the problem by fainting. As was Weber's pleasure, he wrote out an elaborate program that he appended to the score, beginning, "The lady sits in her tower. She gazes sadly into the distance. Her knight has been for years in the Holy Land: Shall she ever see him again . . ."

Casadesus, Turin RAI Symphony Orchestra, Kondrashin: Fonit Cetra FCT ARCD 2051
Demidenko, Scottish Chamber Orchestra, Mackerras: Hyperion CDA 66729

Der Freischütz Overture (1817–21)
Euryanthe Overture (1822–23)
Oberon Overture (1825–26)

These three of the most beloved opera overtures, all staples of concert life, are brilliant resumés of their respective operas. *Freischütz* envelops the ear with its mysterious forest atmosphere; the audience at the opera's premiere demanded an encore. Although *Euryanthe* is not performed today, it influenced not only Wagner but also Schumann in his only opera, *Genoveva* (which is shackled to a poor libretto). In 1847 Schumann wrote of *Euryanthe*, "This music is as yet far too little known and recognized. It is heart's blood, the noblest he had." In *Oberon* we are again made aware of the potential of the orchestra as a great color machine, first pioneered by Weber. The American critic Edward Downes writes, "We sense how he savored the soft glow of the French horn, the velvet caress of the clarinet, the freshness of violin sound, and dozens of subtle combinations."

Philharmonia Orchestra, Järvi: Chandos CHAN 8766
Paris Opera Orchestra, Scherchen: Adès ADE 202692
NBC Symphony Orchestra, Toscanini: RCA 09026-60292-2 (The Toscanini Collection, vol. 16)

OTHER PRINCIPAL WORKS

CHAMBER MUSIC

Quintet in B-flat Major for Clarinet and Strings, J.182, Op. 34 (1815)
Grand Duo Concertant in E-flat Major for Clarinet and Piano, J.204, Op. 48 (1815–18)
Trio in G Minor for Flute, Cello, and Piano, J.259, Op. 63 (1819)*

OPERAS

Abu Hassan (1810–11)
Euryanthe (1822–23)*
Oberon (1825–26)*

ORCHESTRAL MUSIC

Symphony no. 1 in C Major, J.50 (1807)

Symphony no. 2 in C Major, J.51 (1807)

PIANO MUSIC

Momento capriccioso in B-flat Major, J.56, Op. 12 (1808)*

Grand polonaise in E-flat Major, J.59, Op. 21 (1808)

Sonata no. 1 in C Major, J.138, Op. 24 (1812)*

Sonata no. 2 in A-flat Major, J.199, Op. 39 (1816)*

Sonata no. 3 in D Minor, J.206, Op. 49 (1816)

Rondo brillante in E-flat Major, J.252, Op. 62 (1819)*

Sonata no. 4 in E Minor, J.287, Op. 70 (1819–22)*

SOLO INSTRUMENT AND ORCHESTRA MUSIC

Concerto no. 1 in C Major for Piano and Orchestra, J.98 (1810)

Concerto no. 2 in E-flat Major for Piano and Orchestra, J.155 (1812)*

Concerto in F Major for Bassoon and Orchestra, J.127, Op. 75 (1811; rev. 1822)

Concertino in E Minor for Horn and Orchestra, J.188, Op. 45 (1806; rev. 1815)

VOICE WITH PIANO MUSIC

Nearly a hundred works*

GIOACHINO ROSSINI

b. Pesaro, Italy, February 29, 1792

d. Passy, France, November 13, 1868

I take Beethoven twice a week, Haydn four times, Mozart every day. . . . Beethoven is a colossus who often gives a mighty thump in the ribs, but Mozart is always adorable.

Pesaro is a delightful town on the Adriatic in the Marches region of central Italy, which was formerly ruled by the Vatican. The house where Rossini was born remains its chief tourist attraction today. Rossini was an only child of musical parents, Giuseppe and Anna. His father, an inspector of slaughterhouses, moonlighted as the town trumpeter, while his mother sang at various theaters. Unfortunately, Giuseppe supported Napoleon's conquering army and was carted off to prison in 1800. Gioachino was apprenticed to a butcher and a blacksmith, but music was all that interested him. He had a clear soprano voice and helped support the family by singing in churches and theaters. His parents, hoping to preserve his voice, decided to make him a castrato, but they relented at the last minute. Later he would write: "Although still a boy, I was already a great admirer of the fair sex." They decided instead to send Gioachino to study in Bologna, at that city's renowned Liceo Musicale. By eighteen, Rossini had written his first opera, and for the next nineteen years he continued to compose operas at an astonishing rate, producing thirty-eight more.

From the beginning of his career, he was lionized. Lord Byron wrote from Italy in 1816, "The people follow him about, cut off his hair . . . he was shouted and sonnetted and feasted, and immortalized. . . . Think of a people frantic for a fiddler, or at least an inspirer of fiddlers." His airs were whistled and hummed everywhere, and theaters vied to produce his new works. Certainly the first-night audience for *Guillaume Tell* (*William Tell*) at the Paris Opera on August 3, 1829, had no inkling that, at age thirty-seven, Rossini had written his last opera.

Why did he stop? The composer, a lover of mystification, never fully explained. He was wealthy, and perhaps he was simply tired of dealing with difficult theatrical managers and temperamental singers. Certainly he worried obsessively about the decline of singing: "I confess that I have little hope of seeing this divine art emerge from the corruption in which it lies." But it is hard to believe that good or bad singing could keep him from writing operas.

Rossini's first wife, the Spanish mezzo-soprano Isabella Colbran, was one of his finest interpreters. Even after his retirement, he taught talented singers; the best was Marietta Alboni, who learned all of his contralto roles. Many singers in Rossini's day lacked respect for the composer's intentions, adding profuse and often perverse ornamentation that destroyed the musical meaning. Rossini had long waged war on such singers and continued to do so after his retirement. After accompanying the soprano Adelina Patti in one of his arias, the always-witty composer complimented her on her vocal technique but asked, "Could you tell me who composed that aria?"

This is not to say that Rossini was opposed to all ornamentation—indeed, the ornamentation that he himself wrote is usually too difficult for today's singers to navigate. Francis Toye, in his biography of the composer, goes so far as to say, "A strong case, indeed, could be made for eliminating most of the ornamentation in a modern performance of a Rossini opera, for modern singers are mere novices compared with the singers of his day." A singer who is poorly equipped for Rossini's vocal demands offers a worse musical experience than a mediocre pianist performing a Liszt étude on a battered upright.

But singing quality notwithstanding, even after Rossini's retirement his operas were by far the most frequently performed everywhere. He remained highly visible, the lion of Paris, and for years to come, not to be invited to his Saturday evenings where *le tout Paris* mingled was not to have arrived socially. At these events, music and champagne flowed in abundance while guests were treated to myriad delicacies, including Tournedos Rossini. The Italian master dispensed bons mots with dazzling aplomb, telling his guests, "I know of no more admirable occupation than eating, that is, really eating! Appetite is for the stomach what love is for the heart." Mendelssohn encountered him on a visit to Paris: "Rossini, big, fat, in the sunniest frame of mind. I really know few men who can be so amusing and witty as he . . . intellect, animation, and wit, sparkle in all his features and in every word."

When a young composer asked his advice about when to compose an overture, Rossini, gleefully answering from his own experience, told him,

Wait until the evening before opening night. Nothing primes inspiration more than necessity, whether it be the presence of a copyist waiting for your work or the prodding of an impresario tearing his hair out. In my time, all the impresarios in Italy were bald at thirty. . . . I composed the overture to *Otello* in a little room in the Barbaja Palace where the baldest and fiercest of directors had forcibly locked me up with a lone plate of spaghetti and the threat that I would not be allowed to leave the room alive until I had written the last note.

Rossini's marriage had long been in trouble, and in 1832 he met Olympe Pélissier, a beautiful former courtesan who became his devoted mistress. They married in 1846, after his wife died. To the casual observer, Rossini must have seemed blithely carefree, but in reality he was hopelessly neurotic, plagued by nervous ailments and superstitions of all sorts, including the fact that he was born on February 29. When taking his first train ride in 1836, he fainted from fear. The once lithe and handsome composer, even with his refined palate, became larger in girth with each passing year.

Although his opera-composing days were over, Rossini by no means relinquished his art altogether. In 1841 he wrote his *Stabat Mater* and in 1863 the *Petite messe solennelle*, a mass that, despite its name, was nearly an hour long. He had asked the Abbé Liszt, by now an old friend, who was living at the Vatican, to beseech Pope Pius IX to permit "women to sing in church together with men. This would give new life to sacred music, which is in total decline. I am certain that if his Holiness, who so loves music and to whom my name is not unknown, were to issue such a bull, he would win new glory in paradise." Pius paid no heed to his request.

Rossini also wrote nearly 150 piano pieces, many of which he tried out himself at his weekly soirées. Published under the generic title *Péchés de vieillesse (Sins of Old Age)*, they have tongue-in-cheek names like "Italian Innocence," "Harmless Prelude," "French Candor," and "Oh! the Green Peas." *Sins of Old Age* is dedicated "to the pianists of the fourth class, to which I have the honor to belong." When Rossini lay on his deathbed at Passy, the pontiff sent a special nuncio to administer the last rites. The funeral took place at Paris's Trinity Church; the Madeleine was too small for the vast throngs wanting to pay their final respects to the Swan of Pesaro. It was a glorious funeral, and some of the great singers of the age participated in the *Stabat Mater*, while the prayer from *Moïse* (1827) was sung by the chorus of the Paris Conservatory. All of Paris listened to the strains of Beethoven's Funeral March as the cortège followed in procession to Père Lachaise Cemetery. In 1887, after repeated requests from the Italian government, Rossini's remains were moved to Florence's celebrated Santa Croce Church, where they rest with those of no lesser personages than Galileo, Machiavelli, and Michelangelo.

To the writer Franz Werfel, Rossini was "the only creator of truly comic music." Rossini's music is crystal clear: his constructions are tight; the harmony is clever and diatonic; above all, the melodies are easy to remember. His type of melody—simple, rather square, and easily developed in sequence—was the secret of his success. Rossini was the first tunesmith; one might even say that he was the inventor of the pop song. He caught the ear of a growing middle-class public with music that appealed as never before to a mass audience. If his popularity has dwindled considerably, it is because he taught his successors so well how to play on that audience's heartstrings. In 1830 Rossini was far and away the most famous composer in the world. Stendhal, his first biographer, writing as early as 1823, began his biography: "Napoleon is dead; but a new conqueror has already shown himself to the world; and from Moscow to Naples, from London to Vienna, from Paris to Calcutta, his name is constantly on every tongue. The fame of this hero knows no bounds save those of civilization itself." Stendhal would have been astounded to know that today so little of his idol's work is heard.

Rossini's serious operas show an instinctive feeling for drama and action. *Tancredi* (1813), with its ardent aria "Di tanti palpiti," is seldom staged; the same goes for *Semiramide* (1823), which once brought in crowds. *Otello* (1816) is superb melodrama with a silly libretto, but it has been superseded by Verdi's music-drama *Otello*. Lord Byron wrote to a friend in 1818: "They have been crucifying *Othello* into an opera: the music is good but lugubrious; but as for the words, all the real scenes with Iago cut out, and the greatest nonsense inserted; the handkerchief twined into a billet-doux, and the first singer would not black his face, for some exquisite reason." Of the comic operas, *L'Italiana in Algeri* (1813), *Il Turco in Italia* (1814), *La Gazza ladra* (1817), and *La Cenerentola* (1817) all are scintillating if a good cast can be assembled.

Near the end of his career, Rossini was asked what he thought he would be best remembered for. He replied, "My Immortality is dependent on the Third Act of *Tell*, the Second Act of *Otello* and the *Barber*—from one end to the other." He was surely not wrong about *Il Barbiere di Siviglia* (*The Barber of Seville*, 1816). His comic spirit was unique in opera: for Rossini, life is carefree, and the soul is unburdened. No wonder the gloomy philosopher Schopenhauer received daily pleasure by playing Rossini arias on his flute.

Il Barbiere di Siviglia (The Barber of Seville, 1816)

The *Barber*, based on a comedy by Beaumarchais, was a flop on its opening night, February 20, 1816, in Rome. Rossini, sitting in the front row, heard almost nonstop hisses and shouts of disapproval. Perhaps the audience objected to his sheer audacity, for he had based his opera on the same story as Giovanni Paisiello's praiseworthy *Barber*, the most popular comic opera of the day. But despite this rocky beginning, Rossini's *Barber* soon eclipsed Paisiello's piece forever. Rossini, with his usual lightning speed, composed *Barber* in two weeks, using a revised overture from an earlier opera, *Elisabetta, regina d'inghilterra* (1815). The overture and many of the arias, such as the glittering coloratura "Una voce poco fa," Figaro's "Largo al factotum," and "Se il mio nome," are irresistible. In 1822 Rossini met Beethoven, who cried, "Ah, Rossini, you are the composer of the *Il Barbiere di Siviglia*? I congratulate you; it is an excellent *opera buffa*; I read it with pleasure, and it delights me. It will be played so long as Italian opera exists."

Callas, Alva, Gobbi, *Philharmonia Orchestra and Chorus, Galliera: EMI Classics CDCB 47634*

de los Angeles, Alva, Wallace, Cava, *Royal Philharmonic Orchestra and Glyndebourne Festival Chorus, Gui: EMI Classics CDMB 64162*

Battle, Domingo, Lopardo, Gallo, Raimondi, *Chamber Orchestra of Europe, Abbado, Deutsche Grammophon 435763-2*

Overtures (1812–29)

The overture to *Guillaume Tell* (*William Tell*, 1829) is Rossini's finest dramatic overture and perhaps the most famous of all opera overtures. The full *William Tell*, the grandest of his operatic achievements, is tarnished by a horrid libretto and lasts nearly six hours in its original form. Its overture and several others, including those of *La Scala di seta* (1812), *Il Turco in Italia* (1814), *La Gazza ladra* (1817), *Semiramide* (1823), and *Le Siège de Corinthe* (1826), have become concert hall staples.

Montreal Symphony Orchestra, Dutoit: *London 433074-2*
Cincinnati Symphony Orchestra, Schippers: *Vox Box CDX 5141*
Chicago Symphony Orchestra, Reiner: *RCA 60387-4-RG*

OTHER PRINCIPAL WORKS

OPERAS
La Scala di seta (1812)
Tancredi (1813)*

L'Italiana in Algeri (1813)*
Il Turco in Italia (1814)*
Otello (1816)*
La Cenerentola (1817)*
Mosè in Egitto (1818)*
La Donna del lago (1819)*
Semiramide (1823)*
Le Comte Ory (1828)*
Guillaume Tell (1829)*

RELIGIOUS WORKS
Stabat Mater (1832; rev. 1841)*
Petite messe solennelle (1863)*

STRING QUARTETS
Six sonatas for string quartet (c.1804)

VOICE AND PIANO MUSIC
Péchés de vieillesse (*Sins of Old Age*) (1857–68)*

FRANZ SCHUBERT

b. Vienna, January 31, 1797

d. Vienna, November 19, 1828

The latest news in Vienna is that Beethoven is giving a concert, at which his new Symphony, three selections from the new Mass, and a new Overture will be performed. —I too should like to give a similar concert next year, God willing.

Schubert lived his tragically short life exclusively in Vienna. His father, Franz Theodor, was an unassuming schoolmaster who loved music and played the violin passably. His mother, Elisabet, died in 1812. Of her thirteen pregnancies, five children survived, four boys and a girl.

Franz spent his earliest years in pleasant surroundings, with an amiable and loving home life. At five his father taught him to play the violin, and a devoted brother showed him the rudiments of piano playing. To the child's delight, the family played chamber music nightly. Michael Holzer, a respected musician, began instructing the boy when he was about ten. Holzer declared, "If I wished to teach him anything new, he already knew it. So in fact I really gave him no true instruction. I merely talked to him, and watched his musical progress with silent astonishment."

At eleven, because of his fine soprano voice, Schubert was chosen to be a chorister at the renowned Court Chapel and Royal Seminary. There he came under the wing of Mozart's rival Salieri, the Imperial Court music director, who had given composition lessons to Beethoven and was later to teach the prodigy Franz Liszt as well. At the seminary, Schubert had ample opportunity to conduct, play piano, and compose. But life had few comforts: always hungry, he wrote to a brother, "You know from experience that we all like to eat a roll or some apples sometimes, the more so if after a middling lunch one may not look for a miserable evening meal for eight and a half hours. . . . How if you were to let me have a few *kreuzer* a month? You would not so much as know it, while I in my cell would think myself lucky and be content."

In 1813 Schubert's voice broke, forcing the painfully shy boy to leave his sanctuary. Composing had already become his life, but his father now expected him to become an assistant teacher at his suburban schoolhouse. Schubert dreaded the thought, but unable to disappoint his father, he entered a teacher's training school. (His poor eyesight and short stature—he stood only four feet eleven—exempted him from the military service, the lot of most boys his age.) In September 1814 the seventeen-year-old musician qualified as a schoolmaster. From the first moment, the work was sheer drudgery. Only a month after his teaching duties started, his mass was performed at a small church, with Schubert conducting and Salieri himself in attendance.

The performance began a tremendous flood of compositions. Seized by inspiration while reading Goethe's *Faust*, he composed the first of his immortal songs, "Gretchen am Spinnrade" (D.118, 1814). The following year saw the composition of no fewer than 144 songs, including the celebrated "Erlkönig" (D.328, 1815) to Goethe's ballade. In the remaining thirteen years left to him, he wrote six hundred songs to the work of ninety-one poets.

At the seminary, Schubert had become close to Josef von Spaun, a cultivated and sensitive nobleman eight years his senior. Spaun was convinced that Schubert was blessed with genius. Through Spaun, the young composer met an appreciative circle of musicians, painters, and poets who were living a bohemian life in Vienna.

With the spread of dance bands and café nightlife, artists gravitated to the imperial city, where mostly they worked in near poverty and obscurity. Aristocratic patronage was dying out, leaving artists to struggle for their survival; they were beginning to feel alienated from the general society. The Romantic doctrine "art for art's sake" was the slogan of the young. Consecrating one's life to the altar of art had become a worthy ideal.

Much to his father's chagrin, Schubert quit teaching after four years. Yet the abnormally self-conscious composer was not equipped to earn a livelihood as a performer, and selling his compositions was unlikely. This most noncommercial of the great masters was, however, fortunate enough to have a network of friends who realized that he was a genius.

They were a convivial group, meeting regularly at their various homes for what they called Schubertiades. These evenings consisted of chamber music performances, poetry readings, charades, and dancing (with Schubert improvising at the piano). Schubert's newest songs were always featured, often sung by soprano Anna Milder and especially by baritone Johann Michael Vogl, stars of the court opera who loved Schubert and his music. After considerable drinking and merrymaking, Schubert usually stumbled home quite drunk, keeping his spectacles on as he slept so as to begin composing the moment he awoke.

Sometime in 1823 disaster struck: Schubert contracted syphilis. He was acutely embarrassed by the disease and never mentioned it by name. At times his skin was patchy red, and his hair fell out. For some periods the disease went into remission, but he suffered terrible side effects from the medications he took and probably had mercury poisoning. Above all, he was terrified of future insanity. "I feel myself to be the most unhappy creature in the world," he wrote. "Imagine a man whose health will never be good again, and in sheer despair makes things worse and worse, instead of better; imagine a man, whose most brilliant hopes have perished, to whom the felicity of love and friendship have nothing to offer but pain."

Very little is known of Schubert's inner world. He never married, seldom wrote letters, was painfully shy, and was upset enough about his diminutive height and chubby stature that he never danced at the Schubertiades. The composer Anselm Hüttenbrenner wrote, "If I came to see him in the morning, he would play to me what he had already composed. If I praised any song especially, he would say 'yes, that was a good poem; and when one has something good the music comes easily.' " Another close friend observed a distinct private existence: "Anyone who knew Schubert knows he was of two natures foreign to each other and how powerfully the craving for pleasure dragged his soul down to the slough of moral degradation." On good days he could be charming, especially if his work was going well; and there were many good times, especially summers in the countryside, where the scenery inspired him.

Early in 1827 Schubert's idol Beethoven lay on his deathbed. The master had been given nearly sixty of Schubert's songs to read. Struck by the "divine spark," he asked to see the young composer's operas and piano works. One week before Beethoven's death, Schubert was brought to his bedside. For a brief moment, two of the greatest musical geniuses met. At Beethoven's funeral procession, Schubert was one of the thirty-six torch-bearers.

But Schubert himself now had only twenty months to live. They were months of awesome productivity. Only his death stopped the heavenly flow of music. One masterwork after another poured from him as from a magic fountain. In September 1828, during a spell of fever, headaches, and dizziness, he composed for the piano eight impromptus in two sets (D.899, D.935; Opp. 90, 142), three *Klavierstücke* (D.946), Six *Moments musicaux* (D.780, Op. 94), and three gigantic piano sonatas (D.958, D.959, D.960)—in bed. During his final months, he completed eleven works for piano duet, including the F minor fantasy (D.940, Op. 103), perhaps the greatest work for piano four-hands ever composed. For the violin, he wrote the C major fantasy (D.939, Op. 159), as well as the two wondrous piano trios (D.898, D.929; Opp. 99, 100), several choral works, and the E-flat major mass (D.950). For voice, the *Schwanengesang* (D.957) was completed in the summer of 1828, and the great song cycle *Winterreise* (D.911, Op. 89) in 1827. For orchestra, he wrote the mighty C major symphony (D.944), and the sublime C major string quintet (D.956, Op. 163) was completed while he was in desperate pain, days before his death.

Symptoms of the syphilis had flared up badly in September, and the first signs of typhoid fever appeared unexpectedly on October 31. But neither Schubert nor his family and friends probably had any suspicion that nineteen days later he would die. Schubert, who had long been concerned with his sketchy knowledge of counterpoint, arranged for lessons to begin on November 4 with Simon Sechter, a well-known Viennese theorist. These lessons never took place. On November 12, he wrote to a friend, "I am ill. I have eaten nothing for eleven days and drunk nothing, and I totter feebly and shakily from my chair to the bed and back again. If I try to eat I bring it up again at once." Lapsing into delirium, he said his last words to his brother Ferdinand: "Here! This is my end!" While delirious he babbled that Beethoven was not lying close to him. Hearing this, his brother Ferdinand made certain that Schubert was buried almost next to the master he most loved. At his death, Schubert's estate was estimated at sixty-three gulden. The doctor's bill and funeral cost more than a thousand.

The epitaph on Schubert's tombstone, by his friend the poet Franz Grillparzer, reads, "The art of music here entombed a rich possession, but even far fairer hopes. Franz Schubert lies here." At thirty-one, Schubert died younger than any of the great masters. Yet Grillparzer and his contemporaries did not know that the "far fairer hopes" had been more than fulfilled. Throughout Vienna, Schubert's manuscripts lay scattered in the homes of friends and family. In the wake of his death, as his work gradually came to light, the world of music was stupefied by its sheer volume. First performances of his music took place for literally the rest of the nineteenth century. Schubert had supposedly said, "I am in the world only for the purpose of composing!" Schubert biographer M.J.E. Brown wrote: "Schubert's place in the history of music is equivocal: he stands between the worlds of classical and romantic music. He is, however, chiefly to be considered as the last of the classical composers. His music, subjectively emotional in the romantic manner, poetically conceived, and revolutionary in language, is nevertheless cast in the formal molds of the classical school—with the result that in the twentieth century, it was increasingly apparent that Schubert more truly belongs to the age of Haydn, Beethoven, and Mozart than to that of Schumann, Chopin, and Wagner."

Quintet in A Major for Piano and Strings (*Trout*) D.667, Op. 114 (1819)

The *Trout* Quintet (or *Die Forelle*) is Schubert's earliest chamber masterpiece. Nothing but joy exists in its five movements, which burst with vitality. The scoring is unusual; instead of two violins, it uses piano, violin, viola, cello, and double bass. The work is also unusual in that it is cast in five movements. In the third and fourth movements, one hears the energy of peasants dancing. The fourth movement makes use of the famous song "Die Forelle" (The Trout) and five resourceful variations. The piece was composed at a happy time for Schubert, who was on a walking tour in upper Austria with the baritone Johann Michael Vogl.

Curzon, Vienna Octet Members: London 417459-2
Schnabel, Pro Arte String Quartet: EMI Classics CDH 63031
Eschenbach, Koeckert String Quartet: Deutsche Grammophon 427215-2

Symphony no. 8 in B Minor (*Unfinished*), D.759 (1822)

Schubert wrote the *Unfinished* when he was twenty-five, but the world was deprived of hearing it until 1865. Schubert had given the manuscript to his friend Anselm Hüttenbrenner, who released his treasure only when his brother convinced the Viennese conductor Johann Herbeck to conduct Anselm's music. The Eighth Symphony thus received its premiere thirty-seven years after Schubert's death. The two completed movements never fail to weave a magical spell, and are amazingly prophetic of later symphonies of the Romantic era. Why did Schubert leave the work unfinished? Sketches exist of a third movement (though nothing of a finale), and I believe that he simply knew he could not yet write two more movements of equal quality. He simply left it alone, probably realizing that the two completed movements created a perfect emotional unity.

Vienna Philharmonic Orchestra, Walter: Music & Arts MUA 705-2
Boston Symphony Orchestra, Jochum: Deutsche Grammophon 427195-2

Fantasy in C Major for Piano (*The Wanderer*), D.760 (1822)

Completed in November 1822, this fantasy is a formidable piece of musical architecture. All four movements are based on the rhythm of Schubert's song

"Der Wanderer." Technically it is Schubert's most difficult work for the piano. After attempting to play it, the composer is said to have shouted to a friend that perhaps the devil could play it, but he couldn't. The second movement, with its shifting light, is a set of variations on the "Wanderer" theme itself ("O Land where art thou that I call my own"). Schubert never returned to his experiment in thematic transformation, but it bore fruit in the music of Liszt, who so admired the fantasy that he arranged it for piano and orchestra.

Richter: EMI-CDC 747967-2
Pollini: Deutsche Grammophon 447451-2
Kissin: Deutsche Grammophon 445562-2

Rosamunde Overture, Entr'acte no. 3, and Ballet Music no. 2, D.797
(1823)

In eighteen days, Schubert wrote incidental music for a drama, *Rosamunde, Princess of Cyprus.* The play closed after two performances, and the world heard nothing more of *Rosamunde* until 1867, when the English critic George Grove, later the creator of *Grove's Dictionary of Music,* and the composer Arthur Sullivan, later of operetta fame, journeyed to Vienna hoping to discover more unknown Schubert. Although the complete incidental music has been recorded, performances usually include the Overture, Entr'acte no. 3, and Ballet Music no. 2. The Overture has an echo of Rossini, who was all the rage in Vienna at the time. Entr'acte no. 3 is a Rondo, structured ABACA. Schubert also used its main theme, with its gentle lilt, in his B-flat major impromptu and his A minor string quartet. Ballet Music no. 2 is a marchlike piece, invigorating in its freshness.

Berlin Philharmonic Orchestra, Furtwängler: Koch Legacy 370592
Royal Concertgebouw, Szell: Philips 426071-2
Chicago Symphony Orchestra, Levine: Deutsche Grammophon 415137-2

Die schöne Müllerin (song cycle), D.795, Op. 25 (1823)
Winterreise (song cycle), D.911, Op. 89 (1827)

These are two very different song cycles. The twenty songs in *Die schöne Müllerin (The Fair Millmaid)* and the twenty-four in *Winterreise (Winter Journey)* are set to poems by Wilhelm Müller, condemned by history as a fourth-rate poet whom Schubert has ennobled. The songs of the *Müllerin* cycle pass from joy to suicide and possess an elusive charm, their rustic nature warmed by Schubert's sensitivity. If you are among those who consider the harrowing and desolate *Winterreise* to be the greatest of all song cycles, you have plenty of company. Here we find Schubert sodden in despair through the isolation of winter and the burden of a breaking heart. The music critic Harold Schonberg writes: "sad, plaintive, haunting, mounting in melancholy and even desperation to the shattering last song, 'Der Leiermann.' This song is about an organ grinder playing his machine in the winter. Nobody gives him any money, nobody listens to his music, nobody cares. Snarling dogs chase him, but he continues to smile and show no disappointment." Schubert doubtless felt a deep empathy with the organ grinder.

Die schöne Müllerin
Schreier, Schiff: London 430414-2
Fischer-Dieskau, Moore: EMI Classics CDC 56240

Winterreise
Hotter, Moore: EMI Classics CDH 61002
Vickers, Schaaf: VAI Audio VAIA 1007-2
Fischer-Dieskau, Perahia: Sony Classical SK 48237

Lieder (various dates)

Schubert composed his songs almost effortlessly. Poetry automatically affected him with a compulsion to set it to music. In this realm, the last of the Viennese Classicists became Romanticism's first child. At his finest, Schubert had the ability to heighten the meaning of a poem as well as to charge the piano with an unprecedented dramatic responsibility. He was the first great song composer, making possible not only the song recital but domestic music making at its most intimate. Among Schubert's dozens of masterpieces, one may mention "Der Doppelgänger," "Prometheus," "Du bist die Ruh," "Ganymed," "Im Frühling," "Erlkönig," "Gretchen am Spinnrade," "Nacht und Träume," "Auf dem Wasser zu singen," "An Sylvia," "Heidenröslein," "Die Forelle," "Die Stadt," "Am Meer," and "Standchen." Of the poets he set, Johann Wolfgang von Goethe, Friedrich von Schlegel, Johann Mayrhofer, Friedrich Schiller, Wilhelm Müller, Walter Scott, Ludwig Rellstab, Heinrich Heine, Friedrich Klopstock, Friedrich von Matthisson, and Friedrich Rückert were his favorites.

The Hyperion label (33001 to 33029) has the "complete" Schubert songs in twelve volumes, with many celebrated singers and Graham Johnson at the piano. Take a year off, read the poems, and wonder how Schubert achieved it all. His creative life lasted less than fifteen years. Nadia Boulanger exclaimed, "Where did this power come from? . . . Schubert didn't have time. . . . That is why you must say to children every day [in Valéry's words], 'It depends on you, o passer-by, whether I am tomb or treasury.' "

Miscellaneous Collections

Janowitz, Spencer: Nuova Era 6860
Ameling, Baldwin: Philips 420870-2
Battle, Levine: Deutsche Grammophon 419237-2
Souzay, Baldwin: Philips 438511-2
Fischer-Dieskau, Richter: Orfeo C334931
Schwarzkopf, Fischer: Angel CDH 64026

Quartet no. 13 in A Minor for Strings (*Rosamunde*), D.804 (1824)
Quartet no. 14 in D Minor for Strings (*Death and the Maiden*), D.810 (1824)

Schubert had a major syphilitic episode in 1824, and it was then that he courageously but sorrowfully embarked on these two string quartets. His mood, he said, matched that in Gretchen's song: "My peace is gone, my heart is sore, I find it never and never more." To a friend he added, "This is what I should be singing every day, for every night when I go to sleep, I wish never to wake again." The Andante of Quartet no. 13 uses the *Rosamunde* theme.

Quartet no. 14, subtitled *Death and the Maiden*, is permeated with despair. For the second movement, Schubert used the second half of the theme from his song "Death and the Maiden." This quartet and No. 15 in G major (1826) are among the loftiest in the literature and are also among the longest classical string quartets. Unlike the *Lied*, which Schubert mastered easily, the sonata form was a constant agony for him, and he struggled to impose his personal style on it. These string quartets represent Schubert's conquest of a medium that he had begun to wrestle with in 1811 at age fourteen, only two years after Haydn's death.

String Quartet no. 13

Tokyo String Quartet: RCA 7750-2-RC
Budapest String Quartet: Sony Masterwork MPK 45696

String Quartet no. 14
Juilliard String Quartet: Odyssey MBK 42602
Amadeus Quartet: Deutsche Grammophon 427215-2

Trio no. 1 in B-flat Major for Piano, Violin, and Cello, D.898, Op. 99 (1827)
Trio no. 2 in E-flat Major for Piano, Violin, and Cello, D.929, Op. 100 (1827)

Trio no. 1 is more popular, but both are perfect examples of balance between the piano, the violin, and the cello. Of Trio no. 1, English critic William Mann wrote: "It is one of the miracles of the world that Schubert was able to compose this trio at the time he was conceiving the song cycle *Die Winterreise*. There is no trace of melancholy, let alone the black despair that is ascribed to Schubert at this period. . . . It is a blissfully happy work, rich in cheerful melody . . . full of characteristic modulations and key switches." Trio no. 2 is darker, less melodious, and less lovable. Robert Schumann wrote that it is "more active, masculine, and dramatic."

Piano Trio no. 1
Rubinstein, Heifetz, Feuerman: RCA 09026-60926-2
Beaux Arts Trio: Philips 422836-2
Cortot, Thaibaud, Casals: EMI Classics 64057-2

Piano Trio no. 2
Istomin, Stern, Rose: Sony Classical SM2K 64516
Serkin, Busch, Busch: Pearl PEA 9141

Symphony no. 9 in C Major (*The Great*), D.944 (1828)

It was Robert Schumann who, while paying a visit to Schubert's brother Ferdinand on a trip to Vienna in 1838, discovered the existence of the Ninth Symphony. At a glance, Schumann knew that he had struck gold, and he sent it to Felix Mendelssohn, who gave the premiere on March 21, 1839, conducting the Gewandhaus Orchestra of Leipzig. Schubert's last symphony, composed in 1828, is his greatest orchestral score. Perfect in structure, it is the final magnificent utterance of the Viennese Classical symphony, begun by Haydn. From its first breath in the horns, the Symphony no. 9 maintains a relentless sense of motion, fused with Schubert's anguished and bittersweet song.

Berlin Philharmonic Orchestra, Furtwängler: Arkadia 525
Philharmonia Orchestra, Klemperer: EMI Classics CDM 63854
Cleveland Orchestra, Szell: Sony Classical SBK 48268

Quintet in C Major for Strings, D.956, Op. 163 (1828)

The C major quintet, scored for two violins, viola, and two cellos, saw publication only in 1853. In his memoirs, Arthur Rubinstein wrote of the second movement, "This music has always sounded to me like a serene and resigned entrance to death. I have always wished to hear this movement, even on a record, in my own last hour." The String Quintet was Schubert's own requiem. In its depth of expression, he shudders at the proximity of death. Its somber pathos is unrelieved even by the Scherzo; only the finale gives a feeling of hope, in its dancelike themes.

Emerson String Quartet, Rostropovich: Deutsche Grammophon 431792-2
Heifetz, Baker, Primrose, Piatigorsky, Rejto: RCA 7964-2-RG
Juilliard String Quartet, Greenhouse: CBS MK 42383
Cleveland String Quartet, Ma: Sony Classical 39134

Four Impromptus for Piano, D.899 (1827)
Four Impromptus for Piano, D.935 (1827)

The impromptus are the most popular of Schubert's piano music. No. 1 of the first set is the longest, and is severe. No. 2 in E-flat major, with its fleet passagework, makes its way to turbulent heights. No. 3 is a magical Schubert song without words, and No. 4 in A-flat major is unforgettable, with its passionately lyric trio rising to even greater heights. The second set is more complex in tone. The second theme of No. 1 in F minor is a dialogue in the moonlight. No. 2 in A-flat major is contemplative. No. 3 in B-flat major, with its Rosamunde theme, is a set of lighthearted and fetching variations, and No. 4 in F minor is joyous and Gypsy-like in tone.

Schiff: London 425638-2
Fischer: Enterprise ENT SO 530025
Barenboim: Erato 91700-2
Lupu: London 460975

Sonata in C Minor for Piano, D.958 (1828)
Sonata in A Major for Piano, D.959 (1828)
Sonata in B-flat Major for Piano, D.960 (1828)

The Schubert piano sonatas are a golden field to explore. There are the early A major sonata (D.664, 1819) and the superb "unfinished" C major sonata (D.840, 1825). The Sonata in G Major (D.894, Op. 78, 1826) is a work of the most lovable lyricism, and the giant D major (D.850, Op. 53, 1825) is filled with sunlight, yodeling, and the songs and dances of the people. These final three piano sonatas were composed within weeks of Schubert's death and were published posthumously, in 1839. Like the String Quintet and the Ninth Symphony, the last sonatas exhibit a new grandeur and intellectual capacity in their large-scale design. Schubert had grown from being a prodigal, spontaneous fountain of melody to a profound and fully mature composer whose contribution to sonata form was entirely his own, not bound by the sonata-idea as defined by Beethoven. The C minor sonata is somber, stark, and wintry in mood. The A major sonata could not be more different. Perhaps the most amazing of the four movements is the second, an Andantino that rises from sadness to cataclysmic fury. The B-flat major sonata takes forty-five minutes to complete its journey and is of ravishing and visionary beauty. That Schubert was dying painfully at the moment he created these sonatas is almost baffling.

Sonata in C Minor
Lupu: London 417785-2
Shure: Audiofon CD 72010

Sonata in A Major
Schnabel: EMI Classics CDHB 64259
Lupu: London 425033-2

Sonata in B-flat Major
Fischer: Hungaroton HCD 31494
Richter: Music & Arts MUA 642
Schnabel: EMI Classics CDHB 64259

OTHER PRINCIPAL WORKS

ARPEGGIONE AND PIANO MUSIC

Sonata in A Minor (*Arpeggione*), D.821 (1824) (usually played on the cello)*

CHAMBER MUSIC

Trio in B-flat Major (sonata in one movement) for Piano, Violin, and Cello, D.28 (1812)

Quartet no. 12 in C Minor for Strings (*Quartettsatz*), D.703 (1820)*

Octet in F Major for Winds and Strings, D.803 (1824)*

Quartet no. 15 in G Major for Strings, D.887 (1826)*

Notturno in E-flat Major for Piano, Violin, and Cello, D.897 (?1828)*

CHURCH MUSIC

Mass no. 2 in G Major, D.167 (1815)

Mass no. 5 in A-flat Major, D.678 (1819–22)

Mass no. 6 in E-flat Major, D.950 (1828)*

OPERAS

Alfonso und Estrella, D.732 (1821–22)*

Fierabras, D.796 (1823)

ORCHESTRAL MUSIC

Symphony no. 3 in D Major, D.200 (1815)

Symphony no. 4 in C Minor (*Tragic*), D.417 (1816)*

Symphony no. 5 in B-flat Major, D.485 (1816)*

Symphony no. 6 in C Major, D.589 (1817–18)

Overture in C Major ("in the Italian style"), D.591 (1817)

PIANO DUETS

Three *Marches militaires*, D.733 (?1818)

Sonata in C Major (*Grand Duo*), D.812 (1824)

Variations on an Original Theme in A-flat Major, D.813 (1824)

Divertissement à l'hongroise in G Minor, D.818 (?1824)

Andantino varié in B Minor, D.823 (1827)

Fantasy in F Minor, D.940 (1828)*

Rondo in A Major (*Grand Rondeau*), D.951 (1828)

PIANO SOLO MUSIC

Eight *Ecossaises*, D.529 (1817)

Sonata in A Minor, D.537 (1817)

Sonata in B Major, D.575 (1817)

Two *Scherzos*, D.593 (1817)

Sonata in A Major, D.664 (1819)*

Six *Moments musicaux*, D.780 (1823–28)*

Sonata in A Minor, D.784 (1823)*

German dances, D.790 and 820 (1823–24)
Four *Ländler*, D.814 (1824)
Sonata in C Major (*Unfinished*), D.840 (1825)*
Sonata in A Minor, D.845 (1825)*
Sonata in D Major, D.850 (1825)*
Sonata in G Major, D.894 (1826)*
Twelve Waltzes (*Valses nobles*), D.969 (by 1826)
Three *Klavierstücke*, D.946 (1828)*

SONG CYCLE
Schwanengesang, D.957 (1828)*

VIOLIN AND PIANO MUSIC
Three sonatinas, D.384, 385, and 408 (1816)
Sonata in A Major (*Duo*), D.574 (1817)*
Rondo in B Minor (*Rondo brillant*), D.895 (1826)
Fantasy in C Major, D.934 (1827)*

GAETANO DONIZETTI

b. Bergamo, November 29, 1797

d. Bergamo, April 8, 1848

The opera cost me infinite trouble (eleven days). . . . You are re-
quested not to divulge my secrets, as the public won't believe them
anyway, or else imagines the music was tossed off. I leave it to you
whether the author would toss anything off.

Donizetti was born in Bergamo. His parents provided him with a sound education, in the hope that he would become a lawyer (the favored profession among
their set). Gaetano had an excellent talent for drawing, and his parents' second
choice of career for him was architect. Unfortunately for them, the boy's growing ardor for opera drove him to music. In his hometown, he was able to study
with Johannes Simon Mayr, a German-born composer and founder in 1805 of
the Lezioni Caritatevoli di Musica. Mayr taught for free and took Donizetti on
because he was convinced of the boy's talent. Donizetti would always gratefully
acknowledge his debt to Mayr, an unsung hero in the development of Italian
Romantic opera. Mayr's influence from the first decade of the nineteenth century was decisive, and it was his fondness for librettos on French and British
historical subjects that made these subjects the fashion among Italian composers. Mayr was totally forgotten until the revival of bel canto opera in the
twentieth century, but his *Medea in Corinto* (1813) proved him to be a formidable composer.

Legend had it that when Donizetti was about nineteen, he acted on impulse and joined the army. But military life, with its rules and regulations, was
intolerable to him and hardly conducive to creative work. The story goes that

in 1818 several military authorities heard an opera of his and, favorably impressed, gave the budding composer an honorable discharge for the sake of art.

Donizetti led the vagabondish life of an opera composer, roaming Italy and writing furiously. Italian opera houses craved new works, and Donizetti quickly provided them. In less than a dozen years, thirty-one operas flew from his pen. They were produced in Venice, Bergamo, Mantua, Genoa, Milan, Palermo, Naples, Rome, and Florence, and then in smaller towns.

Donizetti has often been criticized for his immense facility—as if composing slowly guaranteed masterpieces. But even the rapid composition of good-quality operas did not guarantee a livable income. Composers of his era seldom saw their work published, royalties were rare, and copyright laws were nonexistent. Various middlemen prevented composers from knowing what their real box-office receipts were. What money they did earn had to be divided with hack librettists. Most impresarios viewed composers and librettists as quickly replaceable commodities—they were far more concerned with the digestion of the prima donna and mood of the tenor than the quality of the opera. Audiences were usually unruly if not outrageous. Talking, eating, smoking, and screaming over high notes were all good sport. A night at the opera could be pandemonium. Berlioz may or may not have been exaggerating when he wrote, of a performance in Milan of Donizetti's sparkling *L'Elisir d'amore*, "The people made so much noise that it was impossible to hear a sound beyond the big drum." On the other hand, even within the general din and commotion, Italian audiences were likely to sense a new opera's value and always relished good singing.

During these first years of frenzied composing, as hard as he may have tried, Donizetti composed nothing that posterity has cared to remember. Perhaps he was too intimidated by Rossini, who wrote his last opera, *William Tell*, in 1829. But in 1828 Donizetti, who had had numerous romantic affairs, found the love of his life and married twenty-year-old Virginia Vasselli. From that moment, his music grew in stature.

In 1830, at age thirty-three, he chose as his subject the seething passions of Anne Boleyn, and to a libretto by Felice Romani, he composed a score appropriate to his genius. Within a few seasons, performances of *Anna Bolena* could be heard from Madrid to St. Petersburg, making Donizetti, like his countrymen Rossini and Bellini, an international figure. In London the basso Luigi Lablache created a sensation with his portrayal of Henry VIII.

Donizetti's gifts now flowered, and in short order he composed many other noteworthy operas, including *L'Elisir d'amore* (1832), packed with melody, pathos, and high comedy. It was followed in 1833 by *Parisina, Torquato Tasso*, and *Lucrezia Borgia*. The last was adapted from Victor Hugo's 1833 play *Lu-*

crèce Borgia, but when it was later staged in Paris, the powerful Hugo disliked the adaptation and prevented it from continuing its run. Romani's libretto also came in for heavy criticism.

Lucia di Lammermoor premiered at the famed San Carlo Theater in Naples on September 26, 1835. It rocked the house. As the mad scene progressed to the sextet, silence pervaded the great theater. At the conclusion, however, tears streaked the faces of the audience in one of operatic history's most celebrated first nights.

In 1837 Donizetti's adored Virginia died while giving birth to their third child, stillborn like the other two. He could not contain his sorrow. Never again would he say her name.

After being refused the directorship of the Naples Conservatory, Donizetti made Paris his headquarters from 1838. Opera followed opera: La Fille du régiment premiered to cheers at the Opéra-Comique in February 1840, and La Favorite received a similar reception at the Paris Opera the following December. These works were favorites of tenors Giovanni Battista Rubini and Giovanni Mario; of sopranos Adelina Patti, Giuditta Pasta, and Jenny Lind; and other stars of the period, making Donizetti the most famous and sought-after composer until Verdi. Composing, like Bellini and Rossini, at the tail end of a great age of vocalism, Donizetti tailored his music to the Italian singers who, at their best, were the finest in the world and through their performances exported Italian opera everywhere.

In 1843 Donizetti capped off his comedic genius with the perennial favorite Don Pasquale. After Pasquale, three more operas would be heard, but the composer's health plunged alarmingly. He had long endured syphilis but by now was experiencing dreadful hallucinations. Strokes and paralysis occurred, and finally he lapsed into complete insanity for nearly three years. A Victorian biographical sketch says that Donizetti, "an incessant worker, had to suffer the penalty of which all must suffer who overtax their brain." After unsuccessful treatment in an asylum outside Paris, he was taken back to Bergamo to die at age fifty-one. Virtually the entire town attended the funeral of its favorite son.

Donizetti when bad is indeed trite and commonplace in both melody and harmony. But when good, his bathos turns into the magical attraction of high melodrama, with lurid and delirious mad scenes in tragedy and a rollicking, high-spirited romp in comedy. He excelled at florid melodies, each of which had its own special shape, and all of which are markedly different from Rossini's topsy-turvy and chaste melodies or the sad long lines of Bellini's themes.

The next chapter of Italian opera would be Verdi's; in the 1840s his Nabucco and Ernani would soon make him famous. Donizetti, a person of charm and generosity, wrote to a friend in 1844, "The world wants new things; others after all have yielded the place to us, so we must yield it to others. . . . I am delighted to yield it to people of talent like Verdi. . . . The Venetians will appreciate him as much as the Milanese, for hearts are everywhere the same." Knowing that, Donizetti would not be surprised to learn that *Lucia* and *Don Pasquale* are still moving human hearts.

Lucia di Lammermoor (1835)

An opera in three acts, with a libretto fashioned from Sir Walter Scott's 1819 novel *The Bride of Lammermoor, Lucia* is one of the indispensable melodramas in opera. As Donizetti's tragic masterpiece, it contains the essence of his dramatic gift. With the mad scene, Lucia has been a coveted role for such glittering sopranos as Adelina Patti, Nellie Melba, Amelita Galli-Curci, Lily Pons, Marcella Sembrich, Luisa Tetrazzini, and more recently Joan Sutherland and Maria Callas (who is presently represented in ten CDs of the complete opera). The tenors Beniamino Gigli and Enrico Caruso were supreme Edgars. The spectacular sextet is the non plus ultra of operatic ensembles, which shows Donizetti's virtuosity in voice placement. It is to be hoped that Donizetti's finest mature operas may be revived and enjoyed, bringing many surprises to opera lovers and further raising his stature.

Sutherland, Pavarotti, Milnes, Ghiaurov, Royal Opera House Orchestra, Bonynge: London 410193-2

Callas, di Stefano, Panerai, Zaccaria, RIAS Symphony Orchestra and La Scala Chorus, Karajan: EMI Classics CDMB 63631

Don Pasquale (1843)

Since its first performance in Paris on January 3, 1843, *Don Pasquale*, Donizetti's last comic opera, has stood with Rossini's *The Barber of Seville* as the most wonderful Italian *opere buffe* of the first half of the nineteenth century. The text was written by Giovanni Ruffini and by Donizetti, who composed the work with his usual quicksilver fluidity (matched in speed only by Rossini himself). The first performance was studded with stars, including baritone Antonio Tamburini, tenor Giovanni Mario, soprano Giulia Grisi, and basso Luigi Lablache. The opera is chock full of enchanting morsels, such as Ernesto's haunting serenade in Act III and his "Sogno soave e casto" (sweet and pure dream), while the role of Norina is a marvelous soubrette. Never had Donizetti written with such lightness of texture. The little overture flies by as light as a feather. Donizetti was once asked which was his best opera. Instantly he replied, "How can I say which? A father always has a preference for a crippled child, and I have so many." One wonders how he felt about *Pasquale*.

Sills, Kraus, Titus, Gramm, London Symphony Orchestra and Ambrosian Opera Chorus, Caldwell: EMI Classics CDMB 66030

Freni, Winbergh, Bruscantini, Nucci, Philharmonia Orchestra and Ambrosian Opera Chorus, Muti: EMI Classics CDCB 47068

OTHER PRINCIPAL WORKS

OPERAS
Anna Bolena (1830)*
L'Elisir d'amore (1832)*
Lucrezia Borgia (1833)*
Maria Stuarda (1835)
Il Campanello di notte (1836)
Roberto Devereux (1837)
La Fille du régiment (1840)*
La Favorite (1840)*
Linda di Chamounix (1842)
Dom Sébastien (1843)*

V I N C E N Z O
B E L L I N I

b. Catania, Sicily, November 3, 1801

d. Puteaux (near Paris), September 23, 1835

Carve in your head in letters of brass: an opera must draw tears, cause horror, bring death, by means of song.

Bellini's father, an organist in Catania, firmly opposed his gifted son's wish to become a musician. Fortunately, in 1819 a wealthy Sicilian patron provided funds for Vincenzo's education in Naples at its celebrated conservatory, where Donizetti and Saverio Mercadante had recently studied. Since the days of Alessandro Scarlatti, Naples, with its great San Carlo Theater, had been a prime center of operatic culture. Neapolitans loved opera and understood the traditions of bel canto singing.

Success came to Bellini when he was just twenty-four, when his first opera, *Adelson e Salvini*, was produced at the Conservatory. Domenico Barbaja, the powerful manager of both the San Carlo and Milan's La Scala, took note and commissioned the composer to write an opera for the San Carlo. At its premiere in May 1826, *Bianca e Gernando* was well received. Pleased, Barbaja asked Bellini to write another for La Scala.

In 1827 Bellini moved to Milan, where his friend Mercadante, whose operas were also becoming known, introduced him to the finest librettist of the day, Felice Romani. Composer and poet would have an enduring collaboration; Romani was Bellini's librettist for seven more of his eight operas. In Milan, Bellini also befriended the singer Giovanni Battista Rubini—the "king of tenors." Rubini's career was soaring, and his association with Bellini would become legendary.

Bellini's first opera for La Scala, *Il Pirata* (1827), catapulted the composer to European fame; the score was soon heard in London, St. Petersburg, Dresden, Vienna, and Madrid. His next operas, *La Straniera* and *Zaira* (both staged in 1829), were followed by *I Capuleti e i Montecchi* (1830), which was staged at Venice's beautiful La Fenice Theater. Bellini's pensive, long-limbed melodies were recognized as a new type, forever after called "Bellinian."

The young composer truly hit his stride with the two-act *La Sonnambula* (1831), an opera unique in its endearing pastoral pathos. It took Milan by storm; the composer wrote, "I say nothing about the music. . . . I can only assure you that Rubini and [Giuditta] Pasta are two angels who enraptured the entire audience to the verge of madness." The Russian composer Mikhail Glinka, who was in the first-night audience, wrote to a friend, "I too shed tears of emotion and ecstasy."

La Sonnambula's gentle light then succumbed to the dark depths of Bellini's next opera, *Norma*. Its opening at La Scala on December 26, 1831, was sabotaged by a certain Countess Samayloff, a supporter of another opera composer, Giovanni Pacini, when she organized a claque to disrupt the performance. Bellini related to a friend, "My poor *Norma* has been persecuted so cruelly—you see they wanted to crush it at birth and all the papers cried failure, utter failure! A powerful faction, supported by the enormous sums of money spent by that madwoman—am I clear?—because in a few days a Pacini opera was to follow—am I clear?" But *Norma* quickly triumphed in the press, and several days later Donizetti wrote, "Everybody is praising the music of my friend, or rather my brother, Bellini to the skies. Everyone is overwhelmed by his sovereign genius, and is discovering in his work undreamed of beauties and treasures of sublime harmony."

Norma, a *"tragedia lirica,"* as its composer subtitled it, is Bellini's undisputed masterpiece. It is blessed with one of the great arias of bel canto opera, "Casta diva," whose swelling lyricism is characteristic of Bellini's gift for pure Italianate song. Romani's libretto is especially felicitous.

The handsome young composer next set out to conquer Paris and settled there in 1833. He moved in the highest social and artistic circles, and the fascinated public noted in detail his every movement and his love affairs. Chopin adored the man and his music, and the Polish master's nocturnes seem to exhale something of the Italian's sensuous and melancholy spirit. As the acute Heinrich Heine later observed, Bellini's "soul was certainly pure and unspotted by any hateful contagion. And he was not wanting in that good-natured, childlike quality which we never miss in men of genius."

Only one more opera was to come from his pen: *I Puritani*, which had its premiere on January 24, 1835, in Paris. Rubini had asked Bellini to write high

D's for him, and when he sang them, he was a sensation. But while Bellini was basking in the golden glow of fame, tragedy struck. Five weeks before his thirty-fourth birthday, the greatest composer ever born in Sicily died of what was probably an abcessed liver. Years before, as a student, Bellini had wept while singing from Pergolesi's *Stabat Mater* and had cried to a friend, "If I too could write such a melody I would not mind dying young." (Pergolesi had died at twenty-six.) Bellini's funeral took place at the Invalides Cathedral; Antonio Tamburini and Giovanni Rubini sang tributes. In 1876 his remains were removed from Père Lachaise Cemetery and taken back to Catania.

In the half-century before Bellini's birth and for a dozen or so years after his death, Italian opera reached its zenith, in terms of number of operas produced and audiences' appreciation of them. At La Scala alone, thirty-eight new operas were produced between 1831 and 1840. After the 1848 Revolution, Verdi notwithstanding, the Italian public would never again be as engrossed in opera. The acclaim given to Rossini, Donizetti, and Bellini, to Mercadante, even to the likes of Pacini, is unsurpassed.

With only slight exaggeration, a commentator in 1869 wrote, "No one who did not live in Italy before 1848 can imagine what the opera house meant in those days. It was the only outlet for public life, and everyone took part. The success of a new opera was a capital event that stirred to its depths the town lucky enough to have witnessed it, and word of it ran all over Italy."

In Bellini's time, opera was still carefree and ephemeral. There were no recordings, no scholarship to speak of, and no authentic editions. It was purely a singer's vehicle—and the singers had an emotional amplitude and technical perfection quite unimagined today. On any given night, in London, Paris, Milan, or Vienna, the public was treated to the likes of sopranos Giuditta Pasta, Henriette Sontag, Jenny Lind, and Giulia Grisi; mezzos Maria Malibran and Pauline Viardot-García; contralto Marietta Alboni; tenors Giovanni Rubini, Gilbert Duprez, Adolphe Nourrit, and Giovanni Mario; baritone Antonio Tamburini; basso Luigi Lablache; and a score of others, all of them great Bellini exponents and all legends in the annals of singing.

By Wagner's maturity in the 1850s, Italian opera had lost a good deal of its prestige. Even Verdi, Wagner's exact contemporary, was considered musically inferior to the creator of *Tristan*. With Wagner's orchestral orientation, the glory of bel canto singing and its technique declined.

Bellini's operas then entered obscurity. In the 1850s, the great painter Eugène Delacroix, a connoisseur of fine vocalism, could still note with surprise, "I have heard *Norma*. I thought I was going to be bored, and the contrary was the case; that music, which I thought I knew by heart and that I was tired of, seemed to me delightful." But in 1935 the critic Edward Dent could write:

Bellini's music is so little known nowadays to the average lover of music that it may
be difficult for him to understand what constitutes its individuality and genius. . . .
Modern listeners can hardly realize how exquisitely subtle and expressive that
melody is, for the art of singing it is almost lost. . . . The airs of Bellini . . . demand
a delicacy and refinement for which modern singers have not the technique. . . .
Cultivating the subtlest elegance of nuance and phrasing, it requires a standard in
these matters which has almost passed out of knowledge among singers and is now
regarded as the province of violinists and pianists.

In the past, pianists have generally been inspired primarily by singers.
Chopin was obsessed with the great singing of his day. Liszt was enraptured
and played in concert with the tenor Adolphe Nouritt, whom some regarded as
the greatest singer of the age. As a child, the pianist Anton Rubinstein heard
Rubini, whose sound haunted him for years: "I formed my idea of noble and
eloquent phrasing almost entirely from the great tenor Rubini."

Not until Maria Callas showered her audiences with bel canto singing in
Italian Romantic operas in the 1950s did a wide public once again deeply respond to and appreciate Bellini's rarefied qualities. The music of Rossini,
Donizetti, Bellini, and Verdi relies on elegant virtuoso vocalism. More than
sixty years after Bellini's death, Verdi wrote, "Bellini is poor, it's true, in instrumentation and harmony, but rich in feeling and in his own individual melancholy. Even in his lesser known operas, such as *La straniera* and *Il pirata*, there
are long, long, long spun-out melodies, like nothing that was ever written before him."

Norma (1831)

A woman once confronted Bellini with the question: "If you were out at sea
with all your scores, and should be shipwrecked and you could save only one
opera, which would you save?" "Oh, Madame," said the composer, looking unhappy, "I would leave the rest and try to save *Norma*." Donizetti, after hearing
the opera's premiere, remarked, "The pieces in *Norma* which struck me most
are: the introduction of the first act where the musical ideas are distributed and
developed with consummate skill and great knowledge of musical technique,
the close of this piece is most original. . . . The 'Casta Diva' is a delicate, enchanting melody. How full of grace and charm is this Cavatina! The melody
lends itself to the most dramatic effects. . . . The duet 'In mia mano alfin tu sei'
is a marvelous example of dramatic melody."

Norma is perhaps the most representative of all bel canto operas. It makes
heavy vocal demands, requiring considerable theatrical power of the soprano

performing the title role. The first Norma, Giuditta Pasta, was a highly regarded actress as well as singer. The most celebrated Norma of the last generation was Maria Callas, but in earlier times, even in the darkest days of Bellini's reputation, the Druid priestess has had legendary advocates in Jenny Lind, Giulia Grisi, Rosa Ponselle, and Lilli Lehmann, who once said that singing three Brünnhildes in a row was easier than one Norma. Bellini's two other important and beguiling operas, *I Puritani* and *La Sonnambula*, are well represented on CD by Maria Callas, Joan Sutherland, and Renata Scotto, and *Il Pirata* by Montserrat Caballé.

Caballé, Cossotto, Domingo, Raimondi, London Philharmonic Orchestra, Ambrosian Opera Chorus, Cillario: RCA 6502-2-RG

Callas, Ludwig, Corelli, Zaccaria, La Scala Orchestra and Chorus, Serafin: EMI Classics CDMC 63000

OTHER PRINCIPAL WORKS

OPERAS

Il Pirata (1827)
La Straniera (1829)
La Sonnambula (1831)*
Beatrice di Tenda (1833)
I Puritani (1835)*

HECTOR BERLIOZ

b. Côte-Saint-André, Isère, December 11, 1803

d. Paris, March 8, 1869

I was in a state of ecstasy. I had just played my first act (Les Troyens) through mentally from beginning to end. Now there is nothing so absurd as an author who, imitating the good Lord, considers his work on the seventh day and finds it good.

Berlioz was the eldest of four children. His father, Louis, was a physician in a small provincial town and took a keen interest in his son's education. He schooled the boy at home and introduced him to ancient and modern poetry, medicine, and Latin. He taught him the rudiments of the flute and guitar, but his sole desire was for his son to follow him into the medical profession. "My father had no intention of making an artist of me," Berlioz later related; "and I dare say he thought that if I learned the piano I should devote myself too passionately to it, and become more absorbed in music than he wished or intended me to be." Hector's mother thought music was a shameful waste of time.

Still, Hector learned whatever he could about music on his own. "I had discovered," he wrote, "Rameau's treatise on harmony . . . and spent sleepless nights in fruitless efforts to unravel its mysteries." As late as 1815, there was not a single piano in town.

When Hector was eighteen, he followed his parents' wishes and moved to Paris to study medicine. The prospect horrified him: "Become a doctor! Study anatomy! dissect! witness horrible operations! instead of throwing myself heart and soul into the glorious and beautiful art of music. . . . It seemed to me the utter reversal of the natural conditions of my life; horrible and impossible. Yet it came to pass." In 1821 he arrived in Paris to enter the École des Medecins.

For three long years, he forced himself to study medicine but spent his free time at the opera and reading musical scores in the library at the Paris Conservatory. At the Conservatory he studied composition privately with Jean-François Lesueur, an eminent composer who saw "genius" in his pupil. Berlioz found his courage and told his much-loved parents that music was his destiny. They summarily disowned him. Undaunted, he plunged into theoretical studies while dreaming of grand musical conceptions and working as a librarian at the Conservatory. For three years, he attempted to win the Prix de Rome, a prize awarded annually by the Académie des Beaux-Arts for composition, among other things; he thought winning it might soften his father's still-boiling wrath. In 1830 the coveted award was his, for a cantata based on Byron's historical drama *Sardanapalus* (1821). The prize consisted of three years of study at the French Academy, housed at the Villa Medici in Rome. His parents were only vaguely pleased.

By then Hector had fallen madly in love with Harriet Smithson, an Irish actress. He first saw her on stage, playing Shakespeare at the Odéon Theater—in English, a language of which Berlioz did not know a word. Berlioz hungrily read Shakespeare in French translation and soon was almost as much in awe of the Bard as he was of Harriet's beauty. Harriet ignored her pursuer, who probably frightened her with his desperate passion. The world gained from her rebuff, however, for Berlioz poured all of his frustrated energy into composing the *Symphonie fantastique* (Op. 14). Its first performance, on December 5, 1830, looms large in the history of Romantic music. Never had music been so pictorial. Never had an orchestra so blazed with such an array of timbres. In Berlioz's first mature work, the opulence of the modern orchestra was born. The audience's reaction was mixed: the older folk were disconcerted, while the young Romantics were excited. Such action and drama had never been represented in an orchestral work. Franz Liszt heard the first performance and hastened to introduce himself to Berlioz. The two young composers were soon fast intellectual companions (they read Goethe's *Faust* together).

After the first performance of the symphony, Berlioz, it seemed, was able to forget Miss Smithson. But he soon fell violently in love again, this time with the beautiful pianist Marie Moke. Shortly before Berlioz left for his three-year stay at the Villa Medici in Rome, the two became engaged. The separation did not prove conducive to romance, and the pianist soon jilted Berlioz to marry a rich piano manufacturer, Camille Pleyel. In a memorable scene in his memoirs, Berlioz tells of his plan to return to Paris disguised as a woman and murder Marie and her mother, and then kill himself.

Though Rome didn't help Berlioz's love life, it offered him some wonderful professional opportunities. There he met Felix Mendelssohn and was impressed by Mendelssohn's prodigious musicianship. The admiration, alas, was not mutual; the conservative German liked Berlioz as a person but thought that the avant-garde Frenchman lacked the talent to match his large ambitions. It was also in Rome that Berlioz composed or began overtures inspired by literature: Shakespeare's *King Lear* (Op. 4, 1831), Scott's *Rob Roy* (1831), and Byron's *Le Corsair* (Op. 21, 1844).

Upon returning to Paris late in 1832, Berlioz once again began to woo Miss Smithson. This time his cause was more successful, though she still knew no French and he no English, and the couple were soon married. But the ardent composer quickly fell from love's grace. All who knew him considered the relationship to be a creation of the composer's extravagant imagination. Smithson was a simple and undistinguished woman who could hardly fulfill her flamboyant husband's need for an ideal love. The marriage produced one son, Louis, in 1834, but by 1842 the couple had separated. Unlike Wagner, whose first marriage was also to a prosaic actress, Berlioz never went on to find his muse.

The marriage was probably not helped by Berlioz's obligations—by 1834 he was swamped with hackwork, debts, and chronic illness. But soon all that was changed when Paganini gave him an unexpected and princely gift of twenty thousand francs—the Italian had recently come into possession of "an admirable Stradivari viola" and wanted Berlioz to compose a work for him for viola and orchestra. The money allowed Berlioz to pay his creditors and to compose without pressure. The result was *Harold en Italie* (Op. 16, 1834). Starting in 1833, he found work as a music critic for various publications.

Unfortunately, Berlioz's gigantic compositions found almost no acceptance in Paris. The public was infatuated with the grand opera spectacles of Daniel Auber, Fromental Halévy, and Giacomo Meyerbeer, all of which Berlioz sharply criticized as banal in his reviews. His uncomprehending audiences were simply not prepared for blazing orchestration and dissonances, as well as the grandiose size of his musical edifices, including the Requiem (Op. 5, 1837), *La Damnation de Faust* (Op. 24, 1846), *Te Deum* (Op. 22, 1849), and *L'Enfance du Christ* (Op. 25, 1850–54). So hostile were the audiences that, at one performance of the opera *Benvenuto Cellini* (1834–37), there was even a riot!

But Paris was not the only possible audience for Berlioz's music. The bitter composer, who was also one of the great pioneers in the art of conducting, took his baton to Germany, England, and Russia. In Weimar, Liszt, a faithful supporter from the beginning of Berlioz's career, gave a weeklong Berlioz festival, with the composer participating. In Russia he made a lasting impression on the younger composers: as the musicologist Elaine Brody notes, "[t]he music of Berlioz took root, flowering abundantly in the music of Mussorgsky, Rimsky-Korsakov, and Borodin, and returning to France via Debussy and Stravinsky, that gallicized Russian."

But in France, Berlioz was a prophet without honor, and it galled him that his countrymen did not understand his art. His last years were a misery of many illnesses. To deaden the mounting pain, he became addicted to laudanum, an opium extract. In 1854, Berlioz's estranged wife Harriet died (after a long and paralyzing illness) and the composer married Marie Recio, his mistress of fourteen years. She was known for her jealousy but took care of him until she died in 1862. In 1867, his adored son Louis died in Havana from yellow fever, at age thirty-three; the death broke his father's spirit. A week later Berlioz dragged himself into his office at the Conservatory and burned a great deal of valuable memorabilia. During the last six years of his life, he composed little. The poet Gautier saw him as an exasperated eagle deprived of the power to soar. Berlioz, who had once possessed an unshakable faith in himself, now was habitually depressed and had become an addict to ease his pain.

On March 8, 1869, the most original French composer of the nineteenth century died. The turnout at the funeral was small but respectable. Berlioz's pallbearers included the composers Charles Gounod, Ernest Reyer, and Ambroise Thomas. He was buried at the Montmartre Cemetery. "But before the body had reached the grave," his biographer Jacques Barzun later wrote, "a final Berliozean incident—never to be believed had it been recorded by a Romantic of 1830—took place. Not far from the goal, the pair of mourning-coach steeds, black and tame as Paris undertakers themselves, suddenly seized the bit in their teeth, plowed through the brass band in front of them, and brought Berlioz alone within the gates."

On his deathbed, Berlioz had predicted that his time would come. He was correct. At the end of the nineteenth century, the French were looking to their recent past for a great master, one perhaps to rival even Wagner. They came upon their long-maligned Berlioz (from whom Wagner, after all, had learned so much). The poet Gautier had always known that Berlioz, along with Delacroix and Hugo, were the three mighty forces of French Romantic art.

Still, it took most of the twentieth century to place Berlioz's art in perspective. He has always irked many people. He refuses to fit into a convenient niche. His works as a whole are not graceful; they do not have the kind of melodies that stick in the mind. His harmonies can sound primitive, and his content empty. But for those who are temperamentally attuned to him, he is shattering. He has a subtlety of construction that goes beyond technique, and his orchestrations have proved to be models for generations to come.

In his memoirs Berlioz explained, "The prevailing characteristics of my music are passionate expression, intense ardor, rhythmical animation and unexpected turns. When I say passionate expression, I mean an expression determined to strengthen or underscore the inner meaning of its subject, even when that subject is the contrary of passion, and when the feeling to be expressed is but gentle and tender, or even profoundly calm." Whenever I hear any of Berlioz's music, I think of the poet Heine's statement: "He is an immense nightingale, a lark as great as an eagle . . . the music causes me to dream of fabulous empires filled with fabulous sins."

Symphonie fantastique, Op. 14 (1830)

The germination of the *Fantastic Symphony*, which became so embedded with Berlioz's adulation for Harriet Smithson, is best recounted in the composer's memoirs.

Berlioz also wrote a long program note for the piece, which begins, "A young musician of morbid sensibility and ardent imagination poisons himself with opium in a fit of amorous despair." The beloved woman became for him a melody, a "fixed idea," that appears in various guises in each of the five movements: 1. Reveries and Passions, 2. A Ball, 3. Scene in the Country, 4. The March to the Gallows, 5. The Witches' Sabbath. The symphony still thrills music lovers with its romantic ardor. The "March to the Gallows" is as audacious today as it was in 1830.

Cleveland Orchestra, Dohnányi: London 430201-2
Boston Symphony Orchestra, Munch: RCA Gold Seal 09026-61721-2
Royal Concertgebouw Orchestra, Davis: Philips 411425-2
French National Radio Symphony Orchestra, Beecham: EMI Classics CDM7 64032-2

Harold en Italie, Op. 16 (1834)

Paganini's entrance into Berlioz's life was not only financially important; it also stimulated him to compose two of the cornerstones of Romantic music, *Harold en Italie* and *Roméo et Juliette*. The first was inspired by Byron's *Childe Harold's Pilgrimage*. Berlioz stated, "I was introducing the viola as a sort of melancholy dreamer." Paganini, however, wanted no part in such an unflashy display of the instrument, and when he saw the score, he declared, "That is not at all what I want. I am silent a great deal too long. I must be playing the whole time." Although it lacks the virtuosity that Paganini desired, *Harold* is the only major symphonic work with viola of the Romantic era.

Cooley, NBC Symphony Orchestra, Toscanini: RCA Gold Seal 60275-2-RG
Bashmet, Frankfurt Radio Symphony Orchestra: Denon CO 73207
Imai, London Symphony Orchestra, Davis: Philips 416431-2

Roméo et Juliette, Op. 17 (1838–39)

From the moment Shakespeare entered Berlioz's artistic world, the composer became a greater artist. In his memoirs, he recalled the effect: "This sudden and unexpected revelation of Shakespeare overwhelmed me. The lightning-flash of his genius revealed the whole heaven of art to me, illuminating its remotest depths in a single flash. I recognized the meaning of real grandeur, real beauty, and real dramatic truth." No other Frenchman of the time understood the great dramatist with such passionate intensity. This passion would culminate years later in a work so original that it still is far from adequately appreciated. Berlioz called his musical ruminations on *Romeo and Juliet* "a dramatic symphony."

Berlioz began *Roméo et Juliette* "caressed by the playful breeze of fancy, beneath the hot rays of that sun of love which Shakespeare kindled." But the huge, ungainly symphony falls into no established form. The music mysteriously highlights and pinpoints aspects of the drama. Concert audiences are most familiar with two excerpts from the seventy-minute score: the "Love Music" and the "Queen Mab Scherzo." However effective these individual selections are, listening to the complete work, with all its depths, is far more engrossing.

Norman, Aler, Estes, Philadelphia Orchestra, Westminster Choir, Muti: EMD EMI Classics
   72640

Le Carnaval romain, Op. 9 (1844)

The Roman Carnival was a first-night success, as conducted by François Habeneck, the conductor of the Paris Conservatory Orchestra. But Berlioz was not satisfied with the slow tempo Habeneck took in the *saltarello* conclusion. Some years later, with Habeneck in the audience, Berlioz himself conducted it "properly." In the green room he told Habeneck, "This is how it *ought* to go!" "Unhappy composers!" Berlioz later admonished. "Learn how to conduct, and how to conduct yourselves well [with or without a pun], for do not forget that the most dangerous of all your interpreters is the conductor himself." The work is in three sections: a brilliant *Allegro*, an amorous section, and a wild Italian dance (*saltarello*).

Although *Le Carnaval romain* is the most familiar of Berlioz's overtures, the listener may want to explore all of them, including especially those to *King Lear* (1831), *Le Corsair* (1844), *Benvenuto Cellini* (1834–37), and *Béatrice et Benédict* (1860–62). *Les Francs-Juges* (1826), *Waverley* (1828), and *Rob Roy* (1831) each has its individual merits.

London Symphony Orchestra, Davis: Philips 442290-2
London Symphony Orchestra, Previn: EMI Classics CDM 64630
Gibson, Scottish National Orchestra: Chandos CHAN 8316

1. Minuet of the Will-o'-the-Wisps
2. Dance of the Sylphs
3. Rákóczy March
from *La Damnation de Faust* (1846)

Berlioz completed his "dramatic legend," *The Damnation of Faust*, in 1846. Its premiere was a disaster. "Nothing in all my artistic career ever wounded me so deeply as this unexpected indifference," the composer wrote. Six years after his death, it was performed in Paris to rousing success. Neither an oratorio nor an opera, it cannot easily be categorized. Berlioz had long been an admirer of Goethe's *Faust*. So was Liszt, who in the 1830s introduced Berlioz to the "Rákóczy March," a Hungarian melody that Berlioz in turn used when he set "his" *Faust* in Hungary. The marvelous "Will-o'-the-Wisps" and "Dance of the Sylphs" have no specific relevance to the Faust legend; Berlioz's musical inspirations always took precedence over the literature that inflamed his imagination.

Three Orchestral Selections
Baltimore Symphony Orchestra, Zinman: Telarc CD 80164
Philadelphia Orchestra, Munch: Sony Classical SBK 53255

Les Troyens (1856–58)

Berlioz's mightiest epic, and arguably one of the greatest of all operas, took five years of effort to gain a full performance. A variety of circumstances, such as its more-than-four-hour length and its demanding score, caused opera producers to turn it down. He had to divide it in two parts for its 1863 premiere, and even then the orchestral interlude "Royal Storm and Hunt" was cut after the first performance. For this mammoth five-act opera, Berlioz fashioned his own libretto from Virgil's *Aeneid*. Incredibly, the first "complete uncut" performance had to wait until 1969. The opera's lack of success was once again a punishing blow to the lonely and bitter composer. It will not automatically fill the listener with warmth, but the more one delves into its vast scheme, the more certain one becomes that Berlioz was one of the great individualists in all art. The poet W. H. Auden once noted that for "whoever wants to know about the nineteenth century, it is essential to understand Berlioz." And to understand Berlioz fully, one must know *Les Troyens*, the culmination of his career as a composer. Every aspect of his personal Romanticism appears in this vast, tumultuous score. It is sweeping in its drama, its compassion, and its tragic impact.

Veasey, Lindholm, Vickers, Glossop, Soyer, Orchestra and Chorus of the Royal Opera House, Covent Garden, Davis: Philips 416432-2

OTHER PRINCIPAL WORKS

CHORAL WORKS WITH ORCHESTRA
Requiem, Op. 5 (1837; rev. 1852 and 1857)*
Grand Symphonie funèbre et triomphale, Op. 15 (before 1840)
Te Deum, Op. 22 (1849)*
L'Enfance du Christ, Op. 25 (1850–54)*

OPERAS
Benvenuto Cellini (1834–37)*
Béatrice et Bénédict (1860–62)*

ORCHESTRAL MUSIC
Waverley Overture, Op. 1 (by 1828)*
Les Francs-Juges Overture, Op. 3 (1826)
King Lear Overture, Op. 4 (1831)*
Marche funèbre pour la dernière scène d'Hamlet, Op. 18/3 (?1848)
Le Corsaire Overture, Op. 21 (1844)*
"Royal Hunt and Storm" from *Les Troyens* (1856–58)*

SONG CYCLE
Les Nuits d'été for Soprano and Orchestra, Op. 7 (1843–56)*

FELIX MENDELSSOHN

b. Hamburg, February 3, 1809

d. Leipzig, November 4, 1847

Genuine music fills the soul with a thousand things better than words. The thoughts which are expressed to me by music that I love are not too indefinite to be put into words, but on the contrary, too definite.

Felix Mendelssohn was a supremely gifted child, the most spectacular musical prodigy after Mozart. He came from a prominent family: his grandfather, Moses Mendelssohn, was a famous Jewish philosopher, and his father, Abraham, was the head of a major Berlin banking firm. His mother, Lea, a sensitive and discriminating woman, was an excellent pianist who organized an elaborate private education for her children. Felix, along with his brother Paul and sisters Fanny and Rebecca, rose daily at five o'clock to begin the arduous daily regime of studying languages, literature, drawing, and many other skills and disciplines. The family lived in a palace on a large estate, fit for a king.

The boy, modest and amiable, took wealth and privilege in stride. By his teens, he had developed into a polished dancer, a master of chess and billiards, a daring horseback rider, an untiring swimmer, a talented watercolorist, and a captivating letter writer. But these and other accomplishments were mere details by comparison with his all-encompassing musical education, complete with hired orchestras to try out the boy's latest compositions. At twelve Felix was an experienced and accomplished composer with an infallible ear and a phenomenal memory.

He played the violin well and the organ brilliantly and eventually became the most important conductor in Europe. As a pianist, he was mentioned among the greatest. At fourteen he took some "finishing" lessons with Ignaz Moscheles, who was known as "the prince of pianists." In his diary, Moscheles recorded: "I gave these lessons without ever losing sight for a single moment of the fact that I was sitting next to a master, not a pupil."

All doors were opened to the handsome youngster. At age twelve, he was the invited guest of Germany's greatest cultural hero, Goethe himself. He spent several days in Weimar, saturating the great poet with music. To his parents, Felix unaffectedly wrote, "Every morning I get a kiss from the author of *Faust* and *Werther*. . . . Think of that! In the afternoon I played to Goethe for over two hours, partly Bach fugues, and partly I followed my own fancies."

Not only was Felix gloriously gifted, but his genius burst early, with immortal masterpieces such as the String Octet (Op. 20, 1825), composed at sixteen, and the overture to *A Midsummer Night's Dream* (Op. 21) the following year. Not even Mozart had created such mature work by that age.

Mendelssohn was one of the first important musicians of his time to be vitally conscious of music's past. His composition teacher, Carl Zelter, had early on introduced him to the works of Palestrina, Handel, Bach, and other "ancient masters," as they were called. Perhaps the most important day in the history of musical resurrection was March 11, 1829, when the twenty-year-old Mendelssohn conducted Bach's *St. Matthew Passion*, which had languished in oblivion since its first full performance in 1736. The performance took place in Berlin's Singakademie. Its success was so great that the *Passion* was repeated ten days later. The performance began the nineteenth-century Bach revival, which led to the publication of the Baroque composer's vast oeuvre.

Wealth and early celebrity allowed Mendelssohn fortunately to escape many of the worst indignities of anti-Semitism. German Jews of his era could rarely attain the peak of their professions without converting to Christianity, and Felix would later become a Protestant. During a rehearsal of the *St. Matthew Passion*, he overheard a choir member say, "Ah, see the Jew boy raising his voice to Christ!" Many years later, in his only known comment on his Jewish origin, he wrote, "It was a Jew who restored this great Christian work to the people," speaking of the *St. Matthew Passion*.

Shortly after the Berlin performance of Bach's *Passion*, Mendelssohn left for a three-year Grand Tour of Europe, as was customary for wealthy young men. He instantly fell in love with Britain, and Britain reciprocated. Mendelssohn had all the right connections, and high society immediately took to the dashing and fashionable young man. Queen Victoria and Prince Albert, both well trained musically, were dazzled by him. In his remaining eighteen years, during ten lengthy visits to the British Isles, he became England's adopted musical son. His two Handelian oratorios, *St. Paul* (Op. 36, 1836) and especially *Elijah* (Op. 70, 1846), with its deep lyricism and dramatic flair, had unrivaled success there. *Elijah* soon rivaled Handel's *Messiah* as a favorite among England's choral societies.

Mendelssohn worked endlessly. Besides founding major musical festivals at Düsseldorf (1833), Birmingham (1837), and elsewhere, he founded the Leipzig Conservatory in 1843, which he served as director. As the tireless conductor of Leipzig's Gewandhaus Orchestra, he presented programs that were uncompromising, and his standards of performance were unequaled. He appeared to find time for everyone and everything. He had a long and outwardly happy marriage to Cécile Jeanrenaud, though it was, as his biographer, Heinrich Eduard Jacob, wrote, "the very model of passionlessness." When courting his bride, Mendelssohn never spoke of love; instead, he simply declared, "And now I am going to get married." Cécile was gentle, lovely to look at, and very undemanding. She bore him five children—three boys and two girls—each of whom grew to undistinguished adulthood. In all truth, the only passion he ever felt for a woman was for his beloved sister, Fanny Hensel, whose very heart seemed to beat to his.

Then, on May 14, 1847, Felix's Fanny, a gifted composer and pianist in her own right, died of a stroke at forty-one. Mendelssohn was devastated. Theirs had been a relationship of rare devotion. Grief was followed by massive depression. Suddenly the years of endless toil took their toll. Within six months of Fanny's death, Mendelssohn, too, was carried to the grave by a stroke. At the time of his death, he was the most celebrated composer in the world.

His premature passing at thirty-eight shocked musical Europe, and his funeral would have befitted a state dignitary. After elaborate services at Leipzig, the coffin traveled to Berlin for interment. The train made numerous stops through the night, with crowds at each station weeping at Mendelssohn's passing. Once in Berlin, the cortège proceeded to the cemetery to the strains of the Funeral March from Beethoven's *Eroica*.

Mendelssohn's music, with its charm, beautifully proportioned Classical forms, and exquisite craftsmanship, was admired over that of other composers in his day. For the average music lover, Berlioz, Chopin, Schumann, and Liszt were too thorny, too harmonically advanced, too complicated, and too often disturbing. The gentlemanly Mendelssohn, by far the most conservative harmonist of the greater early Romantics, was himself often repelled by the music of his friends: Chopin for him could be too sultry and morbid; Liszt too flamboyant; Schumann too weird; and he confessed that after reading a Berlioz score he was impelled to wash his hands. Mendelssohn was the most classical and balanced of the early Romantics; his use of form is impeccable, based on that of composers from Handel to Beethoven. But some of the early Romantics thought he lived too much in the past.

Mendelssohn was truly Romantic in his love for the picturesque. His was not a subjective, personalized Romanticism, but a visual and descriptive one. His imperishable contributions to Romanticism are his unique Scherzo movements, his visions of happy, enchanted worlds, sun-drenched fairy lands of elves and magic spells, in music that travels on gossamer wings. His *scherzando* moods abound throughout his work, appearing in the *Rondo capriccioso* (Op. 14, 1824), *Scherzo a capriccio* (1835–36), "The Spinning Song" (1845), the Scherzo from *A Midsummer Night's Dream* (1842), and many more.

Mendelssohn fed the genteel early-Victorian public's taste for music that was moderate and well-mannered, with genial, distinctive, and delicate melodies. But too often he produced music by the yard, pieces too slick and stolid and, at worst, sickly sentimental, like "On Wings of Song" (1836), which made him the darling of the early-Victorian musical public. By 1900 his works had suffered an almost total eclipse, with only a few remaining in the performance repertoire. To the Wagner-saturated public, Mendelssohn sounded faded and old-fashioned.

Today, however, such criticism has mostly disappeared from discussions of his music, as knowledge of historical style has become more thorough. Recordings have also been kind to Mendelssohn's varied oeuvre. It is refreshing to hear him in context with his contemporaries; his lucidity and fastidiousness and his restrained eloquence, combined with the highest compositional skill and elegance, place him in the first rank. He is what he always was: a great master of his art and the most imitated composer by far of the nineteenth century.

The American composer and critic Daniel Gregory Mason has best summarized Mendelssohn's art: "Violence of contrast, dramatic trenchancy of expression, the over emphasis of hysterical eloquence, he punctiliously avoids. He is always clear, unperturbed, discreet, harmonious. The lavish sensuousness of Schubert, or the impulsive sincerity of Schumann are impossible if not distasteful to this Addisonian temperament; personal sentiment, self-revelation, the autobiographic appeal, he avoids as the purist in manners avoids a blush, an exclamation, or a grimace. If he is romantic in his love of color, and in his fondness for literary motives, his emotional reticence is entirely classic."

Octet in E-flat Major for Strings, Op. 20 (1825)

The glory of Mendelssohn's legendary youth is enshrined in this greatest of all octets for four violins, two violas, and two cellos—composed when he was sixteen! The first movement (Allegro moderato, ma con fuoco), in sonata form, spurts fire. An Andante in C minor follows, opening with a *siciliano* rhythm, with Mozart surely on his mind. Following is the delectable Scherzo, *allegro leggierissimo*. It is as wondrous today as when it leaped from his pen. The English critic Donald Francis Tovey thinks, "Eight string players might easily practice it for a lifetime without coming to an end of their delight in producing its marvels of tone color." The finale, in all its rushing excitement and contrapuntal mastery, is astonishing. No teenage composer in history ever had at his command such depth of compositional technique.

Smetana and Janáček String Quartets: Supraphon Collection 11 0648-2
Cleveland and Meliora String Quartets: Telarc CD 80142
Academy of St. Martin in the Fields Chamber Ensemble: Chandos CHAN 8790

A Midsummer Night's Dream Overture (1826)
Scherzo, Intermezzo, Nocturne, and Wedding March (1842)

The overture was composed by a boy of seventeen, and Mendelssohn's elfin spirit leaps out in his interpretation of Shakespeare's comic masterpiece. With an ethereal shimmer of strings, we enter fairyland and a new conception of orchestral writing. To his sister, Mendelssohn said, "I have grown accustomed to composing in our garden. I am going to dream there the *Midsummer Night's Dream.*" Fifteen years later, King Frederick William IV of Prussia commissioned the composer to write incidental music for the play, which was to be produced at Potsdam. Mendelssohn proceeded to write thirteen pieces, of which the golden Scherzo, Intermezzo, Nocturne, and the indispensable Wedding March are often performed in the concert hall.

Cleveland Orchestra, Szell: Sony Classical SBK 48264
Cincinnati Symphony Orchestra, Susskind: Vox Box CDX 5138

Concerto no. 1 in G Minor for Piano and Orchestra, Op. 25 (1832)

This was the first concerto in three movements to be played without interruption. It is great fun, brilliantly conceived, and sparkling in its orchestration. Energy abounds in the opening, full of fiery octaves. The slow movement is touching, poetic, and nocturnal. From Mendelssohn's first performance of this concerto in Munich in 1831, it caught the fancy of virtuosi. It was so popular in the 1830s that Berlioz dreamed that all the pianos at the Paris Conservatory played the piece late at night, without the help of pianists.

R. Serkin, Philadelphia Orchestra, Ormandy: Sony Classical SBK 46542
Katsaris, Leipzig Gewandhaus Orchestra, Masur: Teldec 9031-75860-2

Hebrides Overture (Fingal's Cave), Op. 26 (1830; rev. 1832)

On his first trip to Scotland in the summer of 1829, Mendelssohn excitedly visited Fingal's Cave. Named for the hero of a Scottish legend, the cave is on the tiny island of Staffa, one of the Hebrides Islands off the west coast of Scotland. The composer was instantly aroused and jotted down the first ten measures of what would be the overture. He immediately sent the theme to his sister, but did not complete the work for three more years. It was first performed at Covent Garden on May 14, 1832. The work has become known as either *Fingal's Cave* or the *Hebrides Overture*. The consummate landscape painter, Mendelssohn transports us to the island. As we listen, we hear the surging waves pushing at the rocks, and the roar of the wind.

Cleveland Orchestra, Szell: Sony Classical SBK 46536
London Symphony Orchestra, Abbado: Deutsche Grammophon 423104
London Philharmonic Orchestra, Haitink: Philips 442661-2

Symphony no. 4 in A Major (Italian), Op. 90 (1833)

Mendelssohn wrote five symphonies. No. 5, *Reformation* (Op. 107, 1832), is rather stodgy, and No. 3, *Scottish* (Op. 56, 1842), often recorded, is suave and effective, while No. 4, *Italian*, basks in sunlight. The twenty-one-year-old composer first set foot in Italy early in October 1830. To his parents he wrote, "The whole country has such a festive air that I felt as if I were a young prince making his entry." In such a mood, this transparent music was composed. The symphony is in four movements of crystal-clear directness, with a Presto Finale in the form of a *saltarello*, an old Italian dance.

Philharmonia Orchestra, Cantelli: Enterprise ENT PD 4158
Royal Philharmonic Orchestra, Kondrashin: Philips 438278-2
Boston Symphony Orchestra, Davis: Philips 420653-2

Forty-eight *Lieder ohne Worte* (*Songs Without Words*) for Piano Solo
Opp. 19, 30, 38, 53, 62, 67, 85, and 102 (various dates)

Each of these eight opuses contains six pieces. Many of the finest, like "Duetto," "Volkslied," "Spinnerlied," "Jägerlied," and the three Venetian boat songs, are characteristic contributions to nineteenth-century piano music and have thousands of imitations. They are watercolors, sketches, or impressions, each impeccably well tailored, of about three minutes in length. These pieces were the joy of the drawing-room pianist. The most famous of them, "Frühlingslied" (Spring Song), became hackneyed almost beyond repair, but even this is once again enjoyed as the delicate and purely Mendelssohnian morsel that it is.

Friedman (ten pieces): Pearl 4 1F2000
Barenboim (complete): Deutsche Grammophon 453061-2
Kyriakou (complete): Vox Box CDX 5077

Variations sérieuses in D Minor for Piano, Op. 54 (1841)

This is one of the finest sets of variations from the Romantic period, and it is charged with emotional intensity. These variations were never equaled by Mendelssohn's other piano music, for they have cohesion of form and passion, and they reveal the composer's remarkable capacity for original and idiomatic keyboard writing. Each tiny eight-measure variation dissolves imperceptibly into the next, and an array of devices such as the two-part canonic writing of Variation 4, the fugal Variation 10, and the constant shifting from light to dark display Mendelssohn's perfect craftsmanship. The word *sérieuses* in the title is thought to reflect Mendelssohn's reaction to the enormous quantity of facile variations on popular opera tunes of the day by Franz Hünten, Henri Herz, and others—those composers whom Schumann called Philistines.

Sofronitsky: Arlecchino ARLA 11
Cortot: Biddulph LHW 002
Horowitz: RCA 60451-2-RG

Concerto in E Minor for Violin and Orchestra, Op. 64 (1844)

The E minor concerto was composed in 1844 for Ferdinand David, the concertmaster of Mendelssohn's Leipzig Gewandhaus Orchestra. David performed the world premiere on March 13, 1845. An ailing Mendelssohn was replaced on the podium by his friend the Danish composer Niels Gade. The concerto has a seamless three-movement sequence, played without interruption, and a haunting, ethereal theme. The violin writing is smoothly graceful, from its autumnal and passionate opening statement to the dancing puckish finale. The concerto's orchestration was endlessly copied by other composers, and most violinists today cannot imagine life without Mendelssohn's concerto.

Kreisler, London Philharmonic Orchestra, Ronald: Pearl PEAS 9362
Menuhin, Berlin Philharmonic Orchestra, Furtwängler: EMI Classics CDH 69799
Elman, Vienna State Opera Orchestra, Golschmann: Vanguard Classics OVC 8034
Mullova, Academy of St. Martin in the Fields, Marriner: Philips 432077-2

OTHER PRINCIPAL WORKS

CHAMBER MUSIC
Quartet no. 5 in E-flat Major for Strings, Op. 44/3 (1838)
Sonata no. 1 in B-flat Major for Cello, Op. 45 (1838)
Trio no. 1 in D Minor for Piano, Violin, and Cello, Op. 49 (1839)*
Sonata no. 2 in D Major for Cello and Piano, Op. 58 (1843)
Trio no. 2 in C Minor for Piano, Violin, and Cello, Op. 66 (1845)*
Quintet in B-flat Major for Strings, Op. 87 (1845)*
Quartet No. 6 in F Minor for Strings, Op. 80 (1847)*

ORATORIOS
St. Paul, Op. 36 (1836)
Elijah, Op. 70 (1846)*

ORCHESTRAL MUSIC
Meeresstille und glückliche Fährt (*Calm Sea and Prosperous Voyage*) *Overture*, Op. 27 (1828)
Die schöne Melusine (*The Fair Melusine*) *Overture*, Op. 32 (1833)
Ruy Blas Overture, Op. 39 (1839)
Symphony no. 3 in A Minor (*Scottish*), Op. 56 (1842)*
Symphony no. 5 in D Major (*Reformation*), Op. 107 (1832)

ORGAN MUSIC
Six Sonatas, Op. 65 (1844–45)

PIANO AND ORCHESTRA WORKS

Capriccio brillant in B Minor, Op. 22 (?1825–26)

Concerto no. 2 in D Minor, Op. 40 (1837)

PIANO MUSIC

Rondo capriccioso in E Major, Op. 14 (1824)*

Capriccio in F-sharp Minor, Op. 5 (1825)

Sonata in E Major, Op. 6 (1826)

Seven *Characteristic Pieces*, Op. 7 (1827)*

Sonata in B-flat Major, Op. 106 (1827)

Three Fantasies, Op. 16 (1829)

  No. 2 Scherzo in E Minor*

Fantasy in F-sharp Minor (*Sonate écossaise*), Op. 28 (1833)*

Three *Capriccios*, Op. 33 (1833–35)

Scherzo a capriccio in F-sharp Minor (1835–36)*

Six Preludes and Fugues, Op. 35 (1836)

  No. 1 in E Minor*

Three Études, Op. 104b (1836–38)*

Six *Kinderstücke*, Op. 72 (1842)

VOICE WITH PIANO WORKS

Eighty songs, which include "Auf Flügeln des Gesanges" (On Wings of Song)

FRÉDÉRIC CHOPIN

b. Zelazowa Wola, March 1, 1810

d. Paris, October 17, 1849

I have five lessons to give today. You will imagine that I am making a fortune—but my cabriolet and white gloves cost me more than that, and without them I should not have bon ton.

Chopin was the second of four children born to Nicolas Chopin, a Frenchman who had left France in 1787 at the age of sixteen. Nicolas served as tutor to the children of the Skarbek family (wealthy aristocrats), and he eventually married one of the family's distant relatives, Tekla-Justyna. The young Frédéric's earliest memory was watching peasants dance the mazurka. The child's health was delicate, and he had symptoms of pulmonary problems as a teenager. His sister Emilia died of consumption (tuberculosis) at age thirteen, and the disease was forever on his mind.

At age six, the boy began to study piano in Warsaw with a local violinist, Adabert Zywny. Frédéric adored Zywny, but his teacher was barely proficient on the instrument and often simply looked on in wonder while his young charge improvised. Zywny did introduce the young musician to the music of Bach, the composer who nourished Chopin more than any other.

After one year of study, Frédéric published his first work, a delightful polonaise. When the boy was eight, Warsaw's music lovers gathered to hear his debut. For weeks the city's residents raved about their "Polish Prodigy." The youngster was oblivious to the attention; when his mother, who had missed the concert because of illness, asked him what the audience had liked best, Frédéric replied, "The white collar you gave me, mama!"

When Chopin was twelve, Józef Elsner, a prolific composer and the director of the Warsaw Conservatory, took him on as a private composition student.
Elsner was to be Chopin's only composition teacher, and like Żywny he seldom stressed rules or imposed his will on Chopin. Elsner told him, "What is
true and beautiful must not be imitated but experienced according to its own
individual and superior laws."

Under Elsner's watchful eye, the boy entered the Warsaw Conservatory in
1826. Late in 1827 he completed his elegant variations on Mozart's "Là ci
darem la mano" (Op. 2). When the work was published two years later, twenty-
one-year-old Robert Schumann reviewed it for a Leipzig journal, beginning
with the prophetic phrase, "Hats off, gentlemen, a genius!" Schumann realized
that in Chopin's fastidious art was a revolutionary new concept of piano technique, demanding from the player novel forms of hand coordination. Chopin
himself was modest about his extraordinary innovations; in 1829 he announced
to a friend, "I have written a big Technical Exercise in my own special manner." The Twenty-four Études (Opp. 10 and 25) have since come to rule the
kingdom of piano playing.

While Frédéric was at the conservatory, he fell in love with a young singer,
Konstancia Gladkowska. She had no idea of his feelings, however, and did not return his infatuation. Instead, he poured his heart into his Second Piano Concerto
(Op. 21), which was premiered at the Warsaw National Theater in October 1830
to resounding success. But Warsaw was a provincial capital, and the young composer needed to expand his horizons. He reluctantly left for Vienna on November 2, not realizing that he would never see his beloved country again.

Mere days after Chopin arrived in Vienna, the tragic 1830 Polish uprising
against Russian rule broke out in Warsaw. Anxious and tormented, the young
man longed to be with his family, but friends and letters from home dissuaded
him from returning. Warsaw fell to Russian forces in September 1831. Meanwhile, musical life in Vienna had disappointed Chopin after ten frustrating
months, and he decided to try his luck in Paris instead.

The variety and liberalism in the French capital attracted Chopin immediately; in an early letter, he described the city: "You find here the greatest splendour, the greatest filthiness, the greatest virtue, and the greatest vice—nothing
but cries, noise, din and mud, past anything you can imagine. One disappears
in this swarming confusion and in one respect it's very convenient: no one in-
quires how anyone else manages to live." In the 1830s, Paris, often called "the
modern Athens," attracted the great and the near great in every branch of the
arts. Authors Honoré de Balzac, Victor Hugo, Théophile Gautier, Alfred de
Musset, and George Sand; poets Heinrich Heine and Alphonse de Lamartine;
painter Eugène Delacroix; ballet dancer Marie Taglioni; singers Maria Mali-

bran and Giovanni Rubini; and composers Gioachino Rossini, Daniel Auber, Luigi Cherubini, Charles Alkan, Hector Berlioz, Franz Liszt, Vincenzo Bellini, and Sigismund Thalberg are only a few of those who lived, loved, and flourished there. Moreover, Paris teemed with Polish exiles, including the poet Adam Mickiewicz.

After several discouraging and financially desperate months, in which Chopin barely avoided a severe cholera epidemic, the young Pole made his debut in the small but prestigious hall of the piano firm of Pleyel on February 26, 1832. (At the time, piano firms regularly hosted piano recitals.) Liszt, Mendelssohn, and many other important pianists were there, and all were intoxicated by his ravishing tone and poetic playing. From that moment on, Chopin held a unique place in the crowded pianistic pantheon of his time.

Chopin's exquisite manners and ethereal playing assured him success at Paris's glittering salons, including those hosted by the Baron Rothschild. He now established himself as a piano teacher. Sought-after and well paid, he was soon able to write to his parents, "I have got into the highest of society; I sit with ambassadors, princes, ministers; and I don't even know how it came about, because I did not try for it."

In spite of his good life in Paris, Chopin was not entirely happy, for he missed his parents and homeland desperately. Returning to Warsaw was out of the question, as the Russian authorities might detain him or withhold his passport. In August 1835 he finally managed to see them during a two-week holiday at Karlsbad. It would be the last time. After Karlsbad he continued on to Dresden to meet the aristocratic Wodziński family, whom he had known well in Warsaw. Although Chopin came from a middle-class background, his talent and public appearances allowed him to associate with the cream of Polish society. In Dresden, he fell in love with the sixteen-year-old Countess Maria Wodzińska. She too was smitten, and Chopin proposed marriage. Only days later, Chopin journeyed to Leipzig, where he renewed his friendship with Mendelssohn and met Schumann for the first time. Mendelssohn noted the "enchanting impression" Chopin's playing made on him, "so very masterly that he may be called a really perfect virtuoso." About a second visit, a year later, Schumann would say that "he played a whole number of new Etudes, Nocturnes and Mazurkas—everything incomparably. It fills you with emotion merely to see him sitting at the piano . . . try to conceive such perfection, a mastery which seems unconscious of itself."

Early in 1837, Chopin fell seriously ill, and Warsaw newspapers even announced his death. The reports reached the Wodziński family, and in these reports Maria's father found an excuse to reject the young suitor. But social barriers probably played a larger role in dissolving the romance. Polish countesses did not usually marry out of the nobility, even to Chopin. Chopin preserved Maria's letters, writing on them, "My Sorrow." But she was soon to be replaced in his life by a woman of much greater fascination and importance.

In 1836 Liszt introduced him to George Sand. Chopin saw her again in 1837, upon his return to Paris from his first visit to London. The prim and proper Chopin was at first repelled by the notorious cigar-smoking, trouser-wearing novelist, who had recently terminated a turbulent affair with the poet Alfred de Musset. Nonetheless, Chopin and Sand formed a romantic relationship, and starting in November 1838, the couple and Sand's two children from a previous marriage spent three months at a monastery in Majorca, where Chopin completed his Twenty-four Preludes (Op. 28). Their romantic idyll turned into a nightmare when Chopin's pulmonary problems increased drastically, and he developed a persistent cough. The islanders, who feared the dreaded consumption, avoided him. Chopin wrote to his friend Julian Fontana that he had seen the "three most famous doctors of the island. One sniffed at what I spat up, the second tapped where I spat it from, the third poked about and listened how I spat it. One said I had died, the second that I am dying, the third that I shall die." From that moment, the islanders ostracized the little group, and Chopin's coughing continued.

Chopin and Sand spent nine years together and broke up in May 1847 over family politics. Chopin took sides with Sand's daughter Solange on many matters, thereby undermining Sand's authority over the children. The couple had spent a good portion of each year at the author's country estate, Nohant, where Chopin composed his greatest music. Sand protected and nursed the increasingly consumptive and irritable composer, attending to his every whim. After their separation, he was a broken man. In the final two and a half years of his life, he composed only a few pages of music.

Chopin played his last concert in Paris on February 16, 1848, one week before the revolution that would depose Louis-Philippe, who had ruled France since 1830. Of Chopin's performance, Chopin's biographer Arthur Hedley wrote, "It was surrounded by every circumstance of elegance and distinction; and marked not only the end of his career in Paris but also the close of an epoch in French artistic life . . . the old days were over and the stage was soon to be set for the brash vulgarities of the Second Empire."

In April, to avoid a cholera epidemic as well as the trials of the Revolution, Chopin set out for England. He spent seven months in the British Isles, playing before Queen Victoria and Prince Albert in London and appearing as well in Manchester, Glasgow, and Edinburgh. His concert in London on November 16 was his last public appearance. He returned to Paris in late November, wasted by consumption (he weighed less than ninety pounds).

Throughout 1849, his health worsened, and since he was too weak to teach, he accepted money from a wealthy former pupil. In August his beloved sister Ludwika, whom he had not seen since 1830, managed a trip to Paris. In September, thinking it would revive his spirits, he moved into a gracious apartment on the fashionable Place Vendôme. He died less than six weeks later. Legend says that George Sand paid a last-minute visit to the composer's deathbed, but in fact the visit never occurred. Many tearful friends did visit, though, and shortly before he died, Chopin asked his close friend the Countess Delphine Potocka to sing an aria by his late friend Bellini. It was the last music the greatest of all Polish composers would hear.

Chopin's funeral was a major event, held at the Madeleine Church. Mozart's Requiem, played at Chopin's request, was heard for the first time in Paris since 1821. Chopin was laid to rest in the Père Lachaise Cemetery, where ever since, it is said, not a day has passed without bouquets of flowers being placed on his grave in grateful homage to the beloved composer.

The world loves him as the poet of the piano. The Russian pianist and composer Anton Rubinstein called Chopin "the piano bard, the piano rhapsodist, the piano mind, the piano soul" and declared that "whether the spirit of the instrument breathed upon Chopin or he upon it, I do not know, but tragic, Romantic, lyric, heroic, dramatic, fantastic, soulful, sweet, dreamy, brilliant, grand, simple, all possible expressions are sung by him upon this instrument."

Twenty-four Études, Opp. 10 and 25 (1829–36)

When the études first appeared, the German critic Ludwig Rellstab advised, "Those who have distorted fingers may put them right by practicing these studies; but those who have not, should not play them, at least, not without having a surgeon at hand." Chopin's Twenty-four Études were the culmination of thirty years of étude writing, starting with Johann Cramer in 1801 and continuing through Ignaz Moscheles in 1828. Chopin learned from them all, but turned the prosaic étude (the study of a specific mechanical technical problem) from prose to poetry. His études were not only for practicing in private but for performing on the concert stage as well. Each one concentrates on a particular technical problem such as staccato, or playing on the black keys, or lightness-of-passage work. As such, they form an encyclopedic methodology, a summary of Chopin's enlarged vision of piano technique.

Backhaus: Pearl PEA 9902
Biret: Naxos 8.550364
Pollini: Deutsche Grammophon 431221-2
Ashkenazy: Melodiya 74321-33215-2

The Mazurkas (1830–49)

The sixty mazurkas are one of the great libraries of ethnically inspired art music. Liszt remarked, "To do justice to the mazurkas, one would have to harness a new pianist of the front rank to each of them." These works explore a new harmonic world with many subtleties in contrapuntal treatment. Every kind of light and shade, of gaiety, gloom, eloquence, and passion is to be found in them. The mazurkas are based on the dance's three main forms: *mazur, oberek,* and *kujawiak.* Chopin at times combines different moods and rhythms of the three dances, often using all three. His first mazurkas, Op. 6, announced his unique Slavic genius to the world. The Chopin biographer Jean Kleczijnski writes, "In these first few mazurkas at once appears that national life from which, as from an inexhaustible treasury, Chopin drew his inspirations." The last piece he wrote in 1849 was a mazurka in F minor (Op. 68/4).

Selected Mazurkas
Kapell: RCA 5998-2-RC
Friedman: Pearl 4-PEA 2000

Complete Mazurkas
Rubinstein: RCA 5614-2-RC
Ashkenazy: London 417584-2

Concerto no. 1 in E Minor for Piano and Orchestra, Op. 11 (1830)
Concerto no. 2 in F Minor for Piano and Orchestra, Op. 21 (1829–30)

The first-numbered concerto was actually composed after the second. These concertos, works of a precocious genius, overflow with melody and extraordinary piano figuration. The slow movements are breathtaking poetic effusions; the Rondo finales are Polish in spirit. Of the slow movement of the First Concerto, Chopin, who seldom described his music, wrote, "It is not meant to create a powerful effect, it is rather a Romance, calm and melancholy, giving the impression of someone looking gently towards a spot which calls to mind a thousand happy memories—it is a kind of reverie in the moonlight on a beautiful spring evening."

Concerto no. 1
Kissin, Moscow Philharmonic Orchestra, Kitaienko: RCA 09026-68378-2
Vásáry, Berlin Philharmonic Orchestra, Semkow: Deutsche Grammophon 429515-2
Zimerman, Los Angeles Philharmonic Orchestra, Giulini: Deutsche Grammophon 415970-2

Concerto no. 2

Haskil, Paris Conservatory Orchestra, Kubelik: Disques Montaigne 2-TCE 8780

Moreira Lima, Philharmonia Bulgarica, Manolov: Vivace 3-E322

Rubinstein, Philadelphia Orchestra, Ormandy: RCA 60404-2-RG

The Nocturnes (various dates)

Nocturne is a poetic word for "music of the night." Chopin's are slow, with a lyrical melody imitating the soprano and a left-hand accompaniment usually spanning a large range of the bass. Chopin inherited the species from the Irish composer John Field and proceeded to replace Field's charming naïveté with his own highly chromatic, sultry genius. In these atmospheric works, Chopin let flow the full power of his voluptuous melodic gift. Each is a love poem of the most rarefied ardor. After Chopin, nocturnes became common in nineteenth-century music, from Liszt to Gabriel Fauré. The American composer and critic Daniel Gregory Mason wrote, "Chopin is one of the supreme masters in the coloristic use of the dissonance. His nocturnes may fairly be said to inaugurate by this means a new era in music, comparable in many respects to the era of impressionism in painting."

Complete Nocturnes

Moravec: Elektra/Nonesuch 79233-2

Rubinstein: EMI Classics ZDHB 64491

The Polonaises (various dates)

The polonaise is a stately Polish processional dance. Chopin wrote sixteen of these pieces, all in moderate three-four time, and his seven mature polonaises form a heroic national epic. Their rhythm was for Chopin a means of expressing his most violent and angry emotions concerning his nation's struggle. These are thrilling in their splendor, rancor, and pianistic invention. Schumann called them "cannon buried in flowers," and they have become symbolic and poignant evocations of an oppressed people. The Polonaise in A-flat Major (Op. 53, 1842) is often called the *Heroic*. Its thrilling martial spirit makes it one of the world's most famous pieces of music. Other polonaises of importance are: the Polonaise in E-flat Minor (Op. 26/2), a tragic tone poem; the Polonaise in A Major, known as the *Military* (Op. 40/1), splendid in its pomp and glory, its chivalry and lean muscularity; the Polonaise in F-sharp Minor (Op. 44), a raw and shattering work; and the *Polonaise-Fantaisie* (Op. 61), music of sublime and visionary power.

Polonaises no. 1–7
Pollini: Deutsche Grammophon 413795-2
Rubinstein: RCA Red Seal 5615-2-RC

The Ballades, Opp. 23, 38, 47, 52 (1831–42)

The American critic James Huneker called the G minor ballade "the odyssey of Chopin's soul." The exquisitely poised lyric theme, stated in three different forms, is intoxicating. The second Ballade, in F major, opens with a slow and magical episode, which turns into a tempestuous Presto con fuoco. The Ballade no. 3 in A-flat Major is the essence of charm and warmth, yet a sense of irony surrounds the second subject. The fourth Ballade, in F minor, is Chopin at his most elevated, most exalted. Its richness overflows into a coda that breaks the tonal boundaries of Chopin's epoch.

Complete Ballades
Cortot: Biddulph LHW 001
Zimerman: Deutsche Grammophon 423090-2
Rubinstein: RCA RCD1-7156

Twenty-four Preludes, Op. 28 (1836–39)

Within these very small frames, Chopin captured a universe of feeling and mood. In the Bachian manner, he wrote a prelude for each major and minor key. Some take less than a minute to play, but each is a masterpiece. No composer had ever written such condensed miniatures. Most of them are technically treacherous for the pianist, such as No. 3 with its dangerous left-hand configuration and No. 16 with its perilous right-hand fingerwork. The preludes express a vast array of emotions, from the deepest gloom to perfect serenity. No. 20 was played at Chopin's funeral. The critic Henry T. Finck goes so far as to say, "If all piano music in the world were to be destroyed, excepting one collection, my vote should be cast for Chopin's Preludes . . . most of them are outbreaks of the wildest anguish and heart-rending pathos. If tears could be heard, they would sound like these Preludes."

Complete Preludes
Bolet: RCA 7710-2 RG
Pogorelich: Deutsche Grammophon 429 227-2
Cortot: Music & Arts MUA 871
Cortot: EMI CDH 7610502

The Scherzos, Opp. 20, 31, 39, and 54 (various dates)

Chopin composed four of his greatest creations under the name *scherzo*, a word that means "joke." Was Chopin being ironic? Schumann was baffled when reviewing the B minor scherzo; "How are seriousness and gravity to be clothed if jest is to go about in such dark-colored garments?" he asked. The scherzos are epics among Chopin's works, each of an incomparable instrumental brilliance. The First Scherzo is feverish, almost repellent, a shriek of despair, with the middle section using the Polish Christmas carol "Sleep, Jesus, Sleep." Schumann compared No. 2 in B-flat minor to a poem by Byron, "so overflowing with tenderness, boldness, love, and contempt." No. 3 in C-sharp minor is volcanic, with a D-flat major, choral-like subject, interspersed with a rainbow of delicate falling arpeggios. No. 4 is more scherzolike, an ethereal work, bathed in light that ripples over the expanse of the keyboard. The Trio is of seraphic lyric beauty.

Rubinstein: EMI Classics CDHE 64933
Katsaris: Teldec 9031-74781-2 AW

The Waltzes (various dates)

The nineteen Chopin waltzes are among the world's most-often-played piano music. The English pianist John Ogdon called them "the brightest jewels in the greatest salons of the time." Arthur Hedley felt that "the Chopin waltzes were never meant to be danced by ordinary mundane creatures of flesh and blood," while Berlioz spoke of their "divine delicacies." The D-flat major waltz, called the *Minute*, has been attempted, it would seem, by everyone who has ever played a piano. The waltzes fall into two styles: gracious and brilliantly decorated, or melancholy. One of the best known is the *Grand valse brillante* (Op. 18), one of Chopin's most extroverted works. It is teasing and high-stepping, beloved of the virtuoso.

Fourteen Waltzes
Lipatti: EMI Classics CDH 69222

Complete Waltzes
Magaloff: Philips 426069-2
Anda: RCA Victrola 7744-2-RV

Sonata no. 2 in B-flat Minor, Op. 35 (1839)

The so-called *Funeral March* Sonata is in four movements. The sonata is fever-ish, a life-and-death struggle. The third movement, Marche funèbre, with its haunting middle section, is the world's most famous funeral march. It is fol-lowed by a short and eerie fourth movement, a shudder of grief that Anton Ru-binstein described as "night winds sweeping over church-yard graves." The work possesses grandeur in its conception.

Michelangeli: Praga PR 250042
Cortot: Biddulph LHW 001
Katsaris: Sony Classical SK 48483
Rachmaninoff: RCA 09026-61265-2 (complete Rachmaninoff recordings)

Sonata no. 3 in B Minor, Op. 58 (1844)

In this late masterpiece, Chopin charted new formal and harmonic paths. The opening subject of the first movement is marked *allegro maestoso*, while the second subject must be the most beautiful ever composed within the confines of the sonata form, unraveling in a lengthy Bellinian coloratura. The second movement is a bubbling, virtuosic Scherzo with a cryptic Trio. The third movement, Largo, opens with a funereal introduction leading to one of the composer's most inward meditations, and the fourth movement, a Rondo, is a volcanic conception whose two subjects are worked out on a grand scale. It is a triumph of primordial power releasing immense energy with its relentless surge. Chopin's piano writing became ever more complex and subtle in his later music.

Michelangeli: Praga PR 250042
Lipatti: EMI Classics CDH 63038
Kapell: RCA 5998-2-RC
Ohlsson: Arabesque 6628

Barcarolle in F-sharp Major, Op. 60 (1845–46)

Chopin played this piece for the first time in public at his last recital in Paris in 1848. It displays the Pole's ornamental genius in full bloom. Ravel wrote, "Through his brilliant passages one perceives profound, enchanting harmonies. Always there is the hidden meaning which is translated into poetry of intense despair. . . . The Barcarolle is the synthesis of the expressive and sumptuous art of this great Slav."

Lipatti: EMI Classics CDH 69802
Perlemuter: Nimbus NI 5038
Rubinstein: RCA 5617-2 RC

OTHER PRINCIPAL WORKS

CHAMBER MUSIC
Trio in G Minor for Piano, Violin, and Cello, Op. 8 (1828–29)
Polonaise brillante for Cello and Piano, Op. 3 (1829–30)
Sonata in G Minor for Cello and Piano, Op. 65 (1845–46)*

PIANO AND ORCHESTRA MUSIC
Variations on Mozart's "Là ci darem la mano," Op. 2 (1827)*
Grand Fantasia on Polish Airs, Op. 13 (1828)
Grand Krakowiak (concert rondo), Op. 14 (1828)
Andante spianato and *Grande polonaise brillante*, Op. 22 (1834) (also for piano solo)*

PIANO MUSIC
Rondo *à la Mazur*, Op. 5 (1826)*
Rondo in E-flat major, Op. 16 (1832)*
Variations brillantes, Op. 12 (1833)*
Bolero, Op. 19 (1833)
Four impromptus, Opp. 29, 36, 51, 66 (1835–42)*
Tarantella, Op. 43 (1841)*
Allegro de concert, Op. 46 (1832–41)
Fantasy in F Minor, Op. 49 (1841)*
Trois nouvelles études (1839)*
Berceuse, Op. 57 (1843–44)*

VOICE WITH PIANO MUSIC
Seventeen Songs, Op. 74

ROBERT SCHUMANN

b. Zwickau, Saxony, June 8, 1810

d. Endenich (near Bonn), Germany, July 29, 1856

I am affected by everything that goes on in the world and think it all over in my own way, politics, literature, and people, and then I long to express my feelings and find an outlet for them in music.

Schumann was the youngest of five children of Johanna and August Schumann. His father was a grocer and an unsuccessful novelist, book publisher, and bookseller who died when Robert was sixteen. Robert began his schooling, including piano lessons, at six. Three years later, he heard the great pianist Ignaz Moscheles play at Karlsbad. The performance made an overwhelming impression on him, and Moscheles's piano style is evident in Schumann's early piano works. Robert loved music and literature equally, and from the age of ten he immersed himself in the often-morbid Romantic literature of the day (especially the novels of the German writer Jean Paul). At around age ten he also began dabbling in composition and in poetry writing. He devoted much time to sitting at the piano, dreamily improvising.

Robert's father had encouraged the boy's artistic pursuits, and after he died in 1826, Robert was left with his formidable mother. He loved her deeply, and she objected (on practical grounds) to his pursuing a career in the arts. Frau Schumann held the family purse strings tightly, and she expected her son to become a lawyer. At eighteen he entered the University at Leipzig to study law, but he seldom attended the lectures. In 1830, hearing Paganini play the violin sparked his ambition to become a piano virtuoso, but with his spotty training this seemed impossible. In 1830, however, he began a course of study with the piano teacher Friedrich Wieck, whose prize pupil was his eleven-year-old daughter, Clara, already a famous piano prodigy. Wieck was impressed by Robert's unusual talent and wrote to Frau Schumann, promising her that if her son worked hard, he could become a pianist equal to the best within three years. Frau Schumann gave in reluctantly, and Robert was released from what he called "[c]hilly jurisprudence with its ice cold definitions, which would crush the life out of me."

On October 20, 1830, the aspiring pianist moved into Wieck's home and began to study music full time, learning piano from Wieck and theory from the respected conductor and teacher Heinrich Dorn. Schumann soon found that he had little use for formal theoretical education; he lasted only six months with Dorn. He later declared, characteristically, that he had learned more about counterpoint from reading a Jean Paul novel than from his formal lessons.

Robert was also dissatisfied with his progress at the piano. Wieck would leave Leipzig for months at a time to accompany his daughter on tour. Robert practiced seven hours a day in Wieck's absence, but he was still discouraged. Hoping to make his fourth finger stronger, he impulsively experimented with an apparatus of his own making that held the third finger back so the other fingers could be exercised. The result was disastrous: he was racked with pain and stiffness in his right hand for more than a year, and the hand was permanently damaged. Never again would he play as well, and his ambition to have a virtuoso career was abruptly ended.

Fortunately, Robert had started composing seriously. Since 1830 he had completed his *Abegg Variations* (Op. 1), the *Papillons* for piano (Op. 2), and his Paganini études (Opp. 3 and 10). By the summer of 1833, he was working on a set of *Impromptus on a Theme by Clara Wieck*. Schumann was fond of the girl, who was nearing fourteen, and she was smitten with the idealistic and romantic twenty-three-year-old.

But the impulsive and often reckless Robert had periods of instability, drank heavily, and often feared for his sanity. He had good reason, for others in his family suffered from mental illness. A much-loved older sister killed herself when Robert was fifteen. After leaving the Wiecks' household in October 1833, he received news that his favorite sister-in-law had died, and the wildly disoriented Schumann attempted suicide by throwing himself out of his fourth-floor apartment window. Though Schumann survived the fall, he developed a lifelong dread of living in upper stories. When his brother died in November, his depression grew worse. A momentary reprieve came in December, when Robert became roommates with a twenty-three-year-old pianist and composer of great gifts, Ludwig Schunke. The two became deeply attached—in Schu-

mann's words, they were "living out a novel the likes of which may never before have been put into a book." Schumann dedicated his great Toccata in
C Major for Piano (Op. 7, completed in 1833) to Schunke, who played it magnificently. A year later Schunke died of tuberculosis, leaving Schumann in despair. But at this time, Schumann became engaged to the beautiful
eighteen-year-old Ernestine von Fricken. "She has a delightfully pure, childlike mind," he wrote to his mother; "she is delicate and thoughtful, deeply attached to me and everything artistic, and uncommonly musical." But the
relationship fizzled out within a year.

Fortunately, Schumann's genius was boiling, in spite of these setbacks in his
personal life. In 1833–35 he composed *Carnaval* (Op. 9), which contained
many portraits of friends, including Ernestine and the fifteen-year-old Clara, as
well as a double portrait of the two sides of Schumann's own personality, the
fiery "Florestan" and the dreamy "Eusebius." The year 1834 was an auspicious
one, in fact, for he also became editor of the *Neue Zeitschrift für Musik*, a bi-
weekly journal of criticism that would prove an ideal format for articulating his
vibrant thoughts on the music of his time. Through 1835, Robert's relationship
with Clara Wieck ripened, and the two stole their first kiss on November 25.

By 1836 Clara's father was becoming uneasy about the girl's infatuation
with Robert. Though Wieck admired Robert's talent, he also considered him
(not without reason) to be a raving lunatic, and he was not about to let his
jewel, whom he had polished and cultivated, fall into the hands of such a man.
Wieck sent the seventeen-year-old girl to Dresden, broke off all relations with
his former student, and forbade Clara to contact him once she returned to
Leipzig. But Clara, whose filial love, respect, and devotion were compelling,
was madly in love with "her Robert." The lovers endured long separations, for
Wieck kept his daughter on concert tours for as long as seven months at a time,
and wrote to each other secretly, through an intermediary.

Schumann's love for Clara inspired some of his greatest music. Of the Fantasy in C Major for Piano (Op. 17, 1836–38), he told her, "I think the first
movement is more impassioned than anything I have ever written—it is a deep
lament for you." After he composed the *Davidsbündlertänze* for piano (Op. 6,
1837), the composer wrote on the title page, "Delight is linked with pain for
ever and ever." And upon completing the *Kreisleriana* (Op. 16, 1838), he
wrote, "You'll smile when you discover yourself there."

Marriage was out of the question: Clara was still underage and by German
law could not marry without her father's consent. Schumann took legal action
to force Wieck to consent to the marriage, and the whole affair blew up into an
awful court battle, with Wieck charging Robert with everything from financial
irresponsibility to alcoholism. Mendelssohn, Liszt, and other friends were wit-

nesses on behalf of Schumann. Clara remained in the middle, naturally ambivalent, for she had always loved her father and was deeply grateful for her pianistic training. Robert was shocked at Wieck's continuous defamation of his character. To make matters worse, his brother Eduard, to whom he had been very close, died. Obsessed by visions of coffins and funerals, Schumann felt he would never win his lady love. Finally, after nearly a year of wavering and agonized waiting, the court sanctioned the marriage. The couple entered matrimony on September 12, 1840, one day before Clara's twenty-first birthday.

For Schumann, 1840 was a year of song. For the ten previous years, he had given his heart and mind to composing for the piano. Now he combined his beloved piano with the poetry he also loved. He wrote no fewer than 140 songs that year, in the greatest creative eruption of song since Schubert.

All was not easy, however. In the following thirteen years, Clara would be pregnant ten times. Each time Robert completed a composition, he struggled with heavy depression, and he often resorted to heavy drinking. The couple had only one piano, and Clara bowed to what she considered Robert's superior creative gift and let his composing take precedence. Clara, one of the great pianists of the time, found this horribly depressing. "Every time Robert composes," she wrote, "my piano playing must be set aside completely. Not a single tiny hour can be found for me all day! If only I don't regress too much." The constant pregnancies left her frustrated and debilitated, and she desperately missed the concert stage as well as the large fees that she could have been earning. In 1844 Clara persuaded her husband to accompany her on a lucrative four-month Russian tour. At a reception, he was asked if he too was a musician. A part of him resented her career and her fame.

In 1850, at age forty, Schumann was prematurely old and often depressed, intolerably withdrawn, and morose. He now attempted to take up his first official position, as conductor of the Düsseldorf Orchestra. But he was a poor conductor and was embarrassed by his dismissal two years later. By 1852 Robert's decline was obvious, and Clara was deeply concerned that the world was seeing her husband as mentally deranged. Robert's condition put tremendous strains on the marriage, though Clara was always loyal and as loving as possible to a man who might not utter a word for days at a time.

On a cold and rainy morning, February 27, 1854, Schumann quietly slipped out of the house while Clara was away and threw himself into the icy Rhine. Fishermen pulled him out, but he fought them desperately. For two weeks he had been living in a psychotic state, one minute hearing divine music, the next feeling that he was being attacked by tigers and hyenas. Schumann begged to be sent to a mental hospital. At first Clara resisted: "He, my glorious Robert, in an asylum! How could I possibly stand it?" But finally she

agreed that he should seek treatment at Endenich, a lunatic asylum outside
Bonn. Schumann left behind six surviving children and another son, Felix
(named after Mendelssohn), soon to be born. He would never see them again,
for he lived only another two and a half years in the asylum. His doctors considered him dangerous and would not let Clara see him until the day before he
died of self-starvation.

Clara wrote, "I stood by the body of my passionately loved husband, and
was calm. All my feelings were absorbed in thankfulness to God that he was at
last set free, and as I kneeled by his bed I was filled with awe. It was as if his
holy spirit was hovering over me—Ah! If only he had taken me with him."
Clara, at thirty-six, was left with a large family to support. She would outlive her
husband by forty-one years, performing his music throughout Europe as one of
the most influential pianists of the nineteenth century.

Schumann, who fought valiantly for many years against insanity, is the most
elusive of the Romantic composers. He is tender, fanciful, autobiographical,
perverse, and daringly original; he has a unique, at times compulsive rhythmic
energy. His harmonic language is as rich as his fragmented, interlaced melody,
woven in a dense, complicated tapestry. No other music ever sounded like
his—it even looked different on the printed page. He invented the Romantic
piano suite, the tying together of smaller musical units into a large form, as in
his *Carnaval*. His biographer Joan Chissell remarked, "His temperament, so
finely attuned to the remoter ways of human experience, had little difficulty in
accepting the mystical and supernatural." In Schumann's music there is something deeply personal. The Norwegian composer Edvard Grieg once exclaimed to an acquaintance, "You love Schumann! Then we are friends." The
French philosopher Roland Barthes once wrote, "Schumann is truly the musician of solitary intimacy, of the amorous and imprisoned soul that *speaks to itself* . . . of the child who has no other link than to the mother. . . . Schumann's
music goes much farther than the ear, it goes into the body, into the muscles."

Schumann has been called the most romantic of the Romantics. His music
formed the springtime of German Romanticism and is among the supreme
manifestations of the Romantic spirit in any art form.

Carnaval for Piano, Op. 9 (1833–35)

Carnaval is subtitled *Scènes mignonnes sur quatre notes* ("small scenes on four
notes"). The four notes are A, E-flat, C, and B, and in German (A, Es, C, and
H) they spell out the name of Ernestine von Fricken's native town, Asch. *Carnaval*, completed in 1835, is Schumann's most frequently played large work.

The richness of its material and its pulsating life make it one of the great half-hours of human fantasy. *Carnaval* is composed of twenty-one pieces; it tells the story of a carnaval where Schumann meets Pierrot, Pantalon and Columbine, Harlequin, Chiarina (Clara), Paganini, Chopin, and others. In the great orgiastic ballroom scene, Schumann reveals his secrets to his assembled friends and lovers. The critic Gary Lemco writes, "Culturally speaking, it was Schumann who, in his piano suite *Carnaval*, gave musical form, in a series of related, anagrammatical, miniature character sketches, to the opposition between the 'artist' and the 'Philistine' as they were conceived by the Romantic sensibility."

Cortot: Biddulph LHW 004
Rubinstein: RCA 5667-2-RC
Arrau: Pearl PEA 9928
Solomon: Testament SBT 1084
Rachmaninoff: RCA 09026-61265-2 (complete Rachmaninoff recordings)

Symphonic Études for Piano, Op. 13 (1834–37)

These piano études, also called by Schumann "*Études en forme de variations*," are based on a theme of great elegiac beauty by Baron von Fricken, an amateur flutist and the father of Schumann's first fiancée. Études no. 3 and 9 and the finale are not derived from the theme; the finale, a regal march, is based on a theme from Heinrich Marschner's 1829 opera *Der Templer und die Jüdin*. Robert warned Clara not to play the whole work in public because of its more than half-hour length. Indeed, he suppressed five variations, which were published posthumously and which are now often included by contemporary pianists. Although Schumann's instinct was to pare down the work for the overall good of the structure, the material of these additional études is of such astounding beauty that not to include them all is to deprive the listener of the fullness of Schumann's treatment. The work is dedicated to the fine English pianist and composer William Sterndale Bennett, who was the first to perform them in England.

Kissin: RCA 60443-2-RC
Cortot: Biddulph LHW 004
Pogorelich: Deutsche Grammophon 410520-2

Fantasy in C Major for Piano, Op. 17 (1836–38)

The Fantasy is dedicated to Liszt, who nearly twenty years later dedicated his B minor sonata to Schumann (who was by that time unable to appreciate the gift). Schumann intended the composition as a tribute to Beethoven and considered calling it *Ruins, Triumphal Arch, Constellation*, but eventually he decided against it. In its constant thematic and tonal ambiguity, the work has little to do with Beethoven's art, but at the end of the first movement Schumann quotes the last song from Beethoven's song cycle *An die ferne Geliebte*. (The opening words are "Take these songs then, my love, that I sang.") For Clara and Robert, Beethoven had special significance, and the Beethoven song was a symbolic link for their love. Schumann's passion boils in the long first movement. The exuberant second movement is a march of vast proportions, ending in a coda of powerful chords and great keyboard leaps. The writer William Newman thought that in performance "one can take a transcendental approach; one can throw oneself into the laps of the gods while gambling on superhuman effort." The finale, an unexpected slow movement, is one of the most heavenly meditations in music. The pianist Harold Bauer wrote, "It would be hard to point to any composition in the entire literature of the piano wherein an expression of intense personal feeling is projected with such compelling and vivid power." On the title page, Schumann appended lines from the poet Friedrich von Schlegel: "Through all the tones of Earth's many-hued dream, one soft-drawn note may be heard by him who listens in secret."

Argerich: Exclusive EXL 48
Horowitz: CBS 3-M3K 44681
Richter (1957): Multisonic 31 0193

Fantasiestücke for Piano, Op. 12 (1837)

Fantasiestücke, one of Schumann's most popular collections, consists of eight piano pieces. In No. 1, "Des Abends" (In the Evening), Schumann lulls us on a fragrant spring evening. No. 2, "Aufschwung" (Soaring), is full of passionate optimism. No. 3, "Warum?" (Why?), is one of his most poetic pieces. In No. 4, "Grillen" (Whims), the tempo marking says "with humor," but it is a humor uniquely Schumann's. No. 5, "In der Nacht" (In the Night), is hauntingly feverish — Schumann fancifully told Clara that it contains the story of Hero and Leander. No. 6, "Fabel" (Fable), is a whimsical tale. No. 7, "Traumes Wirren" (Dream Visions), is the product of a joyous dream. And about No. 8, "Ende vom Lied" (Song's End), Schumann wrote to Clara, "[A]t the close my painful anxiety about you returned, so that it sounds like wedding- and funeral-bells commingled."

Rubinstein: RCA 5667-2-RC
Argerich: EMI Classics CDM 63576
Perahia: CBS MK 32299

Kinderszenen (*Scenes of Childhood*) for Piano, Op. 15 (1838)

Since their creation, these thirteen piano pieces have been favorites of professionals and amateurs alike. No. 7, "Träumerei" (Dreaming), is one of the all-time favorite melodies. The composer Alban Berg once analyzed the piece to show how complex the polyphony of this work actually is. Schumann wrote to Clara that these scenes are "peaceful, tender and happy, like our future. . . . You will enjoy them; but of course you have to forget that you are a virtuoso." Each piece is touched with refinement and tenderness and shows the restraint of which Schumann was capable in his youth.

Moravec: Elektra/Nonesuch 79063-4
Horowitz: CBS MK 42409
Haskil: Music & Arts CD 542

Kreisleriana for Piano, Op. 16 (1838)

These eight untitled piano fantasies, which take thirty-five minutes to play, are dedicated to Chopin, who abhorred Schumann's music as too bizarre and disorganized. Chopin, however, returned the gift by dedicating his Ballade in F Major to Schumann. Johannes Kreisler is a character in a story by E.T.A. Hoffmann, one of the most influential early Romantic writers. In the story, Kreisler is a wild, clever, and eccentric conductor. Schumann identified with him (as did Brahms). The *Kreisleriana* may seem a bewildering maze of fragments and textures. After Schumann completed it (and the work totally drained him), he told Clara, "My music now seems to me so wonderfully complicated, for all its simplicity, so eloquent and from the heart." *Kriesleriana* is the composer's most hallucinatory composition, and it vibrates with disturbing and mysterious chords. Here are the composer's darker aspects, yet Schumann combines them as only he can, with a rare childlike innocence. To Clara he beseeched, "Play my *Kriesleriana* once in a while. In some passages there is to be found an utterly wild love and your life and mine." The work is one of the great touchstones for the poet-pianist.

Argerich: Deutsche Grammophon 410653-2
Horowitz: Deutsche Grammophon 419217-2
Gieseking: Forlane FOR 16590

The Songs (1840)

For the thirty-year-old Schumann, the true beginning of life was his marriage to Clara Wieck. His genius now blazed in the wedding of poetry to music, and he became Schubert's true successor as a master composer of songs. (He was a fitting successor, for when the eighteen-year-old Schumann heard of Schubert's death, he wept through the night.) Schumann's feeling for and comprehension of a poetic text is always a marvel of acute sympathy. In these songs, the piano and voice are inextricably married. Speaking of the songs, Clara flirtatiously asked, "Isn't there perhaps a young nightingale inflaming you?" To which he replied, "I was completely inside you while composing them. You, romantic girl, following me everywhere with your eyes, and I often think that without such a bride one cannot make such music." Such songs as "Widmung," "Die beiden Grenadiere," "Frühlingsnacht," "Du bist wie eine Blume," "Der Nussbaum," and a profusion of others are world famous.

Many of the individually famous songs fall within song cycles or sets such as *Liederkreis* (Op. 39), *Myrthen* (Op. 25), and *Frauenliebe und -leben* (Op. 42). One of the very greatest cycles of all time is the *Dichterliebe* (Op. 48), sixteen powerful settings to Heine. In *Dichterliebe*, the piano at times breaks into heartbreaking sobs, and in fact the ending of the tragic cycle finds Schumann ruminating at length with his piano, singing alone.

Dichterliebe
Fischer-Dieskau, Brendel: Philips 416352-2
Wunderlich, Giesen: Deutsche Grammophon 429933-2

Frauenliebe und -leben
Norman, Gage: Philips 420784-2
DeGaetani, Luvisi: Bridge BCD 9025

Quintet in E-flat Major for Piano and Strings, Op. 44 (1842)

The Quintet, dedicated to Clara, is the greatest of Schumann's many chamber scores—which says much, as the E-flat major piano quartet and D minor trio, for example, are work of high quality. The first movement spurts fire in its

rhythmic verve. The contrasting second theme is a radiant duet for cello and viola. The second movement, in the style of a march, plunges the listener into a
melancholy vortex. The third movement, a Scherzo, has two contrasting trios.
The great finale—a double fugue of amazing design in a contrapuntal flight of
fancy—shows Schumann's ever-growing admiration for Bach.

Budapest Quartet, Serkin: CBS MYK 37256
Pro Arte Quartet, Schnabel: Arabesque Z 6613
Beaux Arts Trio, Bettelheim, Rhodes: Philips 420791-2

Concerto in A Minor for Piano and Orchestra, Op. 54 (1841–45)

The A minor piano concerto is one of the classics of the concerto form. It is lucid, mellow, serene, and joyous, with far less of the mental turmoil evident in
the earlier piano cycles. I would have liked to have attended its first performance at Leipzig on January 1, 1846, with Clara Schumann as soloist and
Mendelssohn conducting. The opening begins with a cascade of descending
chords, which Grieg imitated in his own A minor concerto. The plaintive
opening theme starts with the nasal sound of the oboe and is taken up by
the piano in dialogue. Another, more agitated theme gives depth to the movement that concludes with a penetrating cadenza. The second movement, titled
Intermezzo, is of a gossamer and gracious intimacy, even playful in tone and
transparent in orchestration. The finale opens with a reminiscence of the first-
movement theme, then continues with rhythmically joyous material presenting
the brilliant passagework for the soloist.

Frager, Royal Philharmonic Orchestra, Horenstein: Chesky CD52
Cliburn, Chicago Symphony Orchestra, Reiner: RCA 60420-2-RG
Katchen, Israel Philharmonic Orchestra, Kertész: IMP Collectors Series IMPX 9041

Concerto in A Minor for Cello and Orchestra, Op. 129 (1850)

The Cello Concerto, one of the great works of Schumann's declining years,
was composed in a flurry of creative activity in a mere fifteen days. The score is
humorous and fresh, with melody abounding. The composer interweaves
the cello and orchestral fabric with resounding effectiveness. Schumann
appears young again. The concerto's three movements are played without interruption.

Du Pré, New Philharmonia Orchestra, Barenboim: EMI Classics CDM 64626
Ma, Bavarian Radio Symphony Orchestra, C. Davis: CBS MK 42663
Rose, New York Philharmonic Orchestra, Bernstein: Sony Classical SMK 47609

Manfred Overture, Op. 115 (1848–49)

In Schumann's day, Byron's Romanticism and spirit of revolt captured the hearts of European artists. Schumann had long been enthralled with Byron's 1817 *Manfred*; he broke down with emotion when reading it out loud. He composed the overture in the revolutionary year of 1848 and called it "one of the finest of my brain-children." The score opens slowly, eventually beating with passionate yearning and high-pitched, almost savage intensity.

NBC Symphony Orchestra, Toscanini: RCA Gold Seal 09026-60292-2
Bavarian Radio Symphony Orchestra, Kubelik: Sony Classical SBK 48270

The Four Symphonies
Symphony no. 1 in B-flat Major (*Spring*), Op. 38 (1841)
Symphony no. 2 in C Major, Op. 61 (1845–46)
Symphony no. 3 in E-flat Major (*Rhenish*), Op. 97 (1850)
Symphony no. 4 in D Minor, Op. 120 (1841–51)

Schumann's symphonies have a certain thick awkwardness in the orchestration, so different from the gracious, lucid and meticulous Mendelssohn symphonies, which he admired. They are nevertheless masterworks, indispensable in the history of Romanticism, overflowing with love, torment, and aspiration. After his great song year of 1840, Schumann was intent on conquering the formal symphony. He wrote ecstatically to a friend, "I have completed, at least in outline, a labor which has kept me in a state of bliss, but also exhausted me. Think of it! A whole symphony—moreover, a Spring Symphony! I can hardly believe it myself, that it is finished."

The *Spring* Symphony was written during the winter, but it was the winter when Schumann was flush with the springtime of his marriage to Clara. To the violinist Louis Spohr, he wrote of "the spirit of spring, which seems to possess us all anew every year, irrespective of age." Before the symphony was presented in Berlin, he beseeched the conductor to "breathe into your orchestra, as it plays, some Spring yearning."

The Second Symphony was finished in October 1846 and was immediately performed by the Leipzig Gewandhaus Orchestra, with Mendelssohn conducting. Shortly after Schumann finished it, he described his new work to a visitor: "Yes, indeed, I think it's a regular *Jupiter*." Perhaps the most wonderful movement is the third, an Adagio expressivo of exquisite pathos.

The Symphony no. 3 is the mighty *Rhenish* in five movements, a joyous picture of the Rhenish landscape. On the manuscript of the fourth movement, the composer wrote, "In the character of the accompaniment to a solemn ceremony" and then crossed it out. Schumann, like Goethe before him, was awed by the Romantic architecture of the still-unfinished cathedral at Cologne and once sat through a religious ceremony there with tears streaming from his eyes.

The Fourth Symphony was completed right after No. 1, but after hearing a performance, Schumann was unsatisfied. Ten years later he completely revised it. The D minor symphony in four movements, played without pause, is leaner and more pensive than its companions and breathes its Romanticism with an almost wistful feeling of farewell in the Romanza second movement. The critic Philip Hale wrote, "I know of few more haunting pages in orchestral music than those of the trio in the *scherzo*."

Symphony no. 1
Cleveland Orchestra, Szell: CBS MYK 38468
London Philharmonic Orchestra, Masur: Teldec 2292-46445-2

Symphony no. 2
Baltimore Symphony Orchestra, Zinman: Telarc CD 80182
Berlin Philharmonic Orchestra, Levine: Deutsche Grammophon 423625-2

Symphony no. 3
Detroit Symphony Orchestra, Paray: Mercury 462955
Cleveland Orchestra, C. von Dohnányi: London 421643-2

Symphony no. 4
Boston Symphony Orchestra, Leinsdorf: RCA Victor 09026-61855-2
Vienna Philharmonic Orchestra, Bernstein: Deutsche Grammophon 415274-2

OTHER PRINCIPAL WORKS

CHAMBER MUSIC
Three Quartets for Strings, Op. 41 (1842)
Quartet in E-flat Major for Piano and Strings, Op. 47 (1842)*

Phantasiestücke for Piano, Violin, and Cello, Op. 88 (1842)

Trio no. 1 in D Minor for Piano, Violin, and Cello, Op. 63 (1847)*

Trio no. 2 in F Major for Piano, Violin, and Cello, Op. 80 (1847)

Sonata no. 1 in A Minor for Violin and Piano, Op. 105 (1851)

Trio no. 3 in G Minor for Piano, Violin, and Cello, Op. 110 (1851)

CHORAL WORKS WITH ORCHESTRA

Das Paradies und die Peri, Op. 50 (1843)*

Requiem für Mignon, Op. 98b (1849)

OPERAS

Genoveva, Op. 81 (1847–49)*

ORCHESTRAL WORKS

Julius Caesar Overture, Op. 128 (1851)

Overture, Scherzo, and Finale in E Minor, Op. 52 (1841–48)*

PIANO MUSIC

Abegg Variations, Op. 1 (1829–30)*

Papillons, Op. 2 (1829–31)*

Intermezzi, Op. 4 (1832)*

Davidsbündlertänze, Op. 6 (1837)*

Toccata in C Major, Op. 7 (1829–33)*

Sonata no. 1 in F-sharp Minor, Op. 11 (1832–35)*

Sonata no. 3 in F Minor, Op. 14 (1835–36)*

Arabeske, Op. 18 (1838)*

Humoreske, Op. 20 (1838)*

Novelletten, Op. 21 (1838)*

Sonata no. 2 in G Minor, Op. 22 (1833–38)*

Faschingsschwank aus Wien, Op. 26 (1839–40)*

Album für die Jugend, Op. 68 (1848)*

Waldscenen, Op. 82 (1848–49)*

SOLO INSTRUMENT AND ORCHESTRA WORKS

Conzertstück for Four Horns and Orchestra, Op. 86 (1849)

Introduction and Allegro appassionato for Piano and Orchestra (*Conzertstück*), Op. 92
   (1849)

Introduction and Allegro for Piano and Orchestra, Op. 134 (1853)

Concerto in D Minor for Violin and Orchestra (1853)

FRANZ LISZT

b. Raiding, Hungary, October 22, 1811

d. Bayreuth, Germany, July 31, 1886

Oh, believe me, I beseech you, we must kill the hateful ego within ourselves; and then divine mercy and its truth will shine once again within us when we ask HIM to "forgive us our trespasses as we forgive those who trespass against us. . . ." There are moral sufferings which call for more radical treatment than physical illness. To swerve off course at the key point means losing all.

On the nights before and after Liszt's birth in rural Hungary, a great comet streaked through the sky. The villagers said it was a good omen, that the infant son of Anna and Adam Liszt would have an important place in the world. Anna was a quiet and practical woman. Her husband, a steward on the estates of the Esterházy, the richest family in Hungary, was the musical one; he played the piano and had met Haydn and Hummel. Franz was a sickly child whose life hung in the balance more than once. But between bouts of ill health, he showed an intense interest in music. By Franz's fifth year, Adam knew that his son possessed much more than talent, and he struggled to teach the boy all he could.

After Franz had performed in several places, a few aristocrats pooled together to send Franz and Adam to Vienna. The boy was fortunate enough to have Beethoven's noted pupil Carl Czerny teach him piano, and he studied theory and composition with Salieri. Neither teacher would accept payment, and they quickly spread the word that the charming and beautiful boy was a phenomenal prodigy. Czerny even convinced Beethoven, no lover of prodigies, to meet Franz and hear him play. The boy captivated the great composer, who supposedly told Franz that he would bring much joy to the world.

Franz's eighteen months of lessons with Czerny were the only professional piano instruction he received in his life. Afterward Adam exploited his wonder child: for the next few years the youngster performed continuously, conquering audiences on the Continent and in England. He also began to compose, and his only opera, *Don Sanche,* was heard in Paris (by then the family's home) in 1825. In 1827, after Franz gave a concert at Boulogne, Adam died suddenly of appendicitis. The sixteen-year-old was bereft—his father had been his only companion, guide, and manager. Back in Paris, he went through a deep personal crisis. From his earliest remembrances, the young Liszt had been a soul divided. Music was his life, but he was also deeply attracted to teachings of the Catholic Church. He read hungrily about the lives of the saints; to live the life of a martyr was his ideal. After Adam's death, the boy became disgusted by his life as a circus animal, and he withdrew from society. For some time, Parisians thought their *"petit* Liszt" was dead.

Franz gave piano lessons in order to support himself and his mother, but he spent most of his time praying in church. At eighteen he fell in love with his aristocratic sixteen-year-old student Caroline de Saint-Cricq. Her father, upon discovering their attachment, took immediate action to destroy the budding romance. For Liszt the loss was cataclysmic, and he languished in isolation.

The July Revolution of 1830, which ended the oppressive reign of Charles X and brought the bourgeois king Louis-Philippe to the throne, jolted Franz's sensibilities. Paris was breathing the spirit of Romanticism and freedom of expression. The entire artistic world, it seemed, flocked into the French capital, and Franz soon sketched A *Revolutionary Symphony,* though it was never completed. In March 1831, Paganini arrived for a series of concerts, and his violin playing was a revelation for Liszt. In listening to Paganini's technique, Liszt realized there was no pianist comparable to Paganini as a violinist. The new Romantic music would be of an unprecedented virtuosity and complexity of textures, supported by improvements in the piano.

Liszt stood on the brink of a new era in art, and the enlarged middle-class ticket-buying public waited breathlessly for him. He spent two grueling years practicing and experimenting. He transcribed Paganini's caprices, unlocking the great violinist's secrets. Intoxicated with his newfound power, he declared, "My mind and fingers have been working like two lost spirits—Homer, the Bible, Plato, Locke, Byron, Hugo, Lamartine, Chateaubriand, Beethoven, Bach, Hummel, Mozart, Weber are all around me. I study them, meditate upon them, devour them with fury. Besides this, I practice from four to five hours of exercises, thirds, sixths, octaves, tremolos, repetition of notes, cadenzas, scales, etc. Ah! provided I don't go mad you will find an artist such as you desire, *such as is now required.*"

The presence in Paris of other young musicians inspired him too. When he heard Berlioz conduct his epoch-making *Symphonie fantastique*, the work took Liszt by storm. The two became fast friends and read Goethe's *Faust* together as Liszt transcribed Berlioz's *Fantastic Symphony* for piano. The admiration was mutual, and Berlioz soon declared that "Liszt is the pianist of the future."

Chopin, who arrived in Paris in the autumn of 1831, was another major stimulus for Liszt, who was ravished by Chopin's playing as well as by the poetic passion and refinement of his music. He immediately learned Chopin's études, causing Chopin to write to another pianist, "I write to you without knowing what my pen is scribbling, because at this moment Liszt is playing my études, and transporting me outside of my respectable thoughts. I should like to steal from him the way to play my own études." How fitting that Chopin dedicated his first Twelve Études (Op. 10, published in 1833) to *"mon ami, Franz Liszt."*

Contemporary reports of Liszt's interpretive gifts, virtuosity, sight-reading, and learning abilities border on the incredible. Mendelssohn reported, "I've just witnessed a *miracle*! I was with Liszt at Érard's [a piano firm], and I showed him the manuscript of my concerto. He played it at sight—it's hardly legible—and with the utmost perfection. It simply can't be played any better than he played it. It was miraculous."

In 1833 Liszt met the hypnotically beautiful and cultivated Countess Marie d'Agoult, who was five years older and married with children. Their attraction was immediate and violent. Their elopement in 1835 rocked Paris; married noblewomen did not leave their exalted stations to wander through Switzerland and Italy with semi-impoverished pianists. In Italy their three children were born in quick succession; the middle child, Cosima, would become Wagner's second wife. Throughout this time, Liszt played in public very little but was busy composing what would become his great piano cycle, *Années de pèlinerage (Years of Pilgrimage).*

While in Venice in the spring of 1838, Liszt read that disastrous Danube floods were wreaking havoc in Hungary, his almost-forgotten homeland. The crisis brought Liszt back to the concert stage: between April 18 and May 25, he gave eleven charity concerts in Vienna. The entire proceeds were donated to the flood victims. The concerts were an unprecedented sensation and marked a turning point for Liszt's divided soul. No longer could he suppress his need to perform in public—nor would the world resist hearing him. When Liszt reemerged on the concert stage, the modern concert pianist was born. Wherever he appeared, "Lisztomania" erupted. At Milan in 1839, he performed the first solo piano recital, inaugurating the practice and even coining the term. Piano concerts up to that point had always been mixed affairs, with other instrumentalists and singers. Liszt needed only the piano; exhilarated, he proclaimed, *"Le concert, c'est moi."*

For the next eight years, he toured Europe relentlessly, to acclaim never before enjoyed by any performer, including Paganini. Liszt's was the first truly modern concert career. During these "years of splendor," Liszt broke with the countess, after nine years. In February 1847, he played his last public recitals in Odessa and Elisavetgrad in Russia. The thirty-six-year-old pianist had once again tired of the stage, and he longed to retire, to settle down and compose. The fissure in his soul had widened again, especially after he met his new lover, Princess Carolyne Sayn-Wittgenstein, in Russia. The princess, a fervent Catholic, revived Liszt's dormant religious feelings. She left her husband, a wealthy Russian landowner, and went to live with Liszt in sleepy Weimar, where Liszt became court *Kapellmeister*. Through his baton, he made Weimar into the most musically progressive town in the world of music. He renewed the glorious cultural past of the city, when Goethe and Schiller had lived and worked there.

During his Weimar years, from 1848 to 1861, Liszt composed as in a torrent. Besides a plethora of major piano works, including the B minor piano sonata (S.178, 1852–53), he wrote his thirteen symphonic poems and the *Dante* and *Faust* Symphonies (S.108 and 109, both 1857). His celebrated "master's classes" attracted a constant stream of amazing pianists, all inspired by his example. But this idyllic period ended in 1858, after Liszt conducted the unsuccessful premiere of his disciple Peter Cornelius's opera *Der Barbier von Bagdad* (*The Barber of Baghdad*). Afterward various political tensions erupted and Liszt resigned his position.

At this point Liszt began yet another chapter in his life. His long-projected marriage to the princess was prevented for good when the pope refused to annul her first marriage. In 1859 Liszt's son Daniel died at twenty, and in 1862 his daughter Blandine died at twenty-six. Although the children had lived with their mother, the countess, and he saw them little, he always supported them, wrote them frequently, and was a potent influence on them. More than ever he became immersed in religion and composed a quantity of music for the Church. In 1865 he took several orders of the Church and moved into rooms at the Vatican as the Abbé Liszt.

For the remainder of his life, Liszt divided his time among Rome, Weimar, and Budapest, where as Hungary's most famous personality he helped set Budapest's musical life on solid ground. His health failed in his later years; cataracts deprived him of the ability to read. In 1886 he died of pneumonia at

Bayreuth, where he had gone to see a performance of his late son-in-law Wagner's *Tristan und Isolde*. Once when asked why he had not written an autobiography, as had Wagner, he responded, "It is enough to have lived such a life as mine."

During his life, Liszt became the very symbol of the concert pianist. He was most likely the greatest executant artist the world has known. As teacher, conductor, and composer, his influence was monumental. Nineteenth-century Europeans craved idols, and Liszt gave them a bewildering variety of images to worship: the adorable child prodigy, then the irresistible Don Juan, and still later the abbé, half saint, half Mephisto. For much of his long career, he was the epitome of flaming Romanticism, the very personification of pianistic virtuosity. Even in old age, looking for all the world like an aged Apache chieftain, his magnetism never failed to enthrall.

Never before or since did so many important pianists surround a teacher. From Hans von Bülow and Carl Tausig to Arthur Friedheim, Moriz Rosenthal, Alexander Siloti, and Eugen d'Albert, pianists of every nation nurtured themselves through him. For his master classes, he never charged a penny; his motto was *"Génie oblige."* One student wrote, "He was literally like a sun in our midst." Moriz Rosenthal said, "He played as no one before him, and as no one probably will ever again." And Alfred Reisenauer wrote, "Never have I met a man in any position whom I have no doubt would have proved the inferior of Franz Liszt. . . . Liszt's personality can only be expressed by one word, 'colossal.' "

As a composer, Liszt was known for years chiefly for a few ubiquitous works. The Italian composer and pianist Ferruccio Busoni was one of the first to understand Liszt's magnitude as a composer: "We are all descended from him radically," he wrote, "without excepting Wagner, and we owe to him the lesser things that we can do. César Franck, Richard Strauss, Debussy, the penultimate Russians, all are branches of his tree."

For the present-day music lover, Liszt presents a treasure of unexplored music. His transcriptions of other composers' works to the piano, once anathema to the purist, are again being enjoyed. Indeed, the ability to make such translations is an art form of its own. The critic George Steiner writes, "Liszt's transcriptions for piano from Italian opera, from classical symphonies, from the compositions of his contemporaries, notably Wagner, go a long way to suggest that Liszt's was the foremost critical (if not self-critical) tact in the history of Western music. Together, these transcriptions make up a syllabus of enacted criticism."

The nineteen *Hungarian Rhapsodies* (S.244, 1846–85) are an important compendium of Gypsy material. The *Faust Symphony* and *Mephisto Waltzes* display a daring, diabolically mocking, and ironic spirit. The Twelve Transcendental Études (S.139, 1851) are at the zenith of muscular piano writing. The oratorios and other religious music are uneven; often theatrical but also simple, direct, and humble, they show yet another side of their bewildering creator. Liszt's music describes the world of poetry from Dante, Petrarch, and Torquato Tasso to Johann Wolfgang von Goethe, Lord Byron, Victor Hugo, and Alphonse de Lamartine. He painted in music the fountains of the Villa d'Este and the mystic crooning of its cypresses. He depicted forest scenes, dreams of love, gnomes, saints, and devils. His late works portray old age itself, tonally ambiguous, painfully nostalgic, and elegiac. Liszt in his art encountered the entire world.

Debussy, Bartók, Stravinsky, and a host of twentieth-century composers were influenced by his harmonic audacity in such pieces as *Bagatelle Without Tonality* (S.216a, 1885) and *Nuage gris*, where he pushed tonality as far as a nineteenth-century composer had ever gone. He invented the one-movement symphonic poem and wrote thirteen of them. He understood that the four-movement plan of the sonata was psychologically impossible for program music, or music that describes an extramusical subject. All composers of symphonic poems, from Richard Strauss to Ottorino Respighi, are in his debt. And Liszt saw clearly the piano's suggestive possibilities as nobody before dreamed.

Aaron Copland wrote that Liszt "quite literally transformed the piano, bringing out, not only its own inherent qualities, but its evocative nature as well. . . . The piano as orchestra, the piano as harp (*Un sospiro*), the piano as cimbalom (Hungarian Rhapsody No. 11), the piano as organ, as brass choir, even the percussive piano as we know it (*Totentanz*) may be traced to Liszt's incomparable handling of the instrument. These pieces were born in the piano." Liszt once said, "My sole ambition as a composer is to hurl my javelin into the infinite space of the future." Never has he been more appreciated than today. Finally, he is understood as one of the most innovative composers in history, and a key figure of ninteenth-century Romanticism.

Hungarian Rhapsodies for Piano (1846–85)

Perhaps as famous as Liszt's passionate 1850 love poem, *Liebestraüme* no. 3, is his Second *Hungarian Rhapsody*, which incarnates the Gypsy temperament. In the nineteen *Hungarian Rhapsodies*, Liszt opened the way for a flood of works in national costume. The rhapsodies exhibit Liszt's histrionic nature, and unfortunately the popularity of a few of them has done his reputation more

harm than good. But they remain a unique literature of high-tempered gregar-
iousness.

COMPLETE
Campanella: Philips 438371-2
Szidon: Deutsche Grammophon 453034-2

Les Préludes for Orchestra, S.97 (1848; rev. before 1854)

Liszt invented the one-movement symphonic poem, a landmark in the history
of music. He understood that the literary-minded Romantic composers were seriously hampered by the four-movement abstract symphony. He experimented
with a form that could be flexible in expressing not merely a "programmatic"
story or blatant pictorialism but feelings based on ideas and impressions. In
many of his symphonic poems, he succeeded admirably, as in *Tasso* (S.96,
1849), *Mazzepa* (S.100, 1851), and *Hamlet* (S.104, 1858). But *Les Préludes*,
based on a Lamartine poem, is the most popular by far.

London Philharmonic Orchestra, Solti: London 417513-2
Vienna Philharmonic Orchestra, Furtwängler: Historical Performers HPS 14
Philadelphia Orchestra, Muti: EMI Classics CDC 47022

Concerto no. 1 in E-flat Major for Piano and Orchestra, S.124 (1849; rev. 1853)

Liszt's First Piano Concerto, with its pregnant opening theme followed by
heraldic antiphonal octaves, comprises one continuous movement with four
sections. It is a Romantic concerto par excellence, dramatic, with glittering virtuoso acrobatics and a tender heart on the sleeve. Its world premiere took place
in Weimar in 1855, with Berlioz conducting and Liszt as soloist. What a spectacle it must have been—two of the great progenitors of Romanticism, both
personages of the most striking and picturesque bearing, on the same stage!

Richter, London Symphony Orchestra, Kondrashin: Philips 446200-2
Janis, Moscow Philharmonic Orchestra, Kondrashin: Mercury 432002-2
Sauer, Paris Conservatory Orchestra, Weingartner: Pearl PEA 9403

Twelve Études d'exécution transcendante, S.139 (1851)

The Transcendental Études constitute one of the most exciting cycles in music. They stand as a monument to Romanticism, and their miraculous exploration of piano technique opened new horizons for the instrument. Their powerful chords, sweeping arpeggios, dazzling double notes, and mighty octaves demand that the pianist use his or her shoulders, back, and arms. For example, No. 4, "Mazeppa," is a programmatic work inspired by Victor Hugo's poem of the same title; it portrays a Cossack tied to a wild stallion and is one of the most exhausting works in the piano literature, a monumental workout for wrists and arms. No. 3, "Paysage" ("Landscape"), provides a pastoral setting with a wide vista. No. 5, "Feux follets" ("Will o' the Wisps"), is a shimmering, madcap fairy world. No. 11, "Harmonies du soir," "looks forward," in the late pianist John Ogdon's words, "to the evanescent texture of Debussy and the massive chordal writing of Rachmaninoff." Busoni called No. 12, "Chasseneige," "the noblest example, perhaps, amongst all music of a poetizing nature," as the wind moans, burying in snow the whole world. Listening to the whole seventy-five-minute cycle is also a daunting challenge, but it is most thrilling when heard in its entirety.

Cziffra: Hungaroton HCD 31569
Arrau: Philips 416458-2

Sonata in B Minor for Piano, S.178 (1852–53)

The B minor piano sonata, premiered in 1857 by Hans von Bülow, is one of the glories of the piano literature and Liszt's greatest achievement (along with the *Faust Symphony*) as a musical architect of a high order. When Wagner heard Liszt's pupil Karl Klindworth play it for him privately in London, he wrote to Liszt, "The sonata is beautiful beyond compare; great, lovable, deep and noble, just as you are." Liszt, within one half-hour movement, utilized elements of traditional sonata form along with his own concept of thematic transformation. He built the entire work on five themes, three of them heard at the very beginning of the score. The writer Peter Yates asserts that "Liszt's Piano Sonata in B minor stands isolated as the most successful formal organization of the nineteenth-century stylistic conglomerate."

Pogorelich: Deutsche Grammophon 429391-2
Cherkassky: Nimbus NI 7701

A Faust Symphony, S.108 (1857)

Liszt was never far from Goethe's *Faust*, which he first read with Berlioz in 1830 in French translation by Gérard de Nerval. The Faust story had deep symbolic significance to him. The *Faust Symphony*, which runs for seventy minutes, is divided into three movements that are "character pictures": Faust, Gretchen, and Mephistopheles. The first theme of the Faust movement uses all twelve notes of the chromatic scale enigmatically, with a brooding and tender second melody, followed by a characteristically grandiose theme. This material is then arranged in cunning thematic transformations. The Gretchen movement is a portrait of the ideal woman, one of the finest slow movements of the Romantic age. The Mephistopheles movement presents a crafty, snarling, and sinister devil. A diabolic, sardonic strain threads through many of Liszt's works. The Faust movement concludes with an ecstatic *chorus mysticus*. Its first performance took place in Weimar, with Liszt conducting, on September 5, 1857.

Jerusalem, Chicago Symphony Orchestra and Chorus, Solti: London 417399-2
Young, Royal Philharmonic Orchestra and Chorus, Beecham: EMI CDM 763371-2

Mephisto Waltz no. 1 for Piano, S.514 (1860), and for Orchestra, S.110 (1860)

The piano and orchestral settings of the *Mephisto Waltz* were both composed around 1860. The score, one of Liszt's boldest scenarios, was inspired by the Austrian poet Nikolaus Lenau's 1836 poem *Faust*. The *Mephisto Waltz* is subtitled *The Dance in the Village Inn*. The scene is played out by Faust, Mephistopheles, and Marguerite. The opening, "The Devil Tuning Up His Fiddle," writes the late Hungarian-British pianist Louis Kentner, "is surely one of the most daring things created by any pre-Bartók composer." The middle section, a seductive waltz theme, is gorgeous, halting, languorous, and voluptuous. The directions on the score read, "They sink into the ocean of their own lust." Liszt wrote the orchestral version first, then translated it for piano shortly afterward.

FOR PIANO
Horowitz: RCA 09026-61415-2
Hough: Virgin Classics VC 561439-2
Ashkenazy: Saga EC 3362-2

FOR ORCHESTRA
Philadelphia Orchestra, Ormandy: CBS MLK 39450
Orchestra of Paris, Solti: London 417513-2

OTHER PRINCIPAL WORKS

ORCHESTRAL WORKS
Symphonic Poem no. 2 (*Tasso*), S.96 (1849; rev. 1850–51 and 1854)*
Symphonic Poem no. 4 (*Orpheus*), S.98 (1853–54)*
Symphonic Poem no. 6 (*Mazeppa*), S.100 (1851; rev. 1854)*
Symphonic Poem no. 8 (*Héroïde funèbre*), S.102 (1849–50; rev. 1854)*
Dante Symphony, S.109 (1855–56)

ORGAN MUSIC
Fantasy and Fugue on the Chorale *"Ad nos, ad salutarem undam"* (theme used in
    Meyerbeer's *Le Prophète*), S.259 (1850)*
Prelude and Fugue on the Name BACH, S.260 (1855; rev. 1870)*

PIANO AND ORCHESTRA WORKS
Malédiction for Piano and Strings, S.121 (c.1840)
Concerto no. 2 in A Major, S.125 (1839; rev. 1849–61)*
Hungarian Fantasia, S.123 (c.1852)*
Totentanz, S.126 (1849; rev. 1853 and 1859)*

PIANO SOLO WORKS
Mephisto Waltz no. 2, S.111 (1880–81)*
Six *Études after Paganini*, S.140 (1838)*
Three *Études de concert*, S.144 (c.1848)*
Two *Études de concert*, S.145 (c.1862)*
Apparition no. 1, S.155/1 (1834)*
Années de pèlerinage: Second Year (*Italy*) (set of seven pieces), S.161 (1837–49)
    No. 5, "Sonetto 104 de Petrarca"*
    No. 7, "Dante Sonata"*
Années de pèlerinage: Third Year (set of seven pieces), S.163 (1867–77)

No. 2, "Aux Cyprès de la Villa d'Este"*

No. 4, "Les Jeux d'eau à la Villa d'Este"*

Ballade no. 2 in B Minor, S.171 (1853)*

Six *Consolations*, S.172 (1849–50)*

Berceuse, S.174 (1854–62)*

Harmonies poétiques et religieuses (set of ten pieces), S.173 (1845–52)

No. 3, "Bénédiction de Dieu dans la solitude"*

No. 7, "Funérailles"*

Légendes, S.175 (1863)

"St. François d'Assise: la prédication aux oiseaux"*

"St. François de Paule marchant sur les flots"*

Grosses Konzertsolo, S.176 (?1849)

Scherzo and March, S.177 (1851)

Variations on Themes of Bach: "Crucifixus" *of the B minor mass and Cantata no. 12*
    "Weinen, Klagen, Sorgen, Zagen," S.179 (1859)*

Weihnachtsbaum (*Christmas Tree*) *Suite*, S.186 (1874–76)

Valse impromptu, S.213 (c.1850)*

Four *Valses oubliées*, S.215 (1881–85)

Csárdas macabre, S.224 (1881–82)*

Mephisto Waltz no. 3, S.216 (1883)*

Rhapsodie espagnole, S.254 (c.1863)

Transcriptions for piano of works by Auber, Bach, Beethoven, Bellini, Berlioz, Donizetti,
    Gounod, Halévy, Mendelssohn, Meyerbeer, Mozart, Rossini, Schubert, Schumann,
    Tchaikovsky, Verdi, Wagner, Weber, and many others

SACRED CHORAL WORKS

Christus (oratorio), S.3 (1862–67)

Legend of Saint Elisabeth (oratorio), S.2 (1865)*

Hungarian Coronation Mass, S.11 (1867)

Psalms nos. 13, 18, 23, 116, 129, and 137, S.13–17 (1855–59)

VOICE WITH PIANO WORKS

Nearly seventy songs*

RICHARD WAGNER

b. Leipzig, May 22, 1813

d. Venice, February 13, 1883

Since never in my life have I enjoyed the true happiness of love, I intend to erect a further monument to this most beautiful of dreams, a monument in which this love will be properly sated from beginning to end.

Wagner was legally the son of a police chief, Karl Friedrich, and his wife Johanna, but confusion remains about his actual paternity. Karl Friedrich died when Richard was six months old, and within six months Johanna had married Ludwig Geyer, an actor and painter. Geyer may have been Wagner's natural father; certainly Wagner at times thought so. But modern research has given Karl Friedrich the honor.

If as a child Richard showed any particular aptitude, it was for literature. He came to music at age fifteen, when he heard Beethoven's Ninth Symphony and *Fidelio* and felt an overwhelming desire to compose. Unfortunately, the boy had no skill at playing the piano and knew nothing of the rules of composition. The situation did not improve until he entered the University at Leipzig in 1831. There for a short time he received some instruction in counterpoint from Theodor Weinlig, a musician at the Thomaskirche who also did his best to instill some discipline into the rowdy youth. Weinlig was Richard's only teacher, and it was not until after Richard stopped his lessons that he began to compose. His first efforts were, among other things, a C major symphony (1832), a piano sonata (1832), and the opera *Die Feen* (1833–34), all of them extremely academic if not pedantic. Even as late as his twenty-eighth year, though, Wagner showed few signs of the titanic genius to come.

In 1833 he received his first professional post as chorus master at Würzberg, then in 1834 became musical director at Magdeburg, where he courted and in 1836 married Minna Planer, an actress. Minna, a coarse woman with little education, gained a husband who was moody and temperamental and whose compulsive spending was the bane of their existence. After his third opera, *Das Liebesverbot*, was produced and failed, Minna left him. With creditors demanding payment, Wagner was forced to flee Magdeburg. In the summer of 1837, he found a position as musical director for a theater in Riga and convinced Minna to return to him. There he worked on *Rienzi*, a grand opera that he intended to rival Gaspare Spontini's and Giacomo Meyerbeer's operatic spectacles, which had proved to be financial blockbusters. Wagner hoped that the new opera would bring him fame and fortune.

But while he was working on *Rienzi*, debts mounted quickly, and Richard and Minna soon had to flee Riga, too, this time by sea. They arrived in Paris in April 1842, and their abject poverty while they were there did not help Wagner's attitude toward the city. He disliked Parisians in general and was particularly chagrined by the success of the Jewish opera composers Meyerbeer and Halévy—chagrin that, over the years, fermented into a lasting hatred of Jews. By late 1842, after a year and a half of work, *Rienzi* was finished. The Dresden Opera accepted it and staged it in October 1842. The opera was liked, and if Wagner did not make much money, at least he had been noticed.

He now finished his first mature work, *Der fliegende Holländer* (*The Flying Dutchman*), which he had begun in 1841. Dresden again produced it, at the court opera in January 1843, but much to the composer's disappointment, audiences did not understand the work, and it was performed only four times. This failure did not change the opinions of those in charge of the Dresden Opera, for the company soon offered the thirty-year-old composer a position as second *Kapellmeister*. This post gave him a chance to improve his skills as a conductor and also gave him time to compose. In two years he wrote the libretto and music to *Tannhäuser*, which largely irritated the public at its first hearing in October 1845. Slowly, however, *Tannhäuser* gained admirers and brought Wagner's name to a larger German public.

In 1848 revolutions took place all through Europe as people tried to dispose of monarchies. Wagner took part in the Dresden riots of May 1849, siding with his acquaintance the anarchist Mikhail Bakunin, who had admired Wagner's conducting of Beethoven's Ninth Symphony. It was an unusual moment for Wagner, whose sympathies were normally never aroused by the "vulgar masses," as he called them. (He felt that the "masses" were incapable of appreciating the only thing that mattered to his "amoral" nature—art!) The dire result of his participation in the Dresden revolt was a warrant for his arrest. He fled Saxony and lived in exile in Switzerland for twelve years.

Although Wagner had not liked his years in Paris, they had provided him with one thing that proved crucial in the first days of his exile: the friendship of Liszt. Liszt was the first important artist to realize Wagner's potential, and he provided the fleeing composer with money and a passport to Switzerland. It was also the courageous Liszt who, in Weimar in 1850, presented the world premiere of *Lohengrin*. *Lohengrin* became Wagner's most popular opera, but the exiled composer would not be able to see it performed for a dozen years.

While he was living in Zurich, Wagner was absorbed by new ideas and influences, especially Schopenhauer's philosophy and Teutonic myths. For six years following the completion of *Lohengrin* in 1848, Wagner did not compose a note. He was contemplating a vast tetralogy based on the Nibelungen sagas. After years of contemplation, he began work on the libretto for *Siegfried*, and in 1854 he finished the music to *Das Rheingold*, the opening opera of the four-opera cycle *Der Ring des Nibelungen* (*The Ring of the Nibelungs*).

By this time Wagner was totally at odds with Minna, who wanted her husband to continue writing opera spectacles like *Rienzi* instead of operas that seemed so obscure and complicated. In 1856 he completed work on *Die Walküre* (*The Valkyrie*), the second music-drama of the *Ring* cycle, and became embroiled in a torrid love affair with Mathilde Wesendonk, the wife of his benefactor and patron, Otto Wesendonk, who had given the Wagners a small house on his property near Zurich. At the height of his passion for Mathilde, Wagner interrupted work on the *Ring* to begin his great love story, *Tristan und Isolde*, which he composed between 1857 and 1859. After the heat of *Tristan*, the Mathilde affair churned to a close. In 1860, after a great many attempts, he was allowed to return to any of the German provinces except Saxony. Soon afterward his admirer Princess Augusta of Prussia used her influence with the Saxon government to let him return there too. In 1862 Wagner and Minna separated for the final time, after twenty-six years. By then Wagner had begun an affair with Liszt's daughter Cosima, the wife of the pianist and conductor Hans von Bülow.

Wagner took his *Tristan* to Vienna, where, after dozens of rehearsals, the work was abandoned as unperformable. That failure and Wagner's debts, piling high once again, made the spring of 1864 a particularly dark hour. At the last moment, a princely patron appeared. Ludwig II, the young homosexual king of Bavaria, was wildly in love with Wagner's music. He summoned the composer to join his court at Munich, his capital, and Wagner happily took leave of his old life. The king was ecstatic to meet his "beloved" composer. "I can only adore you," exclaimed Ludwig. "An earthly being cannot requite a divine spirit." On May 5, Wagner wrote, "He offers me everything that I need to live, and to perform my works. I am to be his friend, nothing more: no appointment, no functions to fulfill. It is all I ever wished for."

The king indeed promised Wagner anything and everything, including Wagner's chief desire, the staging of *Tristan*. Wagner convinced Ludwig to make Hans von Bülow court conductor, and the king summoned Hans and Cosima von Bülow to Munich. As von Bülow prepared the production of *Tristan*, the composer and Cosima continued their clandestine affair. The following year, the illicit lovers presented von Bülow with a daughter by Wagner, unabashedly named Isolde. Von Bülow, deeply humiliated, nonetheless carried on with his work on *Tristan*. The disgraced conductor, a very irascible man, bluntly told his friends that he would have shot anyone else. Apparently Wagner was a law unto himself, as von Bülow continued to call him "this glorious, unique man whom one must venerate like a god." Von Bülow's dedication soon paid off, and *Tristan*, much to Wagner's gratification, had its world premiere on June 10, 1865.

The Bavarian coffers were at Wagner's disposal, and his influence and power over the king seemed invincible. He used his powerful position to advantage but soon became embroiled in local and national politics. Before long he had powerful political enemies who reminded the world about the composer's earlier expulsion from Saxony. In 1866 Wagner was asked to leave Munich. He and Cosima complied and moved into the rented Villa Tribschen, near Lake Lucerne, where their third child, Siegfried, was born. Von Bülow granted Cosima a divorce, and the lovers were married on August 25, 1870.

From 1862 to 1867, Wagner, perhaps reacting to the rapturous tensions of *Tristan*, had composed *Die Meistersinger*, his only comedy. It was mounted at the Munich Court Opera on June 21, 1868, under Hans Richter, whom Wagner had personally trained in every detail. On September 22, 1869, *Das Rheingold* (completed in 1854) first saw performance at Munich, and *Die Walküre* (completed in 1856) was heard at the court theater on June 26, 1870. On December 25, 1870, as a surprise birthday present to Cosima, Wagner arranged for a small orchestra to give the first performance of his recently composed *Siegfried Idyll*, on the staircase at Tribschen.

During the next four years Wagner worked intensely to finish the *Ring*. The third component opera, *Siegfried*, was completed in 1871, and the final touches to *Götterdämmerung* (*Twilight of the Gods*) were penned in 1874. It had taken twenty-four years from start to finish, but the *Ring* stands as one of the mighty achievements of the human mind and spirit. With his indomitable energy, Wagner now sought a permanent home where his gigantic works of art, which he called *Gesamtkunstwerk*, or "total artwork," could be staged. He had exacting demands; he needed not only a perfectly adaptable opera house for his many theatrical innovations, but also a shrine where Wagnerian pilgrims could forever come to behold his glory.

Wagner decided that the little Bavarian town of Bayreuth would be perfect.

Against great odds, the Festspielhaus was designed, planned, and built to his every specification. It was the perfect venue to produce his music-dramas as he wished them to be produced, complete with a hidden orchestra pit. King Ludwig contributed funds, as did many others. On August 13, 1876, the first complete performance of *Der Ring des Nibelungen* began. It was the single greatest and most publicized artistic event of the nineteenth century. It put the final stamp on Wagner as the supreme artistic force of the age. He became, after Napoleon, the most written-about person of the nineteenth century.

Wagner, who was in his sixties when he completed his work on Bayreuth, had one more music-drama left to create. *Parsifal* was completed in 1882 and was premiered at Bayreuth on July 26 of that year under the direction of Hermann Levi. Wagner left Bayreuth shortly afterward, hoping that a stay in Venice would restore him to health after the rigors of *Parsifal*. But a heart condition that had plagued him for years got the better of him in the lagooned city. His coffin glided eerily through the Grand Canal and was then transported to his final resting place, in the garden at his Villa Wahnfried in Bayreuth. His death sent shock waves through the world. Later generations of writers tried to assess his impact: American composer Virgil Thomson wrote, "He was everything the bourgeois feared, hoped for, and longed to worship in the artist." And literary critic Allan Bloom wrote that the public "had the religious sense that Wagner was creating the meaning of life and that they were not merely listening to his works but experiencing that meaning."

Wagner fulfilled an age, bringing music to its extremes of emotional amplitude. His greatness went deeper than the thrilling surface magnificence of his works or theoretical discussion about them. The writer Bryan Magee states, "Wagner knew he was making the orchestra express the world of primitive, unbridled inchoate feeling below the level of conscious awareness."

Wagner himself, an autodidact, was deeply in touch with and perfectly trusted his creative consciousness, and he could say in truth to Hugo Wolf that he knew nothing about music. And to an admirer he said, "To me *Tristan* is and remains a wonder! I shall never be able to understand how I could have written anything like it."

Although Wagner considered his librettos to be great poetry, the music of course remains the backbone of the Wagnerian apparatus. It brings the voice, in combination with the orchestra ("that kingdom of subliminal knowledge") to an undreamed-of height of expression. In merging his musical being with the timeless power of myth, Wagner tapped into repressed and unconscious aspects of the psyche. He felt no surprise that his music had the power to unhinge mentally unstable people, touching an exposed nerve. With Schopenhauer, Wagner is the greatest pre-Freudian. Nietzsche declared, "He knows of a chord which expresses those secret and weird midnight hours of the soul, when cause and effect seem to have fallen asunder." Thomas Mann said, "All that I owe to him . . . I can never forget."

Wagner's influence on artists everywhere is unique. Among the poets and writers who adored and promulgated his art were Gérard de Nerval, Théophile Gautier, and Gautier's daughter Judith (a fanatic Wagnerian who had an affair with him while he was composing *Parsifal*), Stéphane Mallarmé, Paul Verlaine, Catulle Mendès, and Charles Baudelaire, who was consumed by him. Legions of painters, from Aubrey Beardsley to Pierre-Auguste Renoir (who sought out the master at Palermo to paint his portrait), were inspired by him. In the twentieth century, James Joyce was powerfully drawn to Wagner and referred to the composer in his novels, as did T. S. Eliot in *The Waste Land*. W. H. Auden proclaimed Wagner "perhaps the greatest genius that ever lived," and Shaw raised monuments of prose to him.

Under his mighty weight, other composers struggled for their identity. Camille Saint-Saëns and Charles Gounod were the first of the French to undertake Wagnerism. When the "Paris version" of *Tannhäuser* failed, Gounod shouted, "God give me a failure like that." César Franck, Jules Massenet, Emmanuel Chabrier, Henri Duparc, and Ernest Chausson were badly and harmfully smitten, and Gabriel Fauré wrote in 1884, "If one has not heard Wagner at Bayreuth, one *has heard nothing*! Take many handkerchiefs because you will cry a great deal! Also take a sedative because you will be exalted to the point of delirium." Debussy attempted to rid himself of the Wagnerian stranglehold, calling him "that old poisoner." But his friend Pierre Louÿs rebuked him: "Wagner was the greatest man who had ever existed. . . . I didn't say that he was God himself, though indeed I may have thought something of the sort."

Among German composers, Bruckner and Wolf did indeed consider Wagner a deity. Schoenberg, whose twelve-tone system was his reaction to Wagner, adored him, and Mahler often said, "There was only Beethoven and Wagner." Strauss blushed with pride when he was called Richard II.

By 1910 the musical world saw a backlash against Romanticism in general and Wagner in particular. Stravinsky, with his primitivism, objectivity, neoclassicism, and fierce anti-Romanticism, was a relief from Wagner's sultry torpor. Through the 1920s and 1930s, Wagner's operas remained widely performed, but his prestige dwindled when Hitler used the composer as a propaganda tool for National Socialism. Wagner was certainly a fanatic pan-German, and his anti-Semitism is the most deplorable aspect of an often-monstrous person. As the poet Auden wrote, "Most nineteenth-century anti-Semites would have been genuinely horrified by Auschwitz but one has the uncomfortable suspicion that Wagner would have wholeheartedly approved." The writer on music Cecil

Gray wrote, "To admire Wagner, except for certain aspects of his technical accomplishment, after the age of about twenty, is a sure sign of arrested development and unfulfilled sexual experience; for the emotional and spiritual content
of his work is that of a substitute for life. . . . The extent to which the National
Socialist Movement had its source and origin in Wagner is still not yet fully
recognized. . . . Quite simply, Wagner was the precursor and creator of the
Nazi order." Over this matter, many music lovers remain in denial, and to read
Wagner's own words on Jews is chilling.

Wagner today, of course, holds his own in the world of music, but since his
death the world has become satiated with cultural and technological wonders
that would have boggled the mind of late-nineteenth-century Wagnerians, who
could not dream of anything more splendid than the *Ring*. To a mass population titillated with gadgets, sports spectacles, scientific marvels, movies, and
space travel, Wagner inevitably has less surface impact than in his day. Stravinsky said, "The thrall of Wagner has abated for reasons as different as the short-
age of Flagstads and the decline of the narcotic effects of the music, owing to
the circulation of stronger drugs." Certainly there has been a massive deteriora-
tion of great Wagner singers since Kirsten Flagstad, Helen Traubel, Frida
Leider, Lilli Lehmann, Friedrich Schorr, Karin Branzell, and others—cause
enough for a decline in Wagner's cultural status. Yet Wagner remains one of
the great composers in history, and it is unlikely that any artist ever again will
have such an all-powerful effect on art itself.

Tannhäuser (1843–45)

In *Tannhäuser* Wagner explores the conflict between spiritual and carnal love
as well as redemption through love, one of his basic themes. For the 1861 Paris
version, he raised the erotic temperature of his 1845 creation, expanding and
modifying the score considerably and adding a passionate bacchanal section.
Both versions are heard today in the world's opera houses; many prefer the
hybrid Paris version, while others the older but in no way crude Dresden version. *Tannhäuser* was the most harmonically advanced opera of the period,
from its long overture with its trembling motive to the Pilgrims' Chorus, the
Hymn to Venus ("Dir töne Lob!"), and the Venusberg Music, the most seductive strains of this very sensual work. In his autobiography, Wagner spoke of
composing the first version: "My whole being was consumed with it, so much
so that I became obsessed with the thought that I was going to die before I completed it and when I had set down the last note, I did feel as if my life had run
its course."

1861 Paris Version

Dernesch, Ludwig, Kollo, Braun, Vienna Philharmonic Orchestra, Vienna State Opera Chorus, Solti: London 414581-2

1845 Dresden Version

Silja, Bumbry, Windgassen, Bayreuth Festival Orchestra and Chorus, Sawallisch: Philips 434607-2

Lohengrin (1846–48)

Lohengrin is still one of Wagner's most popular works. It ends his first phase as a conventional opera composer, when he was still writing formal duets and choruses. The orchestra is very expressive but is not yet central to the work. The prelude to Act I is serenely beautiful. In Act I, after Elsa's Dream, in which Elsa envisions a warrior who rescues her, Lohengrin arrives by a swan-drawn boat. In Act II, she sings "Euch Lüften, die mein Klagen," expressing her love, and the trumpets tell us that it is her wedding day. The prelude to Act III is joyous, preparing the way for the celebrated Wedding March and Bridal Chorus. As in any Wagner work, the music goes far beyond the confines of the story. Lohengrin and Elsa symbolize oneness and separation.

Norman, Randová, Domingo, Fischer-Dieskau, Nimsgern, Vienna Philharmonic Orchestra and Vienna State Opera Chorus, Solti: London 421053-2

Rysanek, Varnay, Kónya, Blanc, Bayreuth Festival Orchestra and Chorus, Cluytens: Myto MCD 890.02

Tristan und Isolde (1857–59)

Tristan is the most-written-about opera ever composed. It is Wagner's most influential work, taking chromatic harmony into new regions where tonality itself is obscured. If one is properly attuned, it has a most staggering effect.

Although Wagner's illicit love affair with Mathilde Wesendonk may have counted for much in the creation of *Tristan*, still there were many other factors, not least his study of Schopenhauer. As Joseph Campbell says, "He had met Mathilde, his Beatrice, two years before. And—what is no less relevant—he had discovered in the language of philosophy, like Dante, the means not only to read in depth the secret of his stricken heart, but also to render the import of its sweetly bitter agony in the timeless metaphors of myth. For, as we learn from his own account in the autobiography, it was in the year of his conception of this monument to a dream that he found the works of Schopenhauer." In Wagner's autobiography, the composer notes, "It was certainly, in part, the serious mood into which Schopenhauer had transposed me and which now was pressing for an ecstatic expression of its structuring ideas, that inspired in me the conception of *Tristan und Isolde*." It is entirely in keeping with Wagner's complex nature that he transformed the misogynist Schopenhauer's thinking into a vast musical structure fueled by passionate love. Each of the three acts has a hypnotic effect, and after four hours, the audience is in a trancelike state. In Act I, because of her hopeless love, Isolde orders a potion that will bring death to both lovers. As they drink, they are overcome by passion. (All of this is predicted in the longing and desire of the famous prelude.) In Act II Isolde realizes that King Mark, her husband, is away hunting and summons her lover to her. The *Liebesnacht* is one of the sublime realizations of desperate love. In Act III Isolde, with her wounded lover in her arms, sings the ecstatic *Liebestod* (Love Death), and the couple together embrace death, the great release.

Dernesch, Ludwig, Vickers, Berry, Berlin Philharmonic Orchestra, German Opera Chorus, Karajan: EMI Classics CDMD 69319

Nilsson, Ludwig, Windgassen, Talvela, Bayreuth Festival Orchestra and Chorus, Böhm: Deutsche Grammophon 419889-2

Flagstad, Thebom, Suthaus, Fischer-Dieskau, Greindl, Philharmonia Orchestra, Royal Opera House Chorus, Furtwängler: EMI Classics CDCD 56254

Die Meistersinger von Nürnberg (1862–68)

Wagner—the creator of music of painful desperation or, as Nietzsche said, "the Orpheus of life's secret pain"—was nevertheless miraculously capable of writing one of the most profoundly moving, warm, and endearing comedies of the ages, ranking next to *Falstaff* and *The Marriage of Figaro*. Like many Wagner works, it was long in gestation, taking six years to write during a continuously stormy and irritating period. In the character of the pedantic and ridiculous Beckmesser, Wagner portrayed his tormenting demon, the Viennese critic Eduard Hanslick, and all the narrow-minded critics of his time. In the original libretto, Beckmesser's name was "Hans Lich." The character of the hero Hans Sachs, an actual cobbler-poet of the sixteenth century, must surely be Wagner's most humble and human creation. A highlight of the gigantic work is the ten-minute Prelude, which draws on five themes from the music-drama. The critic Olin Downes described the incredible Prelude as "[o]ne of

the seven wonders of the musical world." The opera is flooded with charm, celebration, and many famous scenes. Ralph Vaughan Williams was convinced
that "[t]here is no work of art which represents the spirit of a nation more surely
than *Die Meistersinger*." If Tristan and Isolde's love is mad desire, the love between Sachs and Eva in *Meistersinger* is a love of sweetness and light. The
whole score ripples with festive melody. The Prize Song in Act III is the best
known, and the Quintet is one of the great ensembles of opera. Once again this
is no simple story but one that lives on many levels.

*Schwarzkopf, Malaniuk, Hopf, Kunz, Edelmann, Bayreuth Festival Orchestra and Chorus,
Karajan: EMI Classics CDHD 63500*

*Ligendza, Ludwig, Domingo, Laubenthal, Fischer-Dieskau, German Opera Orchestra and
Chorus, Jochum: Deutsche Grammophon 415278-2*

Der Ring des Nibelungen
1. *Das Rheingold* (1853–54)
2. *Die Walküre* (1854–56)
3. *Siegfried* (1856–71)
4. *Götterdämmerung* (1869–74)

The most complex musical-theatrical spectacle of all time is also a monument
to Wagner's tenacious genius. Conceiving the *Ring* as an allegory of human
psychology undoubtedly proves Wagner to be one of the great synthetic minds,
ranking near Shakespeare, Dante, Mozart, Bach, Michelangelo, Beethoven,
Dürer, and Rembrandt.

The *Ring* has been inspected and interpreted from every conceivable van-
tage point, by everyone from materialist capitalists and Shavian socialists to
Jungian analysts. Its music is unfathomably great. Although Rossini (who died
before the *Ring* was produced) had once griped that "Wagner has lovely moments but awful quarters of an hour," all the music in the *Ring* has an elevated
purpose. For those who wait only for familiar thrills like the Ride of the
Valkyries and the Magic Fire, the work will indeed have its longueurs.

To take the *Ring* seriously, one must immerse oneself in the whole thing.
Today far fewer people have the kind of passion or patience that this adventure
requires. W. H. Auden wrote, "Could Wagner revisit the earth . . . he would be
dismayed to learn that the race of Wagnerites has died out, that the opera public listens one night to Wagner and the next, with equal pleasure and admiration, to Verdi, whom he had dismissed as a composer of no account. He would
be right, I believe, in feeling dismay, though not for the reason he would him-

self give. Wagner's operas are freaks, and if we are to appreciate them correctly, we must listen in a way unlike that in which we listen to most operas." Perhaps Auden meant that being a true Wagnerite presupposes dedication verging on fanaticism.

The Nibelungs, a tribe of Rhine warriors of the fifth century, inspired a thirteenth-century epic poem, the *Nibelungenlied*. This courtly and Christian poem (based on pagan and Germanic legends) was Wagner's inspiration for his four music-dramas. Throughout the *Ring*, the composer makes use of *leitmotive*, structural devices that give themes and mottoes to the characters, situations, and moods of the cycle and act as a unifying agent throughout the four music-dramas. The *Ring* is to be performed in four separate evenings, but the cycle should be understood as one work. For Wagner, it was nothing less than an allegory of the human search for power. Only one act serves as a preparation for the other dramas. The long prelude to *Das Rheingold* is built exclusively from an E-flat chord, which swells and surges. Here is the River Rhine itself, and the Rhine maidens jealously guard the lump of gold that has been made into a ring and whose possessor will rule the world.

The *Ring* requires some study to appreciate its vastness, but many extracts have become well known at orchestral concerts. Some of these are the Entrance of the Gods into Valhalla from *Das Rheingold*; the Ride of the Valkyries and the Magic Fire Music from *Die Walküre*; and Siegfried's Death and the Rhine Journey from *Siegfried*. These excerpts were all adapted by Wagner himself to bring aspects of the *Ring* to orchestral audiences. But only by hearing the *Ring* itself, preferably in a theater, does the listener begin to entertain the vast spectacle of Wagner's art.

The *Ring* was first performed at Bayreuth on August 13, 14, 16, and 17, 1876. King Ludwig's financial assistance had once again saved Wagner. The king was given private performances earlier in August and wrote to the composer, "Fortunate century that saw this spirit in its midst! How future generations will envy those who feel the incomparable happiness of being your contemporaries." Wagner hoped for an annual performance of the *Ring*, but the enterprise was at the time too difficult to keep afloat, and he would see and hear it performed only once again in his lifetime.

Nilsson, Flagstad, Crespin, Watson, Ludwig, Madeira, Svanholm, King, Stolze, Windgassen, London, Fischer-Dieskau, Hotter, Frick, Neidlinger, Vienna Philharmonic Orchestra, Solti: London 414100-2

Nilsson, Rysanek, Dvořaková, Burmeister, Bayreuth Festival Orchestra, Bayreuth Festival Chorus, Böhme: Philips 420325-2

Siegfried Idyll (1870)

Wagner was one of the great masters of descriptive, pictorial music, exemplified in dozens of astounding pages of visual impact. But in the *Siegfried Idyll*, he wrote music of an almost beatific calm. The score is a luminous confessional, a tone poem based on themes from the opera *Siegfried*, and surely the most blessed birthday gift ever given by a husband to a wife. Cosima wrote, "As I awoke, my ear caught a sound, which swelled fuller and fuller; no longer could I imagine myself to be dreaming: music was sounding, and such music! When it died away, Richard came into my room with the children and offered me the score of the symphonic birthday poem. I was in tears, but so was all the rest of the household."

That this man, capable of such emotion, was enraged at Bismarck for not burning Paris to the ground will always tantalize and disturb.

NBC Symphony Orchestra, Toscanini: RCA 60264-2-RG
Royal Philharmonic Orchestra, Horenstein: Chesky CD 31
Orpheus Chamber Orchestra: Deutsche Grammophon 431680-2

Parsifal (1877–82)

Wagner's last opera remains his most controversial. Nietzsche hated it, with its "feeble" Christianity. The critic J.W.N. Sullivan wrote, "Wagner, as the fever in his blood grew less, had nothing to express at the end but exhaustion and ineffectual longing." It is indeed a curious mixture of the spiritual and the erotic. By his life's end, Wagner, the ultimate voluptuary, needed an endless array of stimulants. Auden declared, "His tastes in clothes and interior decoration were those of a drag queen." He was surrounded by aromas and scents and silks of an extraordinary variety, as well as by Judith Gautier's ecstatic caresses, all under Cosima's sanctioned gaze—anything to bring to life the master's final utterance. The American composer Charles Ives said, "Richy Wagner is a soft-bodied sensualist-pussy." It is a curious religiosity, this final Wagnerian quest for the Holy Grail. At times *Parsifal* smells of incense, but the work arouses one and makes one uncomfortable but at moments exalted. There are those who unconditionally find this valedictory work to be Wagner's most transcendent achievement. The prelude and Good Friday music are often performed separately. The Prelude is one of Wagner's most advanced pieces—densely chromatic, filled with sorrow. The Good Friday spell is seamless and is Wagner's most moving contemplative music.

"If I only could hear a little Wagner tonight!" wrote Baudelaire in a letter to his idol Wagner. Fortunately, through recordings, we may hear a lot of Wagner every night.

Vejzovic, Hofmann, Van Dam, Moll, Berlin Philharmonic Orchestra, Karajan: Deutsche Grammophon 413347-2

Thomas, Hotter, Talvela, London, Bayreuth Festival Orchestra, Knappertsbusch: Philips 416390-2

Ludwig, Kollo, Fischer-Dieskau, Frick, Vienna Philharmonic Orchestra and Vienna State Opera Chorus, Solti: London 417143-2

OTHER PRINCIPAL WORKS

OPERAS
Rienzi (1838–40)
Der fliegende Holländer (*The Flying Dutchman*) (1843)*

ORCHESTRAL MUSIC
Rienzi Overture (1838–40)
Der fliegende Holländer Overture (1843)*
A Faust Overture (1844)*

SONGS
Five Wesendonk-*Lieder* (1862)*

GIUSEPPE VERDI

b. La Roncole, October 9 or 10, 1813

d. Milan, January 27, 1901

If there is anything in life to be appreciated, it is the bread earned with the sweat of one's own brow.

Verdi's birthplace, the dusty and squalid village of La Roncole (near Busseto, in the province of Emilia-Romagna), had a population of eight hundred in 1813. His parents were semiliterate merchants. When they suspected that their son was musical, they bought him a little spinet. Years later he wrote, "I did my first lessons on the old spinet, and for my parents it was a large sacrifice to get me this wreck, which was already old at that time." The spinet may have been a "wreck," but "having it made [Verdi] happier than a king," and he kept it for eighty years. It was certainly not an auspicious beginning for the boy who would become nineteenth-century Italy's greatest composer.

At age ten he was sent to neighboring Busseto, where a prosperous merchant, Antonio Barezzi (later to become his father-in-law), recognized the boy's gifts. In Busseto he received a fair general education, worked with local music teachers, learned the organ, and occasionally conducted the local orchestra.

Barezzi was like a second father and guardian angel to young Giuseppe, and he knew that the boy must eventually study in Milan. At nineteen Verdi attempted to enter the Milan Conservatory. Much to the future embarrassment of the renowned Conservatory, however, he was refused admittance. Verdi was told he was four years too old, that his piano playing was not good enough, and that he generally lacked sufficient talent. Fortunately Barezzi had confidence in him and helped pay for private instruction.

Verdi's three-year stay in Milan was harsh, for he found it impossible to make a living. During that time he studied with Vincenzo Lavigna, a conductor at La Scala, who awakened Giuseppe to the greatness of Mozart's *Don Giovanni*. After much deliberation and hesitation, the young man wrote an opera. Nobody wanted it, however, and the dejected Verdi returned to Busseto, where he eked out a livelihood as a humble church organist and was grateful to have a job. In Busseto he completed another opera, *Oberto, Conte di San Bonifacio* (1839), and was elevated to the position of *maestro di musica* for the entire town. Giuseppe had long been in love with Margherita, Barezzi's pretty, sensitive, and musical daughter—they had literally grown up together. On May 4, 1836, they were united in marriage.

When La Scala decided to produce *Oberto*, Verdi was jubilant. Immediately he quit his position and moved his family to Milan. Starting on November 17, 1839, *Oberto* had a short but respectable run of fourteen performances. More important, the discerning soprano Giuseppina Strepponi was convinced that the work possessed real dramatic qualities, far above those of the usual operatic potboiler. Also impressed with the opera was the impresario Bartolomeo Merelli, who asked Verdi to compose three operas in two years; the first one was to be a comedy, *Un Giorno di regno*.

After *Oberto*, however, Verdi suffered a series of unbearable personal catastrophes. In August 1838, his young daughter died of an undiagnosed illness; her death was followed in 1839 by that of his son. The terror continued, as Verdi told it: "During the first days of June my young companion and helpmate was stricken with violent encephalitis, and on June 19, 1840, a third coffin was carried out of my home. I was alone! . . . alone . . . I had lost three loved ones. My whole family was gone. . . . And in this terrible anguish of soul, to avoid breaking the engagement I had contracted, I was compelled to write an entire comic opera! *Un Giorno di regno* [produced in 1840] was not successful. Part of its failure was certainly due to the music, but the performance, too, must take part of the blame. My soul rent by the misfortune that had overwhelmed me, my spirit embittered by the failure of my opera, I persuaded myself that I could find no more consolation in art and resolved never to compose again."

Verdi tried to obtain a release from his contract for the two remaining operas. With admirable tact, the impresario Merelli refused to accept Verdi's withdrawal. Instead he handed him a libretto, telling him, "It is superb, magnificent, tense, grandiose, replete with dramatic situations." Merelli pleaded, "I know you have given up composing . . . but read this." Verdi glumly replied, "No, no, I am not able to read a libretto."

"Back home, I threw the manuscript on the table with an almost violent gesture, and remained standing before it. In falling it had opened itself; without realizing it, my eyes clung to the open page and to one special line: 'Va, pensiero, sull'ali dorate' ('Fly oh thought on golden wings') which would become the chorus of the Jews." The libretto of *Nabucco* was staring him in the face. Writing the opera changed Verdi's life and revived the Italian stage, which had been at a low ebb. Except for Donizetti, who was dying, no composer of opera was capable of satisfying Italy's hungry audiences. This situation was changed with the premiere of *Nabucco* on March 9, 1842, where one of the leading roles was sung by Strepponi. *Nabucco* immediately brought Verdi to the forefront of Italian opera.

Only days after Verdi's triumph, he found himself a national hero of the Risorgimento. Those were heated years, when Italy was oppressed and even terrorized by its Austrian overlords, and strong currents of cultural nationalism and political activism (which would eventually result in the unification of Italy) were sweeping through the country. *Nabucco* was a thinly disguised hymn to revolt and freedom, with which the censors could do nothing, since its story was biblical. The magnificent chorus of the subjected Jews became an anthem for the republicanism sweeping through Italy. The day after the premiere, "Va, pensiero, sulle" was sung on every street. Verdi said the opera "was born under a lucky star."

After *Nabucco*, Verdi was on a roll—from 1843 until 1849, no fewer than a dozen of his operas were produced. The finest were *I Lombardi* (1843), *Ernani* (1844), *I Due Foscari* (1844), *Macbeth* (1847), whose sleepwalking scene is a highlight of Verdi's early but enduring interest in Shakespeare, and *Luisa Miller* (1849). Never had Italian opera possessed such a wealth of passionate ensemble singing; Verdi's pen brimmed with duets, trios, quartets, and rousing choruses. Many of these early works brought his name to prominence outside of Italy. Yet even these works would be overshadowed by three of history's most celebrated operas: *Rigoletto* (1851), *Il Trovatore* (1853), and *La Traviata* (1853). The next years were equally productive, culminating in 1871 with *Aïda*, composed for the new opera house in Cairo and the opening of the Suez Canal. Its premiere was world news.

Never had such attention been lavished on a theatrical spectacle. Verdi, a man of humility, was disgusted. "Nowadays, what an apparatus accompanies each opera!" he lamented. "Journalists, soloists, chorus, conductors, players, etc. etc., all must carry their stone to the edifice of publicity, to build up a framework of wretched gossip which adds nothing to the merit of an opera, but merely obscures its real value. This is deplorable, deeply deplorable!!" Verdi had become, along with Garibaldi and Mazzini, a symbol of Italian nationalism, the most famous person in Italy. After most of Italian unification had been accomplished, the great statesman Camillo Cavour convinced Verdi to become a senator, and for several years the composer took seriously his duties in Parliament, until the farce of politics inevitably sickened him.

Verdi was only fifty-eight when he announced that *Aïda* would be his last opera. For many years, he had linked his life with that of Giuseppina Strepponi. After years of living together, the couple finally married in 1859. Verdi retired to his farm in Busetto, where he took pleasure and pride in introducing modern farming methods and tools to the almost-feudal town. He did not completely give up composing, though, and he was especially inspired by the death on May 22, 1873, of the beloved Italian novelist Alessandro Manzoni, author of the seminal 1827 novel *I Promessi sposi* (*The Betrothed*). Verdi wrote his great Requiem in memory of the writer.

After the overwhelming triumph of *Aïda*, however, opera lovers could not understand why Verdi no longer composed for the stage. In the late 1870s, it was suggested that the increasing success of Verdi's exact contemporary, Wagner, had had something to do with his retirement. Although singers loved appearing in Verdi's juicy roles, his music was not considered in Wagner's class. The German composer and his army of Wagnerites (including many influential German critics) all but obliterated the artistic status of any opera composer other than Wagner himself.

Wagner's growing prestige and influence in Italy did make Verdi uneasy, for he felt that each country had its own vital and special way of expressing itself artistically. Before his retirement, Verdi, much to his dismay, had himself been accused of becoming increasingly Wagnerian. In his later operas, he had certainly become more dramatic in his characterizations, and his orchestral forces had been more integrated to the action. But there all similarity ends. Wagner, the eternal egoist, was never known to have paid the Italian a compliment; nor had the two masters ever met. But when Wagner died in 1883, Verdi wrote to his publisher, the director of the Italian music publishing firm Giulio Ricordi, "Sad sad sad! Wagner is dead! When I read this news yesterday, I may truthfully say that I was completely crushed. Let us say no more! It is a great personality that has disappeared. A name which leaves a mighty imprint upon the history of Art."

However, around the time of Wagner's death, Verdi found a new vein of creativity. It was spurred by the appearance in his life of Arrigo Boito, thirty years younger, the extraordinary composer of *Mefistofele* as well as a poet of distinction. Boito had prepared a sensitive adaptation of Shakespeare's *Othello*. In the 1860s, Verdi had composed sketches for an opera of *King Lear*, which he had desperately wanted to write, but the libretto had been weak. Verdi dearly loved Shakespeare; he once told Ricordi, "Ah, Shakespeare, Shakespeare . . . the great poet of the human heart!" Boito pleaded with the old composer, saying that only the great Verdi could make his *Otello* libretto live.

After fifteen years of operatic inactivity, but with one of the finest librettos ever written at his command, Verdi composed with the fervency of youth and the wisdom of age. *Otello* is marvelously fluid in construction. The orchestral writing is as important as in Wagner's operas, but it has Verdi's emphasis on vocal beauty. *Otello* was produced at La Scala on February 5, 1887. It was the first time an opera by Verdi had premiered at Italy's most famous theater since *Giovanna d'Arco* in 1845. (After 1845 he had banned La Scala from premiering his work because of the house's incompetent management.)

The premiere was a heartwarming success. At seventy-three the old master had fulfilled himself by producing the greatest operatic tragedy of his language. Certainly he now felt entitled to peace.

After *Otello* six years passed, years of quiet contentment. But once again Boito appeared; he had written another libretto, a comedy based on Shakespeare's *Merry Wives of Windsor* and the *Henry* plays, which he called *Falstaff*. Verdi, the great tragedian, had composed but one comedy in his career. The failure of that one comedy (*Un Giorno di regno*) in 1840 had always rankled him. Boito once again beseeched the old man to look at his new libretto. Verdi resisted strongly again and again, telling Boito that his great age would never permit such an exertion, that he would probably die before completing it. But as the weeks passed and the master delved deeper into the libretto — a text finer perhaps than even *Otello* — the god of inspiration once again seized him. He cautiously taunted Boito that he was composing a bit for amusement.

Falstaff is a wonderful work of comic genius, the product of a quicksilver mind. It is particularly astonishing for a composer close to eighty whose entire career had been concentrated upon tragedy. The work is radiant and scintillating, as the power of creative genius rejuvenated itself into old age. For an artist at the dusk of an already immortal career to have written two masterworks portraying opposite poles of human nature must remain one of those mysteries of the creative process.

After the premiere of *Falstaff* on February 9, 1893, at La Scala, Verdi lived another eight years and composed two more works, the superb *Te Deum* and *Four Sacred Pieces*; both are sober and beautiful. In 1897 his beloved wife died suddenly. He could not bear the loneliness at his farm after her death and moved to Milan. He refused many honors, including the conferment of nobility by the Italian government and a theater bearing his name. Always keenly aware of poverty and the precarious lot of musicians, he founded a home for old musicians called Casa di Riposo.

His health had been faltering, and he complained that his legs hardly supported him, but still he carried on. At eighty-eight, one evening while dressing for dinner, he bent to look for a fallen shirt stud. He suffered a stroke. Within days the master was dead. "Verdi is dead," Boito wrote; "he has carried away with him an enormous measure of light and vital warmth. We had all basked in the sunshine of that Olympian old age. . . . Never had I experienced such a feeling of hatred against death, of contempt for that mysterious, blind, stupid, triumphant and craven power." Throughout Italy, flags were draped with black ribbon, and schools and theaters were closed.

It was a glorious funeral, with more than 300,000 Milanese lining the street to pay their respects. Toscanini directed a chorus of 820, but throughout the vast throngs of people, flowing spontaneously from the mourners, one softly heard "Va, pensiero" from nearly sixty years before.

Verdi's biographer, Mary Jane Phillips-Matz, wrote, "Few heads of state have been tendered higher honors than Verdi, universally hailed as an artist, a model citizen, and a philanthropist. To the world, as to the nation he helped to found, he left an enduring legacy of music, charity, patriotism, honor, grace, and reason. He was and remains a mighty force for continuing good." The historian Peter Conrad concludes, "Verdi set the entire world to music. . . . The composer is opera's Shakespeare: Verdi the populist is an expert on the human heart. . . . Like the chameleon Shakespeare, Verdi hears everyone at once and distributes music impartially to all men alike . . . as if a god were listening to the polyphonic hubbub of the human race."

Rigoletto (1851)

Rigoletto is based on Victor Hugo's volatile 1832 drama Le Roi s'amuse. An opera of powerful impact, it was theatrically and musically more integrated and dramatic than Verdi's earlier achievements. At thirty-seven Verdi had hit his stride. The title role of Rigoletto, the hunchbacked hero, is a baritone's tour de force. The historian M. Owen Lee wrote, "Rigoletto is not only outwardly deformed. . . . He is not just a jester with a tongue that lashes and cuts—he is inwardly as well as outwardly vile. He is an evil man." The opera contains a quantity of world-famous melodies, from the ubiquitous "La donna è mobile" to "Caro nome" for coloratura and the incomparably effective quartet "Bella figlia dell'amore." Rigoletto was premiered at Venice's La Fenice on March 11, 1851, with resounding success.

Callas, di Stefano, Gobbi, La Scala Orchestra and Chorus, Serafin: EMI Classics CDCB 56327

Tebaldi, del Monaco, Protti, de Palma, Corena, Santa Cecilia Academy Orchestra and Chorus, Erede: London 440242-2

Il Trovatore (The Troubador) (1853)

Less than two years after *Rigoletto*, Verdi followed with *Il Trovatore*, which had its successful premiere in Rome on January 19, 1853. It is perhaps the most melodramatic opera in the living repertoire, with a plot and libretto that almost defy comprehension. The writer James Anderson explains, "The libretto is a by-word for obscurity and confusion, but if the listener attends to Ferrando's narration in the first scene and bears in mind that the old Gypsy Azucena is the central character, the action becomes more logical." The work is flooded with dramatic lyricism in such favorites as the Anvil Chorus, the Miserere, and "Di quella pira."

Sutherland, Horne, Pavarotti, Ghiaurov, National Philharmonic Orchestra, Bonynge: London 417137-2

Price, Elias, Tucker, Warren, Tozzi, Rome Opera Orchestra, Basile: RCA 60560-2-RG

Milanov, Barbieri, Björling, Warren, RCA Victor Symphony Orchestra and Robert Shaw Chorale, Cellini: RCA 6643-2-RG

La Traviata (The Fallen Woman) (1853)

The heroine of *La Traviata* is Violetta, a consumptive and bewitching courtesan who continues to charge our imagination. *La Traviata* was based on the 1848 novel *La dame aux camélias* by the younger Alexandre Dumas, who had been in love with the model for Violetta. The entire opera exudes an aura of glamour, with music of tender lyricism. Verdi is filled with compassion for his "fallen woman." Two of Violetta's arias—"Sempre libera" in Act I and her farewell, "Addio del passato," in Act III—are particularly celebrated. The first performance took place in Venice only weeks after the premiere of *Il Trovatore*, on March 6, 1853. Verdi wrote, "*La Traviata* was an immense fiasco, and worse, people laughed. Still, what do you expect? I am not upset over it. I'm wrong or they are wrong. As for myself, I believe that the last word on *La Traviata* was not said last night. They will see it again, and we shall see!" As usual Verdi was right, and *La Traviata* is one of the best loved of all operas.

Sutherland, Pavarotti, Manuguerra, National Philharmonic Orchestra and Opera Chorus, Bonynge: London 430491-2

Moffo, Tucker, Merrill, Rome Opera Orchestra, Previtali: RCA Gold Seal 4144-2-RG

Aïda (1870–71)

In the years following *Traviata*, Verdi worked with his usual intensity and excellence. *I Vespri siciliani* appeared in 1855, *Un Ballo in maschera* in 1859, *La Forza del destino* in 1862, and *Don Carlos* in 1867. Each one of these operas is entrenched in the repertory today. But the popularity of *Aïda* is equaled only by that of *Carmen* and *La Bohème*. *Aïda* is sure-fire theater, a spectacle equal to Meyerbeer's finest efforts at grandness, but with a musical depth that is as great as its pageantry. The opera literally gushes with beauty. From the great tenor aria "Celeste Aïda" to Aïda's "Ritorna vincitor," the Nile scene where she sings "O patria mia," the wondrous duet for Aïda and Rademes ("Terra, addio"), and the most famous march in Italian opera, *Aïda* never loses its power to enthrall. The music critic Olin Downes wrote, "Characters who never existed in an ancient and unknown past become, through Verdi's powers of divination and expression, human beings caught in a web of passion and circumstance." The premiere on December 24, 1871, in Cairo was exotically colorful: the khedive (the ruler of Egypt) and an extremely large and veiled harem occupied the boxes. The producers had hoped Verdi would attend, but he was worried about the boat trip; he said that if he came, they would probably have to make a mummy out of his remains. From the beginning, *Aïda* was considered a landmark in opera. An excited Mussorgsky, who made a habit of harsh criticism, wrote to the critic Vladimir Stassov, "But *Maestro Senatore* Verdi is quite another matter! This one pushes ahead on a grand scale, this innovator doesn't feel shy. All is *Aida-ai-da!* (Ah, yes!) — outdistancing everything, outdistancing everyone, even himself. He has knocked over *Trovatore*, Mendelssohn, Wagner — and almost Amerigo Vespucci, too."

Ricciarelli, Obraztsova, Domingo, Ghiaurov, La Scala Orchestra and Chorus, Abbado: Deutsche Grammophon 410092-2

Price, Bumbry, Domingo, Milnes, Raimondi, London Symphony Orchestra, Leinsdorf: RCA 6198-2-RC

Requiem (1873–74)

Verdi's is the greatest Requiem since that of Berlioz. Certainly if compared to more pious requiems, Verdi's will smack of high theatricality. But why not? After all, he was Verdi. The Requiem was composed just two years after *Aïda*, his most grandiose opera. It is very great music, moving, profound, and fused with religious spirit, from a creator who had contempt for official religion. After reading a scurrilous review of the Requiem by Hans von Bülow, Brahms studied the score and said, "Bülow has made an ass of himself; Verdi's Requiem is a work of genius." Von Bülow later repented and wrote to Verdi, "Will you forgive me, will you use the sovereign's right to grant pardon?"

Schwarzkopf, Ludwig, Gedda, Ghiaurov, Philharmonia Orchestra and Chorus, Giulini: EMI Classics ZDCB 56250

Sutherland, Horne, Pavarotti, Talvela, Vienna Philharmonic Orchestra and Vienna State Opera Chorus, Solti: London 411944-2

Otello (1887)

Otello, completed sixteen years after *Aïda*, brings us to yet another stage of Verdi's art. Here he probed jealousy and its aftermath, literally dissecting the dangerous emotion as no opera had ever done before. It is no surprise that Verdi, a great soul-psychologist, was an ardent lover of Shakespeare. The opera makes large vocal demands on the leading roles and requires singer-actors of the highest quality.

The critic James Huneker asked, "What is the most surprising thing about *Otello*? I think that it is the fact that it was composed when Verdi was past three score and ten. This seems incredible. It seethes with the passion of middle manhood, with the fervors of a flowering maturity. . . . It is a wonderful thing that Verdi began it at a time when most men are preparing for the great adventure. Reversing the usual processes, this extraordinary Italian wrote younger music the older he grew."

Once again *Otello* thrives on beautiful melody, such as the love duet between Otello and Desdemona "Già nella notte densa," Iago's "Credo in un Dio crudel," Desdemona's famous Willow Song ("Salce, salce"), and her "Ave Maria."

Vickers, Freni, Glassop, Berlin Philharmonic Orchestra, German Opera Chorus, Karajan: EMI Classics CDMB 69308

Tebaldi, del Monaco, Protti, Vienna Philharmonic Orchestra, Karajan: London 411618-2

Scotto, Domingo, Milnes, National Philharmonic Orchestra, Levine: RCA RCD2-2951

Te Kanawa, Pavarotti, Nucci, Chicago Symphony Orchestra and Chorus, Solti: London 433669-2

Jones, di Stasio, McCracken, New Philharmonia Orchestra, Ambrosian Opera Chorus, Barbirolli: EMI Classics CDMB 65296

Falstaff (1893)

Perhaps only Verdi—modest to the core, often disillusioned but never cynical, mentally stable, and even in his old age, as vulnerable and fresh as a spring flower—could have created *Falstaff*. Ernest Newman wrote, "One of the most serious and seemingly least humorous of men bade farewell to the world of art with a comedy of a light-fingeredness unique in that or any other epoch." Verdi's handling of the orchestra in *Falstaff* is light-years away from the approach of his first operas; here the orchestra has become the central figure. Indeed, his winsome characters are completely dependent for their delicious wit and warmth on the orchestral treatment, which is light as snow. *Falstaff* will not reveal itself all at once, but when it does, one judges all comedy from a different angle.

Gobbi, Schwarzkopf, Merriman, Barbieri, Moffo, Philharmonia Orchestra and Chorus, Karajan: EMI Classics CDCB 49668

Bruson, Ricciarelli, Hendricks, Valentini, Nucci, Los Angeles Philharmonic Orchestra and Chorus, Giulini: Deutsche Grammophon 410503-2

OTHER PRINCIPAL WORKS

CHAMBER MUSIC
Quartet in E Minor for Strings (1873)*

OPERAS
Nabucco (1842)*
I Lombardi (1843)
Ernani (1844)*
I Due foscari (1844)
Giovanna d'Arco (1845)
Alzira (1845)
Attila (1846)
Macbeth (1847)*
Il Corsaro (1848)
Luisa Miller (1849)*
I Vespri siciliani (1855)*
Simon Boccanegra (1857)*
Un Ballo in maschera (1859)*

La Forza del destino (1862)*
Don Carlos (1867)*

SACRED CHORAL MUSIC
Te Deum (1896)*
Four Sacred Pieces (1898)*

CHARLES GOUNOD

b. Paris, June 18, 1818

d. Saint-Cloud, October 18, 1893

Liberty is as real as heaven. It is a heaven on earth—the country of the elect; but it must be earned, and conquered, not by oppression, but by self-devotion; not by pillage, but by generosity; not by taking life, but by bestowing it, in the moral as well as the material sense.

Gounod's father, François Louis, was a lithographer and painter of decided talent; he died when Charles was only five. His widowed mother, Victoire, then eked out a livelihood teaching piano and singing, but the family lived in bitter poverty. Victoire was therefore sorry indeed to discover that her son passionately adored music. His first glimpse of opera came when he was taken to see Rossini's *Otello*, starring the great mezzo-soprano Maria Malibran. The boy was beside himself—he never forgot the rapture.

Victoire actively discouraged Charles from following art's wayward path, but he was insistent. At one point she asked her friend Antonín Reicha, a well-known composer and theorist, to teach Charles. She begged Reicha to be brutally hard on the child: "If you can send him back to me hating music, I shall bless you!" But after a year's instruction, Reicha pronounced, "Alas, you must resign yourself. Charles is gifted, nothing puts him off, nothing discourages him. He now knows everything I can teach him."

After acquiring a liberal arts degree from the Lycée Saint-Louis, Charles entered the Paris Conservatory, where he studied with Ferdinando Paer, Jean-François Lesueur (Berlioz's former teacher), and Fromental Halévy, composer of the 1835 opera *La Juive*. He tried three times to win the Prix de Rome—three years of study in Rome at the expense of the French government—and in 1839 he won. Upon winning, he later recalled, "My poor dear mother gave me the full score of *Don Giovanni* as a reward."

Gounod loved Italy, with its balmy climate, easy manners, and abundance of churches. Years later he remarked, "I feel that the land of Rome and Naples is my true, my only country. It is there that I would have wished to live until the end of my days." He had always been deeply attracted to Catholicism and the religious life, and once he was in the Eternal City, pious fervor seized him. Disdaining the tawdriness of the operatic world, he plunged himself in the study of the old polyphonic masters. Palestrina's purity delighted him most. Soon Gounod was composing strict three-part masses.

Gounod stayed at the Villa Medici, the headquarters of the French Academy, where winners of the Prix de Rome studied. He developed a close relationship with the Academy's venerable director, Jean-Auguste Ingres, who was not only a violinist but the greatest classical painter of the age; Ingres had known and admired Gounod's father. He encouraged Gounod to develop not only his musical talent but also his considerable gift for drawing and painting. In Rome, Gounod also met Fanny Mendelssohn Hensel, Felix Mendelssohn's sister and herself a fine pianist, who initiated the Frenchman into Beethoven's piano sonatas. She wrote that Gounod "is passionately fond of music in a way I have rarely seen before." Together they read Goethe's *Faust*, which made an indelible impression.

After completing his three-year term of study in Rome, Gounod visited Vienna, then returned to Paris to look for a position, preferably at a church. He gratefully accepted a post as organist and choirmaster at the Missions Etrangères and immediately introduced Palestrina's music to the parish. In 1846, thinking seriously of entering the priesthood, he started a two-year course at the Seminary of Saint-Sulpice. Gounod had more than a streak of the mountebank in him: although he was only a student, he could not resist donning the cleric's garb. The course satisfied only half of his nature, for Gounod's temperament constantly wavered between religious ecstasies—expressed in theatrical or mystical language—and voluptuous seductions. It was a dissonance in his nature that was never resolved.

Fortunately, Gounod did not neglect his music while he was at the seminary. Instead, he delved into Schubert, Schumann, and the radical Berlioz, who would eventually herald Gounod's gifts in a triumphant review of the composer's 1859 opera, *Faust*. A major turning point came as a result of his regular attendance at the soireés of the mezzo-soprano Pauline Viardot-García, sister of Maria Malibran, the mezzo who had provided Gounod's first introduction to opera. Viardot, who had been admired by Chopin and was at the time loved by the Russian novelist Turgenev, was an extraordinary musician and actress. Captivated by Gounod's talent and personality, she persuaded him to forget his career in the church and compose operas. As a vehicle for Viardot, he composed *Sapho*, produced in 1851. Gounod had long resisted the worldy temptations of opera, with its intrigues, prima donnas, fame, and fortune, and in composing one, he felt that he had fallen from grace. As if to repent, for every opera he composed, he would produce a mass or oratorio. *Sapho* was shelved after four performances at the Paris Opera, but Gounod was hooked. His next opera, *Ulisse* (1852), did well; it was performed forty times—quite exceptional for an unknown composer in Paris. His 1857 *Le Médecin malgré lui*, based on Molière's play of the same name, is touched with light refinement and gentle humor and was a mild success. Yet Gounod's operas made little general impression.

It was Léon Carvalho, director of Paris's Théâtre-Lyrique, who urged Gounod to use Goethe's *Faust* as a subject. Gounod accepted the challenge. *Faust*, which premiered on March 19, 1859, added a golden chapter to the history of opera. It rapidly achieved international repertory status (although the Germans were naturally protective of the integrity of Goethe's masterpiece and retitled the piece *Marguerite* when it was first performed in Germany).

Gounod would never again achieve the triumph he had with *Faust*. His 1867 *Roméo et Juliette* came closest and is today entrenched in the repertory, especially in France. In all he wrote thirteen operas, which met with varying degrees of success. He had fled to London in 1870 with the Franco-Prussian War, an event that deeply shook him. From there he wrote, "Oh, most unhappy earth! Wretched home of the human race, where barbarism not only still exists, but is taken for glory . . . amid the monstrosities of the iron age; and instead of driving their weapons into the earth to benefit their fellow creatures, men plunge them into one another's hearts to decide the ownership of the actual soil. Barbarians! Savages!"

England loved his operas and religious works and was hospitable to Gounod, and he remained there for five years. His personal life was in turmoil in those years, though. In April 1852, he had married Anna Zimmermann, daughter of a well-known piano teacher at the Paris Conservatory. The couple had a son and a daughter. Gounod—in spite of his piety—was an endless womanizer, but for almost two decades Anna had withstood the humiliations. In 1871, however, Gounod began an affair with an intelligent but unstable socialite, Georgina Weldon. The relationship with Georgina lasted some years, but his marriage survived.

Musically, Gounod's stay in England was fruitful. He had turned more and more to religious music, and England's liking for choral music and the high performance standards prevalent there inspired him, as they had Handel, Haydn, and Mendelssohn. For Debussy, the church music "of Gounod and company seems to come from some kind of hysterical mysticism and has the effect of a sinister force." But the formula worked, and the Victorian temper adored the constant flow of Gounod's piety in motets, canticles, cantatas, oratorios, requiems, and masses. Perhaps best known are the oratorios *La Rédemption* (c.1882) and *Mors et vita* (c.1885). Along with his sacred music, he wrote many songs and salon pieces for the piano. One of them, the lugubrious *Funeral March of a Marionette* (1872), which Gounod also orchestrated, was used by Alfred Hitchcock in his television series *Alfred Hitchcock Presents*, with no credit given to the composer.

One of his songs is still occasionally heard, but it is cheap claptrap. Gounod used Bach's chaste C major prelude from Book I of *The Well-Tempered Clavier* as his theme, and he called his song "Ave Maria" or "Méditation religieuse." He also converted it into a piece for solo piano. It brought Gounod a fortune, but eternal damnation from lovers of the Leipzig cantor.

Of the large quantity of songs Gounod composed, many are delightful, while others are dreadfully sentimental. Ravel remarked, "The true founder of song writing in France was Charles Gounod." Gounod was well able to promote his songs as well as write them. He often accompanied himself at the piano, and he had a mellifluous, if fragile, tenor voice, which he used to great effect in the fashionable salons of Paris and London. Jules Barbier, his librettist, said, "There are no singers to equal him, even among tenors who earn 7,000 francs a minute."

Some critics have been unduly harsh on Gounod, but he nevertheless had a potent influence on a long line of French composers, including the early Claude Debussy, Camille Saint-Saëns, Henri Duparc, Ernest Reyer, Gabriel Fauré, Jules Massenet, and Francis Poulenc, all of whom were attracted to his sinuous and specifically French lyricism. Although Gounod is known today by only a fraction of his work, the opera *Roméo et Juliette*, with its seductive charm, continues to delight, and *Faust*, with its magnetic attraction, will be heard as long as opera still has the ability to enchant us.

Faust (1859)

For many English-speaking people, the name *Faust* refers to Gounod's opera first and foremost, before any other literary or musical interpretations of the story. In fact, *Faust* was the most popular opera of the last decades of the nineteenth century. When the Metropolitan Opera first opened its doors in 1883, *Faust* was the work chosen to welcome New York's opera-loving public. Lavish in its arias, the opera also enchants with its waltz, choruses, and ballet. The libretto by Michel Carré and Jules Barbier may seem slight or even ludicrous in relation to Goethe's herculean work, but the very province of opera is to compromise an original drama into a fantasy containing music. Forgotten operas with fine music poorly served by their librettos abound. *Faust* in its way is a masterful adaptation, using Goethe's episode between Faust and Gretchen (Marguerite) as its vehicle.

Faust has become the epitome of grand opera, although, as Gounod's biographer James Harding wrote, "The historical importance of *Faust* is that it sounded a new note in French music. The conventional pomposities of the grand opera that dominated the stage were superseded by a more intimate and poetic approach. The fashion Gounod set was one of conversational exchange rather than declamation. The people in *Faust* sang naturally. They were familiar in their actions. They did not strike flamboyant attitudes."

Sutherland, Corelli, Ghiaurov, London Symphony Orchestra, Ambrosian Opera Chorus, Bonynge: London 421240-2

Freni, Domingo, Allen, Ghiaurov, Paris Opera Orchestra, Prêtre: EMI Classics CDCC 47493

OTHER PRINCIPAL WORKS

CHAMBER MUSIC
Petite symphonie for Nine Wind Instruments (1885)*

OPERAS
Le Médecin malgré lui (1857)*
Mireille (1864)
Roméo et Juliette (1867)*

WORKS FOR ORCHESTRA
Symphony no. 1 in D Major (1855)*
Symphony no. 2 in E-flat Major (c.1856)*

JACQUES OFFENBACH

b. Cologne, June 20, 1819

d. Paris, October 5, 1880

I do not know what I have done to cause God to bestow so much happiness and so much melody upon me.

Offenbach, the seventh child of a Jewish cantor from Offenbach am Main, grew up as Jacob Levy Eberst. Upon embarking on his career, he changed *Jacob* to *Jacques* and took as his last name the name of his father's native town. Jacob was intensely musical from a very young age. His father taught him the rudiments of music, and he was composing by six. Chamber music filled the family's evenings, and Jacob gravitated to the cello, making his debut on that instrument when he was only twelve.

Cantor Eberst wanted his talented son to receive the best possible musical education, and Paris seemed the obvious choice. Unfortunately, the Paris Conservatory excluded foreigners. Jacob's family implored Luigi Cherubini, the venerable director, to make an exception. Cherubini was highly impressed with the fourteen-year-old boy and finally consented to waive the rule.

But the restless Offenbach disliked the Conservatory and left within a year. He was soon hired as a cellist in the Opéra-Comique Orchestra. At the opera he met Friedrich von Flotow, the future composer of the 1847 opera *Martha*. The two collaborated in writing cello pieces, Offenbach composing the melody, Flotow the piano accompaniments. Together they augmented their livelihood by performing these pieces at fashionable salons.

In his twenties, Offenbach, with considerable success, pursued his career as a cellist. One Paris reviewer wrote, "He will be, indeed he already is, the Liszt of the violoncello." He had tours in France, Germany, and London, where he performed for Queen Victoria and Prince Albert. For these concerts, he composed a quantity of cello pieces and his two cello concertos. In August 1844, he converted to Catholicism as a condition of his marriage to Herminie d'Alcain, who went on to give Offenbach four daughters and a son. It was an unusually happy marriage. A friend of the family said, "She deserved well her famous husband." An appointment in 1850 as conductor at the Théâtre Française gave him a chance to compose incidental music for a few plays, and he had also been writing a few operettas as well.

But several theaters refused these works. In 1855 Offenbach had the bright idea of starting his own theater. It was extremely small, but it was on the Champs-Elysées, and he called it the Bouffes-Parisiens. In a short time, his productions were à la mode. Humor, gaiety, wit, and a champagne atmosphere parodying French society and manners prevailed. The shows were harmless spoofs of the pleasure-loving vulgarities of Napoleon III and the Empress Eugénie's Second Empire. In 1858 Offenbach's fame rocketed with the production of the operetta *Orphée aux enfers (Orpheus in the Underworld)*. *Orphée*'s infectious tunes included the naughty and notorious "Can can," which caught the pulse of the era. Each night, audiences waited in line to listen to its giddy quadrilles and gallops and to laugh at the jibes the show poked at them. Offenbach eventually purchased a magnificent summer residence at Etretat and called it Villa Orphée.

Offenbach was prolific during the 1860s and 1870s, when he wrote with amazing speed such operettas as *Barbe-bleue, La Vie parisienne, La Périchole, Vert-vert, Les Brigands, Geneviève de Brabant, La Grande-duchesse de Gérolstein*, and *La Belle Hélène*. The French public could not get enough of Offenbach's mirthful frivolity, and productions in Vienna, London, and New York were sold out as well. Offenbach's operettas are among the finest of all light musical entertainment, resting easily next to those of Gilbert and Sullivan, whom he inspired, and Johann Strauss II, whom he encouraged to write his own operettas.

Naturally some critics lambasted him for writing "fleshly music." One writer thought *La Belle Hélène* (1864) was simply the sexual instinct expressed in melody. For better or worse, Offenbach helped to establish the reputation of Paris as the city of sin. Respectable folks were warned to stay away from the prurience of Offenbach's theatrical demimonde. That prudish teetotaler George Bernard Shaw thought, "Offenbach's music is wicked. It is abandoned stuff; every accent is a snap of the fingers in the face of moral responsibility." As might be expected, Gioachino Rossini, the reigning wit of Paris, loved the operettas dearly, calling Offenbach "the Mozart of the Champs-Elysées." As might also be expected, Wagner, the enemy of Jewish composers and of liberal Paris, called Offenbach's works "a dung heap on which all the swine of Europe wallowed."

The humiliating French defeat in the 1870–71 Franco-Prussian War depressed the composer deeply. Offenbach had become a symbol of Paris and the Second Empire, and he felt thoroughly French. He wrote, "I hope this William Krupp and his dreadful Bismarck will pay for all this. Alas, what terrible people these Prussians are, and what despair do I feel at the thought that I myself was born on the Rhine and am connected with those savages by a number of links! Alas, my poor France, how much do I thank her for accepting me among her children." After the war, with less in their stomachs and in their pockets, the French sobered up considerably. Offenbach's saucy gaiety was wearing thin—so thin that he faced financial ruin. In 1876–77, in a last-ditch attempt to recoup some of his fortune, he took a tour of America. It failed miserably, and on the way back to France, he consoled himself by writing a little book titled *Offenbach in America*, published in 1877. He was relieved to be home, for "[i]n France I became Offenbach again."

By the late 1870s, the composer was gravely ill with an assortment of health problems. He burned with remorse, for he felt he had thrown his talents away on cheap success and the god of money. Before departing this world, he desperately wanted to leave to posterity a work of art—a serious opera. As early as 1851, he had been intrigued by a play by Jules Barbier and Michel Carré, based on stories by the early Romantic German author E.T.A. Hoffmann. Some years after Offenbach first noticed the play, Barbier fashioned an opera libretto from it and sold it to the composer Hector Salomon. Offenbach was in despair. In 1880, in an incredible act of homage and kindness, Salomon, who had almost completed his own opera, relinquished the rights to the ailing Offenbach. The sixty-year-old composer, knowing that death was fast approaching, worked with savage intensity. As the months passed, his doctors found it hard to believe that this shriveled shell of a man, who resembled nothing so much as an eerie character from Hoffmann, could even hold a pen. Only his intense desire to complete the score drove him on, and complete it he did, except for a few details completed by his friend Ernest Guiraud. In June 1880 the production was cast. The composer, always ironical, looked deeply into the eyes of his beloved Russian wolfhound, Kleinzach (named after a character from Hoffmann), and said, "I would give all I have if you and I could be at the first performance." He urged Léon Carvalho, director of the Opéra-Comique, "Hurry, hurry, I have little time left, and my only wish is to see the first performance of my opera." But it was not to be. Ridiculous production delays prevented Offenbach's wish from being granted. He died clutching his manuscript, when a fit of violent choking caused his heart to give out. The opera had its premiere five months after his death, on February 10, 1881. It was the major event of the season, lasting for 101 performances.

Les Contes d'Hoffmann (*The Tales of Hoffmann*) is the crown of Offenbach's life. With this lone opera, the composer of more than one hundred operettas gained entrance into the palace of the immortals.

Les Contes d'Hoffmann (The Tales of Hoffmann) (1880)

In its prologue, three acts, and epilogue, *The Tales of Hoffmann* never flags in its acute musical characterization of an essentially disturbing view of romantic love. The libretto, by Carré and Barbier, is one of the finest of opera texts. The hero of the opera, Ernst Theodor Amadeus (named in tribute to Mozart) Hoffmann (1776–1822), was one of the great characters of his age—poet, scenic designer, novelist, mural painter, caricaturist, lawyer, composer, critic, madman, and one of the chief representatives (in his bizarre stories) of the emerging Romantic spirit. More than thirty operas have been based on his writings. Hoffmann himself composed at least eleven operas, the best being *Undine* (1816), which was admired by Weber. At age thirty-five, Hoffmann fell in love with Julia Marc, a fifteen-year-old girl to whom he taught singing. After her marriage to someone else, he never saw her again, but Julia's image haunted his dreams until his death. In the opera, aspects of Julia are portrayed by the mechanical dancing doll Olympia, the courtesan Giulietta, the doomed singer Antonia, and the actress Stella. The opera possesses a wealth of lovely arias, as well as Offenbach's most famous melodic creation, the Barcarolle, a Venetian boat song sung by gondoliers. In the opera, it is sung by Giulietta and Nicklausse offstage as the curtain rises overlooking the Grand Canal in Act II, "Belle nuit, ô nuit d'amour."

The critic Olin Downes wrote, "*The Tales of Hoffmann* may be accepted as simply a charming, amusing, touching score, full of melody and genius. Or it may appear as being, beneath its surface, the symbol of man's dreams, fears, frustrations and tragical adventures in the search for love. Either way, the opera is unique."

Sutherland, Tourangeau, Domingo, Cuénod, Suisse Romande Orchestra, Bonynge: London
   417363-2
Gruberova, Eder, Domingo, Bacquier, Diaz, Orchestre National de France, Ozawa: Deutsche
   Grammophon 427682-2

Various Overtures

The overtures to Offenbach's operettas are perennial gems. The most popular is the timeless overture to *Orphée aux enfers*.

Berlin Philharmonic Orchestra, Karajan: Deutsche Grammophon 400044-2
Philharmonia Orchestra, Marriner: Philips 411476-2

Gaîté parisienne

In 1938 Manuel Rosenthal ingeniously arranged music from the operettas into a ballet that has become well known and often recorded.

Boston Pops Orchestra, Fiedler: RCA Victrola 7734-2-RV
Pittsburgh Symphony Orchestra, Previn: Philips 442403-2
New York Philharmonic Orchestra, Bernstein: Sony Classical SMK 47532

OTHER PRINCIPAL WORKS

OPERETTAS
Orphée aux enfers (1858)*
La Belle Hélène (1864)*
Barbe-bleue (1866)*
La Vie parisienne (1866)*
Vert-vert (1866)*
La Grande-Duchesse de Gérolstein (1867)*
La Périchole (1868)*
Les Brigands (1869)*
La Fille du tambour-major (1879)

CÉSAR FRANCK

b. Liège, December 10, 1822

d. Paris, November 8, 1890

What is of the first importance is that a composition should be musical, and emotional as well.

Franck was a prodigy on the piano, and his father, a banker with a bent for music, had one desire: to see his son become a concert pianist. César's brother Joseph also showed talent, but far from the level of his brother. Nothing is known of César's relationship with his mother. At eleven the boy was already a veteran of the Belgian concert stage; his father brought César to Paris to study at the Paris Conservatory. He performed brilliantly in all subjects, especially organ playing.

Much to his father's dismay, however, the organ, not the piano, was becoming César's primary interest. He was developing into an introspective and deeply religious man whose glorious organ improvisations seemed to bring to life the spirit of Bach himself. At age twenty-three, he wrote his first choral work, *Ruth*—a biblical eclogue.

During the dark June days of the 1848 Revolution, Franck married an actress, Félicité Desmousseaux, whom he carried over the barricades to the church. Félicité was the daughter of a tragedian, and bringing an actress into the family was the last straw for the elder Franck. Father and son broke off relations. The marriage would last until Franck's death, but the couple remained childless.

In 1861, after stints in two minor organ posts, Franck was appointed chief organist at the St.-Clotilde Church in Paris, a position he would retain until his death, nearly thirty years later. In 1872 he succeeded his former teacher, François Benoist, as organ professor at the Conservatory. His appointment was a surprise, as the unobtrusive Franck was no match for the loud politics at the Conservatory. His colleagues often laughed at him for his lofty ideals, absent-mindedness, and total absorption in his art; when they acknowledged his music at all, it was almost invariably with open hostility. Nothing could stop him from his chosen mission, however, and he rose each morning at five for a few quiet hours of composition before a day of endless activity, most of it frustrating.

Outside of his church duties and organ classes at the Conservatory, a circle of younger composers had been gathering around him: Alexis de Castillon, Henri Duparc, Ernest Chausson, Vincent d'Indy, Augusta Holmès, Albéric Magnard, Guillaume Lekeu, Charles Tournemire, and others. Each was gifted, but each was also, in his way, ill equipped technically. Franck gently but firmly guided them toward musical fulfillment. His teaching became legendary. Later, other composers (including Gabriel Fauré, Paul Dukas, and Emmanuel Chabrier) were also nurtured by him.

Franck himself developed very slowly—his finest music was not written un-til he was into his sixties. Appreciation for his music outside his circle was rare. Saint-Saëns premiered the Piano Quintet (1879) but hated it. After the con-cert, Franck, radiant with joy, offered the manuscript to Saint-Saëns as a token of his appreciation. The next day the janitor found the score still on the piano. After the first performance of the great D minor symphony (M.48, 1888), Gounod, when asked for his opinion, replied, "This symphony was the affirma-tion of incompetence pushed to dogmatic lengths."

In April 1890, to Franck's surprise, the sixty-seven-year-old composer tasted a bit of success for the first time, with his String Quartet (M.9). The next day Franck shyly smiled at Vincent d'Indy and said, "There! You see, the public is beginning to understand me." Only weeks later, when crossing the Pont Royal, he was struck in the chest by a horse-drawn omnibus. From that moment, his health declined rapidly. In the autumn, he caught a cold, which developed into pleurisy. *Père* Franck, as his loving disciples called him, lost all his strength. In a matter of weeks, their master was dead. His last words—"*Mes en-fants! Mes pauvres enfants!*"—were presumably meant for the pupils who had relied so heavily on him.

At the funeral Emmanuel Chabrier said, "*Adieu, Maître, et merci*, for you have done well! We salute in you one of the greatest artists of our century as well as the incomparable teacher whose example has brought into being a whole generation of sturdy, dedicated, and serious-minded musicians thor-oughly equipped to take part in battles often hard and long-disputed. We salute too in you the just and honest man, so human and devoid of self-interest, who never gave advice that was not sound or uttered a word that was not good. *Adieu!"*

A few years after Franck's death, Claude Debussy recalled, "César Franck was a simple-hearted man; even the discovery of a beautiful new chord could fill his day with joy. . . . The genius of Franck has been much discussed without anyone ever mentioning his most personal quality—namely, naïve simplicity. This man had bad luck and he was misunderstood, yet he had the soul of a child so thoroughly good-natured that he could look upon people's wickedness and the disorder of the world without a trace of bitterness."

Franck will always be loved for several instrumental works, each of which displays his structural innovation, which has been called *cyclic form*—the quoting and transformation in the finale of themes from earlier movements. Franck's music is highly chromatic and often has a high-pitched intensity. The Piano Quintet is permeated with an almost oppressive, sweltering emotionalism. His oratorio *Les Béatitudes* (M.53, 1879) combines cloying pages with passages of seraphic beauty. The great *Prelude, Chorale, and Fugue* for piano (M.21, 1884) is haunted by Bach. Franck is less popular today than he was half a century ago, but his music continues to move audiences by its special religious Romanticism, its dark-hued richness, and its glowing faith in humanity. His role in French music during his maturity was, one may say, necessary. Through his organ playing, his pupils on that instrument, his devoted band of composition students, and the high seriousness of his own work, he helped create a true French school of instrumental music that placed the composer, not the singer or instrumentalist, first.

Prelude, Chorale, and Fugue, M.21 (1884)

The *Prelude, Chorale, and Fugue* is the finest large-scale French solo piano work of its period. Like most of Franck's best work, it blends a highly charged mysticism (stated in an intensely chromatic harmonic vocabulary inspired by Wagner) and a lofty, romanticized Bachian sentiment. The richness of the piano writing suggests a feeling of the organ. Once again Franck makes use of cyclic form as he finalizes the work in a burst of radiant light.

Richter: Monitor 72022-2
Rubinstein: RCA 09026-62590-2

Variations symphoniques for Piano and Orchestra, M.46 (1885)

Symphonic Variations, one of the composer's perfect and most economical works, is a masterpiece of variational technique. Within fifteen minutes, an introduction is performed followed by six variations and a finale. In essence, this is a complex one-movement piano concerto. The score is less mystical by far than the usual Franck, with a diamondlike elegance and pianistic glitter. The eminent French pianist Louis Diémer gave the premiere on May 1, 1886, to the displeasure of an aggressively upset audience.

Weissenberg, Berlin Philharmonic Orchestra, Karajan: EMI Classics CDM 64747
Collard, Toulouse Capitole Orchestra, Plasson: EMI Classics CDD 63889

Sonata in A Major for Violin and Piano, M.8 (1886)

This sonata was composed for the Belgian virtuoso Eugène Ysaÿe. It is one of the greatest and most popular Romantic violin sonatas and contains some of Franck's loveliest themes. Sensuous and yearning, it effectively utilizes the composer's cyclic form. A feeling of mystical devotion pervades the opening movement. The second movement is immensely turbulent, followed by a movement called a Recitative-Fantasia, a link to the poetic first movement and the basic vehemence of the second. The theme marked *dramatico* appears in the finale, a masterly movement marked by effective use of the canonic device. The ending is full of joy. The sonata is magnificent in the interplay of the two instruments.

Thibaud, Cortot: EMI Classics CDH 63032
Chung, Lupu: London 421154-2

Symphony in D Minor, M.48 (1886–88)

At its premiere on February 17, 1889, the symphony was a dismal failure. One traditionalist muttered to the composer Vincent d'Indy, "But my dear sir, who ever heard of writing for the English horn in a symphony?" But Franck himself was pleased: "It sounded well, just as I thought it would" was his response to the personal defeat. Rising from darkness to an ever-mounting triumph of blazing light, the symphony has become a staple of the symphonic repertoire. Each of its three movements shows Franck at the apex of his creative and structural power.

Montreal Symphony Orchestra, Dutoit: London 430278-2

Czech Philharmonic Orchestra, Barbirolli: Supraphon Collection 110613-2

OTHER PRINCIPAL WORKS

CHAMBER MUSIC

Quintet in F Minor for Piano and Strings (1878–79)*

Quartet in D Major for Strings, M.9 (1889)*

CHORAL WORKS

Rédemption (symphonic poem), M.52 (1875)

Les Béatitudes (oratorio), M.53 (1869–79)

Psyché (symphonic poem) (1887–88)

ORCHESTRAL WORKS

Les Éolides (symphonic poem), M.43 (1875–76)*

Le Chasseur maudit (symphonic poem), M.44 (1882)

ORGAN MUSIC

Six Pièces pour grand orgue, M.28–33 (1860–62): Fantaisie; Grand pièce symphonique;
    Prélude, fugue et variation; Pastorale; Prière; Final*

Three Pièces pour grand orgue, M.35–37 (1878)

Three Chorales, M.38–40 (1890)

PIANO AND ORCHESTRA WORKS

Les Djinns (symphonic poem), M.45 (1884)*

PIANO SOLO WORKS

Prélude, aria et final, M.23 (1886–87)*

BEDŘICH
SMETANA

b. Litomyšl, Bohemia, March 2, 1824

d. Prague, May 12, 1884

My compositions do not belong to the realm of absolute music, where one can get along well enough with musical signs and a metronome.

Smetana was the eleventh child of František and Barbara Smetana, born in a picturesque town east of Prague. His father ran a brewery, providing the family with an adequate income. František also gave his son a smattering of musical education, and the child learned to play the violin and the piano, which he especially loved. But Bedřich's father would never allow his son to become a professional musician. Bedřich was a dismal student in high school, but he did manage to improve his German considerably. German was then the official language of the Czech provinces, which had been under the political yoke of the Austrian Empire since the Thirty Years War.

In 1840, Smetana left school to devote himself to music. His father stubbornly refused to help him and even slapped the boy on the face when he heard the news. But young Smetana was courageous in his optimism, confiding to his diary, "With God's help and grace, someday I'll be a Liszt in technique, and a Mozart in composition."

Years later he told Liszt, "When I was seventeen, I knew neither what C double sharp nor D double flat was, and harmony was completely an unknown territory to me. Despite that I composed when I was nineteen, I broke the chains that bound me, and with the greatest diligence, devoted myself to music under the direction of a very thorough teacher, Josef Proksch of Prague."

The penniless youngster arrived in Prague in 1843, only to find that he was too old by a year to enter the Conservatory: "I had already been in Prague for two months without being able to obtain a piano, very often I went to bed hungry; once I ate nothing for three days in a row except for a cup of coffee and a roll, then nothing more." But his fortune soon changed. By chance, he met in the street the mother of Kateřina Kolářová, who had been his childhood playmate. In the intervening years, Kateřina had developed into a fine pianist and was on the faculty of Proksch's private music school. She arranged a meeting for Bedřich with Proksch, who had been blind since age thirteen and was one of Prague's best pianists. Proksch perceived Smetana's talent, and for almost four years the young man flourished under his direction, making immense strides in piano playing, conducting, and composition. He earned just enough to survive by teaching privately.

In 1848 most of Europe was in political turmoil, as revolutions spread. Austria's formidable chancellor, Prince Metternich, was forced from power. Smetana, a staunch patriot, helped man the barricades in Prague when Czech citizens rose against their oppressors. In his excitement about the possibility of political liberation, he composed "Song of Freedom." But the revolution was short-lived and brutally suppressed. Smetana was depressed for his fatherland and threw all his energy into founding his own music school. He was desperate for money and even applied to Liszt (whom he had never met) for help. Smetana wrote a melodramatic letter intimating starvation and suicide. Liszt sent no money, but he was impressed by the young composer. Smetana had dedicated his Six *Characteristic Pieces* (Op. 1, 1847–48) to the Hungarian. Liszt heard in them "Smetana's genuine Czech heart," and told him "the pieces are really some of the most excellent, beautifully felt, and finely worked out I have come across recently." Liszt promised "to find a good publisher for a fine work." In the summer of 1848, Smetana finally acquired three rented pianos on credit, and opened his school.

During the last five years Bedřich's relationship with Kateřina Kolářová had bloomed. On August 27, 1849, the couple were married. Kateřina helped at the school, leaving Smetana more time to compose. It was an intense period of composition for him, and a few of these works, especially the charming *Festive Symphony* (c.1850), contain the seeds of Czech nationalism.

Four daughters were born in quick succession, and Smetana adored them. The eldest, Bedřiška, showed unusual musical talent by age three, but she and two of the other girls died in the space of three years, from diphtheria and scarlet fever. To make matters worse, his beloved Kateřina was suffering badly from tuberculosis. In 1855 Smetana composed the lovely G minor piano trio (Op. 15) in memory of his first daughter. It is the first of his compositions to remain in the repertoire and the first important Czech chamber work.

In this difficult period, Smetana was discouraged by the paltry opportunities in Prague. He was therefore glad, in 1856, to accept a post in Göteborg, Sweden, conducting the newly founded Philharmonic Society. There he championed the progressive but little-known music of Berlioz, Schumann, Liszt, and Wagner, which had been critically condemned in conservative Prague. In Göteborg he found appreciation as well as pupils to augment his income. He was composing, too. He produced several nonnationalistic symphonic poems, *Richard III* (Op. 11, 1858), *Wallenstein's Camp* (Op. 14, 1859), and *Hakon Jarl* (Op. 16, 1861), which were influenced by Berlioz and Liszt. At the same time, he was becoming more aware of Czech dances and began composing his unique sets of polkas for the piano. "My intention is to idealize the polka," he wrote, "as Chopin did with the mazurka."

But once again tragedy struck. Early in 1859, Kateřina died. The bereaved composer sought solace with Bettina Ferdinandová, only nineteen years old but already a cultivated painter and singer. Their marriage, only a year after his first wife died, produced a daughter but little personal happiness for the couple.

In 1860 Austria, which had suffered heavy defeats in Italy's quest for independence, loosened its political shackles over the Czech provinces. A surge of nationalism spread, and optimism was in the air. Smetana missed his homeland, and in the spring of 1861, he returned to Prague. It was the decisive step in his creative life. He was caught up in a flurry of activity: writing articles; programming the music of Berlioz, Liszt, and Wagner; conducting a choral society; appearing as a pianist; teaching; and arranging for concerts of his own music. The concerts were poorly attended at first, but slowly the public began to realize that Smetana was a musician who possessed the native stamp.

On January 5, 1866, Czech national opera was born at the new Provisional Theater, with the premiere of Smetana's *The Brandenburgers in Bohemia*. Although the music annoyed the German-oriented critics, the audience liked the patriotic story (and the fact that it was sung in Czech). More important, after the production Smetana was named director and chief conductor at the Provisional Theater. The salary was small, but the honor was great.

The Brandenburgers gave only an inkling of things to come. Within six months (on May 30, 1866) the composer conducted the premiere of another opera, *The Bartered Bride*. Unfortunately, it was little noticed, for Prussian troops had just filled the city in anticipation of war with Austria. Smetana fled the city, but soon returned and conducted another performance. This time pandemonium spread through the theater; the triumph was overwhelming. The simple story of Bohemian village life deeply touched the hearts of the Czech audience. The opera was unmistakably Czech, with its assimilation of folk music and national dances. In its mirth and bobbing happiness, *The Bartered Bride* may be called the "official" opera of the Czech nation.

Smetana's nationalism grew with the years, and he was most comfortable expressing himself in opera. Through opera, he felt, his people would find a more direct way to their national identity. Later in life, he was not pleased that *The Bartered Bride* had received the most attention of all his operas, for he considered it simplistic by comparison with the others. For Smetana, each of his operas was a symbolic act, a creation linking the Czech language to the history and customs of Czech life. In 1868, for the new Prague National Theater, which replaced the Provisional Theater, he produced his tragic opera *Dalibor*, based on the story of a fifteenth-century Czech knight. The public, hoping for a repeat of *The Bartered Bride*, was mystified by the more complex work. Smetana, always conscious of his mission, wrote, "I must give my people all I owe them and carry on in my heart."

Just after his fiftieth birthday, Smetana discovered he was suffering from syphilis: "I have been ill with a pus-oozing ulcer." Complications spread quickly, and by the autumn of 1874, he was experiencing painful hearing problems and hearing irritating noises. In despair the composer wrote, "If only at least the whistling would stop." Then "on the morning of October 20, I awoke stone deaf, unable to hear anything in either the left or the right ear." Conducting, piano playing, and teaching were no longer possible, and Smetana had to leave his position at the theater. Heroically, he kept composing. "I am wholly determined," he wrote, "to endure my sad fate in a calm and manly way as long as I live." That same year his comic opera *The Two Widows* appeared. It is the lightest of his operas, charming and intimate; its composer called it "a conversation piece." *The Two Widows*, like his other operas, has not often been presented outside of Czechoslovakia. *The Kiss* followed in 1876, and *The Secret* in 1878. Both are country tales, but with great subtlety in characterization and mastery of orchestral texture. The year 1881 saw the premiere of Smetana's grandest opera, *Libuše*, a festive work most often performed on high patriotic occasions. Smetana described his last opera, *The Devil's Wall* (1882), as a "comic-romantic opera." During these years he also wrote in other forms, including the string quartets and his monumental *Má vlast (My Country)*, a cycle of six symphonic poems, an orchestral shrine to his fatherland.

In 1876 Smetana left public life and moved with his wife to Jabkenice to live with his daughter Sophie and his son-in-law. At first they searched for a possible cure for his deafness, while he suffered "many dark moments." "If my disease is incurable, I would rather be released from this painful existence," he wrote. But in spite of his harrowing nervous disorders, he continued to compose, even showing increased creative powers. "I keep on composing," he wrote, "only so that people will know what goes on in a musician's head when he is in a condition like mine."

Smetana agonized for years in fear of the insanity that attacks the brain in the tertiary stage of syphilis. In 1883, after bouts of terrible violence, his mind finally snapped. On April 23, 1884, the father of Czech music was confined to a sanatorium and died there nineteen days later.

Outside of his country, Smetana is too little heard. He was primarily a tone painter, a descriptive artist. The critic Geoffrey Clive writes of Smetana's intoxication with Czech woodlands and meadows, "He saw music as a higher visionary force, enabling him to depict the pulse of personal life, or his nation's past glories and legends." "Absolute music," Smetana said, "is impossible for me in any genre. . . . My quartet, *From My Life* [*Z mého života*], does not consist merely of a formal game of tones and motives, by means of which the composer exhibits his skill. On the contrary, my aim was to present to the listener scenes from my life." In his concern for expressing nonmusical concepts in terms of musical sound, Smetana allied himself with Liszt, Berlioz, and Wagner. Many composers, like Brahms and Smetana's compatriot Dvořák, still wrote in established Classical forms.

Smetana was not only the foundation of Czech art music; he seems to have touched the very spirit of his country. It has been said that all Czechs must know Smetana, in order to truly know themselves and the Czech character. No wonder he holds an especially cherished place in the history of Czech culture.

The Bartered Bride (1863–66)

For the many thousands of music lovers who live far from places where live opera performances are held, recordings have been a savior. They have, in no small way, also contributed to keeping alive and well operas from many countries. Opera is one of the primary roads to understanding a culture, but appreciation for an intensely nationalist opera does not easily transcend national borders. Often the problem is language. Opera singers usually learn the main operatic languages and are content to avoid other languages, such as Czech. This has been the case with Smetana's operas, which have held the stage in his own country. Fortunately, Smetana's operas are available on recordings, where we may hear the wonderful effect of the Czech language being sung.

The Bartered Bride, a comic opera in three acts with a libretto by Czech writer Karel Sabina, is so popular in what is today the Czech Republic that by 1952 it had achieved two thousand performances just at the Prague National Theater. For its hundredth performance, Smetana wrote, *"The Bartered Bride* is only a toy and composing it was merely child's play." In the opera Smetana portrays a slice of innocent country life; the vocal writing is artful, and he has an uncanny ability to capture the accent of Czech dance. In *The Bartered Bride* we have a delightful *furiant*, a polka, and a *skočná* (a hop or "jumping dance"), which in the opera is called "The Dance of the Comedians." It opens in a burst of happiness, as the chorus sings, "See the buds burst on the bush." The score abounds in warmhearted arias such as "Gladly do I trust you," "With my mother," "How is it possible," and "How strange and dead."

The Bartered Bride (1866)

Benačková, Dvorsky, Novak, Czech Philharmonic Orchestra and Chorus, Košler: *Supraphon* 103511-2

(soloists unknown), Prague Radio Symphony Orchestra and Chorus, Ančerl (recorded 1947): Multisonic (Prague Opera Collection) 31 0185

The Bartered Bride: Dances (Polka, Furiant, "Dance of the Comedians," and Overture)

Vienna Philharmonic Orchestra, Levine: Deutsche Grammophon 427340-2

Cleveland Orchestra, Szell (without overture): CBS MYK 36716

Royal Liverpool Philharmonic Orchestra, Pešek: Virgin Classics CDC 59285

"The Moldau," Symphonic Poem no. 2 from Má vlast (1874)

The Czech name for this gorgeous tone poem is "*Vltava*," and it is surely the greatest musical depiction of a river. The composer wrote in the preface to his published score, "Two springs pour forth their streams in the shade of the Bohemian forest, the one warm and gushing, the other cold and tranquil. These waters reflect many a forest and castle—witnesses of a bygone age of knightly splendor, and the martial glory of days that are no more." This tone poem is Smetana in all of his magical brilliance. The main theme describing the course of the river is unforgettable. The other five works of *Má vlast* are filled with wonderful pages, especially the tranquil sunlit beauty of "From Bohemian Fields and Groves."

Vienna Philharmonic Orchestra, Kertész: London 417678-2

Cleveland Orchestra, Szell: CBS MYK 36716

RCA Victor Symphony Orchestra, Stokowski: RCA 09026-61503-2

Quartet no. 1 in E Minor for Strings (*Z mého života, or From My Life*) (1876)

In this moving score, Smetana expresses several autobiographical states. The first movement, in sonata form, covers his "inclination to art in my youth—the inexpressible yearning for something which I could not define." The Polka movement tells of "the joyful days of my youth when I composed dance music." The quartet's slow movement, a Largo sostenuto, "recalls the bliss of my first love for the girl who became my devoted wife." In the finale comes "the long-drawn-out note, the fatal whistling in my ear, which in 1874 announced my deafness. I permitted myself this little joke, such as it is, because it was so disastrous to me." In the finale, Smetana briefly brings back themes from the other movements. He said he wrote it "purposely for four instruments, as though in a small friendly circle they are discussing among themselves what so obviously troubles me."

Guarneri Quartet: Philips 420803-2
Talich Quartet: Calliope CAL 9690

OTHER PRINCIPAL WORKS

CHAMBER MUSIC
Trio in G Minor for Piano, Violin, and Cello, Op. 15 (1855; rev. 1857)*
Quartet no. 2 in D Minor for Strings (1882–83)*

OPERAS
Dalibor (1865–67; rev. 1870)*
Libuše (1869–72)*
The Two Widows (1873–74)*
The Kiss (1875–76)*
The Secret (1877–78)*
The Devil's Wall (1879–82)*

ORCHESTRAL WORKS
Festive Symphony (c.1850)
Triumphal Symphony, Op. 6 (1853–54)
Richard III (symphonic poem), Op. 11 (1857–58)
Wallenstein's Camp (symphonic poem), Op. 14 (1858–59)
Hakon Jarl (symphonic poem), Op. 16 (1860–61)

Má vlast (cycle of symphonic poems) (1874–79)
  "Vyšehrad"
  "Šárka"
  "From Bohemian Fields and Groves"*
  "Tábor"*
  "Blaník"
Prague Carnival (symphonic poem) (1883)

PIANO MUSIC
Polkas (various dates)*
Rêves (six characteristic pieces) (1875)
Ten *Czech Dances* (1877)*

ANTON BRUCKNER

b. Ansfelden, Upper Austria, September 4, 1824

d. Vienna, October 11, 1896

I cannot find the words to thank you as I would wish, but if there were an organ here, I could tell you.

Bruckner came from a long line of poor farmers, but his grandfather and father were schoolmasters in the village of Ansfelden, in Upper Austria. The Bruckner scholar and critic Deryck Cooke observed, "He came from the most primitive stratum of European society—the Catholic peasantry. In Metternich's reactionary Austria, this class was unaffected by the growing liberalism and sophistication of European life in general, and its best stock had retained its original characteristics practically unchanged since feudal times—an earthly identification with the vast power of nature, a slow and massive strength of character, a genuine humility, and an unquestioning childlike faith in God."

Anton was the eldest of eleven children, seven of whom died in infancy. When Anton was twelve his father died, and his mother took her children to the nearby town of Ebelsberg. They were poverty stricken, and Frau Bruckner took in washing for their livelihood. Anton had shown musical ability and was admitted as a choirboy at the monastery of St. Florian, where he learned to play the organ. He became an exceptional organist. These were lonely years, during which he caught typhoid and recovered. He wrote his mother, "I cannot describe how sick I am. Only the thought that all God does is for the best keeps me going."

In 1840, at sixteen, Anton moved to Linz, where he received training for a schoolmaster's certificate. He returned to St. Florian in 1845 and took a position at the monastery as teacher and organist, which he held until 1848. In 1855 he became the organist at the Linz Cathedral, a post of some prominence. He would stay there until 1868. He had a fervent desire to compose, but his theoretical training had been spotty. By saving every penny, he managed to spend several weeks each year studying theory and composition in Vienna.

In 1865, when Bruckner was nearly forty, he first heard Wagner's music in Linz. He was overwhelmed. The experience fueled his own need to compose. His latent genius began to ripen, and he composed the D minor mass, an orchestral overture in G minor, and several choruses for male voices. Most important, he began sketching his first symphony, which would be performed at Linz in 1868. Johann Herbeck, an influential Viennese conductor, recognized Bruckner's promise and helped him obtain a position teaching organ and theory at the Vienna Conservatory. Bruckner had at last fulfilled his long-standing dream of living in the Austrian capital. Alas, he did not fit in very well in these sophisticated circles. A thick, provincial dialect, atrocious manners, and ill-fitting peasant clothes hampered the acutely shy Bruckner. His head seemed too large for his meager body, and his bulging eyes held a disturbing and vacant stare. His poverty and general awkwardness were compounded by an unfortunate and desperate propensity for falling hopelessly in love with teenage girls. Many thought him to be a bungling fool.

Poor Bruckner was lonely and miserable—he never married and had no personal life. But music and his unshakable religious faith sustained and nourished him. His face beamed when he played the organ, and he grew ever more confident of his creative power (although his music, when heard, was usually greeted with intense hostility). The press was generally brutal; his chief nemesis was Eduard Hanslick, the most powerful music critic in Vienna. Hanslick, already famous for his antipathy toward Wagner, wrote a scathing review whenever Bruckner's music had one of its rare performances. The composer suffered terribly over these castigations, and he even fell ill when he came upon Hanslick at concerts or at the Conservatory, where the critic taught a course in aesthetics.

Yet Bruckner was desperate to hear his own music played, even badly. Whenever he could, he paid to have his works performed. Once, when he was conducting, nearly the entire audience left in the middle of the piece. Bruckner, rapt in his music, heard neither the footsteps nor the snickering. When he turned to the audience at the conclusion to receive his due applause, he found fewer than ten people remaining. Bruckner left the hall alone and in tears.

On another occasion, much to his elation, the Vienna Philharmonic was to give a rehearsal reading of his Third Symphony. But his elation turned to humiliation when members of the orchestra found the music so odious that they refused to continue. Still, Bruckner's abiding faith kept him going. "When God calls me to him," he wrote, "and asks me 'where is that talent which I have given you?' then I will hold out the rolled-up manuscript of my *Te Deum*, and I know he will be a compassionate judge." Fortunately, although audiences shunned him, Bruckner did receive confirmation of his talent elsewhere — from Wagner himself, in fact. The struggling Bruckner's acquaintance with the master of music-drama sustained him. Bruckner was afraid to ask Wagner to accept the dedication of his Third Symphony, "for I did not wish to desecrate his illustrious name." But upon closely examining the score, Wagner "held out his arms and warmly embraced me," declaring, "dear friend, the dedication is all settled; this composition of yours will give me uncommonly great pleasure."

An excerpt from a letter reveals Bruckner's fawning hero worship: In 1882, "The Master, who was then already suffering, took my hand and said . . . 'Have you been to *Parsifal*? How did you like it?' While he held my hand, I bent down on my knee, kissing and pressing his noble hand to my mouth, and said, 'Oh Master, I worship you!' The Master replied, 'Calm yourself, Bruckner; good night!' The next day the Master, who was sitting behind me at *Parsifal*, rebuked me once because I was applauding too violently. . . . It is my most precious legacy—*until up there!!!*"

By the mid-1880s, Bruckner's works were finding advocates among the great conductors, including Arthur Nikisch, Hans Richter, Felix Mottl, Gustav Mahler, and Hermann Levi. Levi thought the Seventh Symphony was on the level of Beethoven and Schubert. Nikisch agreed; after giving a rousing performance of it in Leipzig, he wrote, "Since Beethoven there has been nothing that could even approach it." After Richter conducted the Fourth Symphony in Vienna, the shaken and bashful composer pushed a coin into the conductor's hand, begging him to drink a beer to his health. Richter had the coin mounted on his watch chain to commemorate "a day on which I wept."

In 1891, after receiving an honorary doctorate from the University of Vienna, Bruckner retired from the Conservatory. His health was failing due to a heart condition, and the Austrian government allotted him a small pension. The Habsburg emperor Franz Josef gave him an apartment in the Belvedere Palace. When the emperor asked if there was anything else he could do, Bruckner, with the innocence of a child, shyly inquired whether his majesty could possibly ask Herr Doktor Hanslick to stop writing so badly about his music.

Bruckner, like Mahler a decade later, was superstitious about composing a Ninth Symphony; he felt it would be an affront to Beethoven: "I do not like to begin the ninth. Beethoven ended his life with his ninth." He struggled mightily with this last symphony, working on it until the very day he died. During the funeral service, Brahms, who had been contemptuous of Bruckner's work, was seen peering through the window. Perhaps Brahms, who was ill, knew he would be the next to go.

Wagner's influence on Bruckner has been too heavily emphasized. Bruckner loved Wagner, but he was in no way an imitator; nor could he have composed anything as worldly as an opera—he was essentially a religious composer. The British composer and musicologist Hans F. Redlich commented that Bruckner's music "is conditioned by the militant faith of the Roman Catholic counter-reformation and fertilized by the potent tradition of devotional music from Palestrina and Lassus to Fux and Caldara. The key to an understanding of his symphonies may best be found in the three grand masses with their colossal dimensions and sudden contrast of mood in the Gloria and Credo sections. The symphonies accept the extended structural and tonal range of Beethoven or Schubert's Ninth Symphonies, increasing their sonority by adding a powerful brass section to the traditional orchestra layout."

The Finnish master Jean Sibelius, a symphonist of a far different cast, related in 1911, "Yesterday I heard Bruckner's B-flat major symphony and it moved me to tears. For a long time afterwards, I was completely transformed. What a strangely profound spirit formed by a religious sense. And this profound religiousness we have abolished in our country as something no longer in harmony with our time."

Within the last two generations, Bruckner's music has steadily climbed in critical and public esteem. In an era alienated from mystery and sacredness, his majestic compositions speak with a deep and humble reverence for life. His slow movements reveal a radiant serenity and vulnerability, and have the power of faith. The Scherzos are rambunctious, and their earthy Trios exhale a rustic purity, harking back to the preindustrial countryside. In his Scherzos, Bruckner was impelled by the spirit of Schubert; he was proud of his heritage from the Classical masters, and he strove to apply and extend aspects of this tradition within his monumental style. If his intentions sometimes exceeded his grasp, producing sections that to some listeners sound heavy, long-winded, and sanctimonious, in many places his work touches a deeply sympathetic chord. For Bruckner, as for Mahler, the symphony was the world itself, and he valiantly attempted to create works of magnificent grandeur and profound solitude, with a unique symphonic sonority. Far more often than not, he succeeded.

Symphony no. 4 in E-flat Major (*Romantic*) (1874; rev. 1878–80)

Bruckner was forever revising his work, and for many pieces, it is impossible to declare a definitive date of composition. In 1930, Robert Haas and the Bruck-

ner Society brought out a close-to-authentic edition of Symphony no. 4. The
title *Romantic* here implies not storm and stress but rather a festive appreciation of the Austrian landscape. The orchestration is replete with rustic horns,
and in the third-movement Scherzo (where Bruckner marked in his manuscript "Dance tune during the hunter's meal"), the composer used the *Länder*,
a traditional Austrian dance. The crown of the composition is the sad second
movement, Andante quasi allegretto, whose climax forms a hymn of thanksgiving. The finale is Bruckner at his most outgoing and majestic. The fourth is the
most directly appealing and easily approachable of Bruckner's symphonies.

Munich Philharmonic Orchestra, Celibidache: Exclusive EXL 23
Vienna Philharmonic Orchestra, Furtwängler: Music & Arts CD 796
Berlin Philharmonic Orchestra, Jochum: Deutsche Grammophon 449718-2

Symphony no. 7 in E Major (1881–83)

The Seventh Symphony was begun in 1881 and completed in September
1883. Unlike Bruckner's earlier symphonies, it was heartily acclaimed from the
beginning. The broad and noble opening theme of the first movement came to
the composer in a dream. The slow Adagio movement is haunted by Wagner.
It is a majestic threnody, or lamentation, which was written in Wagner's memory. Certainly it is one of the most sublime passages in Bruckner. The composer told the conductor Felix Mottl, "I came home and felt sad. I did not think
the Master would live much longer. Then I conceived the adagio in C sharp
minor." Just as he sketched the huge C major climax, the news of Wagner's
death reached him. The third movement finds Bruckner in fine fettle, cheer-
fully observing the Austrian countryside but stopping to be saddened in the
Trio. The finale, with its choral-like theme, ends in glory, circling back to the
theme of the first movement. The Seventh Symphony is dedicated to Wagner's
patron, "His Majesty the King, Ludwig II of Bavaria, in deepest reverence."

Berlin Philharmonic Orchestra, Klemperer: Music & Arts CD 209
Columbia Symphony Orchestra, Walter: Odyssey MB 2K 45669
Berlin Philharmonic Orchestra, Barenboim: Teldec 9031-77118-2
Cleveland Orchestra, Dohnányi: London 430841-2
Berlin Philharmonic Orchestra, Furtwängler: Music & Arts CD 698-1

Symphony no. 8 in C Minor (1884–87)

The Symphony no. 8 is dedicated to "The Imperial and Royal apostolic Majesty Francis Joseph I, Emperor of Austria and apostolic King of Hungary." The score is a mighty conception, lasting approximately one hour and twenty minutes. The work, Bruckner's grandest achievement, finds him at the summit of his powers and contains episodes of visionary, mysterious beauty. Bruckner was always humble and aspired to God's trust with the purity of innocence. He considered the colossal third-movement Adagio to be his greatest creation.

The first performance, which took place on December 18, 1892, in Vienna, was conducted by the venerable Hans Richter. The discrepancies between various editions of the Eighth Symphony are daunting, as one can tell from comparing the various recordings by conductor Wilhelm Furtwängler. This most searching and brooding of Brucknerites was never able to make up his mind; sometimes he used the Haas and Nowak critical editions, and sometimes he used a score that he prepared from earlier versions. Furtwängler wrote, "A work such as the Eighth Symphony cannot be imagined without the dual basis of a mystical and all-encompassing religious sense, and also of a magnificent Baroque heroism."

Vienna Philharmonic Orchestra, Furtwängler: Music & Arts CD 764
Berlin Philharmonic Orchestra, Knappertsbusch: Music & Arts CD 856
Vienna Philharmonic Orchestra, Karajan: Deutsche Grammophon 427611-2

The Other Symphonies

Bruckner listeners will find important music throughout his symphonies. No. 3 in D minor (1873–77) is particularly impressive in its architecture. No. 5 in B-flat major (1875–76), which Bruckner never heard performed, is superb, with its slow introduction to the first movement and the overwhelming might of the finale. The Sixth Symphony is less heroic in scale and thought, but it is characteristically rich in its profusion of material.

Perhaps the finest of these others is his Ninth Symphony—dedicated not, as Bruckner wrote, to earthly majesties, but "to the King of Kings, our dear Lord, and I hope that He will grant me enough time to complete it." Bruckner struggled for two years with the finale and left it incomplete, in six versions. The complete nine symphonies have been recorded by Herbert von Karajan with the Berlin Philharmonic on nine CDs (Deutsche Grammophon 429648-2).

OTHER PRINCIPAL WORKS

CHAMBER MUSIC

Intermezzo in D Minor for String Quintet (1879)

Quintet in F Major for Strings (1879)*

SACRED CHORAL MUSIC

Psalm 114 in G Major (1852)*

Psalm 112 in B-flat Major (1863)*

Mass no. 1 in D Minor for Solo Voices, Organ, and Orchestra (1864; rev. 1876 and 1881–82)

Mass no. 3 in F Minor for Solo Voices, Chorus, and Orchestra (1867–68)*

Motets (various dates)*

Te Deum for Solo Voices, Orchestra, and Organ (1881–84)*

Psalm 150 in C Major (1892)*

JOHANN STRAUSS II

b. Vienna, October 25, 1825

d. Vienna, June 3, 1899

If it is true that I have some talent, then I have to thank for its development my dear city of Vienna, in whose earth my whole strength is rooted, in whose air lie the sounds which my ear gathers, which my heart takes in and my hand writes down. . . . Vienna, the heart of our beautiful, God blessed Austria. . . . To her I give my cheer: Vienna, bloom, prosper and grow!

The Johann Strauss who became famous for his waltzes was actually the second musician by that name. His father, born in 1804, was apprenticed to a bookbinder at a young age but was irresistibly drawn to music, especially the light dance music that was then captivating Vienna. He joined Michael Pamer's famous orchestra, whose dance music quickened pulses in dance halls and beer gardens throughout the city. There Johann Strauss, Sr., met a violinist and composer by the name of Josef Lanner. He joined Lanner's band in 1819.

The post-Napoleonic years in Vienna (from 1815) had given the growing middle class a zest for freedom of expression as well as for lighthearted entertainment—the frothier the better. Could anything be more intoxicating and liberating than the intimate but frenzied waltz, with its graceful but frankly sexual movements? An older, more decorous generation was convinced that the licentious-looking waltz was helping to corrupt Europe's morals.

By the time Johann Strauss, Jr., was born, his father and Lanner were the heroes of Vienna. In 1830 the twenty-year-old Chopin, who was then living in Vienna, wrote home, "Strauss and his waltzes obliterate everything. . . . The lis-

teners are so overjoyed that they don't know what to do with themselves. . . .
It shows the corrupt taste of Vienna." The Strauss-Lanner orchestra was so
popular that it performed regularly in the Prater, Vienna's amusement park.
The Viennese critic Eduard Hanslick later wrote, "There appeared innumerable articles about Lanner and Strauss, enthusiastic, frivolous and serious ones,
and longer, to be sure, than those devoted to Beethoven and Mozart. The
sweetly intoxicating three-four rhythm, which took hold of hand and foot, necessarily eclipsed great and serious music, making the audience increasingly un-
fit for any intellectual effort."

But Lanner and Strauss's domination of the Viennese music scene was not
to continue. After several years, the two were driven apart by petty professional
grievances and parted ways. Each organized his own new orchestra, and
Strauss's, renowned for its virtuosic precision, quickly took the lead in popularity. Invitations to perform poured in from other countries, and in 1833 a major
European tour created a sensation. In Paris, Berlioz was delighted and wrote a
long article extolling Strauss's ingenious use of cross-rhythms. On a later tour
(in 1838), a London newspaper reported, "So perfect a band was never before
heard on this side of the channel."

As Johann Jr. grew up, he and his younger brothers also loved waltzes. But
Johann Sr. did not want his sons to emulate him: for Johann Jr., he chose the career of bond investor. But the boy's mother found a way for him to study the violin in secret. The deceit came to an end when Johann Sr. became involved
with another woman and left home permanently. When he learned of his son's
ambition, the elder Strauss supposedly remarked, "Now the brat Johann also in-
tends to write waltzes, although he has not got a clue about them—and even for
me, being the first in my field, it is terribly difficult to create something new." In
1844, Johann Jr., eager to prove himself, established his own orchestra.

In Vienna in 1849, Johann Sr. died of scarlet fever. Of his 250 waltzes,
polkas, and quadrilles, only a few are still heard, but his *Radetzky March*
(Op. 228, 1848) came to symbolize the Habsburg Empire itself. When asked
about his father forty years later, Johann Jr. said, "My father was a musician by
the grace of God . . . guided by an inner, irresistible impulse."

Johann Jr. proved to be a prolific composer, and in the late 1850s and 1860s
he composed a series of waltzes that far superseded his father's best efforts.
Within a few years, he had become a virtual industry in Vienna, rushing to and
from his six dance orchestras, vigorously conducting with violin in hand. His
gifted brothers, Josef and Eduard, helped keep things running smoothly during
his frequent absences—to, among other places, Russia and (in 1872) the United
States, where he conducted an orchestra of more than one thousand members.

In spite of his frenzied activity as a conductor, Strauss also managed to compose an astonishing amount of music—more than five hundred dances as well as sixteen operettas, two of which, *Die Fledermaus* (1874) and *Der Zigeunerbaron* (1885), are masterpieces of the genre. Unfortunately, Strauss chose librettos carelessly, and hence most of his operettas are no longer staged. His brothers Josef and Eduard were also composers. Josef created some 280 dance pieces, several of which are equal to those of his brother. Johann himself considered Josef to be more gifted; unfortunately, the pale and handsome Josef died in 1870 at the age of forty-three. Strauss's own personal life was often turbulent. He married three times: to singer Henriette Treffz, which ended with her death; to actress Angelika Dittrich, whom he divorced; and to Adele Deutsch. All three alliances were childless.

Musicians of every kind succumbed to Strauss's alluring, insinuating music. Richard Strauss (no relation) recalled "an unforgettable evening" of Strauss waltzes conducted by Hans von Bülow. "Of all the God-gifted dispensers of joy," Richard wrote, "Johann Strauss is to me the most endearing. . . . I also willingly admit to having sometimes conducted the *Perpetuum Mobile* [1862] with far more pleasure than many a four-movement symphony. As for the *Rosenkavalier* waltzes . . . How could I have composed those without thinking of the laughing genius of Vienna?"

When Strauss's wife Adele asked the often ill-tempered Brahms for an autograph, he wrote out the first bars of "The Beautiful Blue Danube," then signed, "Unfortunately not by Johannes Brahms." The Waltz King had become a symbol of Alt Wien (Old Vienna). It was said that when Strauss drew his last breath in 1899, the Habsburg emperor ceased to reign. Strauss's end came swiftly: on May 27 he contracted pneumonia and died a week later. Thousands of disconsolate mourners lined the streets to Vienna's central cemetery, where Strauss is buried not far from Beethoven and Brahms.

In 1896 Oskar Blumenthal, director of Berlin's Lessing Theater, wrote, "For fifty years Johann Strauss has, although unseen, been present at almost every joyous function of the civilized world; wherever parties of happy people have gathered for carefree pleasure Johann Strauss's spirit has pervaded. If we could estimate the amount of happiness and enjoyment contributed to the world by his creations, Johann Strauss would be regarded as one of the greatest benefactors of the century." And so he was—but Strauss himself was unhappy. He wanted what Offenbach had yearned for: immortality through opera. But try as he might, there was no *Tales of Hoffmann* in Strauss. His sole opera, *Ritter Pázmán* (1892), has been shelved forever. He blamed the failure of this opera on the critics, one of whom wrote, "People will go to *Fledermaus* in order to recover from *Ritter Pázmán*." Strauss retaliated by shouting, "They are professors! I shit on all professors of music."

But the title "Waltz King" will more than suffice for Strauss's glory. H. L.

Mencken thought that "there is a mystical something in 'Wiener Blut' or 'Künstlerleben' that fetches even philosophers." Strauss's waltzes exemplified the height of Vienna's glitter and prosperity. They represent a hedonistic city bent on finding pleasure at any cost. The elegance and sophistication of these waltzes meant "Vienna" to the world. Strauss differed from his father and Lanner in his greater sophistication in harmony and in his orchestral mastery. The younger Strauss has no relationship with the early beer-garden, provincial atmosphere of his father's dances. He was a magical melodist, with a gift for writing melodies of a superb rhythmic lift. He took his father's waltz and extended it to symphonic amplitude and perfect organic form.

A most wonderfully ironic footnote: the man who personifies the waltz for all time could not and would not dance himself. To his wife he wrote, "But you know very well that I have never been a dancer, and have to give a decisive 'no' to all the really tempting and attractive 'Invitations to the Dance.' "

Die Fledermaus (The Bat) (1874)

One of the world's beloved theater pieces, Strauss's Fledermaus is the greatest operetta of all time, with his Der Zigeunerbaron (The Gypsy Baron) a close second. Strauss's luminous genius bursts with irresistible rhythmic verve and sensuality and unforgettable melodic appeal. Die Fledermaus was premiered on April 5, 1874, at the Theater an der Wien. Its initial reception was lukewarm, but within a few seasons it had been played in nearly two hundred theaters. When Sir Thomas Beecham performed it in London, he recalled, "Die Fledermaus was the greatest triumph . . . it contained most of the elements dear to the heart, including a large space of that rowdy humor on the stage which is out of place nowhere . . . [and] all the time-honored devices for securing a laugh, such as falling over sofas, squirting water syphons in somebody's face or being carried off to bed in a complete state of intoxication."

Varady, Popp, Kollo, Prey, Rebroff, Bavarian State Opera Orchestra, Kleiber: Deutsche Grammophon 415646-2

Schwarzkopf, Streich, Gedda, Krebs, Christ, Kunz, Philharmonia Orchestra and Chorus, Karajan: EMI Classics CDHB 69531 (mono)

Waltzes and Polkas

Among the Waltz King's most celebrated pieces are "An der schönen blauen Donau" (On the Beautiful Blue Danube), "Kaiserwaltz" (Emperor Waltz),

"Geschichten aus dem Wiener Wald" (Tales from the Vienna Woods), "Frühlingsstimmen" (Voices of Spring), "Wiener Blut" (Vienna Blood), "Rosen aus dem Süden" (Roses from the South), "Künstlerleben" (Artist's Life), "Wein, Weib, und Gesang" (Wine, Woman, and Song), "Tausend und eine Nächter" (A Thousand and One Nights), "Accellerationen" and such favorites as "Perpetuum mobile," "Tritsch-Tratsch Polka," "Annen-Polka," "Über Donner- und Blitz-Schnellpolka" (Thunder and Lightning Polka), and "Pizzicato Polka" (written with his brother Josef).

Vienna Philharmonic Orchestra, Boskovsky: London 417885-2
Vienna Philharmonic Orchestra, Boskovsky: EMI Classics CDC 47052
Vienna State Opera Orchestra, Horenstein: Chesky CD 95
Chicago Symphony Orchestra, Reiner: RCA 09026-68160-2

OTHER PRINCIPAL WORKS

DANCE MUSIC
Quadrilles
Galops
Marches

OPERETTAS
Cagliostro in Wien (Cagliostro in Vienna) (1875)
Eine Nacht in Venedig (A Night in Venice) (1883)
Der Zigeunerbaron (The Gypsy Baron) (1885)*

JOHANNES BRAHMS

b. Hamburg, May 7, 1833

d. Vienna, April 3, 1897

Passions are not natural to mankind, they are always exceptions or excrescences. The man in whom they overstep the limits should regard himself as an invalid and seek a medicine for his life and health. The ideal and the genuine man is calm both in his joy and sorrow.

Brahms was born in a shabby section of Hamburg, the son of Johann Jakob Brahms—a double bass player who was a wastrel and addicted to drink. Johann was twenty-seven when his wife Johanna, already forty-four, gave birth to the second of their three children. Johannes rather disliked his brother and sister: his brother eventually became an undistinguished musician who was deeply jealous of his talented sibling.

The family lived in near poverty—any form of diversion was beyond their means. They did manage to scrape together enough money for music lessons for little Johannes, since his father hoped he would be a child prodigy. Johannes's first piano teacher was Otto Cossel, who immediately realized the child's gift. The boy showed little sign of developing into a prodigy, but within two years he had made enough progress that Cossel thought he was ready to work with his own former teacher, the distinguished theorist, pianist, and composer Eduard Marxsen. Marxsen saw that Johannes was a born composer and therefore gave him an extensive theoretical grounding, laying the foundation for Brahms's later extraordinary discipline and endless curiosity about music past and present.

Johannes had a difficult childhood. His parents, locked into an unhappy marriage and forever quarreling, caused him great anxiety. By the time he reached adolescence, he was forced to help the family scratch out a livelihood. His improvisational skills brought him menial jobs as a pianist, playing night after exhausted night in the dangerous and dreary brothels and taverns of Hamburg's rough waterfront. These were places of appalling depravity, and the exquisitely sensitive youngster may have been abused by prostitutes or brutish sailors. The experience would have profound effects on Brahms's relations with women. Much later in life, in a fit of anger, he told a friend, "You tell me I should have the same respect, the same exalted homage for women that you have! You expect that of a man cursed with a childhood like mine."

During these formative years, the frail youngster's health suffered from poor nutrition and late hours. Fortunately, a local music lover invited him to spend some weeks in the country during the summers of 1847 and 1848. By this time composition had become Brahms's salvation, and these weeks allowed him to give every minute to his work. He early developed a stringently critical view of his own music, and he destroyed most of what he wrote. Around this time, he was able to leave the Hamburg underworld and begin teaching and arranging dance music to earn a living.

After Mendelssohn passed away in 1847, Brahms's revered master Marxsen wrote, "A great master of the musical art has gone, but an even greater one will bloom for us in Brahms." By age eighteen, Brahms composed the first work that he permitted to survive, a powerful Scherzo in E-flat Minor (1851, Op. 4). He had already burned nearly a hundred works. In 1852 he was pleased with some songs as well as with the two extraordinary piano sonatas, in C major (Op. 1) and F-sharp minor (Op. 2). Already it was clear that Brahms had taken the sonata form to heart, especially as it had been conceived by Beethoven. After he performed his Op. 1 sonata in public, a friend remarked that its opening reminded him of Beethoven's titanic *Hammerklavier* Sonata. Legend has it that Brahms gruffly replied, "Any ass can hear that."

In addition to Beethoven, Schumann most attracted his musical spirit. Looking for confirmation of his talent, the young composer sent a few scores to Schumann. They were returned unopened. Fortunately, two young musicians soon came into his life and provided him with encouragement and friendship. The first, the brilliant Hungarian violinist Eduard Reményi, used Brahms as his accompanist on a tour in 1852–53 and introduced him to Gypsy music. While on tour in Hanover, Brahms met twenty-two-year-old violinist-composer Joseph Joachim, already becoming famous as a soloist. Joachim would remain a lifelong friend, and years later Brahms would compose his great Violin Concerto (Op. 77) for him.

Joachim, who had been concertmaster in Liszt's Weimar Orchestra, wrote Brahms a letter of introduction to Liszt. In 1853 Brahms and Reményi traveled to Weimar, where Liszt welcomed both men with open arms. At one of his famous master classes, he examined Brahms's manuscript scores. Then Liszt, who rarely played for his class, proceeded to sight-read the awkward pianism of the Op. 4 scherzo. Liszt was in an especially magnanimous mood that day and decided to play for the assembly his own recently completed B minor sonata. Brahms, most likely exhausted from traveling, tactlessly fell asleep in the middle of the half-hour-long work. Liszt was naturally peeved, but the next day, as Brahms was preparing his departure, the Hungarian warmly embraced him and sent the young man on his way with praise and a gift.

But Brahms and Joachim would soon turn violently away from Liszt's music. Liszt's bold new ideas departed from the traditional values of German music, values that Brahms and Joachim held sacred. In the ensuing years, the conservative faction of German music (headed by Brahms, Joachim, Clara Schumann, and the critic Eduard Hanslick) and the "music of the future" faction (led by Liszt, Wagner, Bruckner, Hugo Wolf, and a host of their followers) battled frequently and vehemently in the press.

From Weimar, Brahms headed to Düsseldorf and an auspicious meeting with Clara and Robert Schumann. Brahms played his sonatas for the couple, who were dumbfounded by his youthful genius. Robert, who had not written any critical articles for several years, returned to print to proclaim Brahms the great hope of German music. "And he has come," exclaimed Schumann, "a young blood at whose cradle graces and heroes kept watch. He is called Johannes Brahms . . . one of the elect." Unfortunately, Brahms came into Schumann's life just as the older composer's mental state was collapsing, and Schumann was taken to an asylum before he could do much more to help Brahms's career.

Brahms was deeply attracted to Clara as a woman and an artist, and during Robert's confinement he was of great comfort and practical help to her and her large family. After Robert's death in 1856, Clara and Brahms remained close friends. There is no evidence that they were ever lovers, but speculation was endless. Perhaps the shadow of Schumann loomed too large, but certainly Clara Schumann remained the most important woman in Brahms's life. His relationship with her may have been one reason that he never married. In 1858, when he was living in Hamburg once again, he fell in love with the singer Agathe von Siebold. He became engaged to Agathe but eventually broke off the engagement, as he would with two other women in the future. Not only did he never marry, he never had (as far as is known) any sexual intimacy with a "respectable" woman. All his life he frequented houses of prostitution, expenses that Brahms, punctilious about money matters, minutely calculated in his account books.

In 1863 Brahms accepted a position as director of the Vienna Sing-akademie. He quit after a year because the job entailed too many administrative duties. Vienna, however, would remain his residence for the rest of his life. He immersed himself in the city's musical life, making friends with conductors, pianists, publishers, and the powerful critic Eduard Hanslick, who never failed to praise him in the press. During his three and a half decades in the Austrian capital, Brahms's life was a nonstop whirlwind of creation, as he composed masterpieces in every form except opera. His self-criticism and his constant desire to learn never ceased, and even in these years of increasing fame, he sought to continue his education—even studying counterpoint with a Viennese theorist just to keep himself flexible.

It was a good life, and as the years went by, he became almost a living monument in a city that fully appreciated its great musical tradition. They were shining years of relative peace and prosperity. The recently enacted copyright laws made Brahms one of the first composers to make a substantial living from his music, and he was spared the toil of constant teaching and concertizing, although he performed fairly often as a conductor and pianist. Through the years he achieved his aim to uphold the great traditions of German music, with music that was basically formal in design, composed in sonata form. His masters were Mozart, Haydn, Beethoven, and Schubert. He, like them, wrote "absolute music," music without programmatic content or stories. Many composers of the time also wrote in the old-fashioned sonata form, but these composers were academic and conventional. Brahms was the only one who could fuse the abstraction of this Classical form with Romantic warmth and ardor. He was greatly embarrassed when the conductor Hans von Bülow dubbed him the third B in the triumvirate of Bach, Beethoven, and Brahms, but he was truly their direct descendant.

Brahms was an honest, abrupt, and difficult man, albeit with a good heart. As a frequent guest at Viennese social functions, his foibles and boorish behavior were gladly overlooked. One evening, leaving a party, at the door Brahms supposedly shouted, "If there is anyone here that I have not insulted, I apologize!"

The 1890s saw the deaths of many dear friends, including his dear Clara Schumann, and Brahms grew increasingly lonely. He himself fell victim to liver cancer and died a month short of his sixty-fourth birthday. He was buried in his adopted city; one of the pallbearers at the funeral was Dvořák, who had cherished Brahms's friendship. The city mourned the composer with tributes and performances (which disguised the fact that the great days of Vienna were fading rapidly). Brahms had loved Vienna, but he had remained a frugal north German at heart, and politically, he was a naïve German patriot, a keen admirer of the "Iron Chancellor" Otto von Bismarck, whose portrait hung in the music room of his small apartment. During the Franco-Prussian War, he was ready to volunteer.

Few artists have worked so hard or so well. The proportion of his music that is still heard today is among the largest of the great masters; he was, quite simply, the foremost architect of instrumental Romantic music. If Brahms, the third B, did not quite attain the absolute spiritual heights that Bach and Beethoven did, he was nonetheless one of the greatest of all composers; his music has a depth and intensity rivaled by few.

Throughout his life, Brahms deliberately covered his biographical tracks, making certain that future biographers would find him a difficult subject. He destroyed many letters and much other evidence of his complex inner life. This insecure and highly sensitive person is partially obscured to us, but his music tells everything of importance. He possessed an emotional intelligence of the highest order. He was pure of heart, a relentless idealist who left behind only the best he had to offer. As a tonal craftsman, he simply defies ordinary analysis; indeed, he possesses no flaws. Deeply intellectual, his music is never dry or pedantic; mysteriously, he enters our innermost sensibilities. His art is a synthesis of many tributaries, yet he is always "Brahmsian," never derivative. Unlike most of the Romantic composers, Brahms was elaborately educated in his art, with almost superhuman self-discipline and a relentless drive for perfection. Not a single Brahms work can be called negligible. How wrong Brahms was when he said, "I know very well the place I shall one day have in music history: the place that Cherubini once had, and has today."

Concerto no. 1 in D Minor for Piano and Orchestra, Op. 15 (1854–58)

Brahms was but twenty-five when he completed this gigantic concerto, a full fifty minutes long. He premiered it on January 22, 1859, with Joseph Joachim conducting. It was poorly received. The composer called it "a brilliant and decided failure. . . . In spite of this, the Concerto will please some day." The musical scholar Donald Francis Tovey wrote, "The tragic mood of this first movement was inspired by the catastrophe of Schumann's illness, on the terrible day when he threw himself into the Rhine. The slow movement is a Requiem for Schumann." The colossal Rondo finale, unlike so many concerto last movements, is in no way inferior to the rest of the work.

Rubinstein, Chicago Symphony Orchestra, Reiner: RCA 09026-61263-2
Serkin, Cleveland Orchestra, Szell: CBS MK 42261
Gilels, Berlin Philharmonic Orchestra, Jochum: Deutsche Grammophon 431595-2

Variations and Fugue on a Theme by Handel, Op. 24 (1861)

Brahms took a spirited tune from Handel's Suite in B-flat Major and subjected it to a dazzling group of piano variations, twenty-five in number, from which emerged a large-scale work ranging in tone from delicately lyrical to thunderous. The last three variations, full of blinding energy, lead to a splendid long fugue, magnificent in sonority and entirely Handelian in its pomp. Op. 24 was a large advance over Brahms's previous large-scale *Variations on a Theme by Schumann* (Op. 9, 1854) and proclaimed Brahms as the greatest living variation composer.

Artymin: Chandos CHAN 8410
Rogé: London 433849-2
E. Petri: APR APR 7024

Variations on a Theme by Paganini, Op. 35 (1862–63)

The Brahms-Paganini, as they are called, are a legend in the piano literature. They are Brahms's tribute to the diabolical violinist who had inspired so many pianists. It was Brahms's intention to compose a work of awesome technical difficulty; in fact, he called these variations "studies." At various times, Brahms played all of his solo piano works and concertos in public—except for the *Paganini Variations*. For his theme, he took the pregnant opening theme of Paganini's Twenty-fourth Caprice in A Minor for solo violin. Each of the thirty variations treats a technical or a rhythmic problem. Most of them sound rather sardonic, and even the occasional lyric variations contain a chill. The critic James Huneker wrote of a further aspect: "These diabolical variations, the last word in the technical literature of the piano, are also vast spiritual problems."

Bachauer: Mercury 434340-2
Michelangeli: Arkadia 903
Biret: Naxos 8.550350
Rodriguez: Elan 2200

Quintet in F Minor for Piano and Strings, Op. 34 (1861–64)

The F minor piano quintet was initially intended as a sonata for two pianos. It is rich in thematic material, as the piano and strings meld in perfect union.

The first movement alone contains five themes that are diversely worked out. The entire movement boils with impetuosity. Here is a full-blooded Brahms in the full sap of youth. The slow movement yields to tender simplicity. The Scherzo is superb in its sonority and sweep. In the finale, Brahms the north German shrouds us in Hamburg fog, then introduces gaiety. The long development is followed by a recapitulation that resolves itself in a triumphant coda. As in all of Brahms's chamber music with piano, he invents a treasury of unique and unforgettable sonorities.

Budapest Quartet, Serkin: Sony Masterworks MPK 45686
Amadeus Quartet, Eschenbach: Deutsche Grammophon 419875-2

Ein deutsches Requiem (German Requiem), Op. 45 (1857–68)

The death of Brahms's mother in 1865 was the profound occasion for finishing the *German Requiem*. Brahms took his text, which is mostly nonliturgical, from Luther's translation of the Bible. H. L. Mencken wrote, "There is not a hint of what is commonly regarded as religious feeling in it. Brahms, so far as I know, was not a religious man. Nor is there the slightest sign of the cheap fustian of a conventional patriotism. Nevertheless, a superb emotion is there—nay, an overwhelming emotion. The thing is irresistibly moving. It is moving because a man of the highest intellectual dignity, a man of exalted feelings, a man of brains, put into it his love for and pride in his country."

Schwarzkopf, Fischer-Dieskau, Philharmonia Orchestra, Klemperer: Angel CDC 47238
Battle, Hagegard, Chicago Symphony Orchestra and Chorus, Levine: RCA 09026-61349-2

Alto Rhapsody, Op. 53 (1869)

Brahms greatly admired Goethe, and for this masterpiece he chose three stanzas from Goethe's *Harzreise im Winter*. The poem is full of gloom and agitation, a Wertherian mood of self-torture. Walter Niemann, Brahms's biographer, explains, "Brahms, the modern master of *Weltschmerz* and resignation in music, was of all people the one who was most likely tempted to set it to music. He chose three stanzas from it, on which are based the three sections of his work." The sections are "But who is that who walks apart," "Who shall heal the pain of him to whom the healing balm becomes poison," and "If his ear can catch a note from Thy lyre, O Father of Love." It is moving, noble music, as Brahms lays bare his heart in music of burnished beauty.

Anderson, Philadelphia Orchestra and Chorus, Ormandy: Pearl PEA 9405
Baker, London Philharmonic Orchestra, John Alldis Choir Male Voices, Boult: EMI Classics
    CDFB 68655
Miller, Columbia Symphony Orchestra, Occidental College Concert Choir, Walter: Sony
    Classical SMK 64469

Variations on a Theme by Haydn, Opp. 56a and 56b (1873)

This piece is known more casually as the Brahms-Haydn variations; both titles reflect the incorrect assumption that the theme Brahms used, marked "Choral St. Antoni," was composed by Haydn. It is now thought to be by Ignace Pleyel, an Austrian composer and founder of the famous Pleyel Piano firm. Brahms copied out the melody in 1870 and then let it simmer for three years. When he finally got back to it, he composed two versions of the work, Op. 56a for orchestra and Op. 56b for two pianos. This magnificent score (along with other works) reveals Brahms as the supreme variationist of his time. It consists of the theme, thirteen variations, and a finale in the form of a Passacaglia (a slow dance of Spanish origin based on an *ostinato* bass motif).

FOR ORCHESTRA
New York Philharmonic Orchestra, Mitropoulos: Arkadia 736
Cleveland Orchestra, C. von Dohnányi: Teldec 2292-44972-2

FOR TWO PIANOS
Perahia, Solti: CBS MK 42625

Concerto in D Major for Violin and Orchestra, Op. 77 (1878)

In seriousness and depth of beauty, this is one of the greatest of all concertos. Brahms dedicated the Violin Concerto to his dear friend Joseph Joachim, who composed the cadenza of the first movement and served as soloist at the first performance on January 1, 1879, with Brahms conducting the Gewandhaus Orchestra of Leipzig. The first movement, Allegro non troppo, is massive in weight. The Tutti announces all material to be worked upon, except a partial first subject that awaits the violin itself to complete it. As usual, Brahms takes all the time necessary to bring to fruition the grave dignity of the movement. The slow movement, Adagio, is of unearthly beauty; Brahms's use of the oboe here is famous. The finale, Allegro giocoso, ma non troppo vivace, is fiery Gypsy music, in Rondo form, building to a marchlike coda.

Menuhin, Lucerne Festival Orchestra, Furtwängler: EMI Classics, CDH 63496
Mutter, Berlin Philharmonic Orchestra, Karajan: Deutsche Grammophon 415565-2
Kreisler, Berlin State Opera Orchestra, Blech: Music & Arts CD 290
Francescatti, New York Philharmonic Orchestra, Bernstein: Sony Classical SMK 47540

Academic Festival Overture, Op. 80 (1880)

In the spring of 1879, the University of Breslau conferred upon Brahms a doctor of philosophy degree. Unimpressed with honors, he thought it sufficient to send a postcard thanking them. A friend suggested that the university should instead be thanked with a composition about student life. The idea appealed to the German master. In 1880 he took a break from composing his *Tragic Overture* (Op. 81, 1880) to write this unique score, which utilizes four student songs as well as original themes and culminates in the rousing "Gaudeamus igitur." Brahms, who persisted all his life in denigrating his own music, called it "a jolly potpourri on student songs à la Suppé." In fact, it is a masterly sonata-allegro movement. The work is dedicated to the University of Breslau.

Cleveland Orchestra, Szell: CBS MYK 37778
Philharmonia Orchestra, Klemperer: EMI Classics CDM 69651

Concerto no. 2 in B-flat Major for Piano and Orchestra, Op. 83 (1878–81)

The Second Piano Concerto, which Brahms gratefully dedicated to his early teacher Eduard Marxsen, is less stormy and conflicted than the first. It is a monumental work in four (instead of the usual three) movements. After the huge and eloquent first movement, Brahms interjected a turbulent Scherzo allegro appassionato. He wrote to a friend that he had composed "a tiny, tiny piano concerto with a tiny, tiny wisp of a scherzo." The long slow movement, a duet for cello and piano, is a dreamy and intimate Andante. (Later Brahms reused the melody for his song "Immer leiser wird mein Schlummer," Op. 105/2.) After three movements of the highest seriousness, in the finale, marked *allegretto grazioso*, Brahms releases us with music of the utmost freshness. At the Budapest premiere on November 9, 1881, the composer himself was the soloist, and later in the month he performed it at Meiningen with Hans von Bülow conducting.

Cliburn, Moscow Philharmonic Orchestra, Kendrashin: RCA 09026-62695-2
Hess, Philharmonic Symphony Orchestra, Walter: Music & Arts MUA 779
Richter, Chicago Symphony Orchestra, Leinsdorf: RCA 07863-56518-2

Symphony no. 1 in C Minor, Op. 68 (1876)
Symphony no. 2 in D Major, Op. 73 (1877)
Symphony no. 3 in F Major, Op. 90 (1883)
Symphony no. 4 in E Minor, Op. 98 (1884–85)

Brahms is considered one of the world's great symphonists, but early in his career he was in awe of the responsibility and took over four years to compose the Symphony no. 1 in C Minor. It is epic in design; the opening Allegro is sublime, heralding a movement of mighty conflicts and dark currents. Surely Brahms felt that the blood of Beethoven had entered his heart. But the self-deprecating Brahms only said, "My first symphony is long and not exactly amiable." The slow movement is a profound Andante sostenuto. The third movement brings relief in a lighter, graceful movement, giving us time to breathe before the battle continues in the anguished and tragic finale, which leads to a theme of ecstatic joy. It was premiered on November 4, 1876, and some days later Brahms directed it in Mannheim. Out of sheer respect for its greatness, Hans von Bülow called it "Beethoven's Tenth Symphony."

The Symphony no. 2 in D Major is a work of deeply felt lyricism and warm well-being; it could be called Brahms's pastoral symphony. He composed much of it at a summer retreat in Carinthia, Pörtschach-am-See at Lake Wörth, which he described as an "exquisite spot." The often ill-tempered composer was happy there, and writing the symphony went smoothly. The first movement has a mellow beauty. Brahms had plumbed the depths in his First Symphony, and as Beethoven had done after turbulent outbursts, he relaxed to explore gentler, more reflective emotions in the next.

The Symphony no. 3 in F Major is infused with a genial lyricism but includes many passages of passionate intensity. The Poco allegretto third movement takes the place of a Scherzo in ABA form; Brahms is relaxed and insinuating. The symphony's premiere took place under the direction of the redoubtable Hans Richter, conducting the Vienna Philharmonic, on December 2, 1883.

Brahms, who had delayed the composition of his First Symphony until he was forty-three, had by age fifty-two completed his fourth essay in the difficult form. The intervening decade was incredibly productive, for Brahms produced thirty opus numbers in those years (including the symphonies). Apparently, when presented with this most enigmatic of his four symphonies, half a dozen of Brahms's closest musical friends could summon little enthusiasm for it. Their response exacerbated his already-stringent self-criticism, and Brahms felt extremely insecure when he sent the score off to von Bülow, who was to prepare the work with the Meiningen Orchestra (though Brahms himself was to conduct the premiere). He was infinitely relieved when von Bülow realized that No. 4 was "incomparable and stupendous." The composition was first conducted by Brahms on October 25, 1885. Shortly afterward, he went on tour with the orchestra and conducted his new work in nine cities. At this time, he was at the summit of his invention.

The Fourth Symphony is a combination of tragic feelings and heart-rending melancholy. Supposedly a reading of Sophocles' *Oedipus Rex* inspired it. Whatever the emotions at play, Brahms, always solving new compositional problems, presents an intellectual tour de force throughout. The fourth-movement finale, Allegro energico e passionato, is one of the mightiest movements in all symphonic literature. It takes the form of a Passacaglia, with an eight-note theme and thirty masterly variations. The more one listens to it, the more enthralled one becomes with the depths of Brahms's mind. In its fusion of musical nobility and mental stamina, the finale is of overwhelming magnitude. Tovey, after an extensive analysis of the score, once declared, "The listener need not worry as to whether he can trace the theme in the variations. If and where he can, that is well; but beauty is skin-deep, though it needs bones to keep it in shape."

The Complete Symphonies

NBC Symphony Orchestra, Toscanini: RCA 60325-2-RG
Vienna Philharmonic Orchestra, Bernstein: Deutsche Grammophon 415570-2
Cleveland Orchestra, Szell: Sony Classical SB3K 48398

Sonata no. 1 in E Minor for Cello and Piano, Op. 38 (1862–65)
Sonata no. 2 in F Major for Cello and Piano, Op. 99 (1886)

These are two of the most important Romantic cello sonatas. From the first movement of No. 1 issues a somber, resigned pathos. Its second movement is charming and, perhaps ironically, was marked by the composer as *allegretto quasi menuetto*, for it lacks any resemblance to the courtly dance. The finale is dense and uses only the lower register of the instrument. The entire piece is fugal and quite peculiarly penetrating. Brahms composed the Second Cello Sonata, consisting of four movements, at Lake Thun. He was always inspired and relaxed in Switzerland, away from the fierce musical tensions of Vienna. The work plays itself out in an atmosphere of passion, and the cellist must produce tonal grandeur. Only the finale brings gracious charm. The sonata was composed for the renowned cellist Robert Hausmann, who premiered it in November 1886.

Du Pré, Barenboim: EMI Classics CDM 63298
Ma, Ax: RCA 09026-61355-2
Rostropovich, Serkin: Deutsche Grammophon 410510-2

Sonata no. 1 in G Major for Violin and Piano, Op. 78 (1878–79)
Sonata no. 2 in A Major for Violin and Piano, Op. 100 (1886)
Sonata no. 3 in D Minor for Violin and Piano, Op. 108 (1886–88)

These three sonatas are indispensable to the violin literature. No. 1 is the most intimately appealing; No. 2 concludes with a fiery Hungarian Rondo; and No. 3 is more restless in character. No. 1 in G major is sometimes called the *Rain-song* because Brahms makes use of his song "Regenlied" in the last movement. Of the A major sonata, the critic Melvin Berger writes, "The radiant music of the A major Sonata is suffused with glowing intimacy, sweetness, and gentility." As Elisabeth von Herzogenberg, a pupil of Brahms, put it, "The whole sonata is a caress." The A major is occasionally called the *Thun* Sonata, as it was conceived in Switzerland at Lake Thun. The powerful Third Sonata, in D minor, is dedicated to Hans von Bülow, whose performances did much to promote Brahms throughout Europe. The Third Sonata is darker and offers a wider emotional landscape than the other two. Berger says, "The glorious, soaring opening theme as played by the two instruments creates the sensation of limit-less space and of compelling sweep and urgency." The Adagio is sparse and re-flective, while the finale is flush with the fevers of a desperate restlessness.

Dumay, Pires: Deutsche Grammophon 435800-2
Perlman, Ashkenazy: EMI Classics CDC 47403
Mutter, Weissenberg: EMI Classics 72093
Laredo, Pommier: Virgin Classics CDZ 59642

Quintet in B Minor for Clarinet and Strings, Op. 115 (1891)

Brahms was close to the clarinetist Richard Mühlfeld, who inspired him to write four important works for his instrument: the Quintet, the Trio, and the two sonatas, which he also arranged for viola. Each of these works contains myriad moods. From the elegiac and mellow to the rhapsodic and cheerful, the Quintet for Clarinet finds Brahms at the summit of his art as a composer of chamber music. The clarinet's blending with strings presents an incomparably fragile tonal coloration. The autumnal elegiac beauty of the Quintet gives to the receptive listener the comprehensive wisdom of Brahms in his final and loneliest period.

Shifrin, *Chamber Music Northwest: Delos DE 3066*
Kell, *Busch String Quartet: EMI Classics CDH 64932*
Leister, *Amadeus String Quartet: Deutsche Grammophon 419875-2*

Seven Fantasias for Piano, Op. 116 (1892)
Three Intermezzos for Piano, Op. 117 (1892)
Six Pieces for Piano, Op. 118 (1892)
Four Pieces for Piano, Op. 119 (1892)

In 1865 Brahms wrote his sixteen charming waltzes (Op. 39). He did not compose for solo piano again until 1878, with the remarkable *Eight Klavierstücke* (Op. 76), followed by the Two Rhapsodies (Op. 79), in 1879. After the rhapsodies, he once again left the field of solo piano music, this time for thirteen years. When he returned in 1892, he produced a series of works that are the last great contribution by any German composer to nineteenth-century piano music. The pianist Arthur Rubinstein wrote, "It is with the late piano works, Op. 116 through 119, that we reach Brahms' most personal music for his chosen instrument. . . . Brahms in his final years produced serene and nostalgic music that was ever more inward in mood. . . . As his own notations in the score indicate, they are so intensely intimate that one cannot really convey their full substance to a large audience. They should be heard quietly, in a small room, for they are actually works of chamber music for the piano." Brahms himself was prompted to remark, "An audience of even one is too many." He titled each of these twenty pieces "Intermezzo," "Capriccio," "Romance," or "Rhapsody." A technical analysis may explain the many compositional devices that Brahms united so deceptively yet rigorously into these miraculous works, but the mystery of their genius will forever remain inexplicable. One of the most profound is the Intermezzo in E-flat Minor (Op. 118/6), a work of visionary beauty and mystery. It seems to express despair, grief, and a desire for atonement. A middle section, beginning in hushed tones, gradually mounts to a marchlike theme, which bursts into a powerful climax.

Complete Piano Works
Katchen: London 455247-2

Op. 116
Gilels: Deutsche Grammophon 419158-2

Opp. 116–19
Kempff: Deutsche Grammophon 437249-2

Opp. 116, 117, 119
Kovacevich: Philips 411137-2

Songs (1851–96)

As a composer of *Lieder*, Brahms ranks near Schubert, Schumann, and Wolf. He composed songs consistently throughout his career, starting with Six Songs (Op. 3), Six Songs (Op. 6), and Six Songs (Op. 7), all in 1851–53 and among the earliest of his published works; His last songs (in 1896) were the magnificent *Vier ernste Gesänge* (*Four Serious Songs*, Op. 121). He permitted 225 songs to see publication; all used poems of German Romantic poets. Melody was one of Brahms's chief glories, and in the songs he used this vital power to the fullest. Many songs are somber or nostalgic; others have the irresistible gaiety of the unique vocal quartet *Liebeslieder* (Op. 52, 1868–69), a series of eighteen waltzes that glorify Vienna itself. He wrote love songs of feverish passion; none are negligible, and among the best are "Sapphic Ode," "Erinnerung" (Memory), "Sonntag" (Sunday), "Regenlied" (Rain Song), "Liebe und Frühling" (Love and Spring), "Immer leiser wird mein Schlummer" (My Sleep Becomes Ever Gentler), "Die Mainacht" (The May Night), and the celebrated "Wiegenlied" (Cradle Song).

The *Four Serious Songs*, composed when Brahms was dying of cancer, are stark and overwhelmingly fatalistic. Brahms was weary, beyond hope, as he set to music words from the Bible, telling a colleague that they were "ungodly ditties." Here the master composed songs of the utmost gentleness. He was ready to depart.

Fischer-Dieskau, Moore: Orfeo C140201
Hotter, Moore: EMI Classics CDH 63198
Norman, Barenboim: Deutsche Grammophon 431600-2
Lipovsek, Spencer: Sony Classical SK 52490

OTHER PRINCIPAL WORKS

CHAMBER MUSIC

Trio no. 1 in B Major for Piano, Violin, and Cello, Op. 8 (1853–54; rev. 1889)*
Sextet in B-flat Major for Strings, Op. 18 (1858–60)*
Quartet no. 1 in G Minor for Piano and Strings, Op. 25 (1861)*
Quartet no. 2 in A Major for Piano and Strings, Op. 26 (1861–62)*

Sextet in G Major for Strings, Op. 36 (1864–65)*
Trio in E-flat Major for Horn, Violin, and Piano, Op. 40 (1865)*
Quartet no. 1 in C Minor for Strings, Op. 51/1 (c.1865–73)*
Quartet no. 2 in A Minor for Strings, Op. 51/2 (c.1865–73)*
Quartet no. 3 in C Minor for Piano and Strings, Op. 60 (1855–75)*
Quartet no. 3 in B-flat Major for Strings, Op. 67 (1876)*
Trio no. 2 in C Major for Piano, Violin, and Cello, Op. 87 (1880–82)*
Quintet no. 1 in F Major for Strings, Op. 88 (1882)*
Trio no. 3 in C Minor for Piano, Violin, and Cello, Op. 101 (1886)*
Quintet no. 2 in G Major for Strings, Op. 111 (1890)*
Trio in A Minor for Clarinet, Cello, and Piano, Op. 114 (1891)*

CLARINET (OR VIOLA) AND PIANO WORKS
Sonata no. 1 in F Minor, Op. 120/1 (1894)*
Sonata no. 2 in E-flat Major, Op. 120/2 (1894)*

CONCERTO
Concerto in A Minor for Violin, Cello, and Orchestra, Op. 102 ("Double Concerto")
    (1887)*

ORCHESTRAL WORKS
Serenade no. 1 in D Major, Op. 11 (1857–58)*
Serenade no. 2 in A Major, Op. 16 (1858–59)*
Tragic Overture in D Minor, Op. 81 (1880, rev. 1881)*

PIANO WORKS
Scherzo in E-flat Minor, Op. 4 (1851)*
Sonata no. 1 in C Major, Op. 1 (1852–53)*
Sonata no. 2 in F-sharp Minor, Op. 2 (1852)*
Sonata no. 3 in F Minor, Op. 5 (1853)*
Variations on a Theme by Robert Schumann, Op. 9 (1854)*
Four Ballades, Op. 10 (1854)*
Sixteen Waltzes, Op. 39 (1865) (also for piano four-hands)*

ALEXANDER BORODIN

b. St. Petersburg, November 12, 1833

d. St. Petersburg, February 27, 1887

I am a composer in search of oblivion; and I'm always slightly ashamed that I compose.

Borodin was the illegitimate son of a sixty-one-year-old prince and Eudoxia An-lonova, a beautiful and cultivated woman of twenty-four (and another man's wife). The boy was given the last name of a serf from the prince's Georgian estate, and was raised by his mother and her husband, an army doctor. The prince died when the boy was just seven. Alexander had delicate health and a gentle disposition, and his mother and her cousin, who lived with them, doted on him. His governess soon realized that he was precocious, especially in languages and science, and she went so far as to set up a laboratory at home, where he conducted experiments, created fireworks, and produced paint. He showed an equal interest in music, and he learned the flute and somewhat later the piano and cello, each in a haphazard way. Without any instruction in theory, he wrote a trio and a concerto for flute and piano. He used as his models Mendelssohn's music and Italian opera, both of which were then popular in St. Petersburg.

By age seventeen, science was edging out music among Borodin's passions, and he entered the St. Petersburg Academy of Medicine and Surgery, performing brilliantly in all classes and specializing in chemistry. He graduated with honors in 1856 and joined the Academy's faculty as an assistant professor. He earned his doctorate in 1858. From 1859 to 1862, he studied science in Heidelberg, Germany, where he met his future wife, Catherine Protopopova.

Catherine was a fine pianist who literally brought Borodin back to music, rekindling his urge to compose. He was thunderstruck when she played works by Chopin and Schumann, who had been unknown to him. The pair married in 1863 and for their honeymoon traveled back to Germany to hear Wagner's operas, which did not fail to make an impact on the young chemist.

During the next few years, Borodin's scientific career flourished. He published several significant papers and made important discoveries about the solidification of aldehydes. In December 1862 he was appointed an assistant professor of organic chemistry at the Academy of Medicine, and in 1864 he became full professor. He was a popular teacher who showed great concern for his students, and he later took the unusual step of initiating courses for women. Under the auspices of the czar's government, he attended and spoke at conferences in Russia and Europe. By his early thirties, he was considered one of Russia's foremost scientists, and his career in theory, practice, and teaching was full and successful.

Yet the musically untutored Borodin would add composition to his life as well. The year 1862 was crucial, for it was then that Borodin met Mily Balakirev, a composer of avowedly national music. Balakirev intended to create a Russian national music and was gathering around himself a group of disciples (who included César Cui, Modest Mussorgsky, and Nikolai Rimsky-Korsakov in addition to Borodin). In a few years the group would be known as the "Mighty Handful" and the "Russian Five."

Balakirev wanted to explore the huge depository of ancient Russian folklore, legends, and dances—the spirit of old Russia—as well as the exotic Asiatic influence of the lands of the Transcaucasus. The Russian heritage had begun to find a characteristic voice in the operas of Glinka, and after Glinka died in 1857, Balakirev continued his pioneer work. In his memoirs, Rimsky-Korsakov commented that the self-taught Balakirev, who knew no musical theory, nonetheless "knew a prodigious quantity of music of all kinds, and could remember, at any moment, every bar he had ever heard or read. . . . He never failed to spot an error or shortcoming. . . . He was so despotic that he insisted upon our music being remodeled in exact accordance with his prescriptions. . . . We simply could not help obeying. He held us absolutely spellbound by his talents, his authority, his magnetism."

Regarding Borodin, Tchaikovsky lamented the fact that "blind fate has led him into the science laboratories instead of a vital musical life . . . and his technique is so poor that he cannot write one measure without assistance." Under Balakirev's instruction, the fledgling composer began to write his First Symphony in 1862. After years of hard work, it was finally performed in 1869, with Balakirev conducting. The Russian press was far from laudatory, but the First

Symphony would find success in several European cities. It was one of the first works to herald the new Russian music abroad.

For the rest of Borodin's relatively short life, stealing precious time for composition was an unsolvable problem. He was absentminded and disorganized, and that, added to his wife's ill health, her relatives, her cats, and his medical and chemistry students, made for a frantic domestic life. In addition, colleagues at the medical school lamented his frequent absences to pursue trivialities. The good-natured Borodin seldom refused to give of his time or do a favor.

To a musical colleague, he mourned, "Days, weeks, months, whole winters pass without my being able to get to work seriously. . . . One must have time to concentrate, to get into the right mood, or else the creation of a sustained work is impossible. For this I have only part of the summer at my disposal. In the winter I can compose only when I am ill and have to give up my lectures and laboratory work. So reversing the usual custom, my friends never say to me: 'I hope you are well,' but 'I hope you are ill.' During Christmas I had influenza and could not go to the laboratory. I stayed home and wrote the Thanksgiving chorus for the last act of *Igor*." Unfortunately he would never complete *Prince Igor*, nor his Third Symphony. (*Igor* would later be completed—and partly orchestrated—by Rimsky-Korsakov and Glazunov.) Yet Borodin handled the dilemma with equanimity, often saying how much "I love my science, the Academy and my students."

In 1884, at age fifty-one, Borodin had the misfortune to contract cholera and seemed to lose all vitality. When he became physically active again, his creative energy seemed dissipated. He often paced his apartment, moaning, "I cannot compose! I cannot compose!"

On February 26, 1887, he wrote to his wife (who was in Moscow) that he was going to attend a fancy dress ball, given by the Academy professors, the next day. Borodin worked well all day on his Third Symphony and was in high spirits. His appearance was dashing, for he dressed in Georgian national costume, and he danced wildly. In the middle of the ball, his heart burst, and he was dead within seconds. He is buried not far from Mussorgsky's tomb in the Alexander Nevsky Cemetery in St. Petersburg. Borodin's beloved wife survived him by just a few months. He left behind their adopted daughter, who would later marry one of his pupils and become the mother of his biographer and editor of his letters.

With such a short life of so many demands, Borodin composed little. His music is the most lyrical in spirit of the Russian Five, and his melodies possess a delicate "oriental" atmosphere. His compositions have a special sweetness as well as a legendary character. In highly charged and picturesque music, Borodin idealized the savage life of the Russian steppes. His pieces have the allure of blazing Tatar blades and Arabian steeds in the heat of battle. It is music that leaps forward and seductively whispers mysterious romances in the slow movements. Borodin was a master of orchestration, and we hear his influence especially in Debussy and Ravel.

Symphony No. 2 in B Minor (1876)

This marvel of orchestration is the finest symphony composed by any of the Russian Five. Borodin's love of medieval Russia charges this stirring epic with a fairytale quality. The structure is powerful and clear-cut, the inspiration sustained throughout. The mighty opening motif dominates the first movement. The Scherzo is a wavering glimmer of light with a folklike Trio. In the slow movement, Andante, the clarinet presents an affable song, a climax ensues, and the movement ends with the clarinet alone. Without pause, the Finale, in sonata form, begins and brings the work to an ebullient ending. The symphony was Borodin's tribute to ancient chivalric Russian tales of maidens and knights, tales that he loved as a child and dreamed of as an artist.

Orchestre de la Suisse Romande, Ansermet: London 430219-2
Stuttgart Symphony Orchestra, C. Kleiber: Memories HR 4410

In the Steppes of Central Asia (1880)

Ravel called this small but perfect tone poem "an ingenuous work whose musicality and impressionism are penetrating." It was written in 1880 to honor the twenty-fifth anniversary of the coronation of Czar Alexander II. Its two main themes are delicately orchestrated, with a program that remarkably fits the music's progress: "Through the silence of the steppes of Central Asia is heard the strain of a peaceful Russian song. Sounds of horses and camels come from the distance, approaching ever nearer and with them the stream of a haunting eastern melody. A caravan is crossing the desert escorted by Russian soldiers. It progresses on its long journey confident in the protection of the soldiers. The caravan disappears into the distant horizon. The song of the Russians blends with that of the Orientals in a common harmony, until both fade away across the plains."

USSR Symphony, Svetlanov, Melodia SUCD10-00155
Gothenburg Symphony, Järvi: Deutsche Grammophon 2-435757-2GH2

Prince Igor Overture and Polovtsian Dances (1869–87)

The full opera, completed by Rimsky-Korsakov and Glazunov, is seldom staged outside of Russia. The story centers on Prince Igor and his son in a campaign against a Tartar people, the Polovtsi. Igor and his son are captured, but the Polovtsi still honor them with a presentation of their tribal dances. *Prince Igor* as a whole lacks dramatic continuity, but the music is thoroughly characteristic of the composer's essence. The overture uses some material from the Polovtsian Dances as well as Igor's aria. In the second act, the opulent and lyrical Polovtsian Dances throb with barbaric splendor.

Atlanta Symphony Orchestra and Chorus, Shaw: Telarc CD 80039
London Symphony Orchestra and Chorus, Solti: London 417689-2

Quartet no. 2 in D Major for Strings (1881)

The second of Borodin's quartets is indispensable to Russian chamber music. The first movement, Allegro moderato, is unusual in that it is lyrical throughout. The second, Notturno, movement rivals in popularity the *Andante cantabile* movement of Tchaikovsky's D major quartet. It was unfortunately used as the basis for the song "And This Is My Beloved" in the Broadway show *Kismet* (which pillaged practically every melody the Russian wrote). The finale begins with an introduction of some weight, moving to a quick tempo. The movement contains a fugal section followed by a long melody. The movement is effectively broken by a reappearance of the Andante theme.

Cleveland String Quartet: Telarc CD 80178
Talich String Quartet: Approche CAL 6202
Borodin String Quartet: EMI Classics CDC 47795

OTHER PRINCIPAL WORKS

CHAMBER MUSIC
Quartet no. 1 in A Major for Strings (1874–79)

ORCHESTRAL WORKS
Symphony no. 1 in E-flat Major (1867)*
Symphony no. 3 in A Minor (*Unfinished*) (1882)

PIANO WORKS
Petite suite (1884) (also an orchestrated version by Glazunov)
Scherzo in A-flat Major (1885)*

VOICE AND PIANO WORKS
Fourteen songs*

CAMILLE
SAINT-SAËNS

b. Paris, October 9, 1835

d. Algiers, December 16, 1921

Of applause
I still hear the noise of applause; and, strangely enough,
in my childish shyness it seemed like mire
about to spot me; I feared
its touch, and secretly shunned it,
affecting obstinacy.

After Mozart and Mendelssohn, Saint-Saëns is probably music's most astonishing prodigy. At two and a half, he was picking out tunes at the piano; by four he had composed; and at five he made his debut as a pianist. The precocious child was also richly gifted in mathematics, science, and languages. A program from 1846 at the Salle Pleyel shows Saint-Saëns performing Mozart's Piano Concerto no. 15 and Beethoven's Third Piano Concerto as well as a formidable group of solo works.

At fifteen he entered the Paris Conservatory, where he claimed prize after prize. His First Symphony (Op. 2, 1853) was performed in Paris when he was twenty. Berlioz reported that Saint-Saëns "knows everything but he lacks inexperience." The versatile musician was also a magnificent organist, and from 1857 to 1876 he was organist at the famed Madeleine Church in Paris. Liszt described his organ playing as "not merely in the front rank but incomparable . . . no orchestra is capable of creating a similar impression." Late in 1877 Saint-Saëns's opera *Samson et Dalila* was given its premiere by Eduard Lassen, under the sponsorship of Liszt at Weimar. Although not seen in Paris until 1892, the opera had splendid success in Europe's major opera houses.

Shortly before finishing *Samson*, Saint-Saëns—by then forty—married nineteen-year-old Marie Laure Emilie Truffot. Three years into the marriage, the couple's two-and-a-half-year-old son was killed falling from the balcony of their Paris apartment. Madame Saint-Saëns, bereft, left town with their seven-month-old son, who died of pneumonia just six weeks after the first tragedy. Saint-Saëns, a man known for his irony and cool restraint, wrote to a friend, "I have lost both of my children in the space of little over a month, and I assure you that my happiness is very much subdued." In 1881, when on vacation with his wife, the composer wrote her a note and left their hotel early one morning. He never returned, and never married again. (Madame Saint-Saëns never re-married either and died near Bordeaux in 1950.)

During his younger years, Saint-Saëns had admired the progressive trends of Berlioz, Wagner, and Liszt. He was especially inspired by Liszt's symphonic poems, and around the time of his marriage he wrote four programmatic works, including the iridescent *Le Rouet d'Omphale* (Op. 31, 1872) and the famous *Danse macabre* (Op. 40, 1874). He was also attracted to Classical forms, and in 1886 he wrote his Third Symphony (Op. 78), the so-called *Organ* Symphony, dedicated to the memory of the recently deceased Liszt. It was his masterwork, and the composer declared, "I gave everything to it I was able to give. What I have here accomplished, I will never achieve again."

The indefatigable Saint-Saëns possessed herculean energy. He edited the then-neglected Mozart sonatas; performed in public the entire cycle of Mozart piano concertos when they were all but unknown; and resurrected and edited the music of Gluck, Rameau, and others. This remarkable artist also dabbled in physics, astronomy, and archaeology, learned one language after another, drew caricatures, and wrote plays and books on painting, aesthetics, criticism, and philosophy. In 1908 he composed history's first film score, *L'assassinat du Duc de Guise*, which premiered at the Salle Charras late that year. His wit and biting sarcasm frightened his enemies and titillated his friends.

From around 1890, Saint-Saëns became almost pathologically restless, and he traveled incessantly. He was French to the core—smartly dressed, correct, lucid, and elegant—but wherever he went (Cairo or New York, Ceylon, Brazil, or Argentina), he imbibed the local color. He wrote a *Caprice andalous* (Op. 122, 1904), an *Egyptian* Concerto (Op. 103, 1896), *Africa Fantasy* for piano and orchestra (Op. 89, 1891), a *Caprice arabe* (Op. 96, 1894), and other tributes to wanderlust. Worldly honors and honorary degrees were lavished upon him; to the world, he represented the summit of French civilization.

But to younger composers, he had become a stuffy "Classic." The once-progressive composer, who had seen Liszt, Berlioz, Wagner, Franck, and Fauré play their music, had become conservative as he aged. After 1910 the music of Mahler, Stravinsky, Scriabin, Ravel, and Schoenberg held no pleasure for him.

Debussy, always acerbic, snapped, "Isn't there anyone who cares enough for Saint-Saëns to tell him that he's written enough music and that he'd be better employed in his recently found vocation of explorer?" George Bernard Shaw, listening to the premiere of Saint-Saëns's opera *Ascanio* (1890), complained, "I need not waste my words on the music of it. There is not an original phrase in it from beginning to end."

Undaunted, and blessed with the energy of youth even in old age, Saint-Saëns continued to compose prolifically, taking little heed of either praise or criticism. He wrote to his dear friend Gabriel Fauré, "The vintage is in! At 85 it is one's right to say no more—and probably one's duty." Changing his mind, however, he proceeded to compose the three superb sonatas, one each for oboe, clarinet, and bassoon. He died in Algiers at eighty-six, playing and conducting in public until the end.

Saint-Saëns summed up his philosophy as a composer with these words: "The artist who does not feel completely satisfied by elegant lines, by harmonious colors, and by a beautiful succession of chords does not understand the art of music." For some decades after his death, his music seemed faded and superficial to many. His pleasant nimble graciousness and cleverness sounded old-fashioned in an ever-more-turbulent century. But today Saint-Saëns has made a comeback. We may admire his slick, pseudo-Classical forms, and their refreshing neatness appeals to us. The freshness of his objective brand of Romanticism keeps alive the Cello Concerto no. 1 (Op. 33, 1872), the Violin Concerto no. 3 (Op. 61, 1880), and the five piano concertos. We enjoy his later compositions too, with their dry, ironic neoclassicism, such as the sonatas for oboe, clarinet, and bassoon (Opp. 166–168, all 1921) and the engaging Septet for Trumpet, Strings, and Piano (Op. 65, 1881).

In every form, he wrote much music good and bad. But even when the music is poor, it reveals enormous zest and a joy in composing. Occasionally his sentimental *tristesse* may provoke a tender smile. Some of his piano pieces, like the *Étude en forme de valse* (*Étude in the Form of a Waltz*, Op. 52/6, 1877), are effervescent, while the severe Fugues for Piano (Op. 161, c.1920), admirable in their contrapuntal skill, are appalling in their intrinsic boredom.

But when Saint-Saëns is in top form, he has an aristocratic reserve, a fund of delightful melody, and an amusing insouciance, all of which are packaged in a streamlined form. The music of Saint-Saëns is for relaxing and smiling, for bright sassy moods, and at times for a precious, almost rococo charm. For music lovers in the twenty-first century, these attractions are far from negligible.

Concerto no. 2 in G Minor for Piano and Orchestra, Op. 22 (1868)

This concerto remains a warhorse of the piano concerto literature. The pianist Sigismund Stojowski thought "it opened like Bach and ended like Offenbach." It lacks a slow movement; Saint-Saëns included instead a puckish Scherzo. It was written in seventeen days and premiered on May 13, 1868. The great pianist Anton Rubinstein conducted and Saint-Saëns played the piano, as he did for the first performances of all five of his piano concertos. Two of his other piano concertos have survived in the repertoire: No. 4 in C minor (1875), musically the finest of the group, and No. 5, the *Egyptian* Concerto (1896), a sparkling audience-pleaser.

Bar-Ilian, Orchestre des Concerts Français, DuBois: Audiofon CD 72006
Rubinstein, Symphony of the Air, Wallenstein: RCA Gold Seal 09026-61496-2

Introduction and Rondo capriccioso for Violin and Orchestra, Op. 28 (1863)

This piece was composed for the fiery Spanish violin virtuoso Pablo de Sarasate. The score has an immediate and irresistible appeal. The work abounds in diamondlike scales and glinting arpeggios. Saint-Saëns is by turns elegant, fetching, and melancholy; here he is a French Mendelssohn. The composer also wrote three violin concertos. The last, in B minor, holds a high place in the history of the French violin concerto.

Stern, Philadelphia Orchestra, Ormandy: CBS MK4 42003
Heifetz, RCA Victor Symphony Orchestra, Steinberg: RCA 7709-2-RG
Friedman, Chicago Symphony Orchestra, Hendl: RCA 09026-61210-2

Danse macabre, Op. 40 (1874)

The third of Saint-Saëns's four symphonic poems is one of his most famous works. The score is modeled on Liszt's one-movement plan; it is concise, clever, and graphic, and it makes delightful use of the xylophone for the rattling bones of skeletons in the cemetery. Saint-Saëns also makes effective use of the Roman Catholic liturgical melody *Dies Irae*. Its satirical appeal and its orchestral savvy continue to delight audiences.

Philharmonia Orchestra, Dutoit: London 414460-2
Royal Stockholm Philharmonic Orchestra, DePreist: BIS CD 555

The Carnival of the Animals (1886)

The Carnival of the Animals is a triumph of humor, graciousness, suavity, and parody, a grand zoological fantasia. One hears a lion, hens, tortoises, roosters, an elephant, a cuckoo, a kangaroo, "pianists," and the celebrated "Swan" (for cello)—fourteen movements in all. There are delicious satires on music by Rossini, Offenbach, Berlioz, Wagner, and Mendelssohn. For reasons unknown, Saint-Saëns refused to have the composition performed during his lifetime. Children who never hear *The Carnival of the Animals* are indeed deprived.

Philadelphia Orchestra, Ormandy: Sony Classics SBK 47655
Boston Pops Orchestra, Fiedler: RCA 6718-2-RG
New York Philharmonic Orchestra, Bernstein: Sony Classical SMK 47596 (with verses by Og-
    den Nash)

Symphony no. 3 in C Minor (*Organ*), Op. 78 (1886)

The spacious Third Symphony has a novel form: it is divided into two parts. Saint-Saëns wrote, "It embraces in principle the four traditional movements, but the first, halted in its development, serves as the introduction to the adagio, and the scherzo is left by the same process to lead to the finale." The use of the organ gives the instrumentation a luscious depth. The Adagio presents a contemplative theme that is magnificently effective, especially when accompanied by the organ. The world premiere took place on May 19, 1886, with Saint-Saëns conducting the London Philharmonic Society.

M. Dupré, Detroit Symphony Orchestra, Paray: Mercury 432719-2
Raver, New York Philharmonic Orchestra, Bernstein: CBS MYK 37255
Alain, Vienna Symphony Orchestra, Prêtre: Erato 2292-45696-2

OTHER PRINCIPAL WORKS

CHAMBER MUSIC

Trio no. 1 in F Major for Piano, Violin, and Cello, Op. 18 (1863)

Quartet in B-flat Major for Piano and Strings, Op. 41 (1875)*

Septet in E-flat Major for Trumpet, Strings, and Piano, Op. 65 (1881)*

Sonata no. 1 in D Minor for Violin and Piano, Op. 75 (1885)*

Trio no. 2 in E Minor for Piano, Violin, and Cello, Op. 92 (1892)

Quartet no. 1 in E Minor for Strings, Op. 112 (1899)

Fantaisie in A Major for Violin and Harp, Op. 124 (1907)*

Quartet no. 2 in G Major for Strings, Op. 153 (1918)

Sonata in D Major for Oboe and Piano, Op. 166 (1921)*

Sonata in E-flat Major for Clarinet and Piano, Op. 167 (1921)*

Sonata in G Major for Bassoon and Piano, Op. 168 (1921)*

OPERAS

Samson et Dalila (1877)*

Henry VIII (1883)

ORCHESTRAL WORKS

Symphony no. 2 in A Minor, Op. 55 (1859)*

Le Rouet d'Omphale, Op. 31 (1872)*

Phaéton, Op. 39 (1873)*

La Jeunesse d'Hercule, Op. 50 (1877)

Suite algérienne, Op. 60 (1880)

PIANO WORKS

Variations on a Theme of Beethoven for Two Pianos, Op. 35 (1874)*

Six Études, Op. 52 (1877)

Étude en forme de valse, Op. 52/6 (1877)*

Suite, Op. 90 (1891)

Six Études, Op. 111 (1899)

Six Études for the Left Hand, Op. 135 (1912)

SOLO INSTRUMENT AND ORCHESTRA WORKS

Concerto no. 1 for Piano and Orchestra, Op. 17 (1858)

Concerto no. 2 for Violin and Orchestra, Op. 58 (1858)

Concerto no. 1 for Violin and Orchestra, Op. 20 (1859)

Concerto no. 1 in A Minor for Cello and Orchestra, Op. 33 (1872)*

Allegro appassionato for Cello and Orchestra, Op. 43 (1875)
Concerto no. 4 for Piano and Orchestra, Op. 44 (1875)*
Concerto no. 3 for Violin and Orchestra, Op. 61 (1880)*
Havanaise for Violin and Orchestra, Op. 83 (1887)*
Africa Fantasy for Piano and Orchestra, Op. 89 (1891)*
Concerto no. 5 for Piano and Orchestra, Op. 103 (1896)*

GEORGES BIZET

b. Paris, October 25, 1838

d. Bougival (near Paris), June 3, 1875

I dreamed last night that we were all at Naples, installed in a charming villa; we were living under a purely artistic government. The senate consisted of Beethoven, Michelangelo, Shakespeare, Giorgione and the likes. The national guard was replaced by an immense orchestra . . . waking up was a cruelly bitter business.

Bizet's first teacher was his father, a singing teacher. The boy exhibited stunning talent and was admitted to the Paris Conservatory at age ten. He was the youngest student there. His ability to sight-read even the most difficult piano scores amazed his colleagues. Several years later, Bizet astonished even Liszt with this ability. The young pianist sight-read one of Liszt's newest pieces in manuscript. The Hungarian was delighted: "My young friend, I thought there were only two men [pianist Hans von Bülow and Liszt] able to surmount the difficulties with which it was my pleasure to adorn this piece. I was wrong. There are three, and in justice I should add that the youngest of the three is perhaps the boldest and most brilliant."

Fromental Halévy, the composer of *La Juive* and Bizet's composition teacher, declared the youngster a great musician. At seventeen he wrote the lovely Symphony in C Major. Two years later, in 1857, he was awarded the coveted Prix de Rome and set off for Italy, where he spent the happiest three years of his life.

When he returned to Paris in 1860, he could have made a living as a concert pianist, but he hoped to succeed as an opera composer. After two operas failed at their premieres in 1863, he wrote *Les Pêcheurs de perles*. The reviews were bad, but Bizet found solace in the comments of Berlioz, who wrote, "The score of *Les Pêcheurs de perles* does M. Bizet the greatest honor." The opera, although uneven, has that special warmth and exotic coloring that are typical of Bizet's genius. The duet for baritone and tenor "Au fond du Temple Saint" never fails to enchant.

In the years following *Les Pêcheurs de perles*, Bizet found himself doing all kinds of disagreeable hackwork. "It is maddening," he wrote, "to interrupt the work I love—to write cornet solos, but one must live!" Two more operas were criticized for being either too Wagnerian or too Verdian. Truthfully, they were mediocre. Saint-Saëns, well aware of the perils of opera production, tried to steer the discouraged Bizet to other forms of music, but Bizet sadly told him, "I'm condemned to the stage for my artistic being."

Late in 1867, he was encouraged by the favorable reviews and amiable audience response to his newest opera, *La Jolie fille de Perth*, whose perky overture is still performed occasionally. Perhaps it was this glimmer of professional hope that convinced Bizet to give up his promiscuous bohemian life and settle down. In 1869 he married Halévy's daughter Geneviève.

With the outbreak of the Franco-Prussian War in 1870, Bizet enlisted in the National Guard. He was deeply distressed by the war and could hardly believe that France had lost, but he was glad to see the corrupt Second Empire fall. In 1871, after his military duty, he composed the delightful suite for piano duet *Jeux d'enfants*, followed the next year by the opera *Djamileh*, which when produced was a fiasco. Shortly afterward he composed incidental music for the play *L'Arlésienne*, which has become one of his best-known scores.

For the next two years, Bizet was completely absorbed in writing a new opera. After many postponements and difficult rehearsals, *Carmen* received its premiere on March 3, 1875. The press reaction was scathing. Bizet's source was a risqué novella by Prosper Mérimée and, although the libretto was considerably watered down, the opera was still considered immoral, even obscene. Its first-night failure was a crushing blow to Bizet, yet in its first season the opera managed to stay open for a respectable thirty-seven performances, although with rather small audiences. Bizet became despondent and increasingly ill—a throat inflammation that had plagued him for years returned, and an abscessed ear caused deafness. Finally the overwrought composer was paralyzed by a stroke. He died on the night of the thirty-third performance of *Carmen*, at the age of thirty-seven. His widow outlived him by almost half a century, and would go on to be immortalized by Proust as Odette, the duchesse de Guermantes, in *Remembrance of Things Past*. His son, Jacques, born in 1872, committed suicide in 1922.

Bizet believed passionately in the dramatic and musical value of *Carmen*, and his work haunts our imagination. "This music is wicked, refined, fatalistic," wrote Nietzsche. "It possesses the refinement of a race. . . . It voices a sensibility that was unknown to us . . . fate hangs over it." Bizet depicted "love as fate, as a fatality, cynical, innocent, cruel . . . Love whose very essence is the mortal hatred between the sexes! I know of no case in which the tragic irony, which constitutes the kernel of love, is expressed with such severity, or in so terrible a formula, as the last cry of Don José with which the work ends: 'Ah! Carmen. It is I who have killed you. My Carmen! My adored!' " The ill-fated composer would be content to know that his masterpiece may well be the most famous and best-loved opera of all time.

Symphony in C Major (1855)

This symphony, a perfect gem written by a barely seventeen-year-old boy, was never performed in the composer's lifetime and was presumed lost until 1933, when it was found in the library of the Paris Conservatory. Felix Weingartner was the first conductor to perform it, in 1935. The score is a wonderful "Classical" symphony, an amalgam of Haydn, Mozart, and early Schubert, as well as Gounod's D major symphony, which Bizet admired and surpassed. The slender orchestration is perfect; the slow movement's oboe solo shows his effortless mastery.

Beecham, French National Radio Symphony Orchestra: EMI Classics CDC 47794
Orpheus Chamber Orchestra (no conductor): Deutsche Grammophon 432624-2

L'Arlésienne, Suites 1 and 2 (1872)

L'Arlésienne (The Girl of Arles), a play by Alphonse Daudet, ran less than three weeks in October 1872. For it, Bizet wrote twenty-seven mostly short selections. From them he rewrote and compiled a four-movement suite, which was a great success at its concert premiere in November 1872. In Suite no. 1 the composer linked together a Prelude, Menuet, Adagietto, and Carillon. Four years after the composer's death, Bizet's Suite no. 2 was adapted by Ernest Guiraud, the composer's close friend, using other selections; it contains a Pastorale, Intermezzo, Menuet, and Farandole. In Suite no. 1 the scoring, especially in the use of woodwinds, is luminous.

Beecham, Royal Philharmonic Orchestra: EMI Classics CDC 47794
Munch, New Philharmonia Orchestra: London 421632-2
Stokowski, National Philharmonic Orchestra: CBS MYK 37260

Carmen (1873–74)

According to Bizet's biographer, Winton Dean, "Carmen is one of the comparatively few operas that are at once a treasure for musicians and a sure success with the public—it owes this position to a rare equilibrium between the musician and the dramatist in Bizet. Just as his musicianship ensured a stylistic balance between *élan* and finish, so in his handling of the drama he could give the fullest expression to the passion of the characters (and in Carmen they tear at the roots of human nature) while standing apart and allowing their fate to move us."

Henri Meilhac and Ludovic Halévy fashioned a flexible and powerful libretto from Prosper Mérimée's novel. At its premiere, Carmen shocked its audience by presenting highly questionable subject matter (at least for that era). In later years, by contrast, the libretto was criticized as too tame. A. W. Raitt, Mérimée's biographer, writes, "To appreciate Carmen at its true worth, it is of course necessary to forget all about Bizet; whatever the musical and dramatic merits of the opera, it is in its basic schema no more than an emasculated and prettified version of Mérimée's tale. What Mérimée wrote has a savage power that the more conventional picturesqueness of Bizet's adaptation cannot match." That may well be true, but it is Bizet's opera that lives on. Indeed, the libretto moves with the music on a high level of dramatic intensity. And the music implies all that Mérimée himself created, but distilled by a superior genius.

The story of Carmen is timeless—hate, love, death, violence, the gory lure of the bullring, scalding sexual passion, the desperation of jealousy, the romance of Gypsy life, and much more. Mérimée's Carmen is a true *femme fatale*, and Bizet's music universalizes the "dangerous woman." In its inevitable and cumulative power, every scene from the dazzling prelude onward is heightened with the throbbing pulse of life.

Tchaikovsky loved Carmen dearly, writing to his patroness Madame von Meck in 1880, "I consider it a chef-d'oeuvre in the fullest sense of the word: one of those rare compositions which seems to reflect most strongly in itself the musical tendencies of a whole generation. . . . I cannot play the last scene without tears in my eyes; the gross rejoicings of the crowd who look on at the bullfight, and side by side with this, the poignant tragedy and death of the two principal characters, pursued by an evil fate, who come to their inevitable end through a long series of sufferings. I am convinced that ten years hence Carmen will be the most popular opera in the world. But no one is a prophet in his own land. In Paris Carmen has had no real success."

Cotrubas, Berganza, Domingo, Milnes, London Symphony Orchestra, Ambrosian Opera Chorus, Abbado: Deutsche Grammophon 419636-2

Bumbry, Freni, Vickers, Diaz, Vienna Philharmonic Orchestra, Vienna State Opera Chorus, Karajan: Arkadia 221

de los Angeles, Micheau, Gedda, Blanc, French Radio Orchestra and Chorus, Beecham: EMI Classics CDS 49240-2

OTHER PRINCIPAL WORKS

OPERA
Les Pêcheurs de perles (1863)*

ORCHESTRAL WORKS
Petite suite (from *Jeux d'enfants*): five pieces orchestrated by the composer (1871)*
Patrie overture (1873)

PIANO WORKS
Variations chromatiques de concert (1868)*

PIANO DUET WORKS
Jeux d'enfants (twelve pieces) (1871)*

MODEST MUSSORGSKY

b. Karevo-Pskov, March 21, 1839

d. St. Petersburg, March 28, 1881

I regard the people as one great being, inspired by one idea. This is my problem. I strove to solve it in this opera.

Mussorgsky was born to a wealthy aristocratic family and early showed an aptitude for music. He had his first piano lessons with his mother. At thirteen he entered the Cadet School in St. Petersburg but continued his piano lessons, studying with Anton Herke, a pupil of the great pianist Adolf von Henselt. The boy made good progress for several years. He received solid training in piano but only a smattering of theory; no surprise, then, that when he tried to write an opera (at sixteen), he failed.

Meanwhile, he had become involved in the rowdy, dissipated life of a Russian army officer as a member of the famous Preobrazhensky guards. At parties the dandified cadet monopolized the festivities by playing salon ditties and operatic potpourri. Alcohol flowed freely, and Mussorgsky rapidly developed an addiction to it. The composer Alexander Borodin later said, "Mussorgsky was at that time a very elegant, dapper little officer . . . he sat at the piano and, coquettishly throwing up his hands, played excerpts from *Trovatore, Traviata*, etc., very pleasantly and gracefully."

A meeting with Mily Balakirev in 1857 changed his life. Mussorgsky was entranced by Balakirev's commanding personality and his ability to impart musical knowledge and confidence. Balakirev talked endlessly about Russian composers' "sacred mission" to free Russian music from the stultifying sterility and feeble imitations of German music and Italian opera. Glinka and Russian folk music were to be their inspirations. The first fledgling composer to come under Balakirev's influence, in 1856, had been the wealthy César Cui, a military engineer who would become known as a composer and critic. Not long afterward Nikolai Rimsky-Korsakov, a young naval officer, entered the little circle, followed by Mussorgsky and finally by Borodin, a chemist. For a time Rimsky-Korsakov was Mussorgsky's roommate. The critic Vladimir Stassov was close to the group, and it was he who eventually called them the *Moguchaia Kutchka*, or "Mighty Handful." (Later they became known as the "Russian Five.") Stassov wrote, "I shall never forget how, when [Rimsky-Korsakov and Mussorgsky] were still young men living together in one room, I would go there early in the morning and find them both still asleep. I would wake them; get them out of bed; give them whatever was necessary for their morning toilet; hand them stockings, pants, robes or jackets and shoes. We would drink tea together and eat the Swiss cheese sandwiches, which we like so much . . . and immediately after morning tea we would start working at what we loved and was so vital to us—music. The piano could be heard and the singing would start, and with great excitement and bustle they would show me what they had composed the previous day, or the day before or the day before that, how wonderful it was."

Under Balakirev's intensive guidance, Mussorgsky analyzed works of Beethoven, Schubert, and Glinka and began composing. In 1858, after a great deal of soul-searching, he resigned his army commission, convinced that he must follow the path of art. His family was, naturally, gloomy about the decision. A career in music was a rarity in upper-class Russian circles, where art was usually reserved for one's spare time.

Leaving the army was, alas, a step toward destruction for the high-strung, unstable, and alcoholic young composer (whose hero was Byron's Manfred). Borodin and others observed that Mussorgsky quickly transformed himself from a self-absorbed fop into an artist possessed. He also became friendly with the composer Alexander Dargomyzhsky and was attracted to his ideas of "truth and naturalism" in music. Like Dargomyzhsky, Mussorgsky experimented with melody based on the inflections of speech. "I foresee a new kind of melody," he wrote, "which will be the melody of life. With great pains I have achieved a type of melody imitating that of speech. Someday, all of a sudden, the ineffable song will arise, intelligible to one and all. If I succeed, I shall be a conqueror in art—and succeed I must."

When Czar Alexander II emancipated the serfs in 1874, Mussorgsky's family fortune rapidly dwindled. For the next two years, he lived at home, trying to salvage the family's failing estates. As Russia left its semifeudal state, many reforms were instituted. Mussorgsky hungrily absorbed the great ferment of liberal thought and was especially enthralled by Darwin's thinking. Late in 1863 it became clear that the family estates could not be saved. The composer was forced to take a job. With great trepidation, he entered the civil service and was assigned to a position as a head clerk at the Ministry of Communications. He despised every minute he spent at the ministry and thought only of composing. He now felt that beauty for the sake of beauty alone was not his goal. For him, the words and music had to be one and the same; art should mirror Russian life in all of its manifestations. In 1868, using a text of his favorite author, Gogol, he began composing an opera, *The Marriage*. Writing to a friend, he said, "The Rubicon will be crossed. . . . This is what I would like. For my characters to speak on the stage as living people speak. . . . My music must be an artistic reproduction of human speech in all its finest shades."

The Marriage was never finished, and in 1868 Mussorgsky turned instead to *Boris Godunov*, destined to be his only completed opera. It was rejected for production in 1869 at St. Petersburg's Maryinsky Theater. A toned-down version was produced at the Imperial Theater on February 8, 1874, but the composer was bitterly hurt at the public's lack of understanding.

In 1874 the unexpected death of Mussorgsky's close friend, the painter and architect Victor Hartmann, had a shattering effect on him. Following an exhibition of Hartmann's works, Mussorgsky, with unusual speed, wrote *Pictures at an Exhibition*, a mighty memorial to his fellow artist. For the following six years, he worked sporadically on two operas, *Khovanshchina* and *Sorochintsy Fair*. Although it was never finished, *Khovanshchina* ranks especially high in his oeuvre. The American author Paul Rosenfeld wrote, "An autumnal ripeness suffuses the deeply sweet melodies. Some of them glow like wines, and they have a grace and an elegance infrequent in Mussorgsky." The opera has rare revivals, but the prelude to Act I, "Dawn on the Moskva River," and the orchestral entr'acte before Act IV, Scene 2 are evocative examples of Mussorgsky the tone painter.

Now the composer's health was deteriorating rapidly. He had first been hospitalized for alcohol problems as early as 1865, but by forty he was losing his ability to function. He had switched jobs, to one at the Forest Ministry, but in 1880 he was forced to resign. His physical and mental condition was frightening. His friends often found him in dives, drunk beyond recognition, his eyes blazing in madness. Every possession he owned had been sold for drink.

On March 18, 1881, the devoted Rimsky-Korsakov conducted Mussorgsky's first major composition, *The Destruction of Sennacherib*, for chorus and orchestra at a concert of Balakirev's Free Music School. Afterward, the composer told an acquaintance that he had no way to survive and would have to beg on the street. Within days he suffered what doctors called an attack of alcoholic epilepsy. After three violent seizures, the composer was taken to the Nikolaev Military Hospital, where Ilya Repin painted a famous portrait of him. His last days were the ravings of a tortured soul. He passed his forty-second birthday on the first day of spring in 1881, and one of the hospital orderlies, against strict orders, brought him some brandy. He lasted until March 28. Repin recalled, "The following day we were supposed to have our last sitting. But when I arrived, he was no longer with us." On the thirtieth he was buried in the Alexander Nevsky Cemetery, not far from where Dostoyevsky had been interred just weeks earlier.

Mussorgsky's art—stark, angular, and often disturbing—was essentially different from that of his colleagues in the Russian Five. The fairyland of Rimsky-Korsakov and the Transcaucasian folk material used by the others had no truth for him. Indeed, in listening to Mussorgsky, one is particularly struck that his work has so little relation to any other music. He was completely anti-academic; he disdained formal training and broke many conventional compositional rules. Those who thought of him as a dilettante did not understand that this was his intention. He was entering Modernism, leaving behind his colleagues and Romanticism. "The artist believes in the future because he lives in the future," he wrote.

But Mussorgsky's impact on later composers, especially Janáček, Debussy, and others of the modern French school, was to be great. In 1901 Debussy, reviewing Mussorgsky's *The Nursery* song cycle, wrote, "Never before has such a refined sensibility expressed itself with such simple means; it is almost as if he were an inquisitive savage discovering music for the first time, guided in each step forward by his own emotions. He composes in a series of bold strokes, but his incredible gift of foresight means that each stroke is bound to the next by a mysterious thread. Sometimes he can conjure up a disquieting impression of darkness so powerful that it wrings tears from one's heart."

At his death, Mussorgsky's manuscripts were in disarray, and they were frequently impracticable in performance. With all good intent, Rimsky-Korsakov tempered (some would definitely say "tampered with") some of Mussorgsky's most scalding and original passages, in some cases prettifying them, in others clarifying the composer's intentions. As Mussorgsky's reputation has grown, Rimsky-Korsakov has often been chastised by scholars for his "good deeds," especially his "restoration" of *Boris Godunov*, arguably the greatest of all Russian operas. After Mussorgsky's death, Rimsky-Korsakov, thinking to make the opera more intelligible and performable, edited the 1874 version, which he considered too rough and unpolished for popular success.

Mussorgsky was severely self-destructive, and his early death was inevitable. His reliance on instinct was an aspect of his personality, as if technical knowledge would limit his search for "truth." He was far more than an artist who merely lacked discipline: he was an idealist incapable of surviving for long in the real world of naked, shattering truth. Like Tolstoy, he was wracked by the violence and heartbreaking injustice inflicted on millions of Russian serfs. Unlike Rimsky-Korsakov, Balakirev, and Borodin, he could not find refuge in Romantic nationalism. He saw strife and bitterness as few of his class did—he acknowledged it and faced it. Nothing in Mussorgsky's art is personal; he dissolved his entire being into the agonized fate of the Russian people, and he saw no hope for the future. His prophetic gaze separated him from his contemporaries. His art is the most elemental, searing, disturbing, and innovative of all nineteenth-century Russian composers. His few compositions reflected the powerful emotions about his country and his people that haunted his mind and heart. To know *Boris Godunov*, it has often been said, is to know the Russian people.

A Night on Bald Mountain (1867; reorchestrated 1886)

A Night on Bald Mountain as we know it is an overhaul by Rimsky-Korsakov, and as such it has become one of Mussorgsky's most famous compositions. In fact, we shall never know the actual materials that Rimsky-Korsakov used in his reconstruction. It should be heard as a joint work of the two composers. Rimsky-Korsakov appended to the score an explanation of the symphonic poem: "subterranean sounds of supernatural voices—appearance of the spirits of darkness, followed by that of Satan himself—Glorification of Satan and celebration of the Black Mass—the Sabbath Revels—at the height of the orgies the bell of the village church, sounding in the distance, disperses the spirit of darkness—Daybreak."

London Symphony Orchestra, Solti: London 417689-2
USSR Symphony Orchestra, Svetlanov: Medlodiya SUCD 10-00138

Boris Godunov (1869)

Boris Godunov, a prologue and four acts based on Pushkin's play of the same name, as well as Nikolai Karamzin's *History of the Russian Empire*, has had a complex history. After Mussorgsky's own revised version appeared in 1874, Rimsky-Korsakov made an edition, which was first staged in St. Petersburg in 1896. A further revision by Rimsky-Korsakov premiered in 1904. It is this version that made the opera famous, along with its greatest Boris, the basso Fyodor Chaliapin. The first "original" performance, using the 1869 score, was performed in Leningrad in 1928. In 1959 there was a version edited by Shostakovich. The controversy over how to do justice to Mussorgsky's sprawling opera will doubtless continue.

Of the Rimsky-Korsakov version, the English writer on music Gerald Abraham goes so far as to say that "he has completely altered its values. It is as if Rubens had repainted a Pieter Breughel. The 'truth' is carefully toned down, the beauty made correspondingly more luscious. It is all very splendid, but it is the negation of that which is Mussorgsky's special and still unique contribution to music in general and to opera in particular." Today the Rimsky-Korsakov version is finally yielding its place to a critical edition of the original version by David Lloyd-Jones.

The musicologist A.J.B. Hutchings points out, "Marvelous is his power, in sparse chords or a few notes, to give full meaning to such ideas as 'Siberia,' when Boris' little son is shown the map. . . . We are moved by terror, humor, pity, and intense pathos; we even accept the horror, shared by Tsar and Serf, that a well-meaning man has arrogated an office invested by divine right in primogeniture. In all opera, nothing is more harrowing than the last call of the Idiot. Boris, forbidding the boyars to drive him away, says, 'Pray for me,' and the Idiot answers, 'No, Boris; that I cannot do.' "

MUSSORGSKY'S ORCHESTRATION
Gedda, Raimondi, Vishnevskaya, Oratorio Society of Washington, National Symphony Orchestra, Rostropovich: Erato 2292-45418-2

RIMSKY-KORSAKOV'S ORCHESTRATION
Ghiaurov, Talvela, Vishnevskaya, Sofia Radio Chorus, Vienna State Opera Chorus, Vienna Philharmonic Orchestra, Karajan: London 411862-2

Pictures at an Exhibition (1874)

Mussorgsky was a fine pianist, and he composed around two dozen piano pieces, which, paradoxically, generally show little gift for piano writing. But his masterwork for the instrument, *Pictures at an Exhibition*, is the greatest piano work of the Russian nationalists. It is stupendously original. A promenade initiates and then links a series of tableaux. The "pictures" are musical adaptations of Hartmann paintings and drawings. A visitor to the exhibition views no. 4, "The Old Castle"; no. 5 is a painting of the Tuileries in Paris, called in

Mussorgsky's composition "The Tuileries"; no. 7 is "Bydlo," meaning "cattle" in Polish. No. 9 is a deftly humorous "Ballet of the Chicks"; no. 10, "Samuel Goldenberg and Schmuyle," is based on a portrait titled *Two Jews: One Rich, the Other Poor*. No. 11 is "Limoges: The Market." No. 12, "Catacombs," represents a drawing of the artist, a colleague, and a guide with a lamp at the Paris catacombs. No. 13, "Cum mortuis in lingua mortua," represents Hartmann's creative spirit. No. 14, "The Hut on Fowl's Legs," represents a drawing of a hut of Baba-Yaga, the witch who eats bone and rides through the sky. No. 15, "The Great Gate of Kiev," depicts Hartmann's design for a gate to the City of Kiev never executed.

The original piano writing has been criticized as bare and awkward. Vladimir Horowitz accepted this verdict and made his own enriched version. But other pianists have treasured the original score. Sviatoslav Richter's recording of a live performance in Sofia, Bulgaria, in 1958 is especially good. The *Pictures* have also become a favorite orchestral work, in a brilliant transcription by Ravel in 1922.

FOR SOLO PIANO
Horowitz: RCA 09026-60526-2
Richter: Philips 420774-2

FOR ORCHESTRA
New York Philharmonic Orchestra, Bernstein: CBS MKY 36726
Berlin Philharmonic Orchestra, Karajan: Deutsche Grammophon 429162-2

OTHER PRINCIPAL WORKS

OPERAS
Khovanshchina (unfinished)*
Sorochintsy Fair (unfinished)

ORCHESTRAL WORKS
Intermezzo symphonique in B Minor (1867; orchestrated by Rimsky-Korsakov)

SONGS
Sixty-three songs, including the cycles *The Nursery* (1868–72), *Sunless* (1874), and *Songs and Dances of Death* (1875–77)*

PETER ILYICH TCHAIKOVSKY

b. Kamsko-Votkinsk, May 7, 1840

d. St. Petersburg, November 6, 1893

Last night I played nearly the whole of Eugene Onegin; *the composer was the only listener, I am ashamed to say so, but I must tell you in secret that the listener was impressed to tears by the music and paid a thousand compliments to the composer. Oh! If only all the members of the future audience could be so impressed and touched by this music as the author was.*

Tchaikovsky came from a well-to-do family. His father was a mining engineer, not particularly cultured, but his mother, of French descent, played piano and sang with a passable voice. Although his parents were only moderately musical, Peter Ilyich was given piano lessons at an early age. In 1850 his mother took the ten-year-old to St. Petersburg, where he was to begin preparation for an eventual law career. She soon returned home, and this first separation from his extravagantly loved mother was traumatic. Four years later, when she died of cholera, Peter Ilyich was inconsolable. Throughout his life he held passionate ties to his family, especially to his brothers and sister and later to his young nephew, Vladimir. After his mother's death, the gloomy adolescent lived a desultory existence. He began his first fairly feeble attempts at composition at about this time, and like most nineteenth-century Russian composers, he had no training to speak of.

At nineteen he graduated from the School of Jurisprudence and took a job as a clerk of the first class at the Ministry of Justice. By 1861 music had become his main solace, and he took the drastic step of resigning his position. Years later he had absolutely no recollection of the two years he spent at the ministry.

In 1862, the pianist Anton Rubinstein, Russia's most prominent international musical celebrity, founded the St. Petersburg Conservatory, and Tchaikovsky enrolled. He had saved a little money and received a small allowance from home. At this time he wrote his sister, "I have entered the newly-opened conservatory. . . . Do not imagine I dream of being a great artist. I only feel I must do the work for which I have a vocation. Whether I become a celebrated composer or only a struggling teacher—'tis all the same." Although skeptical of his own aptitude, and dismayed by his lack of theoretical knowledge and what he called his fearful indolence, he nevertheless zealously studied harmony, counterpoint, and other related subjects and graduated four years later. Anton Rubinstein had observed Tchaikovsky's dedication—and also his poverty: Tchaikovsky's father had just retired from the Technological Institute, and funds at home were low.

In 1866 Nikolai Rubinstein, almost as famous a pianist as his brother, founded the Moscow Conservatory, and Anton recommended the recent graduate to his brother, as a theory teacher for the new Conservatory. Tchaikovsky was desperately frightened of teaching and unhappy about leaving St. Petersburg, but he was nonetheless grateful for the position and its small salary. To make ends meet, for his first few years in Moscow he boarded with Nikolai Rubinstein. He was a conscientious teacher and composed in every spare moment: several piano works, the First String Quartet (Op. 11, 1871), and a First Symphony, subtitled *Winter Dreams* (Op. 13, 1866). Writing the symphony prompted a nervous breakdown, spurred on by insomnia and the fear that he would die before completing it—the first sign of Tchaikovsky's lifelong struggle with his mental health.

During the 1870s, Tchaikovsky made great progress. Nikolai Rubinstein conducted a number of his works, and Muscovites were beginning to know the composer's name. Tchaikovsky's financial problems were alleviated in 1877 by a patroness, Nadezhda von Meck—ten years his senior and the widow of a railroad magnate, with eleven children. Madame von Meck—a romantic, intelligent, eccentric millionaire who controlled a large business empire with an iron hand—fell madly in love with the thirty-seven-year-old composer's music. For the next thirteen years, the two maintained one of music history's most bizarre and curious relationships: by her own wish, the patroness never formally met the composer. But they kept up an intimate correspondence and grew to love one another deeply. Madame von Meck made no demands on Tchaikovsky and gave him a considerable yearly subsidy that made it possible for him to leave the Conservatory and devote all his time to creative work. In her letters, she gave the hypersensitive composer empathy, respect, and the unconditional admiration he desperately needed. She functioned as an idealized mother and also provided him with something resembling an unthreatening female romance.

Early in their friendship, Tchaikovsky had the misfortune to encounter another woman, Antonina Milyukova, who also claimed to worship him and his music and proposed marriage. Against his better judgment, Tchaikovsky agreed, and they were married in 1877. This rash act, perhaps committed in response to his recent good fortune, destroyed the composer's always-precarious mental balance. From their first night together, he felt he had entered a nightmare. As a homosexual, Tchaikovsky was unable to perform in the marital bed, and the hysterical Antonina did not help matters. Tchaikovsky told his brother he was in despair, and two months later he attempted suicide, throwing himself into the Moscow River. He never saw Antonina again, and the marriage was annulled after nine weeks. Antonina continued to haunt his dreams, however, and in real life she tormented him by forever pestering him for money, which he gave to her. Antonina spent years in an insane asylum and died in 1916.

Tchaikovsky could confide in his brother Modest, who was also a homosexual. In Russia homosexual acts were criminal. The brothers were terrified of being exposed, both legally and socially. And Peter Ilyich feared that his "inclination," as he called it, would cause his family pain and embarrassment. After his failed marriage, he felt very uneasy. Marriage was a license to respectability and heterosexual status, while a bachelor of thirty-seven was suspect.

After a year of beneficial travel, the composer's equilibrium was somewhat restored. But composing was necessary for his sanity, and when inspiration eluded him, he was wretched. Nevertheless he was immensely productive during this period, and between 1878 and 1881 he composed his operatic masterpiece, *Eugene Onegin* (Op. 24, 1879); the Violin Concerto (Op. 35, 1878); *Capriccio Italien* (Op. 45, 1880); the Fourth Symphony (Op. 36, 1878); and a great deal more. By now his music had thrilled a large public both in Russia and abroad. Now that Madame von Meck had eliminated his financial strains, Tchaikovsky faced a hard choice between living in Russia and traveling abroad. Away from Russia he wept with longing for his homeland; but within Russia he felt constrained. And even within Russia his mind was divided: when in the city he craved solitude, and in the country he was restless. He wrote, "To be sorry for the past, to hope for the future, never content with the present—that is my life."

Now that Tchaikovsky's music was popular everywhere, he was in demand as a conductor as well as a composer. He was an adequate conductor, but conducting, like everything else, was a torture for him. While he conducted, he grasped his neck to dispel the feeling that his head would topple off. To his nephew he wrote, "I suffer, not only from torments that cannot be put in words, but from a hatred of strangers and an indefinable terror—though of what, the devil only knows."

In December 1890 Tchaikovsky received word from Madame von Meck that she had had severe financial setbacks and would be forced to terminate their relationship. Tchaikovsky was stunned. He assured her that he no longer needed her money—he made a decent living through conducting engagements and the publication of his works—but said that nothing must stand in the way of their friendship. His letters went unanswered. In fact, Madame von Meck's fortune was intact. Had she found out about Tchaikovsky's homosexuality? It seems unlikely that this sophisticated woman had not known every detail about him for many years. But her actual reasons for destroying this unique relationship have never been satisfactorily explained.

Tchaikovsky was deeply depressed by the end of this friendship, and it was many months before he recovered. (His recovery was not helped by the death of his sister Alexandra, a close confidante, around the same time.) He left for New York in April 1891, for the inauguration of Andrew Carnegie's new Music Hall. But nothing—not the triumph of his music, not his financial success, not his delightful time in America—lessened the fact that he desperately missed von Meck's epistolary presence.

During 1891 and 1892, he finished his opera *Iolanta* (Op. 69) and his ballet *The Nutcracker* (Op. 71). Both compositions had glittering premieres in St. Petersburg in December 1892. Beginning in January 1893, he commenced work on his sixth and last symphony, the *Pathétique* (Op. 74), which contains some of his most despairing pages. Tchaikovsky conducted the premiere on October 28, 1893, but the work was only a qualified success.

Early in November, cholera ran rampant in St. Petersburg, gripping the city in fear. One evening Tchaikovsky, who certainly knew about the epidemic and who certainly knew not to drink unboiled water, dined out with a few friends and his nephew—and drank unboiled water. Days later, after terrible suffering, Russia's most celebrated composer was dead at fifty-three from the scourge that had killed his mother. Tchaikovsky had often predicted that he too would die of cholera. In his delirium, he muttered "Nadezhda" over and over. Two months later, Madame von Meck was herself dead of what was called a nervous disease.

Tchaikovsky's music is performed more often than that of any other Russian composer. A dozen of his most famous works have been responsible for bringing many people to classical music. But Tchaikovsky is much more than these dozen works, and for the curious listener, many valuable works remain that have been in the shadow of his best-known ones. He adored opera. "To refrain from writing opera," he wrote, "is the act of a hero . . . the stage with all its glitter attracts me irresistibly." Yet of his eleven operas, only *Pique Dame* (*The Queen of Spades*, Op. 68, 1890) and *Eugene Onegin* are known outside Russia. He also dearly loved the world of ballet. Its highly feminine but boyish ballerinas and homoerotic atmosphere had bewitched him since childhood. No other composer's music is so essentially balletic in spirit.

Tchaikovsky wrote quickly and was frequently self-critical: "My *seams*," he wrote, "always showed and there is no organic union between the separate episodes." But Tchaikovsky was too hard on himself; *Eugene Onegin*, the fantasy-overture *Romeo and Juliet* (1869), the great ballets, and the last three symphonies show a high degree of organizational genius. His melodic gift alone is marvelous, and his inspired melodies are often exquisitely poised. Of course, a great many of his works fall short of first rate; at its worst, his passion is forced, his despair turns to hysterical screams of self-pity, he is noisy and vulgar, and cheap claptrap takes the place of pure sentiment.

Tchaikovsky was Russian to the core of his being: he detested Wagner and Brahms, and today his music sounds no less Russian than that of the Russian Five. But his music in all of its aspects is also a living and glowing self-portrait. It is confessional in nature: he exposes his entire being. And what he found often shakes us profoundly. Early in the twentieth century, the noted critic Rosa Newmarch noted, "He has many things to say which are of the greatest interest to humanity, and he says them with such warmth and intimate feeling that they seem less a revelation than an unexpected effluence from our own innermost being." We will continue to seek comfort from the passion, despair, and faith of his tortured and romantic spirit.

Romeo and Juliet (1869; rev. 1880)

Romeo and Juliet, a fantasy overture, is a masterpiece of suspense, tragedy, and depth of characterization. The love theme is one of Tchaikovsky's most glorious melodies. The structure is solid as stone without resorting to any beatings of the chest. Tchaikovsky beautifully rendered in musical terms the violence of the fighting between the Montagues and Capulets. The slow anguished ending, with its final outburst, is hard to resist. The score throbs with heartfelt passion, and one can imagine Tchaikovsky weeping while reading of Shakespeare's immortal lovers.

Royal Philharmonic Orchestra, Beecham: The Beecham Collection: BEECHAM 1
Chicago Symphony Orchestra, Solti: London 430707-2

Quartet no. 1 in D Major for Strings, Op. 11 (1871)

Tchaikovsky wrote three string quartets. No. 1 is excellent in all four of its movements, but its lovely second movement, Andante cantabile, is particularly fluid, with a rich first subject. The famous Andante is actually based on a folk-song that the composer had heard in the Ukraine. The pizzicato accompaniment is most effective, played over another theme. The third movement is a Scherzo, a fine Russian dance, and it has a rather enigmatic Trio section before returning to the gay proceedings. The finale is a perfect ending—hale and hearty in its first theme, it glides into a Slavic tune. In the coda, the composer takes his four instruments on a last flight of fancy.

Borodin String Quartet: Teldec 90422-2
Emerson String Quartet: Deutsche Grammophon 427618-2

Concerto no. 1 in B-flat Minor for Piano and Orchestra, Op. 23 (1875)

This is perhaps the most popular of all Romantic piano concertos. Hans von Bülow gave it its world premiere in Boston on October 25, 1875. In 1891, with Tchaikovsky conducting, it was the first concerto ever performed in Carnegie Hall. Its famous opening theme (which never returns), the extraordinary interplay between piano and orchestra, its sheer energy, and its Russian coloring continue to keep audiences mesmerized season after season.

Argerich, Bavarian Radio Symphony Orchestra, Kondrashin: Philips 446673-2
Cliburn, RCA Victor Symphony Orchestra, Kondrashin: RCA 07863-55912-2
Horowitz, NBC Symphony Orchestra, Toscanini: RCA 7992-2-RG

Francesca da Rimini, Op. 32 (1876)

Francesca da Rimini, a symphonic poem, was inspired by drawings of Gustave Doré depicting Dante's *Inferno*. In the fifth canto of *Inferno*, Francesca has an illicit affair with her brother-in-law Paolo, and both are put to death. The fateful subject was perfect for Tchaikovsky, who wrote music filled with the pain of the couple's love and the tragedy of their ending. "I have worked on it *con amore*," he wrote, "and believe my love has been successful." Its first performance, on March 9, 1877, was deliriously received, and *Francesca* is one of Tchaikovsky's finest programmatic scores.

Royal Philharmonic Orchestra, Ashkenazy: London 421715-2
Philadelphia Orchestra, Muti: EMI Classics CDC 54338

Marche Slave, Op. 31 (1876)

This piece was composed for a concert to aid wounded soldiers in the Russo-Turkish War of 1877. It comprises five sections, with a half-dozen highly effective themes, including "God Save the Czar." Although this piece has often been dismissed as inconsequential, it is nevertheless stirring, and if performed well, it shows a certain strain of Tchaikovskian sadness. In fact the first three sections are marked *Moderato in modo di marcia funèbre*. Most of the themes are Serbian folksongs, and Tchaikovsky used to great effect the Russian national anthem.

London Symphony Orchestra, Previn: EMI Classics 2-69776
Philadelphia Orchestra, Ormandy: Sony Classical 2-63281

Concerto in D Major for Violin and Orchestra, Op. 35 (1878)

The critic Eduard Hanslick was known for his particularly scathing reviews, and many sensitive musicians were wounded by his barbs. Tchaikovsky was mortified by his condemnation of this concerto at its premiere in Vienna on December 4, 1881 (with Adolf Brodsky as soloist and Hans Richter on the podium). The influential critic wrote, "Friedrich Fischer once asserted in reference to lascivious paintings that there are pictures which 'stink in the eye.' Tchaikovsky's Violin Concerto brings to us for the first time the horrid idea that there may be music that stinks in the ear." When Tchaikovsky showed the work to Leopold Auer, the famed violin teacher called it unplayable. Notwithstanding the comments of these gentlemen, the Tchaikovsky Violin Concerto is one of the most popular of all concertos and will be played as long as there are virtuosi capable of conquering its daunting technical difficulties, including the bruising first-movement cadenza, which demands treacherous skips. The opening theme of the first movement is one of Tchaikovsky's most memorable, worked up to a frenzied and thrilling climax. The slow movement is warmly sensual. The finale is a Russian holiday romp, wild and colorful.

Heifetz, Chicago Symphony Orchestra, Reiner: RCA 5933-2-RC
Mullova, Boston Symphony Orchestra, Ozawa: Philips 416821-2
Francescatti, New York Philharmonic Orchestra, Mitropoulos: Sony Classical MH2K 62339

Symphony no. 4 in F Minor, Op. 36 (1877–78)

The excellent Symphonies no. 1–3 hardly prepare us for the pent-up explosive passion of the Fourth Symphony, dedicated to Tchaikovsky's patroness, Madame von Meck. She loved "her symphony" to the point of delirium, telling Tchaikovsky of her fever when playing it through. The introduction presents a compelling motive of destiny, the "fate" theme that penetrates the whole work. "That is fate," Tchaikovsky wrote, "that tragic power which prevents the yearning for happiness from reaching its goal." Hans Keller calls the Fourth "one of the most towering symphonic structures in our whole literature. Tchaikovsky's individual contribution to the development of symphonic thought was the discovery and integration of new and violent contrasts, of which the opening movement of the Fourth is perhaps the most outstanding example." The composer declared, "I passionately love every manifestation of the Russian spirit. . . . I am Russian in the fullest sense of the word."

Vienna Philharmonic Orchestra, C. von Dohnányi: London 425792-2
London Symphony Orchestra, Markevitch: Philips 438335-2

Eugene Onegin, Op. 24 (1879)

Tchaikovsky's eleven operas are full of wonderful moments, but many of them can be diffuse and meandering. But in two operas, *The Queen of Spades* and *Eugene Onegin,* the composer achieved a high level of unity. Tchaikovsky, a devout lover of Pushkin, had wondered if Pushkin's novel in verse could ever be transformed into a good libretto. Some have argued that Tchaikovsky did not, in fact, find a good libretto. In a 1954 letter, Vladimir Nabokov called it a "vile libretto. Lines from the greatest poetical work ever written in Russian were picked out at random, mutilated at will and combined with the tritest concoctions." Notwithstanding Nabokov, the opera works well theatrically, and Tchaikovsky's scoring is among his most refined and restrained. It sounds like no other opera, with no influence from either Verdi or Wagner. Great arias flow from Tchaikovsky's pen, such as Lensky's "Ya lyublyu vas, Olga" (I love you, Olga) and Tatyana's great letter scene; also famous are the Polonaise and Waltz.

Freni, Schicoff, Otter, Allen, Staatskapelle Dresden, Levine: Deutsche Grammophon 423959-2
Te Kanawa, Bardon, Rosenshein, Hampson, Welsh National Opera Orchestra and Chorus, Mackerras: EMI Classics CDCB 55004

Overture 1812, Op. 49 (1880)

This Tchaikovsky score is one of the most popular. It may not be his finest work—granted, it is filled with cheap thrills—but it can still electrify an audience. The composer thought little of it, but the rousing score also has its gorgeous melody, an outdoor spaciousness, and thrilling climaxes. He uses two national hymns, "God Preserve Thy People," representing the Russians, and "La Marseillaise," representing the French. The *1812 Overture* was written to be played outdoors, using actual artillery, as did the first (1882) performance to commemorate the Battle of Borodino.

Royal Concertgebouw Orchestra, Haitink: Philips 422469-2
Minneapolis Symphony Orchestra, Dorati: Mercury 434360-2

Capriccio Italien, Op. 45 (1880)

The *Capriccio* is a bustling potpourri of Italian tunes dressed *à la Russe*. It has pleased multitudes with its unembarrassed brashness. The opening bugle call was something Tchaikovsky knew well, for he lived near a barracks for a time in Rome. Its orchestration is so vivid and colorful that it fills the ear with Italian warmth and color. It remains a favorite number at symphony concerts, and audiences, while not necessarily deeply moved, are orchestrally well fed and are usually in a good mood afterward.

London Symphony Orchestra, Rozhdestvensky: IMP Classics IMPPCD 875
St. Louis Symphony Orchestra, Slatkin: RCA 09026-60433-2

Symphony no. 5 in E Minor, Op. 64 (1888)

Tchaikovsky's Fifth Symphony was composed eleven years after the Fourth. The first performance, conducted by the composer at St. Petersburg in late November 1888, failed. But the Fifth has since become one of the best-loved symphonies. The first movement is a heroic struggle. Audiences particularly enjoy the ravishing long-breathed theme of the second movement, drenched in the golden sound of the French horn. The third movement introduces (for the first time in the context of a symphony) a Waltz to replace the Scherzo—Tchaikovsky never ceased to love waltzes, and they are strewn throughout his oeuvre. These waltzes are not like those from Vienna, but are mostly aristocratic, balletic, and graceful. The waltz in the Fifth Symphony is elegant and vibrates with an undercurrent of amorous nostalgia. The finale begins as a march and spreads itself through a violent discourse, leading to a coda of superb energy with a reminder of the first movement's main theme.

Cleveland Orchestra, Szell: Sony Classical SB2K 63281
St. Petersburg Philharmonic Orchestra, Temirkanov: RCA 2-09026-61377-2

Ballets
Swan Lake, Op. 20 (1876)
The Sleeping Beauty, Op. 66 (1886)
The Nutcracker, Op. 71 (1892)

We have taken these ballets for granted for so long that we may tend to forget that their scores teem with some of the most wonderful ballet music ever composed. The English composer Humphrey Searle wrote, "Tchaikovsky may be justly described as the ballet composer *par excellence*. He had an extraordinary gift for catching the exact atmosphere needed in a particular dance." The great dancer Rudolf Nureyev once said, "Every morning, every ballet dancer should bow to his portrait."

Like Stravinsky, Tchaikovsky had no problem with composing to prescribed limitations, and the choreographer Marius Petipa asked Tchaikovsky specifically to compose for *The Nutcracker* exact amounts of music for each mood or dance—for instance, 24 bars of joyous music or a march for 64 bars.

The three ballets are filled not only with wondrous melodies and piquant harmonizations but with an inevitable sense of motion, lilt, and lift. Perhaps the greatest of the ballets is *The Sleeping Beauty*, which had a lavish premiere on January 15, 1890, in St. Petersburg, with Czar Alexander III in attendance.

Swan Lake

SELECTIONS
Philharmonia Orchestra, Lanchbery: EMI Classics CDD 64109

COMPLETE
Montreal Symphony Orchestra, Dutoit: London 436212-2

SUITE
Philadelphia Orchestra, Ormandy: RCA Victor 09026-61711-2

The Sleeping Beauty

COMPLETE
London Symphony Orchestra, Previn: EMI Classics CDQB 54814

SELECTIONS
New Philharmonia Orchestra, Stokowski: London 430140-2

The Nutcracker

COMPLETE
St. Louis Symphony Orchestra, Slatkin: RCA 2-09026-61704-2
London Symphony Orchestra, Mackerras: Telarc CD 80137

SUITE
Royal Concertgebouw Orchestra, Dorati: Philips 426177-2

Symphony no. 6 in B Minor (*Pathétique*), Op. 74 (1893)

Tchaikovsky, who endlessly questioned the quality of his music, wrote of the Sixth to his publisher, "I give you my word of honor that never in my life have I been so contented, so proud, so happy, in the knowledge that I have written a good piece." He was at the acme of his power as a symphonic composer. In the first movement, he expresses an almost hopeless weariness with the world. The symphony is a superb amalgamation of forms, from a waltz in five-four time, to a Scherzo and March, to an intriguing slow sonata structure in the last movement—the wailing Adagio lamentoso that has been called his requiem.

NBC Symphony Orchestra, Cantelli: AS Disc 2-AS 503/504
Boston Symphony Orchestra, Koussevitzky: RCA 09026-60920-2
Chicago Symphony Orchestra, Solti: London 430442-2

OTHER PRINCIPAL WORKS

CHAMBER MUSIC
Quartet no. 2 in F Major for Strings, Op. 22 (1874)
Quartet no. 3 in E-flat Minor for Strings, Op. 30 (1876)*

Trio in A Minor for Piano, Violin, and Cello, Op. 50 (1887)*
Souvenir de Florence for String Sextet, Op. 70 (1890)*

CHURCH MUSIC
Vesper Service, Op. 52 (1881–82)*

OPERAS
The Voyevoda, Op. 3 (1867–68)
Undine (1869)
The Oprichnik (1870–72)
The Maid of Orleans (1878–79)
Mazeppa (1881–83)
Pique Dame (The Queen of Spades), Op. 68 (1890)*

ORCHESTRAL WORKS
Symphony no. 1 in G Minor (*Winter Dreams*), Op. 13 (1866; rev. 1874)
Symphony no. 2 in C Minor (*Little Russian*), Op. 17 (1872; rev. 1879–80)*
The Tempest (symphonic fantasy), Op. 18 (1873)
Symphony no. 3 in D Major (*Polish*), Op. 29 (1875)
Manfred (symphony), Op. 58 (1885)*
Suite no. 4 in G Major (*Mozartiana*), Op. 61 (1887)*
Hamlet (fantasy overture), Op. 67 (1888)

PIANO WORKS
More than one hundred short piano pieces
Sonata in G Major, Op. 37 (1878)
Eighteen Pieces, Op. 72 (1893)

SOLO INSTRUMENT AND ORCHESTRA WORKS
Sérénade mélancolique for Violin and Orchestra, Op. 26 (1875)*
Variations on a Rococo Theme for Cello and Orchestra, Op. 33 (1876)*
Concerto no. 2 for Piano and Orchestra, Op. 44 (1879–80)*
Concert Fantasy for Piano and Orchestra, Op. 56 (1884)
Concerto no. 3 for Piano and Orchestra, Op. 75 (1893)

VOICE WITH PIANO WORKS
One hundred songs

ANTONÍN DVOŘÁK

b. Nelahozeves, Bohemia, September 8, 1841

d. Prague, May 1, 1904

Any intelligent and sensitive artist is always very pleased if he can find at least one voice to which he can respond: "Yes, he understands me."

Dvořák was the eldest of eight children. His father was an innkeeper and the proprietor of a small butcher shop. By five, the child was tinkering with music, playing folk tunes on the violin, but he received little training until he was nearly fourteen, when he was sent to the town of Zlonice to live with his uncle. There he was taught by Antonín Liehmann, who realized the boy's great gifts. Liehmann wanted Dvořák to go to Prague, but his father insisted that the boy return home to help support his family, always on the brink of poverty. Fortunately, in 1857 enough money was raised to allow the sixteen-year-old boy to go to the organ school of the conservatory in Prague.

After two years of study, the youth, who knew how to play several instruments, took a job playing viola in the orchestra of the Czech Provisional Theater. He remained with the orchestra until he was thirty years old. Composing was his passion, but he kept the results secret, even from close friends. His early works were competent but show no glimmerings of an individual style. Not until the arrival of his fellow composer Bedřich Smetana, as conductor at the theater, was Dvořák's talent ignited. Like other Czech artists, Dvořák was awakened by Bohemia's growing political and literary consciousness — and he vowed that, like Smetana, he too would be a Czech composer.

In 1874 Dvořák left his comfortable but dull job to become the organist and choirmaster at St. Adalbert's Church in Prague. By then he had married Anna Čermáková, a singer in the chorus of the National Opera. It was a happy marriage, and the couple raised six children.

Shortly after beginning his new job, Dvořák had the good fortune to meet Brahms, who had read through a few of the young man's compositions. Brahms was impressed and became a powerful ally. He also recommended Dvořák to his publisher, hoping to alleviate the young man's financial difficulties. *Moravian Duets* (Op. 32) was the first piece published. Brahms, who had made a good deal of money from his *Hungarian Dances*, then advised his younger colleague to write Czech dances. Dvořák complied, and his *Slavonic Dances* (Op. 46, 1878) scored a substantial success. For Dvořák, Brahms was the great composer of his age, and Dvořák never ceased to be grateful for Brahms's efforts on his behalf.

Through Brahms, Dvořák met many influential musicians, including the conductors Hans Richter and Hans von Bülow and the violinist Joseph Joachim, and it was through their efforts that his music was first performed beyond his native Bohemia. One of the first countries to warm to his music was England, in the 1870s. Dvořák made his first visit there in 1884, to conduct, among other works, his lyrical *Stabat Mater* (which was especially beloved of English audiences). The 1880s were a period of increased creative urgency as well as versatility: Dvořák's music from those years radiates with melodic beauty and piquant harmony. He wrote many enchanting movements in various compositions based on and named after Czech dances, such as the *furiant, polka, skočná* (a type of reel), and *sousedska* (a slow evocative waltz).

As Dvořák's fame grew, he made appearances in Germany and Russia as well. At home he took a prestigious post teaching composition at the Prague Conservatory, and several universities gave him honorary degrees. In 1892 he accepted the splendid salary of fifteen thousand dollars a season to be the director of the new National Conservatory in New York. In America he was shocked at the indifference to the arts and the difficulty of pursuing a career in music. In an article written in 1895 for *Harper's* magazine, he wrote, "It cannot be emphasized too strongly that art, as such, does not 'pay,' to use an American phrase. . . . The great American republic alone, in its national government as well as in the various governments of the states, suffers art and music to go without encouragement. Trades and commerce are protected, funds are voted away for the unemployed, schools and colleges are endowed, but music must go unaided, and be content if she can get the support of a few private individuals." He was convinced that a national school of composition was needed, and he urged American composers to take notice of black and Indian music. Little did he realize that a great African-American music called jazz would become the national school.

Dvořák's American years (1892–95) were happy and, as always, he was productive. He wrote, among other works, the symphony *From the New World*
(Op. 95, 1893), a charming piano suite (*American*, Op. 98, 1895), the E-flat
major string quintet (Op. 97, 1893), the *Biblical Songs* (Op. 99, 1894), the
Cello Concerto (Op. 104, 1815), and the Eight *Humoresques* for piano (Op.
101, 1894), of which the insipid tune of No. 7 became one of the world's best-
known pieces of music.

In the summers during his stay in America, the composer and his family
were refreshed at a Czech community at Spillville, Iowa, which would "remain
a very dear memory to us for the rest of our lives." But Dvořák was very home-
sick, and in 1895 he was ready to go home to Prague. After returning, he composed two operas, *The Devil and Kate* (1898–99) and *Rusalka* (1900), valuable
works that are seldom heard. In 1901 he became director of the Prague Conservatory, where he continued to teach composition. *Armida*, an opera he had
toiled on for two years, had its premiere on March 25, 1904, and was disliked.
A few weeks later at dinner, he had a stroke. At the time of his death, at age
sixty-two, Dvořák was the most celebrated Czech in any field. His funeral on
May 5 was an occasion for national mourning.

Dvořák is the most universally loved Czech composer and one of the most
frequently performed of all national composers. His work is straightforward and
full of feeling, and his musical technique is firm and supple. He prefers the
traditional classical sonata structures of Brahms without the Brahmsian subtlety. Dvořák was one of the memorable melodists of his time, but he seldom
lost sight of the rude peasant environment of his childhood. His nationalism
was natural to him, a point of departure, never a search for an identity. His
spirit was rich and healthy, and his view of the world uncomplicated. The
American composer and critic Daniel Gregory Mason has said, "His music
makes a delightfully frank appeal. It is never somber, never crabbed, never
even profound. It breathes not passion, but sentiment. It is too happily sensuous to be tragic, too busy with an immediate charm to trouble about a remote
meaning." This happiness, stirring and tender, never fails in its radiant message.

Slavonic Dances, Opp. 46 and 72 (1878 and 1886)

In their first version, the *Slavonic Dances*, eight in number, were written for piano duet, which in the nineteenth century was an agreeable pastime for many
amateur musicians. They were later orchestrated, and eight more were added,
in Op. 72. The tunes are sweet, tender, and frolicsome—Czech dances that
burst with joy. Unlike the Brahms *Hungarian Dances*, which used Gypsy

melodies, Dvořák's *Slavonic Dances* use entirely original thematic material. Dvořák's Slav temperament spurts with joyous abandon in Nos. 1, 8, and 15, or with nostalgic sentiment, as in No. 10, where the composer wears his heart on his sleeve.

Royal Philharmonic Orchestra, Dorati: London 430735-2
Scottish National Orchestra, Järvi: Chandos CHAN 8406

Symphony no. 7 in D Minor, Op. 70 (1884)
Symphony no. 8 in G Major, Op. 88 (1889)
Symphony no. 9 in E Minor (*From the New World*), Op. 95 (1893)

Dvořák's first four symphonies fall below the quality of Nos. 5 through 9, and Nos. 5 and 6 are less assured than Nos. 7, 8, and 9. The Seventh Symphony is among Dvořák's stormiest works. Both Dvořák and Hans Richter conducted early performances, without much success. But with Hans von Bülow's performances in October 1889, the symphony took its rightful place as one of the most important symphonies of the last quarter of the nineteenth century. Dvořák wrote to von Bülow, "Glory be to you! You brought this work to life." The symphony's first movement opens and closes quietly, but it is tremendous in its energy—the slow moment finds serenity until a troubled mood breeds stress. The Scherzo is one of Dvořák's *furiants*, with a lighter Trio. The finale is in sonata form, and a grim struggle rages until the symphony ends in a blaze of triumph.

There is nothing quite like the vernal beauty of the Eighth Symphony. The music is by turns festive and serene, laced with the charm of Dvořák's lilting dance rhythms. The listener can almost smell the fresh air of the countryside, and Dvořák floods the score with light. The symphony is in the usual four movements and was premiered by Dvořák conducting the Prague National Theater Orchestra on February 2, 1890.

The overwhelming audience favorite of Dvořák's entire oeuvre is the Symphony no. 9 (*From the New World*). More than a century after its premiere (on December 16, 1893, with Anton Seidl conducting the New York Philharmonic at Carnegie Hall), No. 9 retains its unique appeal, full of pungent musical ideas, rhythmic zest, and symphonic sweep. The work sounds notes of black spirituals, Indian themes, and, as always, Czech folk music. The first movement's second theme invokes the spiritual "Swing Low, Sweet Chariot." The celebrated second movement, Largo, begins pensively and leads to a melody that was later appropriated into the song "Goin' Home." The third-movement Scherzo is a lively affair with an unmistakable Indian flavor, perhaps inspired

by Indians he knew in Iowa. The finale is all jubilation and splendor, a movement of extraordinary muscular power. Dvořák was annoyed when a critic said
he had used American motifs in the symphony. "It is not true," he wrote; "those
motives are my own and I brought some of them to America with me. It is and
it will always be Czech music. It is true that I wrote this music in America and
perhaps it is true that I would never have written it if I had not stayed in America." Dvořák's patriotism was all-encompassing; his motto was "God, Love, and
Country."

Symphony no. 7
London Symphony Orchestra, Kertész: London 433091-2
Los Angeles Philharmonic Orchestra, Previn: Telarc CD-80173

Symphony no. 8
Cleveland Orchestra, Szell: CBS MYK 38470
Royal Concertgebouw, C. Davis: Philips 438347-2
Czech Philharmonic Orchestra, Ančerl: Praga PR 254006

Symphony no. 9
Berlin Philharmonic Orchestra, Kubelik: Deutsche Grammophon 415915-2
Milwaukee Symphony Orchestra, Macal: Koss Classics KC-1010
Philadelphia Orchestra, Ormandy: RCA 60537-4-RV

Quartet no. 12 in F Major for Strings (*American*), Op. 96 (1893)

Dvořák was a prolific composer of chamber music, much of which is bewitching. The *American* Quartet, written in Spillville, Iowa, is Dvořák's attempt to
capture an American Indian spirit. The result is perhaps as much Czech as Native American. The first movement uses three themes reminiscent of Indian
motifs. The quartet's slow movement is the peak of the work, with its sad
melody played by the first violin and accompanied with delicious effect by the
other instruments of the quartet. The Scherzo and finale tell us of Dvořák's
perpetual homesickness for his country in music that is whimsical, airy, and
dancelike. As in most of his chamber music, including the E minor piano trio
and the magnificent A major piano quintet, Dvořák shows here that he is a
master of string writing in combination with the piano.

Emerson String Quartet: Deutsche Grammophon 429723-2
Guarneri String Quartet: RCA 6263-2

Concerto in B Minor for Cello and Orchestra, Op. 104 (1894–95)

This towering, majestic, and melodious concerto is the longest cello concerto in the active repertory. Ever since its first performance in London on March 19, 1896, with Dvořák conducting and Leo Stern as soloist, cellists have gratefully thanked the Czech master. When Brahms read the score, he exclaimed, "Why on earth didn't I know it was possible to write a cello concerto like this? If I had only known, I would have written one long ago." Dvořák had been impressed by Victor Herbert's Cello Concerto, played by Herbert himself at the New York Philharmonic, and he set to work on his own on November 8, 1894, completing the score in three months. It was the last work he wrote in America. The first movement is the most tightly knit of all his concertos, and the piece surpasses the Piano Concerto and the Violin Concerto in the skill of presenting a soloist with an orchestra. The first theme is majestic, leading to a second subject that deeply moved the composer, a penetrating melody sung by a solo French horn. The second movement, Adagio ma non troppo, floods us with the warmth of Dvořák's songfulness. The finale is a combination of rousing country-dance music and a passionate theme that finds itself in a duet for cello and violins. The concerto concludes in a stormy mood. It is a glorious example of Dvořák's prodigality of thematic material perfectly welded into a large-scale form. In the slow movement, he makes a personal farewell to a beloved sister-in-law, quoting from a song he had composed with her in mind thirty years before.

Casals, Czech Philharmonic Orchestra, Szell: EMI Classics CDH 63498
Piatigorsky, Boston Symphony Orchestra, Munch: RCA 09026-61498-2
Rostropovich, Berlin Philharmonic Orchestra, Karajan: Deutsche Grammophon 413819-2

OTHER PRINCIPAL WORKS

CHAMBER MUSIC

Thirteen string quartets (other than No. 12)
Terzetto in C Major for Two Violins and Viola, Op. 74 (1887)
Quintet in A Major for Piano and Strings, Op. 81 (1887)*
Quartet in E-flat Major for Piano and Strings, Op. 87 (1889)*
Trio no. 4 in E Minor for Piano, Violin, and Cello (*Dumky*), Op. 90 (1890–91)*
Quintet in E-flat Major for Strings, Op. 97 (1893)*

CHORAL WORKS WITH ORCHESTRA

Stabat Mater, Op. 58 (1876–78)*
Mass in D Major, Op. 86 (1887)
Requiem, Op. 89 (1890)*

OPERAS
The Devil and Kate, Op. 112 (1898–99)*
Rusalka, Op. 114 (1900)*

ORCHESTRAL WORKS
Symphony no. 5 in F Major, Op. 76 (1875; rev. 1887)*
Three *Slavonic Rhapsodies*, Op. 45 (1878)*
Ten *Legends*, Op. 59 (1880–81) (also for piano duet)*
Symphony no. 6 in D Major, Op. 60 (1880)*
The Water Goblin (symphonic poem), Op. 107 (1896)
The Noonday Witch (symphonic poem), Op. 108 (1896)*
The Golden Spinning Wheel (symphonic poem), Op. 109 (1896)*
The Wood Dove (symphonic poem), Op. 110 (1896)*

PIANO DUET
Ten *Legends*, Op. 59 (1880–81) (also for orchestra)*
From the Bohemian Forest (six pieces), Op. 68 (1883–84)

PIANO MUSIC
Theme with Variations in A-flat Major, Op. 36 (1876)
Eight Waltzes, Op. 54 (1880)*
Thirteen *Poetic Tone Pictures*, Op. 85 (1889)*
Eight *Humoresques*, Op. 101 (1894)
Suite in A Major (*American*), Op. 98 (1895) (also for orchestra)*

SOLO INSTRUMENT AND ORCHESTRA WORKS
Romance for Violin and Orchestra, Op. 11 (1873–77)
Concerto in G Minor for Piano and Orchestra, Op. 33 (1876)*

SONGS
Thirteen *Moravian Duets*, Op. 32 (1880)
Seven *Gypsy Songs*, Op. 55 (1880)
Nine *Biblical Songs*, Op. 99 (1894)*

VIOLIN AND PIANO WORKS
Four *Romantic Pieces*, Op. 75 (1887)
Sonatina in G Major, Op. 100 (1893)

EDVARD GRIEG

b. Bergen, Norway, June 15, 1843

d. Bergen, September 4, 1907

The artist is an optimist. Otherwise he would be no artist. He believes and hopes in the triumph of the good and the beautiful. He trusts in his lucky star till his last breath.

Grieg was born to a middle-class family with a long mercantile tradition, which his father, Alexander, continued. Grieg's maternal grandfather was a provincial governor, and his mother, Gesine, was a poet as well as a good pianist. Edvard was the fourth of five children. At six, Gesine started him on piano lessons. These years of informal instruction were probably the happiest of Grieg's musical education, for the high-strung boy hated formal education and schools in general. When the boy was fifteen, Norway's legendary violinist Ole Bull visited the family, immediately saw Grieg's gifts, and began instilling in him a love for his native land. The boy was enthralled by Bull's own music as well as his worldwide adventures. Years later the composer wrote of his first meeting with Bull, "I felt something like an electric current pass through me when his hand touched mine." Bull persuaded Edvard's parents to send him to Leipzig to study at the Conservatory, which had been founded by Mendelssohn in the year of his birth. He found the school pedantic and stifling and said that it brought out the worst in him. It was also disastrous for his health. Edvard was very small and had always been delicate. In Leipzig he developed pleurisy, which resulted in permanent damage to one of his lungs. In general, he suffered deeply from regimentation: "school life was in the last degree unsympathetic to me," he wrote; "its materialism, its coarseness, its coldness were so abhorrent to my nature that I thought of the most incredible ways of escaping from it, if only for a short time."

After the Conservatory, Grieg returned to Bergen in 1862, but even though he was free from formal instruction, he was still restless and dissatisfied. The music he had composed thus far was derivative, and he knew it. Slowly he began to inch toward his own style. The foremost Danish composer, Niels Gade, urged Grieg to write a piano sonata using his E minor sonata as a model. Grieg did just that, and his Sonata in E Minor (Op. 7, 1865) is much better than Gade's, though it lacks the stamp of Grieg's mature personality.

At twenty-one, the young composer met the major influence of his young life: Rikard Nordraak, a composer one year older than Grieg and a passionate Norwegian nationalist. Upon greeting Grieg for the first time, Nordraak exclaimed, "Well, so we two great men meet at last!" Nordraak told Grieg that the time was ripe and it was their duty to create a truly Norwegian musical art. Together they pored over folk songs and old Norwegian tunes. Grieg was thrilled—this music was his birthright and his destiny, and through Nordraak he had found it. Nordraak, alas, was desperately sick and died of tuberculosis at twenty-four. On the threshold of his career, he had just finished "Yes, We Love the Land That Towers," to words by the poet Bjørnstjerne Bjørnson (which, fittingly, would become Norway's national anthem). The brokenhearted Grieg wrote a funeral march to his colleague's memory.

At age twenty-four, Grieg married his first cousin, Nina Hagerup. Their first few years of married life were difficult, for Grieg found little encouragement for his music and struggled financially. The couple's only child, a daughter, died at thirteen months. Just when things seemed at their worst, though, Grieg received a letter from Franz Liszt in Rome. Liszt, always sensitive to original talent, was charmed by Grieg's Nordic sensibility and had seen promise in the F major violin sonata (Op. 8, 1865). Liszt invited the Norwegian to visit him in Rome. Through Liszt's influence, Grieg was given a government grant and in 1869 headed off to Rome. At their first meeting, the shy Norwegian found Liszt giving one of his famous piano classes. The Hungarian gave his young colleague a warm greeting, introduced him, complimented him on the violin sonata, and proceeded to astonish the composer by playing both the piano and the violin parts of the sonata simultaneously on the piano. Grieg was dumbfounded. He wrote home, "I think I laughed—laughed like an idiot."

At their next meeting, Grieg brought Liszt the manuscript of his just-completed A minor piano concerto (Op. 16, 1868). Liszt, surrounded by adoring students and admirers, asked the composer to play it. "No, I cannot!" Grieg gasped. "I haven't practiced it." Liszt took the manuscript, strode to the piano, and said with a sardonic smile, "Very well, then I will show you that I also cannot play it." Grieg reported, "He played as only he can. . . . In the adagio, and still more in the finale, he reached a climax both as to his playing and the praise he had to bestow. . . . In conclusion, he handed me the manuscript and said, in a peculiarly cordial tone, 'Keep steadily on, I tell you, you have the talent and capacity, but don't let them intimidate you.' "

In the 1870s and 1880s, Grieg's music was applauded everywhere in Europe. The Norwegian government gave him an annual stipend, and he conducted and appeared as a pianist frequently, often with his wife singing his songs. In 1885 they bought Troldhaugen, a villa overlooking a fjord, where Grieg would live for the rest of his life. As he grew more famous, he was heaped with decorations and honors, including a bust at the entrance of the Gewandhaus in Leipzig.

Grieg the man was pure, kind-hearted, and generous, and popular throughout Europe. He traveled frequently to France until the Dreyfus affair's anti-Semitism shocked his democratic sensibilities. When the French conductor Édouard Colonne invited Grieg to once again conduct his orchestra in Paris, he replied, "I regret to say that after the issue of the Dreyfus trial I cannot . . . come to France. I am indignant at the contempt for justice shown in your country, and therefore I am unable to enter into relations with the French public."

In September 1907, on his way to a conducting engagement at England's Leeds Festival, Grieg had a fatal heart attack. He had become the hero of Norway's two million people, and on the day of his funeral, Norwegians lined the streets of Bergen to glimpse their great composer for the last time.

Not everyone cared for Grieg's music. The capricious Debussy wrote, "Grieg is bonbons wrapped in snow." And a small amount of Grieg's work does sink to the level of sticky sentimentality, like the gushing "To Spring," the feeble "Erotik," and the mawkish song "I Love Thee." At times the music is too full of Norwegian folk mannerisms, and his patriotism palls. But to the ears of most of his contemporaries, Grieg's music sounded exotic and harmonically tangy, with a somewhat primitive undercurrent. Young composers like Percy Grainger and Cyril Scott thought him harmonically adventurous; the chromaticism of his G minor ballade (1875) seemed the height of Modernism. The sixty-six *Lyric Pieces* present pictures of Norwegian life in many aspects. Grieg conjured up the Viking world and the Nordic sagas, and his babbling brooks, chilly air, great fjords, and peasant weddings still captivate us. An ethereal tone painter, he captured the mystery of the midnight sun, the eerie kingdom of elves, trolls, and manikins. He had an uncanny ability to infuse his music with the spirit of Norway.

In a late work, the virtually unknown *Slåtter* (Op. 72), he translated to the

piano the harsh screeches and scratches of the Norwegian eight-string hardan-
ger fiddle. His music rings with a native freshness, often bathed in an almost
impressionist harmony. Tchaikovsky, Frederick Delius, Percy Grainger, Jean
Sibelius, and Edward MacDowell loved him and show his influence in their
music to varying degrees. Ravel always acknowledged his admiration for Grieg
as well as his influence. He is one of the most appealing of the nineteenth-
century musical nationalists, and Norway's greatest composer—indeed, the
artist and his country are inseparable. To the world, he has become Norway's
voice.

Concerto in A Minor for Piano and Orchestra, Op. 16 (1869)

Grieg's A minor is one of the most popular of all piano concertos. The score is
a veritable song of Norway, opening in heraldic fashion. The sweeping first
movement inhales delicious mountain air; its long, feverish cadenza seems to
speak of towering pines. The second movement, *Adagio*, is exquisitely tender;
and the finale, interrupted by music charged with melancholy, is an exhilarating peasant dance. The concerto proceeds to an exciting peroration in the
grand manner.

Zimerman, Berlin Philharmonic Orchestra, Karajan: Deutsche Grammophon 431262-2
Lipatti, Philharmonia Orchestra, Galliera: EMI Classics CDH 63497-2
Rubinstein, Philadelphia Orchestra, Ormandy: RCA 09026-60897-2
Curzon, London Symphony Orchestra, Fjeldstad: London 448599-2
Michelangeli, La Scala Orchestra, Galliera (1941): Enterprise AB 78675.76

Ballade in the Form of Variations on a Norwegian Folksong for Piano, Op. 24 (1875–76)

Composed after the death of Grieg's mother, the *Ballade* was written from the
depth of the composer's heart. It is his most important large work for solo piano
and the finest set of Scandinavian variations of the nineteenth century. The
variations, which contain some of Grieg's strangest chromatic harmony, tra-
verse a wide variety of moods and end with the sad folk theme.

Godowsky: APR 7010
Rubinstein: RCA 09026-61883-2

Peer Gynt (incidental music), **Op. 23** (1874–75)
Peer Gynt Suite no. 1, Op. 46 (1874–75)
Peer Gynt Suite no. 2, Op. 55 (1874–75)

Grieg's complete score for Ibsen's *Peer Gynt* contains more than an hour of music, some of it vocal. The incidental music (Op. 23) is extremely effective as part of the play, but it proved unwieldy for concert performances. Grieg wisely chose to create a concert version, which consists of eight numbers arranged in two suites. The first suite is best known; it opens with the sun-drenched "Morning," which is followed by "Ase's Death," "Anatra's Dance," and "In the Hall of the Mountain King." Suite no. 2 consists of "Ingrid's Lament," "Arabian Dance," "Peer Gynt's Homecoming," and "Solvejg's Song," the best known of the four. In all, the selections represent Grieg's distinguished melodic gift and passionate ardor at his best.

Royal Philharmonic Orchestra, Beecham: EMI Classics CDM 64751-2
Berlin Philharmonic Orchestra, Karajan: Deutsche Grammophon 419474-2
San Francisco Symphony Orchestra, Blomstedt: London 425857-2
St. Louis Symphony Orchestra, Slatkin: Telarc CD 80048

Holberg Suite, Op. 40 (1884–85)

This suite began its life as a work for piano and is occasionally still performed in that version, but it was transcribed for string orchestra in 1885. It was composed in tribute to the Norwegian writer Ludvig Holberg, on the two-hundredth anniversary of his birth. Here Grieg wedded his own personal Nordic Romanticism to Baroque classical dances. The piece had an undeniable effect on French composers of the early twentieth century, including Debussy. Its quaint neoclassicism comprises a Praeludium, Sarabande, and Gavotte, followed by an Air and Rigaudon, each of which retains Grieg's individual Norse coloring.

Berlin Philharmonic Orchestra, Karajan: Deutsche Grammophon 419474-2
Orpheus Chamber Orchestra (without conductor): Deutsche Grammophon 423060-2

OTHER PRINCIPAL WORKS

CHAMBER MUSIC

Quartet in G Minor for Strings, Op. 27 (1877–78)*

CELLO AND PIANO WORKS

Sonata in A Minor, Op. 36 (1883)*

ORCHESTRAL WORKS

In Autumn (concert overture), Op. 11 (1866)

Sigurd Jorsalfar Suite, Op. 56 (1872; rev. 1892)

Two *Elegiac Melodies*, Op. 34 (1881)*

Lyric Suite, Op. 54 (1891; four of the six pieces were arranged for orchestra by the composer in 1904)*

Symphonic Dances, Op. 64 (1896–97)

PIANO DUET

Norwegian Dances, Op. 35 (1881)

PIANO SOLO WORKS

Sonata in E Minor, Op. 7 (1865)

Funeral March in Memory of Rikard Nordraak (1866)

Sixty-six *Lyric Pieces*, Opp. 12, 38, 43, 47, 54, 57, 62, 65, 68, and 71 (various dates)*

Slåtter (Norwegian peasant dances), Op. 72 (1902–3)*

SONGS

Nearly 150 songs in twenty-three opus numbers. The eight songs of the *Haugtussa* cycle (Op. 67, 1895) are among the finest.*

VIOLIN AND PIANO WORKS

Sonata no. 1 in F Major, Op. 8 (1865)

Sonata no. 2 in G Major, Op. 13 (1867)

Sonata no. 3 in C Minor, Op. 45 (1886–87)*

NIKOLAI RIMSKY- KORSAKOV

b. Tikhvin, Novgorod District, March 18, 1844

d. Lyubensk, near St. Petersburg, June 21, 1908

Idleness crushes the artist, whose very nature is divided between the creative life, the life of the creative imagination, and real life—between art and the family, and the one can never, under any circumstances, take the place of, much less become one with the other.

Rimsky-Korsakov was born to a family with a long tradition in the Russian navy; his brother, older by twenty years, was an admiral. Nikolai's musical aptitude was noticed early but was not seriously cultivated, for he was expected to follow the family tradition. At age twelve, he was enrolled in the St. Petersburg Naval College in preparation for a naval career, and he took sporadic piano lessons throughout his adolescence. When he was seventeen, he met the nationalist composer Mily Balakirev. He studied for a time with Balakirev, but music had to take a back seat to being a sailor.

In November 1862, Rimsky-Korsakov began a three-year tour of duty on the Russian frigate *Almaz*. They were exciting years, with long periods sailing the Hudson River and the Chesapeake Bay during the American Civil War. "My dreams of artistic activity had entirely faded," he wrote, "and I felt no sorrow over dreams that were gone." In 1865, when his tour was over, he found himself stationed in St. Petersburg, where he again became involved with Balakirev. Under Balakirev's guidance, the twenty-one-year-old plunged into the task of writing a symphony (Op. 1, 1865), which was well received at one of Balakirev's newly instituted orchestral concerts. The composition is probably the first publicly performed Russian symphony.

In 1871 (though he was still in the navy and was required at all times to appear in uniform), Rimsky-Korsakov, much to his surprise, was asked to become professor of composition at the St. Petersburg Conservatory. He was apprehensive about taking the post: under Balakirev he had operated from pure instinct—with his teacher's direct assistance—and he knew next to nothing of harmony and counterpoint, nor of musical forms. He learned what little he could from Nadezhda Purgold, the young pianist and composer who would become his wife in 1872. But he would develop into a teacher and theorist of rare perception. In the years to come, many Russian composers, including Anatoly Liadov, Alexander Glazunov, Mikhail Ippolitov-Ivanov, Alexander Grechaninov, Anton Arensky, and above all Igor Stravinsky, were grateful for his instruction. Rimsky-Korsakov's book on harmony and his remarkable treatise *Principles of Orchestration* have continued to be useful.

Through unrelenting diligence, Rimsky-Korsakov acquired the finest technique by far of his colleagues in the "Russian Five." Years later he wrote, "One must not neglect harmony and counterpoint, and the development of a good technique and clear voice leading. All of us, myself and Borodin and Balakirev, but especially Cui and Mussorgsky, neglected this. I consider that I caught myself in time and made myself get down to work. Owing to such deficiencies in technique, Balakirev writes little; Borodin, with difficulty; Cui, sloppily; Mussorgsky, messily and often nonsensically; and all of this constitutes the very regrettable specialty of the Russian school."

As the years passed, Rimsky-Korsakov suffered from episodes of debilitating depression, partly due to the deaths of two of his three daughters, which prevented him from working. As he recovered from each episode, he would resume composition with singular intensity. During 1887–88, he completed his most popular orchestral works: *Capriccio espagnol* (Op. 34), *Sheherazade* (Op. 35), and the *Russian Easter Festival Overture* (Op. 36). From 1894 through 1907, working at a frenzied pace, he completed the staggering total of ten operas.

The 1905 Russo-Japanese War brought about considerable revolutionary ferment in Russia, and Rimsky-Korsakov sided with Conservatory students who were demanding reforms at the school. As a result, he was dismissed from his position, and his music was banned from public performance. His fellow musicians were outraged, and Liadov, Glazunov, and Felix Blumenfeld resigned in protest.

Although the composer was soon reinstated, he became despondent. In the first decade of the twentieth century, both Russia and the world of music were changing. Music was moving in new directions with Debussy, Scriabin, Ravel, Busoni, and Schoenberg. Rimsky-Korsakov felt he was of a different time. But he and his colleagues had accomplished their mission of creating a Russian nationalist art, and the next generation was profoundly affected by their accomplishment. Rimsky-Korsakov's presence was indelibly inscribed in the music of his foremost pupil, Stravinsky, whose mature work nevertheless would have bewildered his teacher.

In the spring of 1908, Rimsky-Korsakov suffered the first of several heart attacks that would end his highly productive career at age sixty-four. His autobiography, *Chronicle of My Musical Life*, is filled with descriptions of colorful personalities and presents a vivid picture of Russian musical culture in the latter half of the nineteenth century.

Some of the best of Rimsky-Korsakov is contained in his fifteen operas, with their supernatural, pan-Slavic, mythological, and pantheistic symbolism. Unfortunately these operas remain unfamiliar to the vast majority of music lovers. They form an encyclopedic source of a lost, legendary, wild, and exotic Russia. According to the writer V. V. Yastrebtsev, Rimsky-Korsakov confided, "You would scarcely find anyone in the world who believes less in everything supernatural, fantastic, or lying beyond the boundaries of death than I do. Yet as an artist, I love this sort of thing above all else. And religious ceremony? What could be more intolerable? But with what love have I expressed such ceremonial customs in music! No, I am actually of the opinion that art is essentially the most enchanting, intoxicating lie."

Rimsky-Korsakov was one of history's dazzling orchestrators. He knew every instrument's capabilities and invented new tone colors for them. He liked his tone painting to be clear and bright, with nothing murky, and yet he can also be atmospheric. He was capable of creating glistening rays of light and succulent effects. Upon hearing *Sheherazade*, Debussy told Colette he wanted to taste it. When *Sheherazade* was first performed in London, a critic was certain that the clarinet runs in the third movement depicted kisses. Indeed, Rimsky-Korsakov's descriptive powers as an orchestrator are amazing, and in the 1930s and 1940s his music served as a textbook for Hollywood hacks. Rachmaninoff, who loved conducting Rimsky-Korsakov's operas, wrote, "When there is a snowstorm, the flakes seem to dance and drift from the woodwinds and the soundholes of the violin; when the sun is high, all instruments shine with an almost fiery glare; when there is water, the waves ripple and splash audibly."

Rimsky-Korsakov lacked Tchaikovsky's suffering passionate nature, and Mussorgsky's stark and brutal originality, but at his best, he is an inspired storyteller, with a cohesive structure. He was too modest and once told a pupil that he overvalued his teacher; "study Liszt and Balakirev more closely," he said, "and you will see that a great deal in me is—not me." He had his debts, of course, but he is undisputably Rimsky-Korsakov, and he gave his own personal truth to what he wrote. He could be deliriously lyrical and was always fantastic.

He held, in Gerald Abraham's words, "the most superb palette a musician has ever held."

Capriccio espagnol, Op. 34 (1887)

"The Capriccio was to glitter with dazzling orchestra color," Rimsky-Korsakov wrote. And so it does, even after a century and a quarter of use. In a good performance, its effect can be electric. After hearing it, Tchaikovsky wrote to the composer, "Your *Spanish Caprice* is a colossal masterpiece of instrumentation, and you may regard yourself as the greatest master of the present day." The premiere took place on October 31, 1887. There are five movements: "Alborada," "Variations," "Alborada," "Scene and Gypsy Song," and "Fandango of the Asturias." Rimsky-Korsakov reports in his autobiography, *Chronicle of My Musical Life*, that "at the first rehearsal, the first movement had hardly been finished when the whole orchestra began to applaud. Similar applause followed all the other parts whenever pauses permitted. I asked the orchestra for the privilege of dedicating the composition to them."

Montreal Symphony Orchestra, Dutoit: London 430700-2
Czech Philharmonic Orchestra, Ancerl: Supraphon Collection 11 0602-2

Sheherazade (symphonic suite), Op. 35 (1888)

On the score, Rimsky-Korsakov appended this explanation: "The Sultan Shakhriar, persuaded by the falseness and faithlessness of all women, had sworn to put to death each of his wives after the first night. But the Sultana Sheherazade saved her life by arousing his interest in tales which she told him during a thousand and one nights. Driven by curiosity, the sultan put off his wife's execution from day to day and at last gave up his bloody plan altogether. Sheherazade told many marvelous tales to the Sultan. For her stories, she borrowed from poets their verses, from folk songs their words, and she strung together fairy tales and adventures."

The thousand-year-old tale of the thousand and one nights was in vogue in Europe from the eighteenth century on. To Rimsky-Korsakov, the Near East was a live enchantment. Never had his virtuoso brushstrokes painted a more luxuriant canvas. "I had in view the creation of an orchestral suite in four movements," he wrote, "closely knit by the community of its themes and motives, yet presenting, as it were, a kaleidoscope of fairy-tale images and designs of Oriental character." The movements are titled: "The Sea and Sinbad's Ship," "The Story of the Kalander Prince," "The Young Prince and Princess," and "Festival at Baghdad." The last movement, "Festival at Baghdad," has two subtitles, "The Sea" and "The Ship Goes to Pieces Against a Rock Surmounted by a Bronze Statue of a Warrior." The entire score, so gorgeous in fantastic colorations, is achieved by a "normal" orchestra. *Sheherazade* is dedicated to the critic Vladimir Stassov, a father figure to the Russian Five.

Royal Philharmonic Orchestra, Beecham: EMI Classics CDC 47717
Chicago Symphony Orchestra, Reiner: RCA 09026-68168-2
Philadelphia Orchestra, Ormandy: Sony Classical SBT 46537
London Symphony Orchestra, Stokowski: London 417753-2

Russian Easter Festival Overture, Op. 36 (1888)

This overture celebrates both the springtime rebirth of nature and the Resurrection. Rimsky-Korsakov used melodies from the Obikhod, a group of Greek Orthodox canticles, to convey the feeling of Christian ritual with a pagan past. He also attempted to convey the mood of the Russian Easter, "the bright holiday," and attended a great Russian Orthodox cathedral Easter service in order to fully appreciate the religious event. The composer wrote on the score a long explanation adapted from the Old and the New Testaments, which ends, "Resurrect! Sing the chorus of angels in heaven to the sound of the archangels, trumpets and the fluttering of the wings of the seraphim. Resurrect! Clouds of incense by the light of innumerable candles to the chiming of bells." Rimsky-Korsakov conducted the world premiere at St. Petersburg on December 3, 1888. The score is dedicated to the memory of Mussorgsky.

London Symphony Orchestra, Dorati: Mercury 434308-2
New York Philharmonic Orchestra, Temirkanov: RCA 09026-61173-2
Montreal Symphony Orchestra, Dutoit: London 430741-2

OTHER PRINCIPAL WORKS

CHAMBER MUSIC
Quartet in G Major for Strings (1897)
Trio in C Minor for Piano, Violin, and Cello (1897)

CHORAL WORKS
Song of Oleg the Wise, Op. 58 (1899)

CONCERTOS
Concerto in C-sharp Minor for Piano and Orchestra, Op. 30 (1882–83)
Fantasia on Two Russian Themes for Violin and Orchestra, Op. 33 (1886–87)

OPERAS
Mlada (1872)*
May Night (1878–79)*
Snow Maiden (1880–81; rev. 1895)
Christmas Eve (1894–95)
Sadko (1894–96)*
Mozart and Salieri, Op. 48 (1897)
The Story of Tsar Saltan (1899–1900)*
The Legend of the Invisible City of Kitezh (1903–5)*
The Golden Cockerel (1906–7)*

ORCHESTRAL WORKS
Symphony no. 2 (*Antar*), Op. 9 (1868; rev. 1875 and 1897)
Suite from the opera *The Story of Tsar Saltan* (1903)
Suite from the opera *Mlada* (1903)
Suite from the opera *Christmas Eve* (1903)

GABRIEL FAURÉ

b. Pamiers, Ariège, May 12, 1845

d. Paris, November 4, 1924

The artist ought to love life and show us that it is good. Without him, we might have doubts about it.

Fauré was the fifth child of middle-class parents. His father was the principal of a teacher-training college at Montgauzy. "I grew up a rather quiet, well-behaved child in an area of great beauty," Fauré later wrote. ". . . But the only thing I remember really clearly is the harmonium in the little chapel at the college. Every time I could get away I ran there—and I regaled myself. . . . I played atrociously." Soon his unusual talent was detected, and it was decided that it was necessary for him to study music in Paris. "I was nine years old," Fauré recalled. "Imagine sending me to Paris to learn music—what madness!" In 1854 the boy arrived at a small boarding school, École Niedermeyer, where he was given a scholarship and free room and board. "I was there for many years; it was a hard life, but what a delightful one! . . . we made music," Fauré said.

At fifteen he met Camille Saint-Saëns, a teacher at the school. Nothing could have been more fortunate for the boy. At age twenty-five, Saint-Saëns was already an accomplished organist, composer, and conductor and the most comprehensive French musician of his generation. Saint-Saëns took Fauré in hand, helping him to improve his piano and organ playing, and introducing him to eighteenth-century French music as well as the works of Schumann, Liszt, and Wagner. He became the central musical influence of Fauré's young life. The two musicians, essentially different in character and in musical temperament, remained close friends throughout their long lives. In 1920 the eighty-five-year-old Saint-Saëns told Fauré, "You cannot imagine how hard I have been practicing your *Valse-Caprice* in D-flat. . . . When I'm ninety, I shall perhaps be quite sure of it."

At twenty Fauré graduated with honors from the École Niedermeyer. For the next four years, 1866–70, he was church organist at Rennes in Brittany. But he missed Paris and returned just in time to see limited action as a light infantryman in the Franco-Prussian War. After the war, he joined the faculty at his former school and was also assistant to the formidable organist Charles Widor at the prestigious Saint-Sulpice Church. He stayed there until 1872, when he became choirmaster and assistant organist at the even more famous Madeleine Church.

In the early 1870s, he was a suitor for the hand of Marianne Viardot-García, daughter of the great mezzo-soprano Pauline Viardot-García. At the singer's renowned salon, Fauré met the cream of Paris's artistic society. By this time, he had a considerable amount of music to his credit, and a few of his songs and piano pieces were attracting attention. The shy Fauré took four years to propose marriage to Marianne, who accepted, only to break the engagement soon afterward. Fauré, brokenhearted, poured his ardent and frustrated feelings into his A major violin sonata.

In 1879 in Munich, Fauré heard Wagner's operas for the first time. Although he was deeply moved, he never succumbed to the Wagnerian delirium that afflicted other French composers. From the beginning of his career, he knew exactly what his own strengths and limitations were. He lived through the storms of Wagner, the giantism of Mahler, the modulatory and harmonic dissolution of Debussy, the expressionism of Schoenberg, and the extraordinary orchestral virtuosity accomplished by Richard Strauss and Ravel, as well as the varied rhythmic innovations of Stravinsky. In an age of wavering artistic allegiances, Fauré followed his own artistic conscience.

He preferred composing exquisite piano pieces, perfect songs, and classically oriented chamber works. His mission was to produce pure and balanced beauty. With time his music became increasingly original harmonically. As he aged, his inner life grew serene; certainly there is passion in his music, but Fauré fled in horror from theatrical display. His opera *Pénélope* (1913) was dedicated to Saint-Saëns but has nothing in common with the banalities of the composer of *Samson et Dalila*. *Pénélope*, the very model of intimate lyric theater, will never have a large audience. It exists for the most discerning music lover.

In 1883, Fauré married Marie Frémiet, the daughter of well-known sculptor Emmanuel Frémiet. The marriage was solid, and Fauré was solicitous of her fragile health, difficult character, and frustrated artistic ambitions. The couple had two sons, one of whom, Philippe, eventually wrote a biography of his father. By his mid-forties, Fauré was still poor and rather obscure. His activities at the Madeleine were more prestigious than lucrative, and his music was published but seldom purchased. The Fauré who was well known in Paris was the baritone Jean-Baptiste Faure, whose performances of sentimental and religious songs made him wealthy. Our Fauré's fortunes, however, took a turn for the better in 1896, when he became chief organist at the Madeleine and professor of composition at the Paris Conservatory. Fauré was a dedicated and wise teacher, and his pupils held him in the highest regard. The composers Florent Schmitt, Louis Aubert, Jean Roger-Ducasse, Charles Koechlin, George Enescu, and Maurice Ravel studied with him. In 1905 Fauré was appointed director of the Conservatory—but only after a bitter political battle, for many opposed the appointment of one who himself had never studied there. His predecessor, the ultraconservative Théodore Dubois, reminded Fauré that it was his duty to conserve tradition. Fauré paid him little heed, however. The Conservatory had long been encrusted in scholasticism and was completely out of touch with anything progressive in its teaching methods or artistic leanings. Within a few years, Fauré made a clean sweep of the institution, reestablishing its relevance in French musical life.

Unfortunately, by 1903 he was experiencing hearing problems, and what he did hear was horribly distorted. During his Conservatory years, he hid his affliction as best he could. But by 1920 his increasing deafness had caused him much embarrassment, and he resigned. In his remaining years, in spite of deafness and poor health, he composed some of his finest music. The serene String Quartet in E Minor (Op. 121), completed the year of his death, reached new levels of radiance. As with many composers, age did not diminish his creativity. Indeed, the last thirty-five years of his life show a continuous development in subtlety and perfection of form: 1921 saw the creation of the C minor piano quintet (Op. 115); 1921–22, the Thirteenth Barcarolle (Op. 116) and the Thirteenth Nocturne (Op. 119); and 1923, the Piano Trio (Op. 120). The two cello sonatas (Opp. 109 and 117) were composed in 1917 and 1922, and his four songs in the song cycle *L'Horizon chimérique*—settings of poems by the young Jean de La Ville de Mirmont, who was killed in World War I—in 1921–22 (Op. 118). The great pedagogue Nadia Boulanger, who was also his pupil, commented, "His ever-more-frequent physical trials, that had emaciated his handsome face, could not touch his miraculous youthful spirit . . . with the years, he developed an indiscernible serenity . . . giving a sort of heightened fervor to each of his words as to each of his works. Gabriel Fauré made us think that, for certain men, old age marks the liberation of their mental force, its apogee not its decline." The gentle Fauré, a man and artist of deep humility, asked on the last evening of his life, "When I am no longer here, what of my work, will any of it live on?"

Fauré was a composer of the utmost idealism. To his son, he wrote: "The work of the imagination consists in attempting to formulate all that one wants that is best, everything that goes beyond reality. . . . To my mind art, and above all music, consists in lifting us as far as possible above what is." Aaron Copland, a pupil of Boulanger, wrote of a performance of Fauré's music in November 1945, "In a world that seems less and less able to order its affairs rationally, Fauré's restraint and classic sense of order may appear slightly incongruous." In the more than half century since those words were written, Fauré's work has prevailed and, in its fastidious crystalline beauty, provides a deep reservoir of refreshment.

Because of its basically restrained character, Fauré's music has never been as popular as that of Debussy or Ravel. It lacks the "punch" and climactic character of music that makes grandiose statements, as Wagner's does. Nor does it have any of the constant striving for effects and facile novelty with which a great deal of twentieth century music has entertained us, to either our disdain or our pleasure. Fauré's music, it has often been noted, is one of the high points of French artistic civilization. His was the desire to make music that is pure euphonious beauty. In this respect, he was akin to the French aspects of Chopin, whose titles—*ballade, prelude, nocturne,* and *barcarolle*—he would inherit. The lyric vein of Schumann and the sensuous melody of Schubert's song also find their way into the essential delicacy of his music.

But it would be misleading to think of Fauré as a nineteenth-century Romantic who lived too long into the twentieth. He was a patient worker; his development was slow and arduous as he polished and repolished every phrase. By age fifty, he was living in a creatively turbulent Paris, and as a progressive teacher, he experimented with and enriched his harmonic procedures. As the musical writer Jean-Michel Nectoux wrote, "Fauré was thus fully involved in the musical adventure of the twentieth century. His work represents an early attempt to answer what is still a burning question today: how is one to write music after some nine centuries of development in the West? Fauré's answer was an extreme refinement of the Classical tonal system, of which he explored every last possibility, regenerated with the very considerable aid of modality. . . . Clearly the new variety of scales that could be employed and the many possibilities arising out of their combination with different keys resulted in an extraordinary expansion of musical language."

Sonata no. 1 in A Major for Violin and Piano, Op. 13 (1876)

Delicacy, tender passion, and feline grace are hallmarks of this most popular of Fauré's chamber music works. It has been criticized for being similar in mood to César Franck's violin sonata in the same key, but Fauré wrote his score a decade before Franck, causing Charles Koechlin to say, "Render unto Gabriel, and not unto César, that which is Gabriel's." The sonata is in four movements. The first movement uses contrasting themes; the violin writing is especially beautiful, with the melodic line heard above rapid figuration. The slow movement exudes pathos and ends in serenity. The Scherzo is fast and energetic, with a gentle Trio. The finale is full of vigor, growing agitated with an expressive theme that has a tang of Schumann. The sonata ends intensely.

Dumay, Collard: EMI Classics CZS 569261-2
Thibaud, Cortot: EMI Classics CDH 763032-2
Grumiaux, Crossley: Philips 426384-2

Pelléas et Mélisande Suite, Op. 80 (1898)

Fauré wrote very little for orchestra; the medium undoubtedly was too public for his restrained nature. This lack accounts for the long delay it has taken for Fauré to gain his due recognition, since orchestral music is the quickest way to export a composer's work. In June 1898, Fauré went to London to hear his incidental music to Maurice Maeterlinck's play, which was at the same time being set as an opera by Debussy. Fauré discarded most of the music, but he condensed four sections into a suite that is often heard today at symphony concerts. The prelude is subdued, a mysterious and sad prelude to the drama: Mélisande sits at her time-honored spinning wheel. *Siciliana*, an old Italian dance that is also in a version for cello and piano, is a suggestive, slow piece, beguiling in its nine-eight meter. "The Death of Mélisande" is an elegy, which rises in intensity.

Atlanta Symphony Orchestra, Shaw: Telarc CD 80084
Orchestre National de France, Munch: Disques Montaigne MUN 2031

Requiem, Op. 48 (1877; rev. 1900)

Fauré's penetrating masterpiece, with its purity and resignation, is the most beautiful of all requiems. "Everything I managed to entertain in the way of religious illusion I put into my *Requiem*, which moreover is dominated from beginning to end by a very human feeling of eternal rest," the composer wrote. "But it is thus that I see death: as a happy deliverance, an aspiration towards happiness above." In his Requiem, Fauré purposely left out the *Dies Irae* (*Day of Wrath*) section of the mass, refusing to see fear in death or in eternal tortures. Can there be anything more different from the mighty requiems of Berlioz and Verdi? These other composers, writes Émile Vuillermoz, "spared us no painful detail. They stress all the threats contained in the sacred texts." Although Fauré was a church organist and wrote in a few sacred forms, he was a religious agnostic. After reading an article on salvation, he wrote to a friend: "How nice is this self-assurance! How nice is the naïveté, or the vanity, or the stupidity, or the bad faith of the people for whom this was written, printed and distributed."

1900 VERSION

Te Kanawa, Milnes, Montreal Symphony Orchestra and Chorus, Dutoit: London 421440-2

Armstrong, Fischer-Dieskau, Orchestre de Paris, Edinburgh Festival Chorus, Barenboim: EMI Classics CDM 64634

Chilcott, Case, New Philharmonia Orchestra and King's College Choir Cambridge, Willcocks: EMI Classics CDM 64715

Songs (1861–1921)

Fauré was one of the greatest French song composers. His songs are supple in form and have a broad emotional range, from the suggestiveness of "Clair de lune" (Op. 46/2) to the intimacy of "Le Secret" (Op. 23/3) and the tragedy of "Prison" (Op. 83/1). Fauré composed ninety-six songs in twenty-nine opus numbers. The first, "Le Papillon et la fleur" (Op. 1/1), appeared in 1861, and the last, the four songs of the cycle *L'Horizon chimérique* (Op. 118), appeared sixty years later, in 1921. Other famous cycles include four songs in *Mirages* (Op. 113, 1919); eight songs in *Le Jardin clos* (Op. 106, 1914); ten songs in *La Chanson d'Ève* (Op. 95, 1906–10); and nine songs in his most famous cycle, *La Bonne Chanson* (Op. 61, 1892–94), set to love poems by Paul Verlaine. Fauré was a melodist of the first order, never better than in the medium of the *mélodie*, or art song.

La Bonne Chanson

Souzay, Baldwin: Denon CO 2252

Walker, Nash Ensemble: CRD 3389 (with string quintet)

Various Songs

Walker, Martineau: CRD 3476 and CRD 3477
Baker, Parsons: Hyperion CDA 66320

Nocturnes (1883–1922)

Fauré was a master of piano writing. His reflective gentleness and understated passion become more beautiful with repeated and careful listening; he makes his impact gradually. The thirteen nocturnes are among Fauré's finest flights of imagination, displaying many moods and harmonic complexity; they are generally more complicated than the thirteen barcarolles and nine preludes. The nocturnes span almost forty years of Fauré's creative activity. No. 3 (Op. 33) is the most Chopinesque and among the most frequently played. No. 6 in D-flat major (Op. 63) is one of the masterpieces of French piano music; in this nine-minute work, a once-luxuriant form becomes a psychological drama of great depth. With No. 7 in C-sharp minor (Op. 74), Fauré enters the realm of grief. No. 10 in E minor (Op. 99) is very serious, full of asperities. No. 12, also in E minor (Op. 107), expresses gloom. No. 13 in B minor (Op. 119) is Fauré's farewell to the piano, a work of sad nobility, rising to a great climax but ending in calm despair.

Complete Nocturnes

Collard: EMI Classics CZS 569437-2
Lively: Etcetera KTC 1082

Nos. 1, 6, 7, 12, and 13

Perlemuter: Nimbus NI 5165

OTHER PRINCIPAL WORKS

CHAMBER MUSIC

Quartet no. 1 in C Minor for Piano and Strings, Op. 15 (1876–79)*
Quartet no. 2 in G Minor for Piano and Strings, Op. 45 (?1885–86)*
Quintet no. 1 in D Minor for Piano and Strings, Op. 89 (1887–95)*
Quintet no. 2 in C Minor for Piano and Strings, Op. 115 (1919–21)*
Trio in D Minor for Piano, Violin, and Cello, Op. 120 (1923)*
Quartet in E Minor for Strings, Op. 121 (1924)*

OPERA
Pénélope (1913)*

ORCHESTRAL WORKS
Pavane, Op. 50 (1887)*
Masques et bergamasques (suite), Op. 112 (1919)

PIANO MUSIC
Thirteen barcarolles (various opus nos., various dates)*
Theme and Variations in C-sharp Minor, Op. 73 (1895)*
Five impromptus, Opp. 25, 31, 34, 91, 102 (1881–1909)
Dolly Suite for Piano Duet, Op. 56 (1894–97)*
Eight *Pièces brèves*, Op. 84 (1869–1902)
Nine Preludes, Op. 103 (1909–10)*
Four *Valses-caprices*, Opp. 30, 38, 59, 62 (1882–94)

PIANO AND ORCHESTRA WORKS
Ballade in F-sharp Major, Op. 19 (1901)*
Fantaisie, Op. 111 (1919)

SOLO INSTRUMENT AND PIANO WORKS
Berceuse in D Major for Violin and Piano, Op. 16 (1880)
Élégie for Cello and Piano, Op. 24 (1880)*
Fantaisie for Flute and Piano, Op. 79 (1898)
Sonata no. 2 in E Minor for Violin and Piano, Op. 108 (1916–17)*
Sonata no. 1 in D Minor for Cello and Piano, Op. 109 (1917)*
Sonata no. 2 in G Minor for Cello and Piano, Op. 117 (1922)*

LEOŠ
JANÁČEK

b. Hukvaldy, Moravia, July 3, 1854

d. Morava-Ostrava, August 12, 1928

The musically talented person plays and plays again, sings even when he has no words. It is his work, to which no one forces or prompts him. No hour is too late or too early for such work.

Janáček was the tenth of fourteen children, the son of a poor village school-teacher, Jiří, who taught him singing and the piano. He was extremely attached to his mother, Amalie, who was also musical. At age ten he was sent to a monastery in Brno, where he earned his keep as a chorister. He received a well-rounded musical education there from Pavel Křížkovský, Moravia's best-known composer. In 1886 his father died, and the family was supported—albeit in great poverty—by an uncle, a priest. Leoš obtained a state scholarship to the Czech Teachers' Institute and graduated in 1872. He immediately began teaching at the monastery and working as choirmaster of a workingmen's choral society. Another scholarship gave him the chance to study at the Prague Organ School for a year. He was so poor that he could not buy his textbooks or rent a piano. He did manage to meet Dvořák, whose music he had championed in Brno. Dvořák was favorably impressed with some of Janáček's formative scores and helped him with a few awkward passages. With some financial help from friends in Prague, the young composer entered the Leipzig Conservatory. He was unhappy there and left for Vienna after one term. Through all his travels, he wrote daily to Zdenka Schultzová, a girl he had met when he was still in Brno. In 1880, Janáček returned to his homeland, and the next year he married Zdenka, who was not yet sixteen. The marriage, alas, was unhappy, but the couple had two children and remained married until Janáček's death.

The compositions Janáček wrote in his twenties aped Western European models and the Bohemian nationalism of Dvořák and his younger contemporaries, Josef Suk, Zdeněk Fibich, Vitězslav Novák, and Josef Foerster. Even the best of these—the pretty *Idyll* for strings (1878) and *Lachian Dances* (1893)—possess nothing of his later style. He was just past thirty when he started to examine Moravian folksongs, unearthing many old folk melodies. Moravia—both a geographical area and an ethnic term—with its magnificent, romantic scenery, had always bewitched him. There is no separate Moravian language (Czech is spoken there and in Bohemia), but there is a distinct, ancient folk culture, which dug its roots deep into Janáček's heart. For the rest of his life, as a person and a creator, he was endlessly nourished by the land and sounds of northern Moravia. "I have one great joy," he wrote. "Moravia alone is enough to give me all necessary inspiration, so rich are her sources."

Janáček developed slowly as a composer. During the 1890s, he worked on his third opera, *Jenůfa*, which took nine years to complete. During this period, he suffered two major tragedies, the death of his son, Vladimir, at age two, and that of his beloved daughter, Olga, at age twenty-one from typhoid. "She was so loath to die," he wrote, "it was as though someone was tearing my heart out." Soon afterward he wrote an elegy for Olga for mixed voices and piano (1903). At fifty, Janáček, a hardworking provincial musician, was unknown except in Brno. He was grateful that *Jenůfa*, dedicated to Olga, at least won success when it was premiered in Brno in 1904.

He spent the next dozen years composing, teaching violin and organ, and conducting a choral group. By age sixty, Janáček was still unknown and frustrated. His music had now become totally original, and he wrote in many forms. Inspired by a tragic political event in 1905, he composed his heartrending Piano Sonata (*From the Street*). By 1914 he had written his Violin Sonata, a good deal of choral music, and the symphonic poem *The Fiddler's Child*.

Janáček, now sixty-two, desperately wanted *Jenůfa* to be performed in Prague. For over a decade the Prague National Theater had refused the opera because of its unsavory story, which included the murder of a child. Finally in 1916 the National Theater relented. The opera, unexpectedly, was a triumph of major proportions. Suddenly the whole country became aware of Janáček, and other opera houses showed interest as well.

For Janáček, the opera's success was a catharsis. He quickly completed a new opera, *Mr. Brouček's Excursion to the Moon* (1917), which had been languishing half-written for years. "I feel as though I were living in a fairy tale," he wrote. "I compose and compose as though something was urging me on." He was elated with his expanding creativity, and for the rest of his life music flowed nonstop. The extraordinary operas he created are startling in their variety and depth; most of them feature women in tragic circumstances.

During the summer of 1917, Janáček met the great inspiration of his life. Kamila Stösslová, a beautiful, married mother, was thirty-eight years younger than he, but for the rest of his life, he poured out his heart and mind to her in hundreds of ardent letters. Although he remained married, the friendship with Stösslová unleashed powerful feelings that merged into his music. Shortly after meeting her, he composed the erotic song cycle *The Diary of One Who Vanished* (1917–19), about a peasant who abandons his life and family to follow a beguiling Gypsy woman. "While writing the Diary," the composer wrote to Stösslová, "I thought only of you." His ardor never cooled. On December 31, 1927, he wrote, "Kamilka [her nickname] be mine! . . . I'd tremble with pleasure, I'd call you until my heart burst. I'd kiss you until you burned with love and said: 'Be mine, be mine!' . . . and it would be a delight such as no one's ever experienced. We'd burn with passion. . . . To have you, just for that measureless love for you—a love which cannot abide our still being two alongside one another. A love which wants to drown spiritually and physically and merge into one. You don't know where you'd begin and where I'd end."

In the next years, he composed the opera *Kát'a Kabanová* (1921), the story of a woman who commits suicide over unhappy love; *The Cunning Little Vixen* (1923), an allegorical animal opera; and the two great string quartets—the first (1923), subtitled *Kreutzer*, was inspired by Tolstoy's novella *The Kreutzer Sonata*, while the second, *Intimate Pages* (1928), was a confessional work for Kamila. In 1926 he received an invitation to London from the Slavophilic music writer Rosa Newmarch. To his disappointment, none of his operas were performed while he was in London, but he was nevertheless grateful for Newmarch's appreciation. When he returned to Czechoslovakia, he wrote the luminous *Sinfonietta* (1926), which he dedicated to her. It contains none of the tragedy and high-pitched emotion of his operas.

Late in July 1928, Janáček arranged for Kamila, her husband (who had always known of the composer's friendship with his wife), and their eleven-year-old son to visit his home in Hukvaldy. Before the family arrived, Janáček wrote to Kamila, "I've already painted your stay in Hukvaldy so beautifully in my mind that I'm almost frightened that an evil turn of events might thwart these passionate wishes." On August 6 the boy got lost in the forest. The frantic seventy-four-year-old composer exhausted himself in the search and caught a cold that turned into pneumonia. He died six days later.

Since his death, Janáček's reputation has grown. He holds an honored place among twentieth-century composers and is considered one of the great spirits of Czech musical culture. He often expressed his wonder at his own constant musical development. At age seventy-two, he wrote, "Although I am getting on in years, I have a feeling that a new vein is beginning to grow in my work, a new branch—the same thing that happens to the four or five hundred year old trees of Hukvaldy. My latest creative period is also a new kind of sprouting from the soul which has made its peace with the rest of the world and seeks only to be nearest to the ordinary Czech man."

Janáček's music is unlike any other. His is a completely original voice, using an entirely idiosyncratic language based on his folk heritage. He used few traditional compositional devices: "Of all the musical tricks," he once said, "the contrapuntal ones are particularly pitiful." Instead his works have a special kind of polyphonic texture. Janáček's harmonic scheme is complex, but not so far from usual late-nineteenth- and early-twentieth-century harmony. It is not the means but the manner in which he expressed himself that was radical. He wrote within a completely flexible tonality without traditional development of themes. In essence his music is rhapsodic and passionate—and often bittersweet.

Opera gave him great scope for expressing his humanity as well as drawing acute psychological portraits of his beleaguered characters. In Janáček's music, one deeply feels his worship of nature, the buzzing and sounds of the insect world, the language of animals, the mystery of the night, and always the moist dark earth of his Moravia. It is intensely national, but like the music of Bartók nearly thirty years later, it goes far beyond locale. "Each folk song contains an entire man; his body, his soul, his surroundings, everything, everything. He who grows up among folk songs grows into a complete man. Folk songs are made in a single spirit, which gives men the culture of God. . . . Folk songs bind the nation, bind all nations and all people with one spirit, one happiness, one paradise."

Jenůfa (1894–1903)

Jenůfa was the third of Janáček's nine operas. Its story is one of lust, violence, jealousy, and infanticide. The music is intense, excruciatingly lyrical, and passionate, and the orchestra vents both sorrow and love. It is a haunting theatrical experience, but like other Janáček operas, it translates well to recording. Until the 1950s, *Jenůfa* was the only one of his operas to be performed worldwide. Today, however, all of his mature operas have gained currency in the repertoire, and many opera singers have added the study of Czech to their essential education.

Popp, Söderström, Randová, Dvorsky, Ochman, Vienna Philharmonic Orchestra and Chorus,
*   Mackerras: London 414483-2LH2*

Hillebrecht, Varnay, Cox, Cochran, Bavarian State Opera Orchestra and Chorus, Kubelik:
MYTO Records 2MCD 90422

Sinfonietta (1926)

The *Sinfonietta*, once heard, can never be forgotten. It is a masterpiece of orchestration in five movements—Janáček's art at its most sophisticated. The
composer's nationalist roots shine like sunlight, yet as in his other late music,
those roots are universalized. The score is episodic and primitive, with tiny
melodic cells, pungent with its persistent rhythms orchestrated with an almost
unbearable and excruciating lightness, yet using no fewer than fourteen trumpets. The opening movement is a full fanfare and is followed by four other
movements, all constantly shifting their textures to bright, luminous sounds.
The score retains a lyrical impression even as it is fragmented and jerky. The
last movement returns to the fanfare with new instrumental color.

Vienna Philharmonic Orchestra, Mackerras: London 410138-2
New York Philharmonic Orchestra, Masur: Teldec 90847
Berlin Philharmonic Orchestra, Abbado: Deutsche Grammophon 445501-2

Glagolitic Mass (1926)

One spur to Janáček's growing creative powers was the freedom of the independent and united Czech nation after the First World War. The mass is sometimes called the *Slavonic Mass*, because its text uses the early Slavonic
alphabet. All of Janáček's depth of spirit, both religious and aesthetic, shines in
this forty-minute affirmation of his fatherland. The score divides into an introduction, Kyrie, Gloria, Credo, Sanctus and Benedictus, Agnus Dei, organ solo,
and Intrada. Janáček's biographer Ian Horsbrugh wrote, "The *Glagolitic Mass*
is the apotheosis and summary of Janáček's creative work. It embraces the
tragedies of the heroines, his huge compassion for the individual, the wonder of
eternal renewal, the triumph of the spirit in old age. It is expressed in a storm-
ing, hedonistic treatment of the old text, itself a symbol of Czech greatness."

Söderström, Drobkova, Livora, Novák: Czech Philharmonic Orchestra and Chorus, Macker-
ras: Supraphon SUP 103575
Benačková, Palmer, Lakes, Kotcherga, London Symphony Orchestra and Chorus, Tilson
Thomas: Sony Classical SK 47182

OTHER PRINCIPAL WORKS

CHAMBER MUSIC

Quartet no. 1 for Strings (*Kreutzer*) (1923)*

Youth (Mládi) Sextet (1924)

Quartet no. 2 for Strings (*Intimate Pages*) (1928)*

OPERAS

Mr. Brouček's Excursion to the Moon (1917)

Kát'a Kabanová (1919–21)*

The Cunning Little Vixen (1921–23)*

The Makropulos Affair (1923–25)*

From the House of the Dead (1927–28)*

ORCHESTRAL WORKS

Lachian Dances (1893)

The Fiddler's Child (symphonic poem) (1912)

Taras Bulba (rhapsody) (1915–18)*

The Ballad of Blanik (symphonic poem) (1920)

PIANO WORKS

On the Overgrown Path (fifteen pieces) (1901–8)*

Sonata October 1, 1905 (From the Street) (1905)*

In the Mists (four pieces) (1912)*

PIANO AND CHAMBER ORCHESTRA WORKS

Concertino (1925)*

Capriccio (*Defiance*) (1926)*

VIOLIN AND PIANO WORKS

Sonata (1913–21)*

VOCAL MUSIC

The Diary of One Who Vanished (song cycle) (1917–19)*

SIR EDWARD ELGAR

b. Broadheath (near Worcester), June 2, 1857

d. Worcester, February 23, 1934

Music is written on the skies for you to note down. And you compare that to a damned imitation.

Elgar was born in the twentieth year of Queen Victoria's long reign. His father played organ in the village church and ran a music shop. His mother was well read, wrote poetry, and sketched. Although Edward was introduced to a great deal of music, he was not given a thorough foundation. His school education ended at age fifteen, and he was apprenticed to a lawyer. After a year or so, he began pursuing the life of a provincial musician and taught himself. He performed some chamber music and gave a few recitals on the violin, an instrument he hoped to master well enough to become a concert violinist. At a local church, he played organ, led the choir, and did the usual teaching, but he found it difficult to make ends meet. In time he realized he lacked the ability and fortitude to become a brilliant violinist, and in 1879 he settled for a bandmaster's post at the Worcester County insane asylum. He stayed there for five uneventful years, during which he composed several small, insignificant pieces.

The major turning point in Elgar's life came in 1889, when he married Caroline Alice Roberts, a woman nine years his senior, of exceptional qualities and devotion, who believed passionately in her husband's talent. Almost from the beginning of the marriage, Elgar found that he was composing with great facility. A concert overture, *Froissart* (Op. 19), was performed in his hometown in 1890, and he quickly followed with the engaging Serenade in E Minor for

Strings (Op. 20, 1892). Soon afterward he turned his attention to large choral works with orchestra, the most famous being the oratorio *The Dream of Gerontius* (Op. 38, 1899–1900). Another oratorio, *The Light of Life* (Op. 29), was performed at the Worcester Festival in 1896, to local acclaim. But Elgar's first big break came when the great conductor Hans Richter came upon his *Enigma Variations* (Op. 36, 1898–99) while looking for a new English score to perform. Richter gave the first performance on June 19, 1899, in London. Soon Elgar's name was known around the world. His reputation was further enhanced when *The Dream of Gerontius* was given again at the Birmingham Festival on October 3, 1900. After these momentous scores, Elgar turned to lighter fare with the *Pomp and Circumstance Marches* (Op. 39, 1902–7), *Cockaigne Overture* (Op. 40, 1900–1), and the charming *Introduction and Allegro* for Strings (Op. 47, 1904–5). In 1908 he finished the great First Symphony (Op. 55), dedicated to Richter, followed by the Violin Concerto (Op. 61, 1909–10), a Second Symphony (Op. 63, 1909–11), and the remarkable symphonic study *Falstaff* (Op. 68), completed in 1913. Richter saw only a few examples from the *Falstaff* manuscript but wrote about them, "What themes! Unmistakable and genuinely Elgar! . . . Admittedly I can only imagine it, for . . . even one's boldest imagination proves to be far from reality." The composer was knighted in 1904.

Elgar was devastated by World War I. Music became more and more difficult to compose. After the war, Elgar's work became leaner and more withdrawn. Its former optimism vanished. Fine works from this period include the Violin Sonata (Op. 82, 1918), a string quartet (Op. 83, 1918), and the Piano Quintet (Op. 84, 1919). In 1919 he composed his last masterpiece, the anguished Cello Concerto (Op. 85).

Elgar's wife died in 1920, and for the remaining fourteen years of his life, inspiration and the desire to compose eluded him. "I had gone off the boil," he declared. Many honors came his way during these years, however. He was made "master of the king's music" (court composer) in 1924 and a baronet in 1931. His last triumph came at the 1933 Hereford Festival, where he conducted his *Dream of Gerontius*. He died of cancer less than a year later.

Not since Henry Purcell, who died in 1695, had the English nation boasted a composer of international repute. Since then England had been imitating foreign models. Handel and his oratorios dominated in the 1730s and 1740s, Johann Christian Bach reigned later in the eighteenth century, followed by Clementi, Haydn, and Mendelssohn. Their influence overshadowed contemporary English musical talent, including that of Sir William Sterndale Bennett, who impressed both Mendelssohn and Schumann. After Bennett, there emerged an earnest, hardworking community of musicians led by Sir Hubert Parry, Frederic Cowen, Dame Ethel Smyth, and Sir Arthur Sullivan, as well as the Scotsman Sir Alexander Mackenzie and the Irishman Sir Charles Villiers Stanford. Sullivan, by far the best known today, struggled to compose "important" music in keeping with the established church, operatic, and academic traditions, but his collaboration with W. S. Gilbert on operettas was what immortalized them as a twosome. Only when Elgar came of age creatively during the final years of the nineteenth century did England have a musical genius that she could export with pride.

Although Elgar was considered quintessentially English, he had no interest in folk material as such, feeling it was important for a composer to invent his tunes. In all respects, he was a late Romantic, his music characteristic of the period's formal giantism and lofty sentiment. An eclectic, Elgar took what he needed from others, including Handel, Mendelssohn, Richard Strauss, and Brahms. He was influenced by Wagnerian harmony and orchestration and transferred the Wagnerian concept of *leitmotive* to the huge edifices of his oratorios.

In the first decade of the century, Elgar sounded fresh, vital, and new; his melodies went straight to the heart. Themes that he labeled *noblemente* in his scores permeate the *Enigma Variations*, the Violin Concerto, and the two elephantine symphonies. He seemed born to express in music the pride of the British Empire, and his work mirrored the luxuriant materialism of the age. His *Pomp and Circumstance Marches*, especially No. 1 in D major, signified British wealth and the purple patriotism of the epoch. Elgar has been reproached for cheap chauvinism in several of his works, but his music would never have survived if his stirring melodies did not possess that intangible quality that lifts them beyond their own time and place. Michael Kennedy, Elgar's biographer, wrote, "The success of the D major march was no doubt associated with Boer War nationalist fervor. I think the audience immediately recognized that they had heard one of the great melodies of the world, a tune that is at once memorable, stirring, disturbing, and singable." For Elgar, who looked like a Victorian prime minister, England was indeed the land of hope and glory. Britannia would always rule the waves—that was only fair and just. The creator of the "Crown of India March" could never have envisioned a Gandhi.

But even before World War I, as he put the finishing touches to his *Falstaff*, contemporary music was becoming foreign to him. Nothing in Bartók, Debussy, Busoni, Stravinsky, Scriabin, Schoenberg, Satie, or Berg could have meant anything to him. After the war, Ralph Vaughan Williams took over the leadership of the English musical scene. Aside from the *Enigma Variations*, Elgar was considered pompous and stuffy, and the Victorian religiosity of *Gerontius* and his other oratorios sounded sanctimonious, stale, and old-fashioned.

The composer Frederick Delius thought it a nauseating work, and the novelist George Moore called it "holy water in a German beer barrel." In the years to come, to the general public at least, Elgar's *Pomp and Circumstance March no. 1* seemed to be all that was attached to his name, as countless June graduates marched down the aisle. But greatness in art is never totally smothered, and after 1950 a new generation slowly rediscovered Elgar. Today at least a dozen works assure his place in the musical canon.

Enigma Variations, Op. 36 (1898–99)

Hans Richter said he took pride in championing two great composers, Wagner and Elgar. In this composition, a theme and fourteen variations, the composer portrayed his wife and friends. Of the *Enigma*, Elgar, who loved mystification, wrote, "I will not explain, its 'dark saying' must be left unguessed, and I warn you that the apparent connection between the Variations and the Theme is often of the slightest texture; further, through and over the whole set another and larger theme 'goes' but is not played."

Variation IX, "Nimrod," a tribute to August Jaeger (an editor at the music publisher Novello, who was a fierce champion of the composer), was, Elgar wrote, "a record of a long summer evening talk, when my friend grew nobly eloquent (as only he could) on the grandeur of Beethoven, and especially of his slow movements."

Montreal Symphony Orchestra, Dutoit: London 430241-2
London Symphony Orchestra, Boult: EMI Classics CDM 64748
Royal Philharmonic Orchestra, Previn: Philips 416813-2

Pomp and Circumstance Marches, Op. 39 (1902–7)

Each of these five marches smacks of an imperial England whose sun will never set. No. 1 in D major is among the world's most famous marches. Elgar was elated by this composition. Of the trio of the march, he told a friend, "Gosh! Man I've got a tune in my head." For the coronation of Edward VII, Elgar wrote a coronation ode. The king asked the composer if he would use the tune in the ode. Elgar was delighted and fit the melody to words by the poet A. C. Benson. The words and music have since become a second national anthem for England: "Land of hope and glory, Mother of the free, how shall we extol thee, who are born of thee?"

Scottish National Orchestra, Gibson: Chandos CHAN 8429
London Philharmonic Orchestra, Barenboim: Sony Classical SBK 48265

Concerto in B Minor for Violin and Orchestra, Op. 61 (1909–10)

This is the greatest and longest English Romantic violin concerto, which Elgar dedicated to the violinist Fritz Kreisler. The violin writing soars and is consistently imaginative. Here is an intimate, soul-searching Elgar, overflowing with melody, rich in passion. The violin entrance in the opening movement is unforgettable. In the cadenza of the finale, he ingeniously brings back themes from the other movements. The slow movement presents another Elgarian enigma; on the score, he printed in Spanish, "Here, or more emphatically *in here*, is enshrined or simply enclosed—buried is perhaps too definite—*the soul of . . .*"

Menuhin, New Philharmonia Orchestra, Boult, EMI Classics: CDM 64725
Heifetz, London Symphony Orchestra, Sargent: RCA 7966-2-RG
Kennedy, London Philharmonic Orchestra, Handley: EMI Classics 63795

Concerto in E Minor for Cello and Orchestra, Op. 85 (1919)

The Cello Concerto was written after World War I and is filled with sadness and disillusionment. Michael Kennedy writes, "With an artist's vision, [Elgar] saw that 1918 was the end of a civilization. . . . His requiem is not a cosmic utterance on behalf of mankind, it is wholly personal, the musical expression of his bitterness about the providence that was 'against great art' and the heavenly spirit that was 'cruelly obtuse' to individual sorrow and sacrifice. There is no 'massive hope for the future' in this music, only the voice of an aging, shattered man, a valediction to an era and to the powers of music that he knew were dying within him." The concerto is half the length of the effulgent forty-minute Violin Concerto. It is in four movements without a break. An Adagio sets the mood for the larger Moderato movement, which Elgar wanted to be full, sweet, and sonorous. A type of Scherzo, or perpetual motion, forms the second movement, though without gaiety. The crown of the score is the third-movement Adagio, a long lament for cello, soberly Elgarian in its poignancy. The finale, Allegro-moderato-allegro ma non troppo, is a Rondo sonata form where Elgar musters excitement, as if finding his earlier optimism—but all comes to a stop in a slow, sobering chromatic passage. Elgar once again tries to recapture the previous mood but cannot bring himself back. Instead, the meter changes with a new passionate statement, which in its second half becomes the theme of the slow movement. Finally, the soloist brings back the melody of the first movement, and the concerto closes briskly. The last movement is structurally one of Elgar's greatest finales. The concerto as a whole is the composer's most personal testimony.

Du Pré, London Symphony Orchestra, Barbirolli: EMI Classics CDC 56219
Casals, BBC Symphony Orchestra, Boult: EMI Classics CDH 63498
Maisky, Philharmonia Orchestra, Sinopoli: Deutsche Grammophon 431685-2

OTHER PRINCIPAL WORKS

CHAMBER MUSIC
Sonata in E Minor for Violin and Piano, Op. 82 (1918)*
Quartet in E Minor for Strings, Op. 83 (1918)*
Quintet in A Minor for Piano and Strings, Op. 84 (1919)*

CHORAL WORKS
The Dream of Gerontius (oratorio), Op. 38 (1899–1900)*
Coronation Ode, Op. 44 (1902)
The Apostles (oratorio), Op. 49 (1902–3)
The Kingdom (oratorio), Op. 51 (1901–8)
The Crown of India (suite), Op. 66 (1911–12)

ORCHESTRAL WORKS
The Wand of Youth Suites, no. 1 and 2, Op. 1a (1907) and 1b (1908)
Salut d'amour, Op. 12 (1889)
Froissart Overture, Op. 19 (1890)*
Serenade in E Minor for Strings, Op. 20 (1892)*
Imperial March, Op. 32 (1897)
Cockaigne (*In London Town*, overture), Op. 40 (1900–1)*
Introduction and Allegro for Strings, Op. 47 (1904–5)*
In the South (concert overture), Op. 50 (1903)
Symphony no. 1 in A-flat Major, Op. 55 (1907–8)*
Symphony no. 2 in E-flat Major, Op. 63 (1909–11)*
Coronation March, Op. 65 (1911)
Falstaff (symphonic study), Op. 68 (1913)*
Severn Suite, Op. 87 (1930)

ORGAN MUSIC
Sonata in G Major, Op. 28 (1895)

VOICE AND ORCHESTRA WORKS
Sea Pictures, Op. 37 (1897–99)*

GIACOMO PUCCINI

b. Lucca, December 23, 1858

d. Brussels, November 29, 1924

When the fever abates, it ends by disappearing and without fever there is no creation; because emotional art is a kind of malady, an exceptional state of mind, accompanied by over-excitation of every fibre and every atom of one's being.

Puccini was descended from a long line of opera composers and church organists in Lucca, beginning with the humble Giacomo Puccini (born in 1712) and proceeding through the generations to his father, Michele Puccini (born in 1813). Michele died when Giacomo was five, leaving his wife with seven children to raise.

Giacomo was enchanted with opera from a very young age, and he gladly walked the thirteen miles to Pisa just to see a performance. After hearing Verdi's *Aïda* when he was seventeen, he knew that he, too, was destined to write for the theater. Years later he said, "I thought then and there that nothing was so wonderful as to write an opera, to fascinate the public, to move it, to exalt it. How wonderful!"

After musical studies in his hometown, he left for the Milan Conservatory in 1880, on a small subsidy from Queen Margherita of Italy (given to talented sons of poor families). His great-uncle also helped his nephew, who was nearly twenty-two when he passed his entrance exam to the Conservatory. His teacher was Amilcare Ponchielli, the composer of *La Gioconda*. Puccini's 1893 orchestral piece, *Capriccio sinfonico*, was praised at the time, and Puccini later used a striking passage from *Capriccio sinfonico* in *La Bohème*. Upon graduation, he entered a competition for a one-act opera sponsored by a music publisher. *Le Villi* did not win, but the score came to the attention of Arrigo Boito, the brilliant critic, librettist, and composer. Boito arranged for its production in May 1884, with publication soon after by Ricordi. This early taste of success was, alas, the only one for a long time for Puccini—and the years following *Le Villi* were ones of wrenching poverty. For a time, he roomed with fellow composer Pietro Mascagni, and they both subsisted on mostly beans, which later in life Puccini refused to eat at all. When there was a little money, they dined at the Aïda restaurant. Once the young composer pawned his coat, as Colline does in *La Bohème*, for the purpose of dining out with a pretty girl. The amorous Puccini once wrote, "I am almost always in love." In 1885, the composer fell in love with Elvira Gemignani, the wife of a Lucca grocer. The next year, she bore Puccini a son, Antonio, and the family lived together. Because Italian law did not permit divorce, they could not marry until 1904, when Elvira's husband died.

In 1889 the thirty-one-year-old composer finally saw his next opera performed. But Puccini's relief was short-lived—*Edgar*, produced at La Scala, was a flop and was shelved after two performances. Puccini was disgusted with his lack of success and distraught over his heavily mounting debts. He contemplated a move to South America, where his brother was living, for, as he wrote, "I am sick of this eternal struggle with poverty." Fortunately for music, he stayed in Italy, working on a new opera.

Shortly thereafter, Puccini read Abbé Prévost's celebrated eighteenth-century novel *Manon Lescaut*. Puccini had always needed to fall madly under the spell of his heroines, and Manon captivated him. His love must have been great indeed to encourage him to write an opera about her, for Massenet's *Manon* had been a great triumph nine years earlier. Puccini, on contrasting Massenet's opera with his own, declared, "Massenet feels it as a Frenchman, with powder and minuets, I feel it as an Italian, with desperate passion." The world premiere of his opera was held in Turin on February 1, 1893, and Puccini's courage was rewarded with an outstanding success. As an opera composer, he was launched. One Milan newspaper raved, "Puccini's genius is truly Italian. His song is the song of our paganism, of our artistic sensualism. It caresses us and becomes part of us." Three years later to the day, Arturo Toscanini conducted the world premiere of *La Bohème* to a standing ovation. Fame and fortune had now come to Puccini, and they would stay—he died with an estate worth more than four million dollars.

Puccini's most pressing concern was finding stories that could be fashioned into viable librettos. He saw play after play, even in languages he did not understand, always hoping to find plots combining high drama with "the beloved woman." He often said it was a curse to compose for the theater. "If only I could be a purely symphonic writer!" he wrote. ". . . Almighty God touched me with His little finger and said, 'Write for the theater—mind you, only for the theater,' and I have obeyed the supreme command."

One of the plays he saw was Victorien Sardou's *Tosca*, with Sarah Bernhardt's electric performance in the leading role. Puccini was desperately attracted to the heroine, but he discovered to his alarm that the rights to the play had been given to the composer Alberto Franchetti, who had no wish to relinquish them. Puccini tried everything, including a few unsavory intrigues, to convince Franchetti that *Tosca* was not suited to him. Puccini even went to Paris to beg Sardou to let him have *Tosca*. Eventually Franchetti capitulated, and Puccini gratefully began work. Giuseppe Giacosa and Luigi Illica, who had written the *La Bohème* libretto, began *Tosca*. On January 14, 1900, the opera was heard in Rome to rousing acclaim. In the lust and blood of *Tosca*, Puccini showed the world he was capable of naked dramatic force.

Tragedy struck next, in February 1903, when Puccini's automobile missed a curve on the road and overturned. The composer was caught under the car and suffered multiple injuries, from which it took him nearly a year to recuperate. He managed to keep composing, however, and he soon put his librettists to work adapting David Belasco's play *Madame Butterfly*. Never had Puccini composed music of such compassion—yet the premiere at La Scala on February 17, 1904, was a failure with the public and the press. Puccini was unconcerned, for he had unshakable faith in his work and in his heartbreaking heroine. In May 1905, the opera received an overwhelming reception in Brescia, and the next month Toscanini conducted *Butterfly* to ovations in Buenos Aires.

As Puccini's fame increased, New York beckoned. In 1908–9, the Metropolitan Opera commissioned *The Girl of the Golden West* (*La Fanciulla del West*), again based on a play by Belasco. Although Puccini appreciated the novelty of a story from the American West, the material never quite fired him with the enthusiasm of his earlier operas. He wrote, "I live in torment because I do not feel the throbbing life that is essential to the creation of a theatrical work which is to endure and hold." The premiere was held on December 19, 1910, with a cast that included tenor Enrico Caruso and soprano Emmy Destinn, with Toscanini at the helm.

While composing *Fanciulla*, the composer's personal life was a nightmare. His wife, always a difficult and jealous person, became increasingly suspicious of his passing sexual interest in "alluring women," as he called them. Puccini did indeed have affairs, but he vehemently denied having one with Doria Manfredi, their servant at his estate at Torre del Lago, near Florence. Amidst accusations and curses, Elvira drove the girl from the house. All were horrified when, in a paroxysm of despair, the young woman killed herself. The autopsy revealed that she had been a virgin. Puccini shut himself up in a hotel room, desperately weeping. The girl's family brought charges, and Elvira faced the prospect of a five-month prison sentence. The case was eventually settled out of court. The Puccinis did stay together, but the marriage was thereafter in name only.

The years following *Fanciulla* were operatically barren. In 1912 he wrote his compatriot the poet Gabriele D'Annunzio, "I am thirsty for something of yours more than ever. You know what I require! Great love in little souls. But do not forget the grand scene, filled with phonic power and with emotion." For a long time, Puccini had wanted to write in a lighter vein. He finally did so in the delightful *La Rondine (The Swallow)*, but the opera had a lukewarm reception at its premiere at Monte Carlo in 1917. That same year, Puccini was hard at work on *Il Trittico*—three one-act operas titled *Il Tabarro, Suor Angelica,* and *Gianni Schicchi.* He was usually a painfully slow worker and was pleased with the quick progress he was making. The three small operas, each with its own delicate distinction and containing many new details of his art, were produced at the Metropolitan Opera in December 1918. Although they were politely received, *Il Trittico* has not fared well, and the trilogy is seldom staged.

Puccini would write one more opera, *Turandot*, first heard a year and a half after his death. Most of the time he was disheartened while he was composing, and felt he would never finish it. Indeed, it was left unfinished, at the culminating point of the final duet. When Toscanini reached that point at the premiere on April 25, 1926, he stopped abruptly, turned to the audience and said, "Here ends the opera left unfinished by the master, for at this point the master died." An ending derived from Puccini's sketches by Franco Alfano is, unfortunately, customarily used in performances; but Alfano's goodwill could not match Puccini's genius.

While he was working on *Turandot*, the composer was bothered by a throat ailment, which was eventually diagnosed as cancer. (He smoked constantly.) In 1924 he underwent an operation in Brussels. Though doctors were optimistic, Puccini had a fatal heart attack the day after the operation. News of Puccini's unexpected death reached Rome during a performance of *La Bohème*. All action was immediately stopped. After the announcement, the audience stood weeping while the orchestra played Chopin's Funeral March.

With Puccini's death, the world of opera as a living popular art form ended. Certainly, after him great operas have been written, but they are often too complex for wide appeal. Perhaps Puccini said it all late in life: "Melody is no longer produced, or if it is it's vulgar. People believe the symphonic element must rule, and I, instead, believe this is the end of opera. They used to sing."

Since Verdi's death in 1901, Puccini (who claimed he could never rival his mighty compatriot) had worn with honor the mantle of chief practitioner of Italian opera. He was not unaware of his limitations—and considered himself to be a mere mandolin player when compared to Wagner. Puccini was content to write works filled with heartfelt emotion, with characters one could easily imagine. He possessed a perfect instinct for theatrical action and for the exact musical coloration of each situation. Always self-critical, he was relentless on his librettists, too, and would not tolerate one boring moment. Indeed, Puccini at his greatest seems to have had an inexorable rightness in whatever he did. While seeing and hearing *La Bohème*, it is difficult to imagine a more perfect opera. Doubtless there is too much of a family resemblance among his operas, but even at his most sentimental, Puccini is never embarrassing. He has taste, refinement, a golden fund of rapturous melody, a magnificent feeling for the voice, and an infallible sense of his orchestra, which he used at times with extraordinary finesse. For those who love the lyric theater and wonderful stories, Puccini is irresistible. His universal popularity continues unabated—as the receipts of international opera houses have shown for over a century.

La Bohème (1894–95)

Puccini's masterpiece is as forever young as the concept of bohemian life. Puccini was intrigued, as many thousands had been, by Murger's 1848 novel *Scènes de la vie de Bohème*, describing the gaiety, aspirations, and woes of life in Paris's Latin Quarter. Puccini hit his stride with *Bohème*'s intimate appeal. His characters are unforgettable. Arias such as "Che gelida manina" and "Mi chiamano Mimi," the duet "O soave fanciulla," and Musetta's bewitching waltz, "Quando m'en vo'soletta per la via," are deeply moving. In *Bohème*, Puccini touched gently, with heartbreaking tenderness, the transience of life and art. The composer wept when he wrote Mimi's death scene—as does the audience upon hearing it. The vocal writing is so graceful and smoothly wrought that it seems to flow from the voice as easily as talking itself.

de los Angeles, Björling, Merrill, Amara, RCA Victor Symphony Orchestra and Chorus, Beecham: EMI Classics CDCB 47235

Ricciarelli, Putnam, Carreras, Wixell, Royal Opera House, C. Davis: Philips 416492-2

Tebaldi, d'Angelo, Bergonzi, Bastianini, Siepi, Santa Cecilia Academy Orchestra and Chorus, Serafin: London 425534-2

Tosca (1898–1900)

In *Bohème*, Puccini wrote of youth's innocence and idealism. In *Tosca*, without sacrificing his lyric gift, he turned his pen to harsh reality, in a plot wracked by conflict, hatred, and the destruction of love, assaulting our moral sense. So tensely dramatic is the music that he has us in his powerful grip from the opening three bars—the shattering triple *fortissimo* announcing the arrival of the dreaded chief of police, Sarpia—until Tosca's suicide. The opera never fails to thrill the nerves. The atmosphere at the premiere was as tense as the drama itself. The orchestra had only begun when it was silenced by shouting, as people were desperate to hear it, ticket or no. To make things more exciting, Puccini's detractors had written threats to the management, including a bomb scare. The premiere was overwhelming, arias and duets were encored, and Puccini was called to the stage over and over. The great soprano aria "Vissi d'arte" is heard in the second act. Once, when the celebrated soprano Maria Jeritza, the composer's favorite Tosca, fell while singing the aria, she remained on the floor. Puccini was delighted, telling her, "Never do it any other way. It was from God!" From that moment, a tradition began. The opera is replete with famous arias and includes the effective *Te Deum* in the church service, the first act's "Recondita armonia," and Cavaradossi's farewell to Tosca, "E lucevan le stelle."

Callas, di Stefano, Gobbi, La Scala Orchestra and Chorus, de Sabata: EMI Classics CDCB 47174
Freni, Domingo, Ramey, Philharmonia Orchestra and Royal Opera House Chorus, Sinopoli: Deutsche Grammophon 431775-2

Madama Butterfly (1904)

As he was prone to do when embarking on an opera, Puccini did much research. In the case of *Butterfly*, he studied Japanese folk songs. He infused his score with exoticism, especially new sounds using pentatonic scale patterns. In the opening stages of his work, he wrote, "I have had a visit today from Mme. Ohyama, wife of the Japanese ambassador. She told me a great many interesting things and sang some native songs to me. She has promised to send me some native Japanese music. I sketched the story of the libretto for her, and she liked it, especially as just such a story as Butterfly's is known to her as having happened in real life."

Puccini's dear heroine, the one he loved most, is the prototype of innocence and vulnerability. She gives her life, in spite of warnings, to a cad who has played with her emotions. The terrible result is hara-kiri. In *Butterfly* we experience the acme of Puccini's crooning, delirious, and voluptuous lyricism. The aria "Un bel dì, vedremo" is the most famous piece. The passionate "Viene la sera" (their duet after their marriage), "Amore o grillo," "Tutti i fior" (the Flower Duet), "Addio, fiorito asil," and "Tu, tu, piccolo iddio" cast a spell over the theater.

Callas, Danieli, Gedda, La Scala Orchestra and Chorus, Karajan: EMI Classics CDCB 47959

Tebaldi, Bergonzi, Cossotto, Santa Cecilia Academy Orchestra and Chorus, Serafin: London 425531-2

OTHER PRINCIPAL WORKS

OPERAS

Manon Lescaut (1890–92)*
La Fanciulla del West (1910)
La Rondine (1917)*
Il Trittico, consisting of:
  Il Tabarro (1918)
  Suor Angelica (1918)
  Gianni Schicchi (1918)*
Turandot (1921–24)*

HUGO WOLF

b. Windischgraz, Styria, March 13, 1860

d. Vienna, February 22, 1903

There's something gruesome about the intimate fusion of poetry and music, in which, actually, the gruesome role belongs only to the latter. Music has decidedly something of the vampire about it. It claws its victim relentlessly and sucks the last drop of blood from it.

Windischgraz was a small town of mostly Germanic culture in a Slovene region of the Austrian Empire. Philipp Wolf, the composer's father, was by trade in the leather business, but in every spare moment he pursued his passion for music. He had learned several musical instruments and passed this knowledge to his son. His mother, Katharina, was practical and had little patience with the artistic aspects of the household. Hugo was the fourth of eight children and showed precocious talent. At school he did fairly well, but he knew music would be his vocation. Unfortunately, Philipp was unhappy about this choice, as he felt his son would literally starve. But Hugo was undaunted, and when he began studying the symphonies of Haydn and Beethoven in arrangements for duets, a new world opened for him. At fifteen he wrote a tentative piano sonata, which he dedicated to his father. Philipp finally realized that he could not convince his son to become anything other than a musician, and he took advantage of an offer of help from a benevolent aunt in Vienna. Hugo was allowed to enter the renowned Vienna Conservatory.

Vienna was the city of his dreams and he swallowed up the great cultural opportunities of the capital. For a time he lived in a garret with the equally impoverished Gustav Mahler. Like Mahler and most of the other young musicians in Vienna, Wolf was ecstatic about the operas of Wagner. A chance meeting with Wagner confirmed his hero worship; anyone anti-Wagner was in for a tongue-lashing. Wolf was nothing if not intense. When the master of music-drama died in 1883, the twenty-three-year-old Wolf sobbed, "I can hardly believe that the man who changed us lumps of clay into human beings is dead."

Upset with the pedanticism at the Conservatory, Wolf told its powerful director, Josef Hellmesberger, that he forgot more than he remembered from his teachers. Not long afterward, the headstrong youth was expelled, thus ending his formal education. He spent the rest of his teen years teaching a few students and borrowing money from good friends who believed in him. He composed songs to the poetry of Nikolaus Lenau, Adalbert von Chamisso, and especially Heine. Most of them were imitations of Schubert and Schumann. At age eighteen he was taken to one of Vienna's brothels, where he contracted syphilis (which would eventually destroy him). Two years later, he completed his nearly hour-long String Quartet in D Minor (1880), which throbs with intensity. Indeed, no more powerful string quartet has ever come from the pen of a twenty-year-old.

On his twentieth birthday, Wolf was rejected for compulsory military service because of his poor physical development. In the early 1880s, he worked on his symphonic poem *Penthesilea*, inspired by Heinrich von Kleist's poetic drama. These years were racked by poverty and a great deal of mental suffering. Wolf had no patience and little practical aptitude. Fortunately, in 1884, he obtained through a friend a post as music critic for the Vienna *Salonblatt*. For three years, he received a small salary for hurling invective and vitriol at his musical enemies while championing Wagner, Liszt, Berlioz, Bruckner, and others whom he considered worthy.

Wolf despised Brahms with as much passion as he loved Wagner. Of the Brahms D minor piano concerto, Wolf wrote, "One could catch a cold from it. Unhealthy stuff!" In the Fourth Symphony, he claimed, "the art of composing without ideas has decidedly found in Brahms its worthiest representative." And of the Violin Concerto, he reported, "Conspicuous is the crab-like progress in Brahms's output."

Perhaps his mistreatment of Brahms had some personal motivation. As an adolescent, Wolf had sent Brahms a song for criticism, asking him to mark a cross in the score where he thought it poor. Returning the song, Brahms (who was seldom diplomatic) commented, "I don't want to make a cemetery of your composition." Wolf also reported that Brahms told him, "You must first learn something and then we shall see if you have talent."

In 1886 the conductor Hans Richter gave *Penthesilea* a "sight-reading" rehearsal with the Vienna Philharmonic. After the performance, Richter, speaking loudly enough for Wolf to hear, exclaimed, "Gentlemen, I should not have let the piece be played to the end, but I wanted to see for myself the man who dares to write in such a way about Meister Brahms." Henry Pleasants, who translated some of Wolf's music criticism, felt that "Wolf was his own man not only in what he said, but in the way he said it. To read him is to know him." But knowing him reveals a man precariously balanced. In 1881, Wolf became involved with Melanie Köchert, a married woman with three children who developed a dedicated love for the composer, although she remained with her family.

The publication in 1888 of a dozen early songs seemed to be a catharsis. Quite suddenly Wolf, who had always been a sporadic composer, was spurred to action. He was exhilarated by reading Eduard Mörike, a poet of extreme sensitivity, and began composing settings for Mörike's poems. In a three-month blitz beginning in February 1888, he wrote forty-three of the *Mörike-Lieder*. Astonished at his own creative outpouring, he often wept while composing, asking, "Am I one who has been called—Am I really one of the elect?" In the autumn of 1888, he was setting poems by Josef Eichendorff, and in the winter, poems by Goethe.

The outburst continued into 1889, with a new song almost daily and sometimes even two. Describing one of these new songs to a friend, he wrote, "It would lacerate the nervous system of a block of marble." The next day, after composing another, he cried that it "is a million times better, when you have heard this song you can have only one wish—to die!" In just over a year, Wolf was transformed from a promising young composer into a master.

In the spring of 1889, inspiration eluded him. But the composing fever began again in late October, when he started work on the *Spanisches Liederbuch* (*Spanish Songbook*), a group of forty-four sixteenth- and seventeenth-century Spanish poems translated into German by Paul Heyse and Emmanuel Geibel. About this new burst of creativity, he wrote, "I work at a thousand horsepower. . . . I now write for posterity. They are masterpieces. There has been nothing like them since Schubert and Schumann." By April 1890 he had finished the entire set. After a few months of rest, he turned his magical force to Heyse's German translations of various Italian poems, composing the *Italienisches Liederbuch* (*Italian Songbook*). Their composition went more slowly—the first part of the projected series took a little more than a year to finish (until December 1891).

Wolf planned to move on to the second part of the *Italian Songbook*, but suddenly his muse vanished. After four years of periodic but feverish creation, during which he had composed more than two hundred songs, he was "dry."

He wanted to die. "Pray for my poor soul," he told a friend. By the summer of 1893, he was desperate. "I could just as soon begin suddenly to speak Chinese as compose anything at all. What I suffer from not composing I cannot even tell you. I should like to hang myself." The author Romain Rolland wrote, "One may imagine the tortures that this solitary man suffered. His only happiness was in creation, and he saw his life cease without any cause for years at a time, and his genius come and go, and return for an instant, but then go again. Each time he must have wondered anxiously if it had gone forever, or how long it would be before it came back again."

In this period, Wolf lived off the bounty of a group of faithful friends, as well as the loving care that Melanie Köchert somehow managed to give him at all times. But after a decade with Melanie, Wolf fell in love with the soprano Frieda Zerny, who admired his songs, and who he felt would rekindle his dormant creative power. He now loved two women. With this new complication in his life, and not wanting to continue to inflict pain on Melanie, he contemplated leaving for America and began to learn English. "We therefore decided to go to America," he wrote, "to the land of gold, to lay the foundation of a decent existence on a safe basis of dollars." The affair with Frieda fizzled out after three years, and Wolf was again occupied with composing.

Wolf longed to write an opera and was stimulated by and jealous of the success of his friend Engelbert Humperdinck's enchanting *Hänsel und Gretel* in the winter of 1894. He finished *Der Corregidor*, a comedy, in only a year. At Mannheim in June 1896, *Der Corregidor* had a modest success, and the opera, though uneven in quality, is still occasionally staged. Meanwhile, in another surge of composing, from March 25 until April 30, 1896, he had composed the remaining twenty-four songs of the *Italian Songbook*.

Wolf's malady was now progressing into its dangerous stage, and his behavior became erratic and strange. In March 1897 he set a few of Michelangelo's poems to music; they would be his last works. In June he attempted to learn to ride a bicycle but could not stay balanced—a warning that all was not right with his nervous system. By September he had begun to lose his reason. Mahler, whom he had not seen in twenty years, was by then director of the Vienna Court Opera. He showed an interest in mounting *Der Corregidor* but eventually told Wolf that he would not do it. Wolf snapped into insanity, telling everybody he encountered that Mahler was fired and that he was the new director of the opera. In the autumn of 1897, he was taken to an asylum. He now told everyone that he was the head of the asylum. Ironically, there were signs in the musical world of growing recognition of his work. A Hugo Wolf Society was formed in Berlin, and singers everywhere were taking serious notice of his songs. On his thirty-eighth birthday, he received many congratulations and telegrams from various places in Europe. But for him it was too late. His final four and a half years were spent trapped in a blank mind. His eyesight got worse, as did his ability to speak. Occasionally he would howl, "If only I was Hugo Wolf." Throughout this sad period, Melanie Köchert visited three times each week to attend to him. In February 1903 he caught a cold, which moved into his lungs. After violent convulsions, death claimed him at age forty-three. He was buried in Vienna's Central Cemetery, in a plot near Franz Schubert's, whose spiritual heir he truly was.

During his life, Wolf hardly earned a penny from his work. Shortly after his death, the publisher Peters offered his family 260,000 marks for the copyright of his works. But without the brilliant man she had so deeply loved, the faithful Melanie found life meaningless and in 1906 committed suicide.

The high tide of Wolf's creative life had lasted from 1888 to 1897, and the majority of his songs were composed in less than two years. These songs compressed many elements of late-nineteenth-century Romanticism. In a sense, he challenged the boundaries of the *Lieder* of Schubert and Schumann, even of the art of song itself, packing his forms with the aesthetic of Wagnerian music-drama, maintaining a balance of words and music.

Wolf's range of flickering moods and emotional depths is vast. In hymns such as "Um Mitternacht" (Around Midnight) and "Fussreise" (Journey on Foot), his worship of nature brings every particle into perfect focus. His biographer Frank Walker wrote, "There was something elemental about Wolf in his relation to nature, something that made him quiveringly sensitive to her moods . . . always he was absorbing impressions that were later to be reflected in his music. All the wonderful evocations of the open air in the *Mörike-Leider*, the floating clouds, the glowing evening sunlight, the stream murmuring into the night, the music of the birds and bees, the delicate fluttering of a butterfly's wings—are drawn from nature herself and on hearing or singing that last ecstatic cry in *Auf einer Wanderung*, we experience again what Wolf himself must once so intensely have felt, on some blissful evening in his own dear Austrian countryside."

Wolf's songs may often sing of isolation, melancholy, stark tragedy—and in the *Spanish Songbook*, of fearful religious experience. But he also wrote songs of impassioned love, of high and low comedy, of serenity and light-headed happiness, while those that are set to the poems of Eichendorff are filled with an especially delightful variety of characters. The critic Arnold Whittall wrote, "He seems to embody in concentrated form all that is most anguished and self-aware in the Romantic artist—the isolation, the self-doubt, the need to exploit the resources of music to extract maximum intensity from them that is consistent with the preservation of ultimate harmonic coherence. These songs are among the greatest monuments of musical Romanticism."

Lieder

Wolf came at the end of a magnificent century of German *Lieder*: the German art song had reaped an unrivaled harvest from Weber, Schubert, Carl Loewe, Mendelssohn, Schumann, Robert Franz, Adolf Jensen, Liszt, Brahms, and Richard Strauss. The burden of this tradition lay heavily on Wolf, but he was equal to the challenge. He possessed a magnificent sense of the German language, which he dearly loved, and a feeling for characterization so acute that his *Lieder* have been called "psychological songs." In fact they are miniature music-dramas, with the fulsome piano part equal to and at times more important than the vocal line. Although Wolf had been attracted by large forms, instinctively he knew that he was basically a song composer. He needed the poem in order to focus. Like van Gogh, who checked and sublimated his madness in frightening landscapes, Wolf dissolved into a poem's essence, obliterating his own lacerated personality. It was a perilous journey. But as long as German is sung, Hugo Wolf's songs will still be heard.

Spanisches Liederbuch (1889–90)

COMPLETE

Schwarzkopf, Fischer-Dieskau, Moore: Deutsche Grammophon 423934-2

SIXTEEN SONGS

DeGaetani, Kalish: Elektra/Nonesuch 79263-2

Italienisches Liederbuch (1890–91 and 1896)

COMPLETE

Ameling, Krause, Gage: Globe GL 02-5008
Schwarzkopf, Fischer-Dieskau, Moore: EMI CDM 76732-2

Various *Lieder*

Schwarzkopf, Moore: EMI Classics CDC 64905
Kipnis: Music & Arts CD661-2

Italian Serenade (1887)

Wolf found sustained creative work difficult and left many works incomplete. He often composed in a blistering heat of inspiration, as with his *Italian Serenade*, which he created May 2–4, 1887. It was originally prepared as an eight-minute-long movement for a string quartet. Later he sketched out two other in-complete movements, and in 1892 he adapted the score for string orchestra. Both versions are a delight: brightly hued colors of musical levity are mitigated by the occasional solemn moment. The score is infused with light, jocular wit, and a hint of mock melodrama. Throughout we hear Wolf celebrating simple pleasures.

FOR STRING QUARTET
Kolisch String Quartet: Archipon ARC 108

FOR STRING ORCHESTRA
Orpheus Chamber Orchestra: Deutsche Grammophon 431 680-2

OTHER PRINCIPAL WORKS

CHAMBER MUSIC
Quartet in D Minor for Strings (1880)*

OPERA
Der Corregidor (1895)*

ORCHESTRAL WORK
Penthesilea (symphonic poem) (1883–85)

GUSTAV MAHLER

b. Kalište, Bohemia, July 7, 1860

d. Vienna, May 18, 1911

Oh, how lovely it is to live! And only now do I know what it is! Pain has lost its power and death its thorn. Tristan speaks the truth: I am immortal, for how could Tristan's love die?

Mahler was the second of fourteen children born to Jewish parents—Bernhard, a shopkeeper, and Marie. Five of his siblings died in infancy, one at thirteen, and another committed suicide at twenty-five. It was an unhappy childhood, and as an adult, Gustav recalled that his parents "were ill matched as fire and water. He was obstinacy. She was all meekness." Gustav's only solace was music. "From my fourth year on I have always made music. I was composing before I could play scales." A few months after Gustav's birth the family moved to Iglau, a town in Moravia that still had the look of the Middle Ages. There was a military post nearby, where Mahler imbibed the music of the parade ground. Late in life, the composer and some friends were listening on a hilltop to a maze of different sounds coming from several directions: carnival music, military brass bands, organ grinders, and folk singing. "This is polyphony," he exclaimed. "In my earliest childhood in the woods of Iglau I was moved by these sounds and committed them to memory."

It was at the Iglau Municipal Theater that ten-year-old Gustav made his formal debut as a pianist. Immediately afterward he was sent to Prague, where he hoped to receive better training, but the boy did not fare well away from home and returned in 1872. At fifteen he went to Vienna to study at the Conservatory. Julius Epstein, his piano teacher, encouraged him in both piano playing and composition. Another Conservatory faculty member was Anton Bruckner. Although Mahler never formally studied with Bruckner, he found Bruckner's company inspiring and could call himself a Bruckner pupil by spiritual assimilation.

After receiving his diploma from the Conservatory in 1878, the near-destitute Mahler did much-resented hackwork and gave piano lessons to earn a precarious income. Somehow, he also managed to take courses in philosophy at the University of Vienna. At twenty he completed his first important work, a cantata, *Das klagende Lied* (1880). At the Conservatory, it had been clear that he possessed the special qualities of a conductor. In 1881 he was engaged at the opera house in Laibach (present-day Ljubljana), and for the rest of his life, conducting operas and, to a lesser degree, symphony concerts would take up the majority of his time and energy. Although conducting was a necessity to him, financially and emotionally, he complained relentlessly that it took him from his important work of composing.

After Laibach, he moved on to more important posts in Prague (1885–86) and Leipzig (1886–88). In Leipzig, he often came into conflict with the chief conductor, the redoubtable Arthur Nikisch. But he proved to be an indefatigable worker, as demanding on his singers and players as he was on himself. Often arrogant, impatient, irritating, and provocative, he made and kept enemies easily. But he was ethical, could be fiercely loyal, and burned with holy zeal for art as the only road to salvation.

Another important position followed in Budapest (1888–91). In his next post, at Hamburg (1891–97), Mahler consolidated his position as the greatest opera conductor of his time. In 1892 Tchaikovsky came to Hamburg to conduct the German premiere of *Eugene Onegin*. At the rehearsal, he saw Mahler's splendid preparation and production and begged Mahler to conduct for him. Tchaikovsky wrote, "The conductor here is not of the usual kind, but a man of genius." Everywhere Mahler's conducting was admired by conductors and composers alike, from Hans von Bülow to Brahms. But even with all the energy he devoted to conducting, Mahler had hardly neglected composing. He had completed his first masterpiece in 1885, the song cycle *Lieder eines fahrenden Gesellen* (*Songs of a Wayfarer*), followed by the First Symphony in 1888 and the Second in 1894.

During the Hamburg years, the young conductor Bruno Walter first encountered Mahler. "Never before had I seen such an intense person," Walter wrote. "I never dreamed that a terse word, a commanding gesture, and a will directed solely towards a certain goal, could frighten and alarm others and force them into blind obedience." In 1896 Mahler completed the Third Symphony, even larger in scope than the first two. As successful as he was as a conductor, however, his music was generally received with contempt. In 1895 he fell in love with the soprano Anna von Mildenburg. She was the first woman whom Mahler considered to be his intellectual equal, and she greatly inspired him (as he did her). The relationship gradually came to an end, however, probably because of Mahler's difficult and often intractable personality.

In 1897 Mahler took the supreme appointment of his career, as *Kapellmeister* and artistic director at the Vienna Court Opera. It was unthinkable in Vienna for a Jew to command such a prestigious position, and Mahler was forced to convert to Catholicism, the official religion of Franz-Joseph's Austro-Hungarian Empire. Around the time of Mahler's birth, Jews had been given more liberal civil rights, and they had flocked to Vienna from throughout the Empire in search of education and a better life. But that didn't mean that the Viennese accepted them, and most Jews there lived an uneasy, if profitable, existence. The American writer Paul Rosenfeld wrote, "To be born a Jew, particularly in the Austria of the 1860's, was not intensely conducive to the sustainment of that fresh faith in life, that relaxed love of men, from which great song springs. . . . And then, the atmosphere of the Jewish community itself does not make free, healthy living easy. Generation had bequeathed to generation . . . [a] legacy of centuries of uncertain, difficult existence."

Hence for Mahler, an immense sense of anxiety permeated his music and his life. He was as uncomfortable with his Jewishness as he was with everything else. He often said, "I am thrice homeless: as a native of Bohemia in Austria, as an Austrian among Germans, and as a Jew throughout all the world." Only on the conductor's podium did he feel alive and secure.

Mahler had total control of every detail in the opera house, from the hiring of performers, crew, and staff to opera production and direction. No detail was too insignificant for his consideration. After a few years, the opera's enormous deficit became a profit. The Vienna Court Opera shone as never before or since. The conductor Otto Klemperer said, "When he conducted you felt it could not be better and it could not be otherwise. . . . Toscanini was the greatest conductor of his generation, but Mahler was a hundred times greater." Mahler often said, "What is best in music is not to be found in the notes."

Yet through it all, Mahler's symphonies continued to appear with regularity. No. 4 was completed in 1901 and No. 5 in 1902, the year Mahler married the beautiful and intelligent twenty-three-year-old Alma Schindler. Alma was the daughter of a painter and had been surrounded from childhood by artists. She was a composer in her own right. The couple had two daughters, whom he adored. Through his wife, Mahler became friendly with many of Vienna's most progressive artists, such as the stage designer Alfred Roller and the painters Carl Moll and Gustav Klimt. These were busy years, and Mahler's conducting career often took him from Vienna to engagements throughout Europe. His most important work, composing, was possible only in the summertime. During the concert season, he orchestrated and revised constantly.

His music was admired and loved by artists of his own caliber, including the composers Alexander von Zemlinsky, Arnold Schoenberg, Anton Webern, and Alban Berg, and the novelist Thomas Mann, who called Mahler "the man who, as I believe, expresses the art of our time in its profoundest and most sacred form." Few agreed, though, and the many critics who disliked Mahler were usually virulent in their attacks. One Rudolf Louis of the Munich press wrote, "If Mahler's music would speak Yiddish it would be perhaps unintelligible to me. But it is repulsive to me because it *acts* Jewish. This is to say that it speaks musical German, but with an accent. With an inflection, and above all, with the gestures of an Eastern all too Eastern Jew."

In 1901–4, Mahler composed the song cycle *Kindertotenlieder* (*Songs of Dead Children*) to poems of Friedrich Rückert. Even while composing these heartbreaking elegies, he wrote, "I feel sorry for me that I had to write them — and sorry for the world that someday will have to hear them." Mahler's elder daughter, Maria Anna (born in 1902), died of scarlet fever in July 1907. The composer was almost broken by grief. He was deeply superstitious and always believed that in composing the *Kindertotenlieder*, he was responsible for his daughter's death. Around the same time, he was diagnosed with severe heart disease and was told to limit all his activities. This prescription was an impossibility, and with a sense of his own impending death, Mahler worked even harder.

In 1907, after a decade at the Vienna Court Opera during which he had endured jealousy, intrigues, hatred, and vicious attacks from the press, Mahler decided that he had had enough. He resigned on October 15 after a performance of Beethoven's *Fidelio*. The Metropolitan Opera had long hoped for his services, and in December the Mahlers docked in New York. For a brief time the couple yielded to the stimulation of the bustling young city. Mahler admired the Brooklyn Bridge and liked observing the crowds as he walked on Broadway and Fifth Avenue. "The arrival in New York — the harbor and all the sights and scenes and human bustle — so took our breath away that we forgot all our troubles," Alma wrote. "But not for long."

Mahler's duties at the Metropolitan Opera also extended to conducting the New York Philharmonic the following season. This made for a frightful conducting schedule, and at the same time Mahler was revising *Das Lied von der Erde*, which he believed was the most personal music he had written thus far. He was also working on a Ninth Symphony but was terrified that if he completed it, he would be punished for competing with Beethoven. Schubert had died after his Ninth, and the fates had not allowed Bruckner to complete his. Taking stock on his fiftieth birthday, in 1910, he wrote a friend, "It's always difficult to face oneself. Experience is no help at all. Alas, each time it feels as though you have to be introduced to yourself."

Meanwhile, Mahler had become aware that his wife felt neglected and unfulfilled. When he married her, the despotic composer had made her promise not to continue her own composing. Now in the summer of 1910, fearful of losing her to a younger rival, he sought help. On a visit to Leiden, in the Netherlands, Mahler had a three-hour consultation with Sigmund Freud. Freud relieved him by saying that one of the many reasons his wife was attracted to him was that he was older. That evening, Mahler wrote a poem:

> Night shades were dispelled by one powerful word,
> the tireless threat of torment ended.
> At last united in one single chord,
> my timid thoughts and my tempestuous feelings blended.

Although they met only once, Freud wrote years later, "I'd had plenty of opportunity to admire the capability for psychological understanding of this man of genius." The historian Frederic V. Grunfeld feels, "No composer before or since has ever expressed himself more movingly in what Freud calls 'the struggle between Eros and Death, between the instincts of life and the instincts of destruction,' as it works itself out in the human species."

But Mahler's health was failing. Early in 1911, back in New York for a sixty-five-concert season, he collapsed. A streptococcus infection set in, and he and Alma sailed to Paris for treatment. The doctors said it was incurable. Mahler wanted to die in Vienna and was taken back to the city he loved and hated, a city itself on the brink of death, preparing to pass into legend. Mahler died on May 18, 1911, at age fifty-one. The last word he muttered was "Mozart." The gravestone at Vienna's Grinzing Cemetery simply reads: GUSTAV MAHLER. Near the end of his life, Mahler was asked why he had wished nothing on his tombstone but his name, and he answered, "Those who seek me know who I was, and the others do not need to know."

Mahler's life was an endless questioning and questing for truths and meanings. At his most depressed, he could write, "The most consuming yearning for death dominates my heart . . . when the abominable tyranny of our modern hypocrisy has driven me to the point of dishonoring myself, when the inextricable web of conditions in art and life has filled my heart with disgust for all that is sacred to me—art, love, religion—what way out is there but self-annihilation." For a man and an artist who was so often miserable and felt that the lucky ones were deaf and blind, it is amazing that his heart did not burst earlier. Yet his burning spirit was at work almost until his final hour.

Mahler was haunted his whole life by Beethoven's Ninth Symphony and Wagner's *Tristan und Isolde*; for him, greatness meant monumentality. From Bruckner he took his huge dimensions, but he made the symphony ever more flexible and pliable. "To write a symphony is, for me, to construct a world," Mahler declared. He turned the symphony into a human drama, melding the human voice when necessary into a dense polyphonic tapestry, projecting a landscape that is incredibly graphic and ambiguous at the same time. His apocalyptic vision was the last gasp of tonalism. The composer and writer Wilfrid Mellers wrote, "The weeping appoggiaturas of the final pages of Mahler's *Das Lied* imply that the surrender of harmonic consciousness is reluctant; we weep for the self unfulfilled and the world lost, and can find in Mahler . . . a musical synonym for our own alienation and uprootedness." Mahler wrote some of the final and most poignant chapters of the Romantic agony.

After his premature death, music changed radically, and the differing Modernism of Debussy, Schoenberg, Scriabin, Berg, Busoni, Stravinsky, and others inevitably took new directions. Mahler's music was upheld by a few passionately staunch conductors, such as Bruno Walter, Otto Klemperer, and Willem Mengelberg, but performances were rare. His many detractors cited Mahler as tiresomely long-winded, trivial, and vulgar—purple oceans of unbearable, stupefying nostalgia born of unrelenting self-pity. They missed the point. Mahler, in his ninety-minute diatribes on the human condition, attempted to reflect in music everything possible. "Only when I experience intensely do I compose," he once wrote; and "only when I compose do I experience intensely." In this sense, he is the most magnificent failure in all of music. His music opened disturbing, uncharted regions of repressed feelings. Mahler (who often said, "My time will come") has triumphed. A new generation, armed with the long-playing recording, rediscovered Mahler, and in him new conductors found a literature of glory. The young especially, doused in despair, responded passionately to the maelstrom of his deadly military marches, fraught with decay and gore, pain, joy, and ecstasy.

Mahler's music seems to encompass the total range of human emotions. For countless numbers of people, it has become their Bible of sounded emotion. They feel Mahler's elation, rejection, panic, terror, sentimentality, and drunkenness as their own. In short, the music expresses dozens of sensations so pointedly that the true Mahlerite surrenders himself completely, becoming, it seems, at one with the composer's inner world.

Symphony no. 1 in D Major (*Titan*) (1883–88)

Mahler's extraordinary ability to organize his material into large integrated units is quite apparent in this, his most easily digested symphony. The First Symphony is sometimes called the *Titan*, from the inspiration Mahler received from Jean Paul Richter's 1803 novel of the same name. Mahler conducted the world premiere with the Budapest Philharmonic Orchestra on November 20, 1889. He was disappointed with its reception and told the violinist Natalie Bauer-Lechner, "In Pest, where I performed it for the first time, my friends bashfully avoided me afterward; nobody dared talk to me about the performance and my work, and I went around like a sick person or an outcast." The hypersensitive composer locked it away for three years. The first movement begins with a springlike awakening introduction, impressionistic in atmosphere. The whole movement is full of nature, including cuckoo calls. The second movement is a Scherzo; as usual, it is a complex movement, a dance scene in the countryside. Mahler's originality emerges in the extraordinary third movement, where he turns the simple canon "Frère Jacques" into a grotesque funeral march. There is distress and irony in the music. Perhaps the presence of the tragic and the trivial side by side was what disturbed Mahler's audiences, who wished to listen comfortably to traditional forms. Never had they heard such bizarre orchestration, and the constant touches of the grotesque irritated many. Of the third movement, the Austrian musicologist Erwin Stein writes, "He introduces elements of irony and self-persiflage whose pungency makes Berlioz's Witches' Sabbath from the *Fantastic Symphony* sound mild in comparison." Mahler's creative struggle moves inexorably forward throughout the score, culminating mightily in the fourth movement, the finale. (In fact, all of Mahler's symphonies find their complete fulfillment only in the finale.) The music is storm-filled, and the victorious ending stems from the symphony's opening.

Symphony no. 2 in C Minor (*Resurrection*) (1887–94)

The Second Symphony is known as the *Resurrection* Symphony. Mahler told Richard Strauss, "My new work in relation to the one you know (No. 1) is like a man to a newborn baby." The first movement, although very large and thematically complex, is a magnificently balanced sonata form. Mahler called it *Todtenfeier* (funeral rite), and it is a picture of doomsday—the composer was obsessed with death. The theme, as is often true in Mahler, is so long that he had no choice but to compose lengthy movements. The second-movement Andante is lyrically pastoral. The third movement, Scherzo, is made up of Mahlerian satire and humor, with moments of bitter nostalgia. The English critic Michael Kennedy observes, "For the Fourth movement a voice leads the soul to God and in the colossal finale there are the Day of Judgement, resurrection and love. Death and transfiguration, in other words. . . . It's like a resurrection scene painted by Breughel." The huge movement is full of fatal stirrings and portentous effects. The last section of the finale, in Kennedy's words, is "punctuated by distant fanfares and mysterious bird-calls [and] culminates in the magical soft entry of the chorus singing Klopstock's hymn 'Resurrection.'" Mahler himself wrote about this movement, "Why have you lived? Why have you suffered? Has it all been only a huge, frightful joke? We must all somehow answer these questions, if we are to continue living, yes, even if we are only to continue dying. Whoever hears this call must give a reply. And this reply I give in my last movement." Mahler was an artist with a conscious mission. As his biographer Kurt Blaukopf wrote, "He was obsessed by the idea that his compositions were in the truest sense indestructible. Nor was he afraid to assert that art and humanity would be the poorer without his C minor Symphony."

In the first performance, on March 4, 1895, Richard Strauss conducted only three movements with the Berlin Philharmonic Orchestra. The audience was enthusiastic—Mahler, who attended the performance, took five curtain calls after the Scherzo—but the press was hostile. Mahler himself gave the first complete performance in Berlin on December 13, 1895. The conductors Arthur Nikisch, Felix Weingartner, and Bruno Walter were in the audience, and each was deeply shaken.

Symphony no. 3 in D Minor (1895–96)

Mahler called this symphony his "monster." The hour-and-a-half creation is twice as long as Schubert's Ninth Symphony, longer than Beethoven's Ninth, and even reaches beyond the scale of Bruckner's Eighth. It is in six movements, and Mahler was convinced while he was writing it that the composition was taking on a life of its own, totally controlling his heart, mind, and hand. At the time, Mahler was deeply romantically involved with the soprano Anna von Mildenburg, who had complained that he was not writing to her often enough. Mahler's reply is a remarkable description of his creative life:

But I have surely written you that I am at work on a large composition. You cannot believe how this claims one's entire being, and how one is often so deep in it that for the outer world one is as if dead. Try to conceive a work so vast that in it the entire world is mirrored—one is, so to speak, only an instrument on which the whole universe plays. . . . In such moments I no longer belong to myself. . . . These are fearful birth pains, the creation of such works suffers, and before all this organizes itself, builds itself up, and ferments in his brain, it must be preceded by much preoccupation, engrossment with self, a being dead to the outer world. My symphony will be something the world has not yet heard! In it all nature becomes a voice and reveals profound mysteries as one has perhaps surmised only in dreams.

When the work was completed, Bruno Walter was the first to hear it. Mahler played the entire symphony for him on the piano in his summer cottage in Corinthia. Walter would later recall, "The force and novelty of the musical language fairly stunned me, and I was overwhelmed to feel in his playing the same creative fervor and exaltation which had given birth to the work itself. His entire being seemed to breathe a mysterious affinity with nature." The first movement, magnificent in its size, is so ripe with life that its energy overflows; Mahler describes a force of nature. The movement, half the length of the entire symphony, is Mahler's conception of the symphony as an image of the world. He told Anna von Mildenburg, "I could also name the second movement . . . What God tells me." The second movement is a five-part structure of much refinement and charm, reflecting the hum of nature in the summer. A Scherzo follows, then two ingenious vocal movements, the first a sublime piece for contralto singing based on Nietzsche's "Zarathustra's Midnight Song," and the second a happy combination of a boys' and women's chorus. The finale, a deeply felt Adagio, concludes with a variety of lovely thematic material.

Symphony no. 4 in G Major (1899–1901)

Mahler's Fourth is the most shimmering and lyrical of his symphonic incantations. Only around forty-five minutes long, and written for an orchestra of "normal" size, it appears as a resting place before the onslaught of Mahler's remaining work. In the atmospheric Fourth, everything is floating and unburdened. The first movement is relaxed; its opening is a melody jingling in the breeze. Mahler can make a melody seem happy and sad all at once, and here the textures (for him) are light. It is paradoxical music—Bruno Walter called it "of a strangely exalted gaiety." The second movement is a Scherzo, with the violins playing a ghostly and spooky passage showing Mahler's macabre imagery. The Adagio, the third movement, is basically intimate in nature, which is the perfect foil for the soprano soloist in the exquisitely radiant finale. Here Mahler used a text from his beloved *Des Knaben Wunderhorn* (*The*

Youth's Magic Horn, an anthology of German folk poetry), which begins, "All heavenly joys are ours, pleasure of earth we disdain. No worldly strife mars our heavenly life, we live here in sweetest peace." The world premiere took place in Munich on November 28, 1901, with Mahler on the podium, yet even this relatively accessible score received hisses from the audience and bile from the press. Even Alma was not thrilled with it, and Mahler told her, "It is all humorous, 'naïve,' etc., it represents the part of my life that is still the hardest for you to accept and which in the future only extremely few will comprehend." But by 1910, when he conducted it twice in New York, her attitude toward the work had changed to love.

Symphony no. 5 in C-sharp Minor (1901–2)

It was in Cologne on October 18, 1904, that Mahler conducted his Fifth Symphony, known as the *Giant*. Here he returned to purely orchestral forces, with a formal scheme so unusual that it amounts to a new viewpoint on sonata structure. It is in three parts. Part I contains a funereal first movement; its keynote is grief and it proceeds in sheer desperation. The second movement opens with a march and is marked "turbulently rough with great vehemence." The critic Paul Bekker called this movement "a piece of such eruptive strength of passion and intensification of content that one has to count it among the greatest achievements in symphonic art." In Part II of this frightening drama, the third movement, a Scherzo, achieves pure joy in its dancelike momentum. Mahler said, "There is nothing romantic or mystical in it, only an expression of extraordinary strength. It is mankind in the full brightness of day, at the zenith of life." Part III follows, with the celebrated, yearning Adagietto for harp and strings, which was used with telling effect in Luchino Visconti's 1970 film *Morte à Venezia* (*Death in Venice*). Mahler sent it to Alma as a wordless love letter. Richard Strauss wrote to him, "Your fifth symphony again gave me great pleasure, a pleasure only slightly dimmed by the little Adagietto, but as this was what pleased the audience most, you are getting what you deserve." The final movement is a Rondo-sonata movement of uncanny skill, capped off with a quadruple Fugato. It is as if the composer, in all the pride of his mastery, stands chest out and proclaims to the world, "I continually learn from Bach (like a child sitting at his feet) because my way of working is inherently Bach-like."

Writing to Alma on October 16, after a rehearsal, Mahler asked, "What are they to say to this primeval music, this foaming, roaring, raging sea of sound, to these dancing stars, to these breath-taking iridescent and flashing breakers? . . . Oh that I might give my symphony its first performance fifty years after my death!" Mahler's "polyphonic" use of orchestral texture is more complex than ever. The conductor and composer Pierre Boulez has observed, "The more deeply one examines Mahler's work, the denser it becomes. The work acquires this density not by getting thicker but by a multiplicity of lines; polyphony develops through constant and continuous crisscrossing during which the elements attach themselves more and more to a determined theme." In his hands, the orchestra becomes as flexible as a string quartet. While Mahler was composing this work, Debussy was exclaiming that the symphony as a form was no longer valid, especially after Beethoven.

Symphony no. 6 in A Minor (*Tragic*) (1903–5)

The Sixth Symphony, sometimes known as the *Tragic*, is scored for kettledrums, glockenspiel, cowbells, low-pitched bells, bass drum, triangle, snare drum, cymbals, wood blocks, tam-tam, rute, tambourine, whip, hammer, xylophone, two harps, celesta, and huge orchestra. Mahler would probably have been pleased with modern recording technology, for sophisticated stereo reproduction practices are able to bring out clearly the multilayered polyphony of his orchestration, which in many halls can sound blocked or muddied. The A minor symphony, in four movements, was first performed at Essen on May 27, 1906. An extremely tense Mahler felt he gave a poor performance. The *Tragic* is difficult to grasp. Its idiom is enigmatic. Mahler wrote, "My sixth will be asking riddles that can be solved only by a generation that has received and digested my first five." Mahler was never so grim. Many a listener has left the concert hall in dread. Although the symphony is more than eighty minutes long, it moves with inexorable force. The second movement is a horrific Scherzo, demon haunted and eerie. Relief is dispelled in the Andante moderato, but the finale is crushing and alone takes over half an hour to perform. Many hold the Sixth Symphony as Mahler's greatest work.

Symphony no. 7 in E Minor (1904–6)

Mahler first brought his Seventh Symphony to life on September 19, 1908, more than three years after he had completed it. He continued tinkering with the gigantic work up through the dress rehearsal. The Prague audience gave it a cool reception, but Mahler was used to that by now. Once again the symphony is longer than most films, and conductors usually program it alone. Although No. 7 is basically far more Romantic and expansive in nature than

Nos. 5 and 6, it somehow manages an undercurrent of uneasiness, which has kept it the least known of the series. The Mahler scholar Harold Truscott wrote, "The five movements of the seventh are arranged so that the two other ones complement each other, the three middle ones seeming to flow against the main stream. The second and fourth are different types of nocturne, the former not a little like a ghostly army on the march, the latter both sentimental and sarcastic, with the twang of mandolin and guitar. In between them the scherzo slithers like a snake, in opposition not only to the other movements but also to the two nocturnes." The second nocturne, which lasts more than a quarter of an hour, is marked *Andante amoroso.* Tender and alluring, it is a serenade to the beloved, with its transparent orchestration and its sensual message. In the Rondo finale, we move with relief from the boudoir to outdoor revelry.

Symphony no. 8 in E-flat Major (1906–7)

"The Symphony of a Thousand," as it is called, brings Mahler back to solo voice and chorus—three sopranos, two contraltos, tenor, baritone, bass, boys' choir, and two mixed choruses. It is composed in two sections without movements. Part I is based on the ninth-century hymn "Veni, creator spiritus," and Part II on the final scene of Goethe's *Faust,* where the poet interprets immortality and redemption through the love of the eternal feminine (a scene that Mahler thought of as a final fulfillment). He composed it in a fervor of creative ecstasy, feeling it was literally dictated to him. It is the grandest spectacle the concert hall may offer, the Mount Everest of Mahler's exalted aims. In his usual intoxication over his music, he wrote, "I have just completed my Eighth. It is the greatest I have composed. It is so unique in content and form that it does not lend itself to description. These are no longer human voices, but planets and suns that are revolving." No other work of Mahler's, wrote Bruno Walter, "is so saturated with the spirit of fervent affirmation."

The Eighth Symphony is dedicated to Alma and was first performed by Mahler on September 12, 1910, in Munich. A young conductor, Leopold Stokowski, sat awestruck in the audience, vowing to present the score to America, which he did in 1916.

Das Lied von der Erde (1907–9)

Mahler's *Song of the Earth* may be called a symphony in six sections for tenor, contralto, and orchestra. The composer set six Chinese poems from the collection *The Chinese Flute*, translated by Hans Bethge. Here is Mahler at the very summit of his powers. The titles and the words can convey only a morsel of Mahler's message: 1. "The Drinking Song of Earthly Woe," 2. "The Lonely One in Autumn," 3. "Of Youth," 4. "Of Beauty," 5. "The Drunken One in Springtime," 6. "The Farewell." The last is perhaps the most fragile and touching farewell ever penned. Mahler never heard this work performed. His faithful disciple Bruno Walter conducted the world premiere on November 20, 1911.

Baker, King, Royal Concertgebouw Orchestra, Haitink: Philips 432279-2
Miller, Haefliger, New York Philharmonic Orchestra, Walter: CBS MK 42034

Symphony no. 9 in D Minor (1909–10)

No. 9 is a magnificent conclusion to Mahler's symphonic struggles and one of his dearly loved works. It was composed in part in New York, and throughout he was wracked with physical pain, working against the wishes of his doctors and his wife. He completed it on April 1, 1910, thirteen months before his death. Alban Berg, who saw the score shortly before Mahler's death, commented, "The first movement is the most heavenly thing Mahler ever wrote. It is the expression of an exceptional fondness for this earth. The longing to live in peace on it, to enjoy nature to its depths—before death comes. For he comes irresistibly. The whole movement is permeated by premonitions of death." In the second movement, Mahler is captivated by the Austrian countryside, but there is a terrible and slightly gnawing tragic undertone. The third movement, Burleske, is bitter and wild. In the Molto adagio, Mahler bids farewell to life. As with *Das Lied von der Erde*, Mahler never heard his Ninth Symphony performed. Once again, Bruno Walter first conducted it in Vienna in June 1912. With this work, Mahler concluded the great Viennese symphonic tradition. He had forged on heroically, although he believed that "those who are born after such great spirits as Beethoven and Wagner, the epigones, have no easy task. For the harvest is already gathered in, and there remain only a few solitary ears of corn to glean."

In the summer of 1910, Mahler sketched a tenth symphony. In the margins of the score, the dying man wrote, "Have mercy! Oh, Lord, why hast thou forsaken me," and, to his wife, "Almsche, to live for you, to die for you." Mahler completed the bittersweet first movement, Adagio, which is usually performed alone. The English critic and composer Deryck Cooke, with Alma Mahler's permission, re-created from the sketches what he thought Mahler would have written in the four additional movements, but his version is rarely performed. It is extremely unlikely that the fidgety Mahler, a fanatical reviser, would have approved of Cooke's valiant efforts.

Complete Symphonies

New York Philharmonic Orchestra, Vienna Philharmonic Orchestra, Royal Concertgebouw Orchestra, various soloists, choruses, Bernstein: Deutsche Grammophon 435162-2

Bavarian Radio Symphony Orchestra and Chorus, various soloists, Kubelik: Deutsche Grammophon 429042-2

London Philharmonic Orchestra, Tennstedt: EMI Classics ZDMD 64471, ZDMC 64481, and ZDMD 64476

OTHER PRINCIPAL WORKS

CHORUS AND ORCHESTRA WORKS
Das klagende Lied (cantata) (1880; rev. 1892–93)

SONGS AND SONG CYCLES WITH ORCHESTRA
Lieder eines fahrenden Gesellen (song cycle) (1885)*
Lieder und Gesänge aus der Jugendzeit (set of fourteen songs) (1880–90)
Des Knaben Wunderhorn (cycle of twelve songs) (1892–98)*
Kindertotenlieder (cycle of five songs) (1901–4)*
Five songs to poems by Rückert (1901–2)*

ORCHESTRAL MUSIC
Symphony no. 10 in F-sharp Minor (Adagio movement only) (1910)*

FREDERICK
DELIUS

b. Bradford, England, January 29, 1862

d. Grez-sur-Loing, France, June 10, 1934

One can't define form in so many words, but if I was asked, I should say that it is nothing more than imparting spiritual unity to one's thoughts.

Delius was the fourth of fourteen children. As a child, the musically gifted and sickly Delius took piano and violin lessons, but his father, a prosperous wool merchant, expected him to take charge of the family business. Frederick dutifully did his father's bidding but was hopeless as a businessman. He longed for adventure and far-off lands, and when he was twenty-two, his father gave up on his son's ever succeeding in the wool business and bought him a 120-acre orange plantation in Solano Grove, Florida. Neither parent showed any interest in the arts, and even after their son had acquired some renown, they never heard a note of his music.

In 1884, just after he arrived in Florida, he met Thomas Ward, a musician from New York who had come south for his health. Delius invited Ward to stay at his plantation and teach him the mechanics of harmony and counterpoint. Ward was a brilliant teacher, and during his six-month visit his host learned much. At the same time, Delius was falling in love with the lush beauty of Florida. For days at a time, guided by his black workers, he leisurely explored the region by river. But while he composed and read, the oranges, left unattended, rotted. Soon his older brother, Ernest, was sent to Florida to save the family's property. But the budding young musician had never been happier and would later advise artists to go out and live in the wilderness to gain more freedom of expression.

After two isolated years at Solano Grove, Delius felt the need for more musical study, but he was now on his own financially and had to earn money. He was offered a position teaching music at a finishing school for girls in Danville, Virginia. In a year's time, he had saved enough money to attend the Leipzig Conservatory, where he enrolled in 1886. He stayed only eighteen months and was convinced that he had learned nothing and that in the future he must find his own way artistically. Later, he would profess a hatred for any type of traditional study, which, he felt, killed instinct. Delius firmly believed in inspiration first—music, for him, was an outburst from the soul.

One positive result of his time in Leipzig was his acquaintance with Grieg, whose music Delius admired. Grieg saw promise in the Englishman's early songs and invited him for a short visit to Norway, a country that enchanted him. After leaving Norway, around 1889, Delius moved to Paris, where he lived for over a decade. He found much artistic stimulation there—and he also took part in the seamy side of Parisian life. A lover of painting, he helped organize an exhibit for the Norwegian painter Edvard Munch, then unknown in Paris. In 1899 he composed his first important work, *Paris: The Song of a Great City*.

In 1903, Delius, who had often said marriage was fatal for an artist, married Jelka Rosen, a well-to-do painter. She was a devoted wife to the increasingly moody, cynical, contradictory, and even misanthropic composer. The couple bought a home in the French village of Grez-sur-Loing, where Delius lived for the rest of his life.

Until the time of his marriage, Delius had produced little of real importance, but afterward he composed the operas A *Village Romeo and Juliet* (1900–1) and *Fennimore and Gerda* (1909–10) and the large orchestral and choral works *Appalachia* (1898–1903), A *Mass of Life* (1904–5), and *Sea Drift* (1903–4). The orchestral works *Brigg Fair* (1907), *On Hearing the First Cuckoo in Spring* (1912), and several others are among the treasures of late Romanticism. Recognition was slow in coming, however, partly because he lived almost as a recluse and partly because the rarefied quality of his almost amorphous music at first bewildered the public.

Delius's fate was tragic. During his early days in Paris, he had contracted syphilis, and by the early 1920s he was a complete invalid, blind, and increasingly paralyzed. He was in despair over the end of his creative life. In 1928 Eric Fenby, a young Yorkshire musician and a devout lover of the composer's work, donated his services as Delius's amanuensis. Through a torturous process that lasted until Delius's death, Fenby (who often suffered from the composer's abuse) painstakingly notated his compositions. Years later Fenby wrote a memoir, *Delius As I Knew Him*, a little book of delicacy and empathy that records a precious but difficult relationship.

As early as 1906, the conductor Thomas Beecham, deeply moved by Delius's work, became a passionate advocate, championing his music throughout his long career. Just before Delius's death, Beecham persuaded the desperately ill composer to visit England after many years of absence. Beecham organized a weeklong Delius festival. Both audience and composer were thrilled; it was the long-suffering composer's greatest public triumph.

Perhaps Delius is the truest musical impressionist, a master of the imprisoned moment, a nature poet without peer. The Dutch composer Bernard van Dieren wrote, "To all that he touched, he gave a new meaning, a new color, a new outline, a new loveliness, and a new poignancy."

Delius's music explores the evanescence of time and of iridescent sunsets, the momentary life of flowers, the changing colors and scents of the earth. But Delius is far from merely pictorial. His nature worship came from a highly sensitive, fragile soul, isolated by temperament and finally disease. Delius will never appeal to the many; indeed, he repels some. He asks for a special and rarefied taste, but if one has it, the effect may be akin to an addiction.

Brigg Fair: An English Rhapsody (1907)

Delius called *Brigg Fair* a rhapsody, but in fact it is a theme and variations on a folksong, which the pianist, composer, and folksong collector Percy Grainger discovered in a village of North Lincolnshire and showed to Delius. The work was fittingly dedicated to Grainger and was first performed in 1908. It is among Delius's finest orchestral compositions. Less amorphous than a great deal of his music, it realizes various moods and is perhaps his most "English"-sounding work.

Royal Philharmonic Orchestra, Beecham: Sony Masterworks MPK 47680
Welsh National Opera Orchestra, Mackerras: Argo 430202-2
Bournemouth Sinfonietta, Hickox: EMI Classics CDC 49932

In a Summer Garden (1908)

Delius loved his home in his secluded village. For countless hours, he sat in the glow of his garden, living a protected and solitary existence. *In a Summer Garden* is a miraculous piece of musical impressionism. On the top of the score, Delius wrote an unattributed quote: "Roses, lilies, and a thousand scented flowers. Bright butterflies flitting from petal to petal, and gold-brown bees humming in the warm, quivering summer air. Beneath the shades of ancient trees, a quiet river with water lilies. In a boat, almost hidden, two people. A thrush is singing in the distance." Another is by Dante Gabriel Rossetti: "All are my blooms; and all sweet blooms of love. To thee I give while spring and summer sing."

In his biography of the composer, Sir Thomas Beecham writes, *"In a Summer Garden* is not only one of the most completely characteristic efforts of its composer, but is well-nigh flawless in form and orchestration. The mood has an unimpeachable unity and in it as much as in any other single piece may be found the quintessence of Delius."

London Symphony Orchestra, Collins: Dutton Laboratories DUT 2503
Hallé Orchestra, Handley: Classics for Pleasure CDCFP 4568

Summer Night on the River (1911)
On Hearing the First Cuckoo in Spring (1912)

These two scores represent Delius as one of music's wondrous nature poets. Both miniatures capture in sound a tranquil, pacific nature. *On Hearing the First Cuckoo* continues to be his most-often-performed work.

Royal Philharmonic Orchestra, Beecham: Dutton Laboratories CDLX 7011
London Philharmonic Orchestra, Handley: Chandos CHAN 8330

OTHER PRINCIPAL WORKS

CELLO AND PIANO WORKS
Sonata (1917)

CHAMBER MUSIC
Quartet for Strings (1916)

CHORAL WORKS WITH ORCHESTRA
Appalachia (1898–1903)*
Sea Drift (1903–4)*
A Mass of Life (1904–5)*
Songs of Sunset (1906–7)*
A Song of the High Hills (1911)*
Requiem (1914–16)*
Songs of Farewell (1930)*

OPERAS
Irmelin (1890–92)
Koanga (1895–97)
A Village Romeo and Juliet (1900-1)*
Fennimore and Gerda (1909–10)

ORCHESTRAL WORKS
Florida Suite (1887)
Summer Evening (tone poem) (1890)
Prelude to *Irmelin* (1890–92)*
Over the Hills and Far Away (c.1895–97)
Paris: The Song of a Great City (nocturne) (1899)
Walk to the Paradise Garden (from *A Village Romeo and Juliet*) (1900–1)*
North Country Sketches (1913–14)*
Dance Rhapsody nos. 1 and 2 (1908, 1916)*
Eventyr (1917)
A Poem of Life and Love (1918)
A Song Before Sunrise (1918)*

SOLO INSTRUMENT AND ORCHESTRA WORKS
Légende for Violin and Orchestra (1895)
Concerto for Piano and Orchestra (1897–1904)
Concerto for Violin, Cello, and Orchestra (1915–16)
Concerto for Violin and Orchestra (1916)*
Concerto for Cello and Orchestra (1921)

VIOLIN AND PIANO WORKS
Three sonatas (1905–14, 1923, 1930)

CLAUDE DEBUSSY

b. St. Germain-en-Laye (near Paris),
August 22, 1862

d. Paris, March 25, 1918

Generally speaking, I feel more and more that music, by its very essence, is not something that can flow inside a rigorous, traditional form. It consists of colors and of rhythmicized time.

The six generations of the Debussy family preceding Claude's birth seem to have had no trace of musical ability. Achille-Claude (as he was known in childhood) was the eldest of five children. The family was poor, and he received, aside from music, the bare minimum of an education. At seven, losing a brother to meningitis, he and his sister were taken to Cannes to live with their aunt, who decided he should study piano. It was quickly apparent that he was gifted. When the family moved to Paris, he took some lessons with Madame Mauté de Fleurville, who claimed that she had once studied with Chopin. As the Polish master was Claude's favorite composer, he was impressed with his teacher's credentials.

The Paris Conservatory accepted him at age ten. He remained there for eleven years but hated the Conservatory's rigid system of education. He studied piano with the well-known Antoine Marmontel, and although his gifts ripened, he never captured a first prize in piano playing. His parents were disappointed, for they had hoped that their son would eventually earn a living as a professional virtuoso. In harmony class, young Claude was extremely impatient with the stringent rules. When someone asked what rules he followed, he told everyone that he followed only his own pleasure. Considered insolent and constantly at odds with teachers, students, and the institution, Debussy felt himself to be an outsider. Later in life he was to use his caustic and glib tongue and his idiosyncratic critical mind as a delightful if disconcerting music critic.

In 1881 Tchaikovsky's patroness, Nadezhda von Meck, hired Debussy to play chamber music, read new scores, and teach her children for several months in Italy and Russia. She was delighted with his amazing ability to read new music at sight. In Moscow he heard some of the newest Russian music, including Mussorgsky, who would influence his own composing. Later that year, back in Paris, he became romantically involved with Marie-Blanche Vasnier, a married woman twelve years his senior whose husband's friendship he also cultivated. Madame Vasnier sang well, and the young composer dedicated his first songs to her.

In 1884 Debussy won the Prix de Rome, which allotted him three years of study at the French Academy in the Villa Medici. Upset about the victory, he wrote, "I had a sudden vision of boredom, and of all the worries that inevitably go together with any form of official recognition. I felt I was no longer free." He was unhappy about leaving Madame Vasnier and especially Paris, which he loved. As expected, he hated Rome, the "abominable villa," and the mediocrity and dullness of his colleagues in the various arts. He found it so unbearable that he returned to Paris before completing his term of residency. Happy to be home, he lived a casual bohemian existence, frequenting the famous cafés. Poor but free, eager for fresh experience and new friendships, the diffident young composer mingled with artists, poets, and musicians. His friendship with the wealthy Ernest Chausson proved fortunate, as his fellow composer occasionally provided him with money and dinners. Throughout his life, Debussy was constantly in need of money. Early on he acquired a taste for luxuries of every sort, including trinkets, Japanese prints, fine food, wine, and beautiful clothes.

After visiting Bayreuth in 1888 and 1889 to hear Wagner's music-dramas, he was deeply stirred. Instinctively, however, he knew that Wagner was a dead end. He soon found a kindred spirit in Erik Satie, four years his junior. Satie, anti-Teutonic in every fiber of his being, had been composing music stripped bare of pomposity, frills, and grand gestures. Satie talked constantly about writing French music; he once said to Debussy, "We ought to have our own music — if possible without *choucroute* [sauerkraut]."

In 1889, the year of Paris's universal exhibition, Debussy fell in love with the Japanese art on exhibition as well as with the exotic scales and timbres played by the Javanese gamelan orchestras. His own early music had been rather derivative, but after 1890 his personality emerged in a series of extraordinary works, such as the *Fêtes galantes* (1891), song cycle settings of Verlaine poems; the orchestral *Prélude à l'après-midi d'un faune* (1892–94); the nocturnes

(1893–99); and the String Quartet (Op. 10, 1893). In August 1893 he was over-joyed to receive permission to make an opera from Maurice Maeterlinck's play *Pelléas et Mélisande*.

The 1890s were Debussy's happiest years. His music was being published by Georges Hartmann, who showed Debussy warmth and sympathy and helped to alleviate some of his financial worry. (Unfortunately, Hartmann died in 1900.) In 1892 he met Gabrielle Dupont, an attractive woman whom he called Gaby of the Green Eyes, and who was his companion for six years. Yet Debussy thought Gaby slightly disreputable and intellectually inferior and re-fused to take her to respectable and posh households such as the Chaussons'.

In 1899 he jilted Gaby for Rosalie (Lily) Texier, a pretty mannequin- and dressmaker whom he married. Gaby shot herself, recovered, and disappeared. Lily was a devoted wife, but by 1903 Debussy was totally bored by her. Like her predecessor, Lily shot herself, and she too recovered. But the scandal reached the newspapers and alienated many of the composer's friends. He left Lily in 1904 to go live with Emma Bardac, a married woman with children and the former mistress of Fauré. In 1908, after her divorce, they married, but the com-poser always felt hemmed in by domestic life. He did, however, have a daugh-ter with Emma in 1905, an adored girl whom he called Chouchou. (For her he would later write the charming *Children's Corner Suite*.)

After the 1902 premiere of *Pelléas* (which took almost ten years to write and produce) Debussy's fame grew—as did his unhappiness. Basically he was a sad man, whose melancholy moods tormented him. He wrote to Chausson, "Try as I may, I can't regard the sadness of my existence with caustic detachment. Sometimes my days are dull, dark, and soundless like those of a hero from Edgar Allan Poe; and my soul is as romantic as a Chopin Ballade." In 1904 he told a friend, "I feel nostalgia for the Claude Debussy who worked so enthusi-astically on *Pelléas*." In 1908 Debussy, a confirmed Anglophile, visited London twice, to conduct and supervise the English premiere of *Pelléas*. The first signs of the cancer that would kill him appeared in 1909.

In 1910 Debussy was busy conducting in Vienna, Budapest, and elsewhere, and he began writing the incidental music for Gabriele D'Annunzio's mystery play, *Le Martyre de Saint Sébastien*. The years before the war were beset with financial misery, and he returned to musical journalism as well as to conduct-ing in Moscow, St. Petersburg, Rome, the Hague, and Brussels. By 1913 he had completed both books of the twenty-four Preludes for Piano and *Jeux*, a ballet for Diaghilev.

Debussy was increasingly ill and felt devastated by the war. He told Jacques Durand, his publisher, "What I am doing seems so wretchedly small and unim-portant. I can even envy Satie, who, as a Corporal, is preparing seriously to defend Paris." He confirmed his patriotism by calling himself *"musicien français."* To the sixteen-year-old Francis Poulenc, he said, "This is a time when we should be trying to regain a hold on our ancient traditions; we may have let their beauty slip from us, but it has not ceased to exist." For a time, he lost what he called his ability to think in music, and when it returned, he worked against time, knowing that the cancer was growing relentlessly. To make a little extra money, he edited a complete edition of Chopin's music while he was composing his own Twelve Études, dedicated to the memory of Chopin. Elated with his work, he wrote to a friend, "The emotional satisfaction can't be equaled in any of the other arts. Forgive me, I sound as if I've just discovered music."

Late in 1915, after a depleting operation, his physical pain tortured him. Little time remained to him as he planned six sonatas for varied combinations of instruments. In that year, he composed the Sonata for Cello and Piano and the Sonata for Flute, Viola, and Harp. Early in May 1917, in a state of physical torment and spiritual desolation, he finished the third of the group, the Sonata for Violin and Piano, his final work. "By one of those very human contradictions," he wrote, "it's full of happiness and uproar." In May 1917 he played the piano part at its first performance. Late in 1917 his strength failed. He took to his bed and died on March 25, 1918.

In the midst of war, France was hardly aware that one of the greatest of all French artists had died. Chouchou, his remarkable daughter, wrote, "Papa is dead. Those three words, I do not understand them, or rather I understand them only too well." Sixteen months after her father's death, Chouchou herself died, after receiving the wrong treatment for diphtheria. She was fourteen years old.

Debussy was a complex person, enigmatic and secretive, capable of the sweetest affection and tenderness yet also outlandishly selfish. He was often irascible and always inhibited with strangers. When Proust, who had long wanted to meet him, gave a party in his honor, Debussy did not show up.

Debussy founded a new musical vocabulary, but unlike Schoenberg or Stravinsky, his music never occasioned riots. On the contrary, except for arch-conservatives like Saint-Saëns, many listened to Debussy's art with rapt pleasure from the beginning. Its spiritual sensuousness is beguiling and is handled with sophistication and beauty; the composer effortlessly broke any rule he needed to break. The first performance of *Prélude à l'après-midi d'un faune* opened new vistas for music.

His art has been called impressionism, a term with which Debussy was not at all pleased. But he indeed painted in music, as most of his work was inspired by pictorial or poetic themes. He called the nocturnes studies on gray painting, and as the impressionist painters Renoir, Pissarro, Sisley, and Monet let the eye blend the daubs of paint, Debussy let the ear blend the sounds. As Oscar Thompson notes, "In literature, in painting, in music, the aim was to suggest rather than to depict; to mirror not the object, but the emotional reaction of the object; to interpret a fugitive impression rather than to seize upon and fix the permanent reality." But it would be a mistake to give Debussy such a narrow label as impressionist. He was a person of extreme sensitivity and knowledge in many areas, which were all reflected in his art. He enlarged music's color wheel. Hundreds of composers since have been indebted to him.

Debussy brought to music a new harmonic syntax and a breathtaking landscape of unique surface beauties. The American pianist Paul Jacobs stated that he "evolved an extraordinary vocabulary of timbre, which assumes a structural importance often equal to that of the pitch components in a given work. . . . Debussy expressed a new and vast repertory of emotional states, often furtive and fleeting, often mixing pain and pleasure." It is an art luxurious in its rhythmic resources and refinement, a music relying on impressions, suggestiveness, and symbolism. The composer must often have thought of the poet Mallarmé's dictum, "To name an object sacrifices three-quarters of the enjoyment. To suggest it—that is our dream."

With Debussy, the chord itself was freed of its necessity to move and became an experience in itself. With this concept, harmonic progression was no longer required in the traditional sense. Yet Debussy's work is not a formless mass, relying merely on sensation. He is always the subtle architect of pieces that are neither too long nor too short. In the Fifth Piano Prelude, book I, "Des Pas sur la neige" ("Footsteps in the Snow," 1909), he encapsulated within two minutes an incomparable psychological study, and, with only a few notes, painted a picture of complete desolation.

"Historically viewed," Virgil Thomson wrote, "Debussy is the summit toward which . . . French music has risen. . . . Internationally viewed, he is to the musicians of our century everywhere what Beethoven was to those of the nineteenth, our blinding light, our sun, our central luminary." In form, harmony, instrumentation, and subtlety of rhythm, Debussy enlarged the art of music. With his most exquisite sensibility, he created a new sound for the piano, wanting it to sound "hammerless." The critic-poet Léon Fargue remarked, "In playing his own music, he appeared to be giving birth to the piano. He cradled it, talked softly to it." His piano music is thus the most original since Liszt. In his orchestral works, he explored new registers of various instruments, giving rise to new and lovely sonorities. In his vocal music, he achieved a new suppleness in the setting of words. In his exploration of harmony, he broadened its horizons, using all sorts of scale formations as well as Gregorian modes. Most important, he brought to our listening a broader view of consonance and dissonance, which has given us a far wider range in the hearing of music.

In short, Debussy was the most sophisticated musical artist of his age, as well as a nature poet of the deepest perception. His music vibrates with the sounds of the natural world. The pianist E. Robert Schmitz speaks of "clouds, moonlight, passing breezes—either carrying the upper partials of bells of nearby or faraway churches, or the fading notes of military bugles, the wind at sea or in the plains, sunrays on a golden roof, or the shimmering lacquer of a Japanese panel," and much more. In 1971, the year of Stravinsky's death, the Russian-born master asserted, "Debussy is in all senses the century's first musician."

Suite bergamasque (1890)

Debussy added an entirely new dimension to the piano's expressive and evocative power. In the early *Suite bergamasque*, he paid homage to the seventeenth- and eighteenth-century French *clavecinistes*, or harpsichordists. The suite is in four movements: Prélude, Menuet, the ever-popular Clair de lune, and Passepied. Each movement reveals the composer's innate eloquence. The Clair de lune has something of the suavity of Massenet's sensuous melodies.

Paik: Virgin Classics CDZ 59653
François: EMI Pathé Marconi 7473742
Ohlsson: Arabesque Z 6601

Prélude à l'après-midi d'un faune (1892–94)

Debussy completed the score in 1894, based on Mallarmé's long poem of the same name, and it premiered on December 22. The *Prélude*'s gentle languorousness and insinuating sensuousness inaugurated a revolution in music. As the French composer Pierre Boulez wrote, "The art of music began to beat with a new pulse." The faun's desire for a beautiful nymph gives us music of shimmering palpitation and puts us into a rapt, dreamlike trance. The Eastern-sounding scales are voluptuous. Mallarmé was enchanted by the score.

Cleveland Orchestra, Boulez: Deutsche Grammophon 435766-2
Orchestre de la Suisse Romande, Ansermet: London 421171-2
Orchestre de la Suisse Romande, Jordan: Erato 2292-45605-2

Quartet for Strings, Op. 10 (1893)

An early performance of the String Quartet, in 1894, took place in a hall in Brussels, which was also showing an exhibition of impressionist paintings. Critics were already calling Debussy's work impressionism and even musical pointillism. Debussy's only string quartet, composed in 1893, is one of his earliest masterpieces and is the finest string quartet composed since Franck's quartet, which Debussy admired. The first movement, Animé et très décidé, gives the flavor of the ancient Phrygian mode dressed in modern harmony. The movement is long and complex, showing Debussy's amazing grasp of the sonata form. The second movement, Assez vit et bien rhythmé, is a Scherzo and doubtless was heard as pointillism. Great rhythmic vitality holds forth throughout. The third movement, Andantino doucement expressif, is in three sections. The main theme is an especially beautiful melody; the finale (Très modéré) is all finesse. Its light textures are smooth and agreeable.

Guarneri String Quartet: RCA 09026-60909-2
Hagen String Quartet: Deutsche Grammophon 437836-2
Quartetto Italiano: Philips 420894-2

Nocturnes (1893–99)

No. 1, Nuages (Clouds), according to Debussy, "renders the immutable aspect of the sky and the slow, solemn motion of the clouds, fading away in grey tones lightly tinged with white." No. 2, Fêtes (Festivals), is a work of extraordinary ebullience. In the midst of the fête, we hear in the distance a procession announced by a marchlike theme. No. 3, Sirènes (Sirens), is an amazing tonal painting with a chorus of women's voices, which represent the sirens and the sea, silvered by the moon.

Montreal Symphony Orchestra and Chorus, Dutoit: London 425502-2
Detroit Symphony Orchestra and Chorus, Paray: Mercury 434306-2

Pelléas et Mélisande (1892–1902)

On April 30, 1902, Debussy's opera was performed at the Opéra-Comique in Paris, with the Scottish-American soprano Mary Garden singing Mélisande. The most radical opera since Tristan, it was the last word in refined music and used the most sophisticated harmonic palette. Proust could not hear it enough, and the poet Adrienne Monnier and her sister Marie saw it as often as possible: "From the first notes, we would begin to shed tears, and to sniff and sob, with people around us hissing at us for silence. We could not help it, and we wept just the same, every time. That music was '*si mystérieusement . . . émouvante*.' " Debussy had set Maeterlinck's play almost word for word, perfectly fusing the action and music. It has pages of unearthly beauty: "I tried to obey a law of beauty which appears singularly ignored in dealing with dramatic music," Debussy wrote. "The characters of the drama endeavor to sing like an arbitrary language of antiquated tradition. Hence the reproach leveled at my alleged partiality for monotone declamation, in which there is no melody . . . dramatic melody should be totally different from melody in general." To today's ears, Debussy's opera sounds as if it is all melody, but melody so muted, mysterious, and liquid that words and music become as one. In *Pelléas*, he created an ideal dream world.

Söderström, Minton, Shirley, Royal Opera House Orchestra and Chorus, Boulez: Sony Classical SM3K 47265

Alliot-Lugaz, Golfier, Carlson, Montreal Symphony Orchestra and Chorus, Dutoit: London 430502-2

Estampes (1903)

These three works initiate a new era in piano writing. The pieces are *Pagodes* (*Pagodas*), *Soireé dans Grenade* (*Evening in Granada*), and *Jardins sous la pluie* (*Gardens in the Rain*). The title *Estampes* refers to images printed from engraved copper or wood plates. E. Robert Schmitz wrote in the 1930s, "Years of gestation purified these visions to the pungency of an essence." The stimulus for *Pagodas* was the Javanese gamelan orchestra. The Spanish composer Manuel de Falla was dumbfounded by the Spanish authenticity of *Evening in Granada*. This is the first of Debussy's works inspired by Spain, a country he never visited. The final piece, *Gardens in the Rain*, weaves two French nursery songs delicately into its fabric.

Jacobs: Elektra/Nonesuch 71365-2-AW
Moravec: Vox Box CDX 5103

La Mer (1903–5)

Debussy loved and respected the sea. His gorgeous orchestral tribute, *La Mer*, was premiered at a Concert Lamoureux on October 15, 1905. *La Mer* is one of the miracles of musical impressionism; its flashing colors in countless shades need musicians who are painters asking the most of their instruments. The three movements are De l'aube à midi sur la mer (From Dawn Until Noon on the Sea), Jeux de vagues (The Play of the Waves), and Dialogue du vent et de la mer (The Dialogue of the Wind and the Sea). Debussy's admiration for the sea was so great that he once wrote, "To wet in it bodies deformed by the daily life should not be allowed. Truly, these arms and legs which move in ridiculous rhythms—it is enough to make the fish weep. There should be only sirens in the sea."

NBC Symphony Orchestra, Toscanini (vol. 37): RCA 60265-2-RG
Orchestre de la Suisse Romande, Ansermet: London 448576-2
Orchestre National de l'ORTF, Martinon: EMI Classics CDM 69587

Children's Corner Suite (1908)

This suite for solo piano, in six pieces, is a wonderful collection of satire, tenderness, and humor. It begins with *Doctor Gradus ad Parnassum*, which in the composer's words is "a sort of hygienic and progressive gymnastics." No. 2, *Jimbo's Lullaby*, portrays Jimbo, a toy elephant belonging to the composer's daughter. In the final number, *Golliwogg's Cake-walk*, Debussy uses the syncopation of minstrel groups, along with an irreverent quote from Wagner's *Tristan und Isolde*.

Michelangeli: Deutsche Grammophon 415372-2
Rogé: London 417792-2

Twenty-four Preludes for Piano (1910, 1913)

The Twenty-four Preludes furnish the piano with a new, undreamed-of vocabulary. The pianist Claudio Arrau once said of these pieces, "It is like the music of another planet." The titles tell of Debussy's great fund of inspiration, deriving from natural phenomena, landmarks, legends, literature, Spanish rhythms, the music hall, dancers, England, and fireworks. Debussy's biographer Edward Lockspeiser wrote of the preludes, "Soon one is aware of the symbolism in the piano writing. There is no doubt that Debussy shows himself in the Preludes to be not only a clairvoyant but a clairaudient. The music allows the listener to see things and to hear things in a new way."

Gieseking: EMI Classics CDH 61004
Michelangeli: Deutsche Grammophon 413450-2 (Book I); Deutsche Grammophon 427391-2 (Book II)
Zimerman: Deutsche Grammophon 435773-2

Sonata for Violin and Piano (1916–17)

This sonata has recently become a staple in the violin repertoire. Yehudi Menuhin remarked, "The work has been growing on me more than any other composition. I can never get deep enough into it. It's a masterwork. It's a masterpiece of the unpredictable, but with a logic that goes through the unpredictable, that is what fascinates me in it. It's a study of fate in miniature, always bringing the unpredictable event, and yet it makes total sense."

Chung, Lupu: London 421154-2
Heifetz, Bay: RCA 7871-2-RG
Thibaud, Cortot: Pearl PEA 9348

OTHER PRINCIPAL WORKS

BALLET
Khamma (1911–12)
Jeux (1913)*

CHAMBER MUSIC
Première rapsodie for Clarinet and Piano (1909–10)*
Sonata for Flute, Viola, and Harp (1915)*
Sonata in D Minor for Cello and Piano (1915)*

CHORAL WORKS WITH ORCHESTRA
La Damoiselle élue (cantata) (1887–88)

INCIDENTAL MUSIC
Le Roi Lear (1904)
Le Martyre de Saint Sébastien (1911)

ORCHESTRAL WORKS
Le Printemps (1882)
Images (*Gigués, Ibéria,* and *Rondes de printemps*) (1905–12)*

PIANO DUET AND TWO-PIANO WORKS
Petite suite (four pieces) (1886–89)
Six *Épigraphes antiques* (1914)
En blanc et noir (three pieces) (1915)

PIANO SOLO WORKS
Danse (*Tarantelle styrienne*) (1890) (orchestrated by Ravel in 1903)
L'Isle joyeuse (1904)*
Masques (1904)
Images (six pieces in two sets) (1905, 1907)*
Twelve *Études* (1915)*

SOLO FLUTE WORK
Syrinx (1912)

SOLO INSTRUMENT AND ORCHESTRA WORKS
Fantaisie for Piano and Orchestra (1889–90)
Danse sacrée et danse profane for Harp and Orchestra (1904)*
Rapsodie for Alto Saxophone and Orchestra (1901–8)*

SONGS WITH PIANO
Six *Fêtes galantes* (1891)*
Three *Proses lyriques* (1895)*
Three *Chansons de Bilitis* (1899)*
Three *Ballades de François Villon* (1910)*
Three *Poèmes de Stephane Mallarmé* (1913)*

RICHARD STRAUSS

b. Munich, June 11, 1864

d. Garmisch-Partenkirchen, Bavaria,
September 8, 1949

When at night I am stuck at a certain point in my composition, and in spite of all my digging no further profitable work seems possible, I shut the piano or my sketchbook, go to bed, and when I wake up in the morning, the continuation is there.

Franz Strauss, Richard's father, was a well-known horn player in the Munich Court Orchestra, for whom music had ended conclusively with Weber and Mendelssohn. He had an almost irrational hatred of Wagner's music and even caused disruptions at rehearsals in Wagner's presence. When it became clear that his son was brilliantly gifted, the elder Strauss made certain that his boy would not be contaminated by Wagner, Liszt, or any other "music of the future."

Richard and his younger sister grew up in a protected environment, shielded by wealth; his mother was the daughter of the head of the Bavarian brewer Pschorr. At five he was playing piano and violin, and at six he composed a polka. By the time he was a teenager, his music was already being performed. Indeed, the first Horn Concerto (Op. 11), the C minor piano quartet (Op. 13), the B minor piano sonata (Op. 5), and the D minor symphony (all written between 1880 and 1884) are more than merely precocious; they show an extraordinary assimilation of Classical form. A little later, much to his father's disapproval, Richard began to emulate Schumann and especially Brahms.

In 1883 the nineteen-year-old had his first performance outside Munich, when the great pianist and conductor Hans von Bülow conducted his Meinin-

gen Orchestra in Strauss's Serenade for thirteen wind instruments (Op. 7). Von
Bülow observed Strauss's considerable conducting ability and encouraged him
in that direction. By 1885 he had developed brilliantly as a conductor, and von
Bülow made him an assistant at Meiningen. It was then that he broke with his
early musical conditioning.

One of the orchestra members, the young poet and violinist Alexander Ritter, befriended the twenty-one-year-old conductor. Ritter, a passionate Wagnerian, urged Strauss to forget the old-fashioned Classical forms and "absolute
music," to study Wagner, Liszt, and Berlioz, and to compose programmatic
music, highly colored and dramatic. It did not take Strauss long to understand
that he had been merely imitating past models.

In Italy during the spring of 1886, Strauss completed his symphonic fantasy
Aus Italien (Op. 16). Certain that this composition was his "connecting link
between the old and the new methods," he was disappointed that, when he
conducted it in Munich, the audience and critics thought it too discordant.

In the meantime, through various posts, Strauss consolidated his position as
one of Germany's finest young conductors. Constantly searching for a freer
compositional style, he made a great advance with the symphonic poem *Macbeth* (Op. 23). But in 1889 he finally produced his first fully characteristic
score, the tone poem *Don Juan* (Op. 20), inspired by Nikolaus Lenau's lascivious 1844 poem. Here in full bloom was the Straussian melodic phraseology,
with great sweeping melodies soaring into space. It was a new species of
melody, encased in bizarre and gorgeous colors previously unimagined in the
orchestral rainbow.

Within a decade, he wrote five more symphonic poems, each startling in its
effect and descriptive power, which often repelled die-hard conservatives and
mild-mannered Victorian audiences. Strauss seemed to epitomize Modernism,
but in fact he was assimilating the Romanticism of Liszt, Wagner, and Berlioz
into a powerful composite. As the century concluded, the tone poems *Tod und
Verklärung* (*Death and Transfiguration*, Op. 24, 1889), *Till Eulenspiegels
lustige Streiche* (*Till Eulenspiegel's Merry Pranks*, Op. 28, 1895), *Also Sprach
Zarathustra* (*Thus Spake Zarathustra*, Op. 30, 1896), *Don Quixote* (Op. 35,
1897), and *Ein Heldenleben* (*A Hero's Life*, Op. 40, 1897–98) were the most
controversial and most admired works. At thirty-six, Strauss was the world's
most-discussed composer. In this series of spectacular tone poems, he expanded the orchestral firmament to dizzying heights. In his hands, the Lisztian
symphonic poem became almost visual.

Strauss, a discriminating lover of literature, also wanted to compose opera.
In 1894 his first opera, *Guntram* (Op. 25), failed. The heroine was sung by the
soprano Pauline de Ahna, who soon became his wife. (They had one son.) In

1901 Strauss premiered another opera, *Feuersnot* (Op. 50), which was also poorly received. Not until 1905 did he score an exciting sensation with an opera from the notorious Oscar Wilde's *Salome* (Op. 54). Straitlaced German audiences were shocked. Music, it seemed, had become the bedfellow of immorality. An early candidate to sing the title role declined because she was a "decent woman." In no time, however, all of Europe demanded to see and hear the demented *Salome*, and audiences were not disappointed as the eponymous heroine gyrated erotically. In its writhing vulgarity, "The Dance of the Seven Veils" is undeniably irresistible.

In *Elektra* (Op. 58, completed in 1908), Strauss collaborated for the first time with the Austrian poet Hugo von Hofmannsthal. *Elektra* was even more disturbing than *Salome*. Its atmosphere reeked of violence, blood, and evil. Both operas brought an unheard-of realism to musical theater with unparalleled orchestral wizardry. Many people thought *Elektra* outrageous morally, and others found the musical cacophony brutal. Early in the century, Strauss's operas, and not Debussy's ultrarefined *Pelléas et Mélisande*, made the headlines. In France, Saint-Saëns shouted that Strauss had taken music outside of its proper sphere. A disgusted César Cui, member of the Russian Five, wrote, "His absurd cacophony will not be music even in the thirtieth century." But George Bernard Shaw fought for Strauss in the English press. And Paul Dukas, professor of orchestration at the Paris Conservatory, declared that Strauss knew the orchestra better than anyone. One of Strauss's great advocates was England's leading music critic, Ernest Newman, who wrote, "Music, perhaps, will soon be the one art in which a man can show us to ourselves as we really are, without fear of censor or of police. . . . In *Salome* there is more told us of the horror of our bodies and souls than in all the ravings of Saints or Satyrs, or in all the manuals of pathology. And the proof that it is great art is the sense of joyousness it gives us—that sense of clarified understanding of life that it is the business of all tragic art to give."

Interestingly, in "Advice to Young Conductors," the composer instructed: "Direct *Salome* and *Elektra* as if they had been written by Mendelssohn: Elfin music." Here is magnificent irony, yet the subtle statement also shows us that Strauss's early admiration of Mendelssohnian clarity still haunted him throughout the bloodletting of his two monstrous operas. Almost in revulsion, Strauss now turned away from dissecting extremes in human character as well as in modern harmony, feeling that beyond *Elektra*, the human ear would no longer be receptive. His kind of dense chromatic harmony could go no further, and unlike Schoenberg and Scriabin, he was not interested in dissolving tonality. With his bourgeois and materialistic temperament, Strauss refused to enter the uncharted land of atonal music, the single most radical development in twentieth-century music. Strauss believed that a composer of true talent would not and could not deny tonal means. Some progressive critics were disappointed with Strauss's refusal to continue being a pathbreaker. Instead, in *Der Rosenkavalier* (Op. 59, 1909–10), he and Hofmannsthal returned to the world of Mozart and Schubert, enveloped in a luscious Wagnerian harmony and permeated by the allure of the Johann Strauss Viennese waltz. *Rosenkavalier* is a magnificent confection containing some of Strauss's most ravishing music.

During the First World War, Strauss practically disappeared from the international scene as performances of German music were vastly curtailed in the Allied nations. After *Rosenkavalier*, he never again had influence on younger composers. Stravinsky, Bartók, Debussy, Ravel, and Schoenberg were now the leaders of Modernism. But he composed several more operas, mostly with Hofmannsthal, who took libretto writing as seriously as poetry. Hofmannsthal was convinced that Strauss was capable of great subtlety and slowly diverted him from his earlier noisy extravagance.

Gossip about Strauss's marriage made good press; the former Nietzschean "superman" was mercilessly bossed around, publicly and privately, by his wife. Later he even wrote an opera, *Intermezzo* (Op. 72, 1923), that lampooned their relationship. "My wife's a bit rough," he later told Mahler, "but that's what I need." Quite early in his career, Strauss had been obsessed with money. Before World War I, he had become wealthy, receiving larger and larger fees with each conducting engagement. He also made quite a bit of money gambling. He was addicted to the card game Scatt, for which he had an amazing knack. He forced members of the orchestras he conducted to play with him, and the musicians invariably lost large amounts to him. His stinginess and penny-pinching were the source of much laughter. The press found the witty and vain Strauss good copy, but some of his fellow artists were revolted by his combination of art and commerce. It was said that Strauss was spiritually sick—that he was Industrial Man's artist-in-residence. When in New York City, he was criticized for giving two concerts in a department store. The composer countered with good sense, saying, "True art ennobles any hall. And earning money in a decent way for wife and child is no disgrace—even for an artist."

Throughout the 1930s, he was uncomfortably affiliated with the Nazi regime. In 1933, when Toscanini adamantly refused to conduct *Parsifal* at Bayreuth, Strauss readily agreed to take his place. He didn't follow all the Nazi dictums—his prestige and ego were enormous enough that in 1935 he dared to collaborate with the Jewish writer Stefan Zweig—but he was undoubtedly on friendly terms with the regime, although he was aware of their goals. He distanced himself from the Nazis during the war, however, and spent most of it isolated at his beloved villa at Garmisch in the Bavarian Alps. At war's end, he was tried and absolved of any Nazi ties or affiliation. During the Nazi regime, he produced the clearly neoclassical Oboe Concerto (1945), the Horn Concerto no. 2 (1942), and the emotionally charged *Metamorphosen* for twenty-three string instruments (1945).

The once-wealthy composer, with no royalties coming in for years, was now destitute. Although Strauss never regained his earlier popularity, he continued to compose, and created the song cycle *Vier letzte Lieder* (*Four Last Songs*, 1948).

Strauss died in 1949, a few months before his wife. It was generally agreed that, in the thirty-eight years since *Rosenkavalier*, Strauss had shown only flashes of his former greatness. Most critics thought that he relied heavily on his sophisticated technique and had little left to say. But more recently, Strauss has been steadily but cautiously reassessed. At the beginning of the twenty-first century, we no longer believe that, in order to be legitimate, a composer must create in the context of his time. Some feel that his earlier operas *Ariadne auf Naxos* (Op. 60, 1912), *Die Frau ohne Schatten* (Op. 65, 1914–18, Strauss's own favorite), and *Arabella* (Op. 79, 1929–32), as well as the later ones, are his best work, and that in the 1940s he experienced a revitalization of his spirit. Some critics contend that he never dried up but simply went his own way. The terrors of the twentieth century profoundly shocked him. Left alone, he became as oblivious as possible to external reality and to the terrifying events that closely surrounded him. The pianist Glenn Gould, a passionate Straussian, concluded, "The great thing about the music of Richard Strauss is that it presents and substantiates an argument which transcends all the dogmatism of art—all questions of style and taste and idiom—all the frivolous, effete preoccupations of the chronologist. It presents to us an example of the man who makes richer his own time by not being of it; who speaks for all generations by being of none. It is an ultimate argument of individuality—an argument that man can create his own synthesis of time without being bound by the conformities that time imposes."

Don Juan, Op. 20 (1887–88)

This extremely ecstatic score describes three main concepts: (1) the fiery ardor with which Don Juan pursues his ideal woman; (2) the charm of women; and (3) the selfish idealist's disappointment and partial atonement by death. In his 1844 poem, the Austrian poet Nikolaus Lenau is longing to find in one woman all women. Strauss's tone poem was first performed in November 1889 at

Weimar, with Strauss conducting, and it received a huge ovation. Arthur Nikisch conducted it in conservative Boston in October 1891 to less acclaim. Strauss, who took his tone painting seriously, once told a conductor that he had portrayed one of the don's women so realistically that you could see her red hair. Herbert Weinstock wrote, "*Don Juan* is a miracle. *Don Juan* is a whirlwind under control . . . the frantic quality of the hero's search is given ironic emphasis by the sense of impending catastrophe that hovers over the music from the very beginning. Strauss has succeeded in creating an opera without words, cleverly adapting for solo orchestra Wagner's concept of a continuously unfolding music drama."

Minneapolis Symphony Orchestra, Dorati: Mercury 434348-2
San Francisco Symphony Orchestra, Blomstedt: London 421815-2
Bamberg Symphony Orchestra, Horenstein: Vox Legends CDX2 5529

Tod und Verklärung (Death and Transfiguration), Op. 24 (1888–89)

Death and Transfiguration was written only one year after *Don Juan*. This intense tone poem is in four sections, to be performed without pause. It is a direct result of Strauss's love for Wagner's *Tristan und Isolde*. The work describes the last feverish hours of life. Fever and pain blend with dreams. The soul leaves the body, and a magnificent transfiguration takes place. These were Strauss's thoughts when composing the score.

After the first performance in 1890, Strauss's friend Alexander Ritter wrote an elaborate program for each section that so pleased the composer that he had it published on the score. But it is doubtful that Strauss actually had definite detailed stories in mind for his symphonic poems. He considered the division between program music and "absolute music" to be nonsense. To him, the idea that music expressed only music was absurd. Regardless of their imaginary and descriptive intent, the Straussian tone poems are, from a purely musical and formal standpoint, works of a high-level musical mind, with structure and unity always in the forefront.

London Symphony Orchestra, Horenstein: Chandos CHAN 6549
RCA Victor Symphony Orchestra, Reiner: RCA 60388-2-RG
Berlin Philharmonic Orchestra, Karajan: Deutsche Grammophon 439039-2

Till Eulenspiegels lustige Streiche
(Till Eulenspiegel's Merry Pranks), Op. 28 (1894–95)

This scintillating work about a rascal shows us the enormous range of Strauss's temperament and his amazing orchestral fecundity and resourcefulness. *Eulenspiegel* conveys the very spirit of life itself. Strauss subtitled the score "after the old-fashioned roguish manner, in Rondo form." When a conductor asked for a concrete program, he wrote, "It is impossible for me to provide a program for *Eulenspiegel*: If I were to put into words the thoughts which the various incidents suggested to me, they would often make a quite strange impression and might even give rise to offense."

Royal Concertgebouw, Haitink: Philips 412281-2
Berlin State Opera Orchestra, Strauss: Pearl PEA 9366
Cleveland Orchestra, Szell: Sony Classical SBK 48272

Also Sprach Zarathustra (Thus Spake Zarathustra), Op. 30 (1895–96)

Zarathustra was Strauss's next tone poem. With characteristic grandiose candor, the composer asserted, "I did not intend to write philosophical music or to portray in music Nietzsche's great work. I meant to convey by means of music an idea of the development of the human race from its origin, through the various phases of its development, religious and scientific, up to Nietzsche's idea of the superman." The composition is in eight sections. The opening, which was used in Stanley Kubrick's film *2001: A Space Odyssey* and has been repeated ad nauseam in television commercials, is grandiloquent and awesomely effective.

Chicago Symphony Orchestra, Reiner: RCA 6722-2-RG
Philadelphia Orchestra, Ormandy: RCA 60793-2-RV

Don Quixote, Op. 35 (1896–97)

Strauss's ability to tell his story in music is unrivaled, and he always insisted he could depict anything in music—even inanimate objects. He subtitled the tone poem *Don Quixote* "Fantastic Variations on a Theme of Knightly Character for Cello and Orchestra," and the work consists of an introduction, ten variations, and a finale. Each of the ten variations tells of the don's adventures. The work gives the cello almost a soloistic function, and Strauss probably intended it as the voice of the don.

In this long composition, Strauss reached the acme of his orchestral virtuosity. The score spins before the listener in an awesome parade of picturesque settings, as the unhinged Sancho Panza and Dulcinea recount their loves and adventures. Never had even Strauss produced a score of such breathtaking imagination. The American critic James Huneker was the first to write about the score in America in 1899. He said, "Don Quixote is shown as the quotidian type of man whose daydreams are a bridge leading to the sorrowful cell of madness. He is not mocked but tenderly treated by Strauss."

Piatigorsky, Boston Symphony Orchestra, Munch: RCA 09026-61485-2
Ma, Boston Symphony Orchestra, Ozawa: CBS MK 39863

Ein Heldenleben (A Hero's Life), Op. 40 (1897–98)

Strauss composed A Hero's Life when he was drunk on his early success and exulting over his surging creative gift. The Hero is Strauss himself, and in the section "Hero's Works for Peace," he quotes from eight earlier works. The Hero's theme is pregnant with possibilities, and the third section, "The Hero's Courtship," is Strauss at his most giddily amorous, with the violin depicting his loved one in laughter and caresses.

The always-irreverent conductor Sir Thomas Beecham said, "I once spent a couple of days in a train with a German friend. We amused ourselves by discovering how many notes we could take out of Heldenleben and leave the music essentially intact. By the time we finished we had taken out fifteen thousand."

All told, Ein Heldenleben may be Strauss's crowning glory as an orchestral composer. His ample structures are charged with action and tumult. The instrumentation is razor sharp. The colors burn brightly. It is a stupendous finale to the nineteenth-century symphonic poem, as well as the Romantic idea that music was capable not only of presenting psychological states but of evoking stories.

Chicago Symphony Orchestra, Reiner: RCA RCD 1-5408
Vienna Philharmonic Orchestra, Previn: Telarc CD 80180

Salome, Op. 54 (1903–5)

Salome, the most shocking operatic thriller of its day, was first produced at the Dresden Court Opera on December 9, 1906. It rocked the world of opera and made the name of Richard Strauss known to the whole world.

The opera and its subject were talked about everywhere. By March 1907 James Huneker had seen it five times and wrote to a friend, "It is easily the greatest score since *Tristan and Isolde,* even the emotional intensity of Wagner has been surpassed—in *Salome's* final song. Furthermore it follows the book with miraculous exactitude, follows yet interprets. It is the beginning of a new art." Once again, Strauss dazzled the ear with his sumptuous orchestral palette. Never had such hysteria been heard on the stage, and Strauss showed his fine theatrical instinct in his searing psychological portrayals of Salome, Herodias, Herod, and Jokanaan. He wanted his heroine to be played by "a sixteen-year-old princess with the voice of Isolde." Although today nobody is shocked by Salome's dance with the decapitated head, the famous excerpt loses its impact when played as an orchestral piece. Mahler, who heard the opera played on the piano by Strauss before the Dresden premiere, wrote to the composer, "This is your apogee so far! Indeed, I assert that *nothing* that even you have done up to now can be compared with it. . . . Every note is right!" After hearing Strauss conduct it, he wrote, "This is one of the greatest masterpieces of our time."

Nilsson, Hoffman, Stolze, Wächter, Vienna Philharmonic Orchestra, Solti: London 414414-2

Caballé, Resnik, Lewis, Milnes, London Symphony Orchestra, Leinsdorf: RCA 6644-2-RG

Elektra, Op. 58 (1906–8)

More bloodcurdling than *Salome* and more extreme harmonically, *Elektra* was the beginning of Strauss's long collaboration with Hofmannsthal, whose libretto, based on Sophocles, is masterful, a perfect vehicle for the horror, vengeance, and frenzy of the score. *Elektra* is a major landmark in the history of opera, and some consider it Strauss's greatest. To contemporary ears, the score, which moves with fervent speed, is no longer merely discordant but has its own devastating and expressive beauty. Performing it makes overwhelming vocal demands, especially in the title role. The world first heard the opera at Dresden on January 25, 1909, with Ernst von Schuch conducting.

Borkh, Madeira, Schech, Fischer-Dieskau, Dresden Staatskapelle, Böhm: Deutsche Grammophon 445329-2

Nilsson, Collier, Resnik, Stolze, Krause, Vienna Philharmonic Orchestra, Solti: London 417345-2

Der Rosenkavalier (The Knight of the Rose), Op. 59 (1909–10)

Strauss's most loved opera is light, lush, psychologically subtle, and delightfully sophisticated, like both Strauss and Hofmannsthal themselves. Strauss fully realized that for him personally, following the path of *Elektra* would have meant musical destruction. The tonal system would shatter, and he could not have withstood the havoc. Instead, he reverted to the past, to a story set in Empress Maria Theresa's Vienna, yet without losing an iota of his personality. Hofmannsthal's libretto is one of the finest in operatic history, and Strauss was attuned to every nuance of this complex story. The nearly four-hour work has many highlights, including the lovable waltzes, the "Presentation of the Rose," the great trio for three sopranos in Act III, and Sophie and Octavian's duet. When the great critic Ernest Newman heard it in 1913, he was moved to write, "Such warmth of blood, such boldness of flight, and such power of endurance are beyond the scope of any other living musician." Ever since, the opera has captivated audiences with its peculiar magic.

Schwarzkopf, Ludwig, Stich-Randall, Edelmann, Philharmonia Orchestra and Chorus, Karajan: EMI Classics CDCC-56113

Jones, Popp, Ludwig, Domingo, Vienna Philharmonic Orchestra, Bernstein: CBS M3K 42564

Vier letzte Lieder (Four Last Songs) (1947–48)

Strauss, a great song composer, wrote 175 songs throughout his career. "Morgen" (Morning), "Ruhe, meine Seele" (Peace, My Soul), "Heimliche Aufforderung" (Secret Summons), "Ich schwebe" (I Soar), "Allerseelen" (All Soul's Day), "Ständchen" (Serenade), and many more are lovely and often rapturous. They represent the end of the great tradition of German *Lieder*. Strauss wrote for the voice with the same skill as he did for orchestra. The *Four Last Songs* are the eighty-four-year-old master's mellow and thrilling last musical testament. The first three songs are set to poems by Hermann Hesse. The final song, a setting of Eichendorff's "Im Abendrot" (At Sunset), is a farewell to life. Here the composer used to the utmost effect material from *Tod und Verklärung*.

Flagstad, London Philharmonic Orchestra, Furtwängler: Melodram 2 CDM 25009
Schwarzkopf, Berlin Radio Symphony Orchestra, Szell: EMI Classics CDC 47276
Norman, Leipzig Gewandhaus Orchestra, Masur: Philips 411052-2

OTHER PRINCIPAL WORKS

CHAMBER MUSIC

Serenade for Thirteen Wind Instruments, Op. 7 (1881)
Sonata in F Major for Cello and Piano, Op. 6 (1880–83)
Quartet in C Minor for Piano and Strings, Op. 13 (1883–84)
Sonata in E-flat Major for Violin and Piano, Op. 18 (1887)

OPERAS

Ariadne auf Naxos, Op. 60 (1912)*
Die Frau ohne Schatten (*The Woman Without a Shadow*), Op. 65 (1914–18)*
Intermezzo, Op. 72 (1918–23)*
Die Ägyptische Helena (*The Egyptian Helen*), Op. 75 (1923–27)
Arabella, Op. 79 (1929–32)*
Daphne, Op. 82 (1936–37)*
Capriccio, Op. 85 (1940–41)*

ORCHESTRAL WORKS

Macbeth (symphonic poem), Op. 23 (1886–88)
Symphonia domestica, Op. 53 (1902–3)
Eine Alpinensinfonie (*Alpine Symphony*), Op. 64 (1911–15)
Le Bourgeois gentilhomme (orchestral suite), Op. 60 (1918)*
Metamorphosen for Twenty-three Strings (1945)*

PIANO SOLO WORKS

Sonata in B Minor, Op. 5 (1880–81)

SOLO INSTRUMENT AND ORCHESTRA WORKS

Concerto in D Minor for Violin and Orchestra, Op. 8 (1880–82)
Concerto in E-flat Major for Horn and Orchestra, Op. 11 (1882–83)
Burleske in D Minor for Piano and Orchestra, AV85 (1885–86)*
Parergon for Piano Left-Hand and Orchestra, Op. 73 (1924)
Concerto no. 2 in E-flat Major for Horn and Orchestra, AV132 (1942)*
Concerto in D Major for Oboe and Orchestra, AV144 (1945)*

VOICE WITH PIANO WORKS
Eight Songs, Op. 10 (1885)*
Six Songs, Op. 17 (1885–87)*
Four Songs, Op. 27 (1894)*
Five Songs, Op. 41 (1899)*

JEAN SIBELIUS

b. Tavastehus, Finland, December 8, 1865

d. Järvenpää, Finland, September 20, 1957

These symphonies of mine are more in the nature of professions of faith than my other works.

Sibelius was the son of an army doctor who died of cholera when the boy was only two. He was raised by his grandmother and mother and showed sensitivity to music early on. His mother played the piano, and his younger brother and older sister were also musical. By age five, he was engrossed in the piano, endlessly trying out various sounds and chords. At nine he was given piano lessons, and the next year he wrote his first composition, which he titled "Drops of Water." When he was eleven, Sibelius was sent to a private school, but he rebelled against the regimentation. He eventually decided that he preferred the violin to the piano, and at fifteen he began practicing strenuously in the hope of becoming a concert violinist.

After high school, he pursued the study of law at Helsinki University. Music, however, obliterated all else. For a brief period, he studied composition with Ferruccio Busoni, one year his junior, who at the time was teaching at the Helsinki Academy of Music. Somewhat later Martin Wegelius would count as Sibelius's most important teacher. In 1889 Jean won a scholarship to study in Berlin, and later in Vienna.

Sibelius grew up speaking Swedish, which had been the language of the Finnish upper class for more than two centuries. He was not proficient in the Finnish language until his late teens, but he was always full of patriotic zeal. When he returned to Finland in 1891, he began to explore his national heritage. (Finland was then a grand duchy of Russia, despotically ruled by Czar Nicholas II.) On April 28, 1892, he conducted his symphonic poem *Kullervo* (Op. 7), inspired by the Finnish epic *The Kalevalá*. Its success was the turning point in his own life as well as in the art music of his nation. At this auspicious moment, on June 10, 1892, he married Aino Järnefelt, the daughter of one of the major leaders in the quest for Finnish independence. (The couple would eventually raise four daughters.) Shortly afterward he joined the faculty of the Helsinki music academy, where he taught theory and played violin in a string quartet. Although he was given a small lifetime government subsidy, lack of money would plague him for years. In spite of his many woes and his teaching schedule, he managed to find time for composing. The symphonic poem *En Saga* (Op. 9) was performed with resounding success in 1893. Continuing in the Finnish legendary vein, he then wrote the *Karelia Suite* (Op. 11) and *Four Legends from the Kalevalá* (Op. 22). (No. 3 is the exquisite "The Swan of Tuonela.") His most celebrated work, *Finlandia* (Op. 26, 1899), was a sensation at its premiere and instantly became a battle cry for Finnish independence. But in the same year, the Russian autocracy deprived Finns of any representative government and imposed the Russian language on them.

At thirty-five Sibelius was Finland's most famous artist. The First Symphony (Op. 39) was premiered in Helsinki in 1899 to a standing ovation, and the Second Symphony (Op. 43), completed in Italy in 1902, equaled the success of the first. Both works exemplify the heroic-national symphonic tradition, and along with the magnificent Violin Concerto of 1903 (Op. 47), they are among the treasures of Finnish national music. In 1903 he composed *Valse triste* (Op. 44), which became exceedingly popular everywhere. Unfortunately he sold it for a flat fee amounting to $150, after which the publisher grew rich from its worldwide sales. From 1904 to 1907, the composer toiled on a Third Symphony (Op. 52). With this symphony, he entered into a different sphere of musical thought, using a radically condensed form totally devoid of the grand manner of his earlier music.

While working on the Third Symphony, Sibelius experienced dreadful pain in his ear. It finally subsided, and from 1908 he worked on a Fourth Symphony (Op. 63, 1911) and a string quartet (*Voces intimae*, Op. 56, 1909). By then, however, the composer, a heavy cigar smoker, was experiencing terrible pain from a growth in his throat. He suffered through thirteen operations to alleviate the condition. The quartet and especially the symphony reflect his extremely painful existence at the time.

The Fourth Symphony was completed in 1911 and in its arctic loneliness is one of the remarkable compositions of the period, unrelated to anything the composer had previously accomplished. For the critic and Sibelius biographer

Cecil Gray, it was "[t]he outcome of a process of sheer starvation, of a fakirlike asceticism and self denial. It is gaunt, spectral, emaciated almost; the question is no longer one of superfluous flesh, but of any flesh at all—the very bones protrude."

Because of World War I and the Russian Revolution, Finland went to the brink of civil war. The composer lived in constant terror. His brother was murdered, and Jean was placed under house arrest by the Red Army. After the war, with Finnish independence declared, Sibelius embarked on concert tours, where he found himself not only famous but considered one of the great composers of the time. But in 1926, after completing the tone poem *Tapiola* (Op. 112), he abruptly stopped composing. For more than thirty years, he lived an almost completely isolated existence at his villa. The national hero was musically silent and repeatedly denied rumors that he was working on an eighth symphony. In 1930 he wrote to the English critic Rosa Newmarch, "I feel very much alone, there is so much in the music of the present day that I cannot accept. . . . It seems to me that modern music does not progress, that it marks time without getting a step farther."

In the 1930s he had powerful advocates in Cecil Gray in England and Olin Downes in the United States. The composer Constant Lambert wrote, "He alone among modern composers has combined the national intensity of Mussorgsky's operas with the formal intensity of Beethoven Quartets."

It is interesting to note a conversation between Sibelius and Mahler in 1907, when Mahler was conducting in Helsinki. The two master symphonists discussed the symphony as a form. Sibelius said, "I admire its severity and style and the profound logic that creates an inner connection between all the motives. This was the experience I had come to in composing." Mahler replied, "No, the symphony must be like the world. It must embrace everything." As Mahler's symphonies gain in popularity, those of Sibelius are heard less often.

Sibelius's place in music history was once more secure than it is now. Around 1920 in various quarters, he was proclaimed the ideal modern composer and an antidote to the seeming chaos of Schoenberg, Stravinsky, and Bartók. But by the late 1940s, his reputation had begun to decline. The composer Virgil Thomson, listening to the great Seventh Symphony, wrote, "I do not believe for a moment that its gray and dirty-brown orchestral coloring is a depiction of either the Finnish soul or the Finnish landscape. . . . I think Sibelius just orchestrates badly." Thirty years later Harold Schonberg called Sibelius "a dated bore" but conceded for him "an honorable place among the minor composers," while giving to the Danish Carl Nielsen "as much sweep, even more power and a more universal message."

In reality Sibelius was two composers. The first one wrote late Romantic folkloristic music dressed in established forms, such as the Violin Concerto, the first two symphonies, the simpler *Finlandia*, and even the café trifle *Valse triste*. These are the works most listeners like best. From around 1905, however, a second composer emerged in Sibelius and evolved into one of history's great symphonists, the successor of Brahms, reaffirming the importance of the symphony as a major form of intellectual expression. In Symphonies no. 3 to 7, we discover an immense constructive mind and a subtle emotional intelligence at work. Indeed, their high degree of organic unity invites searching study, although the basically disturbing austerity of this music hinders popular appeal. Sibelius remains Finland's greatest composer, but he was also one of the leading composers of the first quarter of the twentieth century (though his lifespan far exceeded his ability to fathom new artistic developments).

Finlandia, Op. 26 (1899)

Far more than a potboiler, Sibelius's most famous work is still capable of stimulating musical glands. The composer's musical patriotism is here at its most public. The work is rightfully treasured by the Finnish people. Its melodies, steeped in Finnish folk quality, are in fact not folksongs but themes of Sibelius's own invention.

Boston Symphony Orchestra, Davis: Philips 446160-2
Swedish Radio Symphony Orchestra, Salonen: Sony Classical SK 46668

The Swan of Tuonela, Op. 22/3 (1900)

The *Swan* was first composed in 1893 and revised in 1897 and 1900. It is a magical piece of orchestration, no. 3 of the *Four Legends* or *Lemminkäinen Suite*. The piece is set in Tuonela, "[t]he Kingdom of Death, the Hades of Finnish mythology," which "is surrounded by a broad river of black water and swift current. On it, in majestic course, floats and sings the swan of Tuonela." The *Swan* is beguilingly sung by the English horn.

Scottish National Orchestra, Gibson: Chandos CHAN 6508
Orchestre de la Suisse Romande, Stein: London 417697-2
Helsinki Radio Symphony Orchestra, Kamu: Deutsche Grammophon 427204-2

Concerto in D Minor for Violin and Orchestra, Op. 47 (1905)

This concerto is one of the grandest of Romantic concertos. Sibelius was dissatisfied with his first version and revised it before giving it to Richard Strauss to
conduct in Berlin in 1905. The famous violinist Maud Powell was soloist when
it had its American premiere at Carnegie Hall in 1906. Sibelius managed to
write a virtuoso concerto in the context of a large-scale symphonic framework;
the work rhapsodizes, broods, and dances in Sibelius's still-extroverted style. It
is the most celebrated Scandinavian violin concerto.

Heifetz, Chicago Symphony Orchestra, Hendl: RCA, RCD1-7019
Oistrakh, Philadelphia Orchestra, Ormandy: Sony Classical SBK 47659
Shaham, Philharmonia Orchestra, Sinopoli: Deutsche Grammophon 437540-2

Symphony no. 1 in E Minor, Op. 39 (1899)
Symphony no. 2 in D Major, Op. 43 (1902)
Symphony no. 4 in A Minor, Op. 63 (1911)
Symphony no. 7 in C Major, Op. 105 (1924)

The twenty-five years from Sibelius's First Symphony to the Seventh form the
composer's essential spiritual journey. The first two are vintage examples of
grand-manner, late-nineteenth-century Romanticism with a definite Finnish
cast, and they are not to be disdained. (I do not include the three-movement
Third Symphony, whose light and restrained manner only seems slight on first
hearing. It is nonetheless a key work in the Sibelius canon.)

The 1911 Fourth Symphony is magisterial. "It stands out as a protest against
the compositions of today," Sibelius wrote. "Nothing, [there is] absolutely nothing of the circus about it." The work finds Sibelius at the crossroads of his career, unable to follow in the wake of Mahler or in the avant-garde spirit of
Stravinsky and Schoenberg. He would continue on his own lonely path
through the one-movement Seventh Symphony and *Tapiola* until that tragic
moment when he had nothing more to say and knew it.

The last five symphonies are astonishing in their tightly packed structure.
Sibelius remained true to his Finnish roots but managed at the same time to
solve some of the thorniest abstract problems of formal design since Brahms.
He slaved over his themes, putting them under a musical microscope, directing
their organic growth with absolute precision.

Sibelius admirers will doubtless want to own the complete symphonies.
The famous set by Colin Davis and the Boston Symphony Orchestra is extraor-

dinary in its spaciousness and restrained majesty on four Philips CDs (446157-
2 and 446160-2). Simon Rattle, a true Sibelian, conducts a lesser but highly re-
sponsive City of Birmingham Orchestra in a more restless version on four EMI
Classics CDs (CDMD 64118). Leonard Bernstein's traversal of the complete
symphonies is an exceptional achievement with his New York Philharmonic
Orchestra on "Bernstein: The Royal Edition" (Sony Classical SM2K 47619
and 47622).

Symphony no. 1

Philharmonia Orchestra, Ashkenazy: London 289455402-2

Vienna Philharmonic Orchestra, Bernstein: Deutsche Grammophon 435351-2

Symphony no. 2

San Francisco Symphony, Blomstedt: London 443376-2

Gothenburg Symphony Orchestra, Järvi: BIS BIS CD 252

Cleveland Orchestra, Levi: Telarc CD 80095

Symphony no. 4

Berlin Philharmonic Orchestra, Levine: Deutsche Grammophon 45865

Royal Scottish National Orchestra, Gibson: Chandos CHAN 6557

Pittsburgh Symphony Orchestra, Maazel: Sony Classical SK 46499

Symphony no. 7

Vienna Philharmonic Orchestra, Bernstein: Deutsche Grammophon 427647-2

Berlin Philharmonic Orchestra, Karajan: Deutsche Grammophon 457748

Tapiola, Op. 112 (1926)

In Finnish mythology, Tapio is the god of the forest. In this monothematic
masterpiece, Sibelius brought his love and awe for the Finnish forests to its ultimate conclusion in music of raw and atmospheric beauty. On the score the
composer appended these four lines:

> *Widespread they stand, the Northland's dusky forests,*
> *Ancient, mysterious, brooding savage dreams;*
> *Within them dwells the forest's mighty God,*
> *And wood-sprites in the gloom weave magic secrets.*

According to the composer and critic Wilfrid Mellers, "*Tapiola* is the *non
plus ultra* of Sibelian technique; and in it the human personality seems to dis-

solve away in nature's infinities of time and space. . . . It is surely one of the most terrifying pieces of music ever written. . . . Perhaps this oneness in Nature is one of the few means whereby an artist may approach religious experiences, in a non-religious materialistic society."

Berlin Philharmonic Orchestra, Karajan: Deutsche Grammophon 445518-2
Helsinki Philharmonic Orchestra, Beecham: Ondine ODE 809

OTHER PRINCIPAL WORKS

CHAMBER MUSIC
Quartet in D Minor for Strings (*Voces intimae*), Op. 56 (1909)*

INCIDENTAL MUSIC AND SYMPHONIC POEMS
En Saga, Op. 9 (1892)*
Karelia Suite, Op. 11 (1893)*
Four Legends from the Kalevalá, Op. 22 (1895)
Kuolema (incidental music; *Valse triste* is one of the numbers), Opp. 44 and 62 (1903–11)
Pelléas et Melisande (incidental music), Op. 46 (1905)
Pohjola's Daughter (symphonic fantasy), Op. 49 (1906)*
Belshazzar's Feast (incidental music), Op. 51 (1906)
Nightride and Sunrise (symphonic poem), Op. 55 (1907)*
Rakastava, Op. 14 (1911)
The Oceanides (tone poem), Op. 73 (1914)*

PIANO MUSIC
Nearly one hundred pieces
Three Sonatinas, Op. 67 (1912)

VOICE AND ORCHESTRA WORKS
Luonnotar (tone poem) for Soprano and Orchestra, Op. 70 (c.1910)

OTHER ROMANTIC COMPOSERS

DANIEL-FRANÇOIS AUBER

(1782–1871) France

In the history of French opera, Auber was the last representative of *opéra comique*. He was equal and often superior to François Boieldieu, Louis Hérold, Adolphe Adam, and others, in a tradition that closed with Jacques Offenbach. His long life was productive as a composer, but he was also the director of the Paris Conservatory from 1842 to 1870. In the majority of his fifty operas, he collaborated with Eugène Scribe, a librettist who seldom failed to make a cohesive drama. His most celebrated opera, *Fra Diavolo* (1830), perfectly represents the spirit of *opéra comique*.

Auber's best work has verve and grace and is very French in its amorous melodic curves. His weightiest opera, *La Muette de Portici* (1828), was admired by Wagner and Liszt. A street in Paris is named for him.

Fra Diavolo (1830)

Mesplé, Berbié, Gedda, Monte Carlo Philharmonic Orchestra and Jean Laforge Ensemble Choir, Soustrot: EMI Classics CDCB 54810

GIACOMO MEYERBEER

(1791–1864) Germany

If a great deal of Meyerbeer's music sounds dated today, it is only because his accomplishments were overwhelmed by those of Verdi and Wagner. But for two decades from 1830, Meyerbeer's name was synonymous with grand spectacle opera. His work contains a whole body of striking effects that were new to the operatic theater, including an extraordinary assimilation of style to the vastly different subject matter demanded by each opera. His librettos were deftly fashioned by Eugène Scribe, the best librettist of the French stage. Musically he was the logical outgrowth of Gaspare Spontini and Carl Maria von Weber; in fact, he and Weber were friends, and had both studied with the Abbé Volger.

In 1831 Chopin, like all of Paris, was astounded by *Robert le diable*: "It is a masterpiece of the modern school. . . . No one will ever stage anything like it! Meyerbeer has made himself immortal!"

The composer was born Jakob Liebmann Beer. Like Mendelssohn, he was the son of a wealthy Jewish banker in Berlin. As the richest composer in the world, he was always at the mercy of spongers. Upon finding out that the poet Heine was going to write critically of him, he confided to his diary, "The true reason for this animosity is that . . . I refused to loan him the 1,000 francs he wanted, after having loaned him many thousands over the years, of which not one penny was ever paid." But, Meyerbeer's most envious enemy was Wagner, who attacked him in his virulent anti-Semitic tract "Judaism in Music." Of his operas, the finest are *Robert le diable* (1831), *Les Huguenots* (1836), *Le Prophète* (1849), and *L'Africaine* (1865), the last of which was produced posthumously. All of Meyerbeer's operas make heavy vocal demands on the singers.

Les Huguenots (1836)
Sutherland, Arroyo, Tourangeau, Vrenios, Cossa, New Philharmonia Orchestra and Ambrosian Opera Chorus, Bonynge: London 430549-2

FRANZ BERWALD

(1796–1868) Sweden

Berwald is the most important Swedish composer of the nineteenth century. He received little recognition in his lifetime, and is still little known. The Sweden of his day was not prepared for a composer of his radical harmonic style. Berwald's four symphonies, with their terse textures and harmonic tension, will be a welcome surprise to lovers of nineteenth-century symphonic music. His chamber compositions are also worthy of attention.

Symphony no. 1 in G Minor (*Sérieuse*) (1842)
Symphony no. 2 in D Major (*Capricieuse*) (1842)
Symphony no. 3 in C Major (*Singulière*) (1845)
Symphony no. 4 in E-flat Major (*Naïve*) (1845)
Gothenburg Symphony Orchestra, Järvi: Deutsche Grammophon 415502-2

ALBERT LORTZING

(1801–1851) Germany

A smattering of Lortzing brings the listener to the youthful humor of the springtime of German Romanticism. Lortzing's operas reflect the manner of Weber, Mendelssohn, and Heinrich Marschner, and theatrically they are precursors of Sir Arthur Sullivan. His most successful opera, produced at Leipzig in 1837, is *Zar und Zimmermann*. Seldom does a season go by with no performance of *Zar*, especially in Germany, where Lortzing has been well loved.

Zar und Zimmermann (selections) (1837)

Popp, Kraus, Prey, Krenn, Bavarian Radio Symphony Orchestra and Chorus, Wallberg: Acanta CD 42424

ADOLPHE ADAM

(1803–1856) France

Adam was born the same year as Berlioz and died in the year of Schumann's death. His father had forbidden him to compose for the theater, but his teacher Boieldieu gave him encouragement. Although he composed both comic and grand opera, Adam lives on each season in his charming ballet *Giselle*, first performed at the Paris Opera in 1841 and a tour de force for every great ballerina since.

Giselle (1841)

Royal Opera House Orchestra, Bonynge: London 417505-2

MIKHAIL GLINKA

(1804–1857) Russia

Glinka, an imposing father figure in the history of Russian music, is dear to the hearts of Russians and their composers. It was his ardent desire to write a Russian national opera, which others had previously attempted unsuccessfully. He finally fulfilled his dream in 1836 with A *Life for the Tsar*, and then in 1842 with the more distinctive *Ruslan and Ludmila*. In the latter opera—stocked with Russian melody, genuine lyricism, and vigorous choruses—one hears much of later Russian opera. *Ruslan and Ludmila* is still staged in Russia but seldom anywhere else, though its overture is known everywhere. Glinka left an engaging book of memoirs.

Ruslan and Ludmila (opera in five acts) (1837–42)

Gorchakova, Diadkova, Bogachova, Masurin, Kirov Opera Orchestra and Chorus, Gergiev: Philips 456248-2

OTTO NICOLAI

(1810–1849) Germany

Nicolai had a considerable conducting career and in 1842 founded and conducted the Vienna Philharmonic Orchestra.

His one enduring work is *Die lustigen Weiber von Windsor* (*The Merry Wives of Windsor*), a comic opera thoroughly enjoyable and lighthearted, and written in a state of inspiration. It was composed in 1844 but was not staged until March 9, 1849, in Berlin, where it had a brilliant success. The composer, weak from illness, conducted the first four performances and died eight weeks later.

Die lustigen Weiber von Windsor (*The Merry Wives of Windsor*) (1849)

Mathis, Wunderlich, Frick, Bavarian State Opera Orchestra and Chorus, Heger: EMI Classics CDMB 69348

CHARLES-VALENTIN ALKAN

(1813–1888) France

Alkan left some of the most inspired piano music of nineteenth-century France and is finally coming to be appreciated as a visionary Romantic. He lived a sad, strange life. Reclusive and basically misanthropic tendencies prevented him from social congress and from bringing his compositions to the public, although whenever he was heard, he was considered to be a great pianist. Late in Alkan's career, the composer Vincent d'Indy heard him and reported that his performance of Beethoven's Piano Sonata no. 31 (Op. 110) "affected me with an enthusiasm such as I have never experienced since." Liszt revered him, recalling that he was never nervous playing for anyone except Alkan.

In the last decades, people have begun to explore Alkan. The pianist Ronald Smith observes, "The very diversity and range of his composition has proved a frustrating obstacle to the filing-cabinet minds. Like Beethoven, he seldom if ever repeats himself. . . . These baffling pages, black with marching regiments of notes, become in performance a Pandora's box of demonic power to which only the most fearless player holds the key."

Alkan's oeuvre forms a vital chapter of nineteenth-century piano music. He was one of the great temperaments of French Romantic art; his vision reminds one of the blazing passion of Géricault, Delacroix, Hugo, and Berlioz. Hans von Bülow called him "the Berlioz of the piano."

His ending was sad. The story, possibly apocryphal, has it that he was reaching for a volume of his beloved Talmud on top of a massive bookcase. The structure toppled over, crushing the emaciated musician to death.

Études, Op. 39/8–10 (1857)
Hamelin: Music & Arts CD 724-1

Various Piano Music
Smith: APR APR 7031

FRANZ VON SUPPÉ

(1819–1895) Austria

The operas that Suppé's overtures once introduced have not been heard since their premieres, but no music collection is complete without a selection of his overtures. *Dichter und Bauer* (*Poet and Peasant*, 1846) was once so popular that it was arranged for more than sixty different combinations. It, along with *Leichte Kavallerie* (*Light Cavalry*, 1879), was a staple item for café orchestras, popular concerts, and seaside bands. Countless amateur pianists played duet versions. These overtures remain a delightful introduction to great music for children.

Poet and Peasant; Light Cavalry; Morning, Noon, and Night in Vienna;
   Jolly Robbers; Beautiful Galatea; Pique Dame
Berlin Philharmonic Orchestra, Karajan: Deutsche Grammophon 435712-2

ÉDOUARD LALO

(1823–1892) France

Lalo was born in Lille and studied at the local conservatory. His teacher, Pierre
Baumann, was proud of the fact that he had played in an orchestra conducted
by Beethoven, and he taught his pupil to love his hero.

But Lalo's father fought his son's artistic inclinations. When Édouard was
sixteen, after a particularly acrimonious quarrel, he fled to Paris. Although he
had no money, he was able to study at the Conservatory, which is a state-
funded institution. Finding the Conservatory distasteful and too academic, he
studied privately, composed, taught, and played violin in chamber groups. After eight years in Paris, however, he was deeply depressed. He had not won the
Prix de Rome; nor could he get his music performed or published. A disheartened Lalo decided to stop composing altogether. Eight years went by without a
single composition. He earned a small income by performing, in a string quartet, music of Haydn, Mozart, and Beethoven, a taste not particularly cultivated
at that time in Paris.

In 1865, however, Lalo inched his way back to his true path, largely because of the encouragement of his new wife, singer Julie de Maligny. (The
couple had one child, Pierre, who became a distinguished music critic.)

Lalo was nearly fifty before he received any recognition as a composer. In
1872 his *Divertissement* was enthusiastically received in Paris. Two years later
his Violin Concerto (Op. 20) was played in London by the brilliant Spanish
virtuoso Pablo de Sarasate, who scored a triumph. In 1875 an even greater triumph came when Sarasate performed Lalo's *Symphonie espagnole* (Op. 21), a
delightful and refined showpiece rich in Spanish flavor that has since become
Lalo's most celebrated score. Bit by bit, his other works saw performance. In
1877 he received ovations for his Cello Concerto, and in 1882 the Paris
Opera produced *Namouna*, a ballet with choreography by Marius Petipa,
Tchaikovsky's collaborator. Lalo arranged a five-movement suite from the ballet, which Debussy called "a masterpiece of rhythm and color." In 1886 his
G minor symphony was performed.

But Lalo's greatest moment came on May 7, 1888, when his opera *Le Roi
d'Ys* scored a sensation at the Opéra-Comique. Hailed as a masterpiece, within
a year it had received one hundred performances. *Le Roi d'Ys* is seldom staged

outside of France, though its overture is occasionally heard at orchestral concerts. It is the best of Lalo's later works, which mostly show little of the freshness of his earlier music: for Lalo's last years were darkened by arthritic paralysis.

Lalo was never profound, nor did he pretend to be. His art is warmly expressive, composed within established classical forms and filled with delightful melodies and exuberant rhythms. He was one of the few French composers of the time unaffected by Wagnerism.

Symphonie espagnole for Violin and Orchestra, Op. 21 (1874)
Perlman, Orchestre de Paris, Barenboim: Deutsche Grammophon 429977-2
Heifetz, RCA Victor Symphony Orchestra, P. Steinberg: RCA Gold Seal 7709-2-RG

Concerto in D Minor for Cello and Orchestra (1877)
Ma, Orchestre National, Maazel: CBS MK 35848
Rose, Philadelphia Orchestra, Ormandy: Sony Classical SBK 48278

LOUIS MOREAU GOTTSCHALK
(1829–1869) United States

Gottschalk, the most famous mid-nineteenth-century American composer, studied piano in Paris as a boy and made his debut as a pianist there in 1844. Berlioz, Chopin, and others were impressed. He toured throughout Europe, where his early piano piece "Bamboula" (Op. 2, composed at sixteen and based on an African-American melody) made a sensation. The New Orleans–born musician returned to America in 1853 and took the country by storm.

During the Civil War this troubadour of the piano performed in both the North and the South to great acclaim, playing such "American"-sounding pieces as "Banjo" (Op. 82, 1853) and "Tournament Galop" (1854). He played his "L'Union" (Op. 48, 1862) at a memorial service for Lincoln shortly after the assassination. Some of his worst pieces are "The Dying Poet" (1864) and "The Last Hope" (Op. 16, 1854), sentimental drawing-room ditties that made him a small fortune. Most of his work is for the piano, and the finest of it is fresh, scintillating, and brash, composed when America itself was the most optimistic of places. In Gottschalk one hears circus bands, Sunday horseraces, Caribbean and Latin American tunes, unabashed sentimentality, sassiness, pianistic hijinks, and hints of the emerging ragtime. Gottschalk's life of only forty years reads like a romance; mystery and legend surrounded him, and even his death was dramatic. He finished a piece called "Morte!!" (Op. 60, 1868), played it at a concert in Rio de Janeiro, fell unconscious at the piano, and died of yellow fever a few days later.

Piano Music
Pennario: EMI Classics CDM 64668-2
Marks: Nimbus NI 5014

KARL GOLDMARK

(1830–1915) Hungary

The son of a poor Jewish cantor, Goldmark was immersed in Viennese musical life as composer and critic. He was a composer of melodic freshness and delightful orchestral coloring. His opera *Die Königen von Saba* (*The Queen of Sheba*, Op. 27, 1875) was once a repertoire piece, and its ballet music was once a pop concert staple. Goldmark's A minor violin concerto (Op. 28, 1877) is warm-blooded and genial, and the sparkling *Ländliche Hochzeit* (*Rustic Wedding*) symphony is perhaps his finest score.

Rustic Wedding (symphony), Op. 26 (1877)
Utah Symphony Orchestra, Abravanel: Vanguard Classics OVC 5002
New York Philharmonic, Bernstein: Sony Classical 61836

AMILCARE PONCHIELLI

(1834–1886) Italy

Ponchielli composed several operas, but only *La Gioconda* has lasted. Its first performance took place at La Scala in 1876, with Arrigo Boito as librettist. Well-known arias are heard throughout, especially "Suicidio!" in Act IV, but its most famous moments occur in the delicious orchestral ballet scene, Dance of the Hours, in Act III.

La Gioconda (1876)
Callas, Cossotto, Companeez, Ferraro, Cappuccilli, Vinco, La Scala Orchestra and Chorus,
   Votto: EMI Classics CDCC 49518

HENRYK WIENIAWSKI

(1835–1880) Poland

The Polish-born Wieniawski was an eminent violinist. His colleague Joseph Joachim noted that other violinists could not fathom the wondrous skill of his left hand. Wieniawski and the pianist Anton Rubinstein toured the United States in 1872, together performing works such as Beethoven's *Kreutzer* Sonata from memory and thrilling audiences with the fury of their performance. Many thought Wieniawski's talent unrivaled, even in a golden age of violinism with such fabulous practitioners as Joachim, Louis Spohr, Ole Bull, Charles de Bériot, Ferdinand David, Pablo de Sarasate, and Henri Vieuxtemps. Before he died of heart disease at forty-four, Wieniawski composed around thirty works for violin. The meltingly beautiful *Légende* (Op. 17, c.1860) is a must for violin lovers, while the warm Second Concerto (Op. 22, 1862) deserves its place in the permanent repertoire.

Concerto no. 2 in D Minor for Violin and Orchestra, Op. 22 (1862)
Heifetz, RCA Victor Symphony Orchestra, Solomon: RCA 09026-60927-2
Stern, New York Philharmonic Orchestra, Kurtz: CBS M4K 42003

LÉO DELIBES

(1836–1891) France

Delibes studied at the Paris Conservatory with Adolphe Adam, composer of the ballet *Giselle*. He is a composer of considerable refinement and charm, with a fund of sensuous melody. His finest opera, *Lakmé* (1883), includes the delectable coloratura aria known as the Bell Song, as well as other favorites—"Dans la Forêt près de nous," "Ah! Viens dans la forêt profonde," and "C'est le dieu de la jeunesse." Delibes's two full-length ballets, *Coppélia* and *Sylvia*, are glories of French Romantic ballet; *Coppélia*, first performed in 1870, is the favorite. Tchaikovsky dearly loved them both. After hearing *Sylvia* (1876), he wrote, "This is the only ballet I know where the music is of the only and vital importance. . . . If I had known this music earlier I would not have written my *Swan Lake*." God forbid!

Coppélia (1870)
National Philharmonic Orchestra, Bonynge: London 414502-2

Coppélia (suite)
Berlin Philharmonic Orchestra, Karajan: Deutsche Grammophon 423215-2

Lakmé (1883)
Sutherland, Vanzo, Bacquier, Monte Carlo Opera Orchestra, Bonynge: London 425485-2

MILY BALAKIREV

(1837–1910) Russia

An impressive composer, Balakirev left a handful of engaging works. Even his flawed compositions contain moments of glowing inspiration. Balakirev took impetus from Glinka's pioneering Russian nationalism and became a propelling force in Russian music. In 1861 he began to assemble a group of nationalist musicians, including César Cui, Borodin, Mussorgsky, and Rimsky-Korsakov, as his pupil-disciples.

Balakirev was a man of passionate extremes. After Balakirev's long absence due to a nervous breakdown, Rimsky-Korsakov wrote, "I found him very much changed. In every room in his home were holy images with a little lamp burning in front of each. He was ever attending services. He had given up wearing furs, smoking, and eating meat. He liked to eat fish, provided it had not been knocked on the head. His love for all living creatures had become so great, that if a noxious insect found its way into his room, he would catch it with care and throw it out the window, wishing it 'God-speed.' "

In time Balakirev's work was overshadowed by that of his pupils. Once, when Rimsky-Korsakov was congratulated for his *Sheherazade*, he responded that the piece was merely a rehashing of Balakirev's symphonic poem *Tamara* (1867–82). His best-known work is *Islamey*, an oriental fantasy for piano (1869). An orchestral version was made by Alfredo Casella.

Islamey (oriental fantasia) (1869)

SOLO PIANO
Barere: Enterprise ENT PL 232

ORCHESTRATED
Philadelphia Orchestra, Ormandy: Sony Classical SBK 62647

Tamara (1867–82)
Philharmonia Orchestra, Svetlanov: Hyperion CDA 66586

MAX BRUCH

(1838–1920) Germany

Bruch was an esteemed German composer. His best-known works are the *Kol Nidrei (Ritual Hebrew Chant*, Op. 47, 1881), adapted for cello and orchestra; the *Scottish Fantasy* for violin and orchestra (Op. 46, 1880); and above all the warm-hearted Violin Concerto in G Minor (Op. 26, 1865), first performed by and dedicated to Joseph Joachim, who considered it among the four greatest violin concertos, the others being by Beethoven, Mendelssohn, and Brahms. Bruch's music derives from Mendelssohn; his form and harmony are conservative. At its best, Bruch's music possesses deep thoughtfulness and melodic richness.

Concerto no. 1 in G Minor for Violin and Orchestra, Op. 26 (1865)
Heifetz, New Symphony Orchestra of London, Sargent: RCA 6214-2-RC
Kennedy, English Chamber Orchestra, Tate: EMI Classics CDC 749663

HERMANN GOETZ

(1840–1876) Switzerland

Goetz was an unpretentious, gentle, elegiac composer whose choral settings and especially his opera *The Taming of the Shrew* might well be revived today. His Piano Concerto (Op. 18, 1867) would be an engaging item for pianists looking for a forgotten Romantic concerto. His songs, piano pieces, and chamber works are rather short of breath, but his Symphony in F Major (Op. 9, 1873) is a gem. In 1893, Bernard Shaw wrote that Goetz's opera and symphony were "two masterpieces which placed him securely above all other German composers of the last hundred years save only Mozart and Beethoven, Weber and Wagner"—an outlandish verdict considering Mendelssohn, Schumann, Brahms, and Bruckner.

Symphony in F Major, Op. 9 (1873)
Monte Carlo Opera Orchestra, Remoortel: Genesis GCD 105

EMMANUEL CHABRIER

(1841–1894) France

Chabrier was born into an affluent family in the Auvergne region. The family moved to Paris in 1856. Chabrier was given piano lessons from age six but was expected to become a lawyer. After he obtained a law degree at age twenty-one, he did not practice but took a position in the Ministry of the Interior, where he worked diligently for more than fifteen years. Music continued to be an avocation, and it was not until 1877 that his operetta *L'Étoile* was performed with success.

In the summer of 1879, Wagner fever was rampant among French intellectuals, indeed in all of Europe. Along with the composer Henri Duparc, Chabrier heard Wagner's *Tristan und Isolde* in Munich. It was a decisive moment in his life. The usually convivial Chabrier sobbed wildly and locked himself in a hotel room after hearing *Tristan*, which surpassed his wildest dreams. "There's music there for a hundred years," he wrote; "he hasn't left us anything to do." In a near-hypnotic state, he returned to Paris, quit his job, and finally devoted his life to composing. He worked furiously at a unique series of piano pieces, Ten *Pièces pittoresques*, and at their premiere in 1881, the composer César Franck declared, "We have just heard something quite extraordinary. This music is a link between our epoch and that of Couperin and Rameau." In 1883 Chabrier visited Spain, found the country exhilarating, and composed *España*, which took Paris by storm when it was premiered that year. He followed *España* with the delectable Three *Valses romantiques* for two pianos (1883). In 1887 his opera *Le Roi malgré lui* was produced in Paris. Stravinsky thought it a masterpiece, but it remains one of the neglected gems of French opera. The last years of Chabrier's relatively short life were bitterly cruel. Advancing syphilis caused an increasing physical and mental paralysis, and he no longer recognized his own music. He had become a well-loved figure in French artistic circles. Manet, who died in his arms, painted him, as did Degas and others.

Chabrier's best work removes all vestiges of German grandiosity. French to the core, he is a harbinger of French Modernism. Indeed, the French pianist Robert Casadesus felt that, with *Bourrée fantasque* (1891), the Modern French school was born. Strutting, seduction, Toulouse-Lautrec-style nightlife, mock sentimentality—all are packed into this boisterous work. *España*, with its riot of orchestral color, was considered the last word in Modernity in 1883. Chabrier is racy, unselfconsciously vulgar, and often tender-hearted. He painted a chivalric portrait of the Belle Epoque. His influence on Satie, Ravel, Poulenc, and others is inescapable. As a teenager, Poulenc one day found himself at the Maison Pathé putting a coin in a machine that played back "Idylle," number six of the Ten *Pièces pittoresques*. Looking back years later, Poulenc declared, "I still tremble with emotion thinking of the miracle that happened then; a new harmonic world opened up before me, and my own music has never forgotten that first *baiser d'amour*."

España: Rhapsody for Orchestra (1883)
Montreal Symphony Orchestra, Dutoit: London 421527-2

Bourrée fantasque (1891)
French National Radio Orchestra, Jordan: Erato ECD 88018

ARRIGO BOITO

(1842–1918) Italy

Besides being a translator, poet, and the creator of the librettos for Verdi's
Otello and *Falstaff*, Boito composed the striking opera *Mefistofele* (1868), based
on Goethe's titanic masterwork. It displays an acute delineation of the conflicts
between good and evil. The critic James Huneker realized, "It is such a
tremendous attempt to embrace all of Goethe's profound world philosophy,
poetry, dramatic symbolism, that it is a failure—a remarkable failure." Yet how
could it be otherwise? But if Gounod's *Faust* is too pretty and frivolous for some
tastes, Boito grips the listener with moments of terrific drama and a truly sardonic leading character. Boito's musical gestations were slow to the extreme: a
second opera, *Nerone*, remained unfinished even after nearly forty years of labor. In the last years of his life, he was elected to the Italian senate.

Mefistofele (1868)
Freni, Caballé, Pavarotti, Ghiaurov, National Philharmonic Orchestra, de Fabritiis: London
410175-241076-2

SIR ARTHUR SULLIVAN

(1842–1900) England

Sullivan was well trained at London's Royal Academy of Music and the Leipzig
Conservatory, and produced the expected symphonies, oratorios, and the like,
each stamped with respectable, stuffy Victorian platitudes. His songs "Onward
Christian Soldiers" and "The Lost Chord" were sung throughout the empire.
Sullivan desperately wanted to scale Parnassus, but it was not to be. Then one
day the solicitor William S. Gilbert, a sour, witty man, ventured to team up
with him to write operettas. Sullivan, with all of the guilt that a serious artist
can experience, collaborated with Gilbert on these "commercial ventures." In
the process, the dowdy Sullivan became touched with musical genius. Together Gilbert and Sullivan ruled the English musical stage. Never before had

there been such a scintillating combination of words and music; never had a ready public received more pleasure. For nearly twenty years, they wrote hit after hilarious hit: *H.M.S. Pinafore* (1878), *The Pirates of Penzance* (1879), *Patience* (1881), *Princess Ida* and *The Mikado* (both 1885), *The Gondoliers* (1886), and *The Yeomen of the Guard* (1888). *Pinafore* and *Mikado* are the most-performed comic operettas ever written.

After its premiere on March 14, 1885, *The Mikado* took London, and soon the world, by storm. All succumbed to its infectious gaiety, and by the end of the year, it was being performed by 150 different companies. On a single night in the United States, it had 117 different performances in various places throughout the nation. H. L. Mencken reported, "The people of the United States were *Mikado* crazed for a year or more, as they had been *Pinafore* crazed some time before. Things Japanese acquired an absurd vogue. Women carried Japanese fans, wore Japanese Kimonos and dressed their hair in some approach to the Japanese manner. The mincing step of Yum-Yum appeared in the land; chop-suey, mistaken for a Japanese dish, became a naturalized victual."

After Sullivan's death in 1900, Gilbert, who lived until 1911, searched in vain for a worthy replacement. Without Sullivan, Gilbert's pen was dry. The two were indispensable to each other. Gilbert and Sullivan made enormous contributions to the pleasure of all musical audiences and left the world merrier than they found it.

H.M.S. Pinafore (1878)
D'Oyly Carte Opera Company, Sargent: Arabesque 28052-2

The Mikado (1885)
D'Oyly Carte Opera Company, Nash: London 425190-2

Overtures
Academy of St. Martin in the Fields, Marriner: Philips 434916-2

JULES MASSENET

(1842–1912) France

Born at Montaud, St. Etienne, Massenet had his first piano lesson (from his mother) on the first day of the 1848 Revolution. Soon afterward the family moved to Paris. The boy clearly had talent, and at age eleven he was accepted at the Paris Conservatory. He was a brilliant pupil and won first prize in piano playing. His teachers, the opera composers Henri Reber and Ambroise

Thomas, composer of the opera *Mignon*, encouraged him, seeing great promise in his work.

In 1863, at twenty-one, Massenet won the Prix de Rome. He was exhilarated to be in Rome, where he met many artists, including Liszt, who introduced Massenet to Constance de Saint-Maire, a beautiful young pianist. The couple married in 1866; it was a long, happy marriage, lasting for forty-six years and producing one child, Juliette. They returned to Paris in 1866, and several of Massenet's works were soon performed. They caused little stir. In 1873 he wrote some feeble incidental music for a play, but one number, "Invocation," struck gold. Massenet changed its name to "Élégie," added words, and arranged the song for cello and piano accompaniment. Sentimental Paris could not get enough of the sadly religious tune with its erotic overtones. He followed it with a religiously ecstatic oratorio, *Marie-Magdeleine* (1873). It, too, was a success. Massenet never had the public far from his heart and told the composer Vincent d'Indy, "I don't believe in all that creeping Jesus stuff, but the public likes it and we must always agree with the public."

Massenet's importance in French music was solidified in the 1880s by a series of operas, tailored to the tastes of the French bourgeoisie in the language they loved—their own. By the time of his death, Massenet sounded faded and artificial to many. A reaction to his immense popularity set in.

In an obituary the day after his death in 1912, Debussy wrote, "He was the most genuinely loved of all our contemporary musicians. His colleagues never forgave him for having such a power to please; it really was a gift. Massenet realized he could better express his genius in pastel tints and whispered melodies in works composed of lightness itself." Massenet never plumbed the depths, but he did not care to. Opera lovers today will find *Werther* (1892), *Thaïs* (1894, with its celebrated "Meditation"), *Sapho* (1897), *Le jongleur de Notre-Dame* (1902), and *Don Quichotte* (1900) to be far more than mere period pieces. Massenet's exquisite masterpiece *Manon*, based on Abbé Prévost's potent eighteenth-century novel of lust and betrayal, had its premiere on January 19, 1884, at the Opéra-Comique in Paris. Sir Thomas Beecham once said he would sacrifice all six of Bach's *Brandenburg Concertos* for *Manon*. Although Puccini's *Manon Lescaut* (premiered in 1893, nine years after Massenet's) has given it competition, *Manon* has had nearly two thousand performances at the Opéra-Comique alone. Nowhere is Massenet's seductive melodic gift more appealing.

Manon (1884)

Sills, Gedda, Souzay, Bacquier, New Philharmonia Orchestra, Ambrosian Opera Chorus, Rudel: EMI Classics CDMC 69831

*de los Angeles, Legay, Dens, Paris Opéra-Comique Orchestra and Chorus, Monteux: EMI
Classics CDMC 63549*

CHARLES-MARIE WIDOR

(1844–1937) France

Although Widor composed in many forms, it is as an organ composer that he is honored worldwide. His grandfather and father were organ builders, and his father gave him a thorough grounding in "the king of instruments." In 1870 he took the coveted position of chief organist at the Church of Saint-Sulpice, in Paris, where he played in the organ loft for sixty-four years. As professor of organ playing at the Paris Conservatory, he was Franck's successor.

Widor's organ music has long been an essential segment of the repertory. From 1876 until 1900, he composed ten large works, which he titled symphonies and which include an enormous variety of movements—marches, toccatas, variations, fugues, and so on, exploring a wide range of technical problems and registration. The Symphony no. 5 contains the popular fifth movement, Toccata.

Symphony no. 5 in F Minor for Organ, Op. 42/1 (1880)
Chorzempa: Philips 410054-2

PABLO DE SARASATE

(1844–1908) Spain

Saint-Saëns, Bruch, Joachim, Dvořák, and Lalo all dedicated compositions to Sarasate, who was one of the most hypnotic violinists ever to walk on the concert stage. In the drawing room, he loved Beethoven and Brahms's chamber music, but on the platform he was the virtuoso, the charmer, his midnight eyes fixed upon his audience. In short, he was the ultimate public performer. "Leave me alone with your symphonic concertos like the Brahms'," he wrote; "I won't deny that it is pretty good music, but do you really think I'll be so insipid as to stand there on stage, violin in hand, to listen while the oboe plays the only melody in the adagio?" He published more than fifty opus numbers, from the graceful Spanish dances to the *Carmen Fantasy* and the *Zigeunerweisen*, producing dashing and idiomatic violinism at its most pleasing.

Zigeunerweisen for Violin and Piano, Op. 20 (1878)
Carmen Fantasy for Violin and Orchestra (after Bizet), Op. 25 (c.1883)
Perlman, Pittsburgh Symphony Orchestra, Previn: EMI Classics CDM 63533

HENRI DUPARC

(1848–1933) France

Duparc was one of music's least prolific masters: he suffered from mental illness and nervous disorders and ceased composing by his late thirties. But he wrote a dozen mature art songs, or *mélodies*, as the French call them. Songs like "Phidylé" (1882) and "Extase" (1884) clearly owe their conception to Wagner but possess Duparc's own definite imprint. The majority of his songs express romantic nostalgia, yearning, grief, and frustrated eroticism.

Complete *Mélodies*
Walker, Allen, Vignoles: Hyperion CDA 66323

Six *Mélodies*
Hendricks, Gardener: EMI CDC 49689-2
Souzay, Baldwin: Denon CO-2252

VINCENT D'INDY

(1851–1931) France

D'Indy's large output adheres to the highest standards of craft, and he is capable of a variety of moods and forms. His chamber music—a Piano Trio (Op. 98, 1929), a Sextet (Op. 92, 1927), three string quartets (Opp. 35, 45, 96, 1890–1929), and a Piano Quintet (Op. 81, 1924)—ranges from the picturesque to the neoclassical, while the numerous orchestral works include the delightful B-flat major symphony (1902), the better-known *Istar Variations* (Op. 42, 1896), and his most popular work, the invigorating *Symphony on a French Mountain Air* for orchestra and piano obligato (Op. 25), composed in 1886.

D'Indy studied composition with César Franck, whom he loved and whose biography he wrote. His theoretical erudition bordered on the fabulous, and he became a renowned teacher. As one of the founders of Paris's Schola Cantorum, a music school that later rivaled the Conservatory, he exerted a profound influence on French musical life. He told the American composer Daniel Gregory Mason, "The principles of art are eternal. They endure," and, "Only the heart can create beauty."

D'Indy is an extremely underrated composer. The English critic Eric Blom observed, "He never has the heated sensuality we find, for example, in Wagner, Liszt, Strauss or Scriabin. . . . He is always admirably cool and fresh in expression." But his reputation for austerity is undeserved. Unfortunately many music lovers define French music by Debussy and Ravel, by Berlioz, Fauré, and Gounod, but d'Indy's music is as French as theirs.

Symphony on a French Mountain Air for Piano and Orchestra, Op. 25 (1886)
C. Collard, Radio France Philharmonic Orchestra, Janowski: Erato 2292-45821-2-ZK
Henriot-Schweitzer, Boston Symphony Orchestra, Munch: RCA 09026-62582-2

Istar (symphonic variations) (1896)
San Francisco Symphony Orchestra, Monteux: RCA 09026-61900-2

ENGELBERT HUMPERDINCK

(1854–1921) Germany

During his creative life, Humperdinck was awestruck by Wagner. His masterpiece is the children's opera Hänsel und Gretel, based on the Grimm brothers' story. Premiered on December 23, 1893, its success was instantaneous. Within a few years, it was staged in every European city with an opera house. By 1902 it was heard throughout South America and reached China by 1909. On June 6, 1923, from the Royal Opera House, Covent Garden, Hänsel und Gretel was the first opera broadcast live in Europe, and on Christmas Day 1931, it inaugurated the famous Metropolitan Opera radio broadcasts. The work, with its heavy Wagnerian orchestration, somehow conveys a magical childlike charm. An enchanting poetry pervades the woodland scene.

Hänsel und Gretel (1893)
Schwarzkopf, Grümmer, Felbermayer, Ilosvay, Schürhoff, Metternich, Philharmonia Orchestra, Loughton High School Chorus, Karajan: EMI Classics CDMB 69293
Gruberova, Jones, Bonney, Oelze, Murray, Ludwig, Dresden Staatskapelle, Davis: Philips 438013-2

JOHN PHILIP SOUSA

(1854–1932) United States

The March King produced a spectacular array of rousing marches that tingle with rhythmic glory and melodic gold. Sousa, one of the great bandmasters and a sterling musician, raised the level of the concert band to unprecedented heights. Beginning his career as conductor of the U.S. Marine Band, he later formed his own ensemble touring the United States and Europe, introducing such favorites as "The Washington Post," "The High School Cadets," "El Capitan," "Hands Across the Sea," "Semper Fidelis," and the immortal "Stars and Stripes Forever." Sousa left more than a hundred marches, fifty songs, ten comic operas, three novels, and a delightful autobiography, *Marching Along*.

Various Marches
Eastman Wind Ensemble, Fennell: Mercury 434300-2

"The Stars and Stripes Forever" (piano arrangement by Vladimir Horowitz)
Horowitz: RCA 7755-2-RG

ANATOLY LIADOV

(1855–1914) Russia

Liadov was a fascinating and remote figure in Russian Romanticism. His indolence was proverbial, but his influence was greater than is usually suspected. His pupil Lazare Saminsky later called him "an important link between Rimsky-Korsakov and the new Russians." He composed slowly and was ever in danger of excessive self-criticism and denial of his own rare gifts. "The world," he said, "was tedious, disappointing, trying, purposeless, terrible." But art was another matter. "Give me fairies and dragons and mermaids, and goblins, and I am thoroughly happy," he declared. "Art feeds me on roast birds of paradise, it is another planet—nothing to do with our earth." His music, from his once-famous piano piece *A Musical Snuffbox* (Op. 32, 1893), to the small symphonic poems *The Enchanted Lake* (Op. 62, 1909), *Kikimora* (Op. 63, 1909), and *Baba Yaga* (Op. 56, 1891–1904), is an essential chapter of the Russian musical heritage. Of his work, the English critic M. D. Calvocoressi remarked, "Its merits are charm, grace, polish, alertness, and moderation. He has neither the power and glow of Borodin and Balakirev, nor the exuberant fancy of Rimsky-Korsakov at his best, nor the energy and abundance of Glazunov; but of the minor poets of music—not only Russian—he remains one of the most lovable."

Orchestral Music
Slovak Philharmonic Orchestra, Gunzenhauser: Marco Polo 8.220348

Variations on a Polish Folk Theme for Piano (1901)
Nikolayeva: Relief CR 911026

ERNEST CHAUSSON

(1855–1899) France

As a boy, Chausson developed a love for literature, painting, and music. At college his wealthy father insisted that he take a law degree, although he had no need to earn a living. In 1879 the young man traveled to Munich to hear Wagner's music. The Bayreuth master had a stunning impact on the young lawyer, and Chausson realized that music, not law, must be his life's work. Unfortunately, he was already twenty-five and sadly deficient in theoretical knowledge. "There is a phrase by Schumann," he wrote, "which is terrible and which resounds in my ears like the trumpet of judgment day: One is only a master of thought when one is the master of forms." Fortunately, he came in contact with César Franck and his disciples Vincent d'Indy, Henri Duparc, Pierre de Bréville, Charles Bordes, and other members of *"la bande à* Franck." Franck, a great and shrewd teacher and a perceptive psychologist, bolstered Chausson's confidence and, within only three years, equipped him with a solid compositional technique.

In 1883 Chausson married Jeanne Escudier, to whom he had dedicated his symphonic poem *Viviane* (Op. 5, 1882). She was refined and musical and provided Chausson with five children and an idyllic marriage. The family lived in grand style at their palatial home at Boulevard de Courcelles, where the couple entertained the cream of Parisian artistic life. Chausson was a man of great kindness and empathy, and he helped many indigent artists financially. He became particularly close friends with Isaac Albéniz and Claude Debussy.

From 1886 until 1895, Chausson labored on his opera, *Le Roi Arthus,* to his own libretto. Wagner haunted him ("that frightful Wagner who blocks my paths"), and *Le Roi* is too impregnated with Wagner. Fortunately, Chausson did not spend all of his time on the opera; these ten years also saw the composition of his most characteristic scores, including the B-flat major symphony (Op. 20, 1889–90), which is one of the best-known French symphonies. It emulates the three-movement structure and cyclic form of Franck's symphony and combines tragic intensity and songfulness with pages of soaring grandeur. Other works during that decade were the concert for violin, piano, and string quartet (Op. 21, 1889–91)—subtle and of aristocratic distinction but also somewhat lacking in cohesion. *Poème de l'amour et de la mer*, for voice and orchestra (Op. 19, 1882–90), has ravishing moments, and his bouquet of lovely songs is mostly melancholic.

Shortly after completing *Le Roi Arthus*, Chausson began his best work, the *Poème* for violin and orchestra (Op. 25, 1896–98), which was performed by the great Belgian violinist Eugène Ysaÿe to critical acclaim. The brooding one-movement *Poème* is one of the most exquisite manifestations of late Romanticism: the violin writing blends seamlessly into the burnished coloring of the rich orchestral fabric, while its shimmering glow is infused with an unfulfilled yearning. It sings a reluctant, elegiac farewell to the opulent fin-de-siècle graciousness of a ripe civilization beginning to decay.

In 1899, tragedy struck. Chausson, an inveterate bicyclist, lost control while riding down a familiar hill. The forty-four-year-old composer smashed into a wall and was killed instantly. At the funeral, the greats of French culture wept. His biographers, Jean-Pierre Barricelli and Leo Weinstein, wrote, "Chausson occupied an almost privileged position between the heavy romanticism of César Franck and the airy impressionism of Claude Debussy. It would be difficult to find in the history of French music a more objectively, a more dispassionately French composer, whose personality, in spite of popular credence, ascertained itself successfully against the forceful influence of Wagnerism, Italianism, and Franckism itself."

Symphony in B-flat Major, Op. 20 (1889–90)
Orchestre de la Suisse Romande, Ansermet: London 433715-2
Boston Symphony Orchestra, Munch: RCA 09026-60683-2

Poème for Violin and Orchestra (1896–98)
Menuhin, Paris Symphony Orchestra, Enescu: Biddulph LAB 058
Francescatti, New York Philharmonic Orchestra, Bernstein: Sony Classical SMK 47548

RUGGIERO LEONCAVALLO

(1857–1919) Italy

At age nineteen, Leoncavallo received his diploma from the famed Naples Conservatory. In his early years, he struggled to make a living, completing an opera, *Tomasso Chatterton* (1876), from Alfred de Vigny's play about the eighteenth-century English poet Thomas Chatterton. Nothing came of it, and he wrote popular songs, accompanied singers, and for several years played piano in cabarets from Amsterdam to Cairo. By thirty-four, he was still unperformed and was distressed by his lack of success. He had heard Pietro Mascagni's 1890 one-act opera *Cavalleria rusticana*, in what was being called *verismo* style—opera depicting contemporary and realistic slices of life. *Verismo* was a reaction against Wagner and sentimental Italian Romantic opera in general. Leoncavallo soon wrote his own libretto based on an incident from his childhood, when a jealous actor killed his wife after a performance. He later said, "This event made a deep and lasting impression on my childish mind, the more since my father was the judge at the criminal's trial." *Pagliacci* was premiered under no less a conductor than Toscanini on May 21, 1892, at Milan's Dal Verme Theater, and it achieved a resounding success. Within months, all of Italy loved it. The opera was performed in Vienna in September 1892, at Covent Garden in London in May 1893, and at the Metropolitan Opera in New York in June 1893.

Opera lovers now hoped for more, but for five years, alas, every opera Leoncavallo wrote encountered disaster. In 1897 it finally looked like another hit was within his grasp. Venice's great La Fenice Theater gave the premiere of Leoncavallo's *La Bohème*, based on Henri Murger's novel of bohemian life. It was well received, but it had the bad luck of vying with Puccini's version of Murger's tale, which had been receiving raves everywhere since it had been produced in Turin sixteen months before. Leoncavallo had started his opera first, and he was hurt and upset by Puccini's success, so much so that he accused Puccini of stealing his idea.

Although he continued writing operas, Leoncavallo was never again able to release the magic that flowed so effortlessly in *Pagliacci* with its wealth of emotion-drenched arias (the most famous of which is the heartrending "Vesti la giubba"). He died a bitter and despondent man at Montecatini-Terme, near Florence, on August 9, 1919.

Pagliacci (1892)

Callas, di Stefano, Gobbi, Panerai, La Scala Orchestra and Chorus, Serafin: EMI Classics CDCC 47981

de los Angeles, Björling, Merrill, Warren, Columbus Orchestra, Robert Shaw Chorale, Cellini: EMI Classics, ZDC 49503

Freni, Pavarotti, Wixell, National Philharmonic Orchestra, Patanè: London 414590-2

MIKHAIL IPPOLITOV-IVANOV

(1859–1935) Russia

Ippolitov-Ivanov was a Russian nationalist who wrote seven operas, many songs, and a good deal of orchestral music. His style is simple, agreeable, graphic, and well orchestrated. Lovers of Russian music would feel deprived without his attractive *Caucasian Sketches* (1894–96), with its star number, "The Procession of the Sardar."

Caucasian Sketches

TWO SUITES, OPP. 10 AND 42 (1894 AND 1896)
Sydney Symphony Orchestra, Gée: Marco Polo 8.220369

SUITE NO. 1, OP. 10 (1894)
Utah Symphony Orchestra, Abravanel: Vanguard Classics OVC 5010

GUSTAVE CHARPENTIER

(1860–1956) France

Charpentier's opera *Louise* is the pinnacle of this long-lived composer's work. It survives by its period charm, the everlasting nostalgia of Parisian bohemia. Its sentimentality is occasionally noxious, but audiences can forgive that for the chance of hearing an aria such as "Depuis le jour." *Louise* also espouses such issues as socialist thought and free love and is thus a compelling document of an era. Virgil Thomson thought that "its intrigue is tightly woven; its characterization is powerful, and the dialogue is simple, direct, and stylistically pure in a way hardly to be expected of a composer who has never shown elsewhere any unusual literary mastery. . . . The opera is built up with clear musical characterization, an intense expression of the atmosphere of its subject, and a sound respect for the plain language of plain people." Today the opera is seldom staged and is slipping from the repertoire. *Louise* has a beauty all its own, however. The opera's symphonic passages and vocal writing are clear as a fresh pond.

Louise (1900)

Cotrubas, Berbié, Domingo, New Philharmonia Orchestra and Ambrosian Opera Chorus, Prêtre: Sony Classical S3K 46429

EDWARD MACDOWELL

(1860–1908) United States

During the 1890s, MacDowell composed some of the most distinctive music in the United States. He headed a group of solid, well-trained composers, including Horatio Parker, George Chadwick, Arthur Foote, and Mrs. H.H.A. Beach. MacDowell was performed frequently—and his fragrant piano lyric "To a Wild Rose" was on every domestic piano. In emerging industrial America, MacDowell yearned for the romance of the sea, old Celtic sagas, and American Indian legends. At his best, he wrote sweet, nostalgic music, scented with lavender harmonies that tell of a vanished age. His four piano sonatas, written late in the century, speak a grittier language and are cast in a heroic mold. MacDowell's best-known score is the Piano Concerto no. 2 in D Minor (Op. 23, 1884–86), a striking concerto in the grand manner and the only nineteenth-century work by an American to claim a small place in the international repertoire.

Concerto no. 2 in D Minor for Piano, Op. 23 (1884–86)
Cliburn, Chicago Symphony Orchestra, Hendl: RCA 60420-2-RG
Watts, Dallas Symphony Orchestra, Litton: Telarc CD 80429

ISAAC ALBÉNIZ

(1860–1909) Spain

Albéniz's childhood reads like an adventure story. He was a musical prodigy, apparently of the Mozartian order, and was composing and playing the piano in public before he was five. His father greedily exploited the boy's gift, but at thirteen Albéniz ran away. He earned a precarious living playing piano in dance halls and bars in Buenos Aires, Costa Rica, Havana, and New York. Within a year, the vagabond musician was found and summarily shipped home.

With the help of a stipend from the Spanish government, he resumed his musical training in Germany at the Leipzig Conservatory. More invigorating was a trip to Budapest to meet Liszt, who gave him a few lessons, worldly advice, and some hardy encouragement. After a few years of roaming Europe, mostly as a piano accompanist, he returned to Barcelona in 1883 to study composition with Felipe Pedrell, Spain's finest teacher and a passionate advocate of Spanish folk music and dance forms. Pedrell was convinced of Albéniz's ability but noted his disgust with theory, indeed with rules of any type. Instead, Pedrell dwelled only on artistic matters and inspired Albéniz to compose Spanish nationalist music.

Albéniz would later say that he wasted years writing poor operas and nearly

250 potboilers for drawing-room consumption. He first began to come into his own in the late 1890s when, like many Spanish artists, he gravitated to Paris. He lived there on and off for the rest of his relatively short life, earning a living as a teacher and pianist. There, inspired by the progressive music of Dukas, Fauré, Debussy, and Ravel, he enlarged his harmonic and pianistic vocabulary. But not until 1906 did Albéniz finally find his creative path. During the remaining three years of his life, he laboriously composed the four books of piano pieces (containing three each) that he proudly called *Iberia* (1906–9). At last he had created a truly Spanish music, the portrait of a magical Spain set mostly in Moorish Andalusia.

Iberia is a ninety-minute cycle of Spanish moods within a rich tapestry of dance forms. It presents a panorama of Spanish life. Debussy felt, "One finds all the atmosphere of those carnation-scented Spanish evenings—the muffled sound of the guitar lamentingly playing to the night." "El Puerto," for example, paints the busy harbor of Santa Maria. "Fête-Dieu à Seville" depicts with joy and pathos a religious procession smoldering with pent-up passion. "Almería" evokes a Spanish port town; the middle section of the score seems to touch the very soul of Andalusia and contains some of Albéniz's loveliest music. In "El Albaicín" the composer describes the Gypsy quarter of Granada. In "Evocación" one almost feels the slow, relentless summer heat.

Albéniz was only forty-nine when he died of Bright's disease, a kidney ailment. His death deprived Spanish music of its first important nationalistic voice; *Iberia* will remain his lasting monument.

Iberia (suite) for Piano (1906–9)
de Larrocha: EMI Classics ZDMB 64504-2
de Larrocha: London 417887-2

CHARLES MARTIN LOEFFLER
(1861–1935) United States

Loeffler was born in Alsace and emigrated to the United States at twenty. A superb violinist, he joined the Boston Symphony Orchestra as assistant concertmaster in 1882 and performed there for two decades. Slowly he built a fine reputation as a composer, assiduously creating refined music, using the harmonic palette of the impressionists but defying actual classification. Loeffler's music is often picturesque; the later work after 1920 differs from the early only in a higher sophistication. Literature inspired him; his most famous composition, the splendid *A Pagan Poem* (Op. 14, 1906) derives from Virgil's eighth eclogue. It is Loeffler at his most supersensuous. The critic Philip Hale wrote of Loeffler, "He has delicate sentiment, the curiosity of the hunter after nuances, the love of the macabre, the cool fire that consumes and is more deadly than fierce, panting flame." The composer Arthur Shepherd wrote to Loeffler, after having read one of his songs, "[I] have experienced that rare feeling—indescribable but permeated with a joyful gratitude—that overtakes one, when suddenly confronted with true beauty."

A Pagan Poem, **Op. 14 (1906)**
Houston Symphony Orchestra, Stokowski: EMI Classics CDM 65074

ANTON ARENSKY

(1861–1906) Russia

Arensky was a distinctive disciple of Tchaikovsky. His suites for two pianos (Opp. 15, 23, 33, 62) are effective, as are the piano études (Op. 74, 1905). The D minor piano trio (Op. 32, 1894) and *Variations on a Theme of Tchaikovsky* (Op. 35a, 1894) continue to charm audiences today.

In 1882 Arensky was appointed professor of composition at the Moscow Conservatory, where he taught no less than Rachmaninoff and Scriabin.

Trio no. 1 in D Minor for Piano, Violin, and Cello, Op. 32 (1894)
Bronfman, Lin, Hoffman: Sony Classical SK 53269

Variations on a Theme of Tchaikovsky **for String Orchestra, Op. 35a (1894)**
London String Orchestra, Barbirolli: EMI Classics CDFB 69361

PIETRO MASCAGNI

(1863–1945) Italy

Mascagni studied with Amilcare Ponchielli (the composer of *La Gioconda* and also Puccini's teacher) at the Milan Conservatory. Although Ponchielli was impressed with his pupil, Mascagni hated the Conservatory and left. Lean years followed as he wandered around Italy conducting in fourth-rate opera houses.

In 1889, at age twenty-six, Mascagni entered a competition for a one-act opera. He quickly composed *Cavalleria rusticana* and won. The opera premiered in Rome on May 17, 1890, and by the conclusion, the unknown composer had become famous. Within months all of Italy fell under the opera's spell, and by the year's end Europe too had succumbed to this lurid and intense work, based on a story of Sicilian life by Giovanni Verga.

In no time, the press was saying that Mascagni had created a new type of opera, soon to be known as *verismo*. This brand of opera featured everyday people, albeit within highly charged situations. The plots were simple, and the characters easy to relate to. Banned were the larger-than-life Valkyries, Wotans, and Siegfrieds of Wagnerian mythology. The realism and simplicity of *Cavalleria* would soon produce a string of *verismo* operas. After Leoncavallo wrote his two-act *Pagliacci* in 1892, opera houses forever teamed them together as "*Cav* and *Pag*," or the "ham and eggs" of opera. Although *Cavalleria* is full of juicy arias, its most famous music is an orchestral intermezzo.

After *Cavalleria*, the opera world looked to Mascagni for another hit. But sadly, none was forthcoming. Mascagni would write fourteen more lackluster operas, but only *L'Amico Fritz* (1891), a comedy, received some recognition.

In later years, the ambitious composer became a devoted apostle of Mussolini, writing music to glorify the dictator's political regime. In 1933, when Toscanini resigned his directorship at Milan's La Scala, Mascagni quickly took over. With Il Duce's collapse in 1943, *Cavalleria*'s composer was publicly vilified for his fascist affiliations, and his possessions and estate were confiscated. Bewildered and bitter, he passed his last years in disgrace in a shabby hotel room in Rome. From his twenty-seventh year, however, *Cavalleria* has been loved by audiences the world over. Mascagni once declared, "It was a pity I wrote *Cavalleria* first. I was crowned before I became king."

Cavalleria rusticana (1890)

Callas, Ticozzi, di Stefano, La Scala Orchestra and Chorus, Serafin: EMI Classics CDCC 47981

Milanov, Smith, Björling, Merrill, RCA Victor Symphony Orchestra, Robert Shaw Chorale, Cellini: RCA 6510-2-RG

Varady, Pavarotti, Cappuccilli, National Philharmonia London Orchestra and Chorus, Gacazzeni: London 414590-2

ALEXANDER GLAZUNOV

(1865–1936) Russia

A prolific composer with touches of genius, Glazunov composed slick, highly skilled Russianized symphonies of Tchaikovskian flavor, adding spices from the oriental splendor of Borodin and Rimsky-Korsakov. A prodigious melodist, he would lavish a three-minute waltz with five different themes.

Glazunov is best known for the ballets *Raymonda* (1897) and *The Seasons* (1899) and the often-recorded Violin Concerto in A Minor (Op. 82, 1904), but he wrote many other attractive pieces. He was a splendid teacher and the director of the St. Petersburg Conservatory until 1928, when he went to Paris, never to return to the Soviet Union.

Concerto in A Minor for Violin and Orchestra, Op. 82 (1904)
Heifetz, RCA Victor Symphony Orchestra, Hendl: RCD1-7019
Oistrakh, USSR State Orchestra, Kondrashin: Vanguard Classics 1025

CARL NIELSEN
(1865–1931) Denmark

Nielsen, Denmark's most distinguished composer, has never appealed to a broad audience. Much of his music is austere, rugged, and uninviting at first. His national opera *Maskarade* (*Masquerade*, 1906) is an exception and is Denmark's best-loved opera. But Nielsen was seldom a nationalist, swaddled in his country's folksongs; rather, he was a late-nineteenth-century Romantic with roots deeply planted in Brahms and other Romantic composers. After 1900 he developed his own terse style, remaining within the traditions of Classical form. His Piano Suite (Op. 45, 1919–20), written for Artur Schnabel, may be the finest Scandinavian piano work of the twentieth century.

Nielsen is best known for his six symphonies, which are of exceptional power and lasting quality, worthy of his better-known Scandinavian contemporary Sibelius.

Symphony no. 3 (*Sinfonia espansiva*), Op. 27 (1911)
Symphony no. 5, Op. 50 (1922)
Royal Danish Orchestra, Bernstein: Sony Classical SMK 47598

PAUL DUKAS
(1865–1935) France

Born in Paris to well-to-do Jewish parents, Dukas received a thorough classical education. At seventeen he entered the Paris Conservatory, where he stayed for eight years. After graduation he served in the military for a year. In 1888, at age twenty-three, he placed second in the Prix de Rome, and from then on his life was filled with teaching and study, a life that, while retiring, made him one of the most erudite musicians in Paris.

With his contemplative nature, Dukas approached the creation of music seriously and cautiously. At age thirty, he produced his first important score, the Symphony in C Major, a three-movement work of Franckian influence, lofty in feeling and crowned by a spacious and lovely Andante movement. The next year was decisive—Dukas became famous. On May 18, 1897, he conducted his symphonic poem *L'Apprenti sorcier* (*The Sorcerer's Apprentice*) at the Société Nationale de Musique. The work created a sensation and quickly entered the repertoire everywhere. It is a symphonic scherzo based on Goethe's ballad "Der Zauberlehrling." At the time it was the last word in orchestral realism. The composer achieved a marvelously graphic rendering of a broom that is transformed into a servant, who continues bringing his master buckets of water until the room is flooded. When Rimsky-Korsakov heard it, he commented, "In terms of orchestration, I think he outshines all of us." Half a century later Walt Disney used the piece in his animated film *Fantasia*, further enhancing its fame.

The public now expected more evidence of his striking talent, but Dukas changed direction. In 1901 and 1903, he produced two large-scale piano works: a sonata, which plays for nearly an hour, and the complex and exquisitely lucid *Variations, interlude, et finale sur un thème de Rameau*. Audiences were disappointed, for both scores lacked the dazzling flair and surface brilliance of *The Sorcerer's Apprentice*.

For the next several years, the composer was immersed in his opera *Ariane et Barbe-bleue*, to a text by Maurice Maeterlinck. It was produced at the Paris Opera in 1907, but there was little enthusiasm for this subtle and recondite work. After *Ariane*, Dukas composed only one other major score, *La Péri* (Fanfare and *Poème dansé*), which premiered in 1912. He died of a heart attack thirty-eight years after the premiere of his *Sorcerer's Apprentice*.

Unfortunately, the few compositions that Dukas permitted to survive have found little favor. The Piano Sonata in E-flat Minor (1901) is the most profound of his works. That its deep humanity has not stirred twentieth-century pianists to enter its dense domain has been a loss to both pianists and the public. The same is true of the touching *Rameau Variations*, a work that absorbs French sensibility from Rameau through the elegance of Fauré and Debussy. *La Péri* is a masterful piece of impressionism and is highly effective; but it, too, has been neglected. Ironically, all of these works are far more characteristic of Dukas's musical mind than *The Sorcerer's Apprentice*, which has taken his name around the world.

L'Apprenti sorcier (*The Sorcerer's Apprentice*) (1896)
Orchestre de la Suisse Romande, Ansermet: London 448576-2
New York Philharmonic Orchestra, Bernstein: CBS MYK 37769
Basel Symphony Orchestra, Jordan: Erato 2292-45819-2

La Péri (1912)
New York Philharmonic Orchestra, Boulez: Sony Classical SMK 68333

PART FIVE

THE AGE OF MODERNISM

It is not possible to declare one perfect turning point into Modernism, a term that has commonly been used for composers living into the twentieth century. When a common language falters, new forms must come into being to provide for new expression; so in the early nineteenth century did rigid Classical forms give way to Romanticism. When Romanticism in turn gave way to Modernism, composers were reacting not so much against rigid forms (after all, many nineteenth- and twentieth-century composers found the sonata form still valid) as against the tonal system. By the third quarter of the nineteenth century, chords had become clogged with different tones. Composers were constantly modulating, hoping always to refresh the ear. Wagner did this most potently, and most composers writing in his wake felt he had left them little more to accomplish. They were right. But composers are, if anything, creative, and many would successfully find their own style in the new century.

No composer of the late nineteenth century was more aware than Liszt that he was working in an exhausted musical vocabulary. Liszt was the first to realize that the major and minor key tonal system would eventually collapse, and by the mid-1870s he was writing small piano pieces that were tonally ambiguous, even titling one of them *Bagatelle Without Tonality*. Nobody wanted to listen to these pieces, and most thought the great virtuoso had gone mad. At the time of his death in 1886, he was the most radical composer in the world.

Liszt set the stage for Modernism, which began in France. Debussy, even as a youngster, was impatient with rules and with thickly textured Romanticism. At the 1889 Paris Exhibition, he heard a Javanese gamelan orchestra and felt released into an entirely new soundscape. Keenly aware of the Wagnerian dead end, and temperamentally antipathetic to the German tradition, Debussy plunged into Modernism both in form and in harmony. In his *Prélude à l'après-midi d'un faune* (1892–94), the fixed forms of the past were replaced by new forms, which were also reflected in new styles of painting, architecture, and poetry. Regularity and balance no longer mattered. Debussy varied his material in the most original and subtle ways, and his forms left behind almost any resemblance to past procedures. No composer within the scope of traditional instruments had ever developed such a heightened sense of timbre. For the diversity and irregularity of his forms (the word *structure* is too rigid to describe them), Debussy needed a revolutionary harmonic system. He used chords as building blocks, shifting them and juxtaposing them for contrast rather than resolution. His impact on music has been felt throughout the century.

Debussy died in 1918. His radical friend, Erik Satie, lived on until 1925. Satie was a far smaller figure, but he served as a catalyst for many young Moderns. His outlook was a severe but necessary reaction to Wagner and Germanic forms in general. His is a touching art, with neither pretension nor caricature. The writer Laurence Davies commented on "Satie's own terrifying willingness to disrobe, shedding all those aids to beauty which the ordinary composer finds indispensable." With his weird titles and pure whimsy, Satie was a breath of fresh air in an age dominated by Mahler and Strauss.

The first generation of composers truly immersed in Modernism were those born in the 1870s, including Scriabin, Vaughan Williams, Ravel, Ives, and Schoenberg. After 1903 Scriabin broke with his early Romanticism. By 1906 he was immersed in mysticism and composed a kind of mystic impressionism, building his chords in fourths; in the Sixth Piano Sonata he dispensed with key signatures and entered a trackless territory of atonality. He was a messianic Theosophist, and his music presents a restless longing to be released from the flesh, to dissolve into the universe.

Ralph Vaughan Williams was an English nationalist who brought new energy to English music as well as some advanced technique. Maurice Ravel, far less progressive than Debussy, was a masterful technician who composed illuminating commentaries on each of the forms he invested with his genius. Charles Ives was a progressive American nationalist who lived in dreadful isolation in a musically conventional environment dominated by the nineteenth-century German tradition. Disillusioned, he stopped composing in 1918. Until that time he was amazingly inventive, using atonality, polytonality, clusters, quarter-tones, and much else. The contemporary use of aleatory music (music characterized by chance), noise, and electronic collage come directly from Ives.

The innovations of Ives still sound pungent, as do those of Arnold Schoenberg. If Debussy's basically nonviolent art was a radical departure from tonality, Schoenberg's far more aggressive (and, to the public at large, ugly and neurotic) art would culminate in a new system of composing altogether. Beginning his career as a Wagnerian, he naturally evolved into atonal expressionism. Through the lean war years, Schoenberg the composer was silent, but the theoretician was hard at work, slowly developing a theory in which all twelve tones of the chromatic scale are equal. It is called the twelve-tone system, or serialism.

The critic Wilfrid Mellers nicely defines the theory of music without tonality: "In chromatic serial music as used by Schoenberg, each note of the composition (chords as well as melodic ideas) must be derived from a preordained sequence, or 'row' of the twelve chromatic semitones, either in the row's original form, or inverted, or backwards, or backwards and inverted. The serial principle is extended by later composers (Boulez, Stockhausen) to rhythm (or rather metrical proportions), dynamic and timbre (the allocation of notes in the series to different instruments)." Naturally, many composers by temperament and conditioning rejected Schoenberg or found this new aesthetic system to be a dreadful error. Debussy, Busoni, Scriabin, and Reger died before Schoenberg's earliest serial works of the mid-1920s, which he wrote when he was already past fifty.

The early 1880s saw the births of Bartók, Webern, Varèse, Berg, and Stravinsky. Bartók in the beginning took from Debussy, Richard Strauss, and Stravinsky but found his personal style in a dissonant, compelling Hungarian nationalism. He ranks near Stravinsky and Schoenberg in searching creativity and perfection of form, though he did not have quite the same impact on music internationally. Berg well showed the flexibility of Schoenberg's system, which he used in his later works. Berg can be called the twelve-tone system's most advanced Romantic, and his music always conveyed a deeply emotional message. Varèse destroyed his earlier work, up to the orchestral piece *Amériques*, composed about 1920. His work would eventually become sound densities, dispensing with any development of ideas and all directionality. He longed for sounds never previously heard or suspected. In his few later tape and electronic compositions with human voice and instruments, he opened up a new world of musical meaning. Webern wrote a complex serial music that captivated composers in the 1950s and 1960s.

For the twentieth-century musical public, Stravinsky was the major figure. He composed in nearly every genre, inventing new rhythms and a vast array of textures, juxtaposing idioms, creating unique harmonic combinations, and so forth. Always a firm tonalist, in his later years he shocked the musical establishment by refreshing his work through serialism.

The above-mentioned are all major innovators, highlights of twentieth-century composition, but many more composers have contributed to the art as well. In a sense, twentieth-century music was a further development of Romanticism, starting with impressionism and ending with minimalism. The diversity has been astonishing, ranging from Szymanowski, Bloch, Respighi, Prokofiev, Hindemith, Poulenc, Barber, Copland, Shostakovich, Kodály, Walton, Schuman, Carter, Gershwin, Sessions, Schnittke, Glass, Crumb, Stockhausen, Ligeti, Bernstein, Babbitt, Rorem, Maxwell Davies, Henze, Corigliano, Dutilleux, and Zwilich, to name only the most celebrated.

How, then, does the world of "classical" music stand at the beginning of the twenty-first century? Oddly, music, with all of this diversity, has been content with instruments that were invented and perfected long ago. No new sound outlets came about until electronic music, and (surprisingly) this development has not been utilized as much as many thought it would be. Only a few composers have experimented with non-Western instruments.

It seems that presently there can be little that is truly new or important, little that can be built upon. The unprecedented market forces of the twentieth century have shown very little concern with promoting classical music. When promoters do focus on classical music, they awkwardly push, over and over, the few most famous works. Over sixty years ago, Virgil Thomson in his book *The State of Music* wrote, "When music shall have become just another consumer commodity like chewing gum, its grand epoch will be over. Already a great deal of it is designed, like central heating, to be merely present. Keeping the rot peripheral, preventing it from infecting the heart, is not going to be easy. Too many people make money out of it."

In the last fifty years, the young have had an unprecedented amount of money to spend, and they have been taught to spend it on bad music—simplistic lyrics set to simplistic music, simulating an orgiastic beat and giving off a constant noise pollution. The "rot" has been getting ever louder and is ever present. Many young people hear classical music only in shopping malls, where it is played to prevent teenage loitering.

Even worse is the shameless way music has become a slave to advertising. We have long been used to hearing never-ending jingles for products, but now television at all times uses a perpetual sound beat, a boom-boom announcing each segment of news or programming, ostensibly to promote excitement but in fact to tame and numb the audience. Crushed forever are the sweet popular songs and dance music of yesteryear's big bands. Since Elvis Presley's death, not a day has passed without his image being broadcast or published. He cannot be avoided. Nothing has emerged to counter the severe damage. Amateur home music-making has all but died out, and the public school system is in a shambles, cutting musical education programs and mostly avoiding any contact with art generally. Indeed, "serious" music has been attacked and is associated with that particularly dangerous word, *elitism*. The white male European product has become the enemy of a multicultural American standard.

The bright side is only this: in a largely uneducated mass and an ever-growing population, there somehow seems to be a place for everything. Classical musicians are now so numerous that they are cultivating a new class of excellent listeners. They teach and are usually aggressive in showing their appreciation of the arts. Looking around the concert halls of the world, I find that audiences are no longer made up only of the elderly. A young lawyer recently asked me, "Who is this Harry Partch? I like his stuff," and people are finally listening to Schoenberg without cringing. Serious composers today—and there are thousands of them—mostly live well from grants, commissions, and university positions, and they continue to pour out their work. Perhaps in the twenty-first century, beauty will make a comeback. For most of human history, it was an integral part of being human. In 1941 the great painting connoisseur Bernard Berenson wrote, "Man is a terrible destroyer, but what a creator! The human past, long before written history begins, is strewn with figured records of his love of beauty and testimonials to his genius as creator. Indeed man seems to have begun as artist and only in the last hundred years has he succeeded in emancipating himself from art completely, exchanging the possible Phidias in him for a Ford."

ALEXANDER SCRIABIN

b. Moscow, January 6, 1872

d. Moscow, April 27, 1915

I will come to dazzle you with the marvel of enchantment re-peated; I will bring you the magical thrill of scorching love and unimagined caresses. Surrender to me in all faith!

Scriabin's father was a diplomat; his mother, a talented pianist, had studied with the celebrated piano teacher Theodor Leschetizky at the St. Petersburg Conservatory. She died sixteen months after Alexander's birth, and the boy was raised by a doting grandmother and an aunt. From the age of six, the piano be-came a fixation. To the hypersensitive child, the instrument was not an inani-mate object; he kissed it, slept under it, and grew agitated if it was moved. At ten he left the spoiled atmosphere of his aunt's home for the Moscow Military Academy. The tiny boy did well in school and was exceptionally popular. As a piano prodigy, he was exempted from strenuous military drills for fear of harm to his hands.

His piano lessons continued while he was at the military academy. More se-rious piano lessons began in 1883, which then led to study with Nikolai Zverev, Sergei Rachmaninoff's teacher. Zverev was a despot who demanded fanatical discipline from his pupils, and Alexander practiced hard. In the winter of 1886, he took theory and composition lessons from Sergei Taneyev, a gifted composer and a former pupil of Tchaikovsky. Already the fourteen-year-old boy had com-posed the beautiful C-sharp minor étude (Op. 2/1). Two years later he gradu-ated from the military school and was admitted to the Moscow Conservatory, where he studied with the pianist and conductor Vasily Safonov, who was en-raptured by the ethereal grace of his pupil's piano playing.

At the Conservatory, Scriabin strenuously devoted himself to becoming a great pianist. The Conservatory had a highly charged and competitive atmosphere with a renowned faculty and an extraordinary group of young pianists of the caliber of Alexander Goldenweiser, Rachmaninoff, and Josef Lhévinne, whose octaves were the envy of his colleagues. Scriabin, not to be outdone, relentlessly practiced such treacherously muscular pieces as Liszt's *Don Juan Fantasy* and Balakirev's *Islamey*. He practiced so hard that he paralyzed his right hand. Doctors offered him little hope of recovery, but Scriabin, with tediously slow practice, somehow brought his injured hand back to life. While recuperating, he wrote his much-loved nocturne for left hand alone (Op. 9/1, 1890).

Because of a conflict with his composition teacher, Anton Arensky, Scriabin left the Conservatory without qualifying for his composer's certificate. The nervous, fastidious, and dandified twenty-one-year-old was now completely on his own, and he began to give recitals. Mitrofan Belayev, an important music publisher, heard him play his Twelve Études (Op. 8, 1894), fell in love with the music, and began publishing everything he wrote.

In 1897 Scriabin married Vera Ivanovna Isaakovich, herself a pianist. The couple lived in Moscow, where Scriabin took a piano professorship at the Conservatory. Although he stayed at the institution for six years, he found teaching to be an odious chore that took him away from his creative work. He completed a First Symphony with a choral finale (Op. 26) in 1900. This work was strongly influenced by the occult, to which Scriabin was increasingly attracted, and it shows the first hints of more esoteric ideas to come.

In January 1902 his Second Symphony (Op. 29) was premiered in St. Petersburg. At the end of the school year, Scriabin resigned from the Conservatory. That summer he worked furiously to complete the Fourth Piano Sonata (Op. 30) and a large number of other piano pieces, all of which enter a rarefied harmonic climate. His piano writing had lost its earlier Chopinesque bearings and was now richer and tighter in texture.

Domesticity never appealed to Scriabin, and by 1903 he grew tired of his wife and four children. After leaving Vera, he saw her only once more, when their daughter Rimma died in 1905 at the age of six. To provide for Vera's living, he taught her all of his own music up to Op. 42. Later, Safonov gave her a professorship at the Conservatory.

In 1904 he fell in love with Tatiana Schloezer, who worshiped him and his art. Although he never married her, they stayed together until his death. For the narcissistic Scriabin, adulation was a necessary component of life. In these years, he became even more enigmatic and mystical, and he soon embraced many ideas of the Theosophical movement. He considered music his path to "divine illumination." On May 29, 1905, Arthur Nikisch conducted his Third Symphony, the *Divin Poème* (Op. 43). Scriabin wrote an elaborate explanation for the composition, attempting to unite the music with his vague pantheistic philosophy. By this time, all music other than his own had ceased to interest him, and he was developing a more modern harmonic vocabulary. "I was once a Chopinist," he said, "then a Wagnerist. Now I am only a Scriabinist."

The young Arthur Rubinstein, who had been a strong advocate of the Russian's music, remembered meeting him in Paris. Scriabin asked the pianist, " 'Who is your favorite composer?' When I answered without hesitation, 'Brahms,' he banged his fist on the table. 'What, what?' he screamed. 'How can you like this terrible composer and me at the same time?' "

With the Fourth Symphony in 1908 (Op. 54), subtitled *Le Poème de l'extase*, Scriabin broke new ground, creating a thoroughly original idiom. Never had orchestral writing so quivered with erotic tension. This time, instead of an explanation, he wrote a long descriptive poem, voluptuously lewd, that contained all sorts of sexualized ravings. His own extravagant verbiage and philosophical jargon seemed to stimulate his musical creativity. With the passing years, his theories grew more fervent and messianic. His conversations and letters were peppered with words such as *fire, light, vertiginous, caressing, venomous,* and *ecstatic,* and he covered his scores with madly evocative directives to the performer. The critic and composer Leonid Sabaneyev described Scriabin listening to his own music thus: "Sometimes he lowered his face rather strangely, his eyes closed and his appearance having an almost physiological enjoyment; then he would open his eyes and look upwards as if wishing to fly; in tense moments of the music he breathed violently and nervously, gripping his seat with both hands."

By 1912 Scriabin believed that he was the Messiah. He strove for purification, writing such works as *Vers la flamme* (Op. 72) and *Flammes sombres* (Op. 73), both in 1914. Occasionally he had "spiritual" setbacks. The Ninth Sonata (Op. 68, 1912–13), called the *Black Mass,* slipped from his subconscious, he believed. He was upset by its creation and refused to play it, for he felt that its grimacing, perfidious, satanic grumbling was a fall from grace.

In his Fifth Symphony, *Prométhée, le poème du feu* (*Prometheus, the Poem of Fire,* Op. 60, 1908–10), he further developed what he called his "Promethean" or "mystery chord" of superimposed intervals of fourths instead of thirds. It was a breakdown of the triadic tonal system. *Prometheus* is a magnificent work—inspired, transparent, and focused. The composer told a friend, "There is not a wasted note, not a wedge where a mosquito could get in and bite."

His plans were now becoming impossibly grandiose. He was convinced that with his music the peoples of the planet would become united forever, through a multimedia festival held at the foot of the Himalayas, combining colors, dance, perfumes, singers, bells, orchestra, and chorus. His "mysterium," or mystery, as he called it, would spawn a new order of the human race. Exactly how this was to be accomplished, he never cared to divulge.

In the spring of 1914, Scriabin went to London to give a series of piano recitals. While he was there, the conductor Sir Henry Wood introduced *Prometheus* to English audiences. Scriabin was delighted and surprised when Wood, after his performance, turned to the audience, told them how important the score was, and immediately repeated the twenty-minute work.

An exhilarated Scriabin returned to his adoring followers in Moscow. For the composer, the beginning of the First World War in August 1914 was an omen telling him that the world was becoming ready for his "mystery." He ranted to his circle that he was the real Messiah, that Christ was not the central Messiah: "The great Messiah is he who will sound the final chord of our race, reuniting it with the spirit." "I shall not die, I shall suffocate in ecstasy after the *mystery*."

He had been working on the text of the "initial act," a preamble to the *mystery*, but after a recital in St. Petersburg, he felt feverish. A carbuncle formed on his lip, and an infection quickly spread, covering his entire face. Blood poisoning and pleurisy set in. At eight A.M., on April 27, 1915, the unfulfilled Messiah died at age forty-three. It was an ignoble passing for such a phantomlike spirit, a man whom Alfred Swan, an early Scriabin biographer, described as "all nerve and holy flame." Scriabin symbolizes the last extravagant faith in the artist as spiritual force and in art as humanity's salvation. World War I profoundly changed the world, but hardly as Scriabin had expected. At his death, his family was destitute, and his gifted son Julian, who had already begun composing in his father's later style, drowned at age eleven.

During his lifetime, Scriabin was a controversial figure, heatedly discussed and debated. Some considered him to be music's savior or at least Debussy's equal. But critics such as Gerald Abraham thought, "The history of Scriabin's creative career is the history of the decline and fall of a remarkable creative talent through unlimited egotism." Others, like the English writer on music Martin Cooper, felt that "he shone like a flame of spirituality, and though such fires may sink so low that they may seem extinguished quite, they never wholly die." After his death, Scriabin's music suffered an eclipse. His volatile personality had been central to his popularity, for people were at least curious about the half-mad composer. In addition, his Theosophical and occult leanings made him unfashionable with the coming Soviet regime. Outside Russia émigrés like

Prokofiev and Stravinsky took center stage. In Germany Schoenberg's twelve-tone technique held sway over the minds of many young composers.

Today Scriabin's sensuous, vaporous music, full of mysterious vibrations and vertiginous nervosity, has for many music lovers regained its pristine appeal. Scriabin was a divine tonal colorist. He thought of each scale as a different color, and he coaxed new and spellbinding sonorities from the piano as well as from the orchestra in the Fourth and Fifth Symphonies. His piano works are deftly refined and breathtaking in their melodic prodigality. His later harmonic vocabulary had a far-reaching impact on the work of numerous composers, from Karol Szymanowski to Charles Griffes.

Piano Music (various dates)

Scriabin's piano music is a perpetual garden of delights. He composed 220 piano works—études, preludes, poems, mazurkas, and so forth—which are contained in sixty-seven opus numbers. The ten piano sonatas are infused with mercurial sensations, breathless palpitations, and new facets of pianistic figuration. They offer a superb overview of Scriabin's evolving style. Paul Rosenfeld was the first American critic fully to comprehend Scriabin's idiom. "Scriabin appears to have awakened in the piano all its latent animality," he wrote in 1920. "Under his touch . . . it cries and chants like a bird. . . . No one has caressed it more lightly, more tenderly, more voluptuously."

Ten *Piano Sonatas* (1892–1913)
Ashkenazy: London 425579-2
B. Berman: Music & Arts CD 605 and CD 621
Szidon: Deutsche Grammophon 3-431747-2

Symphony no. 4 (*Le Poème de l'extase*), Op. 54 (1905–8)

"When you listen to the *Poem of Ecstasy*," Scriabin exclaimed, "look into the eye of the Sun." The work is a marvelous example of his burning genius. It comprises one continuous sonata-type movement, twenty minutes in length. The opening theme for two trumpets is marked *Avec une noble et douce majesté* ("with a noble and gentle majesty"), whereupon the composition builds inexorably to a blazing climax. One listener called it "the obscenest piece of music ever written." At a 1910 performance at London's Gloucester Cathedral, the composer Edward Elgar whispered to the conductor Eugene Goossens, "To think that Gloucester Cathedral should ever echo to such music; it's a wonder the gargoyles don't fall off the tower." The *Poem of Ecstasy* had an indelible influence on several composers. Stravinsky immediately learned from it for his *Firebird*, and Szymanowski's orchestration is indebted to it.

New York Philharmonic Orchestra, Sinopoli: Deutsche Grammophon 427324-2
New York Philharmonic Orchestra, Mitropoulos: Theorema TH 121132

Sonata no. 5 in F-sharp Major, Op. 53 (1907)

This sonata, an outgrowth of the *Poem of Ecstasy*, is a mystic impressionist poem—languorous, impetuous, and sexual. Scriabin said of it, "I do not know by what miracle I accomplished it." The Fifth Sonata came from Scriabin's middle period, when he was purging his art of outside influences. Alfred Swan wrote, "The Fifth Sonata has been likened to a piece of wizardry, a deed of black magic, illuminated by the rays of a black sun. Its impetuosity alternating with a caressing languour, the legerdemain of prestos in their radiant mixture of B major and F sharp major, and the wild orgiastic rhythms of the allegros combine to produce an uncanny impression."

Horowitz: RCA 6215-2-RG
Richter: Arkadia 910
Schumacher: Élan 82242

Sonata no. 9 (*Messe noir*), Op. 68 (1912–13)

Into the nine minutes of the so-called *Black Mass*, the composer compressed the darkest elements of his nature. In the score, he instructs the pianist to play with nascent languor and with "a sweetness gradually becoming more and more caressing." For Alfred Swan, the work is "a veritable picture of Dorian Gray." The Sonata no. 9 is the most accessible of the last five sonatas. In the later ones, Scriabin dispensed altogether with key signatures, and the music dissolves tonality, becoming ever more incandescent, intoxicated, trancelike, and fevered.

Horowitz: RCA 09026-60526-2
Sokolov: Opus 111 OPS 40-9104

OTHER PRINCIPAL WORKS

CONCERTO

Concerto in F-sharp Minor for Piano and Orchestra, Op. 20 (1896)*

ORCHESTRAL WORKS

Symphony no. 3, Op. 43 (*Le Divin Poème*) (1902–4)*
Symphony no. 5, Op. 60 (*Prométhée, le poème du feu*) (1908–10)*

PIANO WORKS

Sonata no. 1 in F Minor, Op. 6 (1892)
Twelve Études, Op. 8 (1894)*
Twenty-four Preludes, Op. 11 (1888–96)*
Sonata no. 2 in G-sharp Minor (*Sonata-Fantasy*), Op. 19 (1892–97)*
Sonata no. 3 in F-sharp Minor, Op. 23 (1897–98)*
Fantasy in B Minor, Op. 28 (1900)*
Sonata no. 4 in F-sharp Major, Op. 30 (1903)*
Poème satanique, Op. 36 (1903)*
Eight Études, Op. 42 (1903)*
Four Pieces, Op. 56 (1907)*
Sonata no. 6, Op. 62 (1911)*
Sonata no. 7 in F-sharp Major (*White Mass*), Op. 64 (1911)*
Three Études, Op. 65 (1912)*
Sonata no. 8, Op. 66 (1912–13)*
Vers la flamme, Op. 72 (1914)*
Five Preludes, Op. 74 (1914)*

RALPH VAUGHAN WILLIAMS

b. Down Ampney, Gloucestershire,
October 12, 1872

d. London, August 26, 1958

The best form of musical appreciation is to try and do it for yourself; to get really inside the meaning of music.

Vaughan Williams was the son of a parson who died when he was three. Josiah Wedgwood, the eighteenth-century potter, was his ancestor, and Caroline Darwin, the sister of the scientist, was his grandmother. His mother encouraged her sons to love music, but Ralph was not considered very talented. He was educated at Trinity College, Cambridge, from 1892 to 1895, and studied at the Royal College of Music in London with Sir Charles Villiers Stanford and Sir Hubert Parry, two of England's most influential musicians and educators. In 1901 he took his first job, as a church choirmaster and organist in South London. By 1906, the thirty-four-year-old musician had shown no indication that he would ever have a significant position in the music world. Although he had attempted a few compositions, his main achievement had been to edit a book of hymns. Nor could he count himself more than a mediocre organist. "The years were passing," he wrote, "and I was adding nothing to the sum of musical invention."

In 1904 he joined a group called the Folk-Song Society, founded in 1899. Avid folklorists such as Percy Grainger, Cecil Sharp, and others feared that, with increasing industrialization, the English folksong heritage would disappear. In order to preserve all they could, they hunted for England's musical roots. Vaughan Williams wrote, "I spent a fortnight in an Essex village only twenty miles from London, and there in the neighborhood I noted down over fifty genuine folksongs. Most of the songs had beautiful and interesting tunes."

For Vaughan Williams, contact with native folk music was a revelation. His creative world was born: he would become a sophisticated and complex composer, but the nourishment he received from the simplicity and sincerity of folk sources would always remain a spiritual necessity. Of folk music he wrote, "Let our composers and performers, when they can spare time from solving some new problem in atonality or exploring the top register of the double-bassoon, refresh themselves occasionally with a draught of that pure water."

Starting in 1905, he used folk material to compose his three *Norfolk Rhapsodies*. He still felt technically limited, though, and decided on further study. He worked first on his own and then studied for a short period in Berlin with Max Bruch. From there, in 1909, he went to Paris and studied for several months with Ravel—who was three years younger than he but already world famous. Pupil and master were totally unalike in temperament, but the contact with the Frenchman was beneficial to Vaughan Williams, who gained a new security in handling orchestration.

During this time, Vaughan Williams was also studying the music of Purcell and the Tudor composers. He composed a touching song cycle, *On Wenlock Edge* (1909), and the atmospheric *A Sea Symphony* (1903–9). In 1910 he finally produced a masterpiece, the *Fantasia on a Theme of Thomas Tallis*, and suddenly he was considered a new force in English music. For many, Vaughan Williams (more than the eclectic Elgar) was the most fundamentally English of composers.

With the onset of World War I, Vaughan Williams insisted on enlisting in the army, although he was forty-two. He served as a hospital orderly in France and Macedonia, then became an artillery officer. After the war, he was able to finish his *A Pastoral Symphony*, which he had begun years before and which was first heard in 1922. The composer Constant Lambert called it "one of the landmarks in modern English music. . . . It is no exaggeration to say that the creation of a particular type of gray, reflective, English-landscape mood has outweighed the exigencies of symphonic form."

From 1920 to 1928, he was busy conducting London's Bach Choir. As with many previous English musicians, choral and church music were ingrained in him. "We pupils of Parry have, if we have been wise, inherited from Parry the great English choral tradition which Tallis passed on to Byrd, Byrd to Gibbons, Gibbons to Purcell, Purcell to Battishill and Greene, and they in turn through the Wesleys to Parry. He has passed the torch to us, and it is our duty to keep it alight," he wrote. The finest of his choral pieces of the 1920s are the unaccompanied Mass in G Minor and the *Te Deum*. The year 1930 saw the completion of *Job*, a "masque for dancing" inspired by William Blake's illustrations for the Book of Job.

With Elgar's death in 1934, Vaughan Williams became the world's best-known English composer. In 1931–34 he composed the Fourth Symphony, which in intent and material is vastly different from the earlier, descriptive *London* and *Pastoral* Symphonies. Its ferocious power surprised his unsuspecting first audiences with its intensity and greater dissonance. "I do not know whether I like it," the composer said, "but this is what I meant."

In London on October 5, 1938, Sir Henry Wood conducted the first performance of the beautiful *Serenade to Music*. On that same program, Sergei Rachmaninoff performed his popular Second Piano Concerto. While listening to the Vaughan Williams score, the Russian wept, and he later told Wood that he had never been so moved.

For the rest of his life, Vaughan Williams's pen seldom rested. His music often encompasses a characteristic serenity touched by a strain of gentle mysticism, and sometimes it is chilled by the horror of the Second World War (as in the bleak Sixth Symphony). In his final symphony, the Ninth, he poignantly takes leave of this earth. The nine symphonies contain much of his greatest music and are among the important contributions to twentieth-century orchestral music.

Vaughan Williams was a lumbering, burly, humble, and uncompromising man, uninterested in awards or honors. He strongly believed in the power of music as the "artistic expression which is natural to everybody." In his book *National Music*, he wrote, "When the United States of the World becomes, as I hope it will, an established fact, those will serve that universal State best who bring into the common fund something that they and they only can bring."

The musician Francis Routh considered Vaughan Williams "both a visionary and a realist. He not only wrestled with the problem of his own musical personality, he also fought passionately to discover the musical soul of his country. His genius was lyrical, religious, like that of William Blake. It is significant that his music speaks with great urgency to those whose outlook is idealistic, striving, unfettered by convention."

Vaughan Williams, a man of high moral and artistic commitment, deeply rooted in his own soil, grew far beyond the confines of a single nation, giving his art to all of humanity. At eighty-one the composer married his secretary, Ursula Wood, and died five years later of a heart attack.

Fantasia on a Theme of Thomas Tallis (1909–10)

This remarkable work, premiered on September 6, 1910, is the composer's most-often-performed composition. In 1567 Thomas Tallis composed nine melodies modeled on church tunes for an English psalter. Vaughan Williams was especially fond of No. 3, which forms the basis of his *Fantasia*. The orchestra, comprising only strings, is divided into three groups: a group of massed strings, a quartet of solo strings, and a group of nine strings. The critic J. A. Fuller-Maitland, reviewing the work in 1910, wrote, "The work is wonderful because it seems to lift one into some unknown region of musical thought and feeling. Throughout its course one is never quite sure whether one is listening to something very old or very new."

London Symphony Orchestra, Frühbeck de Burgos: IMP Classics PCD 930
Royal Liverpool Philharmonic Orchestra, Handley: EMI Classics CDM 64114
New York Philharmonic Orchestra, Bernstein: Sony Classical SMK 47638

Symphony no. 2 (*A London Symphony*) (1911–14)

In 1920 this symphony was revised and dedicated to the composer George Butterworth, who had been killed in the First World War at age thirty-one. The opening, a slow prelude, leads to an Allegro resoluto, which the composer says "may perhaps suggest the noise and hurry of London, with its always underlying calm." The second movement, Lento, is atmospheric and melancholy; the composer used the song "Sweet Lavender" to great effect. Of the third movement, the composer wrote, "If the hearer will imagine himself standing on Westminster Embankment at night, surrounded by the distant sounds of the Strand, with its great hotels on one side, and the 'New Cut' on the other, with its crowded streets and flaring lights, it may serve as a mood in which to listen to this movement." The fourth movement alternates majestic march material with solemn moods culminating with a simulation of Big Ben. *A London Symphony* has different meanings, as various as the endless impressions, images, and moods that the richness of "historical" London evokes. Although London has changed considerably since then, the symphony goes much farther than its descriptive aspects—Virgil Thomson noted around 1950, "It was written in 1913 I believe. It might have been written last month, so actual is its expressive content."

Royal Philharmonic Orchestra, Previn: Telarc 80138
London Symphony Orchestra, Thomson: Chandos CHAN 8629

Symphony no. 4 in F Minor (1931–34)

Dedicated to the English symphonist Sir Arnold Bax, the Fourth Symphony was first performed in London on April 10, 1935. A bitter, violent, even sinister work, it is worlds apart from the Vaughan Williams of folksong, Tudor influence, and pastoral beauty. Ever bountiful in musical material, the composer is here bare and concise, using two small motives as the underlying basis for the four movements. In the first movement, the high-voltage opening material offsets tremendous lyrical passion. The slow movement is in two sections, each ending with a passage for flute. The third movement is basically anxious, with a deftly sarcastic Trio. Vaughan Williams, one of the most learned of English composers, is far more polyphonic than meets the casual ear, and the Fourth Symphony is replete with contrapuntal textures. The finale is marked *con epilogo fugato*. The composer explains it: "the subject of the Fugal epilogue is played first on the trombone and then heard both in its original form and inverted, combined with the other subjects of the finale. The work ends with a reference to the opening bars of the first movement." The fugal epilogue is a tour de force of Vaughan Williams's amazing compositional skill. Every measure is thought through, worked through, and felt through in this work of tremendous complexity and intensity.

New York Philharmonic Orchestra, Bernstein: Sony Classical SMK 47638
London Symphony Orchestra, Previn: RCA Gold Seal 60583-2-RG

OTHER PRINCIPAL WORKS

BALLET
Job (1927–30)*

CHAMBER MUSIC
On Wenlock Edge (song cycle) for Tenor, String Quartet, and Piano (1908–9)*

CHORAL WORKS WITH ORCHESTRA
Toward the Unknown Region (1905–6)
Symphony no. 1 (A *Sea Symphony*) (1903–9)
Five *Mystical Songs* (1911)
Sancta civitas (oratorio) (1923–25)
Flos campi (suite) (1925)*
An Oxford Elegy (1947–49)

CHURCH MUSIC
Mass in G Minor (1920–21)*
Te Deum in G Major (1928)

OPERAS
Hugh the Drover (1910–14)*
Sir John in Love (1929)*
The Pilgrim's Progress (1951–52)*

ORCHESTRAL WORKS
In the Fen Country (symphonic impression) (1904)*
Three *Norfolk Rhapsodies* (1905–6)
The Wasps (incidental music) (1909)
Symphony no. 3 (*A Pastoral Symphony*) (1921)*
Fantasia on "Greensleeves" (1934)
Serenade to Music (1938)*
Five Variants of *"Dives and Lazarus"* (1939)
Symphony no. 5 in D Major (1938–43)*
Symphony no. 6 in E Minor (1944–47)*
Partita for Double String Orchestra (1946–48)
Symphony no. 7 (*Sinfonia antarctica*) (1949–52)
Symphony no. 8 in D Minor (1953–55)*
Symphony no. 9 in E Minor (1956–57)*

SOLO INSTRUMENT AND ORCHESTRA WORKS
The Lark Ascending (romance) for Violin and Orchestra (1914)*
Concerto accademico in D Minor for Violin and Orchestra (1924–25)
Concerto in C Major for Piano and Orchestra (1926–31)
Concerto in A Minor for Oboe and Strings (1944)
Romance in D-flat Major for Harmonica and Orchestra (1951)

VOICE WITH PIANO WORKS
Ninety songs

SERGEI RACHMANINOFF

b. Semyonovo, April 1, 1873

d. Beverly Hills, California, March 28, 1943

Radio cannot really do justice to good music. That is why I refuse to play for it. . . . It makes listening too comfortable. . . . Listening to music is much more demanding than that. . . . You can't fully appreciate it merely by sitting with your feet up and letting it soak into your ears.

Arkady Rachmaninoff, Sergei's grandfather, was an army officer and a wealthy landowner. He was also an amateur pianist and had taken some lessons with the Irish émigré pianist and composer John Field, the inventor of the nocturne. Sergei's father, Vasily, continued the military tradition as a captain in the Imperial Guards and lived a dissipated life of womanizing and liquor. Vasily married Lyubous Boutakovia, whose dowry included five estates. The couple had six children; Sergei was the fourth. Unfortunately, Vasily was financially irresponsible, and by the time Sergei was six, the family had lost its fortune. Sergei was a dreamy, lazy boy who showed abundant musical talent but balked at any sort of discipline. At nine he was sent to school in St. Petersburg. He failed most of his classes and in general had a dismal academic record. Fortunately, in 1885 his cousin, the pianist Alexander Siloti (who had just returned from studies in Weimar with Franz Liszt), took the boy in hand.

Siloti brought the twelve-year-old to Moscow and deposited him at the Moscow Conservatory with his own former teacher, Nikolai Zverev, who was considered to be the best teacher of young pianistic talent in Moscow. Rachmaninoff, with a few other boys, lived with Zverev, a despotic taskmaster. Further indolence was out of the question. The young pianists were up before dawn, practicing a harsh regime of technical exercises. Zverev completely controlled their lives, telling them what to read, what and how to eat and drink at the best restaurants, and how to dress properly. He took them to concerts, museums, and Gypsy camps, to hear Gypsies play and sing. The Moscow intelligentsia had long been enthralled with the Gypsy way of life. Rachmaninoff's first opera, *Aleko* (1892), was based on the story of a man's passionate attraction to a married Gypsy woman.

At Zverev's weekly soirées, the young pianists met Moscow's elite and performed for Tchaikovsky and Anton Rubinstein (head of the St. Petersburg Conservatory and one of the greatest pianists of the nineteenth century, as well as Rachmaninoff's idol). Rachmaninoff admired Tchaikovsky's music above all others, and fifty-six years later the last music he wrote was the exquisite piano transcription of Tchaikovsky's song "Lullaby." Rubinstein's playing also made an indelible impression. Years later Rachmaninoff recalled, "It was less his magnificent technique that held one spellbound than the profound, spiritually refined musicianship that sounded from each work he played." But Zverev, who was interested exclusively in piano playing, thwarted the youngster's attempts at composition. After four tense but productive years, Rachmaninoff parted bitterly with his teacher and mentor.

Siloti, now a respected teacher at the Moscow Conservatory, took charge of his cousin's piano instruction in the autumn of 1888, and Sergei became the star of Anton Arensky's composition class. During his years at the Conservatory, Rachmaninoff was an outstanding pupil, graduating with the gold medal in piano playing and composition. His fellow pupil, the pianist Alexander Goldenweiser, recalled, "Rachmaninoff's talent surpassed any other in my experience—almost unbelievable. . . . I recall how Siloti asked Rachmaninoff to study Brahms's famous *Variations and Fugue on a Theme by Handel*. This was Wednesday, and only three days later Rachmaninoff was already playing them from memory like a master." At nineteen, he was hardworking and serious but desperately prone to melancholy.

After graduation in 1891, Rachmaninoff took his first post as a teacher at a girls' school. While there he completed his opera *Aleko*, a *Trio élégiaque* (Op. 9, written for Tchaikovsky's tragic death in 1893), and, most important, the Prelude in C-sharp Minor (Op. 3/2, 1892), which eventually made him a household name. He premiered the somber, bell-like prelude on September 26, 1892. The next few years were difficult financially, and he lived with his cousins, the Satins. He worked constantly on a symphony and composed his *Six Moments musicaux* (Op. 16, 1896). It was his last work for a long while.

Early in 1897 the composer Alexander Glazunov conducted the young composer's First Symphony in D Minor (Op. 13) in St. Petersburg. The performance was so poor and badly cut that Rachmaninoff was crushed and fled the auditorium. Rumor had it that Glazunov was drunk. To make matters worse, the next day César Cui wrote a scathing review declaring, "If there was a conservatory in hell, Mr. Rachmaninoff's symphony . . . would no doubt thoroughly entertain all of hell's creatures." The hypersensitive young composer was devastated. The performance and the review triggered a terrible depression that lasted nearly four years. During much of this time, Rachmaninoff seemed to lose the will to create.

Princess Alexandra Lieven (famous in Moscow for her social work) had always championed the young composer. Hoping to revive his spirits, she arranged a meeting with Count Leo Tolstoy at the writer's apartment in Moscow. It was not a good match, for by 1900 the author of *War and Peace* was convinced that all art must be predominantly simple and should appeal easily to everyone. Rachmaninoff brought with him his closest friend, the basso Fyodor Chaliapin, soon to become famous. He played a solo piece, after which Tolstoy glared and asked, "Tell me, does anyone want this type of music?" Now it was the nervous Chaliapin's turn. Rachmaninoff played his song "Fate," based on the famous opening of Beethoven's Fifth Symphony, and Chaliapin sang. Tolstoy, who hated Beethoven, pounced on Rachmaninoff, telling him of his distaste for the music.

Early in 1900, Rachmaninoff fortunately sought help from Dr. N. V. Dahl, who was not only an amateur violinist but also a practitioner of psychiatry and hypnosis. Dahl saw Rachmaninoff as a patient but did not charge him. In their sessions, Dahl kept repeating to the composer that he would write a piano concerto, that it would be composed easily, and that it would be of excellent quality. The result was Rachmaninoff's Second Piano Concerto (Op. 18), which almost instantly became one of the most beloved of all concertos. The composer gratefully dedicated it to Dahl. With his creativity revived, he also composed the magnificent Second Suite for Two Pianos (Op. 17) and the luxuriant Cello Sonata (Op. 19).

On April 2, 1902, having overcome formidable legal hassles, Rachmaninoff married his first cousin, Natalia Satina. The next few years were busy, as Sergei composed and conducted both symphonic music and opera. In the summers, the couple stayed at the Satins' estate, Ivanovka, which had become indispensable to the composer's mental well-being. Irina, a daughter, was born there on May 14, 1903. A second daughter, Tatyana, was born on June 21, 1907. Late in 1906, the family moved for the musical season to Dresden, where Rachmaninoff's gifts as a conductor would flourish. His Second Symphony (Op. 27) was highly successful at its premiere in 1908, and offers poured in for Rachmaninoff as composer, pianist, and conductor. In May of that year he performed to wild acclaim in London. In 1909 he arrived in New York with a new concerto, No. 3, written for his first tour of America. In New York, a notable performance of the concerto took place with Mahler conducting. The two great artists were deeply impressed with each other: one the last bastion of Russian Romanticism, the other of German Romanticism.

With money in his pockets, Rachmaninoff returned to Ivanovka in the summer of 1910 and bought the estate from his father-in-law. That summer, while modernizing the estate with new machinery, he put to paper the Thirteen Preludes (Op. 32), which had been brewing in his head, in less than a month. The year 1912 was one of glory, as Rachmaninoff made his debut as conductor of the Moscow Philharmonic. The next three seasons as a conductor were summed up by the important Moscow critic Joel Engel: "Rachmaninoff is a truly 'God-given' conductor who stirs both audience and orchestra. He may be the only great conductor we can compare with such figures in the West as Nikisch, Colonne, and Mahler." Besides his Moscow achievements, he toured in Europe and composed a great deal, including the choral symphony *The Bells* (Op. 35, 1913).

In 1915, after the sudden death of Scriabin, his former classmate, Rachmaninoff played a series of all-Scriabin recitals to help rescue the composer's poverty-stricken family. This was the first time in years that he had learned and performed any piano music but his own.

During the war years, Rachmaninoff, always on the brink of depression, learned to control his black moods. To the poetess Marietta Shaginian, his chief confidante through these years, he wrote, "Here am I, spiritually sick. . . . I am afraid of everything—mice, rats, beetles, oxen, murderers. I am frightened when a strong wind blows and howls . . . when I hear raindrops on the window pane; I am afraid of the darkness, etc. I don't like old attics and I'm even willing to admit there are goblins around."

The 1917 Revolution came as a deep shock. He was in danger at Ivanovka from unruly peasants; eventually the home was looted and destroyed. Russia was a great source of nourishment for Rachmaninoff, and to leave his homeland, his estate, his career, his possessions, and his manuscripts seemed impossible. But he knew he could not stay under such a regime. Fortunately he was still able to leave legally, and he eagerly accepted an offer to play ten concerts in Scandinavia. Early in 1918 he left Russia forever with his family, a few pieces of hand luggage, and the allotted two thousand rubles.

Each passing year, Rachmaninoff missed Russia more. He refused the conductorships of the Boston and Cincinnati Orchestras and decided to make a living performing on the piano. Slowly he learned new music and refurbished his neglected repertoire. In his mid-forties, he began giving concerts, and for the next quarter of a century he played continuously, becoming one of the concert world's biggest box-office attractions. In an interview in London, he lamented, "The whole world is open to me, and success awaits me everywhere. Only one place is closed to me, and that is my own country." In 1931, after he signed an open letter in *The New York Times* condemning the Soviet government, Stalin banned his music from public performance.

For nearly a decade after he fled Russia, no new Rachmaninoff composition appeared. A Fourth Piano Concerto (Op. 40) was finally premiered in 1927, to disappointing reviews. He was deeply discouraged, and five more fallow years followed. In the summer of 1933, the composer moved to a villa in Switzerland that reminded him of his lost Ivanovka. There he composed the *Rhapsody on a Theme of Paganini* (Op. 43, 1934), which was an immediate success. The rest of the 1930s saw the composition of his *Corelli Variations* for piano (Op. 42, 1931), the Symphony no. 3 (Op. 44, 1936, which he later recorded with the Philadelphia Orchestra), and his last major composition, the *Symphonic Dances* (Op. 45, 1940). But he had become increasingly dissatisfied with himself as a composer and even as a pianist. After a long tour of seventy concerts, he told his wife that he had played only two recitals really well. He wrote, "The older we get, the more we lose that divine self-confidence which is the treasury of youth, the fewer are those moments when we believe that what we have done is good."

Now desperately tired, he learned that he had a fast-moving cancer. With his usual tenacity, he performed right up to the end, playing his last solo recital in Knoxville, Tennessee, on February 17, 1943. He died just over a month later, four days before his seventieth birthday. On his deathbed, he lamented that he could not accomplish his daily practice. Looking at his gigantic hands, he said, "My dear hands. Farewell my dear hands." He is buried at Kensico Cemetery in Valhalla, New York. Through the years, many a pilgrim has placed lilacs and daisies, symbols of his two most famous songs, on his tombstone.

Seldom has a musician been so blessed with talent. He was a superb conductor and, as a pianist, among the mightiest in history. The late Francis Robinson, the assistant manager of New York's Metropolitan Opera, wrote, "The fall out at a Rachmaninoff concert was high. . . . The shattering effect began with his first appearance, the austere frame which looked to be as long as his instrument and as gaunt, the angular gait unlike anything that has moved before or since, the withdrawn expression as remote as an icon before centuries of candle smoke." He had an unforgettable stage presence. The English pianist Cyril Smith thought, "Such was the power of his personality that I have seen members of the audience cower down in their seats as his glance passed over them."

Rachmaninoff's recorded legacy is studied by every serious pianist, and his records are priceless treasures of the art of piano playing. As a composer, Rachmaninoff today is more popular than ever. For years he was castigated as old-fashioned, and critics dismissed him as merely a Tchaikovsky epigone, writing music drenched in vodka and melancholia. He told an interviewer, "I feel like a ghost wandering in a world grown alien. I cannot cast out the old way of writing, and I cannot acquire the new. I have made intense efforts to feel the musical manner of today, but it will not come to me."

Never an innovator, Rachmaninoff poured out his heart in a wide variety of established musical forms: songs, operas, concertos, piano and orchestral music—all filled with gorgeous melody, rich harmony, and luscious orchestration, all highly polished. His music offers far more variety than he is usually given credit for. When he died, he was the last effulgent link in the great chain of nineteenth-century Russian Romanticism, which perished forever with the 1917 Revolution.

After his death, the great pianist Josef Hofmann paid him tribute: "Rachmaninoff was made of steel and gold; steel in his arms, gold in his heart. I can never think of this majestic being without tears in my eyes, for I not only admired him as a supreme artist, but I also loved him as a man." The complete recordings of Rachmaninoff, including the concertos and Third Symphony, have been assembled in the Collected Complete Rachmaninoff Recordings (10 discs): RCA 09026-61265-2.

Songs (1887–1916)

Although rather neglected, Rachmaninoff's seventy-five songs are perhaps the most perfect of Russia's song literature. For the discreet Rachmaninoff, they are highly personal. He asked Marietta Shaginian to be on the lookout for poems he might set. In 1912 he wrote her, "Whether it is going to be a contemporary author or one who is dead is immaterial. So long as the piece is original and not in translation and not longer than eight or twelve–sixteen lines at the maximum. Also, the mood should be sad rather than gay; it does not suit me when things go too well."

In his songs, Rachmaninoff's gift for pinpointing and capturing emotion is breathtaking. All he needed from the poetry was an impulse, a suggestion, and the mood was born. It is significant that perhaps his most famous song, "Vocalise" (Op. 34/14), is wordless. The human voice was always his finest inspiration, and the great basso Chaliapin's sound was always with him. Chaliapin's sudden death in 1938 was an agony for Rachmaninoff, although he had not composed for the singer in years. Six of his finest and his last songs, "In My Garden at Night," "To Her," "Daisies," "The Rat Catcher," "A Dream," and "A-u" (Op. 38), were written for Nina Koshetz, another singer whom Rachmaninoff adored (both as a woman and as an artist). In his songs, he asked for the piano to sing equally with the singer. In a 1979 essay, "Rachmaninoff as Songbird," John Russell, best known for his art criticism, wrote, "For Rachmaninoff himself the songs were coded messages from a world of feeling that he did not care to convey more directly. . . . The piano part of Rachmaninoff's songs has a freedom and a momentum of expression that quite often makes it the dominant partner." After 1917, he never again wrote a song; nor in his concert career, from that point, did he perform or record one.

The Complete Songs
Söderstrom, Ashkenazy: London 436920-2
Rodgers, Popescu, Naomenko, Leiferkus, Shelley: Chandos CHAN 9405, 9451, and 9477

Prelude, Op. 3/2 (1892)
Ten Preludes, Op. 23 (1903)
Thirteen Preludes, Op. 32 (1910)

The most famous Rachmaninoff prelude is Op. 3/2 in C-sharp minor. Recordings of it have sold in the millions, but because the nineteen-year-old composer was desperate for money, he sold the rights to it for only a small flat fee. He never made a royalty on one of the most widely sold piano pieces in history. It has been arranged in dozens of ways, from jazz band to saxophone sextet. Even Mickey Mouse played it in the cartoon *Mickey's Opry House*. When Rachmaninoff visited the Disney studios, he told Walt, "I have heard my inescapable piece done marvelously by some of the best pianists, and murdered cruelly by amateurs, but I was never more stirred than by the performance of Maestro Mouse."

In the remaining twenty-three preludes, we encounter the finest of Rachmaninoff's gorgeous piano music, with its exquisite pianistic textures and beguiling melodic appeal. Along with the C-sharp minor prelude, they complete Rachmaninoff's quest to write a prelude in each of the twelve major and minor keys. Throughout, the left-hand figurations make use of bass sonorities that have a physical, almost guttural impact. The composer was convinced that writing miniatures "presents many more problems than a symphony or con-

certo. After all, to say what you have to say, and say it briefly, lucidly, and con-
cisely is still the most challenging problem for the composer."

Ashkenazy: London 414417-2 (Opp. 23 and 32)
Weissenberg: RCA 60568-2-RC (Opp. 3/2, 23, and 32)
Biret: Naxos 8.550466 (Op. 32)

Concerto no. 2 in C Minor for Piano and Orchestra, Op. 18 (1901)

The C minor piano concerto, after the Tchaikovsky No. 1, is a favorite on the
concert stages of the world. The piano writing is intricate, the orchestration is
colorful and subtle, and the soaring melodic lines are ravishing. It was first performed, with the composer at the piano, in Moscow, on November 9, 1901.
The first movement begins with nine chords on the piano, increasing in force
as the first theme swells to ever-mounting passion. The slow movement, with a
luscious nocturnal theme, is finely spun, with an agitated middle section. The
finale opens with dramatic energy, succumbing to a second theme of burning
sensuality, which was pillaged by Tin Pan Alley into "Full Moon and Empty
Arms." This melody rises in triumphant glory in the orchestra as the piano
madly pounds out mighty chords.

The concerto is irresistible: Hollywood has used it over and over as "the
Classical Concerto" in background music. Its seductive power was even used in
a wonderful scene with Marilyn Monroe and Tom Ewell in *The Seven Year Itch*.

Janis, Minneapolis Symphony Orchestra, Dorati: Mercury 432759-2
Kissin, London Symphony Orchestra, Gergiev: RCA 60567-2-RC
Bronfman, Philharmonia Orchestra, Salonen: Sony Classical SK 47183

Symphony no. 2 in E Minor, Op. 27 (1906–7)

The composer conducted the successful premiere of the Second Symphony on
February 8, 1908, at St. Petersburg. It is the full bloom of Russian Romanticism, with melodies of high emotional eloquence, worked out with unerring
skill. Once the diffuse, almost hour-long symphony was played, the composer
sanctioned cuts; but most conductors today prefer it unaltered. The work
speaks with the intensity of Tchaikovsky, but in the language of Rachmaninoff.
Although traditional in design, it is cast in a highly distinct four-movement
form. The first movement (Largo, Allegro moderato) begins with pessimism.

The theme will be disguised throughout the work; the Allegro moderato is more restless and develops like a sonata. The movement is torturously emotional, sparked with great outbursts and strong rhythms. The second movement, Allegro molto, is a Scherzo. It starts with a bold opening tune, then launches into an almost violent episode, then into a short tranquil theme, and finally back to the Scherzo rhythm, which ebbs away into silence. The third movement, Adagio, is full of the Rachmaninoff melodic appeal, in two well-developed themes. The finale, Allegro vivace, blares its material in the bright light of E major. The marchlike first theme is full of energy. The second theme is a subject of glowing passion, which grows and will eventually burst its heart in a magnificent flowering.

Philadelphia Orchestra, Ormandy: RCA Victrola 60132-2 RV
Royal Philharmonic Orchestra, Litton: Virgin Classics CDC 59548
Royal Concertgebouw Orchestra, Ashkenazy: London 400081-2
Royal Philharmonic Orchestra, Previn: Telarc CD 80113

Concerto no. 3 in D Minor for Piano and Orchestra, Op. 30 (1909)

The Third Piano Concerto was composed at Ivanovka for Rachmaninoff's first American tour in 1909. It is terrifyingly difficult, and its challenge has become a legend among pianists. Only a hero of the keyboard should think of working on this exhausting piece, with its huge load of notes and dense harmonies. The pianist Gary Grafmann wishes he had learned it as a youngster, stating that "probably the only time I could have learned that magnificent knucklebreaker would have been when I was still too young to know fear." The work also needs a superlative interpreter who can fully project the almost unbearable nostalgia of Rachmaninoff's lost Russia. The Third Concerto was brought to a wider public in the film *Shine*, about pianist David Helfgott, who was dangerously possessed by the concerto.

The first movement begins with a tender and circumspect theme, which returns in different ways in the other two movements. The gorgeous slow movement, an Adagio titled "Intermezzo" by the composer, is made of two rhapsodic themes. An electrifying passage in octaves leads directly into the brilliant finale, which demands overwhelming sonorous power from the piano.

Cliburn, Symphony of the Air, Kondrashin: RCA 6209-2-RC
Horowitz, RCA Victor Symphony Orchestra, Reiner: RCA 7754-2-RC
Gilels, Paris Conservatory Orchestra, Cluytens: Testament TES SBT 1029
Argerich, Berlin Radio Symphony Orchestra, Chailly: Philips 446673-2

Rhapsody on a Theme of Paganini for Piano and Orchestra, Op. 43 (1934)

A concert-hall staple, the rhapsody is a set of variations, based on the theme of Paganini's Twenty-fourth Caprice for solo violin. The *Dies Irae* (*Days of Wrath*) from the Catholic mass for the dead is also integrated into the rhapsody. Death haunted Rachmaninoff while he was still a child, and the chill of the *Dies Irae* never left the composer's mind and appears in a number of his compositions in various guises. Later in the score, the luscious music of the famous eighteenth variation, Andante cantabile, is an inversion of the Paganini theme. The premiere took place in Baltimore on November 7, 1934. Eugene Ormandy conducted the Philadelphia Orchestra, and the composer appeared as soloist. By the time of its composition, Rachmaninoff, though still true to himself, had pared down both his emotionalism and the density of his music. The sobbing and often indulgent Slavic melancholy of the Third Concerto has drastically diminished. While the rhapsody is of considerable technical difficulty, the structure and the ideas have a new transparency, as well as a more urbane harmonic language.

Gavrilov, Philadelphia Orchestra, Muti: EMI Classics CDC 49966
Katchen, London Philharmonic Orchestra, Boult: London 417880-2
Moiseiwitsch, London Philharmonic Orchestra, Cameron: APR APR 5505

OTHER PRINCIPAL WORKS

CANTATA
Spring, Op. 20 (1902)

CELLO AND PIANO WORK
Sonata in G Minor, Op. 19 (1901)*

CHORAL WORK
Vespers, Op. 37 (1915)*

CONCERTOS
Concerto no. 1 in F-sharp Minor for Piano and Orchestra, Op. 1 (1890–91; rev. 1917)*
Concerto no. 4 in G Minor for Piano and Orchestra, Op. 40 (1926; rev. 1941)*

OPERAS
Aleko (1892)*
Francesca da Rimini, Op. 25 (1900, 1904–5)

ORCHESTRAL MUSIC

Symphony no. 1 in D Minor, Op. 13 (1895)*

The Isle of the Dead (symphonic poem), Op. 29 (1909)*

Symphony no. 3 in A Minor, Op. 44 (1936)*

Symphonic Dances, Op. 45 (1940)*

Vocalise in E Minor, Op. 34/14 (1912) (transcribed for orchestra)

SOLO PIANO WORKS

Six *Moments musicaux*, Op. 16 (1896)*

Various transcriptions of works by other composers*

Sonata no. 1 in D Minor, Op. 28 (1907)

Études-tableaux, Opp. 33 and 39 (eighteen pieces) (1911; 1916–17)*

Sonata no. 2 in B-flat Minor, Op. 36 (1913)

Variations on a Theme by Corelli, Op. 42 (1931)*

SOLOISTS, CHORUS, AND ORCHESTRA WORK

The Bells (choral symphony), Op. 35 (1913)*

TWO-PIANO WORKS

Suite no. 1 (*Fantaisie-tableaux*), Op. 5 (1893)*

Suite no. 2, Op. 17 (1900–1)*

ARNOLD
SCHOENBERG

b. Vienna, September 13, 1874

d. Brentwood, California, July 13, 1951

Music is not merely another kind of amusement, but a musical poet's, a musical thinker's representation of musical ideas; these musical ideas must correspond to the laws of human logic; they are a part of what man can apperceive, reason and express.

Schoenberg was the eldest of three children born to a Jewish family who lived in Vienna's poor Second District. Although the family had no piano, the eight-year-old Arnold began teaching himself on an old violin as best he could. When his father died suddenly in 1890, the youngster was forced to abandon school to help support the family. For five years, he labored unhappily as a bank clerk, struggling to compose bits and pieces of music in his spare time. He had a natural gift, but his efforts were hampered by his insufficient training.

Fortunately, a mentor soon appeared. The gifted young composer Alexander von Zemlinsky, only two years his senior, gave Schoenberg instruction in harmony and counterpoint, which the novice rapidly absorbed. In only two years, Zemlinsky noted that Schoenberg knew as much as he did and was even able to sense what he did not know.

In 1897 Schoenberg completed his first string quartet, which was performed in Vienna a year later. It received little notice. In December 1900 a few of his songs were heard, one of which annoyed the audience. Thereafter Schoenberg's music would seldom please the public: from then on, as Schoenberg later said, "The scandal has never ceased."

Schoenberg's first masterwork, in 1899, was *Verklärte Nacht* (*Transfigured*

Night, Op. 4), a morbidly romantic string sextet. The work's reception was mixed. An unnamed member of the audience shouted, "It sounds as if someone had taken the score of *Tristan* with the ink still wet, and smudged it over."

Ever since *Tristan und Isolde*, Wagner's increasing use of chromatic color chords had made tonal centers more ambiguous. Music's basic grounding was crumbling rapidly, and its older vocabulary was exhausted. The question was when music as previously known would dissolve altogether. This was Schoenberg's dilemma as he and others continued to compose highly charged Romantic but still essentially tonally chromatic compositions, such as the symphonic poem *Pelleas und Melisande* (Op. 5, 1902), *Gurrelieder* (1901–3), the D minor string quartet (Op. 7, 1904–5), and the *Chamber Symphony* no. 1 (Op. 9, 1906). Stuck in a historical impasse, he lingered painfully on.

In 1901 the impoverished composer married Zemlinsky's sister Mathilde, who was already pregnant by Schoenberg. The couple spent two difficult years in Berlin, where he conducted a cabaret orchestra to augment his teaching income, then returned to Vienna in 1903, forming friendships with Mahler and other Viennese artists. Although born Jewish and raised Catholic, Schoenberg had converted to Lutheranism in 1898. His Jewish origin still pursued him, however, and the virulent Viennese anti-Semitism barred him from any official teaching position. Instead, he barely eked out a livelihood teaching composition and theory privately. He did manage to gather around him a group of appreciative pupils, among them Anton Webern and Alban Berg, whom he taught with his characteristic single-minded dedication and intensity.

In January 1905 a performance of *Pelleas und Melisande* riled both critics and audience, but in early 1907, when the D minor string quartet was performed by the renowned Rosé Quartet, hostility turned into a near riot. Mahler pleaded with the giggling, hissing audience to sit and give the work a chance. Both press and public continued to flail at Schoenberg's next ventures, the *Chamber Symphony* and the F-sharp minor quartet (Op. 10, 1907–8). Around the same time, the composer discovered that his wife was having an affair with his close friend the painter Richard Gerstl. Days after Gerstl was told that Schoenberg had learned of the affair, the painter committed suicide by hanging and stabbing himself. A worried Anton Webern convinced Mathilde to stay with Schoenberg for the sake of their two children, who already suffered greatly from their poverty. (Their daughter was malnourished.)

During this vulnerable and desperate period, Schoenberg took his leap into atonal composition. "By avoiding the establishment of a key," he later wrote, "modulation is excluded, since modulation means leaving an established tonality and establishing *another* tonality." He felt he had fallen into an abyss. Schoenberg, a conservative, tradition-minded musician, was forced into becoming a radical. Curiously, just then, almost in justification, he embraced another form of expressionism: he began seriously and passionately painting, especially self-portraits with burning eyes gazing hopelessly into the void. Schoenberg's paintings were admired by Wassily Kandinsky, the leading expressionist painter of the time; his paintings display a moving aspect of Schoenberg's internal world. He painted throughout his entire period of atonal musical expressionism, from 1908 to 1913. In 1909 he composed the song cycle *Das Buch der hängenden Gärten* (*Book of the Hanging Gardens*, Op. 15), to poems by Stefan George; Three Piano Pieces (Op. 11); Five Orchestral Pieces (Op. 16); and the tragic, highly wrought twenty-five-minute one-act monodrama *Erwartung* (Op. 17). The year 1911 brought the Six Little Piano Pieces (Op. 19); No. 6 was influenced by the recent death of Mahler, whose burial was hauntingly depicted in one of Schoenberg's finest paintings.

These latest works continued to be spurned and laughed at. To the Viennese public, entrenched in the status quo, this music was a hostile reminder that their smug, secure world was smoldering with tensions on many levels. By now the vilified composer was becoming used to hearing his work described as "feeding time at the zoo" or "geese strangled," with "cackles," "shrieks," and "caterwauls." Even as late as 1947, Schoenberg wrote to the conductor Hans Rosbaud, "I still yearn that people should know my tunes and whistle them."

All this hostility was merely a warm-up for the first performances of *Pierrot lunaire* (Op. 21) in the autumn of 1912. This piece was written not for a singer but for the actress Albertine Zehme, who used a new kind of vocalization that Schoenberg termed *Sprechgesang* ("speech song"), a no-man's-land between singing and speech. Schoenberg said his intention had been to write in a light, ironic, satirical tone. But the score invites projection on many levels. Pierrot stands as a parable for modern man's desolation in an alienated world. At the first performance, there was near chaos. A woman fainted, a fight broke out, people shouted and screamed. Never had a piece of music so upset an audience, so stirred neurotic feelings.

In February 1913 the monumental oratorio-cantata *Gurrelieder*, composed a dozen years before, was given its first complete performance. This lusciously opulent post-Wagnerian work had an electrifying effect on the Viennese audience, and this time the cheers far exceeded the jeers. Schoenberg, when called to bow, typically refused: instead, he stormed out of the auditorium, yelling bitterly that the audience's appreciation for this early work meant nothing to him. A month later, he conducted a concert of his own music and works by Zemlinsky and Webern, along with Berg's *Altenberglieder*. The last caused such an uproar that the police were called in to stop the concert. Mahler's *Kindertotenlieder*, which was to have concluded the program, was never performed.

Destitute and depressed, despised by many, Schoenberg was now at the end of his atonal—or, as he preferred, "nontonal"—period. Vienna's nerves were on edge as the six-century-old Habsburg Empire reached the end of its life. With the outbreak of World War I, he fell silent, composing very little for nearly seven years. In 1915 he was conscripted and mobilized into the Austrian army. After the war, Schoenberg was surprised to find himself one of the most discussed composers of the day. Yet he did not know how to proceed. What could his future as a composer be? Around the end of 1921, the solution to his dilemma was beginning to appear. Schoenberg had always thought of himself as a respecter of tradition. In his opinion, he became a revolutionary only because he had been forced to do so by a stagnant art. Now he realized that even his atonal compositions were not revolutionary enough. He felt that it was his task to create a new kind of composing, one that was not dependent in any way on the major-minor scales and triads of the tonal system. It would depend, rather, on a new set of rules and a renewed common language, one whose musical vocabulary would be as rich and as traditionally powerful as diatonic Classicism had been.

Finally, Schoenberg codified what he called the *twelve-tone technique*, in which each of the twelve notes of the chromatic scale was of equal value, and a twelve-tone row or "series" was constructed with its inversions. It was the most far-reaching and radical innovation in music history. Swelling with pride, Schoenberg announced, "My technique will assure the supremacy of German music for the next hundred years." The writer Frederic Morton wrote that Schoenberg "would not just revolutionize music but reinvent it." Conductor Otto Klemperer felt, "The great thing that Schoenberg taught us is that there is no real difference between consonance and dissonance." Indeed, with its "emancipation of dissonance," twelve-tone technique allowed for countless new combinations of sounds and rigorous new ways of composing that contributed to the most adventurous twentieth-century music, inescapably affecting Alban Berg, Anton Webern, Olivier Messiaen, Pierre Boulez, Stefan Wolpe, Wallingford Riegger, Luigi Nono, Roberto Gerhard, Luigi Dallapiccola, Milton Babbitt, Luciano Berio, Ernst Krenek, Karlheinz Stockhausen, and dozens of others, giving them the ability to "serialize" pitch, dynamics, harmony, timbre, and rhythm.

Schoenberg completed his Five Piano Pieces (Op. 23) in 1923. The last piece was the composer's first composition to be totally organized on a "row" of the twelve tones. For this epoch-making departure into the new technique, he ironically wrote a waltz, the beloved dance form of his native Vienna. Both Berg and Webern saw new vistas for their own art and immediately followed their master's method. Because of their devoted advocacy, the twelve-tone technique did not appear as the quirk or aberration of one unsatisfied musician but quickly entered music's mainstream, even if public acceptance was rare. When Schoenberg was later asked why he had invented the twelve-tone technique, he replied, "Someone had to."

In 1923 Schoenberg's wife died, and a year later he married Gertrud Kolisch. In May 1933 Hitler's new minister of education dismissed Schoenberg for "Jewish reasons" from his professorship at the Prussian Academy of Fine Arts in Berlin, where he had been teaching composition since 1926. Thereafter he officially returned to the Jewish faith and left Germany for France and then the United States. After various hardships, he settled in Brentwood, California, in 1936, teaching at the University of California in Los Angeles.

In 1932 he had completed two acts of his projected three-act opera *Moses und Aron*, a work of immense power that was left unfinished. The music critic Philip Friedheim wrote that "the story concerns Moses' inability to reveal the essence of his vision of God to his people without destroying it beyond recognition; on another level, Moses becomes the symbol of the modern artist who, faithful only to his inner vision, finds he cannot communicate to his audience."

At age seventy, in 1944, Schoenberg was forced to retire from the university. His pension was only thirty-eight dollars a month, which didn't amount to much with three young children and a wife to support. He applied for a Guggenheim Foundation grant and was refused. As the pianist and writer Charles Rosen wrote, "Recognized internationally as one of the greatest living composers, considered the finest of all by many, acknowledged, with Igor Stravinsky, as one of the two most influential figures in contemporary music since Debussy, Arnold Schoenberg at the end of his life continued to provoke enmity, even a hatred, almost unparalleled in the history of music." Through failing eyesight and a massive heart attack in 1946, somehow he persevered, composing important works to the end. Just as he resumed work on *Moses und Aron*, he died at age seventy-six.

Schoenberg's legacy is vast: he revolutionized musical art, giving all composers the possibility of a new expressiveness through the free use of the chromatic scale. His influence was more than far-reaching; it has proved paramount for achieving a much-needed freedom in musical composition. Possessing this freedom depends on severe discipline, and it was understandable that Schoenberg's great rival Igor Stravinsky, staunch in his elaborate tonalism, would in his long life finally become refreshed through Schoenberg's innovations.

As for Schoenberg's actual music, its high consistency shows an intellectual grasp and a mastery that is at times comparable with that of Bach and Beethoven. Yet except for a few early works, his oeuvre remains very difficult for the majority of music lovers. Perhaps this is best explained by Philip Fried-heim, who observes, "The problem of his music seems to lie in its perpetual complexity and in its compulsion to push every element, including rhythm, form, and texture to its furthest possible limits. His obsessive desire to make every moment count the most, to fill every bar with as much music as possible, to make every inner voice participate in the thematic content, to vary in some way every repetition (even of a single phrase), all ultimately makes staggering demands on the listener. The listener is sometimes bombarded with too much information too quickly; if he does not absorb it fast enough, the composition can become a nerve-wracking experience." But many of Schoenberg's advo-cates—and they are increasing in number every year—find a deep-seated hu-manity, especially in his later music. In recent seasons, audiences have been exalted instead of shocked by *Moses und Aron*, which is finally coming into its own as musical drama of the highest order.

Verklärte Nacht (Transfigured Night), Op. 4 (1899)

The last word in *Tristan*-oriented music, *Verklärte Nacht* absolutely gives one shivers. Its original version for string sextet is superb, but its setting for chamber orchestra is better known. The composition's structure and content are based on the five sections of an 1896 poem by Richard Dehmel about a woman who is pregnant but meets the man she truly loves. She says, "I bear a child and not from you. I walk in sin beside you. I have wronged myself profoundly. I had lost faith in happiness and yet felt such longing for meaning in life, for the joys and the tasks of motherhood that I brazenly gave myself to a stranger's embrace, and thought myself blessed. Now life has taken revenge, for now I have met you." Schoenberg never lost his affection for this youthful score. Many years later he said, "The Supreme Commander had ordered me on a harder road. But a longing to return to the older style was always vigorous in me." Indeed, once at the Hollywood Bowl, after a cheering audience had heard Grieg's Pi-ano Concerto, Schoenberg, longing to communicate on that level, said to the composer Roberto Gerhard, "That is the kind of music I should really like to write."

STRING SEXTET VERSION
Trampler, Ma, Juilliard String Quartet: Sony Classical SK 47690

STRING ORCHESTRA VERSION
Orpheus Chamber Orchestra (no conductor): Deutsche Grammophon 429233-2
New York Philharmonic Orchestra, Boulez: Sony Classical SMK 48464

Chamber Symphony no. 1, Op. 9 (1906)

The *Kammersymphonie* for fifteen solo instruments ended Schoenberg's earliest period, when his music was still related to Wagner and Strauss but possessed its own complex style and inevitable logic. Today it is one of Schoenberg's most frequently performed scores. In 1906, however, Schoenberg reported, "A Viennese conductor made it known to me that he could not perform my *Kammersymphonie* because he did not understand it. I was amused, though; why did he have to pick on me in this sudden burst of wanting to understand, and not on the classical works he blithely conducted year in and year out?"

BBC Symphony Orchestra, Boulez: Sony Classical SMK 48462
Chamber Orchestra of Europe, Holliger: Teldec 2292-46019-2
Southwest German Radio Symphony Orchestra, Horenstein: VoxBox 5529

Gurrelieder (1901–3; orchestrated 1911)

Gurrelieder, a song cycle set to love poems by the romantic Danish writer Jens Peter Jacobsen, is a unique and stupendous score, an hour and a half long. It uses mammoth orchestral forces—138 musicians, five soloists, a chorus, and a speaker-narrator. Before the 1912 premiere, Berg wrote to Schoenberg, "I'm now experiencing the unique joy of immersing myself in the *Gurrelieder*, indeed of being engulfed by it, staggering from one treasure to another like a drunken man." And later: "It's unbelievably magnificent; this is condensed music, as all great works are distinguished from the lesser ones in that they are saturated with music, like full, ripened fruit, ever ready to be savored in complete freshness." The music, in the best Wagnerian mode, describes a love that lives on after death. It contains tone paintings of nature scenes, a horseman riding across midnight skies, and a great array of orchestral colors utilizing twenty-five brass players and a large percussion battery. It is rarely heard in live performance today but is a must for any good collection of CDs.

Norman, McCracken, Troyanos, Boston Symphony Orchestra, Tanglewood Festival Chorus,
   Ozawa: Philips 412511-2
Napier, Minton, Thomas, BBC Symphony Orchestra, Boulez: Sony Classical SM2K 48459

Three Piano Pieces, Op. 11 (1909)
Six Little Piano Pieces, Op. 19 (1911)
Five Piano Pieces, Op. 23 (1923)
Suite for Piano, Op. 25 (1923)

The pianist Paul Jacobs was convinced that "these piano pieces are as important to contemporary piano technique as the Chopin Études were to that of the nineteenth century." Of the Three Piano Pieces (Op. 11), Glenn Gould wrote, "Perhaps no other composition was as crucial to Schoenberg's future. . . . Opus 11 was the first major test of the possibilities of survival in a musical universe no longer dominated by a triadically centered harmonic orbit." The set of Six Little Piano Pieces (Op. 19) continues Schoenberg's adventure in atonality while giving new meaning to musical brevity. The Five Piano Pieces in Op. 23 move closer to twelve-tone technique, and No. 5 embarks on the revolution. The Suite for Piano (Op. 25) is his first completely twelve-tone composition; it includes a Präludium, Gavotte and Musette, Intermezzo, Minuet with Trio, and Gigue. Gould goes so far as to say, "I can think of no composition for solo piano from the first quarter of this century which can stand as its equal."

Helffer: Musique d'Abord HMA 190752
Jacobs: Elektra/Nonesuch 71309-2
Pollini: Deutsche Grammophon 43249-2

Five Pieces for Orchestra, Op. 16 (1909)

How perception changes! Schoenberg's nontonal Five Pieces for Orchestra, once thought to be cacophonous and contemptible, have for many become a vision of beauty and expressiveness. Edward Downes, the critic and program-note annotator for the New York Philharmonic, thinks, "These five books of pieces are as important to contemporary piano technique as the Chopin *Études* were to that of the nineteenth century."

Sir Henry Wood, a conductor who courageously introduced England to much new music, gave the world premiere in 1912. For a later performance in London, Schoenberg appended titles to the pieces. They are: 1. "Premonitions," 2. "Yesteryears," 3. "Summer Morning by a Lake," 4. "Peripetia," 5. "The Obligatory Recitative." The third piece uses no themes, repetition, or any established compositional device. There is no record to show if the descriptive titles helped the audience to navigate in these uncharted waters.

London Symphony Orchestra, Dorati: Mercury 432006-2
Berlin Philharmonic Orchestra, Levine: Deutsche Grammophon 432006-2

Pierrot lunaire, Op. 21 (1912)

At its first performances in 1912, *Pierrot lunaire* was the last word in Modernism. Many thought the composer a lunatic. The great American critic James Huneker attended the fourth performance in Berlin that year and defended Schoenberg: "To call him 'crazy' is merely amusing. No man is less crazy, few men are so conscious of what they are doing, and few modern composers boast such a faculty of attention." That did not mean, however, that the "progressive" Huneker liked the music, for he continued, "Every composer has his aura; the aura of Arnold Schoenberg is, for me, the aura of subtle ugliness, of hatred and contempt, of cruelty. . . . If such music making is ever to become accepted, then I long for Death the Releaser. More shocking still would be the suspicion that in time I might be persuaded to like this music, to embrace it, after abhorring it." Schoenberg was touched that Puccini made a six-hour journey to hear the score and said "some very friendly things to me; that was good, strange though my music may have remained to him."

In its audacity *Pierrot* still astonishes its listeners, yet it remains one of the essential works of twentieth-century art. It is scored for speaker/singer, piano, flute, piccolo, clarinet, bass clarinet, violin, viola, and cello. The speaking-singing voice almost strums and slides through the piece. Its mosaic patterns, which once seemed anarchic, today seem to be a last gasp of expressionistic Romanticism.

DeGaetani, Contemporary Chamber Ensemble, Weisberg: Elektra/Nonesuch 79237-2-ZK
Manning, Nash Ensemble, Rattle: Chandos CHAN 6534

Trio for Strings, Op. 45 (1946)

Schoenberg was quite adamant that his listeners need have no special knowledge in order to understand his twelve-tone works. The trio is a good example of that thought, and it shows the astonishing breadth of his twelve-tone writing. The marvelous polyphonic weaving of the strings is charged with color and a profound rhythmic life. Schoenberg, at seventy-two, remained daring, convinced that his twelve-tone technique had endless possibilities for creative potential. The work is in one movement, which is divided into five sections: Part I, Episode I, Part II, Episode II, and Part III.

Schoenberg had a near-fatal heart attack on August 2, 1946. He was revived by an injection directly into his heart, and he recovered. He wrote the trio immediately afterward, in a weeklong burst of grateful inspiration.

Juilliard String Quartet (members): Sony Classical SK 47690
LaSalle Quartet (members): Deutsche Grammophon 423250-2
Vienna String Trio: Calig CAL 50861

OTHER PRINCIPAL WORKS

CHAMBER MUSIC
Quartet no. 1 in D Minor for Strings, Op. 7 (1904–5)
Quartet no. 2 in F-sharp Minor for Strings with Soprano Solo, Op. 10 (1907–8)*
Serenade for Septet and Baritone, Op. 24 (1923)*
Suite for Woodwinds, String Trio, and Piano, Op. 29 (1925–26)
Quartet no. 3 for Strings, Op. 30 (1927)
Quartet no. 4 for Strings, Op. 37 (1936)*

MONODRAMA
Erwartung, Op. 17 (1909)*

OPERAS
Die glückliche Hand, Op. 18 (1910–13)
Moses und Aron (1930–32)*

ORCHESTRAL WORKS
Pelleas und Melisande (symphonic poem), Op. 5 (1902)*
Variations, Op. 31 (1928)*
Transcription of Bach's Organ Prelude and Fugue in E-flat Major (1928)
Transcription of Brahms's Piano Quartet in G Minor (1937)*

SOLO INSTRUMENT AND ORCHESTRA WORKS
Concerto for Violin and Orchestra, Op. 36 (1935–36)*
Concerto for Piano and Orchestra, Op. 42 (1942)*

SPEAKER AND ORCHESTRA WORKS
Kol Nidre, Op. 39 (1938)
Ode to Napoleon, Op. 41 (1942)
A Survivor from Warsaw, Op. 46 (1947)*

VIOLIN AND PIANO WORK
Phantasy, Op. 47 (1949)*

VOICE WITH PIANO WORK
Das Buch der hängenden Gärten (*Book of the Hanging Gardens*, song cycle), Op. 15 (1908–9)

WIND BAND WORK
Theme and Variations, Op. 43a (1943)*

MAURICE RAVEL

b. Ciboure, France, March 7, 1875

d. Paris, December 28, 1937

All life's pleasure consists of getting a little closer to perfection, and expressing life's mysterious thrill a little better.

Ravel was born in the Basque region of France, near the Spanish border. He adored his mother, a sophisticated, loving woman of Basque descent. His father was a musical amateur who, in Ravel's words, "knew how to develop my taste and to stimulate my zeal at an early age." His first piano teacher, Henri Ghys, was well known as a clever teacher of children. At Maurice's first lesson, on May 31, 1882, Ghys noted in his diary that the boy seemed to be "intelligent."

Ravel entered the Paris Conservatory at fourteen. In the piano class of Charles-Wilfrid Bériot, he met Ricardo Viñes, the Catalan pianist, with whom he formed a lifelong friendship; Viñes later premiered many of Ravel's piano works. The pair had many enthusiasms, including Wagner (Viñes once heard his exceedingly reserved friend's muffled sobbing during a performance of the Prelude and *Liebestod* from *Tristan*) and Emmanuel Chabrier. As a gift to the ailing Chabrier, Viñes and Ravel performed privately for him his Three *Valses romantiques* for two pianos. Another early influence on Ravel was the outlandish Erik Satie, whose piano music had also affected several other French composers.

When Ravel was twenty, he published his first work, the *Menuet antique* for piano. In this work, certain aspects of Ravel's style already sound fully formed—his fastidious design, innate elegance, and free use of ninth chords, for example. Ravel continued at the Conservatory until he was twenty-six, studying counterpoint and orchestration with André Gédalge and composition with Gabriel Fauré, who knew exactly how to extract the best from his pupil. His fellow student Nadia Boulanger was surprised that he was still working at counterpoint exercises after so long, but Ravel never ceased to be a student. In 1901, the year of his graduation, he wrote his shimmering piano piece *Jeux d'eau*, which he dedicated to his beloved Fauré.

From 1900 until 1905, the young composer competed unsuccessfully for the coveted Prix de Rome. The great author Romain Rolland and others considered it ludicrous that he was not given the prize, for in 1905 no young French composer had produced as much important music. Although Rome was denied him, Ravel became one of Paris's leading composers before he was thirty.

It was an exciting time in Paris, and Ravel joined other young artists, such as composers Manuel de Falla and Déodat de Séverac, poets Tristan Klingsor and Léon Paul Fargue, and music critic M. D. Calvocoressi, in a group of sympathetic artists called Les Apaches. The club's signature theme was the main subject of Borodin's Second Symphony. Ravel continued to carefully produce new works: the gracious String Quartet (1903); the five piano pieces titled *Miroirs* (1904–5); the alluring *Introduction et allegro* for harp with flute, clarinet, and string quartet (1905); the *Sonatine* for Piano (1905); *Histoires naturelles* for voice and piano (1906); the orchestral *Rapsodie espagnole* (1908), which was hissed at its premiere; the extraordinary *Gaspard de la nuit* for piano (1908); and the delightful one-act opera *L'Heure espagnole* (1907–9).

Near the end of the decade, the appearance in Paris of the impresario Serge Diaghilev and his Ballets Russes stirred great commotion in the city's social and artistic life. Diaghilev seemed to put almost everyone with talent to work for him. He commissioned Ravel to write a ballet, *Daphnis et Chloé*, which was completed in 1912. In 1911 he also finished the *Valses nobles et sentimentales* for piano and turned *Ma Mère l'Oye*, originally for piano duet, into a ballet. In 1914, as the First World War approached, Ravel completed his Piano Trio.

The dandified five-foot-tall composer was a man-about-town, entertaining friends and prowling Paris at night. To his many acquaintances, he was an enigma; he had no known intimate relationships. Like Debussy, he adored cats. Although he was refused for military service because he was too short and underweight, the composer courageously served France in the war as motor transport driver at the front. What he saw was frightful. Early in 1917, his mother died. The composer was crushed, and he told Falla, "From that moment on, life is transformed." His health began to fail, and later in 1917 he was discharged and sent back to Paris for convalescence. Though he was depressed by the terrors of war and by his mother's death, he completed *Le Tombeau de*

Couperin (1917), each movement of which he dedicated to a friend lost in the war. The piece would be his last work for solo piano.

Ravel began to suffer from insomnia, and he became increasingly taciturn and nervous, even making a public fuss over not accepting the Legion of Honor. The glib Satie told all of Paris that "Monsieur Ravel refuses the Legion of Honor, but all his music accepts it." In 1918 Diaghilev again commissioned a ballet. Ravel finished it in 1920 and played it through for Diaghilev. The impresario told him that *La Valse* was not a true ballet but a portrait of a ballet. Ravel, distressed and hurt, refused to speak to Diaghilev ever again. They met once more, in 1925. The Russian offered Ravel his hand, which the composer declined. The spoiled and impetuous Diaghilev immediately challenged the composer to a duel. Fortunately, the confrontation never took place, but it would have been a unique sight—on the one side the tiny composer in his fashionable spats, on the other the bearlike and affected Russian with his flowing cape.

Ravel was always a slow worker, and during the 1920s he composed even less than before. He completed only the opera *L'Enfant et les sortilèges* (1925, to a libretto by Colette) and his most celebrated composition, *Boléro* (1928). In 1928 he toured the United States, conducting his music with great success. He was delighted by New York and especially enjoyed hearing jazz in Harlem. Despite the alarming decline in his health, he was working simultaneously on a piano concerto and a piano concerto for left hand alone. He took the new concerto for both hands on a European tour, with the famous pianist Marguerite Long as soloist. Upon Ravel's return to Paris, his health further declined, and in 1932, after a taxi accident, he had a nervous breakdown. His last music—three songs, collectively titled *Don Quichotte à Dulcinée*—was completed in 1933. His final six years were terrible. In 1933 he was diagnosed with a rare brain disease. Although he was lucid, his movements were strange; he functioned, but his thought and creative processes were impaired. He still attended the theater and the concert hall, but he appeared oblivious, even to ovations for his own music. At one of the last concerts he attended, after listening to *Daphnis et Chloé*, he wept, telling a friend, "I have so much music in my head, I have said nothing. I have so much more to say." Late in 1937 he heard his music for the last time. After unsuccessful brain surgery, he went into a coma and died days later.

Throughout his career, Ravel was disturbed by the incessant comparisons with Debussy, thirteen years his senior. But Ravel, a Classicist by temperament, was only superficially influenced by Debussy. He was an elegant Apollonian, an exquisite jeweler. His music contains luscious aspects of impressionism, the early influence of Chabrier, poetic symbolism, a fascination with the "Orient," and an attraction to Spanish rhythms. It also holds irony, childlike fantasy, a love for animals, and the waltz form. In addition, Ravel was one of the great orchestrators. His 1922 instrumentation of Mussorgsky's *Pictures at an Exhibition* is a masterpiece of orchestral virtuosity. For Ravel, each work was a new adventure, a new challenge in compositional style and substance. Each composition had an underlying purpose, be it a synthesis of Gypsy music (the Violin *Tzigane*, 1924), a neo-Lisztian portrait of a devilish imp (*Gaspard de la nuit*), a miraculous piano concerto for left hand alone (1929–30), or a bitterly nostalgic portrayal of a dance, a city, and an epoch (*La Valse*, 1919–20). The more one studies Ravel, the more varied and amazing he becomes. Everything he wrote is touched by the hand of a master.

He is France's most frequently performed composer, even more than Debussy. His cool-headed craft achieves absolute perfection in music of a radiant spiritual lightness. Ravel represents French art at its zenith.

Pavane pour une infante défunte for Piano (1899)

The six-minute *Pavane* was the first of Ravel's works to become well known. Tin Pan Alley unfortunately took the theme for a popular song. One might think that a *pavane* for a dead princess would be in a somber minor key, but Ravel used G major and bathed the score in what seems to be a white light, with that peculiarly Ravelian melancholy. In 1910 he orchestrated it.

PIANO VERSION
Casadesus: Sony Classical 2-63316
Thiollier: Naxos 8.550683

ORCHESTRAL VERSION
Chicago Symphony Orchestra, Reiner: RCA 60179

Quartet in F Major for Strings (1902–3)

Ravel's String Quartet is perfect in design, moving swiftly and graciously. After its first performance, Debussy wrote to his younger colleague, "In the name of the gods of music, do not touch one thing in the Quartet." It was dedicated to Fauré and, with Fauré's own String Quartet (composed in 1924) and Debussy's, marks the high point of French music in this pure medium. Although it is an early work, Ravel achieved a breathtaking spontaneity. The opening movement could not be more trim and terse. The Scherzo, which has a touch of Debussy, is all vivacity and rhythmic complexity. The slow movement is a rhapsodic expression, while the finale is Borodin turned Gallic.

Galimir String Quartet: Vanguard Classics OVC 4049
Guarneri String Quartet: RCA Silver Seal 09026-60909-2

Sonatine for Piano (1903–5)

The *Sonatine*, a ten-minute score of supreme polish and perfection of detail, has a thin texture and is the very essence of Gallic lucidity. The first movement is marked *modéré* and is a miniature sonata movement without a development section. The second movement is a neoclassic minuet of exquisite grace with a tiny coda that seems to lift the listener into the air. The third-movement finale, Animé, is the most brilliant, with an admirable use of the keyboard's upper register.

Cortot: Biddulph LHW 006
Körmendi: Naxos 8.550254
Lortie: Chandos CHAN 8647
Perlemuter: Vox Box CDX2 5507

Alborada del gracioso for Piano, No. 4 from Miroirs (1904–5)

The title of this *aubade*, a morning serenade, is perhaps best translated as *Morning Song of the Jester* or *Buffoon*. Each of the five *Miroirs* is a unique excursion into Ravelian impressionism and symbolism. *Alborada* is the best known of the set. Ravel has integrated the glamour of a Liszt rhapsody with Spanish dance rhythms. Ravel's jester and his insinuating guitar strains are hypnotic; the middle section is seduction with a sardonic smile. The composer made a stunning orchestration of it in 1918. Ravel was only an adequate pianist, but as a keyboard explorer, he offers the pianist many cruel exploits, including some incredibly difficult double glissandos in fourths. In all, it is a treacherous battle with the keyboard.

PIANO VERSION
Gilels: Music & Arts CD 747-1
Lipatti: EMI Classics CDH 63038

ORCHESTRAL VERSION

Dutoit, Montreal Symphony Orchestra: London 410010-2

Rapsodie espagnole (1907–8)

Rapsodie espagnole has four sections: Prélude à la nuit, Malagueña, Habanera, and Feria. The Spanish composer Manuel de Falla, who had recently arrived in Paris, was dazzled and thought it genuinely Spanish (unlike the usual paraphrase on Spanish folk themes, such as Liszt's *Rhapsodie espagnole* and Rimsky-Korsakov's *Capriccio espagnole*). Simultaneously in 1907 in Paris, Debussy was working on his *Ibéria*, Falla on his Four *Spanish Pieces*, and Albéniz on his *Iberia*. The premiere of Ravel's *Rapsodie*, the first of his published orchestral works, took place in Paris in 1908. The audience hooted its disapproval and for the moment confirmed the words of the French composer Émile Paladilhe, who said, "M. Ravel may look upon us as old fogies if he pleases, but he will not with impunity make fools of us."

London Symphony Orchestra, Previn: EMI Classics CDD 63887
Chicago Symphony Orchestra, Reiner: RCA 09026-61250-2

Gaspard de la nuit for Piano (1908)

The piano suite was inspired by the poet Aloysius Bertrand's *Histoires vermoulues et poudreuses du Moyen Age*. The three component pieces are "Ondine," "Le Gibet," and "Scarbo." The composition was first performed by the pianist Ricardo Viñes. The pianist Alfred Cortot pronounced, "These three poems enrich the piano repertoire . . . with one of the most extraordinary examples of instrumental ingenuity which the industry of composers has ever produced."

In "Ondine," Ravel portrayed a water nymph attempting the seduction of a mortal. "Nowhere in music," declared the critic Edward Lockspeiser, "and seldom in the Impressionist paintings of this era, have the iridescent images of glistening, transparent water been so convincingly conveyed." "Le Gibet," the gallows, is a study in suspense, evoking an eerie, static, half-lit gruesome scene. "Scarbo," one of the most difficult piano pieces ever written (based on Ravel's microscopic study of Liszt and of Balakirev's *Islamey*), has become a badge of mastery for pianists worldwide. "Scarbo" is a cruel, erotic, macabre, but irresistible goblin.

Gavrilov: EMI CDM 69026
Pogorelich: Deutsche Grammophon 413363-2
Michelangeli: Music & Arts CD 817
Gieseking: Musique D'Abord HMA 190922

Ma Mère l'Oye (Mother Goose) (1911)

Originally composed for piano duet, which two ten-year-old pianists introduced in 1910, the Mother Goose suite is based on seventeenth-century children's rhymes. In 1911 Ravel transformed the enchanting piano score into a
ballet, adding a prelude, a new opening scene, and connecting interludes. As
usual, he crafted a masterpiece of orchestration, using celesta, harp, glockenspiel, tam-tam, cymbals, and other percussion battery for the most charming
and varied effects.

PIANO VERSION
Labèque Sisters: Philips 420159-2

BALLET VERSION
Pittsburgh Symphony Orchestra, Previn: Philips 400016-2

Valses nobles et sentimentales (1911)

"The title Valses nobles et sentimentales sufficiently indicates my intention of
writing a series of waltzes in imitation of Schubert," Ravel wrote. Yet with their
perfectly carved, needlelike detail, and ironic overtones, these seven waltzes
and epilogue are worlds apart from Schubertian innocence. On the title page,
Ravel quoted a line from Henri de Régnier: "The delightful and always novel
pleasure of a useless occupation." Ravel orchestrated the score the following
year for a ballet danced by Natasha Trouhanova.

PIANO VERSION
Michelangeli: Arkadia 904
Rubinstein: RCA Gold Seal 09026-61446-2

ORCHESTRAL VERSION
Detroit Symphony Orchestra, Paray: Mercury Living Presence 434306-2
Cleveland Orchestra, Ashkenazy: London 430413-2

Daphnis et Chloé (choreographic symphony) (1909–12)

Stravinsky called *Daphnis* "one of the most beautiful products in all of French music." His verdict stood throughout the twentieth century. From the complete ballet score, Ravel adapted two suites, the second of which is among the most popular French compositions in the international repertoire. At the ballet's premiere on June 8, 1912, two of the greatest dancers of all time, Vaslav Nijinsky and Tamara Karsavina, danced the principal roles, with Pierre Monteux conducting. The sets were created by the artist Léon Bakst, the choreography by Michel Fokine. The score is Ravel's most intoxicating and sensuous, fully assimilating influences from Rimsky-Korsakov, Balakirev, and Borodin. Ravel wrote that he meant to compose "a vast musical fresco, less thoughtful of archaism than of fidelity to the Greece of my dreams, which identifies quite willingly with that imagined and depicted by late eighteenth-century French artists."

Montreal Symphony and Chorus, Dutoit: London 400055-2
Boston Symphony Orchestra, Munch: RCA Living Stereo 09026-61846-2

Le Tombeau de Couperin (1914–17)

Le Tombeau is a suite of six movements: Prélude, Fugue, Forlane, Rigaudon, Menuet, and Toccata. Ravel said, "The homage is directed less in fact to Couperin himself than to French music of the eighteenth century." Each movement is dedicated to the memory of a friend who was killed during the war. During the darkness of World War I, Ravel, master of logic and reason, looked back with yearning to an earlier age of aristocratic grace. In his attempt to extract every ounce of meaning from his works, he often orchestrated his piano music, as he also did with *Le Tombeau* in 1919. But the Fugue and the golden Toccata, a repeated note (*moto perpetuo*), were left unorchestrated. Even with his unique orchestral mastery, Ravel in his wisdom knew the Toccata would be ruined if separated from its original medium.

PIANO VERSION
Magaloff: Adès ADE 202952
Lortie: Chandos CHAN 8620

ORCHESTRAL VERSION
City of Birmingham Symphony Orchestra, Rattle: EMI Classics CDC 54158

La Valse (choreographic poem) (1919–20)

La Valse, one of Ravel's most popular works, could not be more different from the *Valses nobles et sentimentales*. Even in the late stages of its composing he called it "Wien (Vienna)," and it is considerably darker than the *Valses nobles*. It is desperately nostalgic in its depiction of a recently vanished age. The score is a whirl of misty, ghostlike suffering, possessed by an aura of dissipation. Once again Ravel dazzles us with a delirious essay of orchestral mastery.

Orchestre de la Suisse Romande, Ansermet: London 448576-2
Boston Symphony Orchestra, Ozawa: Deutsche Grammophon 415845-2
NBC Symphony Orchestra, Cantelli: Legend LGD 104

Boléro (1928)

Ravel himself was on the podium for the first concert performance of his most popular work, on January 11, 1930. The Russian dancer Ida Rubinstein, who had commissioned it, danced in the ballet performance on November 22, 1928, at the Paris Opera, to wild enthusiasm. At a Paris performance in Toscanini's hands late in 1930, Ravel was irritated by the too-fast tempo and chastised the conductor afterward. Toscanini lashed back that a bolero is not a funeral march. The two were never again pleased with each other. For a large public, *Boléro*, with its intense buildup and eruptive energy, has always been an anthem to sexuality. In the choreography for the original ballet, Ida Rubinstein, a performer of hypnotic effect, danced upon a round platform with men circling her. As her gyrations became ever more erotic, the audience burst into wild applause at the lust she generated. To Ravel, the composition "constitutes an experiment in a very special and limited direction and should not be suspected of aiming at achieving anything other or more than it actually does."

Philharmonia Orchestra, Sinopoli: Deutsche Grammophon 427644-2
Philadelphia Orchestra, Muti: EMI Classics CDC 47022

Concerto in D Major for Piano Left Hand and Orchestra (1929–30)

This concerto, composed around the same time as the Piano Concerto in G Major, is a miracle of technical savoir-faire; at no time does the listener think that the concerto is for left hand alone. It was composed for the Austrian pianist

Paul Wittgenstein (brother of the philosopher), who had lost his right arm in the war and gave the challenging score its premiere in Paris on November 27, 1931. The concerto, which also uses jazz-inspired material, is more dramatic and grandiose than the G major concerto. The score is in one movement in three sections, highlighted by a tumultuous cadenza for the soloist. The composer restates the main subject with overwhelming orchestral sonority, which leads to a cool theme of slight texture. The middle of the score becomes jazzy, a jaunty tap dance. As is always the case with Ravel, individual instruments of the orchestra are used with ingenious effect.

Cortot, Paris Conservatory Orchestra, Munch: Pearl PEA 9491
Paik, Stuttgart Radio Symphony Orchestra, Bertini: Orfeo 013821
Fleisher, Boston Symphony Orchestra, Ozawa: Sony Classical SK 47188

Concerto in G Major for Piano and Orchestra (1929–31)

The first performance of this piece took place in Paris on January 14, 1932. The composer was on the podium with Marguerite Long, the piano soloist and the dedicatee of the work. Ravel noted that this concerto "is written very much in the same spirit as those of Mozart and Saint-Saëns. The music of a concerto should, in my opinion, be light-hearted and brilliant, and not aim at profundity or at dramatic effects." Ravel's wondrous ability to assimilate different styles of music is here perfectly displayed. In the piano part, the use of alternating hand technique is perfection, allowing for quicksilver speeds. Ravel borrowed jazz and blues elements, yet the concerto is purely Gallic in spirit and still exerts an influence over French musical composition today. The first movement, Allegramente, crackles with emotional brilliance and with light, the piano and the orchestra melding as one. The Adagio assai is of a hypnotic lyricism. The Piano begins with an indescribable nocturne-type theme. Later Ravel uses trills in a luminous manner. The Presto finale flies by at breakneck speed. One hears triangle, gong, wood block, and whip.

Argerich, London Symphony Orchestra, Abbado: Deutsche Grammophon 423665-2
Michelangeli, Philharmonia Orchestra: Gracis: Philips: Great Pianists of the Twentieth Century 456901-2
Bernstein, Columbia Symphony Orchestra, Bernstein: Sony Classical SMK 47571

OTHER PRINCIPAL WORKS

CHAMBER MUSIC

Introduction et allegro for Harp, Flute, Clarinet, and String Quartet (1905)*

Three *Poèmes de Stéphane Mallarmé* for Voice and Ensemble (1913)

Trio in A Minor for Piano, Violin, and Cello (1914)*

Sonata for Violin and Cello (1920–22)

Chansons madécasses for Voice, Flute, Piano, and Cello (1925–26)

Sonata in G Major for Violin and Piano (1923–27)*

OPERAS

L'Heure espagnole (1907–9)*

L'Enfant et les sortilèges (fantaisie lyrique in two parts) (1920–25)*

SOLO PIANO

Menuet antique (1895)

Jeux d'eau (1901)*

La Valse (poème choréographique) (1919–20)*

SONGS WITH PIANO

Histoires naturelles (1906)

VIOLIN AND ORCHESTRA

Tzigane (rapsodie de concert) (1924)*

VOICE AND ORCHESTRA

Shéhérazade (song cycle) (1903)*

BÉLA
BARTÓK

b. Nagyszentmiklós, Hungary, March 25, 1881

d. New York City, September 26, 1945

That man in his misery finds precious comfort in praying to an om-
nipotent being is understandable . . . but how unspeakably feeble!
We should rejoice in life and be interested in everything that goes
on in the world around us. . . . Were I to make the sign of the cross,
I would say, "In the name of nature, of art, and of science."

Bartók's beloved mother, Paula, a piano teacher, gave her son his first lesson at age five. The boy's father, an amateur musician, died when Béla was seven. He had a sister, Elza, four years younger. In 1894 the family settled in Pozsony (now Bratislava), long a capital of culture, where Bartók's talents as a pianist developed rapidly. He was offered a scholarship at the Vienna Conservatory, which he declined in order to attend instead the Budapest Academy of Music. Beginning in 1899, he studied there with the formidable piano teacher István Thomán, a Liszt pupil who had taught the pianist-composer Ernö von Dohnányi.

By 1900 Bartók was composing seriously; his early music was influenced by several composers, especially Richard Strauss, whose symphonic poems dazzled him. From this influence, he would compose *Kossuth* (1903), a symphonic poem inspired by the nineteenth-century Hungarian political leader, followed by his Rhapsody for piano and orchestra (Op. 1, c.1904). In 1905 he won second prize in the Anton Rubinstein piano competition in Paris, losing to Wilhelm Backhaus, who became one of the leading pianists of his generation. The piano remained of the utmost importance to Bartók, who never gave composition lessons but taught the piano throughout his life. Bartók's recordings of his own music are valuable. His eminent pupil György Sándor wrote of Bartók the pianist, "He was technically on the level of Prokofiev, Dohnányi, Rachmaninoff, and Busoni. And as an interpreter, there are no words to describe the fusion of his world with that of the composers he played. . . . His Scarlatti, Bach, Mozart, Beethoven, and Debussy were highly personalized and filled with the spirit and pulsating life of the creative instinct."

In 1904–5 Bartók experienced what he later referred to as a second birth. He had formed a close friendship with his classmate Zoltán Kodály, and together the young composers discovered and explored Magyar peasant music. Their search began when Bartók overheard a servant singing a haunting melody. She said that she learned it from her mother and that such tunes were common in the far province where she was born. Bartók's curiosity was aroused, and he decided to visit several distant villages. Then, with Kodály, he searched in other remote villages in Hungary, Transylvania, and Romania. They persuaded older members of the communities to sing for them while they notated the tunes by ear and used an Edison recording machine. In this manner, they unearthed a treasury of ancient melodies, many of which were based on Greek and religious modes in a variety of fascinating metrics. If an old peasant wondered why Bartók wanted to hear these songs, the composer would explain, "We want to preserve the songs by writing them down. For if we don't write them down, then in years to come no one will know the songs that are being sung here now. You see, even now the young people sing quite different songs; they don't care for the old ones and don't even learn them; and yet they are much prettier than the new ones, aren't they? In fifty years no one will have heard of them if we don't write them down now."

In 1909 Bartók married his sixteen-year-old pupil, Márta Ziegler. He gave her a piano lesson on the day of their wedding; only after the wedding did he tell his mother he was married and that his bride would live with them. Bartók was at times a dictatorial man. Intensely private, he could not easily tolerate intrusions into his personal affairs. In 1910 the couple had a son. The marriage lasted until 1923, when Bartók married another pupil, Ditta Pásztory. Márta, a Catholic, reluctantly gave Bartók a divorce—which Bartók asked for by pointing out that it was better that only one person be unhappy than three. Bartók's second son, Péter, was born in 1924. After Péter's birth, Bartók began composing his 153 small pieces, *Mikrokosmos* (Sz.107), which were graded in difficulty and intended for his son's musical education.

During all these years (from 1908 on), Bartók composed a variety of works, from the String Quartet no. 1 (Op. 7) and the amazingly sonorous Fourteen Bagatelles for piano (Op. 6), both in 1908; to the *Allegro barbaro* for piano and the expressionistic one-act opera *Duke Bluebeard's Castle* (Op. 11), both in 1911; the Fifteen *Hungarian Peasant Songs* for piano (Sz.71) in 1914–18; the ballet *The Wooden Prince* (Op. 13) in 1916; the Second String Quartet in 1914–17; the ballet *The Miraculous Mandarin* (Op. 19, which was damned for its immoral scenario) in 1919; and the *Improvisations on Hungarian Peasant Songs* for piano (Op. 20) in 1920. Still, by 1920 he had received little critical attention as a composer, and he continued to earn a meager living teaching piano at the Academy of Music, as he had since 1907. His first major success occurred in 1923, when Dohnányi conducted his accessible *Dance Suite* for orchestra (Sz.77), which was heard shortly after throughout Europe.

In the next few years, Bartók composed little—his style was undergoing a transformation, and he would later divide his output into works composed before and after *Dance Suite*. By 1926 he was composing in an increasingly original manner, inaugurated by the *Out of Doors Suite* for piano (Sz.81), Nine Little Piano Pieces (Sz.82), and the Piano Sonata (Sz.80). Late in 1927, Bartók toured the United States, giving twenty-six concerts and appearing as soloist in his First Piano Concerto (Sz.83, 1926), which he had recently premiered in Frankfurt with Wilhelm Furtwängler conducting. Audiences were disappointed by a piece that had none of the bravura qualities of the Romantic concertos. The Second Piano Concerto (Sz.95) followed in October 1931 and was conducted in January 1933 in Frankfurt by Hans Rosbaud. Bartók had now reached the acme of his prowess as a pianist. Otto Klemperer, who conducted the Second Concerto in Vienna with Bartók as soloist, wrote, "That was a great experience for me . . . the beauty of his tone, the energy and lightness of his playing were unforgettable. It was almost painfully beautiful. He played with great freedom. He was a strange man—very reserved, very shy, but very sympathetic."

Bartók continued his research into various folk music traditions, visiting Egypt and Turkey in the process. Collecting folksongs was to him "the one thing which is as necessary to me as fresh air is to other people." In the 1930s, his output included the Second Violin Concerto (Sz.112, 1937–38); the Sonata for Two Pianos and Percussion (Sz.110, 1937); the Fifth and Sixth String Quartets (Sz.102, 1934, and Sz.114, 1939); Music for Strings, Percussion, and Celesta (Sz.106, 1936); and the Divertimento for String Orchestra (Sz.113, 1939). During this time, he was in despair over the Nazism contaminating Europe. His letters seethed with frustration over "the imminent danger that Hungary, too, will surrender to this system of robbers and murderers. . . . Hungary, where unfortunately the 'educated' are almost exclusively devoted to the Nazi system: I am really ashamed that I come from this class."

In the fall of 1940, the composer and his second wife fled Hungary for the

United States; Bartók's outspoken hostility to the Nazis had put his life in danger. He was fifty-nine and had almost no money or possessions, telling a friend, "This voyage is, actually, like plunging into the unknown from what is known but unbearable." His life up to that point had been a constant struggle, artistically and financially, and now he was to start over in a new country, hoping to support himself and his family by giving piano lessons and performing in concerts. Bartók felt lost and lonely in a strange society that spoke a different language. In 1943 he received a small research grant from Columbia University and gave a few duo-piano recitals with his wife. But his health was shattered, and he was soon diagnosed with leukemia.

In the summer of 1943, when Bartók was at his lowest point, the conductor Serge Koussevitzky commissioned him to write a piece for the Boston Symphony Orchestra. Though the now eighty-seven-pound composer appeared to have no energy left even to move, miraculously he found his strength and composed his Concerto for Orchestra (Sz.116). Its premiere on December 1, 1944, was a triumph of major proportions: those who knew him had thought, because of his health, that his compositional career was over. But the tiny, emaciated master then managed to compose three more large-scale works—the great Sonata for Solo Violin (Sz.117, 1944), the Viola Concerto (Sz.120, 1945), and the Piano Concerto no. 3 (Sz.119, 1945). He left the last two works a few measures short of completion. After the war, a new government in Hungary begged him to return home, but it was now too late.

Bartók's life had been difficult. Courageously he had faced financial misery, poor health, the misunderstanding of his music, and exile from his beloved homeland and language. He died in a New York hospital of leukemia. A plaque at 309 West Fifty-seventh Street marks the last residence of the great Hungarian composer.

For many years, Bartók's angular, often explosive style, fusing Western European impressionism and expressionism with Eastern European modality and high dissonant content, made him seem to many ears a difficult "Modern" with little regard for an audience's pleasure, and he was frequently greeted with hostility. But at the time of his death, his Concerto for Orchestra was being performed by major orchestras everywhere, and his other music was eagerly studied. A new generation had begun to appreciate him. As the English writer Norman Demuth said as early as 1952, "One can take Bartók in the normal stride of music without any theorizing or philosophical thinking. Idiomatically, he is difficult to explain, but simple to understand. The qualities are distinctly positive, but inexplicable in words. He is one of those who may well be found to form a major part of the basis of the music of the future."

On every form that Bartók touched, he put the stamp of genius. His music presented a new world of sound. The English critic Colin Mason points out, "How important a part of Bartók's art was sheer beauty of physical sound. . . . His instrumental imagination was prodigious. He contrived to draw new sounds from every established instrumental medium." Bartók is rightly described as a Hungarian nationalist composer, but he believed that his work transcended national borders. "My real ideal is the brotherhood of peoples, brotherhood in spite of all wars and conflicts. I try—to the best of my ability—to serve this idea in my music." Although Bartók now sounds "Hungarian," as he intended, he used a compositional vocabulary more extensive than any composer of the twentieth century. He drew from many different musical strains and "Bartók-ized" everything. In the music that appeared after 1920, there is no impression even of his being eclectic, so perfectly does his breathtaking fantasy synthesize his immense erudition, which was always at the service of his technical command and which reveals him to be among the half-dozen supreme craftsmen in history.

The great violinist Yehudi Menuhin stated, "Bartók was one of the greatest men I ever met. . . . He was one of those born scholars—*and yet a creator*. That was his greatness, that he combined the methodical with the creative. There are few people like that." Bartók's motto was "Exactitude above all."

Quartet no. 1 for Strings, Op. 7 (1908)
Quartet no. 2 for Strings, Op. 17 (1914–17)
Quartet no. 3 for Strings, Sz.85 (1927)
Quartet no. 4 for Strings, Sz.91 (1928)
Quartet no. 5 for Strings, Sz.102 (1934)
Quartet no. 6 for Strings, Sz.114 (1939)

The string quartets offer a magnificent overview of Bartók's evolution, ranking high in his overall creative achievement. This is music of penetrating emotional strength, complex and dense—with the broad Romanticism of No. 1; the eerie and impassioned textures of No. 2; the high dissonant quotient in No. 3; the difficult metrics and cellular construction of No. 4, one of Bartók's deepest and most recondite utterances; and the more traditional tonality of the final two quartets. Bartók is a master of asymmetrical phrase groups, irregular meters, and modal melodies—sounding "Modern" but echoing roots that are as ancient as the Magyar psyche. In consistency and artistic qualities, these six works stand high among the greatest chamber music and become ever more rewarding with repeated listening.

Complete String Quartets

Emerson String Quartet: Deutsche Grammophon 423657-2
Chilingirian String Quartet: Chandos CHAN 8588, 8634, and 8660

Music for Strings, Percussion, and Celesta (Sz.106, 1936)

This masterpiece, part symphony and part suite, is one of Bartók's boldest creations. It is unified through a complicated variation technique. Each of its four movements is based on aspects of the opening theme. Bartók here has created a new world of color and sonority with ingeniously complex rhythms. The scoring is for two string sections with side drum without snares, side drum with snares, cymbals, tam-tam, bass drum, kettledrum, xylophone, piano, harp, and celesta. Colin Mason thinks that "the epitome of Bartók's melodic style is to be found in the music for strings, percussion and celesta; where the fugue theme develops during the course of the four movements into the sublime transformation in the finale, where there are marvelous phrase extensions of a beauty rare even for Bartók."

Chicago Symphony Orchestra, Solti: London 430352-2
Montreal Symphony Orchestra, Dutoit: London 421443-2

Concerto no. 1 for Piano and Orchestra, Sz.83 (1926)
Concerto no. 2 for Piano and Orchestra, Sz.95 (1930–31)
Concerto no. 3 for Piano and Orchestra, Sz.119 (1945)

The three piano concertos are now classics of the twentieth-century concerto repertoire. The French composer Poulenc marveled, "One has to go back to Beethoven to find so much fantasy within the rules." No. 1 utilizes a large percussion battery and is an extraordinary stylization of Magyar peasant music. An early reviewer wrote, "The piano becomes a machine, the orchestra a machine workshop, and all in the service of brutal, crudely materialistic noise." In its complex ensemble writing between piano and orchestra, it is very difficult and lacks the lightness of the Second Concerto, which is one of the most technically difficult of all piano concertos, with splashy and dissonant orchestral textures. No. 2 is the most dashing and rhythmically driving of the three. "I wanted to produce a piece which would contrast with the first," the composer wrote: "a work which would be less bristling with difficulties for the orchestra and whose thematic material would be more pleasing." Bartók performed it extensively in London, Vienna, Stockholm, Zurich, and Frankfurt.

Piano Concerto no. 3 lacked a few final bars when Bartók died. He left sketches, which were filled out by his friend the composer Tibor Serly, who found Bartók orchestrating the finale on his last evening at home. The next day he left his New York apartment for the hospital, where he died four days later. The concerto was first performed on February 8, 1946, with Eugene Ormandy conducting the Philadelphia Orchestra and György Sándor as the soloist.

On first hearing, the Third Piano Concerto is by far the easiest to grasp. The style is more relaxed, without the percussive tensions of No. 1 or the driving bravura of No. 2. The work abounds in sparkling dance rhythms, yet remains within a predominantly gentle aura. The slow movement, marked *adagio religioso*, is an unearthly chant interrupted by the nature sounds so integral to Bartók's art.

Three Piano Concertos

Kovacevich: Royal Concertgebouw Orchestra, BBC Symphony Orchestra, and London Symphony Orchestra, Davis: Philips 438812-2

Concerto no. 1

Barenboim, Philharmonia Orchestra, Boulez: EMI Classics CDC 54770-2
Kocsis, Budapest Festival Orchestra, Fischer: Philips 446368-2

Concerto no. 2

Pollini, Chicago Symphony Orchestra, Abbado: Deutsche Grammophon 415371-2
Weissenberg, Philadelphia Orchestra, Ormandy: RCA 09026-61396-2

Concerto no. 3

Donohoe, City of Birmingham Symphony Orchestra, Rattle: EMI Classics CDC 54871
Ránki, Hungarian State Orchestra, Ferencsik: Hungaroton HCD 31036

Concerto no. 2 for Violin and Orchestra, Sz.112 (1937–38)

Menuhin considered this violin concerto to be the greatest of the twentieth century. Bartók started working on it in Budapest in August 1937 and completed it there on December 31, 1938. The Hungarian violinist Zoltán Székely gave its first performance in April 1939 with the great conductor Willem Mengelberg conducting the Amsterdam Concertgebouw Orchestra. It is music of flickering exuberance, composed when Bartók was weeping for the hell that Europe had entered. The three-movement structure is a miracle of virtuoso violin writing and variation form, with orchestration of exuberant color and virtuosity. The first movement, as in many of Bartók's large works, is a sonata-allegro structure of two main subjects and subsidiary ones. The "Magyar" atmosphere is predominant. The movement's lyric theme uses a twelve-tone motif, which some commentators feel is an ironic allusion to Schoenberg—but how well Bartók uses it to establish a clarity of tonality! The slow movement comprises a theme with six variations, which somehow manages to sound improvised. The finale is also a severe Classical form, a dance-like section of savage rhythmic pulse. The recapitulation, in its detailed commentary on the exposition material, is another tour de force. The soloist concludes with a four-note pentatonic motif.

Zukerman, St. Louis Symphony Orchestra, Slatkin: RCA 60749-2-RC
Stern, New York Philharmonic Orchestra, Bernstein: Sony Classical SMK 47511
K.-W. Chung, London Philharmonic Orchestra, Solti: London 425015-2

Concerto for Orchestra (Sz.116, 1943)

Complex and virtuosic, the Concerto for Orchestra has become Bartók's best-known large-scale work. The score, in five movements, is a triumph of Bartók's powers at evoking mystery, excitement, and virtuosity. "The title of this symphony-like orchestral work," Bartók wrote, "is explained by its tendency to treat the single instrument groups in a '*concertant,*' or soloistic manner. . . . As for the structure of the work, the first and fifth movements are written in a more or less regular sonata form. Less traditional forms are found in the second and third movement. . . . The form of the fourth movement—'*intermezzo interrotto*'—could be rendered by the letter symbols C A B A–interruption–B A. The general mood of the work represents—apart from the jesting second movement—a gradual transition from the sternness of the first movement and the lugubrious death-song of the third, to the life-assertion of the last one."

London Symphony Orchestra, Dorati: Mercury 432017-2
Chicago Symphony Orchestra, Boulez: Deutsche Grammophon 437826-2
Chicago Symphony Orchestra, Reiner: RCA 60175-2-RG

OTHER PRINCIPAL WORKS

BALLETS
The Wooden Prince, Op. 13 (1914–16)
The Miraculous Mandarin, Op. 19 (1918–19)*

CHAMBER MUSIC
Sonata no. 1 for Violin and Piano, Sz.75 (1921)*
Sonata no. 2 for Violin and Piano, Sz.76 (1922)*
Sonata for Two Pianos and Percussion, Sz.110 (1937)
Contrasts for Clarinet, Violin, and Piano, Sz.111 (1942)

CHORAL MUSIC
Cantata profana (*The Nine Enchanted Stags*), Sz.94 (1930)*

CONCERTOS
Concerto no. 1 for Violin and Orchestra, Sz.36 (1907–8)
Concerto for Viola and Orchestra, Sz.120 (1945)*

OPERA
Duke Bluebeard's Castle, Op. 11 (1911)*

ORCHESTRAL MUSIC
Two Portraits, Sz.37 (1907–11)
Dance Suite, Sz.77 (1923)* (also for piano)
Divertimento for String Orchestra, Sz.113 (1939)*

PIANO MUSIC
Fourteen Bagatelles, Op. 6 (1908)*
Allegro barbaro, Sz.49 (1911)
Suite, Sz.62, Op. 14 (1916)
Fifteen *Hungarian Peasant Songs*, Sz.71 (1914–18)*
Three Études, Sz.72, Op. 18 (1918)*
Eight *Improvisations on Hungarian Peasant Songs*, Sz.74, Op. 20 (1920)*
Sonata, Sz.80 (1926)*
Out of Doors, Sz.81 (1926)*
Mikrokosmos, Sz.107 (1926, 1932–39)*

VIOLIN WORKS
Forty-four duos for two violins, Sz.98 (1931)
Sonata for Solo Violin, Sz.117 (1944)*

IGOR
STRAVINSKY

b. Oranienbaum (near St. Petersburg),
    June 17, 1882

d. New York, April 6, 1971

I stumble upon something unexpected. This unexpected element strikes me. I make note of it. At the proper time, I put it to profitable use.

Igor's father was Fyodor Stravinsky, a famous bass singer at the St. Petersburg Imperial Opera. Fyodor's career encompassed a quarter century, during which he performed sixty-six roles. He was evidently a better singer than a father, though, for Igor Stravinsky later wrote, "He was affectionate to me only when I was ill." For his mother, Anna, a stern and difficult woman, he had only dutiful feelings. Of his three brothers, he liked only one, Gury, who was killed in World War I. In his autobiography, he recalled that, as a child, "I never came across anyone who had any real affection for me."

In 1890 the eight-year-old Igor was taken to a performance of Tchaikovsky's ballet *Sleeping Beauty* at the Maryinsky Theater where he saw his idol, Tchaikovsky; he was enchanted and never forgot this first impression of an orchestra. The next year he began taking piano lessons and eventually developed into a capable pianist. At fourteen he was able to play Mendelssohn's difficult G minor piano concerto. The youngster enjoyed improvising, but he was often chastised for wasting time instead of practicing his assigned pieces. When he was fifteen, he presented Alexander Glazunov with a piano reduction of one of the composer's string quartets. The youngster was badly discouraged when Glazunov declared him unmusical.

He received no more encouragement from his parents, who expected him to become a lawyer. Law meant nothing to him, but in 1901 he enrolled in the law program at the University of St. Petersburg. Despite his father's death in 1902, Stravinsky continued to study law. Though he attended fewer than fifty class sessions in four years, he somehow received a degree in jurisprudence in 1907.

For some time, Stravinsky had been devoting most of his energy to music and in 1905 studied privately twice a week for free with Rimsky-Korsakov, who equipped him with a fine compositional technique and became a second father to him. A piano sonata of his was performed in 1905, and he began working on his Symphony no. 1 in E-flat Major (Op. 1), which was derivative of Tchaikovsky and Glazunov. In 1906 he married his second cousin Katerina Nossenko (in spite of an imperial edict forbidding consanguineous marriages). Three daughters and a son were born in the next several years. Stravinsky worked with Rimsky-Korsakov until the latter's death in 1908. The composer of *Sheherazade* would be his only teacher. Rimsky-Korsakov said of him, "Igor Stravinsky may be my pupil, but he will never be my or anyone else's follower, because his gift for music is uniquely great and original." In 1908 the impresario Diaghilev heard *Scherzo fantastique* (Op. 3, 1907–8) and *Fireworks* (Op. 4, 1908), two of Stravinsky's short orchestral scores. Diaghilev, who had an astonishing ability to discover new talent, heard in these rather innocuous works the seed of a rare gift. He soon commissioned a ballet, *L'Oiseau de feu* (*The Firebird*), from the twenty-seven-year-old composer. Diaghilev was delighted with the result. On June 25, 1910, with the celebrated ballerina Tamara Karsavina and the Ballets Russes, the most important ballet since Tchaikovsky had its premiere in Paris. As Diaghilev had predicted, Stravinsky became famous overnight. At this point, Stravinsky moved to Paris to be closer to Diaghilev and his ballet company, though he still spent summers in Russia.

Following the lavish *Firebird*, Stravinsky entered Modernism with the ballet *Pétrouchka* (1910–11). Vaslav Nijinsky, the greatest male dancer of the age, performed the title role. Stravinsky was to remark, "As Petrouchka he was the most exciting human being I have ever seen on stage." With Pierre Monteux conducting, *Pétrouchka* was first seen in Paris on June 13, 1911. It was a crucial stepping-stone in Stravinsky's career. Of *Pétrouchka*, Stravinsky wrote, "It gave me the absolute conviction of my ear just as I was about to begin *Le Sacre du printemps*."

On May 29, 1913, his next ballet, *Le Sacre du printemps* (*The Rite of Spring*), was greeted by a riot of booing, whistling, hissing, and fistfighting. Saint-Saëns kept repeating that Stravinsky was crazy and left. The discomfort and hostility were unprecedented even for Paris. The music's primitivism jarred all established sensibility. It was almost as if the first-night audience sensed, in the revolutionary score, a civilization on the brink of war and disaster, the end of a comfortable past and the death of France's Belle Époque. Debussy, a master of irony, thought it "extraordinarily wild. . . . As you might say, it's primitive music with all the modern conveniences!"

In 1914, because of the war, Stravinsky and his family moved from Russia to neutral Switzerland. (He would not see Russia again until 1962.) Thereafter his musical style underwent a complete change, as he eschewed his former large orchestral battery for smaller, leaner-sounding ensembles. Leaving Russia was a profound rupture: "the greatest crisis in my life as a composer," he later said, "was the loss of Russia, and its language not only of music but of words." For the next several years, his music was pervaded by Russian themes. His most famous composition of this period was the ballet *Les Noces* (*The Wedding*, 1914–17). After the war, he returned to France, living there nearly twenty years and becoming a French citizen in 1934.

Another decisive departure for Stravinsky was the composition of yet another ballet, *Pulcinella* (1919–20). Diaghilev had told Stravinsky the time was ripe to look to the past for inspiration and showed him some obscure scores by the eighteenth-century Italian composer Giovanni Pergolesi. "*Pulcinella* was my discovery of the past," Stravinsky later wrote, "the epiphany through which the whole of my late work became possible. It was a backward look of course — but it was a look in the mirror, too." He once stated, "Did not [poet T. S.] Eliot and I set out to refit old ships? And refitting old ships is the real task of the artist. He can say again in his way only what has already been said."

Stravinsky composed prolifically during the 1920s and 1930s, producing a dazzling array of works in what has been called his neoclassical phase. The Piano Sonata (1924), the Concerto for Two Pianos (1931–35), the *Symphony of Psalms* (1930), the Violin Concerto (1931), and the opera-oratorio *Oedipus Rex* (1927), on which he collaborated with Jean Cocteau, were hardly just glances at the past. His music had always been impersonal, a mighty reaction to the emotionalism and the highly charged personal music of the late Romantics. In this neoclassical style, Stravinsky was creating a new and exhilarating idiom — not a pastiche or a refurbishing of the old, but music that was more objective. He wanted to create "significant form" and "aesthetic ecstasy" by perfect arrangement of sounds. Music, he wrote in a famous passage, "is by its very nature powerless to express anything at all, whether a feeling, an attitude of mind, a psychological mood, a phenomenon of nature, etc. *Expression* has never been an inherent property of music."

Written at the very moment when Schoenberg was repudiating the tonal system, Stravinsky's neoclassical works also represented the composer's faith in tonality as the chief framework in Western music. He showed how to create or-

ganic and living forms through the use of bi- and polytonality and the refinement of dozens of compositional devices. As a result, he breathed new life into
and brought renewed confidence to tonality, which invigorated many other
composers.

In 1925 Stravinsky visited the United States, performing as a pianist in his
Concerto for Piano and Wind Orchestra (1923–24). He visited America again
in 1935, receiving a few commissions and many engagements as a conductor of
his own music. In 1939 Stravinsky made the United States his home, and in
1945 he became a citizen.

By the mid-1930s, Stravinsky was unquestionably a household name, and
he was doubtless the most famous living composer. His fame, however, still
rested mostly on his early ballet scores, and he complained that the musical
public "are astonished to hear me speaking in another idiom. They cannot and
will not follow me in the progress of my musical thought. What moves and delights me leaves them indifferent, and what still continues to interest them
holds no further attraction for me."

But if the public did not take Stravinsky's newest work to heart, he had a potent effect on composers everywhere, except for Schoenberg and his disciples.
Nowhere was the Stravinsky force felt more powerfully than in the United
States. Aaron Copland wrote, "With Stravinsky one senses that the place of
each note in the melody and chord has been found for it only after a process of
meticulous elimination, and the place found is usually so unexpected and original that one can imagine the notes themselves being surprised at finding
themselves situated where they are."

The composer's wife had been ill for many years, and a year after her death
in 1939, Stravinsky married his longtime mistress, Vera de Bosset. The couple
settled in Los Angeles, not far from where Arnold Schoenberg lived. For eleven
years, the two leading composers of the time—two leaders of rival camps—
lived in close proximity without ever meeting. They had little in common.

After Stravinsky arrived in California, Walt Disney productions offered him
$5,000 for permission to use Le Sacre du printemps in the animated film Fan-
tasia. Stravinsky, unhappy about this proposal, accepted it only after he was
told that Russian works of art were not protected under U.S. copyright laws and
that Disney would use the music regardless of his response.

During the next years Stravinsky, who was at his happiest when working
with other artists, enjoyed a genial collaboration with W. H. Auden, who wrote
the libretto to his opera The Rake's Progress (1948–51). He also began a longtime collaboration with the great choreographer George Balanchine, which
would give the ballet world such important works as Agon and Orpheus. Another important collaborator was the conductor and writer Robert Craft, who

was just twenty-five years old when he came into Stravinsky's life in 1948. The erudite musician became an indispensable stimulus to the composer. He lived with the Stravinskys for over twenty years and collaborated on a series of books of extraordinary interest. Craft had a foot in each camp, for he not only admired Stravinsky but also was immersed in the music of Schoenberg and Webern. Slowly and astutely, he reversed Stravinsky's antipathy to atonality. Stravinsky became especially attracted to Webern and his compositional procedures.

Craft had helped pave the way, but as always Stravinsky's seemingly endless musical curiosity took nourishment from many sources. Now into twelve-tone music he fit his latest and some of his most profound music: *Canticum sacrum* (1955), *Agon* (1957), *Threni* (1957–58), Movements for Piano and Orchestra (1958–59), Variations for Orchestra (1963–64), and others. They are fitting memorials to his long creative life and are among the finest works from old age of any twentieth-century artist.

Stravinsky was a complicated person, a man of pinpoint intelligence and malicious and witty sarcasm. He was constantly embroiled, often contentiously and litigiously, with the world. He was greedy for money and worked ceaselessly to acquire publicity and disseminate his work. His life and his methods of composing were compulsively ordered. His surroundings were perfectly controlled to accommodate the painful labor he gave to every composition. He loved compositional limitation and restriction. "My freedom," he wrote, "consists in my moving about within the narrow frame that I have assigned myself for each one of my undertakings . . . the more constraints one imposes, the more one frees one's self of the chains that shackle the spirit."

He was also a man of deep religious conviction. In order to compose his religious works, he told Craft, he had to deeply believe in the the Lord, the Devil, and the Church's miracles. Late in life he said, "By temperament and talent I would have been more suited for the life of a small Bach, living in anonymity and composing regularly for an established service and for God."

In his final years, he became an invalid and died in New York, where he had been living. At his request, he was buried in Venice, a city he loved, near Diaghilev, his great benefactor, who had died in Venice in 1929. At the service, Craft conducted the *Requiem Canticles* (1965–66). Afterward, the procession took Stravinsky by funeral gondola to his final resting place on the Island of San Michele, near the grave of Diaghilev.

The American composer David Diamond wrote, "His particular kind of musical discipline is wonderfully creative; it has helped him solve the riddle of lucid thinking within the most extremely compressed musical thought. His art is that mysterious harmony between sensuality, sensitiveness and intelligence. . . . His is music of the longer time; it does not deal with fleeting hours."

Stravinsky's art is among the treasures of the human intellect. Audiences that are still primarily conditioned to Romanticism do not warm to his later, more recondite music easily. If he still remains known by his early works, it is only because music lovers have yet to travel the tremendous artistic distance he traversed in his long creative life. Every work by Stravinsky holds considerable interest. He was an artist of the mind in the sense that his music first and always expresses only musical relationships. But his great spirit is always evident, too, in the perfection of each work, be it lighthearted or sacred. In his religious music particularly, we hear the humility and depth of his being. Stravinsky wrote music "as a form of communion with our fellow man—and with the Supreme Being."

L'Oiseau de feu (The Firebird) (1909–10)

Stravinsky learned well from Rimsky-Korsakov and equaled his master in orchestral opulence. The score is an enchantment, and its individual numbers— from the Infernal Dance to the Berceuse—exude the fragrance of Russianism in the grand tradition, with added dissonant spice. Stravinsky's first important work remains a favorite. The composer later made three suites for orchestra from the ballet; the one usually heard is the 1919 score with a reduced orchestra. The third suite, which contains nine numbers from the ballet, was issued in 1945.

Montreal Symphony Orchestra, Dutoit: London 414409-2
Philharmonia Orchestra, Salonen: Sony Classical 44917
Orchestra of Paris, Ozawa: EMI Classics 2-72664

Pétrouchka (1910–11)

Not far behind The Firebird in popularity is Pétrouchka, a masterpiece of ballet music. The first performance, with Enrico Cecchetti, Tamara Karsavina, and Vaslav Nijinsky, was historic. Nijinsky seemed to have *become* the puppet Pétrouchka. The great actress Sarah Bernhardt was stunned by his instinctive acting abilities.

The rhythms and harmonies are more varied and far more complex than in The Firebird. The bitonal combination of C major and F-sharp major triads has become famous as the "Pétrouchka chord." But the ballet's abundance of chords and chord clusters was highly original in its time. All of the chords, however, are made from triads and can easily be analyzed. In 1921, for his friend Arthur Rubinstein, Stravinsky paraphrased three movements of *Pé-trouchka* for solo piano. It is a remarkable work of exceptional pianistic ingenuity that vividly captures the amplitude of the orchestral score.

Ballet (1910–11)
Leopold Stokowski Symphony Orchestra, Stokowski: Testament 1139
Royal Concertgebouw Orchestra, Chailly: London Classics 443774-2

Three Scenes for Piano (1921)
Pollini: Deutsche Grammophon 47431
Bronfman: Sony Classical SK 46481

Le Sacre du printemps (The Rite of Spring) (1911–13)

Stravinsky later recalled the origin of *Le Sacre du printemps*: "One day I unexpectedly saw before me the picture of a great pagan sacrificial ceremony: the old priests, sitting in a circle, watch the death-dance of a young girl, whom they are offering to the God of spring, in order to placate Him." *Le Sacre du printemps* was at first the most notorious and within a few years the most celebrated of his works; it put Modernism on the map. *Sacre* became the watchword for innovation, and its uninhibited rhythms charged many composers with new life. It is a magnificent exertion; never again would Stravinsky repeat this specific type of primitiveness. It proclaimed him as a revolutionary, but as he wrote, "The tone of a work like *The Rite* may have appeared arrogant, the language that it spoke may have seemed harsh in its newness, but that in no way implies that it is revolutionary in the most subversive sense of the word." Ears change, and today, the *Rite* sounds like part of the tradition of Russian Romanticism.

Philadelphia Orchestra, Muti: EMI Classics CDM 64516
Cleveland Orchestra, Boulez: Deutsche Grammophon 435769-2
Boston Symphony Orchestra, Monteux: RCA 6529-2-RG

Les Noces (The Wedding) (1914–17)

In the spring of 1915, Stravinsky played for Diaghilev the first two tableaux of this score, bringing tears to his eyes. *The Wedding* shows a new Stravinsky, and it took him longer than usual to realize this score to his satisfaction. This ballet, like *Sacre*, is founded on a text offering a young girl in ritual sacrifice. It was composed at the same time that Schoenberg was codifying his twelve-tone technique. Stravinsky was also striving to break the boundaries of established consonance and dissonance but without departing from tonality. *The Wedding*, even saturated in "Russian-ness," is an entirely new adventure in rhythm and sonority. The first performance took place on June 13, 1923, with Ernest Ansermet conducting and choreography by Bronislava Nijinska, Vaslav's sister.

Zimerman, Katsaris, English Bach Festival Orchestra and Chorus, Bernstein: Deutsche Gram-
    mophon 423251-2
The Orchestra of St. Luke and Gregg Smith Singers, Craft: MusicMasters 01612-67086-2

Capriccio for Piano and Orchestra (1928–29)

The Capriccio is an extraordinary piece of compositional virtuosity and a bravura piece of neoclassicism. It is an objective, seemingly lightweight work that draws the listener into the past—a glittering assimilation of J. C. Bach, Hummel, Chopin, and especially Weber (whose *Konzertstück* Stravinsky acknowledged as his model). It has three movements: 1. Presto; doppio movimento, 2. Andante rapsodico, and 3. Allegro capriccioso ma sempre giusto. The composer himself was at the piano at the first performance on December 6, 1929, in Paris's Salle Pleyel; the baton was held by Ernest Ansermet.

Stravinsky, Walther Straram Orchestra, Ansermet: EMI Classics ZDCB 54607
Crossley, London Sinfonietta, Salonen: Sony Classical SK 45797

Symphony of Psalms (1930)

This choral piece is one of Stravinsky's greatest works. With the same trust and awe as Bach or Haydn, Stravinsky dedicated *Symphony of Psalms* "to the Glory of God." Always special is Stravinsky's unique, sonorous imagery, perfectly supporting his musical message. In *Symphony of Psalms*, he composed without violins, violas, and clarinet, which brought to the fore the trumpets, oboes, a contrabassoon, two pianos, a harp, tubas, and trombones. The work bears no resemblance to a traditional symphony; the term is used only to denote its importance. The three movements are performed without pause, and the text, sung in Latin, was taken from the Psalter of the Vulgate.

Atlanta Symphony Orchestra and Chorus, Shaw: Telarc CD 80254
Swedish Radio Symphony Orchestra and Chorus, Ehrling: BIS CD 400
London Symphony Orchestra and Chorus, Tilson Thomas: Sony Classical 53275

OTHER PRINCIPAL WORKS

BALLETS
Pulcinella (1919–20)*
Le Baiser de la fée (The Fairy's Kiss) (1928)*
Apollon musagète (1927–28)*
Jeu de cartes (The Card Party) (1937)
Orpheus (1947)*
Agon (1953–57)*

CHAMBER MUSIC
L'Histoire du soldat (The Soldier's Tale) Suite for Instrumental Ensemble (1918)*
Ragtime for Eleven Instruments (1918)
Octet for Wind Instruments (1922–23)*
Septet (1952–53)*

CHORAL MUSIC
Le Roi des étoiles (King of the Stars) Cantata (1911–12)
Babel Cantata (1944)
Mass (1944–48)*
Cantata (1951–52)
Canticum sacrum (1955)
Requiem Canticles (1965–66)*

CONCERTOS
Concerto for Piano and Wind Orchestra (1923–24)*
Concerto in D Major for Violin and Orchestra (1931)*
Movements for Piano and Orchestra (1958–59)*

DANCE BAND MUSIC
Ebony Concerto (1945)*

OPERAS AND STAGE WORKS
Le Rossignol (The Nightingale) (opera) (1914)
Renard (Reynard the Fox) (1915–16)

L'Histoire du soldat (*The Soldier's Tale*) (1918)*
Mavra (comic opera) (1921–22)
Oedipus Rex (opera-oratorio) (1926–27)*
Perséphone (1933–34)*
The Rake's Progress (1948–51)*
The Flood (biblical allegory) (1962)

ORCHESTRAL WORKS
Symphony in E-flat Major, Op. 1 (1905–7)
Symphonies of Wind Instruments (1920)*
Four Études (1914–18; 1928)
Concerto in E-flat Major for Chamber Orchestra (*Dumbarton Oaks*) (1937–38)*
Symphony in C (1939–40)*
Danses concertantes for Chamber Orchestra (1941–42)
Circus Polka (1942)
Scherzo à la russe (1943–44)
Scènes de ballet (1944)
Symphony in Three Movements (1942–45)*
Concerto in D Major for String Orchestra (1946)*
Monumentum pro Gesualdo di Venosa (*ad CD Annum*) (arrangement of madrigals)
    (1960)*

PIANO MUSIC
Four Études, Op. 7 (1908)*
Piano-Rag Music (1919)*
Sonata (1924)*
Serenade in A Major (1925)*
Tango (1940)*

SONGS
Three *Japanese Lyrics* (1912–13)
Pribaoutki (1914)*
Four *Russian Songs* (1918–19)

TWO-PIANO WORKS
Concerto (1931–35)*
Sonata (1943–44)*

ALBAN BERG

b. Vienna, February 9, 1885

d. Vienna, December 24, 1935

I declare firmly and decisively the great importance which sensuality has for everything spiritual. Only through an understanding of sensuality, only through a profound insight into the "depths of mankind" (or should it rather be "heights of mankind"?) does one arrive at the true idea of the human psyche.

Berg was the third of four children. His family was fairly secure financially, with a father in the export business and a mother who showed some cultivation in the arts. The youngster displayed ability in music and drawing and developed a discerning taste in literature and poetry. Alban took the obligatory piano lessons, but he was no prodigy—indeed, he never became proficient on the piano or any instrument. With his father's death in 1900, the family finances collapsed. It was a difficult time, and young Berg, a nervous, excitable boy, did poorly in high school, failing his exams. Sometime afterward, feeling desperate pangs of unrequited love, he attempted suicide.

From his fifteenth year, music became his dominant passion. Even without instruction, he composed dozens of songs, which were sung at home by his sister. Some of them had been inspired by the *Lieder* of Hugo Wolf, and when Wolf died in 1903, Berg wept bitterly. In the winter of 1904, he unhappily became a government civil servant. A concerned older brother, who realized Berg's frustration at not having adequate training, saw an advertisement for musical theory lessons with one Arnold Schoenberg. Secretly, he gathered a few of Alban's songs and visited Schoenberg, who recognized the young man's talent.

From 1904 until 1910, Berg studied with Schoenberg, his senior by eleven years and his only teacher. Berg had little money, but Schoenberg refused any compensation for his strenuous instruction. Berg was forever grateful to his master, and the two men formed a precious friendship. No fewer than three works of Berg's relatively small output are dedicated to Schoenberg: the Three Orchestral Pieces (Op. 6, 1914–15), the Chamber Concerto (1923–25), and the opera *Lulu* (1929–35).

Like Schoenberg and Webern (Schoenberg's other great pupil), Berg felt that art held life's highest aspirations. No matter what the personal privations, an artist must give all to his "sacred" calling. "Whether I am composing, painting, teaching . . . it is all the same," Schoenberg had written. "I have to do all these things with the same amount of fervor! The same is true of Berg and of Webern . . . and it is probably this that binds us together."

In 1905 Berg, who had given up his civil service position, came into a small inheritance and was lent an attic in a Vienna suburb. Here he worked beyond fatigue and punishing asthma attacks. He drew his shades and shutters so he would not be disturbed even by the changes from day to night. Surrounding himself with the busts of Beethoven, Brahms, and Wagner, the budding composer worked with crushing effort. For him, each note written down was of precious metal.

Vienna in Berg's formative years simmered with new ideas, values, and scientific developments. Numerous artists and intellectuals gathered in the city, including the philosopher Ludwig Wittgenstein and the painters Gustav Klimt and Oskar Kokoschka. The year 1900 saw the publication of Freud's *The Interpretation of Dreams*, a book of shattering consequence. "The people lived in security," Kokoschka wrote about prewar Vienna, "yet they were all afraid. . . . I painted them in their anxiety and pain." Vienna seethed with conflict and restlessness. Musically speaking, as the English critic Martin Cooper remarked, "In Vienna a fury of materialism was offset by a hothouse spirituality cultivated by a minority; . . . only in Russia the spirituality was mystical, often theosophical, whereas in Vienna the emotional world of Wagner lived on, its temperature raised still further, technical complexities increased, and emotions deliberately harrowed to breaking-point." It was in this atmosphere that, in 1908, Berg presented to the world his brooding Piano Sonata (Op. 1). The atonal score, ostensibly wrapped within the key of B minor, has a distinct aroma of decay and *Weltschmerz*, so characteristic of the Viennese fin-de-siècle.

The magnetic conducting of Gustav Mahler dominated musical life in Vienna. Both Berg and Schoenberg venerated Mahler, and upon Mahler's death in 1911, they knew that a great chapter in music history was closed. Only in the autumn of 1910 had Berg come into Mahler's orbit. When Mahler asked his younger colleague if he also conducted, Berg replied, "No!" Mahler, looking at him intensely, said, "Only composing! Yes, that is the only right way." It was a heady musical atmosphere that Berg encountered. Immersed in Schoenberg's atonal works and Strauss's *Elektra*, drinking in Debussy and Dukas's opera *Ariane et Barbe-bleue*, he was aware of his own increasing musical power. Under Schoenberg's strict supervision, he completed the Op. 3 string quartet (1910). His *Altenberg-Lieder* (Op. 4, 1912) caused a scandal at a concert conducted by Schoenberg—which was disheartening but not surprising. In 1911 Berg married Helene Nahowski, who was a great support to him for the rest of his life. The couple had no children.

By the beginning of World War I, Berg had become infatuated with Georg Büchner's pathological 1836 play-fragment *Woyzeck*. In 1915, while fashioning a libretto for his future opera, he was inducted for service into the Austrian army, first in an infantry regiment and then to officer's training school. The regimen, combined with severe bouts of asthma, broke his health. Berg, who had initially supported the war, later described himself as a "fierce antimilitarist," writing to Erwin Schulhoft that "daily for two and a half years from eight o'clock in the morning until six or seven o'clock in the evening I was occupied with the most difficult paperwork under a frightful superior officer (an idiotic drunkard). These long years of suffering endured in the rank of corporal, not composing a note—oh it was dreadful."

Once the war ended, Berg barely survived by teaching several private students and administering a society for modern music that Schoenberg had just founded. Finally he completed the libretto to *Wozzeck*. The music was composed by 1922, and on December 14, 1925, Erich Kleiber conducted the world premiere in Berlin. To Berg's utter amazement, *Wozzeck* was received with tremendous enthusiasm and an understanding remarkable for such a radical work of art. The opera was well suited to the post–World War I malaise of the German world, with its inflation and general hopelessness. *Wozzeck* was then performed throughout Europe. Berg, who detested traveling, even found himself supervising a production in Leningrad, shortly before the Soviets locked the doors of artistic experiment.

Schoenberg's Piano Suite of 1923–25 had codified his radical twelve-tone technique, literally a new form of composing utilizing in various forms each of the twelve notes of the chromatic scale. Berg, who had recently completed his Chamber Concerto, felt he had fully exploited his own atonal expressionism and immediately embraced Schoenberg's innovation in his *Lyric Suite* for string quartet (1925–26). Berg would go on to compose music in his mentor's twelve-tone technique, magnificently shaping the method to his own intensely poetic nature.

In 1928 he began writing a libretto from two of Frank Wedekind's texts, for his second opera *Lulu*. While working on the new opera he completed two other works: "Der Wein" (1929), a fifteen-minute concert aria for soprano and orchestra, based on three poems of Baudelaire's *The Flowers of Evil*; and his final work, the famous Violin Concerto (1935).

Berg was at a breaking point. The once-robust composer's asthma attacks had seriously weakened him. In January 1935, Berg was spurred to creative frenzy by the tragic death of Manon Gropius, the young daughter of his friend Alma Mahler Gropius. Normally a slow worker, he finished the Violin Concerto—written to her memory—in six all-consuming weeks in the summer of 1935. He was exhausted and vulnerable. Above all the strain of his decade-long clandestine affair with Hanna Fuchs-Robettin was taking its toll. Berg met Hanna and her husband in Prague in 1925 when he stayed with them in their home. Although both parties had maintained their separate homes, Berg's wife, Helene, was painfully aware of their relationship. Unfortunately Helene burned Hanna's letters to the composer, although some of Berg's to Hanna were preserved. Berg was fervently inspired by Hanna, and she became inextricably bound to his work, especially the *Lyric Suite* and the opera *Lulu*.

In September 1935, Berg was stung by an insect on his lower back. The pain was excruciating, and the bite became abcessed and developed into a septic ulcer. In the next weeks, his health radically deteriorated. Blood poisoning set in, and an operation took place on December 17. On Christmas Eve the fifty-year-old Berg died of heart failure. Less than a month before, he had written to Schoenberg, who was now living in California, "I am not well. Not well financially . . . not well as regards my health . . . finally I am not well emotionally either." Schoenberg was shocked when he heard of his pupil's death and wrote to Helene, "I still cannot believe that my dear Alban is gone. I still talk to him in my thoughts."

Lulu was unfinished at his death, but the first two acts were performed in Zurich in June 1937. Helene Berg, self-appointed guardian of his memory and immortality, had banned performance of the third act, which she felt revealed too much about Berg's relations with Hanna. It was not until February 24, 1979, that all three acts were finally presented at the Paris Opera. *Lulu* is a psychologically disturbing drama, composed using the twelve-tone technique.

In his comprehensive two-volume study of Berg's two operas, *Wozzeck* and *Lulu*, the American composer George Perle writes,

> Both operas add new dimensions to the dramatic range of the operatic theater and extend its relevance to life and to the world of ideas as radically and significantly as any work—even such a one as *Tristan und Isolde*—of the past. They hold a most important place in the history of music as the first atonal and the first twelve-tone

works to become a part of the repertory and to prove that the revolution in the language of music . . . was not merely a cultist self-centered tendency that could have no significance for musical culture in general.

Berg was a man of the rarest sensibility, kindness, compassion, and charm. Erudite in many areas, he showed an ever-expanding nature, both personally and artistically. His unexpected death was a tragedy for the prestige of the emerging twelve-tone technique and, of course, for the world of art in general. He was a master, and each new work was deeper and more humane. His last composition, the elegiac Violin Concerto, is of heartfelt beauty and astounding compositional mastery.

Wozzeck (1922)

Wozzeck was the most-written-about opera in the last three quarters of the twentieth century. Berg's extraordinary libretto, divided into three acts, is based upon Georg Büchner's 1836 drama *Woyzeck*. Büchner, born in Germany in 1813, was a precocious talent of acute psychological sensitivity. Nihilistic and darkly depressed as well as a rebel against established literary custom, he wrote with a passionate hatred: ironic, pessimistic, and tragic feeling mixed with the macabre. He was dead at twenty-three.

The literary critic George Steiner wrote, "*Woyzeck* is the first real tragedy of low life. It repudiates an assumption implicit in Greek, Elizabethan, and neoclassic drama: the assumption that tragic suffering is the somber privilege of those who are in high places." In the story, Woyzeck, a poor dim-witted soldier, undergoes bizarre dietary experiments conducted by the army doctor. Finding out that Marie, his mistress and the mother of his son, is having an affair with the Drum Major, he slits her throat. Later he returns to the pond to look for the knife he used and drowns. After Marie's body is discovered, the opera ends with their child not understanding that his mother is dead. It is a story of murder and humiliation, of which Martin Cooper observes: "No breath of fresh air even enters this shuttered and permanently darkened world." While in the military during World War I, Berg appeared to relate to the downtrodden Woyzeck. He wrote to his wife in 1918, "There is a bit of me in his character; I have been spending these war years just as dependent on people I hate, have been in chains, sick, captive, resigned, in fact humiliated."

From Büchner's story, Berg created one of the major intellectual achievements in music history. He composed this massively complicated atonal work within classical forms, in a structural organization that is endlessly fascinating.

For further understanding of the work, I recommend George Perle's masterly study in the first volume of *The Operas of Alban Berg*, where Perle analyzes the text's formal design and musical language. Berg was addicted to the symbolism of numbers and divided the three acts into five scenes each. The first act, "Wozzeck in his relation to the world around him," is composed in a Suite, Rhapsody, Military march, Lullaby, Passacaglia, and Quasi rondo. The second act, the "Dramatic development," is arranged as a "symphony in five movements": a Sonata-allegro first movement with exposition, development, and recapitulation; Fantasy and Fugue; Largo; Scherzo; and Rondo con introduzione. The third act, "Catastrophe and epilogue," is a series of Inventions: on a theme, on one note, on a rhythm, on a hexachord, on atonality, and on a regular quaver figure. The high dissonance level present at the beginning completely calms down, and one listens compassionately to music that goes deep into the unconscious.

Lear, Wunderlich, Stoltze, Fischer-Dieskau, Deutsche Opera Orchestra and Chorus, Böhm: Deutsche Grammophon 435705-2

Silja, Winkler, Waechter, Laubenthal, Vienna Philharmonic Orchestra and Chorus, C. von Dohnányi: London 417348-2

Lyric Suite for String Quartet (1925–26)

Berg worked on the *Lyric Suite* from September 1925 to September 1926, putting his heart and essence into this six-movement twelve-tone work. The piece is dark, with disturbed undercurrents, and one can almost imagine Berg meditating over Beethoven's quartets late into the night.

The *Lyric Suite* is a large-scale love poem to Hanna Fuchs-Robettin. Into it Berg poured all the fevered frustration and passion of this affair, which began in 1925 and continued until his death. Berg told her that "I have secretly inserted our initials H.F. and A.B. into the music." He appended to the score, "May it be a small monument to a great love." The philosopher Theodor Adorno felt that the *Lyric Suite* was a "latent opera."

The score is composed tightly, yet it sounds rhapsodic. The movement titles give some indication of the content: 1. Allegretto giovale, 2. Andante amoroso, 3. Allegro misterioso (trio)—estatico, 4. Adagio appassionato, 5. Presto delirando (trio)—tenebroso, 6. Largo desolato. In the fourth movement, Berg quotes from Zemlinsky's *Lyric Symphony*, and in the sixth from Wagner's *Tristan*. Berg admired Freud and was convinced that music reveals the depths of the unconscious as no other art.

Berg later took the second, third, and fourth movements and arranged them for orchestra, in which guise they have become possibly his best-known work.

FOR STRING QUARTET
LaSalle String Quartet: Deutsche Grammophon 419994-2
Artis String Quartet: Orfeo 216901

FOR ORCHESTRA
New York Philharmonic Orchestra, Boulez: Sony Classical SMK 45838 (includes Lulu Suite
with Jessye Norman)

Concerto for Violin and Orchestra (1935)

The twentieth century produced several important violin concertos, such as those by Bartók, Bloch, Hindemith, Stravinsky, Barber, and Khachaturian, but none is greater or of a finer emotional life than Berg's. The composer died four months before its premiere. On the manuscript he wrote, "to the memory of an Angel." The death of the beautiful eighteen-year-old Manon Gropius, the daughter of his friend Alma Mahler Gropius and the famed architect Walter Gropius, was the impetus for writing the concerto. Berg made use of Schoenberg's twelve-tone technique, but he also used with enormous emotional effect the Lutheran chorale "Es ist genug" (It Is Enough), harmonized almost as Bach did in his Cantata no. 60, "O Ewigkeit, du Donnerwort." The concerto was commissioned by the American violinist Louis Krasner, who gave its debut performance at the Barcelona Festival of Contemporary Music on April 19, 1936, with Hermann Scherchen conducting. Of the Violin Concerto the music historian Paul Collaer wrote, "A last arpeggio wings upward and is dissolved on the heights; and then the final adieu of the four open notes of the violin. Alban Berg leaves us, he 'sings' his own requiem. Suddenly everything seems to be resolved, pain, tension, desire, despair, everything which was his personality has gone."

Szeryng, Bavarian Radio Symphony Orchestra, Kubelik: Deutsche Grammophon 431740-2
Perlman, Boston Symphony Orchestra, Ozawa: Deutsche Grammophon 447445-2

OTHER PRINCIPAL WORKS

CHAMBER MUSIC
Quartet for Strings, Op. 3 (1910)*
Chamber Concerto for Piano, Violin, and Thirteen Wind Instruments (1923–25)*

CLARINET AND PIANO WORK
Four Pieces, Op. 5 (1913)

OPERA
Lulu (1929–35)*

ORCHESTRAL WORKS
Three Orchestral Pieces, Op. 6 (1914–15)*

PIANO WORK
Sonata, Op. 1 (1908)*

VOICE AND ORCHESTRA WORKS
Five *Altenberg-Lieder*, Op. 4 (1912)*
"Der Wein" for Soprano and Orchestra (1929)
Lulu Suite for Soprano and Orchestra (1934)

SERGEI PROKOFIEV

b. Sontzovka, Ukraine, April 27, 1891

d. Moscow, March 5, 1953

I work everywhere, always, and I have no need for meditation or privacy.

Prokofiev was an adored only child. His father was an agricultural engineer, his mother a good pianist, and both seriously encouraged young Sergei in his music making. By eleven he was studying harmony and orchestration with the composer Reinhold Glière (whose ballet, *The Red Poppy*, and Third Symphony are still occasionally performed). Glière prepared his young charge for the St. Petersburg Conservatory, which he entered in 1905. Then he studied composition with the composer Anatoly Liadov. The rebellious Sergei could be an unruly pupil, and on one occasion, the exasperated Liadov shouted, "I guess I should be studying with you, not you with me—go to Richard Strauss or Debussy. But for heaven's sake, don't study with me."

At the Conservatory, Prokofiev also received valuable training from Rimsky-Korsakov in orchestration, Alexander Glazunov, and Nikolai Tcherepnin in conducting, and he studied piano with Anna Essipova, one of the finest pianists of the day. Prokofiev complained that she "wanted to fit all of her students into the same mold." Essipova declared, "He is very talented, but rather crude." Nonetheless, Prokofiev developed into an outstanding pianist.

In 1914 he caused a commotion by choosing to play his own First Piano Concerto (Op. 10, 1911–12) instead of a traditional choice, to meet the Conservatory's concerto requirement. Glazunov put his hands over his ears during the performance, and most of the graybeards at the Conservatory were outraged, agreeing that the music was ugly and confused. But if the First Concerto gave displeasure, the Second (Op. 16, 1912–13), written soon afterward, aroused wrath. Even more shocking was his *Scythian Suite* (Op. 20, 1915), which many people despised—though the English composer Bernard Stevens called it "a tour de force in its deliberate concentration on rhythm and sonority and one of the most remarkable examples of 'primitivism' ever composed, all the more remarkable in that it deliberately excluded his greatest quality—that of melodic invention." Some important people began to take notice of the daring young composer, not least the impresario Diaghilev, who commissioned *Chout* (Op. 21, 1915) for his Ballets Russes in Paris.

After the October 1917 Revolution Prokofiev, uneasy about the political climate, decided to leave Russia. In May 1918 he departed for the United States, traveling by way of Vladivostok and Tokyo to San Francisco. He made his American debut in November in New York City, performing his Second Piano Concerto. Audiences were especially delighted, however, with his *Classical Symphony* (Op. 25, 1916–17), and the Chicago Lyric Opera offered him a commission. The result was his best-known opera, *The Love for Three Oranges* (Op. 33, 1919), with its celebrated march. In 1923 he married Lina Llubera, a singer, and the following year their son Sviatoslav was born, followed by Oleg in 1928.

Prokofiev's years in the West were productive, and he found himself one of the most publicized and frequently performed of contemporary composers. But like many other Russians who left their native land, he felt lonely and rootless and yearned to return home. By the early 1930s, much of his music no longer sounded terribly shocking—the jarring motoric rhythms of his earlier years were now merely biting and exciting. The one-armed pianist Paul Wittgenstein commissioned his Fourth Piano Concerto (Op. 53, 1931) but then told Prokofiev, "Thank you very much, but I do not understand a single note of it and I shall not play it." Surely, Prokofiev thought, Russia would herald him as her prodigal son. In 1933 he returned to the Soviet Union. Prokofiev had never been much interested in or involved with politics. But under the collectivist tyranny of Stalin's dictatorship, he found life to be more complicated and tricky than he had anticipated. Still he was glad to be home, and for more than a decade his creativity soared. He composed the Piano Sonatas nos. 6, 7, and 8, known as the *War Sonatas* (Opp. 82–84, 1939–44); the *Alexander Nevsky* Cantata (Op. 78, 1939); the ballet scores to *Romeo and Juliet* (Op. 64, 1934–36) and *Cinderella* (Op. 87, 1940–44); the Fifth Symphony (Op. 100, 1944); and much more. During the Second World War, as Russia became the United States' ally and conductors played less of the usual German classics, Prokofiev's fame in the West increased. After conducting *Alexander Nevsky*, Leopold

Stokowski wrote Prokofiev that he was "deeply impressed by this Russian epic and feel it is one of your greatest works."

In 1941, after years of domestic acrimony and bitterness, Prokofiev left his wife, Lina, his two children, and their spacious Moscow apartment to live with Mira Mendelson, a young Jewish woman of twenty-five. Wartime conditions were desperate, and the couple had to live with Mira's parents. Late in August 1941, however, the Soviet government moved them (for "artistic protection") to an artists' colony in Nalchik in the republic of Kabardino-Balkaria. There, in the Caucasus Mountains, Prokofiev worked on his monumental opera *War and Peace* (Op. 91, 1941–43). Soon the colony was alerted that the Nazis were closing in, and they were all moved to Tbilisi, the capital of Georgia. The couple moved once more in May 1942, when Prokofiev traveled deep into central Asia to work with the great filmmaker Sergei Eisenstein, with whom he had previously worked on *Alexander Nevsky*. This time they collaborated on the film *Ivan the Terrible* (Op. 116, 1942–45), a celebration of Stalin's favorite czar.

After the war, Prokofiev garnered many official honors, including five Stalin Prizes. The Soviets seemed more than pleased to have their internationally celebrated composer as a prime cultural hero. But this feeling did not last. After the sorrows of the war, Stalin grew even more repressive and monstrous.

The year 1948 opened with Prokofiev's marriage to Mira on January 13. Although Lina had refused to divorce the composer, his second marriage was able to take place (after seven years) through a bureaucratic formality in a new law, which dissolved the previous union. Only days after the wedding, Prokofiev was horrified to learn that his first wife, Lina, had been framed as a spy and was sent to Siberia, where she was incarcerated in a labor camp until 1956. The composer's personal prestige could not help her in the slightest. In fact, within weeks of her conviction, he swiftly tumbled from his commanding position in Russian music. The poet Anna Akhmatova had warned the artist, "Worship the night, lest you wake up to be famous."

The purge of Prokofiev himself came in February 1948. Along with such eminent colleagues as Dmitri Kabalevsky, Nikolai Miaskovsky, Vissarion Shebalin, Aram Khachaturian, and Dmitri Shostakovich, Prokofiev was brutally and publicly condemned by the Central Committee of the Communist Party for "formalist perversions," or decadent creative procedures. In Russia, the term *formalist* had commonly been understood as anti-Soviet. "Formalist" painters, poets, writers, and filmmakers in the Soviet Union had been condemned long before, but musicians practiced an art more elusive, to which it was more difficult to attribute political content. Until 1948 they were not watched quite as carefully, and the powerful composers' union had helped protect them. But after the war, musicians were threatened as much as their colleagues in other arts. Dismayed and panicked, Prokofiev penned a sickening public apology, begging forgiveness for his artistic sins. After several pages of ludicrous prose, he wrote, "In conclusion, I would like to express my gratitude to our party for the dear decisions of the resolution, which help me to find a musical language comprehensible to our people and of our great country." But as Vladimir Nabokov once observed, "Even genius does not save one in Russia; in exile, one is saved by genius alone." The composer's health had always been precarious; he suffered from dizziness and headaches and several other ailments that necessitated frequent hospitalizations. But after 1948 he began to decline emotionally as well, and in his last works, such as the Seventh Symphony (Op. 131, 1951–52), one hears his struggle to conform to the system and keep his always fierce artistic integrity intact.

In his last years, Prokofiev believed that he would be best remembered by his seven operas. He hurried to revise *War and Peace*, which had been premiered in 1946 but with which he was not satisfied. With sixty characters and five acts, performed over two evenings, *War and Peace* would, he felt, be his crowning glory.

On New Year's Eve 1953, his second wife, Mira, wrote to a friend, "At midnight we raised our glasses, and then read aloud some letters written by Chekhov, who had recently become very important—even necessary—to Sergei Sergeevich."

On March 5, Prokofiev, only sixty-one, died of a brain hemorrhage. He died just one hour before the seventy-three-year-old Stalin, and of the same affliction. Harlow Robinson, Prokofiev's biographer, relates that on the day of the funeral, Moscow was in chaos because of Stalin's death: "Only forty or fifty people could maneuver through the barricades to attend" Prokofiev's funeral. "David Oistrakh played the first and third movements of Prokofiev's unusually dark F minor Sonata. . . . Flowers were nearly impossible to find, so the pianist Sviatoslav Richter placed a pine branch on the coffin." The press was totally absorbed in Stalin's death, and it would be weeks before the world realized that one of the century's great creators had died the same day.

Prokofiev, with all of his dissonant content and harmonic freedom, was basically a tonal composer, a traditionalist, a master of Classical form, and one who very much sounds his Russian heritage. In his early music, he brought fresh air to the stale and derivative music that was being composed by the followers of Tchaikovsky and the Russian Five.

His art was like a tonic, often tongue in cheek, ever youthful and brash, but tempered with a compelling lyricism. Prokofiev is one of the twentieth century's most-often-performed composers, taking a permanent place in the world's concert repertoire. The *Classical* Symphony is as entertaining as ever. The two beautiful violin concertos are masterful additions for the instrument. *Romeo and Juliet's* emotion overflows. Prokofiev could be powerful and epic, as in the Fifth Symphony, or recondite, as in the Third and Sixth Symphonies. The *Lieutenant Kijé* suite (Op. 60, 1934) is an unfailing piece of buffoonery, the operas *War and Peace* (Op. 91, 1941–43) and *The Fiery Angel* (Op. 37, 1919–23) are powerfully dramatic, and the Third Piano Concerto (Op. 26, 1917–21) is magical. Prokofiev's piano music in general forms one of the important contributions to twentieth-century piano literature. In every genre, he composed wonderful music, and it takes only a moment to recognize his special combination of heart, panache, mockery, biting rhythm, bittersweet melody, and unfailing formal elegance.

Symphony no. 1 in D Major, Op. 25 (*Classical*) (1916–17)

Prokofiev finished his Symphony no. 1 during the heady days before the October Revolution. The composer was intent on writing his first symphony along neoclassical lines, as if he were a composer of Haydn's or Mozart's time. Yet in its wit, angularity, and melodic magic, it is pure Prokofiev to the core. To his early listeners, it sounded like a refreshing break from what was called his "futurist" style. As a Classical symphony, it uses the four-movement plan. The first movement, Allegro, is in textbook sonata-allegro form. The second movement, Larghetto, pretends to be a stately but graceful minuet. The third movement is a perky Gavotte, a dance to which Prokofiev is partial in other scores. The finale is all high spirits. The symphony is far more than a mere stylized imitation of an earlier time: it is an amazing work of irony as well. It was his first attempt at the most difficult of musical structures, the symphony, which would occupy him for the rest of his life.

Philadelphia Orchestra, Muti: Philips 432992-2
Philadelphia Orchestra, Ormandy: Odyssey MBK 39783

Concerto no. 1 in D Major for Violin and Orchestra, Op. 19 (1916–17)
Concerto no. 2 in G Minor for Violin and Orchestra, Op. 63 (1935)

Both of these violin concertos are features of the standard repertoire. The ingratiating First Concerto once again shows the young composer's superb mastery of form and orchestration and an extraordinary understanding of virtuosic violin writing. The concerto's first movement is pervaded by tenderness, but with many imaginative twists of the opening lyric theme. The second movement is one of Prokofiev's relentless but playful Scherzo-type movements, but in a five-section rondo form. The finale resumes a lyrical, serene atmosphere, fused with sunlight and happiness. The concerto, because of the Russian Revolution, was not heard until Serge Koussevitzky conducted it in Paris on October 18, 1923, with violinist Marcel Darrieux.

The Second Violin Concerto was written after Prokofiev's return to the Soviet Union. The first performance took place in Madrid on December 1, 1935. A more serious work than No. 1, it glows with the burnished passion of the *Romeo and Juliet* ballet and scores great melodic curves. The first movement's two themes are kindled by a warm breadth. The slow movement is a jewel, with its pizzicato violin accompaniment against a soulful melody with variations. Only in the finale does Prokofiev's hot blood begin to dance and leap in a movement of wild turbulence.

Violin Concerto no. 1

Szigeti, London Philharmonic Orchestra, Beecham: EMI Classics CDH 64562
Spivakov, Royal Philharmonic Orchestra, Temirkanov: RCA 09026-60990-2

Violin Concerto no. 2

Mullova, Royal Philharmonic Orchestra, Previn: Philips 422364-2
Heifetz, Boston Symphony Orchestra, Munch: RCA Red Seal 09026-61744-2

Concerto no. 3 for Piano and Orchestra, Op. 26 (1921)

One of the most popular twentieth-century piano concertos, the Third Concerto is certainly the most frequently performed of Prokofiev's five superb piano concertos. Even for Prokofiev, the piano part is of exceptional brilliance; the visual aspect of the keyboard writing and the choreography of the hands on the piano are themselves striking. Throughout this perfect score, Prokofiev fused Classical form, motoric energy, Russian-sounding melody, pungent harmony, wit, and gaiety into a gorgeous orchestral frame.

Composed twelve years after Rachmaninoff's Third Piano Concerto, and as distinctly Russian in character, Prokofiev's Third shows the generation gap between the two masters—Rachmaninoff nostalgically embedded in the nineteenth century and Prokofiev avowing the twentieth. The concerto is in three movements. The opening lyric theme of the first movement gives way to impetuous motion. The second movement is a theme and five variations. The finale is once again motoric, with ever-increasing rhythmic energy and force. The composer himself gave the world premiere on December 16, 1921, with Frederick Stock conducting the Chicago Symphony Orchestra.

Argerich, Berlin Philharmonic Orchestra, Abbado: Deutsche Grammophon 415062-2
Graffman, Cleveland Orchestra, Szell: CBS MYK 37806

Lieutenant Kijé (symphonic suite), Op. 60 (1934)

The music was originally written in 1933 for the film *Lieutenant Kijé*. Prokofiev was intrigued with composing for films and once told the director Sergei Eisenstein, "I still consider the motion picture the most modern art." *Lieutenant Kijé* is based on a story by Yuri Tynyanov about the rigidity of military bureaucracy. Kijé, who exists by a bureaucratic mistake, acquires a life and receives an assignment, marries, and dies. The film is set in early-nineteenth-century St. Petersburg. Prokofiev was amused by the character and wrote the music in his best satiric vein. In 1934 he composed a five-movement symphonic suite, using a large orchestra, including a cornet for military sounds and bells to simulate the effect of a troika. The first movement, The Birth of Kijé, is all parody; its offstage fanfare by the cornet presents its military spirit. A drill march is heard with a melody that represents Kijé. The second movement, Romance, is a ballad of mock sentimentality using a delightful Russian-sounding modal theme. Kijé's Wedding, the third movement, opens with a pompous tune, a wedding song, and Kijé's motive, all perfectly welded together. In the finale, The Burial of Kijé, the main themes all parade in a wonderfully gay romp. The suite is one of Prokofiev's best-known works. Bits and pieces are used everywhere, from the hilarious film *The Horse's Mouth* with Alec Guinness, to Woody Allen movies and TV commercials.

Cleveland Orchestra, Szell: CBS MYK 38527
Los Angeles Philharmonic Orchestra, Previn: Telarc CD 80143

Romeo and Juliet, Op. 64 (1936)

Prokofiev began working on his ballet in 1935, but the complete work was not staged until 1940, with the great ballerina Galina Ulanova as Juliet. Long before the first performance, the composer had devised two suites, each consisting of seven movements. The subject gave Prokofiev scope for a work of tragic and dramatic magnitude as well as much jest and comedy. Of course, piercing love is of prime concern, and Prokofiev writes beautifully of the couple's immortal love, issuing a dozen themes depicting the range and character of their emotions. Some of these themes are the loftiest flights of lyricism in Prokofiev's output.

Ballet
London Symphony Orchestra, Previn: EMI Classics CDF 68607

Suites
Cleveland Orchestra, Levi: Telarc CD 80089
Seattle Symphony Orchestra, Schwarz: Delos CD 3050

Peter and the Wolf (symphonic fairy tale for children), Op. 67 (1936)

Prokofiev had no special liking for children, but as a composer he could enter into a fairy tale, a fantasy world of a childlike magical kingdom, and children would respond immediately. Nowhere is this more apparent than in *Peter and the Wolf,* in which the score acquaints the child with the colors of various musical instruments. In a preface to the composition, Prokofiev wrote, "Each character of this tale is represented by a corresponding instrument in the orchestra—the bird by a flute, the duck by an oboe, the cat by a clarinet staccato in a low register, the grandfather by a bassoon, the wolf by three horns, Peter by the string quartet, and the shots of the hunters by the kettle drums and bass drum." Have ever education and fantasy been so artfully merged? *Peter and the Wolf* is a must for children and a perpetual delight. The composer himself wrote the text, and what fun it is to hear various narrators read the tale. Leonard Bernstein, Boris Karloff, Itzhak Perlman, André Previn, Mia Farrow, Cyril Ritchard, Michael Flanders, José Ferrer, Sean Connery, Bea Lillie, and David Bowie are just a few who have entertained children the world over.

Ritchard, Philadelphia Orchestra, Ormandy: Odyssey YT 34616
Gielgud, Academy of London Orchestra, Stamp: Virgin Classics 59533

Sonata no. 7 in B-flat Major for Piano, Op. 83 (1942)

Prokofiev's nine sonatas are the most important Russian sonatas after Scriabin. No. 3, in one movement, is often played, and No. 6 is the most massive. But

No. 7, completed in 1942, is the most popular. Sviatoslav Richter gave the world premiere, and Vladimir Horowitz the first American performance. The magnificently constructed first movement has a characteristic wiry athleticism, contrasted with a lyric subject. The slow movement has a ripe, melodic appeal, and the high-voltage motoric finale is a Toccata, marked *precipitato*, of nonstop energy. In this work and in other sonatas, Prokofiev used the piano's percussive clangorousness, which he greatly popularized, as well as a Schumannesque tapestry of polyphonic textures, infused with great amounts of lyricism and stormy clumps of chords wandering the length of the keyboard.

Pollini: Deutsche Grammophon 419202-2
Horowitz: RCA 60377-2-RG

Symphony no. 5 in B-flat Major, Op. 100 (1944)

Prokofiev's Fifth Symphony was first performed on January 13, 1945. It was the composer's last appearance as a conductor. The symphony is a proclamation, as he said, "of the grandeur of the human spirit." And it is one of the master-pieces of the Russian symphony. The composition is tumultuous and Roman-tic, colorful and rich in melody, and makes a heartfelt effect. It is not difficult in the least to understand at first hearing, although it is epic in design, lasting forty-five minutes or so. Prokofiev is here as Russian as his nineteenth-century forebears and consciously ignites the Russian people during their suffering in a war-torn land. The composer wrote, "The Fifth Symphony was intended as a hymn to free and happy man, to his mighty powers, his pure and noble spirit. I cannot say that I deliberately chose this theme. It was born in me and clamored for expression. The music has matured in me, it filled my soul." Unlike the more profound and gloomy Sixth Symphony, where Prokofiev's grief from the war is far more apparent, this symphony is an affirmation. The Symphony no. 5 is in four movements, but slow tempos predominate in the first-movement Andante and the glorious third-movement Adagio, the crown of the work. Both faster movements offer relief. The second movement is an enchanting Scherzo; the finale, Allegro giocoso, is a perfect foil to the long slow movement and is rhythmically, jauntily thrilling in its use of orchestral tone color.

Leningrad Philharmonic Orchestra, Mravinsky: Russian Disc RUS11 165
Philadelphia Orchestra, Ormandy: Sony Classical SBK 53260
New York Philharmonic Orchestra, Bernstein: Sony Classical SKM 47602

OTHER PRINCIPAL WORKS

BALLETS

Chout, Op. 21 (1915; rev. 1920)
Le Pas d'acier (The Steel Step), Op. 41 (1925–26)
L'Enfant prodigue (The Prodigal Son), Op. 46 (1928–29)
Cinderella, Op. 87 (1940–44)*
The Tale of the Stone Flower, Op. 118 (1948–53)

CHAMBER MUSIC

Overture on Hebrew Themes in C Minor, Op. 34 (1919)*
Quartet no. 1 in B Minor for Strings, Op. 50 (1930)
Sonata no. 1 in F Minor for Violin and Piano, Op. 80 (1938–46)*
Quartet no. 2 in F Major for Strings, Op. 92 (1941)
Sonata in D Major for Flute and Piano, Op. 94 (1943)
Sonata no. 2 in D Major for Violin and Piano, Op. 94 bis (1944) (a transcription of the
     Flute Sonata)

CHORAL MUSIC

They Are Seven (cantata), Op. 30 (1917–18; rev. 1933)
Alexander Nevsky (cantata), Op. 78 (1939)*
On Guard for Peace (oratorio), Op. 124 (1950)

CONCERTOS

Concerto no. 1 in D-flat Major for Piano and Orchestra, Op. 10 (1911–12)*
Concerto no. 2 in G Minor for Piano and Orchestra, Op. 16 (1912–13; rev. 1923)*
Concerto no. 4 in B-flat Major for Piano and Orchestra, Op. 53 (1931)*
Concerto no. 5 in G Major for Piano and Orchestra, Op. 55 (1931–32)*
Sinfonia concertante for Cello and Orchestra, Op. 125 (1950–52)

OPERAS

The Gambler, Op. 24 (1915–17; rev. 1927–28)
The Love for Three Oranges, Op. 33 (1919)*
The Fiery Angel, Op. 37 (1919–23; rev. 1926–27)*
Semyon Kotko, Op. 81 (1939)
Betrothal in a Monastery, Op. 86 (1940–41)
War and Peace, Op. 91 (1941–43; rev. 1946–52)*

ORCHESTRAL WORKS

The Love for Three Oranges (suite), Op. 33 bis (1919; rev. 1924)*
Symphony no. 2 in D Minor, Op. 40 (1924–25)

Symphony no. 3 in C Minor, Op. 44 (1928)

Symphony no. 4 in C Major, Op. 47 (1929–30)

Russian Overture, Op. 72 (1936)

A *Summer Day* (suite), Op. 65 bis (1941)

Symphony no. 6 in E-flat Minor, Op. 111 (1945–47)*

Cinderella (suites 1–3), Opp. 107, 109 (1946)*

Symphony no. 7 in C-sharp Minor, Op. 131 (1951–52)*

SOLO PIANO WORKS

Sonata no. 1 in F Minor, Op. 1 (1909)

Four Pieces, Op. 4 (1910–12)

Toccata in C Major, Op. 11 (1912)*

Sonata no. 2 in D Minor, Op. 14 (1912)*

Five Sarcasms, Op. 17 (1912–14)

Twenty *Visions fugitives*, Op. 22 (1915–17)*

Sonata no. 3 in A Minor, Op. 28 (1917)*

Sonata no. 4 in C Minor, Op. 29 (1917)*

Sonata no. 5 in C Major, Op. 38 (1923)*

Two Sonatinas, Op. 54 (1931–32)

Music for Children (twelve pieces), Op. 65 (1935)

Ten Pieces from *Romeo and Juliet*, Op. 75 (1937)*

Sonata no. 6 in A Major, Op. 82 (1939–40)*

Sonata no. 8 in B-flat Major, Op. 84 (1939–44)*

Sonata no. 9 in C Major, Op. 103 (1947)*

PAUL HINDEMITH

b. Hanau, Germany, November 16, 1895

d. Frankfurt am Main, December 28, 1963

A life in and with music, being essentially a victory over external forces and a final allegiance to spiritual sovereignty, can only be a life of humility, of giving one's best to one's fellow men.

Hindemith was the eldest of three children, born to modest circumstances. His father was a housepainter. From childhood Hindemith burst with musical ability, but formal lessons did not begin until he was nine. Once he started, though, his progress was phenomenal. His younger brother, Rudolf, played violin, and Toni, his sister, the cello, with Paul on the viola. They performed in public as the Frankfurter Kindertrio.

At thirteen Paul entered the Hoch Conservatory in Frankfurt, where he developed his amazing theoretical skills and continued to progress on the viola, on which he would become an internationally renowned virtuoso. In 1915 his father was killed in action in Flanders, and Hindemith took a position as a member of the Frankfurt Opera Orchestra in order to support the family. In 1917 he himself was conscripted and served until the war's end. Starting in the 1920s, his compositions were heard, discussed, and published. In 1921 he was a founding member of the Amar String Quartet, an ensemble that specialized in modern chamber works. The success of the quartet enabled Hindemith to leave the opera orchestra in 1923.

In 1927 he moved to Berlin to become a composition professor at the Hochschule für Musik. Teaching would become essential to his well-being. By the early 1930s, Hindemith was well established as a brilliant musician and one of Germany's foremost composers, championed by conductors of the eminence of Wilhelm Furtwängler. But the Nazi regime would change that. In 1924 Hindemith had married a Jewish woman, Gertrud Rottenberg, daughter of the conductor of the Frankfurt Opera. He refused to sever his ties with his Jewish colleagues, and as a result, he was condemned as a "cultural Bolshevik." Clearly he and his wife would have to leave their homeland. At first he traveled, performing as a viola soloist in Switzerland, then staying for long periods in Turkey, where Licco Amar, the leader of the Amar Quartet, lived. The Turkish government asked him to organize and modernize the country's musical education, and every Turkish music student to this day knows Hindemith's methods. He and his wife finally left Germany in 1939.

They settled in the United States, where for over a decade Hindemith taught composition at Yale University. He was much honored in America, where his incredible erudition was appreciated. In 1946 he became an American citizen. From 1949 he conducted a great deal in Europe, and he taught at the University of Zurich from 1953 until 1955. His health declined after 1960, and he died of a stroke in Frankfurt in 1963. Until the end, he continued to write music with consummate ease and skill.

Through most of his enormously successful career, Hindemith was considered one of the masters of the twentieth century, rivaling even Stravinsky, Schoenberg, Prokofiev, and Bartók. But he overproduced and was uneven. He also composed much functional music, which he called *Gebrauchsmusik*—utility music—whose purpose was to narrow the ever-widening gap between the contemporary composer and his audiences, and to encourage amateur musicians. *Gebrauchsmusik* first emerged in the late 1920s, when the Depression forced some composers to write for the radio and motion pictures. Unfortunately the label *Gebrauchsmusik* has stuck to stereotype Hindemith's music, although it is only one style (and the least important) in his variegated musical vocabulary, which included German folksongs, the popular dances of the 1920s, jazz, and much more.

Hindemith's work has not fared well since his death: today he is more or less in composers' limbo. The musician Howard Boatwright feels "Hindemith held to the mainstream of European classical music, as did Johannes Brahms before him, being neither a simple minded reactionary nor an over-enthusiastic progressive. . . . At the present time Hindemith's music is neither new enough nor old enough to be fashionable." Still, there is no Hindemith work that does not have moments of interest. And when his humor, irony, brilliance, and passion were synchronized, he was a composer of undeniable genius. Dozens of German composers were active from 1920 to 1950. Apart from the later operas of Richard Strauss and a handful of works by Carl Orff and Kurt Weill, Hindemith's output remains the most important German music of the interwar period.

Mathis der Maler (*Matthew the Painter*) (symphony) (1934)

Wilhelm Furtwängler conducted the first performance of *Mathis der Maler* in Berlin on March 12, 1934. It was soon banned by the Nazis as decadent. The symphony, based on parts of an opera of the same name, is one of Hindemith's finest achievements. Its three movements constitute a musical representation of the painter Matthias Grünewald's overwhelming Isenheim Altarpiece at Colmar, in Alsace. Grünewald is the hero of the opera, a deeply symbolic figure for Hindemith, who constructed a libretto about the horrors of the Peasant War of 1524 and the predicament of the artist in an oppressed society. The movements are marked 1. Angelic Concert, 2. Entombment, and 3. Temptation of Saint Anthony. The Temptation is a magnificent example of Hindemith's structural command underlying two chorale themes and concluding in a triumphal celebration of the spirit.

London Symphony Orchestra, Horenstein: Chandos CHAN 6549
Munich Philharmonic Orchestra, Celibidache: Exclusive EXL 37
Israel Philharmonic Orchestra, Bernstein: Deutsche Grammophon 429404-2

Nobilissima visione (dance legend) (1938)

Nobilissima visione, Hindemith's moving ballet on the life of Saint Francis, was commissioned by Diaghilev in 1929 and was first performed in 1938, with choreography by Léonide Massine. The following year, Hindemith recast the music into a three-movement suite. *Noblissima visione* is about Saint Francis's conversion to poverty and sacrifice to humanity. It consists of an Introduction and Rondo, March and Pastorale, and Passacaglia. Norman Del Mar thinks that "[t]he ballet music in particular has, in keeping with its title, a degree of nobility quite unique in Hindemith's work. . . . Hindemith's music describes the meditative fervor and asceticism with consummate understanding. The cadence figure in the second section of the first movement, describing the mystical wedding of the saint with poverty, is extraordinarily affecting in its simplicity."

Ballet suite

San Francisco Symphony Orchestra, Blomstedt: London 433809-2
Royal Philharmonic Orchestra, DePreist: Delos DCD 1006

Ludus tonalis (1942)

Ludus tonalis is the high point in Hindemith's output for piano. It is based upon concepts of expanded tonality that he espoused in his 1937 book, *The Craft of Musical Composition*. He calls the *Ludus tonalis* "studies in counterpoint, tonal organization, and piano playing." There are, he continues, "twelve fugues in as many keys, connected by interludes in free lyric and dance forms, old and new, and framed by a prelude and postlude that have more in common than meets the casual ear." Hindemith is one of the great neoclassicists. This score is rewarding for those seeking intellectual refreshment. At first it may sound somewhat acrid, but its geometry becomes increasingly fascinating on repeated hearings.

McCabe: Hyperion CDA 66824
Mustonen: London 444803-2

OTHER PRINCIPAL WORKS

CHAMBER MUSIC
Quartet no. 1 in F Minor for Strings, Op. 10 (1919)*
Quartet no. 2 in C Major for Strings, Op. 16 (1921)*
Quartet no. 3 in C Major for Strings, Op. 22 (1922)*
Kleine Kammermusik for Wind Quintet, Op. 24/2 (1922)
Sonata for Solo Viola, Op. 25/1 (1922)*
Quintet for Clarinet and Strings, Op. 30 (1923)*
Quartet no. 4 for Strings, Op. 32 (1923)*
Morgenmusik for Brass Ensemble (1932)
Trio no. 2 for Violin, Viola, and Cello (1933)
Sonata for Flute and Piano (1936)
Sonata for Bassoon and Piano (1938)
Sonata in F Major for Horn and Piano (1939)
Sonata for Trumpet and Piano (1939)*
Quartet no. 5 in E-flat Major for Strings (1943)*
Quartet no. 6 in C Major for Strings (1945)*
Sonata for Cello and Piano (1948)
Octet for Winds and Strings (1957–58)*

CHORAL WORKS
When Lilacs Last in the Door-yard Bloom'd: Requiem for Those We Love (1946)
Mass (1963)

OPERAS
Cardillac (1926)
Mathis der Maler (1934–35)*

ORCHESTRAL WORKS
Concerto for Orchestra, Op. 38 (1925)
Concert Music for Brass and Strings, Op. 50 (1930)*
Philharmonic Concerto (1932)
Symphony in E-flat Major for Concert Band (1940)*
Symphonic Metamorphosis on Themes of Carl Maria von Weber (1943)*
Symphonia serena (1946)
Die Harmonie der Welt (*Harmony of the World*) (symphony) (1951)

PIANO MUSIC
1922 Suite, Op. 26 (1922)
Three sonatas (1936)*

SOLO INSTRUMENT AND ORCHESTRA WORKS
Kammermusik nos. 1–7 (concertos) for Various Instruments and Orchestra, Opp. 24/1,
       36/1–4, 46/1–2 (1922–27)
Der Schwanendreher (concerto) for Viola and Orchestra (1935)
Trauermusik for Viola and String Orchestra (1936)*
Concerto for Violin and Orchestra (1939)*
The Four Temperaments (theme and variations) for Piano and Strings (1940)*
Concerto for Piano and Orchestra (1945)
Concerto for Clarinet and Orchestra (1947)
Concerto for Horn and Orchestra (1949)

SONG CYCLE
Das Marienleben (fifteen songs) for Soprano and Piano, Op. 27 (1941 version)*

GEORGE GERSHWIN

b. Brooklyn, New York, September 26, 1898

d. Hollywood, California, July 11, 1937

Try to write some real popular tunes—and don't be scared about going low-brow. They will open you up!

When Gershwin's father Moishe Gershovitz passed through U.S. immigration, his name became Morris Gershvin; George later changed it to Gershwin. America teemed with millions of immigrants, all of whom wanted two things: to become American as quickly as possible and to get rich. The perpetual goal of prosperity, however, eluded poor Morris Gershvin, and in later years he was astonished at the money his son made from his music.

The years of George's New York childhood were the great years of ragtime and the player piano. Sheet music for popular songs was big business, and by the beginning of World War I, phonographs were outselling pianos. After the war, jazz began to emerge. George loved it all. There was no evidence of previous musical talent in the family, and George's first encounter with "classical" music did not occur until he was nine. He was filled with emotion as he stood outside the 125th Street Penny Arcade, listening to Anton Rubinstein's Melody in F—one of the era's popular salon pieces, practiced by countless pianists.

Not until 1910 did the family proudly purchase an upright piano, and it was intended for George's brother Ira. In no time, George appropriated the instrument, and his musical life began. Thereafter he was never far from his beloved piano, and he took every opportunity to play for people. He was an inveterate partygoer, and his mother once chastised him for monopolizing every occasion with his piano playing.

Charles Hambitzer was the boy's first real piano teacher, and although he disdained George's love for popular music, he realized that George was a major talent. Hambitzer wrote, "I have a pupil who will make his mark in music if anybody will. The boy is a genius, without a doubt." George later studied some theory with Rubin Goldmark, who also taught Aaron Copland. He itched to be out in the big world, and he left school at fifteen to become a "song-plugger." His first job was at Remick's publishing house in Tin Pan Alley, playing through the newest songs, hoping to sell them to customers. His first song, "When You Want 'Em, You Can't Get 'Em," was published in 1916. From the beginning, the great song composer Irving Berlin noticed George as a "hot talent." To George's glee and amazement, Max Dreyfus, a power in pop music, gave the young man a job paying thirty-five dollars a week to do nothing but write songs. In no time, he was the Wunderkind of Tin Pan Alley, and before he was twenty-one, he had composed his first Broadway musical, *La La Lucille* (1919). The legendary Al Jolson propelled Gershwin onto the national scene by singing his "Swanee" (1919), which rapidly sold over a million copies.

The rest is theatrical history. From 1920 he wrote song after song to the sophisticated lyrics of his talented brother Ira, who, it seemed, was born to set words to George's beguiling tunes. "The Man I Love," "Embraceable You," "Fascinating Rhythm," "S'Wonderful," "I Got Rhythm," and dozens of others are among the best popular songs ever written, and such musicals as *Funny Face* (1927), *Strike Up the Band* (1927), *Rosalie* (1928), *Show Girl* (1929), *Girl Crazy* (1930), and *Of Thee I Sing* (1931), which won the Pulitzer Prize, are classics of the Broadway musical.

Because of the frenzied success of Gershwin's musicals, Paul Whiteman, the well-known bandleader, asked the composer to write a concert piece for piano and orchestra in the jazz and blues idioms that were sweeping the country (as well as England and France). The composer Erik Satie exclaimed, "Jazz speaks to us about suffering and we don't give a damn. That's why it's beautiful." At first Gershwin was apprehensive about the commission, for he felt insecure about his lack of training in serious forms. The endlessly fertile pop composer could not find an idea. During a train trip to Boston, he kept listening to the throb of the train's hypnotic rhythm, and the seed of *Rhapsody in Blue* was planted. New York greeted *Rhapsody in Blue* with rapture at its premiere on February 12, 1924 (with Gershwin at the piano).

Suddenly the uneducated Tin Pan Alley songwriter had entered the domain of serious music. His stylization of jazz into serious art inspired composers from all over the world to try their hands at the jazz style. Maurice Ravel, William Walton, Aaron Copland, Ernst Krenek, Alexandre Tansman, Kurt Weill, Darius Milhaud, and Constant Lambert are just a few who composed music inspired by jazz and other popular music.

The straitlaced conductor Walter Damrosch of the New York Philharmonic

Orchestra was impressed. He felt that Gershwin was making jazz respectable. He commissioned Gershwin to write a piano concerto; the Concerto in F Major was premiered at Carnegie Hall in 1925. He then completed *An American in Paris* in 1928, Three Piano Preludes in 1926, the Second Rhapsody for piano and orchestra in 1931, the *Cuban Overture* in 1932, the *I Got Rhythm* Variations for piano and orchestra in 1934, and his last work and magnum opus, the opera *Porgy and Bess*, in 1935.

During the 1930s, Gershwin led a strenuous life. He conducted the premieres of his musicals *Strike Up the Band* and *Girl Crazy* in 1930. In 1931 he conducted the premiere of *Of Thee I Sing*, and he was soloist in January 1932 when his Second Rhapsody was given its premiere with the Boston Symphony Orchestra under Serge Koussevitzky. In 1935 he toured the United States as pianist and did a radio series twice a week. While composing *Porgy and Bess*, he painted constantly, which he considered as important to him as composing. He traveled to Europe frequently, was linked to several women, and was seen in all the hot spots of Hollywood and New York.

In February 1937, while performing his Piano Concerto with the Los Angeles Symphony Orchestra, Gershwin suffered a fifteen-second blackout. Doctors concurred that his hectic and strenuous lifestyle had put him under abnormal stress; the blackout and other symptoms, including devastating headaches, were diagnosed as a form of "hysteria." Gershwin, they said, was simply "neurotic." But as the months passed, an awful physical decline was apparent. On July 9, Gershwin lost consciousness. Walter E. Dandy, a renowned brain surgeon, was rushed to Los Angeles, where he operated for five hours. But his efforts were to no avail. Gershwin was dead at thirty-eight from a malignant brain tumor. The nation mourned his passing as the passing of an age. His close friend and great interpreter Oscar Levant wrote, "Up until the six months preceding George Gershwin's death, life for him was just one big, wild, marvelous dream come true."

Gershwin, the all-American boy, the "regular guy," was a classic rags-to-riches story. His personality and music represented complex and powerful aspects of the polyglot American landscape. He was a "natural" in everything he attempted. He was pleasant-looking, slim, bright, brash, and sophisticated, as only a street-wise New Yorker of that period could be; women from waitresses to socialites fell in love with him, with his music, or with both.

The nice Jewish kid was as comfortable with applause on Broadway as at Carnegie Hall, and as comfortable with blacks in Harlem and Charleston as with the swank movie community of Hollywood. He was good at sports and was a terrific dancer who loved imitating Fred Astaire. In the 1930s, Gershwin pursued painting with the same passion as he did composition. The last painting he did was a portrait of his neighbor and frequent tennis partner, Arnold Schoenberg.

As Gershwin's aspirations moved from pop to art, he sought composition lessons from such masters as Ravel, Schoenberg, and Stravinsky. Each refused, on the ground that Gershwin's genius would be cramped. Ravel asked the American composer how much he earned each year. Gershwin shrugged, "Oh, I guess around a half million." Ravel replied, "In that case Mr. Gershwin, you give *me* lessons." The critic Olin Downes felt, "It was only in Gershwin's generation that the American people as a whole took with ardor to good music. He came on the scene just at the time to be a connecting link between the 'serious' and 'popular' composers of America." In naïve America, only an artist with Gershwin's magic touch could be cherished equally for his serious and his popular work. Nobody ever accused George of being "highbrow," a "sissy," or a "pansy." He represented the transfixed Jazz Age as did no other American artist; the *Rhapsody in Blue* sounded the vanishing note of a sweetly sad, brashly energetic, and optimistic time in America. We listen to it with an almost unbearable nostalgia. The same is true for *Porgy and Bess*, whose story of innocence, alienation, and oppression could only have been composed during the demoralized years of the American Depression.

Gershwin was working in the finest hour of American musical culture. American music had come of age, and within a few years of his birth, an amazing group of composers was born. But Gershwin remains America's best-loved composer. Indeed, the affection for him seems only to increase with the years. Oscar Levant wrote, "Music to him was the air he breathed, the food which nourished him, the drink that refreshed him. Music was what made him feel and music was the feeling he expressed. Directness of this kind is given only to great men, and there is no doubt that he was a great composer. What he achieved was not only to the benefit of a national American music, but also a contribution to the whole world."

Rhapsody in Blue for Piano and Orchestra (1924)

On February 12, 1924, luminaries of both popular and serious music gathered at Aeolian Hall in New York to hear the twenty-five-year-old George Gershwin, of Broadway and popular song fame, play his jazz-inspired *Rhapsody in Blue*, with Paul Whiteman conducting his own band. The rhapsody proved then, as it remains today, music of delirious joy, all heart and guts. The slow theme is of an irresistibly sweet lyricism. The piano writing throughout is scintillating.

Tilson Thomas, Los Angeles Philharmonic Orchestra, Tilson Thomas: CBS MK 39699
Levant, Philadelphia Orchestra, Ormandy: Sony Masterworks MPK 47681

Concerto in F Major for Piano and Orchestra (1925)

Although critics have taken Gershwin to task for certain technical shortcomings, especially his rather näive padding of longer works, such faults have little meaning within the larger context of his few breathtaking "serious" compositions. The concerto, with its insistent rhythms and glistening melodies, is spectacular. From the pulsation of the opening Charleston tune, to the nocturnal bluesy slow movement with its beguiling soft-shoe danceability, to the whirling motoric finale (which sounds the note of the modern urban metropolis), the concerto rarely fails to bring the house down. At first, Gershwin thought of calling it *New York* Concerto. Gershwin himself was soloist at the premiere on December 3, 1925, with Walter Damrosch conducting.

Previn, London Symphony Orchestra, Previn: EMI Classics CDC 47161
Wild, Boston Pops Orchestra, Fiedler: RCA 6519-2-RG

An American in Paris (1928)

Gershwin was only twenty-nine when he composed *An American in Paris*. To little-traveled Americans of the Roaring Twenties, the work represented "gay Paree" as a mecca of mystery, foreignness, and free spending. Gershwin, now on his sixth trip to Europe, was rather more sophisticated than average, but he too never got over the exhilaration of the City of Light. On the other hand, he was already a cult figure to many European musicians, who were dazzled by his thoroughly American-sounding music.

Gershwin wrote an elaborate program for this symphonic poem, but he also pointed out that the listener might picture whatever he or she wished and all would be well. For his score, he purchased four taxi horns, which seemed to him to be characteristically Parisian in sound.

New York Philharmonic Orchestra, Bernstein: CBS MK 42264
Pittsburgh Symphony Orchestra, Previn: Philips 412611-2

Porgy and Bess (1935)

"Summertime," "My Man's Gone Now," "Bess, You Is My Woman Now," "I Got Plenty o' Nuttin'," "It Ain't Necessarily So"—these songs are completely integrated into the mainstream of American culture. In *Porgy and Bess*, Gershwin far transcended his merry Broadway shows and composed an opera of greatness. DuBose Heyward and Ira Gershwin adapted the libretto from Heyward's play, which takes place in the 1920s in Catfish Row in Charleston, South Carolina. The first production offered the opera in drastically cut form. The composer Wilfrid Mellers wrote, "Gershwin's *Porgy*, like the operas of Mozart or Verdi, is at once a social act, an entertainment, and a human experience with unexpectedly disturbing implications. Historically it is a work of immense . . . significance. Its historical significance could not, however, exist if it were not the achieved work of art it demonstrably is."

Haymon, Evans, Clarey, White, Blackwell, London Philharmonic Orchestra, Glyndebourne Festival Chorus, Rattle: EMI Classics CDCC 49568

OTHER PRINCIPAL WORKS

CHAMBER MUSIC
Lullaby for String Quartet (1919)

ORCHESTRAL WORK
Cuban Overture (1932)*

PIANO WORKS
Three preludes (1926)*
The George Gershwin Songbook (eighteen songs arranged for piano by the composer) (1932)

PIANO AND ORCHESTRA WORKS
Second Rhapsody (1931)
I Got Rhythm Variations (1934)*

FRANCIS POULENC

b. Paris, January 7, 1899

d. Paris, January 30, 1963

On the radio a lady has just been caterwauling for a quarter of an hour some songs which may very well have been mine!

Poulenc was born near Paris's celebrated Madeleine Church. His father, the head of a chemical firm, was an avid music lover and insisted that his son receive a good classical education. Francis's mother, an accomplished pianist, constantly played for him music of Mozart, Schumann, and Chopin—delightfully, as Poulenc later recalled. He dreamed of becoming a singer, but by fifteen his voice had developed into a croak.

Even as a teenager, he was intrigued by many aspects of contemporary music and took to heart Debussy, Ravel, Schoenberg, Stravinsky, and Bartók. He never attended the Paris Conservatory and instead studied privately—with Ricardo Viñes for piano and with Charles Koechlin for composition. To both of them, he was grateful his whole life. By the time he was eighteen, he had composed his *Rapsodie nègre* (1917) and the *Mouvements perpétuels* for piano (1918), which became popular immediately. His musical training was then interrupted by compulsory military duty.

In 1919 Viñes introduced Poulenc to Erik Satie, long a legend in Parisian artistic circles. The eccentric Satie had recently composed his ballet *Parade*, produced with sets by Picasso, a work that sassed all convention. For the young, *Parade* possessed a liberating irreverence and freedom to experiment. Even before the war ended, Poulenc had met Darius Milhaud, Georges Auric, Arthur Honegger, Louis Durey, and Germaine Tailleferre. These composers were very

different from one another, but they had in common a horror of Germanic influence, and of the academic and conservative Schola Cantorum. Even such
former heroes as Debussy and Ravel were now considered too rarefied. For inspiration, the young composers looked to popular dance music and jazz, to
street music, and to the Paris circus and music halls. Satie, their new musical
hero, told them to forget about sacred cows and lampooned the establishment.

In 1920 the music critic Henri Collet baptized the group "Les Six." The
young Jean Cocteau became an effective propagandist for them. Cocteau was
pleased with their unpretentious music. Les Six wrote many pieces in the insouciant new Dadaist image, and other composers followed suit. Nostalgia and
sentimentality—even vulgarity and blather—were their banners.

Most of the music of this era is now faded and sounds trivial, but Poulenc's
work still sounds invigorating and stylish. Works such as the Sonata for Clarinet
and Bassoon (1922); the Piano Impromptus (1920); the piano suite Napoli
(1925); the Sonata for Trumpet, Horn, and Trombone (1922); and the song cycle Le Bestiaire (1919) are examples of his happy-go-lucky Parisian boule-
vardier style.

Inevitably, Poulenc came to Diaghilev's attention, and the great impresario
commissioned a ballet. In Monte Carlo, on January 6, 1924, the Ballets Russes
premiered the twenty-five-year-old composer's Les Biches, with rousing success.
Once again Diaghilev had launched a young composer. Poulenc's adroit and
sophisticated mastery of ragtime and jazz idioms as well as his delightful lyric
gift give Les Biches a permanent place in the ballet repertoire.

During the Roaring Twenties, Poulenc—who had an exuberant personality—knew everyone in the Parisian musical world. Wanda Landowska's harpsichord playing inspired him to compose the wonderful Concert champêtre
(1927–28) for her. Arthur Rubinstein remembers, "Poulenc played to me much
of his piano music and I picked some of his pieces right away for my repertoire.
They were refreshing in their subtle simplicity. Because they always seemed to
remind you of something, I sometimes accused them of being simple pas-
tiches. But later I learned better. Poulenc was one of the bravest musicians of
his time. He accepted all the influences without qualms but somehow a striking personality emerged."

In the 1930s, Poulenc collaborated with the baritone singer Pierre Bernac.
Poulenc was a splendid pianist, and the two musicians gave countless recitals
together, becoming lifelong lovers and companions. Poulenc's songs are among
the best known of his works, wherein his infallible settings of poetry and unforgettable melodies are perfectly wedded to rich piano accompaniments. Also in
the 1930s, his music deepened, and he composed his tender-hearted Two-
Piano Concerto in 1932 and the grander Organ Concerto in 1938. In 1936 he

was shocked by the death of his friend the composer Pierre-Octave Ferroud in an auto accident. It abruptly awakened in him a deeper understanding of the fragility of life, and he reembraced the Catholic faith of his youth and began composing religious scores, which would continue for the remainder of his life: highlights are the Mass in G Major (1937), the *Stabat Mater* (1950), and the *Gloria* (1959). His religious opera *Dialogues des Carmélites* (1953–56) is all light and compassion. In 1958 he composed music to Cocteau's monodrama *La Voix humaine*, a telephone conversation with a silent lover who has ended the affair. As Poulenc aged, his high spirits and elegance were combined with deeper issues, even gravity. In his religious music, he sounds like a modern Machaut.

Poulenc loved people, but he also craved solitude, and loved to retreat from the high life in Paris to his house at Noizay in Touraine. From the late 1930s he also spent a good deal of time in church. He had deep friendships with a host of people and many famous performers. He often mentioned that the three major artistic encounters of his life, in different ways, were with the harpsichordist Wanda Landowska, the singer Pierre Bernac, and the poet Paul Éluard. Poulenc died suddenly of a massive heart attack in his Paris apartment, leaving no incomplete work.

Perhaps he was thinking of himself when in 1950 he spoke to the music historian Roland Gelatt on the character of French music: "You will find sobriety and dolor in French music just as in German or Russian. But the French have a keener sense of proportion. We realize that somberness and good humor are not mutually exclusive. Our composers, too, write profound music, but when they do, it is leavened with that lightness of spirit without which life would be unendurable." In its always engaging, disarming manner, Poulenc's music has proved to be highly resilient. He is the most enduring and endearing French composer since the 1920s and by far the most frequently performed of Les Six. Poulenc once said, "Above all do not analyze my music—love it!"

Concerto in D Minor for Two Pianos and Orchestra (1932)

This is the most successful two-piano concerto of the twentieth century. It was commissioned by the music patroness, painter, pianist, and organist Princess Edmond de Polignac, the eldest daughter of Isaac Singer, of the American Sewing Machine fortune. The first performance took place in Venice on September 5, 1932, with Poulenc and his close friend Jacques Février as soloists. The concerto is all wit and high style, touched by the elegance of Mozart and the insouciance of Chabrier. It is a delightfully sophisticated work in three movements; the Allegro ma non troppo is saucy and humorous. The spirit of the café concert and the popular music hall dominates. The Larghette is all heart-on-sleeve, with a rather agitated middle section. The finale, Allegro molto, is all verve, with a delightfully conscious sentimentality. The American composer Ned Rorem summarized Poulenc's harmonic style thus: "Take Chopin's dominant sevenths, Fauré's plain triads, Debussy's minor ninths, Mussorgsky's augmented fourths. Filter these through Satie by way of the added sixth chords of vaudeville (which the French called le music-hall), blend in a pint of Couperin to a quart of Stravinsky, and you get the harmony of Poulenc."

Poulenc, Février, Paris Conservatoire Orchestra, Prêtre: EMI Classics 72435694662
Rogé, Deferne, Philharmonia Orchestra, Dutoit: London 436546-2
Labèque, Labèque, Boston Symphony Orchestra, Ozawa: Philips 426284-2
Gold, Fizdale, New York Philharmonic Orchestra, Bernstein: Sony Classical SMK 47618

Le Bal masqué (1932)

Le Bal masqué, subtitled by the composer *Cantate profane*, is based on poems by Max Jacob, with the unusual scoring for voice, oboe, clarinet, bassoon, cornet, violin, cello, percussion, and piano. Here is the ebullient Poulenc with the world at his feet, freshness personified; the piece's charm, goodwill, and clean, clear textures make it one of the highlights of the younger Poulenc. Virgil Thomson wrote, "It was composed in 1932, about the last year anybody in Europe was really carefree, and it's musical high jinks from beginning to end. Its pasticcio of urban banalities, melodic and rhythmic, is rendered interesting by the extreme elegance of the vocal lines and of the instrumental texture . . . its wit and poetry . . . is as fresh as the day the piece was written."

Van Dam, Lyon Opera Orchestra, Nagano: Virgin Classics CDC 59236
Allen, Nash Ensemble CRD CRD 3437
Bernac, Poulenc, Paris Opera Orchestra Soloists, Frémaux: Adès ADE 202522

Concerto in G Minor for Organ, Strings, and Timpani (1938)

This work was also commissioned by the generous Princess Polignac, and the composer himself thought highly of it. It is characteristic Poulenc in its combination of various materials. It has a quality of medievalism and the French cathedral, cleverly mixed with earthier elements. The inventive structure divides its single movement into seven sections. The opening, with organ alone, is a grand reminiscence of the glory of the Baroque organ. The concerto was premiered on June 10, 1941, by the great organist and composer Maurice Duruflé and the Paris Symphony Orchestra, conducted by Roger Désormière, the composer's favorite conductor.

Murray, *Atlanta Symphony Orchestra, Shaw: Telarc CD 80104*
Duruflé, *French National Radio Symphony Orchestra, Prêtre: EMI Classics CDC 47723*

Sonata for Flute and Piano (1956)

Flute sonatas of all kinds have proliferated since the 1920s, but none has so captivated the fancy of flutists and the public alike as Poulenc's twelve-minute, three-movement sonata, which piquantly displays the instrument, framed by a perfect piano accompaniment. The finale, Presto giocoso, displays Poulenc's sophisticated jest and joyousness. The piece was composed for the celebrated flutist Jean-Pierre Rampal. If one knows Poulenc's *Dialogues des Carmélites*, one will hear a few melodic borrowings from that opera.

Baker, *Emenheiser Logan: VAI Audio VAIA 1022*
Wilson, *O'Riley: Etcetera KTC 1073*
Rampal, *Poulenc: Adès ADE 202522*

Gloria in G Major for Soprano, Chorus, and Orchestra (1959)

The celebrated composition teacher Nadia Boulanger once observed, "Poulenc's personality was much more complex than met the eye. He was entirely paradoxical. You could meet him as easily in fashionable Parisian circles . . . or at mass." Poulenc wrote, "I've not the slightest philosophical conception of life . . . outside the religious faith which is instinctive and hereditary. I have no preconceived idea. I compose as seems best to me." The *Gloria* is once again immersed in eclectic influences, the foremost being Stravinsky and Ravel. The score is a heartfelt and original treatment of a liturgical form by a twentieth-century master.

Battle, *Boston Symphony Orchestra, Tanglewood Festival Chorus, Ozawa: Deutsche Grammophon 427304-2*

Blegen, New York Philharmonic Orchestra, Westminster Choir, Bernstein: Sony Classical
   SMK 47569

Carteri, French National Radio Symphony Orchestra, Prêtre: EMI Classics CDC 47723

Songs (1916–62)

Poulenc's songs are an indispensable part of his oeuvre and were often initially performed by the baritone Pierre Bernac, to Poulenc's own superb accompaniment. On their EMI recording, we hear their collaboration in such well-known songs as "C" (1943) and "Dans le jardin d'Anna" (1938). *Tel jour, telle nuit* (1937), to nine poems of Éluard, is one of the great song cycles by a French composer. Among the other poets whose poems Poulenc set are Guillaume Apollinaire, Pierre de Ronsard, and Max Jacob.

Complete Songs
Ameling, Souzay, Baldwin: EMI Classics CDMD 64087
Bernac, Poulenc: EMI Classics CDC 54605

OTHER PRINCIPAL WORKS

BALLETS
Les Biches (1923)*
Les Animaux modèles (1940–41)*

CHAMBER MUSIC
Sonata for Clarinet and Bassoon (1922)*
Sonata for Trumpet, Horn, and Trombone (1922; rev. 1945)*
Trio for Piano, Oboe, and Bassoon (1926)*
Sextet for Piano and Woodwind Quintet (1932–39)*
Sonata for Violin and Piano (1942–43)*
Sonata for Cello and Piano (1948)
Sonata for Oboe and Piano (1962)*
Sonata for Clarinet and Piano (1962)*

CHAMBER MUSIC WITH VOICE
Le Bestiaire (1918–19)*
Cocardes (1919)
Chansons villageoises (1943)*

CHAMBER ORCHESTRA WORKS
Rapsodie nègre (with voice) (1917; rev. 1933)*
Aubade for Piano and Eighteen Instruments (1929)*
Suite française (1935)
Deux marches et un intermède (1937)

CHORAL MUSIC
Mass in G Major (1937)*
Four *Motets pour un temps de pénitence* (1938–39)
Exultate Deo (1941)
Stabat Mater (1950)*

CONCERTOS
Concert champêtre for Harpsichord and Orchestra (1927–28)*
Concerto for Piano and Orchestra (1949)

OPERAS
Les Mamelles de Tirésias (opéra bouffe) (1944)*
Dialogues des Carmélites (1953–56)*
La Voix humaine (tragédie lyrique) (1958)*

ORCHESTRAL WORK
Sinfonietta (1947)*

PIANO DUET AND TWO PIANOS
Sonata for Piano Four-Hands (1918)*
Sonata for Two Pianos (1952–53)*

PIANO SOLO WORKS
Three *Mouvements perpétuels* (1918)*
Six Impromptus (1920)
Suite in C Major (1920)
Promenades (1921)
Napoli (1925)*
Three *Pièces* (1928)*
Nocturnes no. 1–8 (1929–38)*
Les Soirées de Nazelles (1930–36)*
Valse-improvisation sur le nom de Bach (1932)
Intermezzo in A-flat Major (1943)

SONG CYCLES

Poèmes de Ronsard (1924–25)

Five *Poèmes de Jacob* (1931)*

Five *Poèmes de Éluard* (1935)*

Tel jour, telle nuit (1936–37)*

Banalités (1940)*

Two *Poèmes d'Aragon* (1943)*

AARON
COPLAND

b. Brooklyn, New York, November 14, 1900

d. North Tarrytown, New York,
    December 2, 1990

*The process of music and the process of life will always be closely
conjoined. So long as the human spirit thrives on this planet, music
in some living form will accompany and sustain it and give it
expressive meaning.*

Copland's parents were Russian-Jewish immigrants whose name had been Kaplan. "I was born on a street in Brooklyn that can only be described as drab," he later wrote. Aaron was the youngest of five children. His father, Harris, was the owner of a small department store, and the family lived above the store. His mother, Sarah, "might best be described as everything a maternal parent should be," Copland remembered in his old age. "She was affectionate, and a very nice mother to have. . . . I must have inherited some of my own comparative evenness of temperament from my mother."

The boy was irresistibly drawn to music. Though a brother played the violin and a sister the piano, Aaron was not to have piano lessons until he was thirteen, for his parents felt they had already spent too much money on the other children's lessons. Soon after his first lessons, he began composing part of a song he titled "Lola." By the time he was sixteen, he had come "to the daring decision to spend my life as a musician. It was so startling an idea that I dared not share it with anyone." But he badly needed solid training and in 1918 found himself taking the subway to Manhattan to study harmony and composition with Rubin Goldmark, with whom Gershwin also studied.

After high school, Copland concentrated totally on music: instead of going to college, he continued with Goldmark until 1921. Unfortunately, Goldmark was a musical "old fogy" who kept the young man away from any of the "contaminating" Modern influences. For some time, the fledgling composer felt musically isolated. He took many odd jobs and carefully saved his money. By 1921 he had enough to sail for Europe to enroll at the newly established American Conservatory at Fontainebleau, near Paris. Shortly after arriving, he happened to hear a theory class given by Nadia Boulanger. It changed his life. The impression she made on him was overwhelming. For the next three years he studied privately with Madame Boulanger. Copland was the great teacher's first American pupil, and for the next half century hundreds of other talented Americans crossed the ocean to receive her musical wisdom as well.

By 1924 Copland was out of money. The time had come to return home, but Boulanger surprised him with a vote of confidence: she commissioned him to write a piece for organ and orchestra, which she would premiere the following season. Copland worked speedily the rest of the year, and on January 11, 1925, the New York Symphony Orchestra, conducted by Walter Damrosch, premiered the Symphony for Organ and Orchestra at Aeolean Hall. As Copland reports it, "At the conclusion, there was considerable applause, and when Mr. Damrosch pointed to the upper box where I was seated, I rose to bow. As things quieted down, Mr. Damrosch advanced to the footlights and to everyone's surprise, addressed the audience. 'Ladies and Gentlemen,' he began, 'I am sure you will agree that if a gifted young man can write a symphony like this at twenty-three,'—and here he paused dramatically, leaving the audience to expect a proclamation of a new musical genius—then continued, 'within five years he will be ready to commit murder!' "

Whatever that enigmatic remark meant, Aaron Copland's career was launched. Boulanger was pleased with the score. When she asked another of her students, Virgil Thomson, if he liked the symphony, he replied, "I wept when I heard it." "But why did you weep?" Boulanger asked. "Because I had not written it myself." Thomson commented, "The piece that opened the whole door to me was that Organ Symphony of Aaron's. I thought that it was the voice of America in our generation."

Next, Serge Koussevitzky, the great conductor of the Boston Symphony Orchestra, heard the symphony and was convinced that Copland could create an authentic American musical language. Koussevitzky commissioned him to write a score, and Copland obliged with the jazz-inspired suite Music for the Theater (1925). When Koussevitzky conducted the piece in Boston and in New York, it was wildly applauded. But even a performed composer must have a means to survive, and Copland was barely making ends meet. A Guggenheim Fellowship briefly alleviated his financial struggle, enabling him to concentrate on the Piano Concerto (which also used jazz elements), completed in 1926. Again Koussevitzky introduced it, with Copland as soloist.

Early in the Depression, Copland began to write stark, lean, dissonant, abstract music, perhaps as a grim reminder of alienated industrial society. Characteristic of this style is the Piano Variations (1930), considered one of the seminal works in the American piano repertoire. Composers throughout the world were affected by the Depression. Many, like Copland, came to feel that an unprecedented gulf lay between the modern composer and the audience. "It seemed to me," Copland wrote, "that we composers were in danger of working in a vacuum. Moreover, an entirely new public for music had grown up around the radio and the phonograph. It made no sense to ignore them and to continue writing as if they did not exist. I felt it was worth the effort to see if I couldn't say what I had to say in the simplest possible terms."

From the mid-1930s, he produced some of his most popular scores. For a high school orchestra, he wrote *An Outdoor Overture* (1938). He wanted to write "the kind of brilliant orchestral piece that everyone loves," so he next composed two Latin American scores, *El Salón Mexico* (1933–36) and *Danzón cubano* (1944). In 1938 he wrote the first of his ballet "classics," *Billy the Kid.* Few composers have ever managed popular material with such panache and quality.

In the 1940s, Copland's creative capacities expanded. The delightful ballet *Rodeo* was completed in 1942, followed in 1944 by his ballet masterpiece, *Appalachian Spring*. At the same time, he composed such splendid instrumental compositions as the Violin Sonata (1942–43) and the Piano Sonata (1939–41). Copland himself gave the first performance of the Piano Sonata in Buenos Aires. One month after its completion in 1946, Koussevitzky gave the world premiere of the Third Symphony. The conductor was elated with the work, and was convinced that it was the greatest symphony written by an American.

Hollywood also called to the busy composer. Composing for films was often considered hackwork, but Copland took the medium seriously. His music for *Of Mice and Men* (1939), *Our Town* (1940), and *The Red Pony* (1948) shows a rare understanding of this tricky medium. For his perceptive score to *The Heiress* (1948), he received an Academy Award.

From the beginning of his musical life, Copland had been a staunch tonalist. But in the 1950s, he began searching for new directions. Finding himself attracted to dodecaphonic procedures, he wrote, "I found twelve-tone writing to be especially liberating in two respects: It forces the tonal composer to unconventionalize his thinking with respect to chordal structure, and it tends to freshen his melodies and figurational imagination."

With his rich diversity and his unusual ability to move from one style to another, some listeners ask, "Which is the real, the truest Copland?" The answer is that each style of his varied output is an authentic expression of this particularly wide-ranging master. His distinctive voice is always pure Copland, be it the populist *Lincoln Portrait* (1942) or the experimental Piano Fantasy (1952–57).

In the late 1960s, Copland's creative spring dried up and he caught "the conducting bug," as he called it. He developed into a good conductor, making guest appearances in many countries. He conducted American music in general and especially his own music, which he also recorded. When not active in the musical world, Copland lived quietly at his home on the Hudson River at Peekskill, New York. He was homosexual and never married. His physical health remained good, but his final years were crippled by Alzheimer's disease.

Throughout his career, Copland was the guiding light of American music. Very few have served their art so unstintingly. Once, when speaking of Copland's music, Leonard Bernstein exclaimed, "It's the best we've got, you know!" But Copland was more than "the best we've got"—he touched greatness in many forms. A healthy amount of his invariably highly finished output will survive, representing his nation more completely than that of any other composer.

Variations for Piano (1930)

This fifteen-minute set of variations is Copland at his most uncompromising. It depicts a stark, bare, often grim industrial landscape, and it is also a study of intense logic. The theme, twenty variations, and coda remain as rugged and abstract as on the day they were finished. The piece was a landmark in Copland's musical development, as well as in the history of American music. Surprisingly, this "difficult" work has been frequently played and appreciated from its inception.

Marks: Nimbus NI 5267
Tocco: Pro Arte CDD-183

El Salón Mexico (1933–36)

Copland's *El Salón Mexico* stemmed from his 1932 visit south of the border. Copland finished the piece in 1934 in Minnesota, but he did not orchestrate it until he was in Mexico again in 1936. For this electric orchestral sizzler, Copland appropriated Mexican tunes, reinforcing them with his own sense of vigor and gaiety. It was first performed in Mexico City by Copland's great friend, the composer Carlos Chávez, on August 27, 1937. Copland was nervous before the performance, wondering how the Mexican audience would feel about a "gringo" taking their native tunes. His worries were assuaged nine minutes later with a triumph.

New York Philharmonic Orchestra, Bernstein: CBS MYK 37257
New Philharmonia Orchestra, Copland: CBS MK 42429
Minneapolis Symphony Orchestra, Dorati: Mercury 434301-2

Billy the Kid Suite (1938)

Billy the Kid is a nostalgic ballet about the outlaw folk hero, otherwise known as William Bonney. The suite contains two-thirds of the complete ballet score. With *Billy* and *Rodeo*, Copland added an American accent to the fantasy world of ballet, and the American ballet stage had long awaited such works. Both of them go beyond the merely folkloristic. *Billy* opens and closes on the open prairie, with a feeling of deep desolation and loneliness. Cowboy songs are brilliantly integrated into the orchestral fabric, such as "Great Grand-Dad," "The Old Chisholm Trail," "Get Along Little Doggies," and "The Dying Cowboy." The composer had said, "It is a delicate operation to put fresh and unconventional harmonies to well-known melodies without spoiling their naturalness."

New York Philharmonic Orchestra, Bernstein: CBS MYK 36727
St. Louis Symphony Orchestra, Slatkin: EMI Classics CDM 64315

Lincoln Portrait for Speaker and Orchestra (1942)

The *Lincoln Portrait* was composed on a commission from the conductor André Kostelanetz, at a time when the morale of the nation was at a low ebb. Copland extracted a text from Lincoln's letters and speeches that opened with "Fellow citizens! We cannot escape history," then, with an uncanny sense of timing, gave us a portrait of substance and sincerity. The composer said, "I hoped to suggest something of the mysterious sense of fatality that surrounds Lincoln's personality . . . and something of his gentleness and simplicity of spirit." He created a patriotic piece without rival, a work of popular appeal with his musical fingerprint on every bar. It is entertaining to hear recordings of the various celebrities who have narrated the piece—and one of the best was Copland himself. Adlai Stevenson, with Eugene Ormandy conducting the Philadelphia Orchestra, is perfectly solemn. The first performance had an overwhelming effect. It took place on July 4, 1942, on a barge in the Potomac, with the Lincoln Memorial in plain sight. Kostelanetz conducted, and the famous poet and Lincoln biographer Carl Sandburg narrated. Members of the audience wept and simply forgot to applaud.

Fonda, London Symphony Orchestra, Copland: CBS MK 42431
Hepburn, Cincinnati Pops, Kunzel: Telarc CD-80117

Fanfare for the Common Man (1942)

In 1942, while Copland was composing his *Lincoln Portrait*, Eugene Goossens, then the conductor of the Cincinnati Symphony Orchestra, asked him and other composers to compose a fanfare for his concerts during the 1942–43 season. Copland, always successful at producing music to order, wrote a most wondrous fanfare. Within three minutes, one experiences the isolation of the American prairie and the desolation of the industrial city. Copland also utilized the *Fanfare* most tellingly in his Symphony no. 3. The most effective recording is Bernstein's (Deutsche Grammophon 419170-2, which also contains the ethereal *Quiet City*).

Philadelphia Orchestra, Ormandy: CBS MLK 39443
London Symphony Orchestra, Copland: CBS MK 42430
Boston Pops Orchestra, Williams: Philips 412627-2

Appalachian Spring Suite (1944)

The ballet *Appalachian Spring* was composed for Martha Graham, one of the great figures in the history of dance. It is a work of immense appeal and subtlety, telling the story of "a pioneer celebration in spring around a newly-built farmhouse in the Pennsylvania Hills in the early part of the last century." The Shaker tune "Simple Gifts" is used ingeniously in the score. In its original version, Copland used only thirteen instruments: flute, clarinet, bassoon, piano, and strings. Copland himself conducted the complete ballet in its original version in 1973 (CBS MK 42431). The premiere of the full ballet took place on October 30, 1944, at the Coolidge Auditorium of the Library of Congress. The orchestral suite was premiered a year later, on October 4, 1945, in New York.

Los Angeles Philharmonic Orchestra, Mehta: London 417716-2
Los Angeles Philharmonic Orchestra, Bernstein: Deutsche Grammophon 431048-2

Concerto for Clarinet and Strings, Harp, and Piano (1947–48)

Commissioned by the famous clarinetist Benny Goodman, the Copland Clarinet Concerto was given its world premiere by Goodman with Fritz Reiner conducting the NBC Symphony Orchestra on November 6, 1950. The concerto immediately became a staple work for clarinetists, with its sweet and mellow jazz feeling and pure Coplandesque harmony. It is cool refreshment for the ear. In its layout, the concerto comprises two movements: the first, marked "slowly and expressively," has a waltz feeling. Copland uses the orchestra with his usual skill and delicacy. The movement ends as the clarinet takes center stage in a wonderful cadenza, which inaugurates melodies to come in the next movement, marked "rather fast." Copland next gives us a Brazilian tune that he heard while visiting the country. The piano (having been dormant on stage for the first movement) enters in the second movement. Jazz rhythms erupt, and we are in the world of Goodman's "swing" music, with sides of boogie-woogie.

Stoltzman, London Symphony Orchestra, Leighton Smith: RCA 09026-61360-2
Drucker, New York Philharmonic Orchestra, Bernstein: Deutsche Grammophon 431672-2

OTHER PRINCIPAL WORKS

ORCHESTRAL MUSIC
Music for the Theater (suite) (1925)
Short Symphony (1932–33)*
An Outdoor Overture (1938)*
Letter from Home (1944)
Danzón cubano (1944)*
Symphony no. 3 (1944–46)*
Dance Panels (1959)
Connotations (1962)
Three Latin American Sketches (1972)

BALLET
Rodeo (1942)*

CHAMBER MUSIC
Vitebsk: Study on a Jewish Theme for Cello, Violin, and Piano (1928)*
Sonata for Violin and Piano (1941–42)*
Quartet for Piano and Strings (1950)*
Duo for Flute and Piano (1971)

PIANO MUSIC
Passacaglia for Piano (1921–22)
Four Piano Blues (1947, 1934, 1948, 1926)
Sonata for Piano (1939–41)*
Piano Fantasy (1952–57)*

OPERAS
The Second Hurricane (1936)
The Tender Land (1952–54)*

SOLO INSTRUMENT AND ORCHESTRA MUSIC
Symphony for Organ and Orchestra (1924)*
Concerto for Piano and Orchestra (1926)*
Quiet City for Trumpet, English Horn, and Orchestra (1939)*

FILM MUSIC
Of Mice and Men (1939)*
Our Town (1940)
The Red Pony (1948)*
The Heiress (1948)*

SONGS
Twelve *Poems of Emily Dickinson* (1949–50)*
Old American Songs (two sets) (1950–52)

DMITRI SHOSTAKOVICH

b. St. Petersburg, September 25, 1906

d. Moscow, August 9, 1975

I'm not a militant atheist, and I feel people can believe as they wish. But just because a person has a particular set of superstitions doesn't prove anything good about him. Just because a person is religious, he does not automatically become a better person.

Shostakovich was the second of three children. His father was an engineer, and his mother taught him piano from age nine. His childhood was blighted by the 1917 Revolution, which brought terrible deprivation to St. Petersburg. There was little food, money, or fuel; Dmitri later remembered that he always felt cold. In his memoirs, the composer recalled, "I was sickly as a child. It's always bad to be sick, but the worst time to be sick is when there's not much food."

Dmitri entered the Petrograd Conservatory in 1919, studying composition with Maximilian Steinberg and piano with Leonid Nikolaiev. At the Conservatory, he developed into a formidable pianist and took advantage of every opportunity to learn, especially from the Conservatory's revered director, Alexander Glazunov. While still a student, he composed for the piano the Three *Fantastic Dances* (Op. 1, 1922), which had a small vogue. During this time, his father died and the family's poverty became crushing. His mother took a job as a cashier. To make matters worse, Dmitri suffered from tuberculosis. Still he pressed on, earning a little money playing the piano for silent movies.

In 1925, at nineteen, he graduated from the Conservatory. For his graduation piece, he wrote his First Symphony (Op. 10). It was an unexpected triumph, and overnight Shostakovich became a hero of Soviet music, lauded as the first illustrious artistic child of the Revolution. Word spread of the high quality of the symphony, and it was soon heard in Europe and the United States, conducted by such luminaries as Otto Klemperer, Bruno Walter, and Leopold Stokowski. In 1927 the government commissioned him to write a Second Symphony (Op. 14) to celebrate the tenth anniversary of the October Revolution. Many new compositions followed rapidly: the satiric opera *The Nose* (1927–28), based on Gogol's novel; the Third Symphony (Op. 20, 1929); the ballet *The Golden Age* (Op. 22, 1927–30), with its piquant polka; the ballet *Bolt* (Op. 27, 1930–31); two film scores; Twenty-four Preludes for Piano (Op. 34, 1932–33); and the Piano Concerto with Trumpet (Op. 35, 1933), so characteristic of the composer's youthful high spirits. Shostakovich's music was performed worldwide and made a deep impression on many listeners. The conductor Serge Koussevitzky went so far as to say, "There has never been a composer since Beethoven with such tremendous appeal to the masses." His position in Soviet art appeared secure.

Although he lived in poverty, he married Nina Varzar in 1933, after a three-year engagement. A daughter, Galya, was born in 1936, and a son, Maxim, who would become a conductor, in 1938. In 1934, after three years of work, his opera *Lady Macbeth of Mtsensk* (Op. 29) was first staged in Leningrad. Productions quickly followed in New York, Cleveland, Prague, London, Zurich, Copenhagen, and elsewhere. By 1936 Leningrad had seen *Lady Macbeth* eighty-three times and Moscow ninety-seven. Unfortunately, early that year Stalin attended a performance. The dictator was shocked by what seemed to him the repugnant, incestuous, murderous plot and stormed out. Unlike Lenin, Stalin had little tolerance for artists and indeed feared them deeply.

In January 1936, a scathing attack on the opera appeared in the official newspaper, *Pravda*, under the headline: "Chaos Instead of Music." The next week another article condemned Shostakovich's recent ballet *The Limpid Stream* (Op. 39, 1934–35), disapproving of the composer's handling of its collective farm subject matter and criticizing its ideological "falsehood." Stalin, who had a particular taste for grand spectacles, saw opera and ballet as valuable propaganda tools. He listed the qualities that a Soviet opera should have: a libretto that extolled socialist realism, and music, based on folk music, that spoke clearly and realistically, without dissonance or complexity. The heroes should be characteristic of Soviet aspirations, and there should be a properly happy ending for all. The *Pravda* article was a personal attack on Shostakovich, but the anonymous writer made it clear that petty-bourgeois innovations in painting, poetry, teaching, and science were also not to be tolerated.

Shostakovich, fearing arrest, quickly mended his ways. He withdrew his recondite Fourth Symphony (Op. 43, 1935–36) from a scheduled performance.

Little did he know that it would not be performed for a quarter century. On November 21, 1937, his Fifth Symphony (Op. 47), marking the twentieth anniversary of the Soviet Republic (a commission he had received prior to the *Pravda* article), received a huge ovation. Apparently Stalin himself found pleasure in the uplifting score. Shostakovich appeared to have been rehabilitated. In the next few years, he composed a Sixth Symphony (Op. 54, 1939), several more film scores, and the Piano Quintet (Op. 57, 1940), for which he won the prestigious Stalin Prize in 1940.

During the war, because of poor eyesight, Shostakovich was forbidden to join the Red Army, though he tried three times. In the horrifying siege of Leningrad from September 1941 to January 1944, at least a third of the city's three million inhabitants died. Shostakovich was reluctantly evacuated to safer ground, where he finished his Seventh Symphony (Op. 60, 1941), subtitled *Leningrad*. He exclaimed, "The Nazi barbarians seek to destroy the whole of Slavonic culture." While composing the symphony, he wrote, "Never in my life have I dedicated my compositions to anyone. [This wasn't true.] But this symphony—if I succeed in its realization—I shall dedicate to Leningrad. For all that I wrote into it, all that I expressed in it, is tied up with that beloved native city of mine, is connected with the historic days of its defense against fascist oppressors."

Long before the symphony was performed in Leningrad, the giant score was put on microfilm and flown by the military to the United States, where, on July 19, 1942, Arturo Toscanini conducted a performance by the NBC Symphony Orchestra as millions listened on the radio. Within nine months, it had been performed sixty-two times in the United States alone. The poet Carl Sandburg called it music "written with the heart's blood." The *Leningrad* Symphony, with its graphic march in the finale, became emblematic of victory; audiences stood through the movement. Shostakovich became a heroic figure, even appearing on the cover of *Time* magazine on July 20, 1942. He wore a firefighter's helmet, symbolizing Russian resistance to Hitler's onslaught. The composer himself resented being turned into a symbol.

After the war, some were optimistic that Soviet artists would have new freedom, but dark clouds were gathering for Shostakovich. His next symphonies were found to have ideological weakness. In 1948 the Central Committee of the Communist Party wiped out any vestige of hope for artistic freedom for all Russian artists by viciously attacking Prokofiev, Khachaturian, Vissarion Shebalin, Gavryil Popov, Miaskovsky, Shostakovich, and others. "Bourgeois formalism," "anti–working class deviation," and "counterrevolutionary music, not in the best interests of the Soviet people," were the primary charges. All of the accused composers, fearing the loss of their positions or even arrest and banishment, made public confessions of their guilt. In 1954, Nina died, and in 1956 the composer impulsively remarried. He barely knew his new wife, Margarita, who had no understanding of the composer, and the marriage lasted for four years of misery. In 1962 he remarried again to a woman named Irina, and the relationship was a happy one.

In later years, Shostakovich's position as a Soviet artist stabilized, but even after Stalin's death in 1953, life could be hazardous. Throughout his career, Shostakovich, because of his international reputation, was forced to be a mouthpiece for the government, delivering speeches written by others. As late as 1968, he uttered nonsense that was written for him. His last years were a constant battle with ill health, primarily renal failure and lung cancer. He died in a Moscow hospital in 1975 and was buried in Novodevichy Cemetery in Moscow.

Four years after the composer's death, the Russian musicologist Solomon Volkov published *Testimony: The Memoirs of Shostakovich*, on which Volkov and Shostakovich had worked together. The world read the composer's shattering condemnation of the Soviet system and his hatred for Stalin. "I have thought that my life was replete with sorrow and that it would be hard to find a more miserable man," Shostakovich related. "But when I started going over the life stories of my friends and acquaintances I was horrified. Not one of them had an easy or a happy life. Some came to a terrible end, some died in terrible suffering, and the lives of many of them could easily be called more miserable than mine."

Shostakovich's worst music is drearily ponderous; his use of satiric themes, marchlike tunes, and sarcasm in general has dated badly. Sometimes the bitterness that festers in his slow movements sounds too self-conscious. But at his best, his music flows with buoyant lightness, sardonic humor, bleak pessimism, and deathly anguish. The musicologist Boris Schwarz wrote, "Shostakovich was true to himself. Whether introvert or extrovert, neoclassic or neo-banal, in Shostakovich's musical make-up, Bach and Offenbach had always been friendly neighbors." Of primary importance, said Schwarz, Shostakovich was the last great symphonist: "This composer preserved and reaffirmed almost single-handedly the grandeur of the symphonic genre, the Mahlerian vision of the world within a score."

Shostakovich's finest work encompasses greatness. His pain is palpable, yet he reveals no self-pity. His art meant everything to him; it was his salvation. He was speaking of himself when he wrote, "Music illuminates a person through and through and it is also his last hope and final refuge."

Concerto no. 1 in C Minor for Piano, Trumpet, and Strings, Op. 35 (1933)

This is one of the best-known twentieth-century piano concertos, blazing with youthful brazenness and mockery and with touching heart-on-the-sleeve moments in the slow movement. The concerto is in the usual three movements. The use of the solo trumpet is electric. The piano writing is often percussive, especially in the finale, with its delightful and effective cadenza. The American premiere took place in 1934, with Eugene List as piano soloist and Leopold Stokowski at the helm of the Philadelphia Orchestra.

Kissin, Moscow Virtuosi, Spivakov: RCA 7947-2-RC
Argerich, Württemberg Chamber Orchestra, Faerber: Deutsche Grammophon 39864
Ogdon, Academy of St. Martin in the Fields, Marriner: London Classics 448577-2

Symphony no. 1 in F Minor, Op. 10 (1924–25)
Symphony no. 5 in D Minor, Op. 47 (1937)
Symphony no. 6 in B Minor, Op. 54 (1939)
Symphony no. 8 in C Minor, Op. 65 (1943)
Symphony no. 9 in E-flat Major, Op. 70 (1945)
Symphony no. 10 in E Minor, Op. 93 (1953)
Symphony no. 14 in G Minor, Op. 135 (1969)
Symphony no. 15 in A Major, Op. 141 (1971)

Together the fifteen symphonies add up to one of the noble contributions to symphonic culture. In toto they paint a comprehensive autobiography of a composer with awesome technical equipment and an unfailing sense of orchestral timbre. They brim with cleverness, quotations of all sorts, goodly amounts of blather and bloat, arresting *scherzando* pages, true pathos, and an irritating bathos, at times with an almost embarrassing effectiveness. Shostakovich can and does often sweep his listeners off their feet in feats of emotional manipulation; certainly the once-lauded Seventh Symphony gives one a thrill on first contact, but with repeated hearings, its inherent vulgarity makes one shudder.

The First Symphony, now more than three quarters of a century old, is still popular. It is crystal clear, lyric, and jaunty; the last movement delights in its momentum. The Fifth Symphony is the best known and can be overwhelming; its slow movement moves to a thrilling climax. The Sixth Symphony opens with a spacious Largo, one of the composer's greatest utterances, which takes up half the length of its three movements. The Eighth Symphony, from 1943, is a powerful creation, a chilling reaction to the war. The Ninth Symphony is filled with cheer and goodwill and was a much-needed respite from the hour-long Seventh and Eighth Symphonies. The Ninth has five movements but runs less than half an hour and brims with all sorts of felicities. The Tenth is one of the composer's finest, another complex self-portrait, yet exceptionally accessible.

The Fourteenth Symphony is a symphony–song cycle for soprano and bass in eleven somber movements: four movements call for soprano, four for bass, and three for both. The text, concerning death, is poetry by Lorca, Rilke, Apollinaire, and Brentano. The orchestra of strings and percussion is splendid. The composer told Solomon Volkov, "I don't feel that writing and thinking about death are symptomatic of illness and I don't think that writing about death is characteristic only of old men. I think that if people began thinking about death sooner they'd make fewer foolish mistakes." The Fifteenth Symphony is a curious and enigmatic work. It contains self-quotations as well as quotations from Rossini's *William Tell* Overture and Wagner's *Götterdämmerung*.

Symphony no. 1

New York Philharmonic Orchestra, Bernstein: Sony Classical SMK 47614
NBC Symphony Orchestra, Toscanini: RCA 09026-60323-2
Royal Philharmonic Orchestra, Ashkenazy: London 425609-2

Symphony no. 5

Philadelphia Orchestra, Muti: EMI Classics CDC 54803
London Symphony Orchestra, Previn: RCA 6801-2-RG

Symphony no. 6

Vienna Philharmonic Orchestra, Bernstein: Deutsche Grammophon 419771-2
Leningrad Philharmonic Orchestra, Mravinsky: ICONE 9404

Symphony no. 8

Leningrad Philharmonic Orchestra, Mravinsky: Philips 422442-2
National Symphony Orchestra, Rostropovich: Teldec 9031-74719-2-ZK

Symphony no. 9

Royal Philharmonic Orchestra, Ashkenazy: London 430227-2
Milan RAI Symphony Orchestra, Celibidache: Arkadia 765
Dallas Symphony Orchestra, Mata: Dorian DOR 90169

Symphony no. 10

Leningrad Philharmonic, Mravinsky: Erato 45753
Berlin Philharmonic Orchestra, Karajan: Deutsche Grammophon 39036
London Symphony, Rostropovich: Telarc 74529

Twenty-four Preludes and Fugues for Piano, Op. 87 (1950–51)

These works are Shostakovich's major contribution to the piano literature, teeming with ingenuity and fugal flights of fancy and encompassing a wide range of feelings. In 1950, for the commemoration of the bicentennial of Bach's death, the composer visited Leipzig, where he began sketching a modern *Well-Tempered Clavier* in each of the twelve major and minor keys. They were premiered in Leningrad in 1952 by Tatiana Nikolaeva.

Nikolaeva: Hyperion CDA 66620
Jarrett: ECM New Series 78118-21469-2

Quartet no. 8 in C Minor for Strings, Op. 110 (1959–60)

The fifteen string quartets reveal Shostakovich's most personal thoughts. Within the enclosed solitude of this demanding form, he confided some of his grimmest, most cryptic, and most desolate thoughts, culminating in the six movements of unrelenting gloom that make up No. 15 in E-flat minor (Op. 144, 1974). The quartets in sum are his crucifixion under the Soviet regime. On the title page of the Eighth Quartet, one of the finest, Shostakovich dedicated it to "the memory of the victims of Fascism and war." It is a gripping testament, in five movements, in which Shostakovich bares his broken heart as he quotes from earlier works. The fifteen string quartets rank near the finest string quartet writing of the twentieth century. The Borodin String Quartet has, admirably, twice recorded the complete set.

Borodin String Quartet (fifteen quartets): Melodiya 74321-40711-2
Brodsky String Quartet: Teldec 2292-44919-2-ZK
Medici Quartet: Nimbus NI 5077

OTHER PRINCIPAL WORKS

BALLETS

The Golden Age, Op. 22 (1927–30)*

Bolt, Op. 27 (1930–31)

CHAMBER MUSIC

Trio no. 1 in C Minor for Piano, Violin, and Cello, Op. 8 (1923)

Quintet in G Minor for Piano and Strings, Op. 57 (1940)*

Trio no. 2 in E Minor for Piano, Violin, and Cello, Op. 67 (1944)*

CONCERTOS

Concerto no. 1 in A Minor for Violin and Orchestra, Op. 99 (1955)*

Concerto no. 2 in F Major for Piano and Orchestra, Op. 102 (1957)*

Concerto no. 1 in E-flat Major for Cello and Orchestra, Op. 107 (1959)*

Concerto no. 2 for Cello and Orchestra, Op. 126 (1966)

Concerto no. 2 in C-sharp Minor for Violin and Orchestra, Op. 129 (1967)

FILM MUSIC

The Golden Hills, Op. 30 (1931)

The Unforgettable Year 1919 (1951)

The Gadfly, Op. 97 (1955)

Hamlet, Op. 116 (1963–64)*

King Lear, Op. 137 (1970)*

OPERAS

The Nose, Op. 15 (1927–28)

Lady Macbeth of Mtsensk, Op. 29 (1930–32)*

PIANO MUSIC

Three *Fantastic Dances*, Op. 1 (1922)

Sonata no. 1, Op. 12 (1926)

Aphorisms (ten pieces), Op. 13 (1927)

Twenty-four Preludes, Op. 34 (1932–33)*

Sonata no. 2, Op. 61 (1942)

ORCHESTRAL WORKS

Ballet Suites no. 1–4 (1949–53)

Festive Overture, Op. 96 (1954)

SOLO INSTRUMENT AND PIANO WORKS

Sonata in D Minor for Cello and Piano, Op. 40 (1934)*

Sonata for Violin and Piano, Op. 134 (1968)

Sonata for Violin and Piano, Op. 147 (1975)*

SONG CYCLES

Six Songs from Japanese Poems, Op. 21 (1928–32)

From Jewish Folk Poetry, Op. 79 (1948)*

BENJAMIN BRITTEN

b. Lowestoft, Suffolk, November 22, 1913

d. Aldeburgh, December 4, 1976

Music demands . . . from a listener . . . some preparation, some effort, a journey to a special place, saving up for a ticket. . . . It demands as much effort on the listener's part as the other two corners of the triangle, this holy triangle of composer, performer, and listener.

Britten dearly loved his native Suffolk and derived lifelong stimulation from the county. When he was honored by his hometown in 1951, he said, "Suffolk, the birth place and inspiration of Constable and Gainsborough, the loveliest of English painters, the home of Crabbe, that most English of poets; Suffolk, with its rolling intimate countrysides, its heavenly Gothic churches, big and small; its marshes, with those wild sea-birds; its grand ports and its little fishing villages, I am firmly rooted in this glorious country."

Britten's father was a dental surgeon, his mother a talented amateur singer. From the moment he could reach the keys, Benjamin monopolized the piano, showing prodigious ability. Already in childhood, he was scribbling down music. He retained some of these melodies, and when he was twenty-one, he utilized them in his *Simple Symphony* (Op. 4, 1934).

At London's Royal College of Music, which he entered in 1930, Britten studied with the notable composers John Ireland and Arthur Benjamin. But his most influential teacher was Frank Bridge. The two formed a rich friendship, and Bridge provided Britten with a powerful compositional technique. It was Britten's splendid *Variations on a Theme of Frank Bridge* (Op. 10), first performed in 1937, that brought the young composer to an international audience.

After leaving school, he earned a livelihood by writing music for film documentaries. He did this rather effortlessly from 1935 until 1939, composing his "serious" music on the side. Because of his pacifist beliefs, he left England in 1939 for Brooklyn, New York, moving into an apartment he shared with the tenor Peter Pears and with W. H. Auden, the leading English poet of his generation. Auden had an incalculable influence on Britten's literary taste, revealing to him many avenues of English literature and poetry.

While Britten was in the United States, he wrote the deeply felt *Sinfonia da requiem* (Op. 20, 1941) and a delightful operetta titled *Paul Bunyan* (Op. 17, 1940), with a libretto by Auden. When the latter was staged at Columbia University, the composer remarked that the audience "politely spat at it." (When the New York City Opera performed it in 1998, by contrast, it was greatly enjoyed.)

War was raging in 1941, and Britten became increasingly concerned about England's plight. One day while visiting California, the young composer happened to pick up a magazine with an article by E. M. Forster on the Suffolk poet George Crabbe; it read, "To think of Crabbe is to think of England." Overcome with nostalgia and guilt, the composer quickly resolved to return home. He was still an unflinching pacifist, however, and he and his companion Peter Pears had to appear before the Tribunal of Conscientious Objectors. They were exempted from military service, but as a public service they were obliged to give song recitals in hospitals, bombed villages, or wherever needed. At this point, the two began their lifelong public musical collaboration. Britten was a formidable pianist, and Pears developed into one of the most musicianly tenors of the century. Their closely knit relationship, both personally and professionally, ended only with Britten's death.

On June 7, 1945, the Sadler's Wells Opera Company in London produced Britten's opera *Peter Grimes* (Op. 33). Critical opinion unanimously acknowledged the opera's high quality. The great American literary critic Edmund Wilson was there and wrote, "The opera seizes on you, possesses you, keeps you riveted to your seat during the action and keyed up during intermissions, and drops you, purged and exhausted, at the end." Within the year, Leonard Bernstein conducted it at Tanglewood, and in 1948 the Metropolitan Opera produced it. Within a few years, *Peter Grimes* was translated into a dozen languages. After *Grimes*, Britten composed three more operas—*The Rape of Lucretia* (Op. 37, 1946), *Albert Herring* (Op. 39, 1947), and *Billy Budd* (Op. 50, 1951), all of them successful. His operas were the first by an English composer to become staples in the international repertoire. Nor did Britten neglect other forms. The delightful *Young Person's Guide to the Orchestra* (Op. 34,

1946) and the *Spring Symphony* (Op. 44, 1949) became popular. By his mid-thirties, Britten was one of the most famous composers in the world. Each of his works had a compelling, poetic meaning. He could be Romantic, acrid, or explosive; polyphonically complex or simple; and although he was dissonant when necessary, he was always accessible and basically tonal.

In a 1947 essay, Aaron Copland wrote, "I know of no other composer alive today who writes music with such phenomenal flair. Other composers write with facility, but Britten's is breathtaking. He combines an absolutely solid technical equipment with a reckless freedom in handling the more complex compositional textures. The whole thing is carried off with an abandon and verve that are irresistible."

The year 1947 saw Britten move to the village of Aldeburgh, and in 1948 he and Pears established the Aldeburgh Festival, which continued through the twentieth century. In the next decades, Britten continued to compose music of an astounding range and variety. He loved nothing better than to incorporate music from the past. The critic Erwin Stein wrote, "Purcell is as near to him as Verdi, and Handel as near as Berg. . . . He is free to draw directly from all the sources that are music's springs. And the tradition he carries on comprises the whole of European music." Thus *Lachrymae* (Op. 48, 1950) revives the Elizabethan world of John Dowland, while Henry Purcell's English Baroque spirit lives in the *Young Person's Guide*. In using the anonymous medieval verse "Sumer is icumen in" for his *Spring Symphony*, Britten went back to the very foundation of English music. In other pieces, such as the *Soirées musicales* (Op. 9, 1936), Rossini shows up, and in others echoes of Mahler to Milhaud. His setting of texts from Rimbaud in the original French or from John Donne and Thomas Hardy are incomparable. Rarely does an artist feel such complete empathy with so many sources without being tainted by imitation. Indeed, Britten's adventurousness while manipulating musical material into unified conceptions is astonishing.

Britten also composed several works for children, including the masterful *Noye's Fludde* (Op. 59, 1957), based on the Chester miracle play. The violinist Yehudi Menuhin, who knew him well, thought Britten had "a wonderful sensitivity for children. He was a very young person. One had the feeling, with Ben, that one was in the presence of a tremendous creative genius who never grew up. . . . He had a tireless avidity for life, for feeling and experiencing, and he was often excessive . . . and with it all, Ben, who was so kind, so touching, was also an elusive person, a sprite. But above all he had a hunger for something great. He was always striving for it. He was a wonderful pianist, oh, the way he played Schubert songs, the *Winterreise* with Peter Pears was unbelievable. The way he accompanied me—incomparable!"

Britten, who had heart surgery in 1973, died at only sixty-three, in 1976. He was undoubtedly the major influence on postwar British music, and his presence was a boon to such diversely gifted composers as Ronald Stevenson, Nicholas Maw, Richard Rodney Bennett, Peter Maxwell Davies, and David Bedford, to name a few. Britten has proved to be the most exportable of any English composer born in the twentieth century. A great deal of his work will survive, for it reaches deep levels of emotion, heightened by an acute sense of human drama. He was the first British composer raised to the peerage, becoming Lord Britten of Aldeburgh in 1976.

Variations on a Theme of Frank Bridge for String Orchestra, Op. 10 (1937)

This piece is one of the finest examples of string orchestra writing. Britten is by turns satiric, gentle, and perky. Each of the ten variations sails by in a breeze. Among the variations are a clever march, an outrageous parody of a Rossini aria, a Viennese bonbon in waltz time, an emotional funeral march, and a fugal finale. The Bridge theme comes from the second of his three idylls for string orchestra, a perfect foil for Britten, who gallivants around and through the theme.

London Symphony Orchestra, Britten: London 417509-2
Norwegian Chamber Orchestra, Tomler: Virgin Classics CDC 45121
English String Orchestra, Boughton: Nimbus NI 5025

Sinfonia da requiem, Op. 20 (1940)

During his fruitful American sojourn, Britten composed the expressive Violin Concerto (Op. 15, 1939); the song cycle *Seven Sonnets of Michelangelo* (Op. 22, 1940); another song cycle, the incandescent *Les Illuminations* (Op. 18, 1939); and the *Sinfonia da requiem*. The *Requiem* was premiered by the New York Philharmonic Orchestra under Sir John Barbirolli on March 29, 1941. It is a poignant expression of the composer's sorrow at the war. The movements are Lacrymosa, Dies irae, and Requiem aeternam. The composer explained, "The scheme and the mood of the work are indicated by the Latin titles which are taken from the Requiem Mass; but the connection to the great Catholic ceremony is more emotional than liturgical."

City of Birmingham Symphony Orchestra, Rattle: EMI Classics CDM 64870
London Philharmonic Orchestra, Slatkin: RCA 90926-61226-2

Serenade (song cycle), Op. 31 (1943)

Britten used poetry by Nathaniel Cotton, Tennyson, Blake, Jonson, and Keats in this masterpiece. The settings are "The day's grown old" by Cotton, "The splendour falls" by Tennyson, "O rose, thou art sick" by Blake, "Lyke-Wake Dirge" (anonymous), "Hymn to Diana" by Jonson, and "To Sleep" by Keats. In its diversity of mood, it is among Britten's most haunting creations. The Canadian composer Godfrey Ridout writes, "The role of the horn is twofold: at times it plays in duet with the voice (recalling the obbligato instrumental part in baroque arias) and at others, as a color added to the string orchestra sound that produces an effect far greater than the sum of the two ingredients. The results are stunning, especially in the Nocturne, where the strings produce a continuous echo effect. . . . In the Hymn the horn assumes its historic function of an essential appurtenance of the hunt."

Pears, Tuckwell, London Symphony Orchestra, Britten: London 417153-2

Peter Grimes, Op. 33 (1944–45)

Grimes remains Britten's most popular opera. It is based on George Crabbe's 1810 poem *The Borough* and was written for Pears in the lead role. Its subject is the place of the outsider in a society that he despises and yet yearns to be part of. "It is also a portrait of the sea—for most of my life," the composer wrote, "I have lived closely in touch with the sea. My parents' house on Lowestoft directly faced the sea, and my life as a child was colored by the fierce storms that sometimes drove ships on our coast and ate away whole stretches of neighboring cliffs. In writing *Peter Grimes*, I wanted to express my awareness of the perpetual struggle of men and women, whose livelihood depends on the sea—difficult though it is to treat such a universal subject in theatrical form." Britten extracted *Four Sea Interludes* ("Dawn," "Sunday Morning," "Moonlight," and "Storm," Op. 33a) and his powerful Passacaglia (Op. 33b) from the opera. They have often appeared on symphonic programs. The opera itself, however, is a must for lovers of the form, as are the comic opera *Albert Herring, Billy Budd, Gloriana* (Op. 53, 1953), and *Death in Venice* (Op. 88, 1973).

Complete Opera

Watson, Pears, Evans, Pease, Orchestra and Chorus of the Royal Opera House, Covent Garden, Britten: London 414577-2

Four Sea Interludes and Passacaglia
New York Philharmonic Orchestra, Bernstein: Sony Classical SMK 47541

The Young Person's Guide to the Orchestra, Op. 34 (1946)

The *Guide* was originally composed for a 1945 documentary, *Instruments of the Orchestra*. It has been performed both with and without narrator. To introduce a child to the orchestra, the narrator is educative, but the "straight" version is musically more satisfying and far afield from mere functional music. The theme Britten used comes from Purcell's *Abdelazer*. In thirteen splendid variations, the orchestral battery presents itself. The fugue brings back each of the instruments in a superbly crafted and effective peroration.

WITH NARRATOR
Connery, Royal Philharmonic Orchestra, Dorati: IMP Collectors Series IMPX 9002

WITHOUT NARRATOR
London Symphony Orchestra, Britten: London 417509-2
Royal Philharmonic Orchestra, Previn: Telarc CD 80126

War Requiem, Op. 66 (1961)

All his life Britten, an avowed pacifist, was perplexed and disgusted that humanity had still not cured its illness of waging war. The title page of this mighty antiwar document reads, "My subject is war, and the pity of war.—The poetry is in the pity.—All a poet can do is warn." The words are by Wilfred Owen, killed in action at age twenty-five, one week before the end of World War I. The *War Requiem*, in eighty minutes, is scored for soprano, tenor, baritone, chorus, boys' choir, orchestra, chamber orchestra, and organ.

Söderström, Tear, City of Birmingham Symphony Orchestra and Chorus, Rattle: EMI Classics CDC 47033
Vishnevskaya, Pears, Fischer-Dieskau, London Symphony Orchestra and Chorus, Britten: London 414383-2

OTHER PRINCIPAL WORKS

BALLET

The Prince of the Pagodas, Op. 57 (1957)

CELLO SOLO WORKS

Suite no. 1, Op. 72 (1964)*

Suite no. 2, Op. 80 (1967)

Suite no. 3, Op. 87 (1972)

CHAMBER MUSIC

Quartet no. 1 in D Major for Strings, Op. 25 (1941)

Quartet no. 2 in C Major for Strings, Op. 36 (1945)

Lachrymae for Viola and Piano, Op. 48 (1950)

Quartet no. 3 for Strings, Op. 94 (1975)

CHORAL WORKS

A Ceremony of Carols for Treble Voices, Harp, and Chorus, Op. 28 (1942)*

Rejoice in the Lamb (cantata), Op. 30 (1943)

Festival Te Deum for Organ and Chorus, Op. 32 (1944)

Spring Symphony, Op. 44 (1949)*

Noye's Fludde, Op. 59 (1957)*

Missa brevis for Boys' Choir and Organ, Op. 63 (1959)

Welcome Ode for Young People's Chorus and Orchestra, Op. 95 (1976)

GUITAR SOLO WORK

Nocturnal after John Dowland, Op. 70 (1963)*

OBOE SOLO WORK

Six *Metamorphoses after Ovid*, Op. 49 (1951)

OPERAS

The Rape of Lucretia, Op. 37 (1946)

Albert Herring, Op. 39 (1947)*

Billy Budd, Op. 50 (1951)*

Gloriana, Op. 53 (1953)*

The Turn of the Screw, Op. 54 (1954)

A Midsummer Night's Dream, Op. 64 (1960)

Curlew River, Op. 71 (1964)

Owen Wingrave, Op. 85 (1970)

Death in Venice, Op. 88 (1973)*

SOLO INSTRUMENT AND ORCHESTRA WORKS

Concerto in D Major for Piano and Orchestra, Op. 13 (1938)*

Concerto in D Minor for Violin and Orchestra, Op. 15 (1939)*

Diversions for Piano Left-Hand and Orchestra, Op. 21 (1940)

Symphony for Cello and Orchestra, Op. 68 (1963)

SOLO VOICE AND ORCHESTRA WORKS

Les Illuminations for Tenor or Soprano and String Orchestra, Op. 18 (1939)*

Nocturne for Tenor and String Orchestra, Op. 60 (1958)*

SONG CYCLES WITH PIANO

Seven Sonnets of Michelangelo, Op. 22 (1940)*

The Holy Sonnets of John Donne, Op. 35 (1945)*

A Charm of Lullabies, Op. 41 (1947)

Winter Words, Op. 52 (1953)

Songs and Proverbs of William Blake, Op. 74 (1965)*

OTHER MODERN
COMPOSERS

ERIK SATIE

(1866–1925) France

A fascinating and amusing character, Satie is brilliantly captured in Roger
Shattuck's classic volume *The Banquet Years*. Often associated with such movements as Dadaism and surrealism, Satie occupies a pivotal position in French
music. He detested Wagnerism and Germanic "giantism," creating instead a
music devoid of heroics or heavy emotionalism, even one that mocked such
sentiments. Virgil Thomson, who was musically indebted to his predecessor,
wrote that "Satie's music is as simple as a friendly conversation and in its better
moments exactly as poetic and as profound."

In the preface to his composition *Sports et divertissements* (1914), Satie
wrote, "Turn the pages of this volume with an amiable and smiling hand, for
this is a work of fantasy and does not pretend to be anything else. For those who
are dried up and stultified, I have written a chorale which is serious and respectable. This chorale is a sort of bitter preamble, a kind of austere and un-
frivolous introduction. I have put into it everything I know about boredom. I
dedicate this chorale to those who do not like me—and withdraw." The composer Darius Milhaud, among others, considers this composition to be one of
the characteristic works of modern French music. For those looking for cool refreshment, Satie offers music so guileless that on first hearing, it may seem to
lack substance. Soon, however, the childlike lyricism emerges, as well as its
satire.

The main body of Satie's work is for piano, with unique titles such as *Em-
bryons desséchés* (1913), *Pièces froides* (1897), and Three *Véritables préludes
flasques* (1912).

Various Piano Works
Ciccolini: EMI Classics CDC 49714
Rogé: London 421713-2

FERRUCCIO BUSONI

(1866–1924) Italy

The restless, multifaceted Busoni is one of Modernism's germinative figures. His brilliant essays, letters, and music show him to be prophetic, perplexing, and full of contradictions. One of the supreme pianists in history, he was Mediterranean by temperament but German by training and intellect.

Bachian polyphony was a primary influence on his work, the basis of his musical speech: a universalistic neoclassicism in which freedom and form were to achieve an eloquent balance. He reached maturity during the last days of nineteenth-century Romanticism, and he was fully aware of the new problems facing a twentieth-century composer. But he had difficulty freeing himself from the grand manner of late Romanticism, as exemplified by his huge Piano Concerto (Op. 39, 1904). He began purging Romantic elements by immersing himself in the late works of Liszt. In 1907 he composed the Seven Elegies for piano; he went on to compose *Berceuse élégiaque* for orchestra (Op. 42, 1909), the Second Sonatina (1912), and the opera *Arlecchino* (Op. 50, 1916), moving beyond traditional notions of consonance and dissonance during the same years that the younger Schoenberg was contending with these issues.

Busoni said that music was born free, and he wanted to help emancipate the art from structures that would choke it. He experimented with new scales and sounds. His 1907 book, *Sketch of a New Aesthetic of Music*, was widely read by musicians and anticipated the thinking of much of twentieth-century music. "I almost think that in the new great music, machines will also be necessary and will be assigned a share in it," he wrote. His ideas and advice influenced musicians as dissimilar as Varèse, Sibelius, Otto Luening, Hindemith, and Schoenberg. He taught Kurt Weill, Egon Petri, Philipp Jarnach, and many others. Busoni once commented, "I should like to catch hold of a corner of the coming art of music and, where possible, sew a seam in it myself."

His opera *Doktor Faust* (1919–24), completed by Jarnach, contains the essence of the mature Busoni. He wrote to his wife, "Infinity lives in the spirit of all beings; that each being is illimitably great and illimitably small: the greatest expansion is like a point; and that light, sound, movement and power are identical, and each separate and all united, they are life." In *Faust*, Busoni's own Faustian nature is expressed in one of the masterful operas of the twentieth century.

Concerto for Piano, Male Chorus, and Orchestra, Op. 39 (1904)
Ohlsson, Cleveland Orchestra and Men's Chorus, C. von Dohnányi: Telarc CD 80207
Thiollier, Nice Philharmonic Orchestra, Schønwandt: Kontrapunkt 32057

Doktor Faust (1919–24)
Fischer-Dieskau, Hillebrecht, Cochran, Kohn, Bavarian Radio Symphony Orchestra and Chorus, F. Leitner: Deutsche Grammophon 427413-2

UMBERTO GIORDANO

(1867–1948) Italy

Although Giordano's opera *Fedora* (1898) was once popular, his enduring success is *Andrea Chénier*, produced in Milan in 1896. Like Mascagni and Leoncavallo just before him, Giordano became an overnight celebrity and never again wrote anything comparable. *Andrea Chénier* is a bloodcurdling tale of duels, prison, and passion. Each of the four acts contains well-known arias, especially the Act III soprano aria, "La mamma morta."

Andrea Chénier (opera in four acts) (1896)
Caballé, Pavarotti, Nucci, National Philharmonic Orchestra, Chailly: London 410117-2

ENRIQUE GRANADOS

(1867–1916) Spain

In Barcelona, the young Granados had the good fortune to study composition with Spain's finest piano teacher, Joan Baptista Pujol. When he was fifteen, he took first prize in piano playing at the Barcelona Conservatory and came in contact with Felipe Pedrell, the eminent folksong collector and musicologist whose ideals for a Spanish national school live through his three great pupils, Granados, Albéniz, and de Falla. Granados worked with Pedrell until he was twenty, when he left Barcelona for the excitement of Paris. After two years, he missed Spain deeply, and in 1889 he returned to Barcelona. In 1891 he married Amparo Gal, with whom he would have six children. In the next two decades he performed and taught a great deal, opened a piano academy in Barcelona, and composed a few unsuccessful operas and some significant piano music, including the Ten *Spanish Dances* (1892–1900).

By 1910 Granados, himself a gifted painter, had become transformed by his veneration for the Spanish painter Francisco Goya. He even fell in love with Goya's models, his loves and flirtations. He yearned for *Madrilenismo* (the spirit of eighteenth-century Madrid) and translated the atmosphere of the great painter's works into his undisputed masterpiece, the epic seventy-five-minute piano cycle *Goyescas* (1911–14). In this suite of six pieces, with their coquettish sensuality, gallantry, and turbulence, subtly enmeshed within Spanish dance forms, Granados's luxuriant piano style fully bloomed.

Granados's music was becoming known, and the Paris Opera commissioned him to adapt *Goyescas* into an opera, but the Great War prevented its first performance there. The opera had its premiere instead in New York, where it was the first opera by a Spaniard ever staged at the Metropolitan Opera. Despite his phobia of traveling by water, Granados came to New York to assist in preparations for the production. It was heard on January 26, 1916, and was only a mild success. The opera has seldom been revived.

Only days before Granados and his wife were to return to Europe, the composer received an invitation from President Woodrow Wilson to give a recital at the White House and attend a reception in his honor. Such an invitation could not easily be refused. Granados canceled his tickets on a neutral Dutch ship and gave the recital in Washington. He and his wife then crossed the Atlantic on the British steamer S.S. *Sussex*, but the ship was torpedoed by a German submarine. The couple perished in each other's arms in the freezing water of the English Channel.

The English critic Ernest Newman lamented, "The death of Granados was the greatest loss the artistic world of Europe has sustained by reason of the war." He continued, "The texture of Granados' music is of the kind that makes you want to run your fingers over it, as over some exquisite velvet; the flavor of it is something for the tongue almost, as well as the ear; to play through some of his pages is like a joyous wading knee-deep through beds of gorgeous flowers, always with a sure way through and the clearest of light and air around us." In *Goyescas*, Granados blended tragedy and amorous love, using Spanish dances such as the *jota* and *fandango*, with consummate skill. The fourth piece, "Laments, or The Maiden and the Nightingale," is a supremely poetic evocation with an unforgettable melody, a mirror of Iberian beauty.

Goyescas (suite of six pieces) for Piano (1911–14)

de Larrocha: London 448191-2
de Larrocha: EMI Classics CDMB 65424
Battersby: Koch International Classics KIC 7062-2

SCOTT JOPLIN

(1868–1917) United States

The creator of "classic" notated ragtime was an authentic genius, a black itinerant pianist in the Tenderloin districts of the Missouri Valley states. Here, where pianists were hired to entertain in brothels and were quaintly called "professors," ragtime was born. Joplin's syncopated jewels created a sensation from his very first hit, "The Maple Leaf Rag" (1899), which pioneered the formal basis of the genre. It was the first piece of sheet music ever to sell more than one million copies, and Joplin was called the King of Ragtime. Joplin fought for the purity of piano ragtime and considered the genre properly as art music; he lived to see its essence proliferate in the popular music of the day. But the classic ragtime of Joplin, James Scott, and others lasted for less than twenty years, after which it was ousted by its own child, jazz. Joplin had early contracted syphilis and eventually went insane. At his funeral John Stark, his publisher, declared, "Here is the genius whose spirit was filtered through thousands of cheap songs and vain imitations."

Joplin's fifty-five rags, such as "The Entertainer," "The Ragtime Dance," "Elite Syncopations," "Gladiolus Rag," and "Bethena," are affirmations of an ebullient spirit. Here joyous melodies and irresistible rhythmic verve are perfectly matched.

The Complete Rags
Albright: MusicMasters 7061-2-C

HANS PFITZNER

(1869–1949) Germany

Pfitzner was a large talent with larger ambitions, and his music can be strained and overblown—but it does possess some marvelous pages. He had a lyric gift, a richness in his orchestral fabric, and a mastery of late Romantic chromatic procedures, which he often used adventurously. Wearing the mantle of nineteenth-century tradition, he bitterly fought such progressives as Busoni and Schoenberg. One of his finest works is the large-scale Romantic cantata *Von deutscher Seele* (*The German Soul*, 1922). For the fourth of his five operas, *Palestrina* (1912–15), he wrote his own libretto, and it is considered by some to be the greatest German opera since *Parsifal*.

Palestrina (opera in three acts) (1912–15)
Jurinac, Ludwig, Wunderlich, Frick, Vienna State Opera Orchestra and Chorus, Heger: MYTO Records 3 MCD 92259

ALBERT ROUSSEL

(1869–1937) France

Roussel will never attain the popularity of Debussy or Ravel, as his work lacks sensuous appeal. He was not Parisian, yet he was a compelling and important French composer. Upon repeated listening, his music becomes more and more intriguing because of its subtle rhythmic vitality. He can be alternately brilliant, astringent, tender, biting, dry, and humorous. His splendid Suite for Piano (Op. 14, 1911) shows his mastery of old dance forms. The ballet scores *Le Festin de l'araignée (The Spider's Feast,* Op. 17, 1913) and *Bacchus et Ariane* (Op. 43, 1931) are vibrant and pictorial, while the Third and Fourth Symphonies are among the finest contributions to the French symphony.

Symphony no. 3 in G Minor, Op. 42 (1930)
Detroit Symphony Orchestra, Järvi: Chandos CHAN 8996
New York Philharmonic Orchestra, Bernstein: Sony Classical MHK 62352

Symphony no. 4 in A Major, Op. 53 (1934)
Detroit Symphony Orchestra, Järvi: Chandos CHAN 9072
Orchestre National de France, Munch: Valois 4832

FRANZ LEHÁR

(1870–1948) Hungary

After writing several mediocre operas, Lehár found his real metier in operettas. He composed more than twenty examples. *Der Graf von Luxemburg (The Count of Luxembourg,* 1909), *Das Land des Lächelns (The Land of Smiles,* 1929), and above all, the radiant *Die lustige Witwe (The Merry Widow,* 1905), with its beguiling melodies, are in a class near Strauss's *Die Fledermaus.* Lehár also composed many waltzes, such as the ravishing "Gold and Silver," that continue to give enjoyment.

Die lustige Witwe (*The Merry Widow*) (1905)
Schwarzkopf, Steffek, Gedda, Wächter, Philharmonia Orchestra and Chorus, Matačič: EMI Classics CDCB-47177

ALEXANDER VON ZEMLINSKY

(1871–1942) Austria

Zemlinsky worked in Vienna as a conductor and teacher as well as a composer; he was Schoenberg's early mentor. His complex late Romantic work was influential among Viennese composers in the first decades of the twentieth century. Berg paid homage to him by using a theme from Zemlinsky's *Lyric Symphony* (Op. 18, 1923) in his *Lyric Suite*. The *Lyric Symphony* is Zemlinsky's most-performed creation.

Lyric Symphony, Op. 18 (1923)
Söderström, Duesing, Berlin Radio Symphony Orchestra, Klee: Koch Schwann CD 311053

MAX REGER

(1873–1915) Germany

Almost fiendishly prolific in his short life, the German composer Reger was essentially a post-Romantic, with a scholastic penchant for Baroque and Classical forms. Many of his dense, often ponderous works are stuffed with notes and accidentals, resulting in fearsome-looking pages! He also wrote many smaller works of simple charm. Reger was arguably the most important variationist after Brahms. Rudolf Serkin championed and recorded the *Variations and Fugue on a Theme by J. S. Bach* (Op. 81, 1904), and the F minor piano concerto (Op. 114, 1910).

Some of his organ compositions have become staples for organists, and Rosalinde Haas has recorded the complete organ music on twelve CDs (MD+G MDG 3350 to MDG 3361). Recently Reger has received more attention in public performance as well as in recording. *Variations and Fugue on a Theme of J. A. Hiller* (Op. 100, 1907) is a good introduction and is one of Reger's most attractive larger compositions.

Variations and Fugue on a Theme of J. A. Hiller, Op. 100 (1907)
Bavarian Radio Symphony Orchestra, C. Davis: Orfeo C090841
Royal Concertgebouw Orchestra, Järvi: Chandos CHAN 8794

GUSTAV HOLST

(1874–1934) England

In what amounts to a personal credo, the self-effacing Holst told a friend, "It's a great thing to be a failure. If nobody likes your work, you have to go on just for the sake of the work. And you're in no danger of letting the public make you repeat yourself. Every artist ought to pray that he may not be 'a success.' If he's a failure he stands a good chance of concentrating upon the best work of which he's capable." Holst was anything but the fire-breather of his uncharacteristically bold orchestral work *The Planets* (Op. 32, 1914–18). He fits more comfortably into the English choral tradition, writing part songs for mixed voices and choral hymns. His opera *The Perfect Fool* (Op. 39), composed in 1918–22, mocks grand opera. One of his best orchestral scores, *Egdon Heath* (Op. 47, 1927), was booed when Pierre Monteux first conducted it in Paris and it never gained popularity. Holst was convinced that *Egdon Heath* and his *First Choral Symphony* (Op. 41, 1923–24), not *The Planets*, were his finest achievements. In his student days, he formed a deep friendship with Vaughan Williams, whose insight into English folksong helped wean Holst from his early heavily Romantic style. Later in life, Eastern philosophy, the ancient Indic language, and Sanskrit interested him. Standing between Elgar and Vaughan Williams, Holst holds a special place in English music.

The kaleidoscopic *Planets* has seven movements: "Mars, the Bringer of War"; "Venus, the Bringer of Peace"; "Mercury, the Winged Messenger"; "Jupiter, the Bringer of Jollity"; "Saturn, the Bringer of Old Age"; "Uranus, the Magician"; and "Neptune, the Mystic," which ends in an offstage, wordless women's chorus. Holst composed these movements during World War I. Earth itself is not depicted, and Pluto had not yet been discovered when Holst conceived the cycle. The first public performance took place in 1919 with Adrian Boult conducting. During his career, Boult recorded it eleven times.

The Planets, Op. 32 (1914–18)

London Philharmonic Orchestra, Boult: EMI Classics CDM 64748
Montreal Symphony Orchestra, Dutoit: London 417553-2
Royal Philharmonic Orchestra, Previn: Telarc CD 80133

CHARLES IVES

(1874–1954) United States

Ives's life has taken on an almost mythic cast. He has become something of a New England "Yankee" folk hero—a curmudgeon and misunderstood genius living in an isolated cultural wasteland surrounded by brutes and mediocrity. Ives suffered from poor health and constant musical disappointment, and he eventually stopped composing and went into the insurance business. He even wrote a book on insurance: the iconoclastic Ives had many radical and intriguing ideas on property and government. Finally, after years of severe neglect, his music started being played in the 1940s. For his centenary in 1974, every orchestra in America and some in Europe seemed finally to be giving him proper recognition. But since then "live" performances of his extraordinary work have declined alarmingly, and one must rely on recordings to hear it.

Ives was a true innovator, and the first American composer to venture into uncharted regions of sound. It seems incredible that his music was composed against the background of the genteel East Coast composers' establishment (such as Edward MacDowell, Horatio Parker, and Henry Holden Huss). If ever a man was frustrated with the music of his day, it was Ives. He wanted to "kick out the softy ears" and shouted, "Stand up and use your ears like a man." As the twentieth century dawned, Ives the musical pioneer was using polytonality, tone clusters, aspects of atonality, quarter-tones, and much more. For creative pianists, the two mammoth sonatas are fascinating. In 1939 Lawrence Gilman called the Piano Sonata no. 2 (1909–15), subtitled *Concord, Mass., 1840–1890*, "the greatest music composed by an American." Ives viewed his performers as partners in creation. "In fact," he wrote, "these notes, marks, and near pictures of sounds, etc. are for the player to make his own speeches on."

His work—particularly *Central Park in the Dark* (1898–1907), *The Unanswered Question* (1906), and *A Symphony: Holidays* (1904–13)—is breathtakingly original, bizarre, quirky, and often unexpectedly touching.

Sonata no. 2 for Piano (*Concord, Mass., 1840–1890*) (1909–15)
Kalish: Elektra/Nonesuch 71337-2-J

Symphony no. 4 (1910–16)
Chicago Symphony Orchestra and Chorus, Tilson Thomas: Sony Classical SK 44939

JOSEF SUK

(1874–1935) Czech Republic

Suk is especially powerful in his epic Second Symphony, *Asrael* (Op. 27, 1905–6). At nineteen he composed a piano piece, "Love Song" (Op. 7/1), that became popular. Later his music grew more cryptic in such piano cycles as *Things Lived and Dreamed* (Op. 30, 1909). Suk was married to Dvořák's daughter, and from 1892 to 1933 he was second violinist in the Czech Quartet. He was professor of composition at the Prague Conservatory from 1922 until his retirement.

Symphony No. 2 in C Minor (*Asrael*), Op. 27 (1905–6)
Russian State Symphony Orchestra, Svetlanov: Russian Disc RCDC 11011

Serenade in E-flat Major for String Orchestra, Op. 6 (1892)
Orpheus Chamber Orchestra: Deutsche Grammophon 447109-2

REINHOLD GLIÈRE

(1875–1956) Russia

Glière, who was of Belgian descent, was a talented disciple of the great Russian nationalist tradition. In the Soviet Union in 1938, he was elevated to master status—a "people's artist" who upheld nineteenth-century Russian nationalism against twentieth-century Western decadence. He was born at a time when late-nineteenth-century Russian Romanticism still had something left of its potent flavor. Unfortunately, through the years his music became more and more fabricated and vapid. But his best work is patently effective in its smooth lyricism, peppered with Russian color, and there are still devotees of his *Red Poppy* ballet (1927), with its "Russian Sailors' Dance," and of the overripe Third Symphony (Op. 42, 1909–11).

Symphony No. 3 in B Minor (*Il'ya Muromets*), Op. 42 (1909–11)
BBC Philharmonic Orchestra, Downes: Chandos CHAN 9041

FRITZ KREISLER

(1875–1962) Austria

As with most successful performers, Kreisler's gifts appeared early, and his success throughout his career was constant; indeed, he was one of the most appreciated and beloved violinists in history. For many years, he perpetuated a hoax. He told the world he had discovered a treasure trove of neglected music by Vivaldi, Padre Martini, Gaetano Pugnani, and others—a whole slew of forgotten eighteenth-century composers—when in fact they were his own pieces, dressed in antique garments. It caused much comment, and in 1935 the New York critic Olin Downes brought the fun to an end by exposing the hoax. Kreisler took it casually, telling all that these gross imitations, the dessert of his recitals, would have been less appreciated if the public had known he composed them. His questionable ethics were quickly forgiven, and both his "fakes" and his own original pieces still give enjoyment. In our more sophisticated day, we find that the fakes have almost nothing specific in style to their alleged composers, whose names Kreisler doubtless culled from a dictionary.

Original Pieces and Transcriptions for Violin
Szeryng, C. Reiner: Mercury 434351-2
Perlman, Sanders: EMI Classics CDC 47467

JOHN ALDEN CARPENTER

(1876–1951) United States

Carpenter was that rare creature, a man who managed to combine composing and a career in business (from 1909 to 1936). He was a conservative composer strongly influenced by impressionism, but he wrote with flair. The Concertino for Piano and Orchestra (1915), Danza for Orchestra (1937), and the ballets *Krazy Kat* (1921) and *Skyscrapers* (1923–29) are especially fetching. His best-known score is the 1914 suite *Adventures in a Perambulator*. Today Carpenter is seldom performed, but his charm and his breezy humor are real.

Adventures in a Perambulator (suite) (1914)
Eastman-Rochester Orchestra, Hanson: Mercury 434319-2

MANUEL DE FALLA

(1876–1946) Spain

Falla was born to cultivated parents; his mother was his first piano teacher. He concentrated on becoming a pianist until 1902, when he met Felipe Pedrell, the legendary teacher of Albéniz and Granados. Pedrell's impact on Falla was decisive and electric.

Like other Spanish artists of the time, Falla wanted to visit Paris. He arrived in the French capital in 1907, intending to stay for a short time. But Paris enchanted and stimulated him, and he remained for seven years. There he found his compatriot Albéniz desperately ill, and he dedicated to Albéniz his glorious set of piano pieces, Four *Pièces espagnoles* (1902–8).

At the beginning of the war, he returned to Spain. His ballet *El Amor brujo* was first performed in Madrid in 1915, and contains the obsessive *Ritual Fire Dance*, the most famous piece Falla composed. The score shows Falla's astounding mastery of Gypsy and Spanish elements. The year 1916 saw the first performance of the bewitching and atmospheric *Noches en los jardines de España* (*Nights in the Gardens of Spain*), with its taut piano part as a foil for lustrous orchestration.

The early deaths of Albéniz in 1909 and Granados in 1916 left Falla as Spain's leading composer. On July 22, 1919, his ballet *El Sombrero de tres picos* (*The Three-Cornered Hat*), commissioned by Diaghilev, was premiered in London (with costumes and scenery by Picasso and choreography by Léonide Massine) with enormous success. That year he also completed the large solo piano work *Fantasía bética* (*Bética* being the Roman name for present-day Andalusia). *Bética* is a work of scorching power, a bleak vision of Spanish antiquity, composed for Arthur Rubinstein.

During the 1920s Falla's always-slow production slowed further. In 1923 came the premiere of *El Retablo de maese Pedro* (*Master Peter's Puppet Show*), a "puppet opera" based on an episode in *Don Quixote*. Falla's work was becoming spare and more brittle. His striving for economy and purity of sound made his musical language seem starkly brutal compared with Albéniz's and Granados's Romanticism. His last important work, the Harpsichord Concerto (begun in 1923 and completed in 1926), has nothing in common with the lush *Nights in the Gardens of Spain*. The concerto's scoring is frugal, making use only of a flute, oboe, clarinet, violin, cello, and harpsichord.

In 1936, at the outset of the Spanish Civil War, the fatal shooting of his dear friend the poet Federico García Lorca by Franco's soldiers brought home to Falla the terrors of their uprising. But during the tumult of the war, Falla, a fervent Catholic, took no side, wishing to uphold traditional Spanish Catholicism. Unable to live any longer in his beloved country, he left for Argentina, never to return. He composed little after 1936 and left unfinished at his death (in 1946) a kind of epic cantata he had begun in 1926.

Falla was an austere man. People who knew him found him either saintly or difficult and hypochondriacal, with beliefs that were a strange mixture of deep faith and absurd superstition. He was especially fearful of the effects of the full moon. Stravinsky, himself devoutly religious, wrote that Falla's "nature was the most unpityingly religious I have ever known and the least sensible to manifestations of humor." He left only a handful of works, but each one is master-ful, perfectly chiseled, exhibiting the musical soul of his homeland.

El Amor brujo (Love the Magician) (ballet in one act) (1915)
Tourangeau, Montreal Symphony Orchestra, Dutoit: London 430703-2

El Sombrero de tres picos (The Three-Cornered Hat) (ballet in two scenes) (1919)
DeGaetani, New York Philharmonic Orchestra, Boulez: Sony Classical SMK 68333

Noches en los jardines de España (Nights in the Gardens of Spain) for Piano and Orchestra (1909–15)
de Larrocha, Montreal Symphony Orchestra, Dutoit: London 430703-2
Rubinstein, San Francisco Symphony Orchestra, Jorda: RCA 60046-2-RG

ERNÖ VON DOHNÁNYI

(1877–1960) Hungary

Dohnányi was once labeled the "Hungarian Brahms." For many years his works received more performances than those of Kodály or Bartók. He was a great musician, an influential teacher, and one of the leading pianists of the world until around 1940. Today it is the 1914 *Variations on a Nursery Song* (Op. 25) that keeps his name alive in the international repertoire. The work, for piano and orchestra, was made "for the enjoyment of lovers of humor and the annoyance of others," the composer explained. After the portentous intro-duction, we hear the French nursery rhyme "Ah, vous dirai-je, maman" and are treated to eleven variations of impressive inventiveness. But there is more to Dohnányi than this score. Writing of his chamber music, the English critic Donald Francis Tovey stated, "In his compositions we have art in which the form arises organically from the matter. We also have mastery, describable in academic terms and traceable beyond anything that academies have codified."

Quintet no. 1 in C Minor for Piano and Strings, Op. 1 (1895)
Manz, Gabrieli String Quartet: Chandos CHAN 8718

Variations on a Nursery Song for Piano and Orchestra, Op. 25 (1914)
Katchen, London Symphony Orchestra, Solti: London 448604-2

OTTORINO RESPIGHI

(1879–1936) Italy

Respighi, who came from a musical family, developed into a good violinist at Bologna's Liceo Musicale, where he acquired diplomas in violin playing and composition. In 1900 he got a position in St. Petersburg, playing viola in the opera orchestra. In the Russian capital, he studied composition and orchestration with Rimsky-Korsakov, from whom he learned many secrets of orchestral writing. Before returning to Italy, he spent some time in Berlin working with Bruch. From 1903 until 1908, he played violin as a member of the Mugellini String Quintet. During these years he also composed a good deal and received some recognition.

In 1917, Toscanini conducted his symphonic poem *Le Fontane di Roma* (*The Fountains of Rome*), first in Italy and later in America. This piece brought Respighi international recognition. Seven years later, another symphonic poem, the sumptuous *I Pini di Roma* (*The Pines of Rome*) rivaled *The Fountains* in popularity.

Although his best works are instrumental, Respighi, a true Italian, did not neglect the stage. He composed nine operas, of which a lyric comedy, *Belfagor* (1921–22), became well known for a short time. In the 1930s—a period when Italian composers such as Alfredo Casella, Gian Francesco Malipiero, and Ildebrando Pizzetti were also composing important music—Respighi was Italy's best-known composer. Respighi and his colleagues were intent on unearthing their early Italian heritage of instrumental music, from Monteverdi to Vivaldi, and composing instrumental music as well. Respighi died of a heart attack at age fifty-six. His funeral, a national occasion, was attended by the king and by Mussolini.

Besides his symphonic poems, he wrote fifty songs and a fine violin sonata (1916–17). He was a brilliant adapter and arranger of other composers' music. His ballet *La Boutique fantasque*, composed for Diaghilev, was first produced in London in 1919 to overwhelming success. It is based on Rossini piano pieces, and Respighi's orchestration is scintillating. Respighi had a painter's eye. *The Fountains of Rome* is a brilliant evocation of four of Rome's most famous fountains. *The Pines of Rome* is even more fulsome than *The Fountains*; in it, Respighi paints the great pine trees that grow in various places in the city. He learned well from Rimsky-Korsakov's bright orchestrations, as well as from the symphonic poems of Richard Strauss. But these influences are always buttressed by his own piquant touches, and by a deep awareness of Debussy's impressionist harmony. Respighi, when not slick and banal, displays an irresistible and cunning virtuosity that gives his work a sure-fire appeal and pictorial directness. Several of his orchestral scores are literally textbooks of orchestral effects, and as such they have been used by many lesser composers for their excursions into "realistic" tone painting.

Le Fontane di Roma (The Fountains of Rome) (1914–16)
London Symphony Orchestra, Kertész: London 425507-2
Minneapolis Symphony Orchestra, Dorati: Mercury Living Presence 432007-2
Montreal Symphony Orchestra, Dutoit: London 410145-2

La Boutique fantasque (ballet) (1918)
Academy of St. Martin in the Fields, Marriner: Philips 420485-2
Boston Pops Orchestra, Fiedler: RCA 61847

I Pini di Roma (The Pines of Rome) (1923–24)
Philadelphia Orchestra, Ormandy: GBS MYK 38485
Atlanta Symphony Orchestra, Lane: Telarc CD 80085

FRANK BRIDGE
(1879–1941) England

The English composers John Ireland, Peter Warlock, Constant Lambert, and Cyril Scott all wrote consequential music. But among this group, Frank Bridge, Benjamin Britten's teacher, stands out as one of the extraordinary musicians of his generation. After World War I, his work took on a deeper cast than its conventional nationalism of before the war. For example, the 1921–24 Piano Sonata, Bridge's reaction to the horrors of the war, is arguably the finest English piano sonata of the 1920s. It is harsh, nervous, and introspective, at times agonizing in its tragic impact. The sonata, like Bridge's chamber music, took on more dissonance than had his earlier pieces, including at times polytonality—but it was always tailored in intelligible forms.

Suite for String Orchestra (1908)
English Chamber Orchestra, Tate: EMI Classics CDM 64200

Quartet no. 3 for Strings (1926)
Endellion String Quartet: Virgin Classics CDC 59026

NIKOLAI MEDTNER

(1880–1951) Russia

Medtner is an important composer who nevertheless remains at the fringes of the repertoire. Most admired for his fourteen piano sonatas and smaller piano pieces, he also composed three fine piano concertos and dozens of songs. Many find him to be a more intellectual Rachmaninoff who lacks the immediacy of Rachmaninoff's melodic gift. But Medtner can offer music of a penetrating and grave beauty, beautifully chiseled and rhythmically subtle. Early in the century, the critic Ernest Newman described his music as "not always easy to follow at first hearing, but not because of any extravagance of thought or confusion of technique; it is simply because this music really does go on thinking from bar to bar, evolving logically from its premises."

Concerto no. 2 in C Minor for Piano and Orchestra, Op. 50 (1920–27)
Demidenko, BBC Scottish Symphony Orchestra, Maksymiuk: Hyperion CDA 66580

ERNEST BLOCH

(1880–1959) Switzerland

Bloch was born into a family of Swiss Jews. His mother bought him a flute when he was six, but the family frowned upon music as a profession. Bloch was already fourteen when he had his first formal musical studies. At seventeen he went to Brussels to study with the great violinist Eugène Ysaÿe, but it was already too late for him to build a virtuoso violin technique. Composing started to occupy most of his time, and by 1902 he had completed a symphony that won the admiration and encouragement of Romain Rolland, the novelist and biographer of Beethoven. Under family pressure, Bloch entered the family's clock business, but he continued to compose. By 1910 the thirty-year-old composer's opera *Macbeth* (1904–9) was performed at the Paris Opera. Around 1912 Bloch, who had previously been influenced by Wagner, Richard Strauss, and Franck, began composing music inspired by Jewish sources.

"It is the Jewish soul that interests me," he wrote, "the complex, glowing, agitated soul that I feel vibrating throughout the Bible . . . the sacred emotion of the race that slumbers far down in our soul." During the next few years, he composed his *Israel Symphony* (1912–16), the *Baal Shem Suite* (1923), and above all the celebrated *Schelomo* for cello and orchestra (1915–16). He emigrated to the United States in 1916 and became the director of the Cleveland Institute of Music in 1920, and later the director of the San Francisco Conservatory (1925–30). In the United States, he composed many works of non-Jewish inspiration such as the Piano Quintet no. 1 (1921–23), Concerto Grosso no. 1 (1924–25), and the remarkable five string quartets (1916, 1945, 1952, 1953, 1956). They are very neglected, but they are among the most magnificent string quartets of the twentieth century. Bloch's music, like the man himself, was brooding, introspective, and passionately intense. He used his art to probe his psychological states. His seventy-five published compositions are clearly the work of an artist of lofty feeling, often with an agonized sense of suffering humanity.

Schelomo (Hebrew rhapsody) for Cello and Orchestra (1915–16)
Feuermann, Philadelphia Orchestra, Stokowski: Biddulph LAB 042
Rostropovich, Orchestre National de France, Bernstein: EMI Classics CDC 49307

GEORGE ENESCU

(1881–1955) Romania

The best-known Romanian composer, Enescu had a remarkable career. He was long acknowledged as a violinist of the first rank, and he was also a first-rate pianist and an inspiring teacher. After an early musical education in Vienna (1888–93), he absorbed French influences while studying at the Paris Conservatory with André Gédalge and Fauré. The full value of his music has never been appreciated except for the two *Romanian Rhapsodies* (Op. 11, 1901), of which No. 1 in A major is world famous. Composed when he was twenty, it subsequently eclipsed his other work. He spent a decade on his opera *Oedipe* (Op. 23, 1921–31), which contains Romanian folk elements bound to an impressionist technique. The opera is subtle and worthy of study.

Yehudi Menuhin, who studied with Enescu, said, "He was unique and unapproachable as a musician; a delicate mixture of elements . . . with the folk and Gypsy roots of Rumania and Hungary blended with the high cultivation of Western Europe. Enescu, the man, was a true aristocrat: polished, educated, refined, and a musician the likes of whom I have never seen equaled, with a musical memory that cannot be described."

Romanian Rhapsodies nos. 1 and 2, Op. 11 (1901)
London Symphony Orchestra, Dorati: Mercury 432015-2 and 434326-2

Sonata no. 3 in A Minor for Violin and Piano, Op. 25 (1926)
Menuhin, Menuhin: Biddulph LAB 066

KAROL SZYMANOWSKI

(1882–1937) Poland

Szymanowski has never quite achieved the recognition he deserves. He produced highly significant work throughout his career, notably a large amount of piano music, three symphonies (Opp. 15, 19, 27, 1906–16), two violin concertos (Opp. 35, 61, 1916, 1933), the *Stabat Mater* (Op. 53, 1926), two string quartets (Opp. 37, 56, 1917, 1927), the opera *King Roger* (Op. 46, 1924), and numerous songs. Also remarkable are the Twenty Mazurkas for piano (Op. 50, 1924–25) and the *Symphonie concertante* for piano and orchestra (Op. 60, 1932). His art is often florid and heavily textured, exuding a fairy-tale atmosphere with hypnotic rhythms and floating textures. Yet he can also be biting and fairly dissonant, making it difficult to categorize his various styles. Early influences of Scriabin, Richard Strauss, and Reger give way to music of a rare and individual personality.

Concerto no. 1 for Violin and Orchestra, Op. 35 (1916)
Oistrakh, Leningrad Philharmonic Orchestra, Sanderling: Forlane FRL 16589
Juliet, Montreal Symphony Orchestra, Dutoit: London 436837-2

JOAQUÍN TURINA

(1882–1949) Spain

Turina is a delightful composer of picturesque music, offering authentic Spanish rhythms and colors. Although a regionalist, he studied in Paris with d'Indy, who gave him an unusual grasp of his material and assured him a depth beyond the touristic picture-postcard type of Spanish music. Although he is not of the rank of Albéniz or Falla, his best music deserves more frequent performance.

Danzas fantásticas, Op. 22 (1920)
Bamberg Symphony Orchestra, Almeida: RCA 09026-60895-2

PERCY GRAINGER

(1882–1961) Australia

Grainger's reputation and musical stock have risen greatly in the past two decades. His music definitely speaks louder and more joyously than ever; its bracing goodwill and generally folklike character give it a multicultural flavor. Grainger wanted to bring "all the world's music to all the world." He grew up in colonial British Australia, in a young country that heralded democratic ideals, which stayed with him forever.

At the beginning of the twentieth century, Grainger was the golden boy of the pianistic world. His playing created a sensation; Grieg wrote that it was "like the sun breaking through the clouds." Grainger also participated in the vigorous folksong collecting that was taking place in many countries. The fear that industrialization would destroy the great repository of folksong was a real concern of Cecil Sharp, Vaughan Williams, Bartók, Kodály, Pedrell, and many other composers.

Grainger loved with an exuberant passion folk music of every context, and he was convinced that European civilization had become artistically too rarefied, having lost its earthiness and animal vitality. He disliked the intellectuality of the sonata form and often actively denounced the Viennese Classical school, having a special temperamental antipathy toward Beethoven. His music exploited folk music of many nations, in many instrumental combinations (often using xylophone, saxophone, marimba, harmonium, and many other "exotic" instruments). Some of his best-known folksong settings for piano are *Country Gardens* (1918), *Shepherd's Hey* (1911), *Spoon River* (1919–22), and *Molly on the Shore* (1918). The *Colonial Song* (1914), Grainger's finest tribute to the land of his birth, gives expression to feelings aroused by the landscape of Australia.

As a pianist, Grainger was unapproachable in his own music; the keyboard sizzles and spurts, and the punch of his playing, its rhythmic dynamism, is inimitable. From 1915 he lived in the United States.

Piano Works
Grainger: Nimbus NI 8809

Orchestral Works
Bournemouth Sinfonietta, Montgomery: Chandos CHAN 6542

ZOLTÁN KODÁLY

(1882–1967) Hungary

Both of Kodály's parents were amateur musicians. His father was a railroad master, and the composer later said his first teachers were his father's violin, the music of Gypsies, and the rhythms of the great trains. Without much knowledge of harmony, the teenage boy started composing. After high school, he received a scholarship to the university in Budapest. At the same time, he took a few courses at Budapest's Academy of Music, where he met Béla Bartók in 1905.

Both young musicians were absorbed in Hungarian folk materials, which they hoped would free Hungarian music from the all-pervading German influence. At the time, to most outsiders, Hungarian music meant little more than Brahms's *Hungarian Dances*, Gypsy tunes, and Liszt's *Hungarian Rhapsodies*. Together Kodály and Bartók took to the countryside, collecting and writing down the Magyar folk melodies they uncovered by the thousands.

In these early years, Kodály also composed a string quartet (Op. 2, 1908–9), the Sonata for Cello and Piano (Op. 4, 1909–10), and seven Piano Pieces (Op. 11, 1910), all showing an ear for Debussy's impressionist innovations. These early works found advocates, and Kodály began to be performed outside of Hungary as well.

In the 1920s his reputation continued to grow. The choral work *Psalmus hungaricus* (Op. 13, 1923), based on a sixteenth-century text, is one of his most profound scores. *Háry János* (Op. 15), a delightful folk opera, was an instant hit when premiered in Budapest in October 1926. The ebullient Háry János is a character in Hungarian folklore, a beloved scoundrel, and a liar in the grand manner. Kodály's folk opera about him is Hungary's most-loved national opera.

Besides composing and teaching composition at the Budapest Academy, Kodály made other indelible contributions to music education: for one, he devised an ingenious system of sight-singing that became renowned as the Kodály method.

Kodály and Bartók would forever remain linked to Magyar folk music. Bartók became increasingly more experimental and dissonant, while Kodály, by nature more conservative, changed little musically during his long life. His C major symphony (1930–61), completed at eighty, sounds younger than his early works. Essentially he was a rhapsodic bard. His music is never trite, and its buoyancy and energy are invigorating. At times he transports the listener back to a remote past, a fairy-tale Hungary, where the air is clear and the peasants are dancing and happy.

Háry János Suite (1926)
Seattle Symphony Orchestra, Schwarz: Delos DE 3083
Cleveland Orchestra, Szell: CBS MYK 38527

Variations on a Hungarian Folksong (*The Peacock*) (1938–39)
Chicago Symphony Orchestra, Dorati: Mercury 434397
Vienna Philharmonic Orchestra, Solti: London 452853-2

ANTON WEBERN

(1883–1945) Austria

Webern's art has been a most significant influence on post–World War II composition. Indeed, it cannot be overestimated. Webern wrote thirty-two compositions, fifteen of which adopt Schoenberg's twelve-tone technique. For listeners conversant with twelve-tone music, Webern's work is not only subtle but poetic, pure, and lyrical. Webern is a "radical" in his extreme paring down of music to its bare essentials. In Eric Salzman's words, "The minimum materials are endowed with their maximum meaning." Francis Routh writes, "Tonality had been the chief means of creating unity and of building a musical structure. Before tonality, this had been achieved by polyphony; now, to use Webern's words, 'Just as ripe fruit falls from the tree, music has quite simply given up the formal principle of tonality.' "

All of Webern's serial or twelve-tone music is intense and aphoristic, a perfect geometry of sounds related only to each other. He took the elements of pitch, rhythm, duration of note values, and rests and totally predetermined their place in the musical scheme. Webern's obsession with formal purity and sound for its own sake attracted Stravinsky, Boulez, Babbitt, Stockhausen, and many others as well, as a means to new musical adventure.

Webern's earliest composition, the Passacaglia for Orchestra (Op. 1, 1908), is an intense post-Wagnerian affair. The Six Pieces for Orchestra (Op. 6, 1909), the Six Bagatelles for String Quartet (Op. 9, 1911–13), and other works that preceded the adoption of twelve-tone technique are expressionist, yet they differed from those of Webern's teacher, Schoenberg, and his close friend Alban Berg. At the end of World War II, while going out to get cigarettes after the curfew, Webern was shot in the back by an American serviceman.

Passacaglia for Orchestra, Op. 1 (1908)
Six Pieces for Orchestra, Op. 6 (1909)
Symphony for Chamber Orchestra, Op. 21 (1928)
Berlin Philharmonic Orchestra, Karajan: Deutsche Grammophon 423254-2

Variations for Piano, Op. 27 (1936)
Pollini: Deutsche Grammophon 447431-2

SIR ARNOLD BAX

(1883–1953) England

Bax called himself "a brazen romantic—by which I mean that my music is the expression of emotional states. I have no interest whatever in sound for its own sake, or in any modernist 'isms or factions." The chief influence on his work was his love for Irish landscape, folklore, and all things Celtic. In 1942, he became "master of the king's music," an honor he retained until his death. During the war, he composed one of the finest of all film scores, for director David Lean's *Oliver Twist*. Those who find Bax's rhapsodic, nature-loving music appealing will be most rewarded by many pages of his seven symphonies, composed between 1921 and 1939. His more accessible symphonic poems, such as *Tintagel* (1917–19), *The Garden of Fand* (1913–16), *November Woods* (1917), and *Overture to a Picaresque Comedy* (1930), are moody and memorable.

Tintagel (1917–19)
Philharmonia Orchestra, Barbirolli: EMI Classics CPM 65110

ALFREDO CASELLA

(1883–1947) Italy

Casella was a musician of wide outlook and fierce integrity. In his early music, one hears the strong influence of post-Romantic composers; these works are reminiscent of the restlessness of Busoni, and Casella often used neoclassical schemes informed by Bach. Such works as the *Due Ricercari sul nome BACH* (*Two Ricercari on the Name BACH*, Op. 52, 1932) are darkly intense. He experimented with polytonality and even atonality but bowed to the seductions of impressionism and Debussy in the outstanding piano piece *A notte alta* (Op. 30, 1917). His later work was brighter and used aspects of his Italian heritage.

Paganiniana for Orchestra, Op. 65 (1942)
La Scala Orchestra, Muti: Sony Classical SK 53280

EDGARD VARÈSE

(1883–1965) France

Varèse was born in Paris, where he studied mathematics and science, as well as conducting with Vincent d'Indy and composition, counterpoint, and fugue with Albert Roussel at the Schola Cantorum. Meeting Busoni in 1909 greatly influenced his thinking. Moving to New York in 1915, he was fascinated by the sounds of the city. Varèse already dreamed of a new music. "In my own work," he wrote, "I have always felt the need of new mediums of expression. I refuse to submit myself to sounds that have already been heard." By 1937 the sounds at his disposal no longer filled his need, and Varèse stopped composing.

In the early 1950s, with the advent of electronic reproduction, Varèse set to work again, now calling himself "a worker in intensities, frequencies and rhythms." At the 1958 Brussels World Fair, his *Poème électronique*, a composition entirely for tape, performed through hundreds of tiny speakers, helped inaugurate the tape-electronic music to come. He suppressed all of his work composed before the 1920s. Each of his dozen published scores represents a unique musical thinker, a courageous path-breaker, creating music that broadened the *sound* possibilities of the art.

His works fall more or less into three groups. The first are those that have some link with this century's musical production, such as *Offrandes* for soprano and small orchestra (1921), which stems from the most atmospheric French impressionism. *Amériques* for orchestra (1918–22) celebrates his new country, and the stunning orchestral *Arcana* (1925–27) calls for 120 musicians, with eight percussionists playing forty percussion instruments.

The second group are those that depart from known melodic and harmonic procedures: *Hyperprism* (1922–23), *Octandre* (1923), and *Ecuatorial* (1933–34). *Ionisation* (1929–31), for thirty-five percussion instruments, scandalized music lovers when first heard in 1931. The last piece of this second group was the expressive *Density 21.5* for flute (1936). The third period began with *Déserts* for fourteen winds, piano, percussion, and taped sounds (1950–54), a work of haunting power. All of his music has been recorded, but it is infrequently performed.

Arcana for Orchestra (1925–27)
Royal Concertgebouw Orchestra, Chailly: London 436640-2

CHARLES TOMLINSON GRIFFES

(1884–1920) United States

In the words of the critic Lawrence Gilman, Griffes lacked "the priceless instinct for publicity." He led a difficult life, fighting hard for a livelihood and for the small recognition he achieved. He was the most sensitive impressionist tone-poet America ever produced. The American composer Deems Taylor called his early death, at thirty-five, "the greatest musical loss this country has sustained." He left only a handful of precious works. His most popular piece is the evocative *The White Peacock* (1915); his most painful and frenzied score is the masterful Piano Sonata (1917–18), which fully reveals the composer's magnificent ear for piano sonority and color. Wilfrid Mellers thinks, "This disturbingly powerful sonata is an American parable in musical terms telling us what happens to the ego alone in the industrial wilderness." In his half dozen years of musical maturity, Griffes absorbed all of the most progressive tendencies of his time, merging them into a fully realized personal style.

Sonata for Piano (1917–18)
Tocco: Gasparo GS 233

The Pleasure Dome of Kubla Khan (Op. 8, 1917)
Boston Symphony Orchestra, Ozawa: New World NW 273-2

Poem for Flute and Orchestra (1918)
Mariano, Eastman-Rochester Orchestra, Hanson: Mercury 434307-2

GEORGE BUTTERWORTH

(1885–1916) England

Around 1904, Butterworth met Vaughan Williams and the folksong collector Cecil Sharp, both of whom introduced him to the English folksong heritage. From that moment, his art was English to the core, and his orchestral works *A Shropshire Lad* (1912) and *The Banks of Green Willow* (1913), as well as some of the songs, are engaging and nostalgic of a far-off time. Butterworth was killed at thirty-one, at the Battle of the Somme, and he maintains a small but special place in English music.

A Shropshire Lad (rhapsody) for Orchestra (1912)
Royal Liverpool Orchestra, Llewellyn: Argo 436401-2

MARCEL DUPRÉ

(1886–1971) France

By age twelve, Dupré was organist at the Church of Saint-Vivien in Rouen, his birthplace. At the Paris Conservatory from 1902 to 1914, he worked with the great organist Charles Widor. In 1920 all of musical Paris went to the conservatory to hear Dupré perform in ten recitals, from memory, the complete organ music of J. S. Bach; the feat had never before been accomplished. His success was repeated in London and in annual world tours. By 1953 Dupré had performed nearly two thousand organ recitals. In 1934 he succeeded Widor at the Saint-Sulpice Church in Paris.

The French organ tradition has a long history of secularization, and Dupré's performing and lordly improvisations enormously helped to bring his instrument to universal solo recital status. Dupré's ample output for organ is chromatically conceived and impressively idiomatic; the music is constructed as solidly as rock.

Organ Music
Dupré: Motette MOT 60011
Filsell: Guild GMCD 7131

HEITOR VILLA-LOBOS

(1887–1959) Brazil

Villa-Lobos learned his art haphazardly and as a result developed a lifelong aversion to conventional education. His first musical impressions came from his father, an amateur cellist, who taught him the cello. At sixteen the boy left home, wandering Brazil with his cello, earning a pittance wherever he could find work with a café orchestra. He took dangerous journeys down the Amazon River and was captivated by Brazilian popular music, dances, and Indian music that would influence his later compositions. Before Villa-Lobos, serious Brazilian music paid scant attention to the country's multiracial folk heritage of African, Portuguese, and indigenous Indian music.

For the next ten years, he struggled to master his musical materials. Contact with the young French composer Darius Milhaud, who was in Brazil as secretary to diplomat-poet Paul Claudel, was a revelation. Milhaud introduced Villa-Lobos to the music of Satie, Ravel, Stravinsky, and Schoenberg. Soon afterward, in 1918, he met the renowned pianist Arthur Rubinstein, who was performing in Rio and happened to hear a piece by Villa-Lobos. Rubinstein was captivated by its strange rhythms, sensuous melody, and lush textures and was soon performing Villa-Lobos's piano music and providing contacts to help his career. In 1926 Villa-Lobos would complete a large, colorful, and massive piano work, *Rudepoema* (*Rough Poem*), as a musical portrait of the pianist.

A government travel grant allowed Villa-Lobos to go to Paris for three years starting in 1923. In that year, the conductor Leopold Stokowski introduced his music to Paris. Slowly, throughout the 1920s, his music became known. He had evolved a new musical form derived from the *chôro*, a kind of ensemble piece popular in Rio. He called these works *chôros* and eventually produced fourteen examples, some of which require a battery of native percussion instruments. These pieces cleverly combine various types of Brazilian music.

In 1930 Villa-Lobos created another genre, which he titled *Bachiana brasileira*. Once again it is a synthesis, this time using counterpoint, combining Bachian flavor and Brazilian-sounding folk music (though, as always, his melodies are original). "A truly creative musician," the composer wrote, "is capable of producing, from his own imagination, melodies that are more authentic than folklore itself." The most famous of the nine *Bachiana brasileira* is No. 5, for soprano and eight cellos (1938–45). For many listeners throughout the world, the score has come to epitomize Brazilian music.

Villa-Lobos was amazingly prolific. It is estimated that he produced three thousand works, the majority of which are still in manuscript. That portion of his work that is known is uneven in quality. But some of his music is unique: strange, eerie, savage, exotic, and picturesque in the deepest sense. He created new sounds and painted immense and inhuman aspects of rain forests and jungles. Above all he contributed to Romantic nationalism in art music: it was Villa-Lobos alone who put Brazil on the world's musical map.

Bachiana brasileira no. 5 (1938–45)
Gomez, Pleeth Cello Octet: Hyperion CDA 66257
Hendricks, Royal Philharmonic, Bátiz: EMI Classics CDC 47433
Moffo, American Symphony Orchestra, Stokowski: RCA 7831-2-RG

Concerto for Guitar and Orchestra (1951)
Romero, Academy of St. Martin in the Fields, Marriner: Philips 416357-2
Bream, London Symphony Orchestra, Previn: RCA 6525-2-RG
Williams, English Chamber Orchestra, Barenboim: CBS M2K 44791

JACQUES IBERT

(1890–1962) France

Ibert's work is full of light charm and wit. A transparent and clever orchestrator, he wrote slender neoclassic chamber music; the Three *Pièces brèves* for wind quintet (1930) have become a "classic." *Histoires* (1922), a set of ten piano pieces, is characteristic; *The Little White Donkey* (1940) was once played with frequency. Also well known are the Flute Concerto (1934) and the infectious *Divertissement* for chamber orchestra (1930). Ibert could also be sensuous, as in *Escales* (*Ports of Call*, 1922), which describes Palermo, Tunis-Nefta, and Valencia.

Escales (1922)
Orchestre National de France, Martinon: EMI Classics CDM 64276

Three Pièces brèves (1930)
Pro Arte Wind Quintet: Nimbus NI 5327

BOHUSLAV MARTINŮ

(1890–1959) Czech Republic

Martinů left his east Bohemian homeland in 1923, and for seventeen years he lived in Paris, composing with passionate intensity. He eventually wrote more than four hundred compositions. In 1940 he made the United States his home, then returned to Europe in 1953. Although little Czech folk music appears in his work, one is very aware of its Czech nature. In a great deal of it, he used traditional forms modified by his demands; sonatas, trios, variations, and quartets abound, as do Baroque forms. The six symphonies and five piano concertos are very successful. All of his music possesses a tremendous impulse, but many of the works fizzle out for lack of sustained inspiration. Music obviously poured from him, and although he was a master craftsman, he was insufficiently self-critical.

Concerto for String Quartet and Orchestra (1931)
Cleveland Orchestra, C. von Dohnányi: London 443173-2

Sonata for Flute and Piano (1945)
Válek, Hála: Supraphon SUP 0096

Symphony no. 6 (*Fantaisies symphoniques*) (1951–53)
Czech Philharmonic Orchestra, Ančerl: Supraphon 11 1932

FRANK MARTIN
(1890–1974) Switzerland

Martin wrote music of compelling value. He composed in many media and forged his own passionate musical diction, which combined French clarity of texture with German harmonic idioms. From 1933 on, Martin integrated something of Schoenberg's twelve-tone system into his own highly emotional chromaticism. His rhythms are often original, such as the *Étude rhythmique* for piano (1965), an homage to the composer Émile Jaques-Dalcroze. In it, Martin demands a nine-eight meter from the right and a three-four meter from the left.

Mass for Double Chorus (1922–26)
Christ Church Cathedral Choir, Darlington: Nimbus NI 5197

Petite symphonie concertante (1944–45)
Orchestre de la Suisse Romande, Jordan: Erato 2292-45694-2

Le Mystère de la nativité (oratorio/spectacle) (1957–59)
Ameling, Heynis, Cuénod, Devos, Tappy, Orchestre de la Suisse Romande, Ansermet: Cascavelle CVL 2006

ARTHUR HONEGGER
(1892–1955) France

Honegger, a member of the Parisian composers' group Les Six, was born in Le Havre to Swiss parents. The 1921 oratorio *Le Roi David* (*King David*) brought him international renown. Honegger was versatile in form and idiom. He produced twenty-one stage works, forty-four film scores, thirteen piano works, fifty songs, and fifty chamber and symphonic pieces. His style emphasized counterpoint. He said that his model was always Bach, and a strong architectural sense is apparent in his works, which use rhythmic ostinatos, polytonality, and polyrhythms.

Pacific 231, a symphonic poem describing a locomotive (1923), is cleverly constructed on a *canto fermo* and once had a vogue. His works have received relatively few live performances since his death. The best of Honegger is in his five symphonies.

Le Roi David (dramatic psalm) (1921)

Davrath, Preston, Sorenson, Utah Symphony Orchestra, Abravanel: Vanguard Classics OVC 4038

Symphonies no. 1–5 (1930, 1941, 1945, 1946, 1951)

Toulouse Capitole Orchestra, Plasson: EMI Classics CDM 64274 and CDM 64275

FERDE GROFÉ

(1892–1972) United States

Like Gershwin, Grofé was brought up on popular music and jazz. He became an adroit pianist and arranger and worked with Paul Whiteman and his orchestra. It was Grofé who first orchestrated Gershwin's *Rhapsody in Blue* in 1924. (Gershwin was still a novice at the craft but later orchestrated it himself.) Grofé composed a good deal, but only his blockbuster *Grand Canyon Suite* (1931) is now performed. The score was often conducted and recorded by Toscanini and continues to be well represented in CD catalogs. Of the five movements, the languid, cowboylike atmosphere of the third movement, On the Trail, is best known. In the Kunzel rendition, the fifth movement, Cloudburst, utilizes an actual thunderstorm.

Grand Canyon Suite (1931)

Cincinnati Pops Orchestra, Kunzel: Telarc CD 80086
New York Philharmonic, Bernstein: CBS MYK 37759

DARIUS MILHAUD

(1892–1974) France

Milhaud was a member of the group of Parisian composers called Les Six. For years he taught composition, both at the Paris Conservatory and at Mills College in California. By the time of his death, he had written some fifteen hundred compositions. It will take a long time to sort out such a large oeuvre, but already there are many who think that Milhaud was one of the great French composers of the twentieth century.

He was a complex composer who incorporated many styles and devices into his work, even writing one electronic score, *Étude poétique*. He remains best known for his wonderful jazz-influenced ballet *La Création du monde* (Op. 81, 1923), for *Saudades do Brasil* (Op. 67, 1920–21), and for the infectious surreal ballet accompaniment to Cocteau's *Le Boeuf sur le toit* (Op. 58, 1919).

La Création du monde (ballet), **Op. 81 (1923)**
French National Orchestra, Bernstein: EMI Classics CDC 47845
Boston Symphony Orchestra, Munch: RCA 09026-60685-2

WALTER PISTON

(1894–1976) United States

The music of Walter Piston has aged extremely well. He is considered a stable academic composer; he taught at Harvard and wrote well-known textbooks on harmony and counterpoint. Piston was always well respected but was typecast as a bit stuffy. Upon investigation, however, his output is discovered to be not only impeccably crafted but deep, sane, virile, and satisfying. He was a confirmed Classicist, and most of his work fits into sonata form. He produced high-level music, almost all of it instrumental, crowned with his eight symphonies.

The Incredible Flutist (ballet) (1938)
St. Louis Symphony Orchestra, Slatkin: RCA 60798-2-RC

Symphony no. 4 (1950)
Philadelphia Orchestra, Ormandy: Albany TROY 256

MARIO CASTELNUOVO-TEDESCO

(1895–1968) Italy

Castelnuovo-Tedesco was born in Florence to Jewish parents and studied with the renowned composer Ildebrando Pizzetti. His work was often performed through the 1920s and 1930s and was much admired by Toscanini and Heifetz. It is music warm in tone, and impressionistic. His piano music derives from Chopin. He was influenced by various sorts of Italian music and was also interested in Spanish and Jewish folk music. Because of Mussolini's racial laws, he emigrated to the United States in 1939. Today, his best-known work, the Guitar Concerto no. 1, is a staple of that instrument's repertoire.

Piano Music
Ciccolini: Phoenix Classics 97301

Concerto no. 1 in D Major for Guitar and Orchestra, Op. 99 (1939)
Romero, Academy of St. Martin in the Fields, Marriner: Philips 416357-2

CARL ORFF

(1895–1982) Germany

Orff wrote textbooks on music education, invented percussion instruments for children, and devised gymnastic movements that were to be performed in combination with music. As a composer he is famous only for his dramatic cantata *Carmina burana* (1935–36), based on medieval Latin verse. Through its colorful timbres and primitivism, *Carmina burana* became one of the popular works of the twentieth century. Countless people have been drawn to "classical" music through its visceral, hypnotic rhythms and its power to invigorate. Parts of the score are heard everywhere, from television commercials to movies.

Carmina burana (scenic cantata) (1935–36)

Janowitz, Stolze, Fischer-Dieskau, Berlin German Opera Orchestra and Chorus, Jochum: Deutsche Grammophon Galleria 423886-2

Armstrong, English, Allen, London Symphony Orchestra and Chorus, St. Clement Danes Boys' Chorus, Previn: EMI Classics CDC-47411

VIRGIL THOMSON

(1896–1989) United States

Thomson was born in Kansas City and studied at Harvard and with Nadia Boulanger in Paris. He was in Paris during the 1920s and 1930s and took part in the wide cultural life of that city, meeting everyone from Picasso to Gertrude Stein, who would write the librettos for his operas *Four Saints in Three Acts* (1927–28) and *The Mother of Us All* (1947). From 1940 to 1954 Thomson, always a gifted prose stylist, wrote for the *New York Herald Tribune* the most clever, most perceptive, and most influential music criticism ever written in America. His music was influenced by a variety of sources: the Baptist hymns of his youth, the harmony of Debussy, and the insouciant style of Satie. It is simple sounding but at the same time complex in craft and highly polished; yet there is a blowsy, unfinished sense to some of his work, having none of the climactic energy of Copland. His music is exceptionally clever in the contrapuntal devices that garnish it, and its milklike diatonic framework is mixed here and there with a glassful of bitonal and polytonal syrups. If a taste for him is acquired, Thomson is appealing and can be unexpectedly refreshing. His operas are great theater and, if performed well, seldom fail to give pleasure. *Four Saints in Three Acts* is as madcap and exuberant today as it was when first performed in Hartford, Connecticut, in 1934. Thomson, a great wit, was once asked why he chose Paris over Germany to complete his studies: "I preferred to starve where the food is good," he replied.

Four Saints in Three Acts (opera) (1934)
Soloists, Orchestra of Our Time, Thome: Elektra/Nonesuch 79035-2

HOWARD HANSON

(1896–1981) United States

A native of Wahoo, Nebraska, Hanson was director of the Eastman School of Music in Rochester, New York, from 1924 to 1964 and conductor of the Eastman-Rochester Orchestra. He developed into a fine conductor who helped promote the cause of American music. He won the 1944 Pulitzer Prize (for his Fourth Symphony) and garnered thirty-five honorary degrees. The essential quality of Hanson's work is a vibrant, warm-hearted Romanticism, which seldom fails to stir listeners even though his conservative language has long been entirely out of fashion.

The Lament for Beowulf for Orchestra and Chorus, Op. 25 (1925)
Seattle Symphony Orchestra and Chorale, Schwarz: Delos DE 3105

Symphony no. 2 (Romantic) Op. 30 (1930)
Eastman-Rochester Orchestra, Hanson: Mercury 432008-2

ROGER SESSIONS

(1896–1985) United States

Sessions is a composer not necessarily friendly upon introduction but is well worth pursuing. Intellectual, formal, focused, and often lofty in thought, Sessions is certainly not an American master who found his roots in native soil.

All of his music demands penetrating listening, and the majority of his major works are technically difficult to perform. The three piano sonatas (1930, 1946, 1965) are tremendous contributions to the pianist's world. The pianist Rebecca La Brecque once said to the composer that she thought No. 1 was the most difficult of the three. Sessions responded, "If I practiced nothing else for two years, I could probably play my third sonata. If I practiced nothing else for one year, I could play my second sonata. If I wanted to play the first, I would have to be sixteen years old, maybe fourteen, and practice only Czerny,

Chopin, and Bach for the next twenty years." His nine symphonies (from 1927 to 1978) show much of his evolution and are among the most important symphonies composed in the United States.

Sessions wrote, "The key to the understanding of contemporary music lies in repeated hearing; one must hear it till it sounds familiar, until one begins to notice false notes if they are played: one must make the effort to retain in one's ear, and one will always find that the accurate memory of sounds heard coincides with the understanding of them. In fact, the power to retain sounds by memory implies that they have been mastered. For the ear by its nature seeks out patterns and relationships, and it is only these patterns that we can remember and that make music significant for us."

Concerto for Violin and Orchestra (1930–35)
Zukofsky, French Radio-TV Philharmonic Orchestra, Schuller: CRI CD 676

Sonata no. 1 for Piano (1930)
O'Reilly: Albany TROY 038

Symphonies no. 6 (1966), no. 7 (1967), and no. 9 (1978)
American Composers Orchestra, Davies: Argo 444519-2

ERICH WOLFGANG KORNGOLD

(1897–1957) Austria

Korngold, born in Brno, was the son of the Viennese music critic Julius Korngold. Reams of newspaper copy told of the young Korngold's prodigious exploits as a composer, and naturally he was hailed as the new Mozart. Artur Schnabel premiered the twelve-year-old's Piano Sonata no. 1 (1908), and the musical world was opened to him. When he was twenty-three, his sensational opera *Die tote Stadt* (Op. 12, 1920) played the major opera houses, and it remains an outstanding late Romantic opera. With Hitler's annexation of Austria, Korngold, like many other European artists, made Los Angeles his home. He proceeded to write some of the most memorable and invigorating film scores in Hollywood history, with a mastery of graphic orchestration that brought him wealth and two Academy Awards (for *The Adventures of Robin Hood* and *Anthony Adverse*). At the same time, he pursued his serious work in a lush post-Romantic manner. Perhaps his best composition from his American years is the Violin Concerto (Op. 35, 1945). For all of Korngold's late Romantic excesses, he was surprisingly unenterprising as a harmonist.

Concerto in D Major for Violin and Orchestra, Op. 35 (1945)
Heifetz, Los Angeles Philharmonic Orchestra, Wallenstein: RCA 7963-2-RG
Shaham, London Symphony Orchestra, Previn: Deutsche Grammophon 439886-2

ROY HARRIS

(1898–1979) United States

Harris is a major figure in American music, and his symphonies were land-marks in building an American school. Born in a log cabin in Lincoln County, Oklahoma, on Abraham Lincoln's birthday, he studied with Arthur Farwell, who had collected Native American folk music. In 1927, at Copland's sugges-tion, he sailed to Paris and studied composition with Nadia Boulanger. His out-put is fairly large and uneven; his harmonic language is basically tonal, with smatterings of polychords and dissonant content. His best music has a certain spaciousness and ruggedness, mixed with a meditative quality. His polyphonic writing and asymmetrical rhythms need close listening. For this listener, his Third Symphony (1937) is one of the significant symphonies of the twentieth century in America and anywhere.

Symphony no. 3 (1937)
New York Philharmonic Orchestra, Bernstein: Deutsche Grammophon 419780-2
Boston Symphony Orchestra, Koussevitzky: Pearl PEA 9492

SILVESTRE REVUELTAS

(1899–1940) Mexico

The short-lived Revueltas died on the night of the premiere of his ballet *El Re-nacuajo paseador*. Although he studied music as a child, he did not compose seriously until after he was thirty. He differs from Carlos Chávez, Mexico's other prominent composer, in his more apparent local Mexican flavor and his biting humor. But Revueltas is not a "touristic" composer by any means, and his work can be subtle and complex, as well as boisterous, depicting urban street life. His outstanding works are the *Homenaje a Federico García Lorca* (1935), whose exciting dance rhythms are laced with dissonance, and the ebul-lient tone poem *Sensemayá* (1938).

Homenaje a Federico García Lorca for Chamber Orchestra (1935)
Ensemble 21, Weisberg: Summit DCD 122

Music of Revueltas
Mexican State Symphony Orchestra, Lozano: Forlane FRL 16614

CARLOS CHÁVEZ

(1899–1978) Mexico

Chávez is indisputably Mexico's most revered composer. Usually dissonant, taut, and stoic, he also can be colorful and intensely nationalistic. His vision is fired with the internal throbbing of pre-Hispanic Mexico in such powerful orchestral works as the *Sinfonía india* (1935–36) and *Sinfonía de Antígona* (1933). Although he is primarily a symphonist, he also wrote much piano music, which requires an adventuresome pianist to perform. His ballets are also of interest, especially *Caballos de vapor* (*Horse Power*, 1926–27), with its finale, "Dance of Men and Machines." Diego Rivera designed the sets and costumes for the premiere of *Horse Power*. Like his friend Aaron Copland, Chávez had a populist period, but he was more secure as a composer in a more "difficult" idiom. In such works as the Piano Concerto (1938–40), he blended Mexican and abstract elements. In its day, the concerto was considered cacophonous; today we hear a work filled with color that evokes landscapes of ferocious power. "Chávez's music is extraordinarily healthy," Copland writes. "It is music created not as a substitute for living but as a manifestation of life. It is clear and clean-sounding, without shadows or softness. . . . It propounds no problems, no metaphysics."

Symphony no. 2 (*Sinfonía india*) (1935–36)
London Symphony Orchestra, Mata: Vox Box CDX 5061

GEORGE ANTHEIL

(1900–1959) United States

Antheil, born in Trenton, New Jersey, headed the 1920s musical avant-garde in Paris with his *Airplane Sonata* for Piano (1922) and the notorious *Ballet mécanique* (1923–25), which caused a riot. The poet Ezra Pound touted him as the ideal modern artist. Later his style calmed down, and in Hollywood he composed film scores and even books on criminology. He wrote a delightful autobiography, *Bad Boy of Music* (1945), filled with literary heroes and Hollywood celebrities. Antheil's music has dazzling moments of inspiration, rhythmic vitality, and instrumental brilliance. Few of his works are unblemished—trivial bridge passages often have a paste-up quality. But many of the works reveal a genuine zest and love of life.

A Jazz Symphony (1923–25)
New Palais Royale Orchestra, Peress: MusicMasters 01612-67094-2

KURT WEILL

(1900–1950) Germany

The German-born Weill studied with Busoni in Berlin. He wrote several expressionist chamber pieces, a violin concerto (Op. 12, 1924), and his first symphony (1921) before his remarkable collaboration with Bertolt Brecht. Weill and Brecht's *Die Dreigroschenoper* (*Threepenny Opera*, 1928) is a work of social consciousness that has been compared to the drawings of Georg Grosz. Weill's modernized version of John Gay's 1728 *The Beggar's Opera*, with jazz and pop-oriented bittersweet lyricism, biting rhythm, and trenchant depiction of social corruption, influenced a long line of composers, including Gershwin, Menotti, and Marc Blitzstein, as well as Leonard Bernstein.

The *Threepenny Opera* was followed by an even more ambitious and cynical Brecht-Weill collaboration, *The Rise and Fall of the City of Mahagonny* (1930). In 1933 the Nazi press denounced the works of Weill, a Jew, and on March 21, upon learning that the Gestapo was about to arrest him, he fled to France and later, in 1943, to America, where he wrote more conventional musicals.

Die Dreigroschenoper (*The Threepenny Opera*) (1928)
Lenya, Neuss, Hesterberg, Trenk-Trebitsch, Southwest German Radio Orchestra and Chorus, Brückner-Rüggeberg: CBS MK 42637
Lemper, Milva, Tremper, Berlin RIAS Sinfonietta and RIAS Chamber Choir, Mauceri: London 430075-2

HARRY PARTCH

(1901–1974) United States

Partch was a true sound explorer, and as early as 1930 he created his own method of music making, based on a forty-three-tone scale. He built an entire band of new instruments to play his work. Although his music needs trained performers on "his" instruments, it has found many admirers. Partch believed "in musicians who are total constituents of the moment, irreplaceable, who may sing, shout, whistle, stamp their feet; in costume always, or perhaps half naked and I do not care which half."

Barstow, 8 Hitchhiker Inscriptions from a Highway Railing at Barstow, California (stage piece) (1941)

Wendlant, Partch, Charnstrom, Hoiby, and others: Innova MN 401 (includes interviews with Partch)

The Letter (1943)

Partch, Ensemble: CRI CD 7000

GERALD FINZI

(1901–1956) England

London-born Finzi's brand of music is for some a taste acquired; for others, his gentle tone gives pleasure and comfort from the first. Finzi is very English in spirit—not in any folksy sense, but in his well-tailored reticence and handling of musical texture. The Dies natalis, a distinguished cantata for soprano and orchestra (Op. 8, 1926), continues to secure performances. Finzi permitted fewer than twenty compositions to see the light, and each has a peculiar fascination.

Concerto in C Minor for Clarinet and Strings, Op. 31 (1948–49)

Stoltzman, Guildhall String Ensemble, Salter: RCA 60437-2-RC

JOAQUÍN RODRIGO

(1901–1999) Spain

Rodrigo, who at age three became permanently blind, was a Spanish nationalist who composed steadily throughout his very long life. In 1927, like Albéniz, Granados, Falla, Joaquín Turina, and Federico Mompou before him, he traveled to Paris seeking inspiration and instruction. Rodrigo studied with Paul Dukas and was forever grateful to the composer of The Sorcerer's Apprentice.

In 1939 he composed his Concierto de Aranjuez for guitar and orchestra. It became the most popular guitar concerto in history. Its slow movement has been used shamelessly to sell products of all sorts. Although he composed many delightful scores, this idiomatic concerto remains his signature piece. The composer said that when he composed, he imagined an instrument "that would combine the soul of a guitar, the tail of a piano, and the wings of a harp." The *Concierto de Aranjuez* is named for the site of Philip II's royal summer palace, on the shore of the River Tagus not far from Madrid.

Concierto de Aranjuez for Guitar and Orchestra (1939)
Parkening, Royal Philharmonic Orchestra, Litton: EMI Classics CDC 54665
Williams, English Chamber Orchestra, Barenboim: CBS MK 33208

MAURICE DURUFLÉ

(1902–1986) France

Duruflé came from the long line of French organ virtuosi, and as a pupil of Charles Tournemire and Louis Vierne, he was one of the finest organists of his time. He studied composition with Dukas, and like his master, he composed slowly and with difficulty, believing himself incapable of adding anything significant to the piano, song, or chamber literature. In his long life, he left about a dozen works, of which the beautiful Requiem (Op. 9) has surely deserved its acclaim.

Requiem, Op. 9 (1947)
Blegen, Morris, Atlanta Symphony Orchestra and Chorus, Shaw: Telarc CD 80135

SIR WILLIAM WALTON

(1902–1983) England

Both of Walton's parents were singers, and as a child he sang in his father's church choir. At ten he received a scholarship to Oxford's renowned Christ Church Choir. Although he grew up surrounded by music, his training was haphazard, and in composition he was virtually self-taught. He nevertheless managed, by his sixteenth year, to produce a piano quartet that already showed his finely expressive nature.

At Oxford he seldom attended to his academic curriculum and left in 1920 without a degree because he had failed some necessary classwork. He became friendly with Sacheverell Sitwell, the highly musical youngest member of the literary family of Edith and Osbert, and they invited him to live with them in London. In their stimulating household, he met such brilliant musicians as Bernard van Dieren, Peter Warlock, and Constant Lambert.

Working closely with Edith Sitwell, in 1922 he composed the first version of *Façade*. This suite, for narrator and six instrumentalists, was conceived as an accompaniment to Sitwell's avant-garde poetry. The score is frivolous, consisting more of sounds than of actual words. It was an age for such experimentation: *Façade* seemed artistically chic and as up-to-date as Gertrude Stein and the Dadaists. Much to Walton's surprise, it earned him a certain notoriety. Shortly afterward his bright overture *Portsmouth Point* (1924–25) added to his growing reputation.

A slow and painful worker, by 1929 he had composed the beautiful Viola Concerto, first performed by the composer Paul Hindemith, who was also a first-class violist. But it was with *Belshazzar's Feast* (1930–31) that Walton achieved international acclaim. The oratorio harks back to Walton's childhood days, when he so often took part in singing Handel's works, the daily bread of the still-flourishing English choral tradition. *Belshazzar's Feast*, with its explosively glowing barbaric sweep, is theatrical in the best sense of the word. It uses material from the Bible, as adapted by Sir Osbert Sitwell.

Walton, now thirty-one, was planning to compose a symphony. He was highly conscious of the symphonic tradition and labored for more than three years. The Symphony no. 1 in B-flat Minor was first performed on November 6, 1935, and remains one of the landmark English symphonies since the 1930s. The conductor Sir Henry Wood wrote, "What a work, truly marvelous; it was like the world coming to an end, its dramatic power was superb; what orchestration, what vitality and rhythmic invention—No orchestral work has ever carried me away so much."

In 1938–39 Walton composed his lovely Violin Concerto for the great violinist Jascha Heifetz. With the war raging, Walton found release in writing *Scapino* (1940), a comic overture inspired by a character from the commedia dell'arte. In 1942 Oxford honored him with a doctorate of music.

In 1943–44 he collaborated with Laurence Olivier on the film *Henry V*. Olivier wrote, "William knocked out the most fantastic score for Henry V. . . . It's the most wonderful score I've ever heard for a film."

Knighthood was bestowed on Walton in 1951. In his last decades, Sir William continued composing fitfully and slowly, but he had lost confidence in his talent. For his eightieth birthday, England paid him homage as one of the most frequently performed composers of his generation. On the morning of March 8, 1983, he had a fatal heart attack. He once said, "I seriously advise all sensitive composers to die at the age of thirty-seven. I know I've gone through the first halcyon period, and am just about ripe for my critical damnation."

It is true that Walton was at his best in his earlier works, such as the flamboyant *Belshazzar*, the full-blown, emotional First Symphony, and the effervescent *Façade*. Later he wrote in a concise neoclassicism, as in the Partita and the Second Symphony. His later, closer-knit idiom sounds self-conscious and lacks his youthful vigor. In all, he is a composer of distinguished craft, whose best music is among the finest by an English composer of the 1920s and 1930s.

Belshazzar's Feast (1930–31)

Stone, Atlanta Symphony Orchestra and Chorus, Shaw: Telarc CD 80181

Luxon, Royal Philharmonic Orchestra, Collegeum Musicum of London, Previn: RPO Records
   7013

Symphony no. 1 in B-flat Minor (1932–35)

London Symphony Orchestra, Previn: RCA 7830-2-RG

Royal Philharmonic Orchestra, Ashkenazy: London 433703-2

ARAM KHACHATURIAN

(1903–1978) Armenia

Khachaturian is the foremost Armenian composer. He knew next to nothing of the theory or literature of European music when, at age seventeen, he left his birthplace of Tiflis (now called Tibilisi, in Georgia) to study music in Moscow. At the Gnesin Music Academy, he was taught cello and piano, and after graduation in 1929 he continued his studies at the Moscow Conservatory, with the venerable symphonist Nikolai Miaskovsky. From the first, his objective was to write "Armenian" music, and he studied thoroughly the rich treasury of his country's folklore and song. After 1930 he crystallized his style, producing the brilliant Piano Concerto (1936), the Violin Concerto (1940), and the ballet *Gayane* (1940–42), with its riveting "Sabre Dance," which made him world famous. In 1948, along with many of his colleagues, he was attacked by the Central Committee of the Communist Party for indulging in what was called decadent formalism. As did his colleagues, he made a public confession of artistic wrongdoing, but in the end, he weathered the storm, continuing to do what he had always done. He composed music solely from the inspiration of his Transcaucasian background of Armenia, Georgia, and Azerbaijan, often imitating the rhapsodic and improvisatory style of the ancient Armenian troubadours, called *ashugs*. His work is a branch of the great musical tradition of nationalism begun in the nineteenth century. Khachaturian's output is extremely uneven, but at his best he sings his colorful musical heritage with an authenticity that rings true. Armenia is proud of him, the composer of her national anthem. He died of a heart attack on May 1, 1978, and is buried in the Pantheon in Yerevan, the capital of Armenia, among his distinguished compatriots.

Gayane (ballet in three acts) (1942)
USSR Symphony Orchestra, Khachaturian: Russian Disc RUS 11018

Gayane Suite no. 1 (1943)
Vienna State Opera Orchestra, Golschmann: Vanguard Everyman Classics OVC 5010

Concerto in D-flat Major for Piano and Orchestra (1936)
Kapell, NBC Symphony Orchestra, Black: VAI Audio VAIA/IPA 1027
Atamian, Seattle Symphony Orchestra, Schwarz: Delos DE 3155
Yablonskaya, Moscow Symphony Orchestra, Yablonsky: Naxos 8.550799

DMITRI KABALEVSKY

(1904–1987) Russia

Kabalevsky was one of Soviet Russia's foremost composers. He created music of many moods, technically ingenious, and often with exuberant melodies, some of which were derived from folk sources. He composed brilliantly for the piano, including dozens of suggestive pieces for children. The Sonatina no. 1 in C Major (Op. 13, 1930) has attained "classic" status among piano students for its light heart. It has too often been said that Kabalevsky's music was overly influenced by Prokofiev, but Kabalevsky is no mere imitator; he was capable of profundity of feeling, which was never secondhand.

The Comedians (symphonic suite), Op. 26 (1940)
London Philharmonic Orchestra, Slatkin: RCA 09026-60968-2

Sonata no. 2 in E-flat Major for Piano, Op. 45 (1945)
Horowitz: RCA 62644

SIR MICHAEL TIPPETT

(1905–1998) England

After Benjamin Britten's death, Tippett assumed the position of England's leading composer. In later decades, he decidedly became one of the world's most respected composers. He developed slowly; he was already seventeen before he first heard a symphony orchestra, and his first works did not appear until late in his twenties. As a boy, Tippett reacted painfully to World War I, becoming a pacifist in the 1930s. When he was called for military service in 1940–41, he registered as a conscientious objector, for which he suffered a period of imprisonment during World War II.

Tippett is a complex and often stylistically difficult composer, incorporating various styles in his work including jazz, neoclassicism, African-American spirituals, and English madrigals. He has been influenced by the poetry of Yeats and Eliot and the psychology of Jung. He has studied ancient Greek literature, and his opera *King Priam* (1958–61) is one of the most intriguing operas of Modernism. His mature works include four symphonies, four piano sonatas, four string quartets, four operas, several orchestral works, and the oratorio *A Child of Our Time* (1939–41).

Fantasia concertante on a *Theme of Corelli* for String Orchestra (1953)
Bath Festival Orchestra, Tippett: EMI Classics ZDMB 63522

ELLIOTT CARTER

(1908–) United States

Thorny, dense, and formidably intellectual, Carter's music is either fervently admired or as fervently disliked. Carter studied with Nadia Boulanger in Paris and produced his formative compositions in the 1930s. This music, though accessible, has small vitality compared to, say, that of Sessions or Copland. In the mid-1940s, Carter began writing more "advanced" music, initiating this period with the Sonata for Piano (1945–46). With each new work, Carter's intricate music brought him new accolades.

Some of Carter's significant compositions are the Variations for Orchestra (1954–55), the Concerto for Orchestra (1969), the *Night Fantasies* for Piano (1980), and the four stellar string quartets, composed from 1951 to 1986. A good introduction to Carter's style is the Concerto for Piano and Orchestra (1964–65), about which the composer states, "It employs no preestablished form, but is a series of short, usually overlapping episodes, mosaics of fragments, that derive from parts of the basic material."

Concerto for Piano and Orchestra (1964–65)
Oppens, Cincinnati Symphony Orchestra, Gielen: New World NW 80347-2

Quartets for Strings no. 1–4 (1951–86)
Juilliard String Quartet: Sony Classical S2K 47229

OLIVIER MESSIAEN

(1908–1992) France

At his death, Messiaen was considered France's most illustrious composer, as well as one of the most influential composers since World War II. He was a renowned theorist and teacher whose pupils included Pierre Boulez, Iannis Xenakis, Karlheinz Stockhausen, Jean Barraqué, and other important composers. Some find his music interminably long-winded and totally undigestible. Others claim that he was one of the major composers of the twentieth century, even the greatest after Debussy himself: an ecstatic, inspired visionary and a monumental experimenter in the tradition of Berlioz, whom he greatly admired.

He once called himself a "sound color" composer, and he added many new sounds to music through his "superchords," using "layers" of harmony within fascinating and complex rhythms. Not the least aspect of his art is his reverence for the Catholic faith, which has inspired some of his best works, which are frequently shrouded in symbolism.

As an ardent lover of birdsong, Messiaen added to the piano literature his *Catalogue d'oiseaux* (1956–58), a work of astounding pianistic ingenuity and daunting technical demands, based on birdsongs that he notated in the field. His most frequently performed piano work is *Vingt regards sur l'enfant Jésus* (1944), a complete performance of which lasts over two hours. Messiaen, a profound student of music from plainsong to Hindu ragas, composed music that can give the impression of timelessness. Some listeners have reported that it is capable of inducing a trancelike state.

For the novice Messiaen listener, the gargantuan, ten-movement *Turangalîla-Symphonie* (1946–48) is a splashy, voluptuous beginning. The title, meaning "lovesong," is of Hindu origin, and the huge score contrasts mystical and physical love. Messiaen's use of various orchestral instruments in combination with the piano is audacious.

Turangalîla-Symphonie (1946–48)

City of Birmingham Symphony Orchestra, Rattle: EMI Classics CDCB 47463
Philharmonia Orchestra, Salonen: Sony Classical SMK 53473

GRAŻYNA BACEWICZ

(1909–1969) Poland

After studies at the Warsaw Conservatory, Bacewicz worked in Paris with Nadia Boulanger in the early 1930s. A violin virtuoso, she left the concert stage in 1955 to devote more time to composition.

Bacewicz's music is strong, compact, and dissonant and deserves to be well known. Her chamber music has found advocates, and her piano music, especially the études and the two sonatas, is powerful and compactly constructed.

Piano Sonata no. 2 (1953)
Zimerman: Olympia OLY 392

SAMUEL BARBER

(1910–1981) United States

Barber was born in Pennsylvania; his mother was musical, and his aunt, the famous contralto Louise Homer, taught him singing. At fourteen he was accepted at the recently founded Curtis Institute of Music in Philadelphia, where his gifts were recognized. After graduation in 1932, he finished his delightful overture to *Sheridan's School for Scandal* (Op. 5). In Italy he met Toscanini, who performed his *Essay* no. 1 (Op. 12, 1937) and the Adagio for Strings (Op. 11, 1936) to much acclaim. During the war, he served in the Air Corps and composed little. In 1946 he set up housekeeping at Mt. Kisco, New York, with his longtime companion, composer Gian Carlo Menotti.

Barber was the golden boy of American music; commissions poured in, and he was twice awarded the Pulitzer Prize (in 1958 and 1962). His music is romantic, and to many experimental composers of the 1960s and 1970s, he seemed a musical reactionary. But for the majority of concertgoers, Barber's high gloss gives an agreeable sense of satisfaction, a pleasant feeling that old values like emotional, and occasionally teary-eyed, melody, with a shapely and well-defined structure, are still plausible. The composer and writer Wilfrid Mellers feels, "It is not extravagant to say that his music is meaningful to comparatively large numbers of people precisely because it is not experientially 'mature.' His appeal depends on qualities that his music shares with Tchaikovsky and Puccini. It matters because it is deeply felt, never second-hand: and its awareness of adolescence strikes deep into the American experience." Indeed, a great quantity of his work contains a striking nostalgia, a longing for an evergreen past. Childhood and nostalgia, however, are time-honored and legitimate reservoirs of inspiration. Such works as the Violin Concerto (Op. 14, 1931–40), the Piano Sonata (Op. 26, 1949, composed for Horowitz), *Dover Beach* (Op. 3, 1933), the Cello Concerto (Op. 22, 1946), and *Knoxville: Summer of 1915* (Op. 24, 1947)—as well as the celebrated Adagio for Strings (Op. 11, 1936), with its unforgettable elegiac beauty and lyrical headiness—will, I believe, stand the severe test of time.

Adagio for Strings, Op. 11 (1936)
Los Angeles Philharmonic Orchestra, Bernstein: Deutsche Grammophon 431048-2

Sonata for Piano, Op. 26 (1949)
Horowitz: RCA 60377-2-RG
Browning: MusicMasters 01612-67122-2

ALAN HOVHANESS

(1911–2000) United States

Hovhaness was born in Massachusetts, but his art was inspired mainly by his Armenian roots and by the Middle East generally, with smatterings of the Far East. He used Chinese, Japanese, Korean, and Balinese instruments in some compositions. He attempted to combine his exotic material into traditional Western forms, using ostinato rhythms, highly colored chromaticism, and above all improvisatory and rhapsodic traits. His music is often interesting in detail, although many of the large-scale works are static and monotonous. But there is much to choose from among his three hundred works. *Khaldis*, for piano, four trumpets, and percussion (Op. 91, 1951); *Meditations on Orpheus* for orchestra (Op. 155, 1957); *Fantasy on Japanese Woodprints* for xylophone and chamber orchestra (Op. 211, 1965); and *Alleluia and Fugue* for string orchestra (Op. 40b, 1941) are compelling. The best introduction to this composer is his masterful Symphony no. 2, *Mysterious Mountain* (Op. 132, 1955).

Symphony no. 2 (*Mysterious Mountain*), Op. 132 (1955)
American Composers Orchestra, Davies: MusicMasters 7021-2-C
Chicago Symphony Orchestra, Reiner: RCA 5733-2-RC

GIAN CARLO MENOTTI

(1911–) United States

In 1924, the Italian-born Menotti immigrated to the United States with his mother. By 1950, he had become the most celebrated opera composer of the time. In 1958 he founded the annual Spoleto Festival in Italy. For many, his music sounds dated, so Menotti has become increasingly involved with stage direction. His best operas, however, should indeed be revived. *The Saint of Bleecker Street* (1954), the once-popular *The Consul* (1950), *The Telephone* (1946), *The Medium* (1945), *The Old Maid and the Thief* (1939), and the little Christmas opera *Amahl and the Night Visitors* (1951) are all very entertaining and vocally effective, conveying Menotti's considerable dramatic flair.

Concerto in F Major for Piano and Orchestra (1945)

Wild, Symphony of the Air, Mester: Vanguard Classics OVC 4029

The Telephone (1946)

Ommerle, Holmes, New York Chamber Ensemble, Radcliffe: Albany TROY 173

Amahl and the Night Visitors (1951)

Rainbird, Haywood, Dobson, Watson, Royal Opera House Orchestra and Chorus, Menotti:
*   Jay 1303*

JOHN CAGE

(1912–1992) United States

During his career, the Los Angeles–born Cage made plenty of noise for the publicity machine, but many of his auditors also thought he made much noise "musically" speaking, notwithstanding his celebrated 4'33" (1952)—silent music for piano in three movements. Indeed, he became a celebrity and had a major influence on many composers. For the piano, Cage explored new sounds, and his invention of the "prepared piano," in which various objects are put into the piano between the strings to alter the sound, has given the instrument new means of expression. His belief that all sounds are equal, his play with chance and randomness, give an extended outlook on form and color. He wanted to depersonalize music, but instead, through his screws and bolts, he added new and distinctive sonorities to it. Cage's music has often disturbed or refreshed listeners, but few remain indifferent.

Sonatas and Interludes for Prepared Piano (1946–48)

SONATAS 1, 5, 10, 12
Miller, Interlude 2: New World NW 80203-2
Berman: Naxos 8559042

MORTON GOULD

(1913–1996) United States

Gould was an undervalued American master who skirted from Broadway to movies, broadcasting, ballet, and band music and who used American vernacular music with delightful flair. He was famous early for his *Latin-American Symphonette* (1941), *Spirituals* for orchestra (1941), *Interplay* for piano and orchestra (1943), and the ballet *Fall River Legend* (1947). He was a master orchestrator, and his best music has style and zing, sweetness and character. His later works are rather more astringent and complex.

Spirituals for Orchestra (1941)
Eastman-Rochester Orchestra, Hanson: Mercury 432016-2

WITOLD LUTOSŁAWSKI

(1913–1994) Poland

During Lutosławski's later years, he was, along with Messiaen, the most famous living composer in an age when no composers' names were universally recognized; Stravinsky and Shostakovich had been the last household names. Lutosławski's work has been fairly well documented on CD, and the adventurous listener may choose to hear *Funeral Music* for string orchestra (1958), the four symphonies, *Venetian Games* for chamber orchestra (1961), or the two quartets for strings (1964, 1984), each of them digging deeply into the musical psyche. Lutosławski's least important but best-known score is the clever six-minute *Variations on a Theme of Paganini* for two pianos (1941).

He can be a difficult composer, especially in his music after 1960, when he occasionally uses aleatory processes, much dissonance, and quickly changeable sonorities. In such works as the 1987 Piano Concerto, his textures grew light and swift—so different from the neo-Bartókian Concerto for Orchestra of nearly thirty-five years earlier.

Chain 2 for Violin and Orchestra (1984)
Mutter, BBC Symphony Orchestra, Lutosławski: Deutsche Grammophon 423696-2

Concerto for Orchestra (1950–54)
Cleveland Orchestra, C. von Dohnányi: London 425694-2

GEORGE PERLE

(1915–) United States

Born in Bayonne, New Jersey, Perle had a distinguished teaching career at Queens College. His later years have been devoted to composition and the writing of an extraordinary series of books, which include *The Operas of Alban Berg*, a two-volume work on Berg's *Wozzeck* and *Lulu*, as well as his influential *Twelve-Tone Tonality* (1978). One of the most searching of theorists, he was deeply influenced by Schoenberg's twelve-tone system, which he used as the foundation of his own expanded tonality.

Perle's music stems from the mind of a lucid and aristocratic thinker: he possesses formal elegance, subtlety, and a superb sense of motion. Each tone fits into a luminous pattern, and every work is created with the pain of labor, artfully concealed. His manner is beguiling, and he writes his music to last.

In each decade since the 1940s, Perle has written fine music, but it is the works of his old age—such as the three piano concertos—that are among the significant and fulfilling compositions from the twentieth century's final years.

Serenade no. 3 for Piano and Chamber Orchestra (1983)
Goode, Music Today Ensemble, Schwarz: Elektra/Nonesuch 79108-2

Six New Études for Piano (1994)
Boriskin: New World NW 80342-2

MILTON BABBITT

(1916–) United States

Babbitt's control of his musical materials goes beyond his chief influences, Schoenberg and especially Webern. The compression of music takes on new meaning in his work; he is one of the most intellectual musicians of his generation.

For some listeners, Babbitt's work is mere "paper" music. It does not easily

attract or light the emotions; this goes for his electronic work as well. His eventual importance may well be theoretical. He has taught many composers, first
at Princeton (where for a time he also taught mathematics) and later at Juilliard. Those who are attracted to Babbitt's elegant and noble constructions will
find distinction on every page, pervaded by a clarity that can be grasped surprisingly well even by the uninitiated.

Concerto for Piano and Orchestra (1985)
Feinberg, American Composers Orchestra, Wuorinen: New World NW 80346

ALBERTO GINASTERA

(1916–1983) Argentina

Ginastera is the best known of Argentina's many serious composers. His earliest
music stemmed from his country's folklore. The effective *Panambi*, a 1937 ballet, is stark and forceful in rhythm, infused with folk elements. The Piano Concerto no. 1 (1961) and First Piano Sonata (1952) are less performed now than
twenty years ago. Ginastera's instrumental writing is virtuosic; he is comfortable with traditional forms, and his craft is impeccable. He often creates
swatches of color by employing a variety of percussion instruments. His operas
Don Rodrigo (1963–64) and *Bomarzo* (1966–67) caused a good deal of comment at the time of their premieres. Although they have had no revival, they
are the two most significant Latin American operas of their time.

Concerto for Harp and Orchestra, Op. 25 (1956)
Masters, City of London Sinfonia, Hickox: Chandos CHAN 9094

Milena for Soprano and Orchestra, Op. 37 (1971)
Curtin, Denver Symphony Orchestra, Priestman: Phoenix USA PHCD 107

LOU HARRISON

(1917– 2003)

An ingenious composer of many facets, Harrison is a student of various subjects, including the language of Esperanto, which he uses for his vocal scores.
He has written serial music and has delved into Korean and Chinese music,
producing some of the finest Western "classical" music of Asian inspiration.
His opera *Rapunzel* (1954) is fascinating and was first sung by Leontyne Price.

Harrison has been prolific. His music is varied and eloquent. As Virgil Thomson put it, it is "really sensitive and elaborate and lively and not about anything in the world but how beautiful the materials of music can be when handled with tenderness and with intelligence."

Concerto for Piano and Orchestra (1985)
Jarrett, New Japan Philharmonic Orchestra, Otomo: New World NW 366-4

Symphony on G (1948–61)
Royal Philharmonic Orchestra, Samuel: CRI CD 715

LEONARD BERNSTEIN

(1918–1990) United States

Bernstein was one of the most famous musicians of the twentieth century, and a composer of startling inspiration. As a confirmed tonalist, he drew from Stravinsky, Copland, jazz, rock—whatever pleased him. His music can be fun-loving, mocking, sentimental, restless, or religious, and is punctuated by brash rhythms, dance elements, and high theatricality. In the 1957 musical *West Side Story*, Bernstein by turns is tender, sordid, and tensely sexual, depicting the pent-up tensions of the city street. High among his achievements are the ballet *Fancy Free* (1944), the Symphony no. 2 for piano and orchestra (*The Age of Anxiety*, 1949), and the *Chichester Psalms* for chorus and orchestra (1965). His overture to *Candide* (1956) ranks with Rossini. As one of the finest conductors of his time, his performances of his own music were never less than captivating.

Symphony no. 2 for Piano and Orchestra (*The Age of Anxiety*) (1949)
Foss, Israel Philharmonic Orchestra, Bernstein: Deutsche Grammophon 445245-2

West Side Story (1957)
Te Kanawa, Troyanos, Carreras, Ollmann, chorus and orchestra unknown, Bernstein: Deutsche Grammophon 415963-2

KAREL HUSA

(1921–) Czech Republic

Husa is able to extract new timbres from traditional means. Since 1954 he has lived in the United States, earning a living as a conductor and teacher.

His work has many influences—Bartók, Stravinsky, Schoenberg, Berg, and Janáček—all finely distilled. He is a serious artist worthy of special investigation.

Apotheosis of This Earth for Orchestra and Chorus (1970)
Louisville Orchestra and University of Louisville Concert Choir, Husa: Louisville LCD 005

IANNIS XENAKIS
(1922–2001) Romania

Xenakis was trained in engineering and studied composition in Paris with Messiaen. His music is made up of complex structures and a dense web of unique sonorities, which has strongly attracted composers as different as Lutosławski, Yuji Takahashi, and Henryk Górecki. The critic Bernard Jacobson wrote, "Whereas John Cage and many other users of aleatory processes in music have sought to eliminate the primacy of the composer by pursuing the ideal of indeterminacy, Xenakis has maintained the dominance of the composer and of the principle of determinacy. His aim is nothing less than the expression in music of the unity he sees as underlying all activity, human and nonhuman, artistic and scientific."

Chamber Music (1955–90)
Helffer, Arditti String Quartet: Montaigne MO 782005

Thalleïn for Fourteen Instruments (1984)
SONOR Ensemble of the University of California at San Diego, Steiger: Neuma 450-86

GYÖRGY LIGETI
(1923–) Hungary

The most widely known Hungarian composer since Bartók and Kodály, Ligeti writes music that is sonorously original. His ear for refined and distilled detail is amazing. His piano études are rewarding for the virtuoso pianist, and his chamber music uses the instruments with dazzling effect. Ligeti's use of microintervals, amorphous textures, and delicate wind-tones is especially effective. In the late 1960s, *Atmosphères* (1961), used by Stanley Kubrick in the film *2001: A Space Odyssey*, brought Ligeti's name and music to an international audience.

Atmosphères for Orchestra (1961)
Lontano for Orchestra (1967)
Vienna Philharmonic Orchestra, Abbado: Deutsche Grammophon 429260-2

NED ROREM

(1923–) United States

Rorem composes everything from organ music and piano études to operas and symphonies, but his best-known productions are his more than two hundred songs. His acute ear for poetry, his deep intelligence, and his unusual understanding of the voice give him a high place in the art song of the second half of the twentieth century. Rorem the writer—of diaries, autobiography, and books of criticism—forms a valuable adjunct to Rorem the composer.

Songs
Curtin, Wolff, Gramm, Rorem: Premier PRCD 1035

LUCIANO BERIO

(1925–2003) Italy

Berio graduated from the Music Academy of Milan and later studied with the composer Luigi Dallapiccola. With the composer Bruno Maderna, he co-founded the first electronic music studio in Italy at the Milan radio station in 1955. Since 1955 Berio's music has had frequent performances. His work offers many elements: serialism, electronic technology, texts, and indeterminacy. His work at all times is inventive and adventurous.

Continuo for Orchestra (1989–91)
Chicago Symphony Orchestra, Barenboim: Teldec 4509-66596-2

PIERRE BOULEZ

(1925–) France

Boulez is one of the most influential musicians of the second half of the twentieth century, as composer, conductor, and polemicist. After studying mathematics at Lyons, he studied intensively with Messiaen at the Paris Conservatory and became well known by his mid-twenties. Boulez's work has extended serial technique into enlarged and flexible regions. *Eclat* (1965), the three piano sonatas (1946–57), and *Pli selon pli* (1957–62) are considered classics of contemporary music. Boulez's moving *Rituel* (1974–75), composed in memory of Bruno Maderna, is one of his most accessible works. A slow worker, he has experimented at times with electronic music and indeterminacy. He has been deeply influenced by the poet Mallarmé as well as by the writings of Joyce and the compositions of Debussy, Schoenberg, and Webern.

Sonata no. 2 for Piano (1948)
Pollini: Deutsche Grammophon 419202-2

Rituel (1974–75)
BBC Symphony Orchestra, Boulez: Sony Classical SMK 45839

HANS WERNER HENZE

(1926–) Germany

After training in Germany, Henze traveled to Paris and Darmstadt, where he met and learned much from the Schoenberg disciple René Leibowitz. By his late twenties, he was one of the most discussed and performed of younger composers. He is deeply political and has written various polemics reflecting the turmoil of the age. Henze has flatly rejected any dogmatism and has connections with Italian music, Stravinsky, the Viennese School, rock, Baroque, and electronic music, and much else. He is a virtuoso orchestrator, and his music is full of captivating timbres. His catalog in each medium—from ballet and opera to chamber music and concertos—deserves careful exploration. Henze is one of the most significant composers of the second half of the twentieth century.

Symphony no. 7 (1983–84)
City of Birmingham Symphony Orchestra, Rattle: EMI Classics CDC 54762

Elegy for Young Lovers (opera in three acts) (1959–61)
Schudel, Morgan, Richard, Bernhofen, Berlin Chamber Opera Orchestra, Jones: Deutsche Schallplatten 2 DS 1050

KARLHEINZ STOCKHAUSEN

(1928–) Germany

Stockhausen studied piano from 1947 in Cologne and composition in 1950 with the Swiss composer Frank Martin. His early music exhibits strains of Bartók, Schoenberg, and Stravinsky; pivotal in his development was meeting Boulez and Messiaen, with whom he studied in Paris in 1952–53. He also experimented at the *musique concrète* studio of the French radio.

As Stockhausen developed, his point of departure became the later music of Webern. As musical scholar and composer Jonathan Kramer points out, "It was Webern's techniques rather than his esthetics or musical gestures that were important. As Stockhausen discovered the systematic control of independent elements in Webern's music, he realized that the traditional hierarchy of these elements might be challenged, and he embraced the idea that every sound is uniquely determined by five parameters or dimensions: pitch, intensity, duration, timbre, and position in space. All other elements of music (tempo, rhythm, instrumentation, melody, density, harmony, register, meter, etc.) were derivable from the five basic parameters, and Stockhausen classified them as compositional parameters because their relevance in a musical context is controlled by the composer." Within this context, Stockhausen set off on one of the great adventures of post-Webern music. When he worked with electronic music, he expanded his horizons in various ways. In his piano music, he has limited his sound scope, writing, "From time to time I have concentrated again on 'piano pieces,' on composing for a single instrument, for ten fingers, with minute nuances of timbres and structures. They are my 'drawings.'" He has also written, "In a world bombarded by images the function of music is to awaken the inner man."

Stimmung for Six Vocalists, no. 24 (1968)

Flowers, Walmsley-Clark, Long, Covey-Crump, Rose, Hillier: Hyperion CDA 66115

Mantra for Two Pianos + Woodblock + Crotales and Two Ring Modulators, no. 32 (1969–70)

Bevan, Mikhashoff, Orsted: New Albion NAR 025

GEORGE CRUMB

(1929–) United States

Crumb was a composition pupil of the American composer Ross Lee Finney and also for a time of the German composer Boris Blacher. Crumb has been in the compositional limelight since winning the 1968 Pulitzer Prize for his orchestral work *Echoes of Time and the River*. The critic Richard Wernick writes, "Crumb's mature style . . . does not follow an established convention or 'ism.' It possesses an unpretentious musicality best expressed in the composer's remark that 'music can exist only when the brain is singing.' " Crumb has bowed to his influences, especially those of Webern and Debussy. Symbolism plays a large role in his music, with a spice of medievalism now and then. He writes in a free dissonant manner, which brings to his work a feeling of improvisation. Adventurous pianists have been fond of *Makrokosmos I* and *II* (1972 and 1973), subtitled *Twenty-four Fantasy-Pieces after the Zodiac*, for amplified piano. In this seventy-minute cycle, the composer is indebted to Bartók and Debussy, which he notes but says, "The spiritual impulse of my music is more akin to the darker side of Chopin, and even to the child-like fantasy of early Schumann."

Ancient Voices of Children for Soprano and Chamber Ensemble (1970)
DeGaetani, Contemporary Chamber Ensemble, Weisberg: Elektra/Nonesuch 79149-2

Makrokosmos I, II (1972–73)
Henz-Diémand: Musiques Suisses MGB CD 6091
Jacob: Centaur CRC 2050

TORU TAKEMITSU

(1930–1996) Japan

Takemitsu enjoyed a major career as Japan's foremost composer and traveled widely as a lecturer. He produced a body of work of unorthodox structural patterns and unusual and evocative textures. Takemitsu's music is of exceptional rhythmic complexity; in an orchestral score, he pits one instrumental group against another; each group has its own time scheme, giving the music a wonderful rhythmic sway.

Quartet no. 1 for Strings (A Way a Lone) (1980)
Tokyo String Quartet: RCA 09026-61387-2

November Steps no. 2 for Orchestra (1967)
Saito Kinen Orchestra, Ozawa: Philips 432176-2

RODION SHCHEDRIN

(1932–) Russia

Shchedrin, one of the best-known Russian composers of his generation, is also a powerful pianist. His First Piano Concerto (1954), written as a graduation piece from the Moscow Conservatory, is delightful—a stew filled with Prokofiev, Gershwin, Ravel, and whatnot. The story differs considerably by the time we get to the grinding, dissonant Third Concerto (1973), as the composer struggles to release his pent-up originality. His ballet in one act, *Carmen* (1968), written for his wife—the famed ballerina Maya Plisetskaya—shows the wizardry of his orchestral technique.

Concertos no. 1–3 for Piano and Orchestra (1954, 1968, 1973)
Shchedrin, USSR Symphony Orchestra, Svetlanov: Russian Disc RUS 11129

Carmen (ballet, after Bizet) for Strings and Percussion (1968)
Bolshoi Theater Orchestra, Rozhdestvensky: Melodiya 74321-36908-2

KRZYSZTOF PENDERECKI

(1933–) Poland

Penderecki is presently the best known and most often performed of contemporary Polish composers. After being influenced by Boulez, he came into his own with works that are novel in their sonorous imagery, especially evoking different string textures or even using noise at times. Much of his music sounds spontaneous and possesses high drama, stimulated by literary sources. The *St. Luke Passion* caused a stir when it first appeared.

St. Luke Passion (1963–65)
van Osten, Roberts, Rydl, Lubaszenko, Polish National Radio Symphony Orchestra, Cracow Boys Choir, Penderecki: Argo 430328-2

SIR PETER MAXWELL DAVIES

(1934–) England

One of the most creatively restless of contemporary composers, Maxwell Davies has used many different media. With an avid interest in history and literature, he has set to music various texts, from medieval to modern. *Eight Songs for a Mad King* (1969) combines stage action with vocal and instrumental effects.

Maxwell Davies's compositions are highly intense and are sometimes striking in their unconventional sounds; they often use percussion with great effect. Salient examples of his work include *Ricercar and Doubles on "To Many a Well"* for eight instruments (1959) and the dramatic work *Revelation and Fall* (1965–66). Listeners at first may find themselves unsettled by the howling in *Eight Songs for a Mad King*, based on the period of insanity in the life of King George III, but the music soon becomes strangely engrossing.

Eight Songs for a Mad King for Baritone and Ensemble (1969)
Eastman, Fires of London, Maxwell Davies: Unicorn-Kanchana DKP CD 9052

Miss Donnithorne's Maggot for Mezzo-Soprano and Ensemble (1974)
Thomas, Fires of London, Maxwell Davies: Unicorn-Kanchana DKP CD 9052

ALFRED SCHNITTKE

(1934–1998) Russia

Schnittke was trained in Moscow at the famed Conservatory, where he also taught from 1961. Shostakovich, Stravinsky, and the Viennese serialists were paramount in his formative stages; later Stockhausen, Cage, and Ligeti came within his orbit, fueling his restless creativity. No other Russian composer of the last thirty years has made such a deep impression on an international public. The listener will note the deep emotionalism permeating his scores, with almost shocking sudden effects whose impact does not fade upon repeated hearing.

Concerto no. 3 for Violin, Viola, Cello, and Orchestra (c.1989)
Kremer, Bashmet, Rostropovich, Moscow Soloists, Bashmet: EMI Classics CDC 55627

The History of Dr. Johann Faustus (opera in three acts) (1992)
Schwarz, Raunig, Büchner, Freier, Hamburg State Philharmonic Orchestra and Opera Chorus, Albrecht: RCA 09026-68413-2

ARVO PÄRT

(1935–) Estonia

Pärt graduated from the Tallinn Conservatory in 1963. At first he wrote neo-classical works, then changed to twelve-tone works, tone clusters, and various collage-type pieces. The compositions that have made him well known date from after 1985 and are mostly accessible and Romantic, with the heart on the sleeve. These winning qualities are appreciated by his mounting legion of listeners, and he has been much recorded.

Summa for Orchestra (1991)
Philharmonia Orchestra, Järvi: Chandos CHAN 9134

PHILIP GLASS

(1937–) United States

Glass is a minimalist. The term is derived from sculpture and painting, and in music the minimalist label (like most popular terms) unfortunately typecasts much good music. Like his fellow minimalist composers, La Monte Young, John Adams, and Terry Riley, Glass utilizes concentrated sound units, stating their material over and over, with only gradual changes in tonality, texture, and other traditional devices. For some the effect is moronic; for others, hypnotic. Glass's career has been sensational, and he has become a culture hero for some. His early music was a reflection of his teachers, first William Bergsma and Vincent Persichetti, later Darius Milhaud, and finally, in Paris, Nadia Boulanger, the mother-figure for many significant American composers.

In Paris in 1966 he also worked with the celebrated Indian sitarist Ravi Shankar and began forming his individual style, which in 1970 he described as repetitive and reductive. His encounter with the director and writer Robert Wilson was cathartic, and their opera *Einstein on the Beach* (1974–76) was a smash success. The opera brought together many of the avant-garde theater and musical aspirations of the 1950s, 1960s, and 1970s and packaged them in an imaginative collage. Glass has composed a good deal of film music, orchestral scores, and chamber pieces, but his operas *The Juniper Tree* (1985), *The Fall of the House of Usher* (1988), *The Making of the Representative for Planet 8* (1985–88), *Satyagraha* (1980), and *Akhnaten* (1983) have usually caused more delight than hostility.

Today, after a quarter century of exposure and imitation, the work as a whole has lost its first freshness. It remains, however, representative of a school of musical activity that was given much publicity.

Concerto for Violin and Orchestra (1987)
Kremer, Vienna Philharmonic Orchestra, C. von Dohnányi: Deutsche Grammophon 437091-2

Einstein on the Beach **(opera in four acts) (1976)**
Glass Ensemble: CBS M4K 38875

WILLIAM BOLCOM

(1938–) United States

Bolcom was a pupil of Milhaud and of Leland Smith. Perhaps he is best known for his piano rags from the late 1960s, but Bolcom is a typical American of his generation, and he incorporates anything and almost everything into his music, which is generous in spirit. He has flair and zest; some of his music is gutsy, some serious. His career has been well publicized, and he won a Pulitzer Prize in 1989 for his Twelve Études.

Twelve New Études for Piano (1977–86)
Hamelin: New World 354-2

A BRIEF GLOSSARY
OF MUSICAL TERMS

SOURCE LIST

NAME INDEX

A BRIEF GLOSSARY OF
MUSICAL TERMS

Absolute music—music that is not set to words and has no literary, pictorial, or descriptive nature; that is, instrumental music. The term applies to the abstract forms of the sonata, fugue, and the like. It is the opposite of *program music*.

A cappella—unaccompanied vocal music.

Accelerando—quickening the tempo; speeding up.

Accidental—a sign that alters a note by raising or lowering it. A sharp (♯) sign raises a note by a half tone; a flat (♭) lowers it by a half tone; a double sharp (𝄪) raises it by a whole step; a double flat (𝄫) lowers it by a whole step. A natural (♮) negates the sharp or flat that appears in the key signature, or it restores a note that has been sharpened or flattened to its original position in the key signature.

Acoustics—the physical science pertaining to sound waves. The word is often used to refer to the sound properties in concert halls.

Adagio—at ease; at a slow tempo. *Adagio* is usually a tempo indication, but it may also be the title of a piece; for example, Mozart's Adagio in B Minor, or Barber's Adagio for Strings. *Adagietto* is occasionally used to denote a tempo somewhat faster than *adagio*, although, unless a composer gives a metronome marking, it is a subjective indication.

Agitato—restless; agitated. The word is very often used in tempo markings, such as *allegro agitato*.

Alberti bass—a device by which the notes of a triad or chord are played separately instead of together. The device was used by Domenico Alberti (1710–40) in his keyboard music and became common during the Classical period. Haydn's and Mozart's sonatas abound in examples.

Aleatory music—Music, especially of the avant-garde, in which the notation leaves many musical decisions to the performer's choice.

Allegretto—not as fast as *allegro*.

Allegro—literally, "cheerful"; fast but not excessively fast.

Allemande—a dance in a graceful moderate tempo with four beats per measure, consisting of two sections. The Baroque suite often begins with an allemande, if it does not open with a nondance prelude. The greatest examples of the allemande are in Bach's suites.

Andante—literally, "moving, going"; a moderate tempo, but now more often understood as a slower tempo. Andantino, its diminutive, was originally used to denote a slower pace than andante, but since andante is now used as a slow tempo the andantino marking has come to mean a slightly faster tempo.

Antiphony—Music in which two or more groups of instruments, voices, or both, are separated in space to make contrasts or echo effects.

Appassionata—a common marking, usually indicating that a passage is to be played in an ardent, impassioned way.

Appoggiatura—from appoggiare, "to lean"; a note that is a whole or half step above or below the melody note. The appoggiatura note is played within the proper tempo of the melody, but it is not a part of the melody. It is the most common of all ornaments and is used to give poignancy and/or a sense of dissonance to the melody.

Arabesque—a term that comes from Moorish architecture, meaning a piece of music that is meant to be decorative in quality rather than deep. The title does not pertain to a specific form, however; Schumann's Arabeske, for example, is in a modified Rondo form.

Aria—literally, "air." In the late seventeenth and early eighteenth centuries, an aria was a vocal form that comprised three sections, the third being a repetition of the first and the second a contrasting theme known as da capo. Today it is a commonly used name for any vocal piece in an oratorio and especially in opera.

Arpeggio—literally, "harplike"; a chord that is played in a broken manner, often starting from the bottom and proceeding upward and then back downward, usually at a rapid speed for one or more octaves. Arpeggiation is a basic device of piano technique.

Augmentation—a compositional device that lengthens a musical phrase, usually by doubling the note values; the opposite of diminution.

Augmented—an adjective applied to an interval that has been widened by a half tone or minor second. For example, the interval C–F (a perfect fourth) becomes C–F# (an augmented fourth). In early music, an augmented fourth was called Diabolus in Musicus, "the devil tuning his fiddle."

Bagatelle—a short piece, usually of a light or frivolous character.

Ballad or ballade—originally, an old popular song or folk melody set to words or a sentimental love song. In medieval France, a ballade had a refrain. By the time of Chopin and Liszt, the term ballade was also used for large-scale piano pieces with a narrative atmosphere.

Bar or bar line—the vertical line drawn through the music stave to indicate the metrical divisions of the music. The space between two bar lines is often called a measure.

Barcarolle—a boat song, usually of a kind sung by Venice's gondoliers. A barcarolle is in six-eight time. The most famous example is Offenbach's Barcarolle in Tales of Hoffmann.

Baritone—from the Greek for "a deep sound"; the masculine voice between tenor and bass.

Bass—the lowest of the adult male vocal ranges.

Bel canto—literally, "beautiful song"; a style of singing with perfect intonation and tone, and clean and perfect articulation. It originated in Italy and culminated around 1850.

Berceuse—a cradle song, a lullaby. Grieg, Chopin, and Liszt all composed berceuses.

Binary form—music in two sections. The first section ends in something other than the principal key (usually the dominant), and the second section opens in something other than the principal key. Neither section alone gives a sense of completion. The dances of Bach's suites are examples, as are Scarlatti's harpsichord sonatas.

Bolero—a Spanish dance in three-four time, usually with a triplet on the second half of the first beat. The most famous example is Ravel's orchestral work of that name, consisting of one theme repeated over and over.

Boogie-woogie—a jazz idiom, stemming from ragtime, that uses a continuous *ostinato* bass for the left hand with melodic formulation for the right, often improvised by the performer. Morton Gould wrote an exciting "Boogie-Woogie Étude."

Bourrée—a French dance in a fast two-two or four-four time, often found in the Baroque suite.

Bravura—literally, "courage, bravery"; a marking for a passage or work to be played with swagger, virtuosity, or fearlessness.

Brio—literally, "fire, spirit." It is usually used in the marking *con brio*.

Cabaletta—the fast-moving, usually brilliant last section of an aria of several sections.

Cadence—the closing to a melodic or harmonic phrase. A cadence usually closes on the tonic or "home" note. A cadence that approaches that note through the dominant harmony is called a *perfect cadence*. One that approaches it through the subdominant harmony is called a *plagal cadence*.

Cadenza—a display of vocal or instrumental technical prowess, based on a composer's thematic material. From the seventeenth through the early nineteenth centuries, cadenzas were improvised by the performer. In Classical concertos, they appear near the end of the first movement and sometimes in the finale.

Canon—an important compositional device in which one voice or instrument introduces a subject, then a second voice repeats it, followed by others in succession. The entrance of each new voice occurs before the previous one is completed. There may be canons in unison on the same notes. The entrances may be inverted. The canon is the foundation for the fugue.

Cantata—usually, an extended work based on a text, for one or more voices and chorus, often with orchestral support. There are church cantatas and secular cantatas.

Castrato—an artificial soprano or alto; a eunuch. Castrati became the preferred choice for choruses because women were not allowed to sing in church. Castrati were outlawed in France around Gluck's time, but they continued in Italy into the nineteenth century.

Chamber music—originally, domestically performed music, usually instrumental, with one player for each part, as in a trio for cello, violin, and piano, or any other combination. The string quartet consists of two violin parts, a viola, and a cello. Chamber music today is heard mostly in concert halls and on recordings.

Chord—Three or more pitches struck together.

Chromatic—from the Greek *chroma*, meaning "color." The chromatic scale proceeds by half steps until all twelve tones are used. Chromatic notes are those outside the main key or scale used in a particular piece. The heavy use of "color" chords finally undermined Classical tonality.

Clavier—a German word for keyboard instrument.

Color—tonal variety produced by different sound intensities; also called tone color.

Concerto grosso—Baroque musical form in which a small body of instruments plays in alternation, contrast, and combination with a larger group; *grosso* meaning "grand."

Consonance—an intonation of notes that produces a concord; a group of tones that sound agreeable.

Counterpoint—a mode of composition that is polyphonic or "many voiced," combining several melodies, subjects, or themes (each with its own musical texture). The intersection of the various parts provides harmony.

Courante—a popular two-part dance of the seventeenth century in three-two time, often used in Baroque suites. The name means "the running one."

Crescendo—increasing in loudness.

Da capo—Italian for "from the beginning." A direction to the performer to return to the opening of the composition and play it again.

Diatonic—the opposite of chromatic. A diatonic scale uses only the established notes for a given key, in either major or minor. Example: the E major scale must use F#, G#, C#, and D# as well as E, A, B.

Dies Irae ("Day of Wrath")—a Latin hymn that is a sequence in a Mass for the Dead, appearing between the Epistle and the Gospel.

Diminuendo—decreasing in loudness.

Diminution—repetition of a subject in notes of shorter duration.

Dissonance—intonation of notes that produces discord; a group of unstable tones that may sound harsh, disagreeable, and in need of resolution to a consonance.

Divertimento—a style of light music often in more than four movements, for various instrumental groups or orchestra. The form does not use any dance movements except the minuet. The first movement is often in sonata form. The terms serenade and cassation were used by Mozart and Haydn for the same type of piece.

Dodecaphonic—see serialism.

Dominant note—the fifth tone of a scale and the most important note of the scale after the tonic, to which it "wants" to move.

Duet—a composition for two instruments or singers. A vocal duet may be accompanied by instruments or not. An unaccompanied duet for string or wind instruments is a duo. Piano duets were once a popular form of domestic music making.

Dynamics—the loudness or softness of a piece of music; its contrasts, crescendos, diminuendos, and the like.

Electronic music—Sounds usually produced under laboratory conditions; the sounds are recorded on tape and may then be integrated into a conventional musical work, or they might stand on their own. Since the 1950s, it has been used by "advanced" composers such as Varèse and Babbitt. The term is also used to describe music made by electronic instruments such as electronic keyboards.

Embellishment—decorative material, usually of the melody—a trill, grace note, and so on; also known as an ornament.

Equal temperament—the tuning of an instrument, especially a keyboard instrument, by dividing the octave into twelve half-tones, each with exactly the same ratio of vibrations.

Étude—an instrumental exercise often based on a specific technical aspect, such as scales, arpeggios, or chords. Many études are written for pedagogical purposes, but Chopin, Liszt, Debussy, and others united technical problems with artistic quality.

Fandango—a Spanish dance of early-nineteenth-century origin, in animated triple time. A folk fandango uses guitar and castanets.

Fermata—a sign that directs the performer to pause: ⌢.

Finale—the last movement of a symphony, concerto, quartet, or other musical work; or the closing scene of an opera.

Fine—Italian for "end."

Fioritura—embellishment of a melody; a term generally used for vocal music and in particular for sopranos.

Flat—*see* accidental.

Form—a general term for the structure of the work: sonata form, dance form, and so on.

Forte—loud. The symbol used by composers is *f*. The symbol for *fortissimo*, or very loud, is *ff*. Composers have used up to *fffff*.

Fugue—a contrapuntal form using one or more subjects, introduced at first by a part called a voice. The voice introducing the subject is then answered by another voice giving the same subject a fifth higher or a fourth lower. The fugue is the most complex and elaborate of contrapuntal forms, often using devices such as augmentation, diminution, and inversion. The rules are strict, based on long usage, but the great composers (especially Bach) often broke the rules for artistic purposes.

Galant—an eighteenth-century style of C.P.E. Bach, Johann Christian Bach, and the Mannheim school of Johann and Carl Stamitz, displaying a kind of superficial elegance.

Gavotte—French dance in four-four time, beginning on the third beat and in two sections. Gavottes occur frequently in Baroque suites, but the form has intrigued countless composers, from François Gossec and Ambroise Thomas to Moderns such as Prokofiev, in his Gavotte from the *Classical* Symphony.

Gebrauchsmusik—Hindemith's term for music composed for utilitarian or practical use.

Gigue—an old English dance in binary form, usually in six-eight or twelve-eight time. It is an important part of the Baroque suite, usually (as in Bach's invariably brilliant examples) the concluding dance.

Gregorian chant—liturgical music of the medieval Roman Catholic Church, associated with the sixth-century Pope Gregory I, who supervised its organization based on plainchant, a plainsong sung in unison without measured rhythms.

Ground bass—a subject appearing in the bass, continually repeated.

Habanera—a dance form that originated in Africa and traveled to Spain via Havana, Cuba. It is in two-four time, with the first eighth note dotted. Bizet's Habanera in *Carmen* is the most celebrated example, but Ravel, Debussy, and Saint-Saëns all wrote within this dance form.

Harmony—the use of chords and combinations of chord progressions.

Heldentenor—literally "heroic tenor"; a male tenor voice of huge size, fit for Wagnerian roles.

Homophony—a kind of music consisting of a single tune with an accompaniment; the opposite of *polyphony*.

Impressionism—originally, a school of painters (Monet, Pissarro, Renoir, and others) who tried to evoke subjective states and sensory impressions rather than depict objective reality directly. The term was then appended to the music of Debussy, Ravel, Cyril Scott, Delius, Scriabin, and others. It may be considered an outgrowth and a harmonic refinement of late-nineteenth-century Romanticism.

Impromptu—an instrumental piece that suggests spontaneity or a feeling of improvisation. The Chopin impromptus are good examples.

Improvisation—playing music from one's imagination, without the aid of any printed notes. Improvisation flourished in art music until the early nineteenth century. In the twentieth century, the practice was revived on a high level with the best jazz musicians. Another word for it is *extemporization*.

Instrumentation—the art of writing for various instruments in a way that brings out their special qualities, especially in context to the whole orchestral fabric. It is also known as *orchestration*.

Intermezzo—a small theater piece played between the acts of an opera or a short instrumental work such as Brahms's Intermezzos for Piano.

Inversion—a compositional device in which ascending intervals of the melody are inverted to become descending intervals. In harmonic inversion the bass voice is put on the top of the chord.

Jota—a quick Spanish dance in three-eight time from Aragon and Navarre, dating to as early as the twelfth century. Originally it was accompanied by percussion, tambourine, and castanets.

Key signature—the major or minor key, with its sharps or flats, in which a musical work is set, written at the beginning of each stave. A work with a key signature of C major means that it was composed in that key and that the main tonality of the piece will be in that key.

Largo—literally, "spacious"; a tempo indicating a slow movement in broad style, slower than *adagio*. *Larghetto* means not quite as slow as *largo*.

Leitmotiv—a short theme that portrays a character or place. Wagner popularized the term, and in his music dramas the use of leading motives amounts to a complex structural device.

Libretto—the text of an opera.

Lied—a German art song with piano accompaniment; a self-contained song set to poetry.

Linear counterpoint—a kind of counterpoint in which the voices move totally independently of any harmonic relationship to one another.

Madrigal—a work, usually for five voices, that originated in Italy during the Renaissance. They are often secular, but there are religious madrigals as well.

Magnificat—the Latin hymn to the Virgin Mary, sung as a Vesper canticle in the Roman Catholic Church service, and as part of the evening service in the Anglican Church. It has been universally cultivated, from Palestrina to Vaughan Williams.

Major interval—For example, the interval from C to E is a major third. To create a minor third from C, lower the E one half tone to E-flat. C to E is two full tones; C to E-flat is one and a half tones.

Ma non troppo—a performance indication in Italian meaning "but not too much."

Mass—the chief liturgical service of the Roman Catholic Church. Its musical setting falls into five sections: Kyrie, Gloria, Credo, Sanctus, Benedictus, and Agnus Dei. It has been one of the greatest and most fertile of musical forms, often written for solo voices, chorus, and orchestra.

Mazurka—a sixteenth-century Polish national dance in three-four time, usually in moderate tempo. Chopin's sixty mazurkas are among the first important examples of nationalist music.

Mediant—the third note of a major or minor scale.

Meter—the rhythm produced by the notes of varying lengths. Each bar or measure contains a specific number of pulses, or beats, grouped in different patterns of whole notes, half notes, quarter notes, eighth notes, etc.

Mezzo-soprano—the female vocal range between soprano and contralto.

Minimalism—the music of Philip Glass, John Adams, Steve Reich, and other composers since the 1960s; repetition of phrases is often artfully used to create a type of unity.

Minuet—a French dance. The word means "small"; Lully popularized the form in his ballets and operas. It is a moderate, elegant, courtly dance in three-four time with a contrasting Trio section, after which the first section is repeated. It is also used in the Baroque suite and is the only dance movement contained in the sonata. Beethoven often replaced the minuet of the sonata with a Scherzo movement.

Mode—an arrangement of the tones of an octave according to a fixed scheme of intervals. Modes were established in the Middle Ages and were used until the sixteenth century. They were supplanted by the major-minor scale system.

Modulation—within a composition, harmonic movement into a new tonality or key.

Monody—a song for a single voice, with or without accompaniment.

Motet—a polyphonic sacred vocal composition, set to a Latin text.

Music-drama—a term invented by Wagner to differentiate his later stage works from other operas, for he considered them to be a synthesis of drama, poetry, philosophy, singing, and orchestral music.

Nationalism—in music, the use of folk music, national history, and dance forms in compositions that are inspired by and express aspects of a particular country. From around the second half of the nineteenth century until well into the twentieth, nationalism was one of the prime motivating factors in composition.

Neoclassicism—a twentieth-century reaction to self-absorbed Romanticism, in which many composers returned to the more objective spirit of Baroque and Classical forms.

Nocturne—an atmospheric night piece. Chopin's nineteen are the most renowned examples.

Nuance—light, shading, and color in a delicate variant of expression.

Octave—a perfect interval consisting of eight diatonic tones, for example, C to C.

Oeuvre—French for "work"; a body of compositional work or the entire output of a composer's work.

Opus—the Latin word used to number the works of many composers, usually in order of their composition or publication. It is often used in abbreviation: Op.

Oratorio—a large-scale work for solo voices, chorus, and orchestra, usually dealing with a biblical subject, but presented without scenery or costumes.

Overture—an orchestral work preceding an opera or oratorio, often using motives and themes from the opera itself; later in the nineteenth century, an overture could be an autonomous concert piece in its own right, not tied to a larger work.

Partita—a suite of dances. Bach's Six Partitas for Keyboard and three for solo violin are among his most imposing suites. In the twentieth century, the term was revived by Alfredo Casella, Vaughan Williams, Walton, Luigi Dallapiccola, and others.

Passacaglia—a composition based on a ground bass motive that is heard throughout, though not necessarily always in the bass. The finale of Brahms's Fourth Symphony is a passacaglia, and the Organ Passacaglia in C Minor of Bach is a supreme example.

Passion or passion music—a musical composition that relates the story of the passion of Christ, as given by Matthew, Mark, John, and Luke.

Pianissimo—very soft. The sign for it is: *pp.*

Piano—soft. The sign for it is: *p.*

Pizzicato—a violin technique in which the strings are plucked instead of bowed.

Polka—a dance dating from about 1830, originating in Bohemia. It is danced by couples in two-four meter with an accent on the second beat. Like the waltz, the polka, which became one of the best-loved dance forms, began its life criticized as a scandalous and licentious dance.

Polonaise—a stately, processional Polish dance in triple time, dating back to the sixteenth century. Bach, Beethoven, and Weber wrote polonaises, while the great polonaises of Chopin express his Romantic patriotism.

Polyphony—a kind of music in which two or more voices or subjects are played or sung simultaneously. Music that makes use of counterpoint is polyphonic.

Polytonality—a twentieth-century compositional procedure in which three or more keys are used simultaneously, usually making for dissonance. *Bitonality* is the use of two keys that clash together.

Presto—very fast, faster than *allegro*. *Prestissimo* means faster still.

Program music—instrumental music that is inspired by a work from another art or by history, autobiography, nature, or something else outside music. The use of extramusical and literary apparatus became increasingly sophisticated during the nineteenth century as composers became more adept at depicting a variety of musical moods and subjects. Program music is the opposite of *absolute music*.

Quartet—a musical work for four instruments or voices, such as a string quartet.

Quintet—a musical work for five instruments or voices, such as piano with a string quartet.

Ragtime—a style of African-American piano music in which tunes are "ragged" through syncopation. Developed in the 1890s, it culminated with the classic ragtime of Scott Joplin and James Scott.

Range—the distance between the top and bottom limitations of an instrument or human voice.

Recital—a concert that is given by a solo pianist, another instrumentalist and a pianist, or a singer and a pianist.

Recitative—sung speech that is used to advance the plot of an opera or oratorio. It is a form of declamation without a definite time signature or bar lines. *Recitativo secco* is recitative with a harpsichord accompaniment, used frequently in eighteenth-century opera.

Requiem—the Catholic mass for the dead, used at funeral services.

Rhapsody—music without a specific form, often using several themes. The *Hungarian Rhapsodies* of Liszt are good examples.

Ritardando—reducing speed. *Rallentando* is the same.

Rondo—an important Classical form, sometimes used alone but appearing more frequently as the finale of a sonata, quartet, concerto, or symphony. Its main theme appears at least three times, alternating with contrasting material. The structure may be ABACADA or a similar combination.

Saltarello—a lively Italian dance with jumps *(salti)*, in three-four or six-eight time. It was used as the finale in Mendelssohn's *Italian* Symphony and Berlioz's *Roman Carnival Overture*.

Sarabande—a dance of Spanish origin from the sixteenth century, introduced to the French court in 1588. The sarabande is slow, in three-two time, and often grave in mood. It is one of the main dances in the Baroque suite, along with the allemande, courante, and gigue.

Scale—a consecutive series of diatonic notes.

Scherzo—Italian for "joke"; usually the third movement of a four-movement sonata, quartet, or symphony, replacing the Minuet movement. In 1796 Beethoven first used the Scherzo in his Piano Sonata in A Major. It is normally in three-four time with a Trio section, then returning to the first section. The Romantics used the form as a separate entity. Mendelssohn's scherzos are usually light and airy.

Septet—a musical work for seven instruments or voices.

Sequence—the repetition of a melody or motive, transposed up or down.

Serialism—also called twelve-tone technique, or dodecaphonic method; a system of composition that arranges pitches in a sequence of the twelve tones of the chromatic scale, with no note repeated. The series of pitches is called a *tone row*, and it remains constant throughout the work. Twelve-tone music's major effect is the abolition of tonality. Instead of notes within the major and minor scale being powerful tonal centers, each note in a tone row is of equal importance. Serialism was invented by Schoenberg and was used or adapted by many twentieth-century composers. It had a revolutionary effect on music after 1925.

Sextet—a musical work for six instruments or voices.

Signature—a notation at the beginning of a musical work indicating the key and meter.

Sonata—a musical form that was developed during the eighteenth century from C.P.E. Bach through Beethoven and Schubert. It began as a work for piano (or solo instrument with piano) in four movements or fewer, though there are exceptions (Brahms's Piano Sonata no. 3 in F Minor is in five movements, for example). The first movement is often in sonata-allegro form. The second is a slow, songlike movement. The third is a Minuet or Scherzo, and the finale is a Rondo. A set of variations may be incorporated into the plan.

Sonatina—a short sonata, usually in three movements, without elaborate development in the first movement.

Song cycle—a group of songs with connected subject matter or any other unifying feature. Beethoven's *An die ferne Geliebte* is an early example, as is Schubert's *Winterreise*. Many composers have created some of their most personal music using the song cycle.

Soprano—the highest female voice range. The voice of a boy soprano may extend as high as a female's. Sopranos are called *dramatic, lyric,* or *coloratura,* based on their compass and sound or tonal quality. The range normally is from about B-flat below middle C to the C two octaves above middle C.

Stabat Mater—a widely used musical form; part of the liturgy of the Roman Catholic Church.

String quartet—the Classical sonata form written for an ensemble of two violins, viola, and cello.

Subdominant—the pitch of the fourth degree of a musical scale.

Subject—the theme of a fugue (where it can be as short as two notes) or the theme group in sonata-allegro form.

Submediant—the pitch of the sixth degree of a musical scale.

Suite—a form of instrumental music comprising a group of contrasting dance forms strung together. Suites from the sixteenth to the eighteenth century used one tonality or key. Dance forms often used include the hornpipe, gavotte, musette, minuet, bourrée, allemande, sarabande, and gigue. During the nineteenth and twentieth centuries, suites were frequently adapted excerpts from operas or incidental music for plays.

Supertonic—the pitch of the second degree of a musical scale.

Symphonic poem—a free orchestral work, usually in a single movement. The form was first introduced by Liszt, whose symphonic poems were inspired by literary or pictorial sources, and it was used by many subsequent composers. Some (like Dukas, in *The Sorcerer's Apprentice*) used it more literally, while others (like Richard Strauss in *Also Sprach Zarathustra*) used it more philosophically.

Symphony—from the Greek, "sounding together"; a multimovement sonata for orchestra that, from Haydn through Shostakovich, was the major orchestral form.

Syncopation—the unexpected displacement of regular metrical accents.

Tarantella—a Neapolitan dance, usually in six-eight time and increasing in speed. In its earliest stages, it was danced by couples. Tarantula stings were said to cause a delirium that made one dance, and this dance form developed to ward off the madness. Rossini, Chopin, Liszt, and many others wrote tarantellas.

Tempo—Italian for "time"; the speed of the basic beat of a musical work.

Tenor—the highest range of the male voice.

Toccata—from the Italian verb *toccare*, "to strike" or "to touch." In Bach's Baroque toccatas, keyboard virtuosity shines. Since the nineteenth century, composers have used the term to describe a small virtuoso piece of regular rhythm, such as Schumann's or Prokofiev's toccatas.

Tonic—home key or chord; the first note of a musical scale.

Triad—a chord made of three pitches, separated by intervals of a third. For example, C–E–G is a major triad. The triad is the foundation for harmony in Western music.

Trill—a musical embellishment that quickly alternates between the notes of a major or minor second, producing a vibratory sensation.

Trio—a sonata for three instruments; also, the middle section of a musical work or movement in ABA form.

Triplet—a group of three notes that are written to be sounded within the timing of two notes. A triplet is the most important deviation from regularity of beat.

Twelve-tone technique—*see* serialism.

Unison—a melody line repeated exactly by both hands playing an instrument, or sung exactly the same by two or more performers without harmony.

Variations—one of music's most ancient and viable forms—taking a melody and transforming it in many ways. The simplest variation is merely to vary the melody of a theme. Many sets of variations, such as Bach's *Goldberg* and Beethoven's *Diabelli*, go deeper into structure, theme, bass line, harmony, and so on, to produce a far more complex intellectual form.

Vibrato—a slight fluctuation of pitch, vocal or instrumental, to produce warmth and added expressivity.

Virtuoso—a performer of great technical skill.

Vivace—lively, bright; often used in conjunction with the term *allegro*.

Waltz—a dance in three-four time derived from earlier folk dances, especially the Austrian *Ländler*. The waltz was developed by Schubert and transformed by Weber, Lanner, and Johann Strauss, Jr., into a popular ballroom dance. The first beat is followed by two repeated chords from the upper harmony of the bass—*um pah pah*. The waltz became the most glamorous dance form in history.

SOURCE LIST

Acknowledgments

xv "I've always felt that . . .": "Writers at Work," *The Paris Review*, ed. George Plimpton, series two (New York: Penguin Books, 1963), pp. 72–73.

Epigraphs

xvii "The study of the history of music . . .": Richard Lewis, *In Praise of Music* (New York: Orion Press, 1963), p. 67.

xvii "Music is a higher revelation . . .": Nat Shapiro, *An Encyclopedia of Quotations about Music* (Garden City, NY: Doubleday, 1978), p. 6.

xvii "As neither the enjoyment . . .": Charles Darwin, *The Descent of Man* (Princeton, NJ: Princeton University Press, 1981), 2:333.

Introduction

4 "Mary had a little lamb . . . aback in my life": Roland Gelatt, *The Fabulous Phonograph: 1877–1977* (New York: Collier, 1977), p. 21.

5 "a special stupidity . . .": Aaron Copland, *Copland on Music* (New York: Norton, 1960), p. 124.

5 "Music itself . . . conjuring up . . .": Bernard Berenson, *Sketch for a Self-Portrait* (London: Robin Clark, 1991), p. 113.

7 "a melody is not merely . . .": Aaron Copland, "A Modernist Defends Modern Music," *New York Times Magazine*, December 5, 1949, p. 11.

8 "Music 'says' things about the world . . .": Aldous Huxley, *Music at Night and Other Essays* (1931; reprinted by London: Triad Grafton, 1986), p. 41.

PART I: THE MEDIEVAL, RENAISSANCE, AND ELIZABETHAN AGES

11 "that musical notes and rhythm . . .": Charles Darwin, *The Descent of Man* (Princeton, NJ: Princeton University Press, 1981), 2:336.

12–13 "music was not a set of compositional . . .": Iain Fenlon, *Man and Music: The Renaissance* (London: Macmillan, 1989), p. 1.

13 "I envy those jacks . . .": William Shakespeare, *The Norton Shakespeare*, ed. Stephen Greenblatt (New York: Norton, 1997), p. 1966.

Giovanni Pierluigi da Palestrina

17 "one senses that the technique . . .": Charles Gounod, *Mémoires d'un artiste* (Paris: Calmann-Lévy, 1896), p. 100.

17 "composed with continuous application . . .": Eric Blom, ed., *Grove's Dictionary of Music and Musicians*, 5th ed. (New York: St. Martin's Press, 1964), 6:512.

William Byrd

18 "Byrd, though the creator of . . .": Glenn Gould, *The Glenn Gould Reader*, ed. Tim Page (New York: Alfred A. Knopf, 1984), p. 13.

18 "Reasons briefely set downe . . .": William Byrd, *The Collected Works of William Byrd* (London: Stainer and Bell, 1950), 14:1.

Giovanni Gabrieli

19–20 "Palestrina and Lassus inherited and perfected . . .": Alfred Einstein, *A Short History of Music*, 3rd ed. (New York: Dorset Press, 1986), p. 67.

Carlo Gesualdo

20 "Gesualdo's music is so strange . . .": Aldous Huxley, *Gesualdo: Variations on a Musical Theme* (New York: Harper and Brothers, 1959), p. 182.

John Dowland

21 "Whose heavenly touch upon the lute . . .": A. L. Bacharach, ed., *The Music Masters*, vol. 1, *From the Sixteenth Century to the Time of Beethoven* (Baltimore: Penguin, 1957), p. 144.

21 "The position of John Dowland . . .": ibid.

Gregorio Allegri

22 "of a singular gentleness . . .": Blom, *Grove's Dictionary*, 1:115.

PART II: THE AGE OF THE BAROQUE

27 "one of the most excellent and important . . .": Will Durant and Ariel Durant, *The Age of Louis XIV* (New York: Simon and Schuster, 1963), p. 32.

27 "I have honored them . . .": ibid., p. 33.

27 "It was . . . not so much a masterpiece . . .": ibid., pp. 91–92.

27 "I was of a low and inconsiderable . . .": ibid., p. 208.

28 "so far surpassed whatever . . .": ibid., p. 267.

30 "What strikes me most markedly . . .": Aaron Copland, *Copland on Music* (New York: Norton, 1960), p. 37.

George Frideric Handel

31 "Whether I was in my body . . .": Romain Rolland, *A Musical Tour Through the Land of the Past* (New York: Henry Holt, 1922), p. 48.

32–33 "Some say, that Signor . . .": A. L. Bacharach, ed., *The Music Masters: After Beethoven to Wagner* (Baltimore: Penguin, 1957), 2:197.

33 "I reached here on . . .": written on the score of *Jephtha*, February 13 and 23.

33 "in the hope of rejoining . . .": Wallace Brockway and Herbert Weinstock, *Men of Music: Their Lives, Times, and Achievements* (New York: Simon and Schuster, 1966), p. 83.

34 "To him I bend the knee . . .": Ludwig van Beethoven, *Beethoven: The Man, and The Artist as Revealed in His Own Words*, ed. Friedrich Kerst and Henry E. Krehbiel (New York: Dover, 1964), p. 54.

34 "On Wednesday Evening at about 8 . . .": Edward Downes, *The New York Philharmonic Guide to the Symphony* (New York: Walker, 1976), p. 376.

35 "Handel's oratorios thrive . . .": Ian Crofton and Donald Fraser, *Dictionary of Musical Quotations* (New York: Schirmer, 1985), sec. 208.8.

35 "the most gigantic effort . . .": Romain Rolland, *Handel* (New York: Henry Holt, 1916), p. 178.

36 "I think I did see all Heaven . . .": Paul Henry Lang, *George Frederic Handel* (New York: Norton, 1966), p. 336.

36 "there are at all times . . .": L. B. Urbino, *Biographical Sketches of Eminent Musical Composers* (Boston: Oliver Ditson, 1876), p. 58.

Johann Sebastian Bach

39 "I was obliged to work . . .": Crofton and Fraser, *Dictionary of Musical Quotations*, p. 11.

39 "It appeared self-evident that . . .": Albert Schweitzer, *A Treasury of Albert Schweitzer*, ed. Thomas Kiernan (New York: Gramercy, 1945), p. 200.

41 "born musicians": Gertrude Norman and Miriam Lubell Shrifte, comps. and eds., *Letters of Composers: An Anthology, 1603–1945* (Westport, CT: Greenwood Press, 1979), p. 26.

41 "a good clear soprano": ibid., p. 26.

41 "my gracious prince who . . .": ibid., p. 24.

41 "1. the position is not nearly . . .": ibid., p. 25.

42 "I worked hard": Hans T. David and Arthur Mendel, eds., *The Bach Reader* (New York: Norton, 1945), p. 334.

42 "a manifestation, on the plane of art . . .": Norman and Shrifte, *Letters of Composers*, p. 779.

43 "the most stupendous miracle . . .": Milton Cross and David Ewen, *Encyclopedia of the Great Composers and Their Music* (Garden City, NY: Doubleday, 1953), 1:15.

43 "a sheaf of pages . . .": Pablo Casals, *Joys and Sorrows: Reflections by Pablo Casals as Told by Albert E. Kahn* (New York: Simon and Schuster, 1970), pp. 46–47.

44 "The *Brandenburg Concertos* are the purest . . .": Schweitzer, *Treasury of Albert Schweitzer*, p. 198.

44 "I humbly pray for you not . . .": Norman and Shrifte, *Letters of Composers*, p. 24.

45 "a treasury of musical scholarship . . .": Ernest Hutcheson, *The Literature of the Piano: A Guide for Amateur and Student*, 3rd rev. ed. (New York: Alfred A. Knopf, 1964), p. 39.

46 "If Bach continues to play . . .": Crofton and Fraser, *Dictionary of Musical Quotations*, p. 12.

46 "It is as though eternal harmony . . .": ibid., p. 12.

46 "The *Orgelbüchlein* is not only . . .": Schweitzer, *Treasury of Albert Schweitzer*, p. 197.

47 "Bach's *St. Matthew Passion* is perhaps . . .": Anton Ehrenzweig, *The Hidden Order of Art: A Study in the Psychology of Artistic Imagination* (Berkeley and Los Angeles: University of California Press, 1967), p. 161.

47–48 "Any shades of crescendo . . .": David Dubal, *Reflections from the Keyboard: The World of the Concert Pianist* (New York: Summit, 1984), p. 23.

48 "Dear Goldberg . . .": Norman Lebrecht, *The Book of Musical Anecdotes* (New York: Free Press, 1985), p. 22.

48 "The elegance of the *Goldberg* . . .": David Matthews, ed., *Keyboard Music* (New York: Praeger, 1972), p. 95.

Domenico Scarlatti

50 "Dear reader, whether you are . . .": David Dubal, *The Art of the Piano* (San Diego: Harcourt Brace, 1995), p. 398.

50 "This son of mine is an eagle . . .": Ralph Kirkpatrick, *Scarlatti: Sixty Sonatas* (New York: Schirmer, 1953), p. 21.

51 "till he had heard . . . of its powers": Ralph Kirkpatrick, *Domenico Scarlatti* (Princeton, NJ: Princeton University Press, 1953), p. 33.

52 "an agreeable man in society . . .": Eric Blom, ed., *Grove's Dictionary of Music and Musicians*, 5th ed. (New York: St. Martin's Press, 1964), 4:152–57.

52 "my music master who has followed . . .": Kirkpatrick, *Domenico Scarlatti*, p. 72.

52 "this greatest of keyboard . . .": Sacheverell Sitwell, *Baroque and Rococo* (New York: G. P. Putnam's Sons, 1967), p. 294.

52 "Spain fired the imagination . . .": Wanda Landowska, *Landowska on Music*, ed. Denise Restout and Robert Hawkins (New York: Stein and Day, 1964), p. 246.

53 "There is hardly an aspect . . .": Kirkpatrick, *Domenico Scarlatti*, pp. 114–15.

Jean-Baptiste Lully

56 "I do not believe that there . . .": David Ewen, *Encyclopedia of Musical Masterpieces: An Incomparable Concert and Record Guide* (New York: Grosset and Dunlap, 1944), p. 330.

Arcangelo Corelli

57 "It looks deceptively simple . . .": David Dubal, *Conversations with Menuhin* (London: William Heinemann, 1991), p. 46.

Henry Purcell

58–59 "Poetry and painting . . .": Louis C. Elson, ed., *Modern Music and Musicians*, vol. 3, *The Great Composers* (New York: University Society, 1918), p. 29.

59 "Here lyes Henry Purcell . . .": Blom, *Grove's Dictionary*, 6:1001.

59 "Masters as great as he . . .": Eric Blom, *A Musical Postbag* (London: J. M. Dent & Sons, 1949), p. 41.

François Couperin

61 "Couperin's language differs . . .": Landowska, *Landowska on Music*, p. 260.

Jean-Philippe Rameau

63–64 "It is certain that harmony can arouse various . . .": Blom, *Grove's Dictionary*, 7:34.

64 "Rameau was lyrical, and . . .": Claude Debussy, *Debussy on Music*, ed. Richard Langham Smith (New York: Alfred A. Knopf, 1977), p. 230.

PART III: THE AGE OF CLASSICISM

73 "In the music of a master slowness . . .": Donald Francis Tovey, *The Forms of Music* (New York: Meridian, 1956), p. 220.

75 "that great giant whose steps I always hear . . .": Robert Simpson, ed., *The Symphony*, vol. 1, *Haydn to Dvořák* (Baltimore: Penguin, 1966), p. 318.

75 "Man only plays when in the full . . .": Norman O. Brown, *Life Against Death* (Middletown, CT: Wesleyan University Press, 1970), p. 33.

Christoph Willibald Gluck

77 "It is sometimes necessary . . .": Piero Weiss, ed., *Letters of Composers Through Six Centuries* (Philadelphia: Chilton, 1967), p. 84.

78–79 "I begged him . . . into our music": Alec Robertson and Denis Stevens, eds., *The Pelican History of Music*, vol. 3, *Classical and Romantic* (Baltimore: Penguin, 1968), p. 41.

79 "I now strive to be a poet . . .": Gertrude Norman and Miriam Lubell Shrifte, eds. and comps., *Letters of Composers: An Anthology, 1603–1945* (Westport, CT: Greenwood Press, 1979), p. 45.

79 "I think it is my duty . . .": ibid., p. 45.

79 "I have striven to restrict . . .": Eric Blom, ed., *Grove's Dictionary of Music and Musicians*, 5th ed. (New York: St. Martin's Press, 1964), 3:679.

79 "I love money more . . .": L. B. Urbino, *Biographical Sketches of Eminent Musical Composers* (Boston: Oliver Ditson, 1876), p. 79.

80 "little nightingale": A. L. Bacharach, ed., *The Music Masters* (Baltimore: Penguin, 1959), 4:175.

80 "No one has ever stirred up . . .": Norman and Shrifte, *Letters of Composers*, p. 50.

80 "Happy people! . . .": Harold Schonberg, *The Lives of the Great Composers* (New York: Penguin, 1947), p. 56.

80 "I do not know whether . . .": Robertson and Stevens, *Pelican History of Music*, 3:37.

80 "He thrust the doors open . . .": Milton Cross and David Ewen, *Encyclopedia of the Great Composers and Their Music* (Garden City, NY: Doubleday, 1953), p. 297.

81 "as many rehearsals . . . insupportable of all": Norman and Shrifte, *Letters of Composers*, p. 45.

81 "I read and reread Gluck's . . .": Hector Berlioz, *Memoirs of Hector Berlioz, from 1803 to 1865*, trans. Rachel Holmes and Eleanor Holmes, ed. Ernest Newman (New York: Dover, 1966), p. 22.

81 "I believe that if Gluck were to . . .": The Arts Council, *Berlioz and the Romantic Imagination* (London: The Arts Council and the Victoria and Albert Museum in Cooperation with the French Government, 1969), p. 22.

Franz Joseph Haydn

83 "Oh, God, how much is still . . .": Ian Crofton and Donald Fraser, *Dictionary of Musical Quotations* (New York: Schirmer, 1985), p. 76.

83 "more floggings than food": Schonberg, *Lives of the Great Composers*, p. 62.

84 "no conjuror on any instrument": ibid., p. 63.

84 "a delightful grove . . .": Blom, *Grove's Dictionary*, 4:150.

85 "My Prince was always satisfied . . .": ibid., 4:151.

85 "We shall not ever meet again": Cross and Ewen, *Encyclopedia of the Great Composers*, p. 370.

85 "[preferred] people of [his] own class": Schonberg, *Lives of the Great Composers*, p. 61.

85 "Because whenever I think of God . . .": David Dubal, *Conversations with Menuhin* (London: William Heinemann, 1991), p. 9.

86 "I knelt down every day . . .": Blom, *Grove's Dictionary*, 4:159.

86 "One moment I was cold as ice . . .": ibid.

86 *"The Seasons* gave me the finishing stroke": ibid., 4:160.

86 "I have only just learned in my old age . . .": ibid., 4:162.

86 "I know that God has bestowed . . .": ibid., 4:163.

87 "Haydn compels our study just because . . .": Daniel Gregory Mason, *Beethoven and His Forerunners* (New York: Macmillan, 1904), p. 195.

89 "Oh, Papa, you have no education . . . language": Crofton and Fraser, *Dictionary of Musical Quotations*, sec. 20.5.

90 "Haydn shows himself to be . . .": Edward Downes, *The New York Philharmonic Guide to the Symphony* (New York: Walker, 1976), pp. 426–27.

90 "one of the grandest compositions . . .": ibid., p. 434.

93 "is the greatest splendor . . .": C. G. Burke, *The Collector's Haydn* (Philadelphia, PA: J. B. Lippincott, 1959), pp. 243–44.

Wolfgang Amadeus Mozart

95 "People are wrong who think . . .": Joseph Solman, *Mozartiana* (New York: Vintage, 1990), p. 14.

97 "This boy will consign us all . . .": ibid., p. 23.

98 "I did not know . . .": ibid., p. 7.

98 "I will never have anything more . . .": Blom, *Grove's Dictionary*, 5:934.

99–100 "a delicate and lovable soul . . .": Solman, *Mozartiana*, p. 40.

100 "We cannot despair about mankind . . .": Marian McKenna, *Myra Hess: A Portrait* (London: Hamish Hamilton, 1976), p. 165.

100 "he learned for himself the taste . . .": Saul Bellow, *It All Adds Up: From the Dim Past to the Uncertain Future: A Nonfiction Collection* (New York: Viking, 1994), p. 14.

100 "The whole concerto is an object lesson . . .": Ralph Hill, ed., *The Concerto* (Harmondsworth: Penguin, 1952), p. 115.

101 "with a sense of proportion and dramatic . . .": Charles Rosen, *The Classical Style: Haydn, Mozart, Beethoven* (New York: Viking, 1971), p. 210.

101 "Suddenly with the A minor sonata . . .": David Dubal, *The Art of the Piano* (San Diego: Harcourt Brace, 1995), p. 375.

102 "No concerto andante of Mozart's . . .": C. M. Girdlestone, *Mozart and His Piano Concertos* (London: Cassell, 1978), p. 251.

103 "Christ inspires truly and exclusively . . .": Modeste Tchaikovsky, *The Life and Letters of Peter Ilich Tchaikovsky*, trans. Rosa Newmarch (New York: Vienna House, 1973), pp. 117–18.

103 "I tell you that your son . . .": Blom, *Grove's Dictionary*, 6:936.

104 "We will never get an idea like that": Dubal, *Art of the Piano*, p. 373.

105 "Combining grace and majesty . . .": Girdlestone, *Mozart and His Piano Concertos*, p. 352.

105 "The Finale, *allegro assai*, is euphoric . . .": Dubal, *Art of the Piano*, p. 374.

105 "In its sustained imaginative power . . .": Hill, *Concerto*, p. 95.

106 "a long summer day spent in a . . .": Sir Thomas Beecham, *A Mingled Chime: An Autobiography* (New York: G. P. Putnam's Sons, 1942), p. 154.

106 "Every number in *Figaro* is for me . . .": Solman, *Mozartiana*, p. 144.

106 "The characters in *Figaro* are not the characters . . .": W. J. Turner, *Mozart: The Man and His Works* (London: J. M. Dent, 1939), p. 338.

107 "*Don Giovanni* [was] the best of operas . . .": Daniel Cory, *Santayana: The Later Years* (New York: George Braziller, 1963), p. 145.

107 "*Don Giovanni* was the first music to produce . . .": Norman and Shrifte, *Letters of Composers*, p. 259.

107–8 "The G minor Quintet is the most poignant . . .": J.W.N. Sullivan, *Beethoven: His Spiritual Development* (New York: Alfred A. Knopf, 1944), p. 64.

108 "In his chamber music Mozart fascinates . . .": Tchaikovsky, *Life and Letters of Tchaikovsky*, p. 260.

108 "Here they talk about nothing . . .": Solman, *Mozartiana*, p. 139.

109 "What a piece! No amount of analysis . . .": ibid., p. 111.

110 "*The Magic Flute* is life itself . . .": Wilhelm Furtwängler, *Notebooks of Wilhelm Furtwängler: 1924–54*, ed. Michael Tanner (New York: Quartet, 1995), p. 193.

111 "Since death, strictly speaking, is the true end . . .": Wolfgang Amadeus Mozart, *Letters of Mozart*, ed. Hans Mersmann (New York: Dorset Press, 1986), p. 233.

111 "The death of Mozart before . . .": Solman, *Mozartiana*, p. 184.

Ludwig van Beethoven

114 "Blessed is he who has overcome all . . .": Friedrich Kerst and Edward Krehbiel, eds., *Beethoven: The Man and the Artist* (New York: Dover, 1964), p. 91.

114 "Keep your eyes on him . . .": John N. Burk, *The Life and Work of Beethoven* (New York: The Modern Library, Random House, 1946), p. 20.

115 "receive the spirit of Mozart from . . .": Denis Matthews, *Beethoven* (New York: Vintage/Random House, 1988), p. 12.

115 "Not Handel or Mozart in earlier times . . .": Joseph Kerman, *The Beethoven Quartets* (New York: Norton, 1966), p. 5.

115 "Beethoven's magnificent playing . . .": Matthews, *Beethoven*, p. 23.

115–16 "It is amazing that the cultured . . .": Ernest Hutcheson, *The Literature of the Piano* (New York: Alfred A. Knopf, 1948), p. 81.

116 "It was impossible for me . . .": Sullivan, *Beethoven*, p. 110.

116 "I will take Fate by the throat": ibid., p. 107.

117 "Love alone—yes only love . . .": ibid., p. 123.

117 "It was by no means an enjoyment . . .": Frederick Freedman, ed., *Spori's Autobiography* (New York: Da Capo Press, 1969), p. 189.

117 "Submission, absolute submission . . .": Sullivan, *Beethoven*, p. 170.

117 "Deep within himself the artist . . .": ibid., p. 105.

117–18 "He lived in a universe richer than ours . . .": ibid., p. 24.

118 "Truly, a hard lot has fallen . . .": Ludwig van Beethoven, *Beethoven: Letters, Journals, and Conversations*, ed. Michael Hamburger (New York: Doubleday Anchor, 1960), p. 270.

118 "No words of comfort could . . .": Sullivan, *Beethoven*, p. 257.

118 "[H]ad we a Beethoven among us . . .": Wilfrid Mellers, *Beethoven and the Voice of God* (New York: Oxford University Press, 1983), p. 368.

118 "Beethoven brought three startling innovations . . .": Aaron Copland, *Copland on Music* (New York: Norton, 1960), p. 39.

119 "The essence of Beethoven . . .": Louis Kentner, *Piano* (New York: Schirmer, 1976), p. 106.

120 "a flower between two abysses": Donald Francis Tovey, *Beethoven* (London: Oxford University Press, 1945), p. 80.

120 "It is a flash of genius . . .": Kempff's notes for his Deutsche Grammophon recordings of the Beethoven sonatas, 1970.

120 "Now you have a sonata that . . .": written by Beethoven on Sonata no. 29.

120 "The immensity of this composition . . .": Hutcheson, *Literature of the Piano*, p. 124.

120 "The Fugue is an almost insensate . . .": Sullivan, *Beethoven*, p. 44.

121 "This work has won me . . .": Cross and Ewen, *Encyclopedia of the Great Composers*, p. 72.

121 "Beethoven's *Fidelio* . . . combines the profoundest . . .": Howard Mills, ed., *Memoirs of Shelley and Other Essays and Reviews* (New York: New York University Press, 1970), p. 177.

121 "[scale] the greatest heights . . .": Stephen Spender, *World Within World: The Autobiography of Stephen Spender* (New York: St. Martin's Press, 1994), p. 72.

122 "cobbler's patch": John Gillespie, *Five Centuries of Keyboard Music* (New York: Dover, 1972), p. 192.

123 "All three movements demonstrate . . .": Donald Francis Tovey, *Essays in Musical Analysis*, vol. 3, *Concertos* (London: Geoffrey Cumberlege/Oxford University Press, 1936), p. 76.

125 "mysterious in radiantly happy . . .": Matthews, *Beethoven*, p. 179.

125 "there's something of the same . . .": Lawrence Durrell to Henry Miller, *The Durrell-Miller Letters, 1935–1980* (New York: New Directions, 1988), p. 18.

126 "Everything that I had thought and been . . .": André Maurois, *Memoirs: 1885–1967* (New York: Harper and Row, 1970), p. 72.

126 "So just another tyrant . . .": Blom, *Grove's Dictionary*, 1:542.

126 "Composed to celebrate the memory of a great man": Godfrey Ridout and Gordon V. Thompson, *A Concert Goer's Companion to Music* (Toronto: G. V. Thompson Music, 1996), p. 56.

126 "the infallible logic that guides him . . .": Norman and Shrifte, *Letters of Composers*, pp. 352–53.

127 "a slender Greek maiden": Matthews, *Beethoven*, p. 157.

127 "more the expression of feeling . . .": ibid., p. 162.

127 "[A]lmighty one, in the woods . . .": Kerst and Krehbiel, *Beethoven*, p. 1964.

127 "the apotheosis of the Dance": Cross and Ewen, *Encyclopedia of the Great Composers*, p. 60.

128 "For all its revolutionary aspect . . .": Matthews, *Beethoven*, p. 167.

128 "Finished with God's help": Mellers, *Beethoven and the Voice of God*, p. 11.

128 "Blessed and blessing, this music is . . .": Aldous Huxley, *Music at Night and Other Essays* (1931, reprinted by London: Triad Grafton, 1986), p. 41.

129 "Do you think I worry about . . .": Kerman, *Beethoven Quartets*, p. 119.

130 "Even Shakespeare . . . never wrote his C-sharp . . .": Sullivan, *Beethoven*, p. 259.

130 "All art exists to communicate . . .": ibid., pp. 228–29.

130 "there was the exploration . . .": Spender, *World Within World*, p. 71.

Giuseppe Tartini

134 "One night I dreamed that I had sold my soul . . .": Boris Schwarz, *Great Masters of the Violin* (New York: Simon and Schuster, 1983), p. 75.

134 "In the history of violin playing . . .": ibid., p. 22.

Giovanni Battista Pergolesi

135 "All Paris divided into two . . .": Jean-Jacques Rousseau, *The Confessions of Jean-Jacques Rousseau*, trans. J. M. Cohen (Baltimore: Penguin, 1954), p. 257.

135 "Only *The Village Soothsayer* could . . .": ibid.

Carl Philipp Emanuel Bach

136 "This music presents the most . . .": Alfred Einstein, *A Short History of Music*, 3rd ed. (New York: Dorset Press, 1986), pp. 154–55.

137 "Of Emanuel Bach's pianoforte works . . .": Ludwig van Beethoven, *Beethoven's Letters*, ed. A. Eaglefield-Hull (New York: Dover, 1972), p. 90.

Pietro Nardini

137 "The beauty, purity and equality . . .": Blom, *Grove's Dictionary*, 6:10.

Luigi Cherubini

140 "The guillotine was kept . . .": Bacharach, *Music Masters*, 4:254.

140 "I understand; you like music . . .": ibid.

141 "In spirit I am often with you . . .": Beethoven, *Beethoven: Letters*, p. 296.

Johann Nepomuk Hummel

143 "my old man certainly . . .": Ernst Berger, *Franz Liszt: A Chronicle of His Life in Pictures and Documents* (Princeton, NJ: Princeton University Press, 1989), p. 152.

PART IV: THE ROMANTIC AGE

148 "Mozart's melodies may be brilliant . . .": Aldous Huxley, "The Young Archimedes," in *Collected Short Stories* (Chicago: Ivan R. Dee, 1992), p. 239.

148 "Heard melodies are sweet . . .": Keats, "Ode on a Grecian Urn," *Immortal Poems of the English Language,* ed. Oscar Williams (New York: Washington Square Press, 1992), p. 325.

149 "[a] vague, mellow tone-cloud . . .": Arthur Loesser, *Men, Women, and Pianists* (New York: Dover, 1990), p. 340.

149 "Chopin's music was as destructive . . .": Charles Rosen, *Arnold Schoenberg* (New York: Viking, 1975), p. 27.

149–50 "Chopin could appeal not only to listeners . . .": Norman Davies, *Europe: A History* (Oxford: Oxford University Press, 1996), p. 820.

152 "I believe that *Die Meistersinger* . . .": Mark N. Grant, *Maestros of the Pen* (Boston: Northeastern University Press, 1998), p. 133.

152 "I have become a completely different fellow . . .": Arnold Whittall, *Romantic Music* (London: Thames and Hudson, 1987), p. 101.

Nicolò Paganini

159 "I am neither young nor handsome . . .": Renée de Saussine, *Paganini* (New York: McGraw-Hill, 1954), p. 117.

160 "I can teach you nothing . . .": Boris Schwarz, *Great Masters of the Violin* (New York: Simon and Schuster, 1983), p. 177.

161 "No one ever asks if you have . . .": Derek Watson, comp., *The Wordsworth Dictionary of Musical Quotations* (Ware, Hertfordshire: Wordsworth Editions, 1994), p. 173.

162 "I heard the singing of an angel": de Saussine, *Paganini,* p. 120.

162 "Never in my life have I heard . . .": Leslie Sheppard and Dr. Herbert R. Axelrod, *Paganini* (Neptune City, NJ: Paganinia, 1979), p. 284.

162 "At last a dark figure . . .": Heinrich Heine, *The Prose Writing of Heinrich Heine,* ed. Havelock Ellis (London: Walter Scott, n.d.), pp. 200–1.

162 "What a man . . .": Alan Walker, *Franz Liszt* (New York: Alfred A. Knopf, 1983), p. 174.

163 "Paganini's genius for composition . . .": Milton Cross and David Ewen, *Encyclopedia of the Great Composers and Their Music* (Garden City, NY: Doubleday, 1953), 2:571.

164 "The sinister, cadaverous . . .": Wilfrid Mellers, *Man and His Music* (New York: Schocken, 1969), 4:33.

164 "They opened up a world . . .": Schwarz, *Great Masters of the Violin,* p. 177.

Carl Maria von Weber

167 "To judge a contemporary work . . .": Sam Morgenstern, ed., *Composers on Music* (New York: Pantheon, 1956), p. 97.

168 "a wandering minstrel . . . winning all hearts . . .": Eric Blom, ed., *Grove's Dictionary of Music and Musicians,* 5th ed. (New York: St. Martin's Press, 1964), 9:203.

168 "no more fruitful source . . .": Morgenstern, *Composers on Music,* p. 100.

168 "That usually feeble little man . . .": John Warrack, *Carl Maria von Weber* (New York: Macmillan, 1968), p. 220.

169   "I am going to London to die": ibid., p. 307.

169   "I heard the lid close upon his coffin": ibid.

169   "It was the greatest success . . .": Wallace Brockway and Herbert Weinstock, *Men of Music* (New York: Simon and Schuster, 1966), p. 223.

169   "In my youth, I had learned . . .": Warrack, *Carl Maria von Weber*, p. 347.

169   "The Briton does you justice . . . all German composers": Cross and Ewen, *Encyclopedia of the Great Composers*, p. 889.

170   "An angel passes through the sky": David Dubal, *The Art of the Piano* (San Diego: Harcourt Brace, 1995), p. 267.

172   "In my exclusive worship of . . .": Hector Berlioz, *Memoirs of Hector Berlioz, from 1803 to 1865*, trans. Rachel Holmes and Eleanor Holmes, ed. Ernest Newman (New York: Dover, 1966), p. 58.

172   "The *Konzertstück* is a keystone . . .": Warrack, *Carl Maria von Weber*, p. 238.

172   "The lady sits in her tower . . .": ibid., pp. 237–38.

173   "This music is as yet . . .": ibid., p. 269.

173   "We sense how he savored . . .": Edward Downes, *The New York Philharmonic Guide to the Symphony* (New York: Walker, 1976), p. 1032.

Gioachino Rossini

175   "I take Beethoven twice a week . . .": Francis Toye, *Rossini: The Man and His Music* (New York: Dover, 1987), p. 233.

175   "Although still a boy . . .": Herbert Weinstock, *Rossini* (New York: Limelight, 1987), p. 16.

175   "The people follow him about . . .": Jacques Barzun, *Pleasures of Music* (New York: Viking, 1951), p. 539.

176   "I confess that I have little hope . . .": Gertrude Norman and Miriam Lubell Shrifte, comps. and eds., *Letters of Composers: An Anthology, 1603–1945* (Westport, CT: Greenwood Press, 1979), p. 110.

176   "Could you tell me who . . .": Weinstock, *Rossini*, p. 276.

176   "A strong case, indeed . . .": Toye, *Rossini*, p. 248.

176   "I know of no more admirable . . .": Norman Lebrecht, comp., *The Book of Musical Anecdotes* (New York: Free Press, 1985), p. 105.

176   "Rossini, big, fat, in the sunniest . . .": Felix Mendelssohn, *Letters*, ed. G. Selden-Goth (New York: Pantheon, 1945), p. 260.

177   "Wait until the evening before . . .": Ray Robin, *Words on Music* (New York: Beaufort, 1984), p. 93.

177   "women to sing in church . . .": Norman and Shrifte, *Letters of Composers*, p. 114.

177   "to the pianists of the fourth class . . .": Weinstock, *Rossini*, p. 469.

177–78 "the only creator of truly comic music": Cross and Ewen, *Encyclopedia of the Great Composers*, p. 639.

178   "Napoleon is dead; but a new conqueror . . .": Stendhal, *Life of Rossini*, trans. Richard N. Coe (Great Britain: Criterion Books, 1957), p. 1 of preface.

178   "They have been crucifying *Othello* . . .": Barzun, *Pleasures of Music*, p. 539.

178   "My Immortality is dependent on . . .": Lebrecht, *Book of Musical Anecdotes*, p. 107.

179   "Ah, Rossini, . . .": Toye, *Rossini*, p. 120.

Franz Schubert

181 "The latest news in Vienna . . .": Norman and Shrifte, *Letters of Composers*, p. 119.

181 "If I wished to teach . . .": Blom, *Grove's Dictionary*, 7:537.

182 "You know from experience . . .": ibid., 7:552–53.

183 "I feel myself to be the most unhappy . . .": ibid., 7:550.

183 "If I came to see him in the morning . . .": Cross and Ewen, *Encyclopedia of the Great Composers*, p. 680.

183 "Anyone who knew Schubert . . . degradation": Harold Schonberg, *The Lives of the Great Composers* (New York: Norton, 1970), p. 109.

184 "I am ill . . . This is my end!": Blom, *Grove's Dictionary*, 7:558.

184 "The art of music here entombed . . .": ibid.

184 "Schubert's place in the history . . .": *Encyclopaedia Britannica* (Chicago: William Benton, 1968), 19:1191.

187 "sad, plaintive . . .": Schonberg, *Lives of the Great Composers*, p. 114.

188 "Where did this power come from? . . .": Bruno Monsaingeon, *Mademoiselle: Conversations with Nadia Boulanger*, trans. Robin Marsack (Boston: Northeastern University Press, 1988), p. 40.

188 "This is what I should be singing . . .": Norman and Shrifte, *Letters of Composers*, p. 118.

189 "It is one of the miracles . . .": Alec Robertson, ed., *Chamber Music* (Baltimore: Penguin, 1957), p. 163.

189 "more active . . .": Robert Schumann, *On Music and Musicians* (New York: Pantheon, 1946), p. 121.

190 "This music has always sounded to me . . .": Arthur Rubinstein, *My Many Years* (New York: Alfred A. Knopf, 1980), p. 494.

Gaetano Donizetti

194 "The opera cost me infinite . . .": Piero Weiss, *Letters of Composers Through Six Centuries* (Philadelphia: Chilton, 1967), p. 172.

195 "The people made so much noise . . .": Berlioz, *Memoirs of Hector Berlioz*, p. 183.

196 "an incessant worker . . .": L. B. Urbino, *Biographical Sketches of Eminent Musical Composers* (Boston: Oliver Ditson & Co., 1876), p. 282.

197 "The world wants new things . . .": Weiss, *Letters of Composers Through Six Centuries*, p. 274.

198 "How can I say which? . . .": Lebrecht, *Book of Musical Anecdotes*, p. 114.

Vincenzo Bellini

199 "Carve in your head . . .": Watson, *Wordsworth Dictionary of Musical Quotations*, p. 325.

200 "I say nothing about the music . . .": Charles Osborne, ed., *The Dictionary of Composers* (New York: Taplinger, 1981), p. 42.

200 "I too shed tears . . .": ibid.

200 "My poor *Norma* has been persecuted . . .": Norman and Shrifte, *Letters of Composers*, p. 121.

200 "Everybody is praising the music . . .": Morgenstern, *Composers on Music*, pp. 110–12.

200 "soul was certainly pure . . .": Heine, *Prose Writing of Heinrich Heine*, p. 195.

201 "If I too could write . . .": Schonberg, *Lives of the Great Composers*, p. 215.

201 "No one who did not live . . .": John Roselli, *Music and Musicians in Nineteenth Century Italy* (Portland, OR: Amadeus Press, 1991), pp. 70–71.

201 "I have heard *Norma* . . .": Eugène Delacroix, *The Journal of Eugène Delacroix*, trans. Walter Pach (1937; reprinted by New York: Grove, 1961), 8:357.

202 "Bellini's music is so little known . . .": Edward J. Dent, *The Rise of Romantic Opera*, ed. Winton Dean (Cambridge, UK: Cambridge University Press, 1976), pp. 164–65.

202 "I formed my idea of noble . . .": Henry Pleasants, *The Great Singers* (New York: Simon and Schuster, 1966), p. 134.

202 "Bellini is poor, it's true . . .": Osborne, *Dictionary of Composers*, p. 263.

202 "If you were out at sea . . .": Urbino, *Biographical Sketches of Eminent Musical Composers*, p. 294.

202 "The pieces in *Norma* which . . .": Morgenstern, *Composers on Music*, p. 111.

Hector Berlioz

204 "I was in a state of ecstasy . . .": Letter dated February 5, 1875, in The Arts Council, *Berlioz and the Romantic Imagination* (London: The Arts Council and the Victoria and Albert Museum in Cooperation with the French Government, 1969).

204 "My father had no intention . . .": Berlioz, *Memoirs of Hector Berlioz*, pp. 13–14.

204 "I had discovered . . .": ibid., p. 11.

204–5 "Become a doctor! . . . came to pass": ibid., p. 16.

207 "[t]he music of Berlioz took root . . .": Elaine Brody, *Paris: The Musical Kaleidoscope, 1870–1925* (New York: George Braziller, 1987), p. 6.

207 "But before the body had reached . . .": Jacques Barzun, *Berlioz and His Century* (Chicago: University of Chicago Press, 1982), p. 412.

208 "The prevailing characteristics . . .": Berlioz, *Memoirs of Hector Berlioz*, p. 220.

208 "He is an immense nightingale . . .": Cross and Ewen, *Encyclopedia of the Great Composers*, p. 82.

208 "A young musician of morbid . . .": Godfrey Ridout and Gordon V. Thompson, *A Concert Goer's Companion to Music* (Toronto: Gordon V. Thompson Music, 1996), p. 90.

208 "I was introducing the viola . . .": Berlioz, *Memoirs of Hector Berlioz*, p. 202.

208–9 "That is not at all what I want . . .": Barzun, *Berlioz and His Century*, p. 202.

209 "This sudden and unexpected revelation . . .": ibid., pp. 66–67.

209 "caressed by the playful breeze . . .": ibid., p. 320.

209 "This is how it *ought* to go!": Berlioz, *Memoirs of Hector Berlioz*, p. 223.

209–10 "Unhappy composers! . . .": ibid.

210 "Nothing in all my artistic career . . .": ibid., p. 421.

211 "whoever wants to know . . .": Barzun, *Berlioz and His Century*, p. 11.

Felix Mendelssohn

212 "Genuine music fills the soul . . .": Mendelssohn, *Letters*, ed. Selden-Goth, p. 313.

213 "I gave these lessons . . .": Dubal, *Art of the Piano*, p. 169.

213 "Every morning I get . . .": Mendelssohn, *Letters*, ed. Selden-Goth, p. 22.

213 "Ah, see the Jew boy . . .": Cross and Ewen, *Encyclopedia of the Great Composers*, p. 473.

213 "It was a Jew . . .": Blom, *Grove's Dictionary*, 5:675.

214 "the very model of . . .": Heinrich Eduard Jacob, *Felix Mendelssohn and His Times* (Englewood Cliffs, NJ: Prentice-Hall, 1963), p. 139.

215 "Violence of contrast, dramatic . . .": Daniel Gregory Mason, *The Romantic Composers* (London: Macmillan, 1917), pp. 176–77.

216 "Eight string players might . . .": Alec Robertson, ed., *Chamber Music* (Baltimore: Penguin, 1957), p. 178.

216 "I have grown accustomed . . .": Ian Crofton and Donald Fraser, *Dictionary of Musical Quotations* (New York: Schirmer, 1985), p. 93.

217 "The whole country has . . .": Felix Mendelssohn, *Letters of Mendelssohn* (New York: Vienna House, 1971), p. 109.

Frédéric Chopin

221 "I have five lessons . . .": Frédéric Chopin, *Selected Correspondence of Fryderyk Chopin*, ed. Bronislaw E. Sydow and Arthur Hedley (New York: McGraw-Hill, 1963), p. 115.

221 "The white collar . . .": Arthur Hedley, *Chopin* (New York: Collier, 1962), p. 21.

222 "What is true and beautiful . . .": Chopin, *Selected Correspondence*, p. 97.

222 "Hats off, gentlemen . . .": Schonberg, *Lives of the Great Composers*, p. 154.

222 "I have written . . .": Chopin, *Selected Correspondence*, p. 36.

222 "You find here the greatest splendour . . .": ibid., p. 93.

223 "I have got into the highest of society . . .": Frédéric Chopin, *Chopin's Letters*, comp. Henryk Opienski, trans. and ed. E. L. Voynich (New York: Dover, 1988), p. 168.

223 "enchanting impression . . . virtuoso": Hedley, *Chopin*, p. 61.

223 "he played a whole number of new . . .": Chopin, *Selected Correspondence*, p. 134.

224 "three most famous doctors . . .": Chopin, *Chopin's Letters*, p. 186.

224 "It was surrounded by every . . .": Chopin, *Selected Correspondence*, p. 306.

225 "the piano bard . . . upon this instrument": Catherine Drinker Bowen, *"Free Artist": The Story of Anton and Nicholas Rubinstein* (Boston: Little, Brown, 1939), p. 316.

225 "Those who have distorted fingers . . .": G. C. Ashton Jonson, *A Handbook to Chopin's Works* (London: William Reeves, c.1910), p. 96.

226 "To do justice to the mazurkas . . .": Dubal, *Art of the Piano*, p. 311.

226 "In these first few mazurkas . . .": ibid.

226 "It is not meant to create . . .": Chopin, *Selected Correspondence*, p. 24.

227 "Chopin is one of the supreme . . .": Mason, *Romantic Composers*, p. 211.

227 "cannon buried in flowers": James Huneker, *Chopin: The Man and His Music* (New York: Dover, 1966), p. 181.

228 "the odyssey of Chopin's soul": James Huneker, *Chopin* (New York: Charles Scribner's Sons, 1900), p. 200.

228 "If all piano music in the world . . .": Henry T. Finck, *Chopin and Other Musical Essays* (New York: Charles Scribner's Sons, 1889), p. 51.

229 "How are seriousness and gravity . . .": Dubal, *Art of the Piano*, p. 321.

229 "so overflowing with tenderness . . .": Robert Schumann, *On Music and Musicians* (New York: Pantheon, 1946), p. 138.

229 "the brightest jewels in . . .": ibid., p. 311.

229 "the Chopin waltzes were never . . . divine delicacies": ibid., p. 32.

230 "night winds sweeping over church-yard . . .": Dubal, *Art of the Piano*, p. 323.

231 "Through his brilliant passages . . .": ibid., p. 307.

Robert Schumann

232 "I am affected by . . .": Joan Chissell, *Schumann* (New York: Collier, 1962), p. 60.

233 "[c]hilly jurisprudence . . .": ibid., p. 25.

234 "living out a novel . . .": Peter F. Ostwald, *Schumann, Music and Madness* (London: Victor Gollancz, 1985), p. 105.

234 "She has a delightfully . . .": Chissell, *Schumann*, p. 52.

234 "I think the first . . .": ibid., p. 58.

234 "Delight is linked . . .": Dubal, *Art of the Piano*, p. 407.

234 "You'll smile when . . .": Chissell, *Schumann*, p. 64.

235 "Every time Robert composes . . .": Joan Chissell, *Clara Schumann: A Dedicated Spirit—A Study of Her Life and Work* (New York: George Braziller, 1987), p. 70.

235 "He, my glorious Robert . . .": Robert Haven Schauffler, *Florestan* (New York: Henry Holt, 1945), p. 251.

236 "I stood by the body . . .": Chissell, *Clara Schumann*, p. 138.

236 "His temperament, so finely . . .": ibid., p. 63.

236 "You love Schumann! . . .": Louis C. Elson, ed., *Modern Music and Musicians* (New York: University Society, 1918), p. 197.

236 "Schumann is truly the musician . . .": Dubal, *Art of the Piano*, p. 402.

237 "Culturally speaking . . .": Gary Lemco, "Nietzsche and Schumann," *Journal of the Nietzsche Society* 1 (1996).

238 "one can take a transcendental approach . . .": Dubal, *Art of the Piano*, p. 407.

238 "It would be hard . . .": Robert Schumann, *Fantasia* in Op. 17, preface, ed. Harold Bauer (New York: Schirmer, 1946).

238 "Through all the tones . . .": ibid.

238–39 "[A]t the close my painful . . .": Schauffler, *Florestan*, p. 322.

239 "peaceful, tender and happy . . .": Dubal, *Art of the Piano*, p. 402.

239 "My music now seems . . .": ibid., p. 406.

239 "Play my *Kreisleriana* . . .": Schauffler, *Florestan*, p. 326.

240 "Isn't there perhaps . . .": Ostwald, *Schumann, Music and Madness*, p. 157.

242 "one of the finest . . .": Robert Schumann, *The Letters of Robert Schumann*, ed. Karl Storck (New York: Benjamin Blom, 1971), p. 247.

242 "I have completed . . .": Downes, *New York Philharmonic Guide to the Symphony*, p. 834.

242 "the spirit of spring . . .": Schumann, *Letters of Robert Schumann*, p. 239.

242 "breathe into your orchestra . . .": Schauffler, *Florestan*, p. 166.

243 "Yes, indeed, I . . .": Philip Hale, *Philip Hale's Boston Symphony Programme Notes: Historical, Critical, and Descriptive Comment of Music and Composers*, ed. John N. Burk (Garden City, NY: Doubleday, Doran, 1936), p. 282.

243 "I know of few more . . .": ibid.

Franz Liszt

245 "Oh, believe me, I beseech . . .": Franz Liszt, *The Letters of Franz Liszt to Olga von Meyendorff, 1871–1886* (Cambridge, MA: Harvard University Press, 1979), pp. 121–32.

246 "My mind and fingers have been . . .": Alan Walker, ed., *Franz Liszt: The Man and His Music* (New York: Taplinger, 1970), p. 27.

247 "Liszt is the pianist . . .": Alan Walker, *Franz Liszt*, vol. 1, *The Virtuoso Years, 1811–1847* (New York: Alfred A. Knopf, 1983), p. 232.

247 "I write to you without knowing . . .": Chopin, *Chopin's Letters*, p. 171.

247 "I've just witnessed . . .": Dubal, *Art of the Piano*, p. 169.

248 "*Le concert, c'est moi*": Schonberg, *Lives of the Great Composers*, p. 182.

249 "It is enough to have lived . . .": Walker, *Franz Liszt*, vol. 1, *The Virtuoso Years*, p. 18.

249 "He was literally like a sun . . .": Dubal, *Art of the Piano*, p. 167.

249 "He played as no one . . .": ibid., p. 169.

249 "Never have I met a man . . .": ibid.

249 "We are all descended from . . .": Ferruccio Busoni, *The Essence of Music and Other Papers* (New York: Dover, 1957), p. 139.

249 "Liszt's transcriptions for piano . . .": George Steiner, *Real Presences* (Chicago: University of Chicago Press, 1989), p. 20.

250 "quite literally transformed . . .": Dubal, *Art of the Piano*, p. 169.

250 "My sole ambition . . .": Geoffrey Hindley, *Larousse Encyclopedia of Music* (New York: Excalibur Books, 1981), p. 320.

252 "looks forward . . . to the evanescent texture . . .": Dubal, *Art of the Piano*, p. 352.

252 "the noblest example . . .": Busoni, *Essence of Music*, p. 162.

252 "The sonata is beautiful beyond . . .": Dubal, *Art of the Piano*, p. 169.

252 "Liszt's Piano Sonata in B minor . . .": ibid., p. 357.

253 "is surely one of the most . . .": Walker, *Franz Liszt*, vol. 1, *The Virtuoso Years*, p. 101.

Richard Wagner

256 "Since never in my life . . .": Richard Wagner, *Selected Letters of Richard Wagner*, ed. Stewart Spencer and Barry Millington (New York: Norton, 1980), p. 323.

258 "I can only adore you . . .": Brian Magee, *Aspects of Wagner*, rev. ed. (New York: Oxford University Press, 1988), p. 32.

258 "He offers me everything that I need . . .": Wagner, *Selected Letters*, p. 600.

259 "this glorious, unique man . . .": Magee, *Aspects of Wagner*, p. 32.

260 "He was everything the bourgeois feared . . .": Virgil Thomson, *A Virgil Thomson Reader* (Boston: Houghton Mifflin, 1981), p. 238.

260 "had the religious sense that Wagner . . .": Allan Bloom, *The Closing of the American Mind* (New York: Simon and Schuster, 1987), p. 68.

260 "Wagner knew he was making . . .": Magee, *Aspects of Wagner*, p. 36.

260 "To me *Tristan* is and remains . . .": Crofton and Fraser, *Dictionary of Musical Quotations*, p. 154.

260–61 "He knows of a chord which . . .": W. H. Auden, *Forewords and Afterwords* (New York: Vintage, 1989), p. 255.

261 "All that I owe to him . . .": Magee, *Aspects of Wagner*, p. 31.

261 "perhaps the greatest genius . . .": ibid., p. 48.

261 "God give me a failure like that": ibid., p. 51.

261 "If one has not heard Wagner at Bayreuth . . .": Crofton and Fraser, *Dictionary of Musical Quotations*, p. 155.

261 "that old poisoner": ibid.

261 "Wagner was the greatest man . . .": Magee, *Aspects of Wagner*, p. 31.

261 "There was only Beethoven and Wagner . . .": ibid., p. 51.

261 "Most nineteenth-century anti-Semites would . . .": Auden, *Forewords and Afterwords*, p. 247.

262 "To admire Wagner, except for certain aspects . . .": Cecil Gray, *Musical Chairs* (London: Hogarth, 1985), pp. 86–87.

262 "The thrall of Wagner has abated . . .": Igor Stravinsky and Robert Craft, *Themes and Conclusions* (Berkeley and Los Angeles: University of California Press, 1982), p. 247.

262 "My whole being was consumed with it . . .": M. Owen Lee, *First Intermissions* (New York: Oxford University Press, 1995), p. 83.

263–64 "He had met Mathilde, his Beatrice . . .": Joseph Campbell, *The Master of God: Creative Mythology* (New York: Penguin, 1968), p. 71.

264 "It was certainly, in part, the serious . . .": ibid.

264 "the Orpheus of life's secret pain": ibid., p. 225.

264–65 "[o]ne of the seven wonders of the musical world": Olin Downes, *On Music* (New York: Simon and Schuster, 1957), p. 292.

265 "[t]here is no work of art which . . .": John Wilson, ed., *The Faith of an Artist* (London: George Allen and Unwin, 1962), p. 171.

265 "Wagner has lovely moments but . . .": Crofton and Fraser, *Dictionary of Musical Quotations*, p. 154.

265–66 "Could Wagner revisit the earth . . .": Auden, *Forewords and Afterwords*, p. 253.

266 "Fortunate century that saw this spirit . . .": Ernest Newman, *The Life of Richard Wagner*, vol. 4, *1866–1883* (Cambridge: Cambridge University Press, 1946), p. 182.

267 "As I awoke, my ear caught a sound . . .": Downes, *New York Philharmonic Guide to the Symphony*, p. 1019.

267 "Wagner, as the fever in his blood grew . . .": J.W.N. Sullivan, *Beethoven: His Spiritual Development* (New York: Alfred A. Knopf, 1944), p. 62.

267 "His tastes in clothes and interior decoration . . .": Auden, *Forewords and Afterwords*, p. 246.

267 "Richy Wagner is a soft-bodied sensualist-pussy": Crofton and Fraser, *Dictionary of Musical Quotations*, p. 155.

267 "If I only could hear a little Wagner tonight!": Charles Baudelaire, *Selected Letters of Charles Baudelaire*, ed. Rosemary Lloyd (London: Weidenfeld and Nicolson, 1986), p. 145.

Giuseppe Verdi

269 "If there is anything in life . . .": Giuseppe Verdi, *Letters of Giuseppe Verdi*, ed. Charles Osborne (New York: Holt, Rinehart and Winston, 1972), p. 142.

269 "I did my first lesson on the old spinet . . .": Mary Jane Phillips-Matz, *Verdi: A Biography* (Oxford: Oxford University Press, 1993), p. 18.

270 "During the first days of June . . .": Giuseppe Verdi, *Verdi: The Man in His Letters*, ed. Franz Werfel and Paul Stephan (New York: L. B. Fisher, 1942), pp. 86–87.

270–71 "It is superb, magnificent, tense . . .": ibid., p. 89.

271 "was born under a lucky star": ibid., p. 92.

271 "Nowadays, what an apparatus accompanies . . .": Verdi, *Letters of Giuseppe Verdi*, p. 184.

272 "Sad sad sad! Wagner is dead . . .": ibid., p. 219.

272 "Ah, Shakespeare, Shakespeare . . .": Verdi, *Man in His Letters*, p. 310.

273–74 "Verdi is dead . . .": Frank Walker, *The Man Verdi* (London: J. M. Dent, 1962), p. 509.

274 "Few heads of state have been tendered . . .": Phillips-Matz, *Verdi*, pp. 765–76.

274 "Verdi set the entire world to music . . .": Peter Conrad, *A Song of Love and Death: The Meaning of Opera* (London: Hogarth, 1989), p. 147.

274 "Rigoletto is not only outwardly deformed . . .": Lee, *First Intermissions*, p. 19.

275 "The libretto is a by-word for obscurity . . .": James Anderson, *The Complete Dictionary of Opera and Operetta* (New York: Wing Books/Random House, 1995), p. 584.

275 "*La Traviata* was an immense fiasco . . .": Phillips-Matz, *Verdi*, pp. 765–76.

276 "Characters who never existed in an ancient . . .": Olin Downes, *Ten Operatic Masterpieces* (New York: Charles Scribner's Sons, 1952), p. 10.

276 "But *Maestro Senatore* Verdi is quite another matter . . .": Weiss, *Letters of Composers Through Six Centuries*, p. 356.

277 "Bülow has made an ass of himself . . .": ibid., p. 575.

277 "Will you forgive me . . .": Phillips-Matz, *Verdi*, p. 712.

277 "What is the most surprising thing . . .": James Huneker, *Overtones: A Book of Temperament* (New York: Charles Scribner's Sons, 1904), p. 269.

278 "One of the most serious and seemingly least . . .": Ernest Newman, *More Stories of Famous Operas* (Philadelphia: Blakiston, 1946), p. 363.

Charles Gounod

280 "Liberty is as real as . . .": Norman and Shrifte, *Letters of Composers*, p. 207.

280 "If you can send him back . . . I can teach him.": James Harding, *Gounod* (New York: Stein and Day, 1973), p. 28.

281 "My poor dear mother gave . . .": Charles Gounod, *Mémoires d'un artiste* (Paris: Calmann-Lévy, 1896), p. 56.

281 "I feel that the land . . .": Harding, *Gounod*, p. 125.

281 "is passionately fond of music . . .": ibid., p. 42.

282 "Oh, most unhappy earth! . . .": Norman and Shrifte, *Letters of Composers*, p. 206.

283 "of Gounod and company seems . . .": Claude Debussy, *Debussy Letters*, ed. François Lesure and Roger Nichols (London: Faber and Faber, 1987), p. 14.

283 "The true founder of . . .": Frits Noske, *French Song from Berlioz to Duparc* (New York: Dover, 1970), p. 160.

283 "There are no singers to equal . . .": Harding, *Gounod*, p. 97.

284 "The historical importance . . .": ibid., p. 114.

Jacques Offenbach

285 "I do not know what . . .": Siegfried Kracauer, *Orpheus in Paris: Offenbach and the Paris of His Time* (New York: Alfred A. Knopf, 1938), p. 89.

285–86 "He will be, indeed . . .": Crofton and Fraser, *Dictionary of Musical Quotations*, p. 101.

286 "She deserved well her . . .": Kracauer, *Orpheus in Paris*, p. 90.

286 "fleshly music": Schonberg, *Lives of the Great Composers*, p. 308.

286 "Offenbach's music is wicked . . .": Crofton and Fraser, *Dictionary of Musical Quotations*, p. 101.

286 "the Mozart of the Champs-Elysées": Schonberg, *Lives of the Great Composers*, p. 307.

287 "a dung heap on which . . .": Downes, *Ten Operatic Masterpieces*, p. 239.

287 "I hope this William Krupp . . .": Kracauer, *Orpheus in Paris*, p. 308.

287 "[i]n France I became . . .": Cross and Ewen, *Encyclopedia of the Great Composers*, p. 320.

287 "I would give all . . .": Downes, *Ten Operatic Masterpieces*, p. 239.

287 "Hurry, hurry . . .": ibid.

288 "*The Tales of Hoffmann* may be . . .": ibid., p. 236.

César Franck

290 "What is of the first importance . . .": Crofton and Fraser, *Dictionary of Musical Quotations*, p. 67.

291 "This symphony was the affirmation . . .": Hale, *Philip Hale's Boston Symphony Programme Notes*, p. 148.

291 "There! You see . . .": Blom, *Grove's Dictionary*, 3:467.

291 "*Mes enfants! Mes pauvres enfants!*": Laurence Davies, *César Franck and His Circle* (Boston: Houghton Mifflin, 1970), p. 243.

291 "*Adieu, Maître, et merci* . . .": Rollo Myers, *Emmanuel Chabrier and His Circle* (Rutherford, NJ: Fairleigh Dickinson University Press, 1969), p. 102.

292 "César Franck was a simple-hearted . . .": H. L. Mencken, *H. L. Mencken on Music*, ed. Louis Cheslock (New York: Schirmer, 1975), pp. 172–73.

293 "But my dear sir . . . It sounded well . . .": Cross and Ewen, *Encyclopedia of the Great Composers*, p. 278.

Bedřich Smetana

295 "My compositions do not belong . . .": Ernest Rychnowsky, *Smetana* (Stuttgart: Deutsche Verlagsanstalt, 1924), p. 263.

295 "With God's help and grace . . .": Anton Neumayr, *Music and Medicine* (Bloomington, IL: Medi-Ed Press, 1997), 3:144.

295 "When I was seventeen . . .": ibid., p. 183.

296 "I had already been in Prague . . .": ibid.

296 "Smetana's genuine . . . for a fine work": ibid.

297 "My intention is to idealize . . .": ibid., p. 180.

298 "I must give my people . . .": ibid., p. 183.

298 "I have been ill . . . whistling would stop": ibid., p. 170.

298 "on the morning of October . . .": Bedřich Smetana, *Letters and Reminiscences*, ed. F. Bartos (Prague: Artia, 1955), p. 150.

298 "I am wholly determined . . .": Cross and Ewen, *Encyclopedia of the Great Composers*, p. 752.

298 "many dark moments . . . condition like mine": Neumayr, *Music and Medicine*, p. 185.

299 "He saw music as . . .": Geoffrey Clive, *The Romantic Enlightenment* (New York: Meridian, 1960), p. 49.

299 "Absolute music is impossible . . . from my life": Morgenstern, *Composers on Music*, p. 207.

299 "*The Bartered Bride* is only a toy . . .": Watson, *Wordsworth Dictionary of Musical Quotations*, p. 122.

300 "Two springs pour forth . . .": written on the original score.

301 "inclination to art in my youth . . . obviously troubles me": Norman and Shrifte, *Letters of Composers*, pp. 217–18.

Anton Bruckner

303 "I cannot find the words . . .": Derek Watson, *Bruckner* (New York: Schirmer, 1975), p. 41.

303 "He came from the most . . .": Robert Simpson, ed., *The Symphony*, vol. 1, *Haydn to Dvořák* (Baltimore: Penguin, 1966), p. 248.

303 "I cannot describe . . .": Neumayr, *Music and Medicine*, 3:481.

305 "When God calls me to him . . .": Cross and Ewen, *Encyclopedia of the Great Composers*, p. 154.

305 "for I did not wish . . . great pleasure": Norman and Shrifte, *Letters of Composers*, pp. 220–21.

305 "The Master, who was then . . .": ibid., p. 221.

305 "Since Beethoven there . . .": Erwin Doernberg, *The Life and Symphonies of Anton Bruckner* (London: Barrie and Rockliff, 1960), pp. 91–92.

305 "a day on which I wept": Cross and Ewen, *Encyclopedia of the Great Composers*, p. 155.

305 "I do not like to begin . . .": Ridout and Thompson, *A Concert Goer's Companion to Music*, p. 169.

306 "is conditioned by the militant . . .": Blom, *Grove's Dictionary*, 1:971.

306 "Yesterday I heard . . .": Wilfrid Mellers, in *The Listener* (London), Dec. 1955.

307 "I came home and felt sad . . .": Ridout and Thompson, *A Concert Goer's Companion to Music*, p. 165.

308 "A work such as the Eighth . . .": Wilhelm Furtwängler, *Notebooks of Wilhelm Furtwängler, 1924–54*, ed. Michael Tanner (New York: Quartet, 1995), p. 188.

308 "to the King of Kings . . .": Watson, *Bruckner*, p. 42.

Johann Strauss II

310 "If it is true that . . .": Peter Kemp, *The Strauss Family: Portrait of a Musical Family* (London: Omnibus Press, 1989), p. 140.

310–11 "Strauss and his waltzes obliterate . . .": Chopin, *Chopin's Letters*, p. 129.

311 "There appeared innumerable articles . . .": Schonberg, *Lives of the Great Composers*, p. 229.

311 "So perfect a band . . .": *The Morning Post* (London), April 18, 1838.

311 "Now the brat . . .": Kemp, *Strauss Family*, p. 33.

311 "My father was a musician . . .": ibid., p. 15.

312 "an unforgettable evening . . . genius of Vienna": Schonberg, *Lives of the Great Composers*, p. 304.

312 "Unfortunately not by Johannes Brahms": Kemp, *Strauss Family*, photo section.

312 "For fifty years Johann Strauss has . . .": ibid., p. 153.

312 "People will go to *Fledermaus* . . .": ibid., p. 132.

312 "They are professors! . . .": ibid., p. 436.

313 "there is a mystical something . . .": Mencken, *H. L. Mencken on Music*, p. 126.

313 "But you know very well that . . .": Kemp, *Strauss Family*, p. 143.

313 "*Die Fledermaus* was the greatest . . .": Sir Thomas Beecham, *A Mingled Chime: Leaves from an Autobiography* (New York: G. P. Putnam's Sons, 1943), p. 157.

Johannes Brahms

315 "Passions are not natural to mankind . . .": Letter to Clara Schumann, in Malcolm MacDonald, *Brahms* (New York: Schirmer, 1990), p. 49.

316 "You tell me I should have the same . . .": Jan Swafford, *Johannes Brahms* (New York: Alfred A. Knopf, 1998), p. 29.

316 "A great master of the musical art . . .": ibid., p. 27.

317 "And he has come . . .": Swafford, *Brahms*, p. 84.

319 "I know very well . . .": Brockway and Weinstock, *Men of Music*, p. 469.

319 "a brilliant and decided failure . . .": ibid., p. 95.

319 "The tragic mood of this first movement . . .": Donald Francis Tovey, *Concertos and Choral Works* (New York: Oxford University Press, 1935), p. 89.

320 "These diabolical variations . . .": James Huneker, *Mezzotints in Modern Music* (New York: Charles Scribner's Sons, 1899), p. 57.

321 "There is not a hint of what is commonly . . .": Mencken, *H. L. Mencken on Music*, p. 49.

321 "Brahms, the modern master . . .": Walter Niemann, *Brahms* (New York: Alfred A. Knopf, 1929), p. 434.

323 "a jolly potpourri . . .": Hale, *Philip Hale's Boston Symphony Programme Notes*, p. 93.

323 "a tiny, tiny piano concerto . . .": Swafford, *Brahms*, p. 464.

324 "My first symphony is . . .": Watson, *Wordsworth Dictionary of Musical Quotations*, p. 24.

324 "exquisite spot": Hale, *Philip Hale's Boston Symphony Programme Notes*, p. 81.

325 "The listener need not worry . . .": Tovey, *Concertos and Choral Works*, p. 225.

326 "The radiant music of the A major . . .": Melvin Berger, *Guide to Sonatas* (New York: Anchor, 1991), p. 76.

326 "The whole sonata is a caress": ibid.

326 "The glorious, soaring opening theme . . .": Berger, *Guide to Sonatas*, p. 77.

327 "It is with the late piano works . . .": Dubal, *Art of the Piano*, p. 301.

327 "An audience of even one is too many . . .": ibid.

328 "ungodly ditties": Watson, *Wordsworth Dictionary of Musical Quotations*, p. 48.

Alexander Borodin

330 "I am a composer in search . . .": Crofton and Fraser, *Dictionary of Musical Quotations*, p. 46.

331 "knew a prodigious quantity . . .": M. D. Calvocoressi and Gerald Abraham, *Masters of Russian Music* (New York: Alfred A. Knopf, 1936), p. 113.

331 "blind fate has led him . . .": Modeste Tchaikovsky, *The Life and Letters of Peter Ilyich Tchaikovsky*, trans. Rosa Newmarch (New York: Vienna House, 1973), p. 250.

332 "Days, weeks, months . . .": Norman and Shrifte, *Letters of Composers*, p. 228.

332 "I love my science . . .": ibid., p. 228.

332 "I cannot compose! . . .": Calvocoressi and Abraham, *Masters of Russian Music*, p. 172.

333 "an ingenuous work whose . . .": Arbie Orenstein, ed., *A Ravel Reader* (New York: Columbia University Press, 1990), p. 346.

333 "Through the silence of the steppes . . .": David Ewen, *Encyclopedia of Musical Masterpieces: An Incomparable Concert and Record Guide* (New York: Grosset and Dunlap, 1944), p. 102.

Camille Saint-Saëns

336 "Of applause / I still hear . . .": Romain Rolland, *Musicians of To-day* (New York: Henry Holt, 1915), p. 97.

336 "knows everything but he lacks . . .": Schonberg, *Lives of the Great Composers*, p. 329.

336 "not merely in the front rank . . .": *Letters of Franz Liszt to Olga von Meyendorff*, p. 301.

337 "I have lost both . . .": Michael Stegemann, *Camille Saint-Saëns and the French Solo Concerto, 1850–1920* (Portland, OR: Amadeus Press, 1984), p. 38.

337 "I gave everything . . .": Stegemann, *Camille Saint-Saëns*, p. 42.

338 "Isn't there anyone who cares . . .": Debussy, *Debussy on Music*, p. 54.

338 "I need not waste my words . . .": George Bernard Shaw, *London Music in 1888–89 as Heard by Corno di Bassetto* (New York: Dodd, Mead, 1937), p. 361.

338 "The vintage is in! . . .": Gabriel Fauré, *Gabriel Fauré: His Life Through His Letters*, comp. Jean-Michel Nectoux, trans. J. A. Underwood (New York: Marion Boyars, 1984), p. 311.

338 "The artist who does not feel . . .": Cross and Ewen, *Encyclopedia of the Great Composers*, p. 657.

339 "it opened like Bach . . .": Dubal, *Art of the Piano*, p. 395.

340 "It embraces in principle . . .": Downes, *New York Philharmonic Guide to the Symphony*, p. 785.

Georges Bizet

343 "I dreamed last night . . .": Winton Dean, *Bizet* (London: J. M. Dent and Sons, 1948), p. 86.

343 "My young friend . . .": ibid., p. 44.

344 "The score of *Les Pêcheurs* . . .": ibid., p. 52.

344 "It is maddening . . .": ibid., p. 55.

344 "I'm condemned to the stage . . .": ibid, p. 54.

344–45 "This music is wicked": Downes, *Ten Operatic Masterpieces*, p. 179.

345 "love as fate . . .": Henri Meilhac and Ludovic Halévy, *Carmen* (New York: Park Lane Press, 1996), last words of Act IV.

346 "*Carmen* is one of the comparatively few . . .": Dean, *Bizet*, pp. 204–5.

346 "To appreciate *Carmen* . . .": A. W. Raitt, *Prosper Mérimée* (New York: Charles Scribner's Sons, 1970), pp. 191–92.

346 "I consider it a chef-d'oeuvre . . .": Tchaikovsky, *Life and Letters of Tchaikovsky*, p. 382.

Modest Mussorgsky

348 "I regard the people as . . .": Crofton and Fraser, *Dictionary of Musical Quotations*, p. 98.

348 "Mussorgsky was at that time . . .": Calvocoressi and Abraham, *Masters of Russian Music*, pp. 180–81.

349 "I shall never forget how . . .": Alexandra Orlova, ed., *Musorgsky Remembered*, trans. V. Zaytzeff and F. Morrison (Bloomington: Indiana University Press, 1991), p. 17.

349 "I foresee a new kind of melody . . .": Cross and Ewen, *Encyclopedia of the Great Composers*, p. 551.

350 "The Rubicon will be crossed . . .": Jay Leyda and Sergei Bertensson, trans. and eds., *The Musorgsky Reader* (New York: Norton, 1947), pp. 111–12.

350 "An autumnal ripeness . . .": Paul Rosenfeld, *Discoveries of a Music Critic* (New York: Vienna House, 1972), p. 128.

351 "The following day we were . . .": Orlova, *Musorgsky Remembered*, p. 75.

351 "The artist believes in the future . . .": Schonberg, *Lives of the Great Composers*, p. 348.

351 "Never before has such a refined . . .": Debussy, *Debussy on Music*, p. 348.

352 "subterranean sounds . . .": Downes, *New York Philharmonic Guide to the Symphony*, p. 601.

353 "he has completely altered its values . . .": A. L. Bacharach, ed., *The Music Masters*, vol. 3, *The Romantic Age* (New York: Pelican, 1958), p. 345.

353 "Marvelous is his power . . .": Alec Robertson and Denis Stevens, eds., *The Pelican History of Music*, vol. 3, *Classical and Romantic* (Baltimore: Penguin, 1968), p. 184.

Peter Ilyich Tchaikovsky

355 "Last night I played nearly the whole . . .": Peter Tchaikovsky, *Letters to His Family*, trans. Galina von Meck (New York: Stein and Day, 1981), p. 167.

356 "I have entered the newly-opened . . .": Tchaikovsky, *Life and Letters of Tchaikovsky*, p. 42.

357 "To be sorry for the past, to hope . . .": Tchaikovsky, *Letters to His Family*, p. 169.

358 "I suffer, not only from torments . . .": H. C. Colles, ed., *Grove's Dictionary of Music and Musicians*, 3rd ed. (New York: Macmillan, 1941), 3:287.

358–59 "To refrain from writing opera . . .": ibid., 3:290.

359 "My *seams* always showed . . .": ibid., 3:292–93.

359 "He has many things to say which . . .": ibid., 3:293.

360 "I have worked on it *con amore* . . .": Tchaikovsky, *Life and Letters of Tchaikovsky*, p. 42.

361 "Friedrich Fischer once asserted . . .": Hale, *Philip Hale's Boston Symphony Programme Notes*, p. 361.

362 "That is fate, that tragic power . . .": Edwin Evans, *Tchaikovsky* (New York: Avon, 1960), p. 98.

362 "one of the most towering . . .": Simpson, *The Symphony*, vol. 1, *From Haydn to Dvořák*, pp. 346–47.

362 "I passionately love every manifestation . . .": Gerald Abraham, ed., *The Music of Tchaikovsky* (New York: Norton, 1946), p. 35.

362 "vile libretto. Lines from the greatest . . .": Vladimir Nabokov, *Vladimir Nabokov: Selected Letters 1940–1977*, ed. Dmitri Nabokov and Matthew J. Bruccoli (San Diego: Harcourt, Brace, Jovanovich, 1989), p. 148.

364 "Tchaikovsky may be justly described as the ballet . . .": Humphrey Searle, *Ballet Music* (London: Constable, 1958), p. 68.

364 "Every morning, every ballet . . .": Interview of Nureyev by dance critic John Gruen, 1970.

365 "I give you my word of honor . . .": Hale, *Philip Hale's Boston Symphony Programme Notes*, p. 351.

Antonín Dvořák

367 "Any intelligent and sensitive artist . . .": Otakar Dvořák, *Antonín Dvořák: My Father* (Spillville, IA: Czech Historical Research Center), p. 460.

368 "It cannot be emphasized too strongly . . .": Antonín Dvořák, "Music in America," *Harper's Magazine*, February 1895.

369 "remain a very dear memory . . .": Norman and Shrifte, *Letters of Composers*, p. 274.

369 "His music makes a delightfully frank . . .": Daniel Gregory Mason, *From Grieg to Brahms* (New York: Outlook, 1903), p. 94.

370 "Glory be to you! . . .": Downes, *New York Philharmonic Guide to the Symphony*, p. 325.

371 "It is not true . . .": Dvořák, *Antonín Dvořák: My Father*, p. 169.

372 "Why on earth didn't I . . .": Ralph Hill, ed., *The Concerto* (Baltimore: Penguin, 1961), p. 242.

Edvard Grieg

374 "The artist is an optimist . . .": Norman and Shrifte, *Letters of Composers*, p. 45.

374 "I felt something like an electric . . .": John Horton, *Grieg* (London: J. M. Dent and Sons, 1974), p. 6.

374–75 "school life was in the last degree . . .": ibid., p. 5.

375 "Well, so we two great men meet . . .": ibid., p. 19.

375 "I think I laughed . . .": Walker, *Franz Liszt*, p. 18.

375–76 "No, I cannot! . . . 'Keep steadily on . . . don't let them intimidate you' ": Percy Grainger, Preface to the musical score of Grieg Piano Concerto (New York: Schirmer, 1919).

376 "I regret to say that after the issue of the Dreyfus . . .": Norman and Shrifte, *Letters of Composers*, p. 276.

376 "Grieg is bonbons wrapped in snow": Schonberg, *Lives of the Great Composers*, p. 376.

Nikolai Rimsky-Korsakov

380 "Idleness crushes the artist . . .": V. V. Yastrebtsev, *Reminiscences of Rimsky-Korsakov*, ed. and trans. Florence Jonas (New York: Columbia University Press, 1985), p. 85.

380 "My dreams of artistic activity . . .": Nikolai Rimsky-Korsakov, *My Musical Life*, trans. Judah A. Joffe, ed. Carl van Vechten (New York: Tudor, 1936), p. 51.

381 "One must not neglect harmony . . .": Leyda and Bertensson, *Musorgsky Reader*, p. 406.

382 "You would scarcely find anyone . . .": Yastrebtsev, *Reminiscences of Rimsky-Korsakov*, p. 280.

382 "When there is a snowstorm . . .": Oskar von Riesemann, *Rachmaninoff's Recollections* (New York: Macmillan, 1934), p. 141.

382 "study Liszt . . .": Calvocoressi and Abraham, *Masters of Russian Music*, p. 423.

383 "the most superb palette . . .": ibid., p. 422.
383 "The Capriccio was to glitter . . .": Rimsky-Korsakov, *My Musical Life*, p. 244.
383 "Your *Spanish Caprice* is a colossal . . .": Hale, *Philip Hale's Boston Symphony Programme Notes*, p. 250.
383 "at the first rehearsal . . .": Rimsky-Korsakov, *My Musical Life*, p. 246.
383 "The Sultan Shakhriar, persuaded . . .": written on the score of *Scheherazade*.
383–84 "I had in view the creation . . .": Hale, *Philip Hale's Boston Symphony Programme Notes*, p. 248.
384 "Resurrect! Sing the chorus . . .": written on the score.

Gabriel Fauré

386 "The artist ought to love life . . .": Crofton and Fraser, *Dictionary of Musical Quotations*, p. 64.
386 "I grew up a rather quiet . . .": Fauré, *Gabriel Fauré*, p. 12.
386 "I was nine years old . . .": Fauré, *Gabriel Fauré*, p. 12.
387 "You cannot imagine how hard . . .": ibid., p. 307.
388–89 "His ever-more-frequent . . .": Léonie Rosenstiel, *Nadia Boulanger: A Life in Music* (New York: Norton, 1982), p. 176.
389 "When I am no longer here . . .": Schonberg, *Lives of the Great Composers*, p. 399.
389 "The work of the imagination . . .": Fauré, *Gabriel Fauré*, p. 278.
389 "In a world that seems less and less . . .": Mencken, *H. L. Mencken on Music*, p. 126.
389 "Fauré was thus fully . . .": Fauré, *Gabriel Fauré*, p. 348.
390 "Render unto Gabriel, and not unto César . . .": Melvin Berger, *Guide to Sonatas* (New York: Doubleday, Anchor Books, 1991), p. 96.
390–91 "Everything I managed to entertain . . .": Fauré, *Gabriel Fauré*, p. 314.
391 "spared us no painful detail . . .": Émile Vuillermoz, *Gabriel Fauré*, trans. Kenneth Schapin (Philadelphia: Chilton, 1969), p. 75.
391 "How nice is this self-assurance . . .": ibid., p. 74.

Leoš Janáček

394 "The musically talented person . . .": Leoš Janáček, *Janáček's Uncollected Essays on Music*, ed. Mirka Zemanová (London: Marion Boyars, 1989), p. 77.
395 "I have one great joy . . .": ibid., p. 33.
395 "She was so loath to die . . . my heart out": Ian Horsbrugh, *Leoš Janáček* (New York: Charles Scribner's Sons, 1982), p. 80.
395 "I feel as though I were . . .": ibid., p. 123.
396 "While writing the Diary . . .": ibid., p. 139.
396 "Kamilka [her nickname] be mine . . .": Leoš Janáček, *Intimate Letters of Leoš Janáček to Kamila Stösslova*, ed. John Tyrrell (Princeton, NJ: Princeton University Press, 1994), p. 179.
396 "I've already painted your stay . . .": ibid., p. 344.
396–97 "Although I am getting on in years . . .": Horsbrugh, *Leoš Janáček*, p. 213.
397 "Of all the musical tricks . . .": ibid., p. 201.
397 "Each folk song contains . . .": ibid., p. 49.
398 "The *Glagolitic Mass* is the apotheosis . . .": ibid., p. 215.

Sir Edward Elgar

400 "Music is written on the skies . . .": Michael Kennedy, *Portrait of Elgar* (London: Oxford University Press, 1968), p. 136.

401 "What themes! . . .": Christopher Fifield, *True Artist and True Friend: A Biography of Hans Richter* (Oxford: Oxford University Press, 1993), p. 445.

401 "I had gone off the boil": Blom, *Grove's Dictionary*, 2:915.

402 "The success of the D major . . .": Kennedy, *Portrait of Elgar*, p. 169.

403 "holy water in a German beer barrel": Crofton and Fraser, *Dictionary of Musical Quotations*, p. 59.

403 "I will not explain . . .": Kennedy, *Portrait of Elgar*, p. 84.

403 "a record of a long summer . . .": ibid., p. 92.

403 "Gosh! Man I've got a tune . . .": ibid., p. 168.

404 "Here, or more emphatically . . .": Ridout and Thompson, *A Concert Goer's Companion to Music*, p. 239.

404 "With an artist's vision . . .": Kennedy, *Portrait of Elgar*, p. 283.

Giacomo Puccini

407 "When the fever abates . . .": Giacomo Puccini, *Letters of Giacomo Puccini*, ed. Giuseppe Adami, trans. Ena Makin (Philadelphia: Lippincott, 1931), p. 270.

407 "I thought then and there . . .": Downes, *Ten Operatic Masterpieces*, p. 325.

408 "I am almost always in love": Cross and Ewen, *Encyclopedia of the Great Composers*, p. 500.

408 "I am sick of this . . .": ibid., p. 588.

408 "Massenet feels it as . . .": Mosco Carner, *Puccini* (New York: Alfred A. Knopf, 1959), p. 57.

408 "Puccini's genius is . . .": Giacomo Puccini, *Letters of Puccini* (New York: Vienna House, 1973), p. 67.

409 "If only I could be . . .": Puccini, *Letters of Giacomo Puccini*, ed. Adami, p. 265.

409 "I live in torment because . . .": ibid., p. 21.

410 "I am thirsty . . .": Weiss, *Letters of Composers Through Six Centuries*, p. 427.

410 "Here ends the opera . . .": ibid., p. 436.

410–11 "Melody is no longer produced . . .": ibid.

412 "Never do it any other way . . .": Schonberg, *Lives of the Great Composers*, p. 410.

412 "I have had a visit . . .": Puccini, *Letters of Giacomo Puccini*, ed. Adami, p. 146.

Hugo Wolf

414 "There's something gruesome . . .": Weiss, *Letters of Composers Through Six Centuries*, p. 395.

415 "I can hardly believe . . .": Frank Walker, *Hugo Wolf* (New York: Alfred A. Knopf, 1952), p. 139.

415 "One could catch a cold . . .": Schonberg, *Lives of the Great Composers*, p. 291.

415 "the art of composing . . . Brahms's output": Hugo Wolf, *The Music Criticism of Hugo Wolf*, trans. and ed. Henry Pleasants (New York: Holmes and Meier, 1978), p. 186.

415 "I don't want to make . . .": Crofton and Fraser, *Dictionary of Musical Quotations*, p. 157.

415 "You must first learn . . .": Walker, *Hugo Wolf*, p. 84.

416 "Gentlemen, I should . . .": ibid., p. 183.

416 "Wolf was his own man . . .": Wolf, *Music Criticism*, p. xiv.

416 "Am I one who . . .": Walker, *Hugo Wolf*, p. 200.

416 "It would lacerate . . .": ibid., p. 203.

416 "is a million times . . .": ibid.

416 "I work at a thousand . . .": Romain Rolland, *Essays on Music* (New York: Dover, 1959), p. 329.

417 "Pray for my . . . hang myself": ibid., p. 352.

417 "One may imagine . . .": ibid., p. 351.

417 "We therefore decided . . .": Walker, *Hugo Wolf*, p. 335.

418 "If only I was Hugo . . .": ibid., p. 462.

418 "There was something elemental . . .": ibid., p. 99.

418 "He seems to embody . . .": Arnold Whittall, *Romantic Music* (London: Thames & Hudson, 1987), p. 173.

Gustav Mahler

421 "Oh, how lovely it is . . .": Alma Mahler, *Gustav Mahler: Memoirs and Letters*, rev. and ed. Donald Mitchell, trans. Basil Creighton (New York: Viking, 1969), p. 338.

421 "were ill matched as . . .": Kurt Blaukopf, *Mahler*, trans. Inge Goodwin (New York: Limelight, 1985), p. 16.

421 "From my fourth year . . .": ibid., p. 22.

421 "This is polyphony . . .": Frederic V. Grunfeld, *Prophets Without Honor: A Background to Freud, Kafka, Einstein and Their World* (New York: Holt, Rinehart and Winston, 1979), p. 40.

422 "The conductor here is not . . .": Blaukopf, *Mahler*, p. 93.

422 "Never before had I . . .": Michael Kennedy, *Mahler* (New York: Schirmer, 1998), p. 41.

423 "To be born a Jew . . .": Paul Rosenfeld, *Musical Chronicle, 1917–1923* (New York: Benjamin Blom, 1972), pp. 244–45.

423 "I am thrice homeless . . .": Mahler, *Gustav Mahler*, p. 109.

423 "When he conducted you felt . . .": Bruno Walter, *Gustav Mahler* (New York: Greystone Press, 1941), p. 81.

423 "What is best in music . . .": Jonathan Carr, *Mahler* (New York: Overlook Press, 1998), p. 62.

424 "the man who, as I believe . . .": Mahler, *Gustav Mahler*, p. 342.

424 "If Mahler's music would . . .": Nicolas Slonimsky, *Lexicon of Musical Invective: Critical Assaults on Composers Since Beethoven's Time* (Seattle: University of Washington Press, 1953), p. 121.

424 "I feel sorry for me . . .": Grunfeld, *Prophets Without Honor*, p. 43.

424 "The arrival in New York . . .": Mahler, *Gustav Mahler*, p. 342.

425 "It's always difficult . . .": Blaukopf, *Mahler*, p. 8.

425 "Night shades were dispelled . . .": ibid., p. 11.

425 "I'd had plenty of opportunity . . .": ibid., p. 12.

425 "No composer before or since . . .": Grunfeld, *Prophets Without Honor*, p. 41.

425 "Those who seek me . . .": Carr, *Mahler*, p. 3.

425 "The most consuming . . .": Gustav Mahler, *Gustav Mahler: Selected Letters*, ed. Knud Martner (New York: Farrar, Straus and Giroux, 1979), p. 54.

426 "To write a symphony . . .": Joseph Machlis, *Introduction to Contemporary Music* (New York: Norton, 1979), p. 58.

426 "The weeping appoggiaturas . . .": Wilfrid Mellers, *Caliban Reborn: Renewal in Twentieth-Century Music* (New York: Harper and Row, 1967), p. 53.

426 "Only when I experience . . .": Machlis, *Introduction to Contemporary Music*, p. 55.

427 "In Pest, where I performed . . .": Constantin Floros, *Gustav Mahler: The Symphonies* (Portland, OR: Amadeus Press, 1993), p. 27.

427 "He introduces elements . . .": Erwin Stein, *Orpheus in New Guises* (London: Rockliff, 1953), pp. 7–8.

427 "My new work in relation . . .": Floros, *Gustav Mahler*, p. 56.

428 "For the Fourth movement . . .": Kennedy, *Mahler*, p. 121.

428 "punctuated by distant . . .": ibid., p. 124.

428 "Why have you lived? . . .": Floros, *Gustav Mahler*, p. 54.

428 "He was obsessed . . .": Blaukopf, *Mahler*, p. 101.

428–29 "But I have surely . . .": Mahler, *Gustav Mahler*, p. 162.

429 "The force and novelty . . .": Walter, *Gustav Mahler*, pp. 27–28.

429 "I could also name the . . .": Floros, *Gustav Mahler*, p. 89.

429 "of a strangely exalted . . .": Walter, *Gustav Mahler*, p. 116.

430 "It is all humorous . . .": Mahler, *Gustav Mahler*, p. 276.

430 "a piece of such eruptive . . .": Floros, *Gustav Mahler*, p. 145.

430 "There is nothing romantic . . .": ibid., p. 153.

430 "Your fifth symphony . . .": Gustav Mahler and Richard Strauss, *Mahler–Strauss Correspondence, 1888–1911*, ed. Herta Blaukopf (Chicago: University of Chicago Press, 1997), p. 75.

430 "I continually learn from . . .": Floros, *Gustav Mahler*, p. 145.

430–31 "What are they to say . . .": ibid., p. 209.

431 "The more deeply one . . .": *The New York Review of Books, An Anthology* (New York: New York Review of Books, 1976), pp. 150–51.

431 "My sixth will be asking . . .": Floros, *Gustav Mahler*, p. 161.

432 "The five movements of the . . .": Robert Simpson, ed., *The Symphony*, vol. 2, *Elgar to the Present Day* (Baltimore: Penguin, 1967), p. 43.

432 "I have just completed . . .": Floros, *Gustav Mahler*, p. 213.

432 "is so saturated . . .": Walter, *Gustav Mahler*, p. 116.

433 "The first movement is the most . . .": Downes, *New York Philharmonic Guide to the Symphony*, p. 565.

433 "those who are born after . . .": Kennedy, *Mahler*, epigraph.

433 "Have mercy! Oh, Lord . . .": Downes, *New York Philharmonic Guide to the Symphony*, p. 568.

Frederick Delius

435 "One can't define form . . .": Eric Fenby, *Delius As I Knew Him* (Cambridge: Cambridge University Press, 1936), p. 120.

437 "To all that he touched . . .": Cross and Ewen, *Encyclopedia of the Great Composers*, p. 206.

438 "All are my blooms . . .": ibid., p. 214.

438 *"In a Summer Garden* is not only . . .": Sir Thomas Beecham, *Frederick Delius* (New York: Alfred A. Knopf, 1961), p. 167.

Claude Debussy

440 "Generally speaking, I feel more . . .": Debussy, *Debussy Letters*, p. 184.

441 "I had a sudden vision . . .": ibid., p. 211.

441 "We ought to have our own . . .": Myers, *Chabrier and His Circle*, p. 32.

442 "Try as I may, I can't . . .": Debussy, *Debussy Letters*, p. 51.

442 "I feel nostalgia for the Claude . . .": ibid., p. 149.

442–43 "What I am doing seems so . . .": Myers, *Chabrier and His Circle*, p. 49.

443 "This is a time when . . .": Debussy, *Debussy Letters*, p. 307.

443 "The emotional satisfaction can't be . . .": ibid., p. 302.

443 "By one of those very human . . .": ibid., p. 324.

443 "Papa is dead . . .": Edward Lockspeiser, *Debussy: His Life and Mind* (Cambridge: Cambridge University Press, 1978), 2:224.

444 "In literature, in painting . . .": Oscar Thompson, *Debussy: Man and Artist* (New York: Dodd, Mead, 1937), p. 21.

444 "evolved an extraordinary vocabulary . . .": liner notes to *Debussy Piano Music* (New York: Nonesuch Records, 1977).

444 "To name an object sacrifices . . .": Dubal, *Art of the Piano*, p. 333.

444 "Historically viewed . . .": E. Robert Schmitz, *The Piano Works of Claude Debussy* (New York: Dover, 1966), p. ix.

444 "In playing his own music . . .": Dubal, *Art of the Piano*, p. 328.

445 "clouds, moonlight, passing . . .": Schmitz, *Piano Works of Debussy*, pp. 11–12.

445 "Debussy is in all senses . . .": John Vinton, ed., *Dictionary of Contemporary Music* (New York: E. P. Dutton, 1974), p. 179.

445 "The art of music began to beat . . .": Debussy, *Debussy Letters*, p. 324.

446 "renders the immutable . . .": Léon Vallas, *Claude Debussy: His Life and Works*, trans. Maire O'Brien and Grace O'Brien (New York: Dover, 1973), p. 112.

447 "From the first notes, we would . . .": Katherine Anne Porter, *The Collected Essays and Occasional Writings of Katherine Anne Porter* (New York: Delacorte Press, 1970), p. 108.

447 "I tried to obey a law of beauty . . .": Ewen, *Encyclopedia of Musical Masterpieces*, p. 172.

447 "Years of gestation purified . . .": Schmitz, *Piano Works of Debussy*, p. 82.

448 "To wet in it bodies . . .": Hale, *Philip Hale's Boston Symphony Programme Notes*, p. 93.

448 "a sort of hygienic . . .": Dubal, *Art of the Piano*, p. 330.

448 "It is like the music of another . . .": David Dubal, *Reflections from the Keyboard: The World of the Concert Pianist* (New York: Summit Books, 1984), p. 14.

448–49 "Soon one is aware of the symbolism . . .": Dubal, *Art of the Piano*, p. 333.

449 "The work has been growing . . .": David Dubal, *Conversations with Menuhin* (New York: Harcourt Brace Jovanovich, 1992), pp. 45–46.

Richard Strauss

451 "When at night I am . . .": Morgenstern, *Composers on Music*, p. 338.

452 "connecting link between . . .": Blom, *Grove's Dictionary*, 8:124.

453 "His absurd cacophony . . .": Crofton and Fraser, *Dictionary of Musical Quotations*, p. 143.

453 "Music, perhaps, will soon . . .": Ernest Newman, *Testament of Music* (London: Putnam, 1962), p. 102.

453 "Direct *Salome* and *Elektra* . . .": Richard Strauss, *Betrachtungen und Erinnerungen* (Zurich: Atlantis, 1949), p. 44.

454 "My wife's a bit rough . . .": Crofton and Fraser, *Dictionary of Musical Quotations*, p. 143.

454 "True art ennobles . . .": Brockway and Weinstock, *Men of Music*, p. 223.

455 "The great thing about the music . . .": Glenn Gould, *The Glenn Gould Reader* (New York: Alfred A. Knopf, 1984), p. 92.

456 "*Don Juan* is a miracle . . .": Brockway and Weinstock, *Men of Music*, p. 558.

457 "It is impossible for me . . .": Downes, *New York Philharmonic Guide to the Symphony*, p. 901.

457 "I did not intend . . .": Hale, *Philip Hale's Boston Symphony Programme Notes*, p. 317.

458 "Don Quixote is shown as . . .": Huneker, *Overtones*, p. 14.

458 "I once spent a couple of days . . .": Crofton and Fraser, *Dictionary of Musical Quotations*, p. 144.

459 "It is easily the greatest . . .": James Huneker, *The Intimate Letters of James Gibbons Huneker* (New York: Charles Scribner's Sons, 1930), p. 75.

459 "a sixteen-year-old . . .": Ernst Krause, *Richard Strauss* (Boston: Crescendo, 1969), p. 304.

459 "This is your apogee . . .": Mahler, *Gustav Mahler*, p. 201.

459 "This is one of the greatest . . .": ibid.

460 "Such warmth of blood . . .": Newman, *Testament of Music*, p. 110.

Jean Sibelius

463 "These symphonies of mine are more . . .": Norman and Shrifte, *Letters of Composers*, p. 324.

465 "[t]he outcome of a process of sheer . . .": Cecil Gray, *Sibelius* (London: Oxford University Press, 1946), p. 240.

465 "I feel very much alone . . .": Norman and Shrifte, *Letters of Composers*, p. 325.

465 "He alone among modern . . .": Constant Lambert, *Music Ho!* (New York: October House, 1967), p. 162.

465 "I admire its severity . . .": Kennedy, *Mahler*, p. 81.

465 "I do not believe for a moment . . .": Virgil Thomson, *The Musical Scene* (New York: Alfred A. Knopf, 1945), p. 49.

465 "a dated bore . . .": Schonberg, *Lives of the Great Composers*, pp. 385–87.

466 "[t]he Kingdom of Death . . .": Downes, *New York Philharmonic Guide to the Symphony*, pp. 862–63.

467 "It stands out as a protest against . . .": Melvin Berger, *Masters of Modern Music* (New York: Lothrop, Lee and Shepard, 1970), p. 101.

468 "Widespread they stand . . .": Wilfrid Mellers, *Man and His Music: The Story of Musical Experience in the West* (New York: Schocken, 1969), pp. 129–30.

468–69 *"Tapiola* is the *non plus ultra* . . .": Cross and Ewen, *Encyclopedia of the Great Composers*, p. 248.

Giacomo Meyerbeer

472 "It is a masterpiece of the modern . . .": Chopin, *Selected Correspondence*, pp. 100–1.

472 "The true reason for this animosity . . .": Heinz Becker and Gudrun Becker, *Giacomo Meyerbeer: A Life in Letters*, trans. Mark Violette (Portland, OR: Amadeus Press, 1989), p. 107.

Charles-Valentin Alkan

475 "affected me with an enthusiasm . . .": Ronald Smith, *Alkan: The Enigma* (New York: Crescendo, 1976), 1:101.

475 "The very diversity and range . . .": ibid.

Édouard Lalo

476 "a masterpiece of rhythm . . .": Claude Debussy, *Debussy on Music*, comp. François Lesure, ed. and trans. Richard Langham Smith (New York: Alfred A. Knopf, 1977), p. 114.

Léo Delibes

479 "This is the only ballet . . .": Tchaikovsky, *Letters to His Family*, p. 126.

Mily Balakirev

480 "I found him very . . .": Calvocoressi and Abraham, *Masters of Russian Music*, p. 134.

Hermann Goetz

481 "two masterpieces . . .": Stanley Weintraub, ed., *Bernard Shaw: The Diaries* (University Park: Pennsylvania State University Press, 1986), 1:35.

Emmanuel Chabrier

482 "There's music there for . . .": Myers, *Chabrier and His Circle*, p. 27.

482 "We have just heard something . . .": ibid., p. 33.

482 "I still tremble with emotion . . .": ibid., p. 35.

Arrigo Boito

483 "It is such a tremendous . . .": Huneker, *Overtones*, p. 273.

Sir Arthur Sullivan

484 "The people of the United States . . .": Mencken, *H. L. Mencken on Music*, pp. 117–18.

Jules Massenet

485 "I don't believe in all . . .": Schonberg, *Lives of the Great Composers*, p. 332.

485 "He was the most . . .": Debussy, *Debussy on Music*, p. 114.

Pablo de Sarasate

486 "Leave me alone with your symphonic . . .": Schwarz, *Great Masters of the Violin*, p. 237.

Vincent d'Indy

488 "The principles of art . . .": Daniel Gregory Mason, *Music in My Time and Other Reminiscences* (New York: Macmillan, 1938), p. 242.

488 "He never has the heated . . .": Eric Blom, *Classics Major and Minor* (London: J. M. Dent and Sons, 1958), p. 149.

Anatoly Liadov

489 "an important link between Rimsky-Korsakov . . .": Lazare Saminsky, *Music of our Day: Essentials and Prophecies* (New York: Thomas V. Crowell, 1932), p. 175.

489 "The world was tedious . . .": Calvocoressi and Abraham, *Masters of Russian Music*, p. 425.

489 "Give me fairies and dragons . . .": ibid.

489 "Its merits are charm, grace . . .": ibid., p. 430.

Ernest Chausson

490 "There is a phrase by Schumann . . .": Jean-Pierre Barricelli and Leo Weinstein, *Ernest Chausson* (Norman: University of Oklahoma Press, 1955), p. 9.

490 "that frightful Wagner . . .": ibid., p. 38.

491 "Chausson occupied . . .": ibid., p. 111.

Ruggiero Leoncavallo

492 "This event made . . .": Henry Edward Krehbiel, *A Second Book of Operas* (Garden City, NY: Garden City, 1917), p. 110.

Gustave Charpentier

493 "its intrigue is tightly woven . . .": Thomson, *Musical Scene*, pp. 161–62.

Isaac Albéniz

495 "One finds all the atmosphere . . .": Debussy, *Debussy on Music*, p. 301.

Charles Martin Loeffler

496 "He has delicate sentiment . . .": Ewen, *Encyclopedia of Musical Masterpieces*, p. 329.

496 "[I] have experienced . . .": Ellen Knight, *Charles Martin Loeffler: A Life Apart in American Music* (Urbana: University of Illinois Press, 1993), p. 210.

Pietro Mascagni

497 "It was a pity . . .": Pietro Mascagni, *Mascagni: An Autobiography*, ed. David Stivender (White Plains, NY: Pro/Am Music Resources/London: Kahn and Averill, 1988), p. xi.

Paul Dukas

499 "In terms of orchestration . . .": Yastrebtsev, *Reminiscences of Rimsky-Korsakov*, p. 376.

PART V: THE AGE OF MODERNISM

504 "Satie's own terrifying willingness . . .": David Dubal, *The Art of the Piano* (San Diego: Harcourt Brace, 1995), p. 396.

505 "In chromatic serial music . . .": Wilfrid Mellers, *Caliban Reborn: Renewal in Twentieth-Century Music* (New York: Harper and Row, 1967), p. 190.

506 "When music shall have become . . .": Virgil Thomson, *The State of Music* (New York: Vintage Books, 1962), p. 225.

507 "Man is a terrible destroyer . . .": Bernard Berenson, *Sketch for a Self-Portrait* (London: Robin Clark, 1991), p. 113.

Alexander Scriabin

509 "I will come to dazzle . . .": Faubion Bowers, *Scriabin* (Tokyo: Kodansha International, 1969), p. 134.

511 "I was once a Chopinist . . .": ibid., p. 220.

511 "Who is your favorite . . .": Arthur Rubinstein, *My Young Years* (New York: Alfred A. Knopf, 1973), p. 1969.

511 "Sometimes he lowered his face . . .": M. D. Calvocoressi and Gerald Abraham, *Masters of Russian Music* (New York: Alfred A. Knopf, 1936), p. 486.

511 "There is not a wasted note . . .": Bowers, *Scriabin*, p. 204.

512 "The great Messiah is he . . .": Calvocoressi and Abraham, *Masters of Russian Music*, p. 494.

512 "all nerve and holy flame": Alfred J. Swan, *Scriabin* (New York: Da Capo, 1969), p. 20.

512 "The history of Scriabin's . . .": Calvocoressi and Abraham, *Masters of Russian Music*, pp. 496–97.

512 "he shone like a flame of . . .": A. L. Bacharach, ed., *The Music Masters*, vol. 4, *The Twentieth Century* (Baltimore: Penguin, 1957), p. 345.

513 "Scriabin appears to have awakened . . .": Paul Rosenfeld, *Musical Portraits* (New York: Harcourt Brace and Howe, 1920), pp. 178–79.

513 "When you listen to the *Poem* . . .": Bowers, *Scriabin*, p. 135.

513 "the obscenest piece . . .": Derek Watson, comp., *The Wordsworth Dictionary of Musical Quotations* (Ware, Hertfordshire: Wordsworth Editions, 1994), p. 188.

513–14 "To think that Gloucester . . .": Eugène Goossens, *Overture and Beginners: A Musical Autobiography* (London: Methuen, 1951), p. 193.

514 "I do not know by what . . .": Bowers, *Scriabin*, p. 176.

514 "The Fifth Sonata has been likened . . .": Swan, *Scriabin*, p. 93.

514 "a sweetness gradually becoming . . .": written on the score.

514 "a veritable picture of Dorian Gray": Swan, *Scriabin*, p. 106.

Ralph Vaughan Williams

516 "The best form of musical . . .": John Wilson, ed., *The Faith of an Artist* (London: Allen and Unwin, 1962), p. 165.

516 "The years were passing . . .": Milton Cross and David Ewen, *Encyclopedia of the Great Composers and Their Music* (Garden City, NY: Doubleday, 1953), p. 813.

516 "I spent a fortnight . . .": Lewis Foreman, ed., *From Parry to Britten: British Music in Letters, 1900–1945* (Portland, OR: Amadeus Press, 1987), p. 30.

517 "Let our composers and performers . . .": Ralph Vaughan Williams, *National Music* (London: Oxford University Press, 1934), p. 47.

517 "one of the landmarks . . .": Constant Lambert, *Music Ho!* (New York: Scribner, 1934), p. 134.

517 "We pupils of Parry have . . .": Harold Schonberg, *Lives of the Great Composers* (New York: Penguin, 1947), p. 493.

518 "I do not know whether I like it . . .": Francis Routh, *Contemporary Music* (London: English Universities Press, 1968), p. 151.

518 "artistic expression which is natural . . .": Wilson, *Faith of an Artist*, p. 160.

518 "When the United States of the World . . .": ibid., p. 169.

518 "both a visionary and a realist . . .": Routh, *Contemporary Music*, p. 146.

519 "The work is wonderful . . .": Edward Downes, *The New York Philharmonic Guide to the Symphony* (New York: Walker, 1976), p. 992.

519 "may perhaps suggest the noise . . .": ibid.

519 "If the hearer will imagine . . .": ibid.

519 "It was written in 1913 . . .": Virgil Thomson, *A Virgil Thomson Reader* (Boston: Houghton Mifflin, 1981), p. 191.

520 "the subject of the Fugal . . .": Robert Simpson, ed., *The Symphony* (Baltimore: Penguin, 1967), p. 120.

Sergei Rachmaninoff

522 "Radio cannot really do justice . . .": Julian Haylock, *Sergei Rachmaninoff* (London: Pavilion, 1996), p. 72.

523 "It was less his magnificent technique . . .": Sergei Bertensson and Jay Leyda, *Sergei Rachmaninoff: A Lifetime in Music* (London: Allen and Unwin, 1965), pp. 12–13.

523 "Rachmaninoff's talent surpassed any other . . .": Haylock, *Rachmaninoff*, p. 69.

524 "If there was a conservatory . . .": ibid., p. 25.

524 "Tell me, does anyone want . . .": Bertensson and Leyda, *Rachmaninoff*, pp. 88–89.

525 "Rachmaninoff is a truly 'God-given' . . .": ibid., p. 182.

525 "Here am I, spiritually sick . . .": Gertrude Norman and Miriam Lubell Shrifte, *Letters of Composers: An Anthology* (Westport, CT: Greenwood Press, 1979), pp. 339–40.

526 "The whole world is open to me . . .": Haylock, *Rachmaninoff*, p. 73.

526 "The older we get . . .": ibid., p. 75.

526 "My dear hands . . .": Bertensson and Leyda, *Rachmaninoff*, p. 381.

526 "The fall out at a Rachmaninoff . . .": Dubal, *Art of the Piano*, p. 212.

526–27 "Such was the power of his personality . . .": Haylock, *Rachmaninoff*, p. 69.

527 "I feel like a ghost . . .": ibid., p. 82.

527 "Rachmaninoff was made of steel . . .": CD booklet, *Collected Recordings of Rachmaninoff* (RCA 09026-61265-2).

527 "Whether it is going to be a contemporary . . .": Victor I. Seroff, *Rachmaninoff* (New York: Simon and Schuster, 1950), p. 136.

528 "For Rachmaninoff himself the songs . . .": John Russell, *Reading Russell: Essays 1941–1988* (New York: Harry N. Abrams, 1989), pp. 213–14.

528 "I have heard my inescapable piece . . .": Bertensson and Leyda, *Rachmaninoff*, p. 372.

528–29 "presents many more problems . . .": Haylock, *Rachmaninoff*, p. 49.

530 "probably the only time I could . . .": Gary Graffman, *I Really Should Be Practicing* (New York: Doubleday, 1981), p. 45.

Arnold Schoenberg

533 "Music is not merely . . .": Arnold Schoenberg, *Style and Idea: Selected Writings of Arnold Schoenberg*, ed. Leonard Stein (Berkeley and Los Angeles: University of California Press, 1975), p. 220.

533 "The scandal has never ceased": Charles Rosen, *Arnold Schoenberg* (New York: Viking Press, 1975), p. 4.

534 "It sounds as if someone . . .": Downes, *New York Philharmonic Guide to the Symphony*, p. 804.

534 "By avoiding the establishment . . .": Schoenberg, *Style and Idea*, p. 217.

535 "I still yearn that people . . .": Watson, *Wordsworth Dictionary of Musical Quotations*, p. 115.

536 "My technique will assure . . .": Joseph Rufer, *The Works of Arnold Schoenberg: A Catalogue of His Compositions, Writings, and Paintings*, trans. D. Newlin (London: Faber and Faber, 1962), p. 48.

536 "would not just revolutionize . . .": Frederic Morton, *A Nervous Splendor* (New York: Penguin, 1973), p. 18.

536 "The great thing that . . .": Peter Heyworth, ed., *Conversations with Klemperer* (London: Camelot Press, 1973), p. 74.

537 "Someone had to": Willi Reich, *Schoenberg*, trans. Leo Black (New York: Praeger, 1971).

537 "the story concerns Moses' . . .": John Vinton, ed., *Dictionary of Contemporary Music* (New York: E. P. Dutton, 1974), p. 660.

537 "Recognized internationally . . .": Rosen, *Arnold Schoenberg*, p. 2.

538 "The problem of his music . . .": Vinton, *Dictionary of Contemporary Music*, p. 661.

538 "I bear a child . . .": Downes, *New York Philharmonic Guide to the Symphony*, p. 805.

538 "The Supreme Commander": Schoenberg, *Style and Idea*, p. 109.

538 "That is the kind of music . . .": Rosen, *Arnold Schoenberg*, p. 37.

539 "A Viennese conductor . . .": Schoenberg, *Style and Idea*, p. 97.

539 "I'm now experiencing . . .": Alban Berg and Arnold Schoenberg, *The Berg-Schoenberg Correspondence*, ed. Juliane Brand (New York: Norton, 1987), p. 61.

539 "It's unbelievably magnificent . . .": ibid., p. 94.

540 "these piano pieces . . .": Dubal, *Art of the Piano*, p. 398.

540 "Perhaps no other composition . . .": ibid., p. 399.

540 "I can think of no . . .": ibid.

540 "These five books of pieces . . .": ibid., p. 398.

541 "To call him 'crazy' . . .": James Huneker, *Ivory, Apes, and Peacocks* (New York: Sagamore Press, 1957), p. 65.

541 "Every composer has his . . .": ibid.

541 "some very friendly things . . .": Schoenberg, *Style and Idea*, p. 97.

Maurice Ravel

544 "All life's pleasure . . .": Arbie Orenstein, ed., *A Ravel Reader* (New York: Columbia University Press, 1990), p. 1.

544 "knew how to develop my . . .": ibid., p. 29.

544 "intelligent": ibid., p. 33.

545 "From that moment on . . .": ibid., p. 193.

546 "Monsieur Ravel refuses . . .": Joseph Machlis, *Introduction to Contemporary Music* (New York: Norton, 1963), p. 123.

546 "I have so much music in my head . . .": Orenstein, *Ravel Reader*, p. 12.

547 "In the name of the gods . . .": Alec Robertson, ed., *Chamber Music* (Baltimore: Penguin, 1957), p. 383.

549 "M. Ravel may look upon us as old . . .": Downes, *New York Philharmonic Guide to the Symphony*, p. 744.

549 "These three poems enrich . . .": Dubal, *Art of the Piano*, p. 389.

549 "Nowhere in music . . .": ibid.

550 "The title *Valses nobles et . . .*": Arbie Orenstein, *Ravel: Man and Musician* (New York: Columbia University Press, 1975), p. 175.

550 "The delightful and always novel . . .": ibid.

551 "one of the most beautiful products . . .": Orenstein, *Ravel Reader*, p. 177.

551 "a vast musical fresco, less . . .": ibid., p. 60.

551 "The homage is directed less . . .": ibid., p. 32.

552 "constitutes an experiment in a very . . .": Downes, *New York Philharmonic Guide to the Symphony*, p. 734.

553 "is written very much in the same spirit . . .": Orenstein, *Man and Musician*, pp. 101–2.

Béla Bartók

555 "That man in his misery finds . . .": Béla Bartók, *Béla Bartók Letters*, ed. János Demény (New York: St. Martin's Press, 1971), p. 81.

556 "He was technically on the level . . .": David Dubal, *Reflections from the Keyboard: The World of the Concert Pianist* (New York: Summit Books, 1984), p. 312.

556 "We want to preserve the songs . . .": ibid., p. 71.

557 "That was a great experience . . .": Heyworth, *Conversations with Klemperer*, p. 88.

557 "the one thing which is as necessary . . .": Bartók, *Bartók Letters*, p. 153.

557 "the imminent danger that Hungary . . .": ibid., p. 153.

558 "This voyage is, actually, like . . .": ibid., p. 284.

558 "One can take Bartók in the normal stride . . .": Norman Demuth, *Musical Trends in the Twentieth Century* (Westport, CT: Greenwood Press, 1975), p. 276.

559 "How important a part of Bartók's art . . .": Eric Blom, ed., *Grove's Dictionary of Music and Musicians*, 5th ed. (New York: St. Martin's Press, 1964), 1:159.

559 "My real ideal is the brotherhood . . .": Bartók, *Bartók Letters*, p. 201.

559 "Bartók was one of the greatest men . . .": David Dubal, *Conversations with Menuhin* (London: Heinemann, 1991), p. 39.

559 "Exactitude above all": Bartók, *Bartók Letters*, p. 209.

560 "the epitome of Bartók's melodic style . . .": Blom, *Grove's Dictionary*, 1:479.

560 "One has to go back to Beethoven . . .": Francis Poulenc, *Selected Correspondence: 1915–63*, trans. and ed. Sidney Buckland (London: Victor Gollancz, 1991), p. 299.

560 "The piano becomes a machine . . .": Ian Crofton and Donald Fraser, *A Dictionary of Musical Quotations* (New York: Schirmer, 1988), p. 13.

560 "I wanted to produce a piece . . .": Béla Bartók, *Béla Bartók Essays*, ed. Benjamin Suchoff (Lincoln: University of Nebraska Press, 1992), p. 57.

562 "The title of this symphony-like orchestral work . . .": ibid., p. 43.

Igor Stravinsky

564 "I stumble upon . . .": Howard Gardner, *Creating Minds: An Anatomy of Creativity* (New York: Basic, 1993), p. 219.

564 "He was affectionate . . .": Igor Stravinsky and Robert Craft, *Memories and Commentaries* (Berkeley: University of California Press, 1959), p. 19.

564 "I never came across . . .": Igor Stravinsky, *Stravinsky: Chronicle of My Life* (London: Victor Gollancz, 1936), p. 7.

565 "Igor Stravinsky may be my . . .": Stravinsky and Craft, *Memories and Commentaries*, p. 192.

565 "As Petrouchka he was . . .": ibid., p. 38.

565 "It gave me the absolute . . .": Gardner, *Creating Minds*, p. 199.

566 "extraordinarily wild . . .": Claude Debussy, *Debussy Letters*, ed. François Lesure and Roger Nichols (London: Faber and Faber, 1987), p. 270.

566 "the greatest crisis . . .": Watson, *Dictionary of Musical Quotations*, p. 195.

566 "*Pulcinella* was my discovery . . .": Igor Stravinsky and Robert Craft, *Expositions and Developments* (Berkeley and Los Angeles: University of California Press, 1959), p. 113.

566 "Did not [poet T. S.] Eliot and I . . .": Gardner, *Creating Minds*, p. 217.

566 "is by its very nature . . .": Stravinsky, *Chronicle of My Life*, p. 91.

567 "are astonished to hear . . .": Cross and Ewen, *Encyclopedia of the Great Composers*, p. 784.

567 "With Stravinsky one senses . . .": Aaron Copland, *Copland on Music* (New York: Norton, 1963), p. 94.

568 "My freedom consists in . . .": Igor Stravinsky, *Poetics of Music* (Cambridge, MA: Harvard University Press, 1942), p. 65.

568 "By temperament and talent . . .": Igor Stravinsky and Robert Craft, *Dialogues* (Berkeley and Los Angeles: University of California Press, 1982), p. 123.

568 "His particular kind . . .": Norman and Shrifte, *Letters of Composers*, p. 416.

569 "as a form of communion . . .": Stravinsky, *Poetics of Music*, p. 142.

570 "One day I unexpectedly . . .": Humphrey Searle, *Ballet Music* (New York: Dover, 1973), p. 102.

570 "The tone of a work . . .": Stravinsky, *Poetics of Music*, p. 10.

Alban Berg

574 "I declare firmly and decisively . . .": Mosco Carner, *Alban Berg* (New York: Holmes and Meier, 1975), pp. 6–7.

575 "Whether I am composing . . .": Willi Reich, *Alban Berg* (New York: Vienna House, 1994), pp. 29–30.

575 "The people lived . . .": Allan Janik and Stephen Toulmin, *Wittgenstein's Vienna* (Chicago: Ivan R. Dee, 1996), p. 101.

575 "In Vienna a fury of . . .": Bacharach, *Music Masters*, p. 36.

576 "No! . . . the only right way": Reich, *Alban Berg*, p. 34.

576 "daily for two and a half . . .": George Perle, *The Operas of Alban Berg* (Berkeley and Los Angeles: University of California Press, 1980), p. 21.

577 "I am not well . . .": Berg and Schoenberg, *Berg-Schoenberg Correspondence*, p. 467.

577 "I still cannot believe . . .": ibid., p. 471.

577–78 "Both operas add new . . .": Perle, *Operas of Alban Berg*, p. xiv.

578 "*Woyzeck* is the first real tragedy . . .": George Steiner, *The Death of Tragedy* (New York: Alfred A. Knopf, 1961), p. 274.

578 "No breath of fresh air . . .": Bacharach, *Music Masters*, p. 38.

578 "There is a bit of me in . . .": Perle, *Operas of Alban Berg*, p. 71.

579 "I have secretly inserted . . .": Melvin Berger, *Guide to Chamber Music* (New York: Doubleday, 1985), p. 78.

579 "latent opera": ibid., p. 77.

580 "A last arpeggio wings . . .": Paul Collaer, *A History of Modern Music* (Cleveland, OH: World, 1961), p. 113.

Sergei Prokofiev

582 "I work everywhere . . .": Harlow Robinson, *Sergei Prokofiev* (New York: Paragon House, 1988), p. 234.

582 "I guess I should be studying . . .": Israel V. Nestyev, *Prokofiev*, trans. Florence Jonas (Stanford, CA: Stanford University Press, 1960), p. 26.

582 "wanted to fit all of her students . . .": Robinson, *Sergei Prokofiev*, p. 72.

582 "He is very talented . . .": ibid.

583 "a tour de force . . .": Howard Hartog, ed., *European Music in the Twentieth Century* (New York: Praeger, 1957), p. 220.

583 "Thank you very much . . .": Nestyev, *Prokofiev*, p. 238.

584 "deeply impressed by this Russian epic . . .": Robinson, *Prokofiev*, p. 414.

584 "Worship the night . . .": ibid., p. 467.

585 "In conclusion, I would like to express . . .": Jacques Barzun, *Pleasures of Music* (New York: Viking, 1951), p. 380.

585 "Even genius does not save . . .": Robinson, *Prokofiev*, p. 157.

585 "At midnight we raised . . .": ibid., pp. 491–92.

585 "Only forty or fifty people . . .": ibid., pp. 2–3.

588 "I still consider . . .": Nestyev, *Prokofiev*, p. 249.

589 "Each character of this tale is . . .": ibid., p. 279.

590 "of the grandeur of the human spirit": Robinson, *Prokofiev*, p. 432.

590 "The Fifth Symphony was intended . . .": Boris Schwarz, *Music and Musical Life in Soviet Russia, 1917–1981* (New York: Norton, 1972), p. 197.

Paul Hindemith

593 "A life in and with music . . .": Wilson, *Faith of an Artist*, p. 135.

594 "cultural Bolshevik": Hartog, *European Music in the Twentieth Century*, p. 68.

594 "Hindemith held to the mainstream of European classical . . .": Vinton, *Dictionary of Contemporary Music*, p. 321.

595 "[t]he ballet music in particular has . . .": ibid., pp. 67–68.

596 "studies in counterpoint, tonal . . . meets the casual ear": Dubal, *Art of the Piano*, p. 347.

George Gershwin

598 "Try to write some real popular . . .": Edward Jablonski, *Gershwin Remembered* (London: Faber and Faber, 1992), p. 66.

599 "I have a pupil who will make . . .": David Ewen, *The Story of George Gershwin* (New York: Henry Holt, 1956), p. 27.

599 "Jazz speaks to us about . . .": Erik Satie, *Erik Satie: Écrits* (Paris: Éditions Champs Libres, 1981), p. 166.

600 "Up until the six months . . .": Oscar Levant, *Memoirs of an Amnesiac* (New York: G. P. Putnam's Sons, 1965), p. 149.

601 "Oh, I guess around a half million . . .": Norman Lebrecht, *The Book of Musical Anecdotes* (New York: Free Press, 1985), p. 296.

601 "It was only in Gershwin's generation . . .": Olin Downes, *Downes on Music* (New York: Simon & Schuster, 1957), p. 235.

601 "Music to him was the air . . .": Oscar Levant, *A Smattering of Ignorance* (Garden City, NY: Garden City, 1942), pp. 209–10.

603 "Gershwin's *Porgy*, like the operas of . . .": Wilfrid Mellers, *Music in a New Found Land* (New York: Hillstone, 1975), p. 413.

Francis Poulenc

604 "On the radio a lady . . .": Watson, *Wordsworth Dictionary of Musical Quotations*, p. 104.

605 "Poulenc played to me much of . . .": Arthur Rubinstein, *My Many Years* (New York: Alfred A. Knopf, 1980), p. 105.

606 "You will find sobriety and dolor . . .": "A Vote for Francis Poulenc," *Saturday Review of Literature* (1950), p. 57.

606 "Above all do not analyze . . .": Pierre Bernac, *Francis Poulenc* (New York: Norton & Company, 1977), p. 13.

607 "Take Chopin's dominant sevenths . . .": Ned Rorem, *Music from the Inside Out* (New York: George Braziller, 1967), p. 276.

607 "It was composed in 1932 . . .": Thomson, *Virgil Thomson Reader*, pp. 316–17.

608 "Poulenc's personality was much more complex . . .": Bruno Monsaingeon, *Mademoiselle: Conversations with Nadia Boulanger*, trans. Robin Marsack (Boston: Northeastern University Press, 1988), p. 103.

608 "I've not the slightest . . .": Francis Poulenc, *My Friends and Myself: Conversations Assembled by Stéphane Audel* (London: Dennis Dobson, 1963), p. 59.

Aaron Copland

612 "The process of music and the process . . .": Copland, *Copland on Music*, p. 72.

612 "I was born on a street in Brooklyn . . .": Aaron Copland and Vivian Perlis, *Copland: 1900 through 1924* (New York: St. Martin's/Marek, 1984), p. 16.

612 "might best be described . . .": ibid., p. 18.

612 "to the daring decision to spend . . .": ibid., p. 25.

613 "At the conclusion, there was . . .": ibid., p. 104.

613 "I wept when I heard it . . . in our generation": ibid., p. 104.

614 "It seemed to me that we composers . . .": ibid., p. 316.

614 "the kind of brilliant orchestral . . .": Copland, *Copland on Music*, p. 133.

614 "I found twelve-tone writing . . .": From a brochure introducing Copland's year-long series, *Aaron Copland's Comments*, on WNCN. Produced by David Dubal, New York, 1969.

615 "It's the best we've got . . .": Thomson, *Virgil Thomson Reader*, p. 459.

616 "It is a delicate operation . . .": Copland and Perlis, *Copland*, p. 279.

616 "I hoped to suggest something . . .": ibid., p. 342.

617 "a pioneer celebration in spring . . .": Godfrey Ridout and Gordon V. Thompson, A *Concert Goer's Companion to Music* (Toronto: G. V. Thompson Music, 1996), p. 184.

Dmitri Shostakovich

620 "I'm not a militant . . .": Dmitri Shostakovich, *Testimony: The Memoirs of Shostakovich*, ed. Solomon Volkov (New York: Harper and Row, 1979), p. 9.

620 "I was sickly . . .": ibid.

621 "There has never been . . .": Cross and Ewen, *Encyclopedia of the Great Composers*, p. 725.

622 "The Nazi barbarians . . .": Schwarz, *Music in Soviet Russia*, p. 176.

622 "Never in my life . . .": ibid., p. 178.

622 "written with the heart's blood": ibid., p. 179.

623 "I have thought that my life . . .": Shostakovich, *Testimony*, p. 277.

623 "Shostakovich was true . . .": Schwarz, *Music in Soviet Russia*, p. 174.

623 "This composer preserved . . .": ibid.

623 "Music illuminates . . .": Shostakovich, *Testimony*, p. 232.

625 "I don't feel that writing . . .": ibid., p. 138.

Benjamin Britten

629 "Music demands . . .": Benjamin Britten, *On Receiving the First Aspen Award* (London: Faber and Faber, 1964); his acceptance speech.

629 "Suffolk, the birth place and inspiration . . .": Bacharach, *Music Masters*, 4:48.

630 "politely spat at it": Cross and Ewen, *Encyclopedia of the Great Composers*, p. 142.

630 "To think of Crabbe is to . . .": Eric Walter White, *Benjamin Britten* (Los Angeles: University of California Press, p. 1948), p. 35. The article first appeared in *The Listener*, May 29, 1941.

630 "The opera seizes on you . . .": Edmund Wilson, *Europe Without Baedeker* (New York: Farrar, Straus and Giroux, 1966), p. 187.

631 "I know of no other composer . . .": Copland, *Copland on Music*, pp. 225–26.

631 "Purcell is as near to him as Verdi . . .": Erwin Stein, *Orpheus in New Guises* (London: Rockliff, 1953), p. 150.

631 "a wonderful sensitivity for children . . .": Dubal, *Conversations with Menuhin*, p. 25.

632 "The scheme and the mood of the work . . .": Cross and Ewen, *Encyclopedia of the Great Composers*, 1:148.

633 "The role of the horn is twofold . . .": Ridout and Thompson, *Concert Goer's Companion to Music*, p. 152.

633 "It is also a portrait of the sea . . .": Downes, *New York Philharmonic Guide to the Symphony*, p. 204.

634 "My subject is war . . .": Jonathan Buckley, ed., *Classical Music on CD* (London: Penguin, 1994), p. 77.

Erik Satie

637 "Satie's music is as . . .": Dubal, *Art of the Piano*, p. 396.

637 "Turn the pages of this . . .": Satie, *Sports and Divertissements*, composed to accompany drawings by Charles Martin (New York: Dover, 1979), preface.

Ferruccio Busoni

638 "I almost think that . . .": article on Busoni by David Dubal, WNCN *Program Guide*, Feb. 1969, p. 6.

638 "I should like to catch . . .": ibid.

638 "Infinity lives in the spirit . . .": Ferruccio Busoni, *The Essence of Music and Other Papers* (New York: Dover, 1965), p. 189.

Enrique Granados

640 "The death of Granados . . .": Ernest Newman, *Testament of Music* (London: Putnam, 1962), p. 193.

Scott Joplin

641 "Here is the genius . . .": James Haskins with Kathleen Benson, *Scott Joplin* (New York: Doubleday, 1978), p. 196.

Gustav Holst

644 "It's a great thing . . .": Imogen Holst, *Holst* (London: Faber and Faber, 1974), p. 54.

Charles Ives

645 "kick out the softy ears . . .": Dubal, *Art of the Piano*, p. 348.

645 "the greatest music . . .": ibid.

645 "In fact, these notes . . .": ibid.

Manuel de Falla

648–49 "nature was the most unpityingly . . .": Stravinsky and Craft, *Memories and Commentaries*, p. 80.

Ernö von Dohnányi

649 "for the enjoyment . . .": Dubal, *Art of the Piano*, p. 334.

649 "In his compositions . . .": Donald Francis Tovey, *The Main Stream of Music and Other Essays* (New York: Meridian, 1959), p. 302.

Nikolai Medtner

652 "not always easy to follow . . .": Dubal, *Art of the Piano*, p. 364.

Ernest Bloch

652 "It is the Jewish soul . . .": Bacharach, *Music Masters*, 4:45.

George Enescu

653 "He was unique and unapproachable . . .": Dubal, *Conversations with Menuhin*, p. 36.

Percy Grainger

655 "all the world's music . . .": Wilfrid Mellers, *Percy Grainger* (Oxford: Oxford University Press, 1992), p. 9.

655 "like the sun . . .": Dubal, *Art of the Piano*, p. 104.

Anton Webern

657 "The minimum materials . . .": Dubal, *Art of the Piano*, p. 430.

657 "Tonality had been the chief . . .": Francis Routh, *Contemporary Music: An Introduction* (London: The English Universities Press Ltd., 1968), p. 108.

Sir Arnold Bax

658 "a brazen romantic . . .": Blom, *Grove's Dictionary*, p. 510.

Edgard Varèse

659 "In my own work . . .": David Dubal, "Varèse," WNCN *Program Guide*, Feb. 1969, p. 1.

659 "a worker in intensities . . .": ibid.

Charles Tomlinson Griffes

660 "the priceless instinct . . .": Edward Maisel, *Charles T. Griffes: The Life of an American Composer* (New York: Alfred A. Knopf, 1984), p. 334.

660 "the greatest musical loss . . .": ibid., p. 331.

660 "This disturbingly powerful sonata . . .": Mellers, *Music in a New Found Land*, p. 148.

Heitor Villa-Lobos

662 "A truly creative musician . . .": Nat Shapiro, ed., *An Encyclopedia of Quotations About Music* (Garden City, NY: Doubleday, 1978), p. 65.

Virgil Thomson

668 "I preferred to starve . . .": Kathleen Hoover and John Cage, *Virgil Thomson: His Life and Music* (New York: Thomas Yoseloff, 1959), p. 49.

Roger Sessions

668–69 "If I practiced nothing else . . .": Dubal, *Art of the Piano*, p. 420.

669 "The key to the understanding . . .": Roger Sessions, *The Musical Experience of Composer, Performer, Listener* (Princeton, NJ: Princeton University Press, 1950), p. 99.

Carlos Chávez

671 "Chávez's music is extraordinarily healthy . . .": Aaron Copland, *The New Music: 1900–1960* (New York: Norton, 1968), p. 146.

Harry Partch

673 "in musicians who are total constituents . . .": Vinton, *Dictionary of Contemporary Music*, p. 556.

Joaquín Rodrigo

673–74 "that would combine the soul . . .": Victoria Kamhi de Rodrigo, *Hand in Hand with Joaquín Rodrigo* (Pittsburgh, PA: Latin American Literary Review Press, 1992), p. 325.

Sir William Walton

675 "What a work, truly marvelous . . .": Susana Walton, *Behind the Façade* (New York: Oxford University Press, 1988), p. 83.

675 "William knocked out . . .": ibid., p. 94.

675 "I seriously advise . . .": Shapiro, *Encyclopedia of Quotations*, p. 127.

Elliott Carter

678 "It employs no preestablished . . .": Dubal, *Art of the Piano*, p. 304.

Samuel Barber

680 "It is not extravagant to say . . .": Mellers, *Music in a New Found Land*, p. 160.

Lou Harrison

686 "really sensitive and elaborate . . .": Virgil Thomson, *Music Reviewed, 1940–1954* (New York: Vintage, 1967), p. 314.

Iannis Xenakis

687 "Whereas John Cage and many other . . .": Vinton, *Dictionary of Contemporary Music*, p. 327.

Karlheinz Stockhausen

690 "It was Webern's techniques rather than . . .": Vinton, *Dictionary of Contemporary Music*, p. 708.

690 "From time to time I have concentrated . . .": Dubal, *Art of the Piano*, p. 421.

690 "In a world bombarded by images . . .": ibid.

George Crumb

691 "Crumb's mature style . . .": Vinton, *Dictionary of Contemporary Music*, p. 156.

691 "The spiritual impulse of my music . . .": Dubal, *Art of the Piano*, p. 326.

NAME INDEX

Listings in boldface indicate composers with entries in the book.